PRAISE FOR *CONFLICT*
AND LEADERSHIP FOR MANAGERS

"This third edition is one of the best innovations for the field of conflict management and even beyond. Raines offers an expanded exploration of conflict management for managers across practical settings, making it an instructive read for managers interested in learning how to best help others manage conflict, especially after the pandemic and those experiencing cultural and generational differences. This text can be useful for both advanced managers and those just starting out."
—Brittany Foutz, Salisbury University; senior research fellow, Bosserman Center for Conflict Resolution; and United Nations Co-Secretariat, RCE Salisbury

"This textbook presents basic concepts and skills necessary to prevent and proactively resolve common workplace conflicts. It's appropriate for use in an undergraduate course on conflict resolution and a great resource for future organizational leaders. There are skill-building exercises on difficult conversations, conducting performance reviews, and negotiating with employees and other managers while navigating through difficult times." **—Jody A. Worley, associate professor, University of Oklahoma**

"This book offers information that will stand any manager in good stead. It gives managers the language to talk about conflict and the grounding to identify conflict when it happens. Knowing conflict is there and knowing how to talk about it are the first important steps toward resolving or managing conflict. The discussion questions and exercises at the end of each chapter offer an opportunity to reflect on conflict management strategies in a risk-free environment."
—Daniel Rainey, principal, Holistic Solutions, Inc.; fellow, National Center for Technology and Dispute Resolution; and editor-in-chief, *International Journal of Online Dispute Resolution*

"Whether you are seeking insight into your organizational conflict culture or practical conflict management approaches, this book has it all. This book is a great teaching and training resource for individuals seeking to understand and improve their conflict management skills. There are excellent workplace examples and thought-provoking discussion questions throughout, which I love to use as conversation starters in my own classroom." **—Erica Knotts, senior instructor, Southern Oregon University**

"*Conflict Management and Leadership for Managers* reviews central issues in preparing for and addressing myriad types of conflict that occur in organizational settings. The book covers micro, interpersonal conflicts that occur among supervisors and employees such as giving performance feedback, as well as group-level interactions and macro-level considerations such as designing systems for organizational conflict management that protect employees and organizations from harm and promote organizational justice." **—Jessica Jameson, professor and head, department of communication, North Carolina State University**

Conflict Management and Leadership for Managers

Knowledge, Skills, and Processes to Harness the Power of Rapid Change

Third Edition

Susan S. Raines, PhD

ROWMAN & LITTLEFIELD
Lanham • Boulder • New York • London

Acquisitions Editor: Michael Tan
Assistant Acquisitions Editor: Hollis Peterson
Sales and Marketing Inquiries: textbooks@rowman.com

Published by Rowman & Littlefield
An imprint of The Rowman & Littlefield Publishing Group, Inc.
4501 Forbes Boulevard, Suite 200, Lanham, Maryland 20706
www.rowman.com

86-90 Paul Street, London EC2A 4NE

British Library Cataloguing in Publication Information Available

Library of Congress Cataloging-in-Publication Data

Names: Raines, Susan, author.
Title: Conflict management and leadership for managers : knowledge, skills, and
  processes to harness the power of rapid change / Susan S. Raines, PhD.
Description: Third edition. | Lanham : Rowman & Littlefield, [2024] | Includes
  bibliographical references and index.
Identifiers: LCCN 2023019073 (print) | LCCN 2023019074 (ebook) | ISBN
  9781538177969 (cloth) | ISBN 9781538177976 (paperback) | ISBN 9781538177983
  (epub)
Subjects: LCSH: Conflict management. | Interpersonal relations. | Personnel
  management—Psychological aspects. | Customer relations. | Conflict management—
  Case studies.
Classification: LCC HD42 .R35 2024 (print) | LCC HD42 (ebook) | DDC 658.4/053—
  dc23/eng/20230523
LC record available at https://lccn.loc.gov/2023019073
LC ebook record available at https://lccn.loc.gov/2023019074

To my young people: Kennedy, Thomas, and Will, for keeping me humble, making me laugh, and challenging me to grow every day. Thank you for supporting my inconvenient dreams. Do not waste energy coming up with reasons not to chase your heart's desire. Go forth boldly, in faith that your dreams contain your purpose.

The future belongs to those who believe in the beauty of their dreams.

—Anonymous

Brief Contents

Contents

PART II. THE PREVENTION AND RESOLUTION OF INTERNAL ORGANIZATIONAL CONFLICTS

Boxes, Figures, and Tables

BOXES

FIGURES

TABLES

Acknowledgments

There is a widely held misperception that writing books is a solo endeavor. Instead, writing a book requires collaboration from start to finish. Thank you to those who made this largely new creation possible:

Will S. White: You shared your superior education and intellect with me, which I repeatedly used to improve my training, consulting, writing, parenting, and leadership. "Iron sharpens iron, and one man sharpens another" (Proverbs 27:17). You make me better every day.

Troy Patterson: Thank you for sharing your fortress of solitude and peace that facilitated the deep, undisturbed concentration necessary to finish this book. You are the balmy calm in the storm.

Mark Kerr: Your enthusiasm, encouragement, and support are like water in the desert. Thank you for reinvigorating my creative spirit after COVID.

Sarah E. Rinehart: Your heavy lifting turns coal into diamonds. Thank you for elevating this work.

I also wish to thank the following reviewers, whose thoughtful comments and expertise guided my writing and revisions for the development of this book. As always, any errors and omissions are my own.

Frank Dukes, *University of Virginia*

Wayne A Durr, *Western New England University*

Clare Fowler, *University of Oregon School of Law*

Kenneth H. Fox, *Hamline University*

Jessica Jameson, *North Carolina State University*

Cheryl Jamison, *Tufts University*

Erica Knotts, *Southern Oregon University*

Eren Ozgen, *Florida State University*

Dulce Pena, *La Sierra University*

Elva Resendez, *Purdue University Fort Wayne*

Colin Rule, *Santa Clara University Law School*

Jeffery Shepardson, *Cornell Law School*

Lori Silverman, *Golden Gate University*

Gregory Stephens, *Texas Christian University*

Ann-Marie Vigano

Maria Volpe, *John Jay College of Criminal Justice—City University of New York*

Jody Worley, *University of Oklahoma*

Introduction to the Third Edition

If you don't like change, you're going to like irrelevance even less.

—Eric Shinseki

Change. The second edition of *Conflict Management for Managers (CMM)* was published in 2019. That world is gone. There is no going back. This version is focused on providing current and future leader-managers with the tools they need to respond effectively to the challenges facing their teams and organizations so they can thrive during periods of upheaval in rapidly evolving environments. Leaders, managers, and rank-and-file employees must be nimble in their response to constant change because it isn't slowing down anytime soon: pandemics; the Great Resignation; environmental and climate change; economic disruptions that defy expert predictions; the largest generation gap seen since the 1960s; and the redefinition of social identities and hierarchies based on gender, race, disAbility,* geography, and more. When physical environments rapidly change, animal species adapt or die. Ours is no exception. Will you change fast enough to survive? To thrive? Will your organization? How can you make your work life more humane, fulfilling, and even joyful? As the quote from Eric Shinseki demonstrates, and as this text will instruct, we cannot stop the pace of change. However, we control our reaction to change, or lack thereof. The longer we spend in denial, focused on the way things "should be" rather than the way they are, the less likely we are to come out on top. Change hurts because it causes growing pains. We can do hard things with the right outlook and skills. Let's work together to master both.

By learning how to adapt to a changing world, you will change your world for the better. But how? That is the focus of the chapters to follow. In these pages, you will learn how to cope with change, but more importantly, this text will teach you how to surf the waves of change for the betterment of your organization, your team, your career, and your sanity.

---

*The capitalization of the A puts an intentional focus on an individual's abilities.

REFRAMING THE HUMAN-ORGANIZATION RELATIONSHIP

Organizations need people and people need organizations. Yet, instead of con-sciously focusing on the creation of mutually beneficial, humane, and produc-tive relationships between humans and organizations, there is a tendency to feed the flames of opposition. We create "us-them" dichotomies, implying that our individual and collective success are mutually exclusive. Yet we ARE the organization. Can you think of any other interdependent relationship in which each side consistently puts their needs above the other's? This mindset predicts an inevitably painful ending to the relationship (e.g., resignation, termination, alienation, abandonment, divorce, etc.). Use the strategies in this book to re-frame unhealthy organizational relationships—at all levels. From interpersonal relationships between coworkers, to intergroup interactions between unions and boards, to the curation of the organization's public image, which is key to earn-ing the loyalty of both employees and customers. We must turn from adversarial competition to cooperative collaboration. We cannot succeed without healthy, productive employees working in ethical, innovative, and nimble organizations led by competent, caring managers. I choose not to live and work like that. You?

Like children, organizations are created by well-intentioned people, but then they take on a life and character of their own. Sometimes they reflect well on the founders of the organization, sometimes not so much. Yet, bad organizational decisions are made by human beings, especially leaders of those organizations. This is a conundrum worthy of deep reflection.

The need is great. In tumultuous times, specialists in conflict and collabo-ration are busy. Effective, kind, creative managers are in high demand and add incredible value. They are not found, they are made. In that vein, you may notice that this book is written at the nexus of conflict management and leadership. All managers are conflict managers. The best managers develop their leadership skills to lead teams, organizations, and their careers strategically. The book's unifying theme revolves around the specific behaviors, systems, and (conflict) management habits needed to enhance collaboration and mission achievement, using the skills and processes gained through decades of experience working with organizations of all types, sizes, missions, and cultures.

About the Author and This Book

My PhD in Public Policy (Indiana University) leads me to examine the incen-tives that shape human behavior. In graduate school, mostly through serendip-ity, I began to study mediation and conflict resolution. This led to a long career as a professor of conflict management, but equally importantly, as a mediator and organizational consultant. I've mediated more than 17,000 cases, including matters related to workplace and employment, contract and business, divorce and family, environmental pollution, special education, international trade, and even medical malpractice. As a consultant, I've worked with many U.S. state and federal government agencies, multinational corporations, international financial institutions, chambers of commerce, professional associations, supreme courts, universities, and CEOs seeking to improve their ability to lead and collaborate effectively, especially in response to challenging circumstances. While my preference is to train, equip, and intervene *before* scandals occur, I'm frequently called upon to assist organizations as they seek to respond effectively after damage to their brand name, corporate image, and/or the career trajectory of their leaders. For organizations to learn, recover, and remake their organizational cultures, there must be a willingness to look deeply at things they have *tried not to see*. It requires a willingness to engage in the hard work of changing behaviors to ensure they align with espoused values, even when no one is looking. Unfortunately, some leaders prefer to go through the motions. They give lip service to change, while internally planning to continue business as usual. These leaders will fail, often dragging their teams and companies down with them. It is not "if" they will fail, but "when" and at what cost.

Using this book as a tool kit and guide, you can improve your ability to become a great leader-manager as well as identifying the strengths and weaknesses of others who may seek to lead you.

As George Patton said, "Lead me, follow me, or get the hell out of my way."

A TALE OF TWO MANAGERS

John and Elise are managers who strive to apply the principles and practices of conflict management in their everyday working environments.[1] They come from vastly different organizations, yet both recognize the importance of proactively addressing conflict. By observing them, we can see the techniques from this book at work.

MEET JOHN, DIRECTOR OF THE STATE BUREAU OF RECLAMATION

Almost every day, John dreads coming to work. As soon as he walks through the door to the State Bureau of Reclamation, his administrative assistant practically tackles him and regales him with the emergency du jour. It is these constant interruptions and daily emergencies that keep him from doing his real job, which is shaping and leading his department so that it can fulfill its regulatory mandate in an efficient and productive manner. What are these "daily emergencies"? They tend to fall into one of three categories.

Workplace Problems

Inevitably someone on John's staff calls in sick or announces that he or she is leaving for a position in private industry. Pay for government workers simply has not kept up with recent inflation and wage increases in the private or even the not-for-profit sectors. Staff members are stressed as they often are asked to do the jobs of two or three people, due to the prevalence of empty positions. Newer employees are not adequately mentored, trained, or even onboarded effectively so they often do not stay long. John's employees often compete over scarce resources, blame each other for missed deadlines, or avoid talking altogether even when they are supposed to work on team-based projects. Occasionally employees file union grievances or discrimination complaints with the Equal Employment Opportunity Commission (EEOC). John's organization "wins" the vast majority of these cases, but the paperwork and drama wear him down and cost his agency tens of thousands of dollars per year. He wants his agency to be a fair and pleasant place to work but he struggles to change the existing culture and the resulting disgruntlement. It doesn't feel good to work at the Bureau of Reclamation.

Customer Complaints

John's agency is part of the state's Department of Natural Resources. Specifically, the Bureau of Reclamation issues licenses for coal mines and ensures that all coal mines operating in the state are doing so within the bounds of applicable state and federal environmental regulations. Because the turnover in John's department is high, it is difficult to meet deadlines for issuing permits and conducting mandatory audits. Sometimes his department loses applications altogether or makes mistakes in the paperwork, so the applicant must start the process over again. Every day that a mining company cannot work because of a missing license application means idle and unpaid employees as well as lost tax revenue. Calls come in nearly every day from citizens and companies who believe that the Bureau is not doing its job quickly enough. When the call comes from a state legislator's office, then John knows things have really gotten bad. Honestly, if he cannot turn around his agency, John might leave too. He cares deeply about the mission, but the stress is not healthy for him or his family life.

Regulatory Challenges

On really bad days, one of the mining companies will be in the news for some environmental mess they created or other violation of the state or federal laws that John's agency is supposed to enforce. The alleged violator will likely feign ignorance of the broken rule or law and try to avoid taking responsibility for the damage caused. The violator's legal counsel might threaten to sue the agency. Lawsuits are inevitable and unavoidable. If John does his job right, then the corporations he regulates want to sue him for his overzealous enforcement of state and federal mining laws. If he backs off a bit, then citizens' groups sue him for not adequately enforcing the laws. It is a no-win situation. No wonder turnover and absenteeism are so high.

Something Has to Give

John has passion for the mission of his organization, and he views himself as a committed public servant with good people skills who knows the mining industry inside and out. This should be the perfect job for him. So why is it that the bureau has not improved since he assumed command six months ago? John got this job by sharing some of his ideas for improvement with the agency's director, who quickly recognized John's passion and competence. So far, none of those ideas have been implemented due to the nonstop crisis management style in which the Bureau seems to function. How can John focus on "fire prevention" when he is so busy "putting out fires" every day?

MEET ELISE, FOUNDER AND CEO OF MAIN STREET BAKERIES

Elise started with a good idea: provide local, organic, fresh foods to people in a café-bookstore atmosphere. Customers buy freshly prepared foods, healthy groceries, and gourmet items; get one-on-one consultations from certified nutritionists; and listen to guest speakers on various topics. Her stores have become gathering places for the communities in which they operate. Her company is widely reputed to be environmentally friendly and socially conscious, a reputation gained through innovations in environmental management and significant charitable giving. She started in the early 1980s in California and has ridden the green wave into the 21st century by expanding from one shop to 425 stores throughout the United States and Canada. Elise plans to expand into European markets next year if she can overcome supply chain problems. Her company is consistently rated as one of the best places to work by *Fortune* magazine and *Working Mother* magazine. *Consumer Reports* rates Main Street Bakeries as having the highest customer satisfaction of any grocery store chain. Unfortunately, this sparkling image has recently been tarnished by a high-profile manager accused of serial bullying and harassment.

Managing the Chaos

From supply-chain issues to turnover during the Great Resignation, to helping employees and managers maintain healthy work-life balance, Elise is tired. Every day she arrives at work with a long to-do list, only to find that the crisis du jour interferes with her ability to get the work done and meet important deadlines. She has even thought of selling the business, but in the end, she loves this work. Or at least she used to love it and wants to do so again. Elise needs help to avoid burnout and run a growing, thriving business that delivers value to both its customers and its employees. But how can she survive in the midst of constant change and chaos?

★　★　★

Throughout this book we will return to John and Elise to learn how they grapple with the challenges of leading teams and organizations through change in ways that promote their organizational missions and their personal sanity. We will watch John as he transforms his work group into one that is less riddled with unproductive conflict and more successful at accomplishing its regulatory mission despite the ever-present shortage of resources common to public agencies. By implementing the processes, strategies, and techniques in this book, John, Elise, and you will learn the skills necessary to be proactive conflict managers even in chaotic times.

HOW TO USE THIS BOOK

You are reading this book because you are, or you hope to become, a leader who productively manages conflict to the benefit of your organization, your career, and—let's face it—your sanity. Whether you acknowledge it or not, all managers are conflict managers. Whether you work in the private, public, or nonprofit sector, you are likely to spend most of your day dealing with conflicts between employees; disputes with clients, suppliers, or vendors; or relationships with myriad regulatory agencies. Until you positively change the culture of your team, you will repeatedly face the same problems with disappointing outcomes.

The question is not *if* managers deal with conflict but *how* managers deal with conflict. Those who do not recognize it, analyze it, and design better methods for conflict prevention and resolution end up like John at the Bureau of Reclamation (but there is still hope for John, so don't quit reading now). The goal is to become adept at fostering and facilitating collaboration within your work teams and organizations to proactively avoid destructive conflict and harness the power of constructive change.

Conflict is not inherently negative. It is how we handle conflict that makes it a positive or negative force for our relationships, our careers, our families, and our organizations. Don't you want to handle conflict in ways that improve, rather than harm, you and others? Lean into the positive power for change inherent in conflict.

This book will provide readers with a knowledge base and a set of skill-building opportunities so they can reclaim their time and make their workplaces enjoyable, productive, mutually supportive, and a place where people want to work. Even in difficult economic times, during crises, scandals, or recessions, there will always be managers who use these challenges as opportunities to shine. It is not the good times that test or showcase your skills as a leader-manager.

Each chapter includes exercises designed to allow you to practice these skills in your current work environment, while setting goals for continual improvement. The text can be read as part of a course or group-based training, or it can be used by individual managers seeking to improve their skills and work lives.

You need not be the CEO, like Elise, to make changes within your own work unit, as we will see from John's example. Managers at any level can positively impact their work teams and improve mission achievement. The costs of unproductive conflict are too high to remain unaddressed. Look at your most successful competitors and you are likely to find that they have put into place systems and people who manage conflict and collaboration well. Mission achievement requires trust, accountability, and commitment within teams. It also requires workplaces that feel affirming, welcoming, and joyful. Let's remake our workplaces together.

Public-Sector Managers

You may be thinking, "OK, but the public-sector work environment is nothing like the private sector." Although differences exist, managers across sectors have more in common than not. They need to be attentive to the organization's cultural norms, keep customers and stakeholders in powerful positions satisfied, solve problems efficiently, design and use tools to track progress toward goals, give and receive feedback effectively, lead productive meetings, coach and mentor employees, and strategically foster a collaborative team environment. Managers in large, unionized corporations may have more in common with public-sector managers than they have in common with small businesses. And yes, public-sector managers sometimes face problems or environments that are more rule-bound and more open to public scrutiny, and have more accountability than some private-sector managers.

Regulatory agencies are usually a part of the executive branch of the government at the federal or state level, and they have statutory authority to perform their functions with oversight from the legislative branch. Regulatory authorities are commonly set up to enforce standards and safety, regulate commerce, and oversee public goods such as national defense or clean air. Regulatory agencies deal in the area of administrative law—regulation or rulemaking. A **public good** is something that, by its nature, is supplied either to all people or to none, regardless of whether each individual has paid his or her fair share of that good. For example, national defense, clean air, roads, and libraries are all public goods: if they exist for anyone, then they exist for everyone. The problem with public goods is that many people try to gain the benefit of the goods without paying for them (via taxes, usually). Also, because they are owned by everyone and no one, they may not be adequately supplied or protected without governmental action.

It is undeniable that government workers (i.e., public-sector employees) face challenges that are slightly different from those working in commercial enterprises (i.e., private-sector employees) or for nonprofit organizations. For an organization to operate efficiently, its managers need to develop strategies and skills for collaboratively managing relationships with overlapping levels of regulatory agencies as well as with myriad vendors, suppliers, and others within their supply chains. This book will help you map out those necessary relationships for the success of your unit, your organization, and ultimately your career, regardless of the size or type of your organization.

Private-Sector Managers

The private sector is far from monolithic. Managers in small companies face challenges at a different scope and level than managers in Fortune 500 organizations. Small companies are nimbler and more open to changing as needed, whereas large ones seem slow to respond to rapidly changing environments we see post 2020. Examples throughout the book are used to illustrate the ways in which the techniques and ideas may be applied in varying contexts—from huge U.S.-based airlines to a family-owned restaurant or a dentist in private practice. Most of the material presented in this book can be applied to businesses of all sizes but the relative costs of implementation for some interventions may be proportionately higher in small organizations. When this is the case, it will be noted and ideas for overcoming or reducing costs will be discussed.

Nonprofit-Sector Managers

Nonprofits often combine the biggest challenges from the other two sectors. Like the private sector, nonprofits can be as small as a one-employee shop or as large as Blue Cross Blue Shield Association, with tens of thousands of employees across the United States. Similar to the private sector, nonprofits generally must find streams of revenue to support their work, often through grants, government contracts, and fundraising events. The persistent state of budgetary uncertainty is a source of stress among employees and can lead to burnout and departure for one of the other two sectors. Nonprofits are generally involved with supplying public goods or private goods for which the market is not well suited, such as health care for the poor, emergency housing, humanitarian relief, transportation for the disabled or elderly. The importance of the mission means that most nonprofit employees care deeply about those served by their organization, yet employees may disagree strongly about the best way to serve their clientele. Nonprofits must keep their administrative costs down and their brand name sparkling if they are to compete for scarce funds—thereby increasing the importance of intra-office collaboration and the need to reduce the costs of conflict. Case studies and illustrations from the nonprofit sector are used throughout the book to show how collaboration and conflict management can be applied in these challenging and diverse environments.

Not a Manager Yet?

What if you are not a manager yet? The material contained in this book will empower you to attain and display critical leadership and management skills to get you noticed, promoted, and into the roles you seek. You will learn how to take ownership of your performance, ways to motivate those around you to reach their highest potential, and how to create a working environment that is happy and healthy for yourself and your coworkers.

If you are reading this book as part of a university course, you will likely have opportunities to discuss and apply the skills and concepts with your classmates. If you are reading the book on your own, I encourage you to seek out one or more managers within your company or outside it in order to fully benefit from the skill-building exercises, role-plays, surveys, discussion questions, and goal setting tasks supplied at the end of each chapter. Old habits die hard, and practicing your new skill set will improve your ability to transfer these practices from the book and classroom into the boardroom and break room.

ORGANIZATION OF THE BOOK

The book is organized into three parts. The first part introduces the primary knowledge, skills, and processes of conflict management on which the rest of the book depends. This edition of *CMM* focuses more deeply on the incredible breakthroughs from neuroscience that have shed light on practical strategies for building collaborative, high-impact teams and fun, affirming workplaces where people feel a sense of belonging and efficacy. This edition also delves deeper into issues of managing conflict across generations.

Part II examines sources of conflict internal to an organization, such as employment disputes, turnover, dysfunctions within a team, working with union leaders, the creation of a strong organizational culture, and the common skills and practices used by ombudsmen at work. This edition focuses on addressing the roots of dysfunctional organizational cultures that give rise to negative behaviors including harassment, bullying, discrimination, disengagement, litigation, brand damage, and scandals. These are the sources of conflict that eat up managers' days, leaving them less time to build their businesses, respond to customers, and mentor their employees. A house divided will not stand.

Part III examines conflicts external to an organization, meaning those involving clients, customers, patients, vendors, and regulators. Additionally, this part provides skill-building and process knowledge used to facilitate effective meetings and large-group collaboration such as staff and board meetings as well as regulatory negotiation.

Each chapter begins with a fictional illustration of the challenges facing two very different organizations—the Bureau of Reclamation, headed by John, and Main Street Bakeries, led by Elise. These examples are used to illustrate common sources of conflict faced by managers and then apply the concepts and tools from each chapter. The learning objectives at the beginning of each chapter serve to outline the concepts and skills covered. You may wish to come back to these at the end of each chapter to evaluate the extent to which the learning objectives have been achieved.

Note that "he/she/they" will be used alternatively throughout the book. The terms "organization," "corporation," "agency," and "company" will be used throughout, even though some readers will work in the for-profit, not-for-profit, or public sectors.

LESSONS OF THE GREAT RESIGNATION: GENERATIONAL DIFFERENCES IN TURNOVER AND WORKPLACE EXPECTATIONS

The **Great Resignation** is an economic trend in which employees have voluntarily resigned from their jobs en masse, beginning in early 2021 in the wake of the COVID-19 pandemic. Among the most cited reasons for resigning include wage stagnation amid rising cost of living, limited opportunities for career advancement, hostile work environments, lack of benefits, inflexible remote-work policies, and long-lasting job dissatisfaction. The most likely to quit have been workers in hospitality, health care, and education.[2] While some elements of employee turnover are due to macroeconomic forces, such as variations in the unemployment rate, great managers make all the difference when it comes to turnover and productivity. The good news is that your organization and its competitors face the same macroeconomic conditions. How you choose to respond to those conditions will determine your brand as a manager and your company's image, more broadly. The key is to focus on what you can control. When it is easy to find a "better" job, then we can expect higher rates of employee turnover. "Better" includes obvious factors such as higher pay, comprehensive health and retirement benefits, and flexible work arrangements. Recent research indicates employees are likely to seek out or stay put in organizations with healthy organizational cultures as reflected in their approaches to issues like employee empowerment versus micromanaging, clear paths for career advancement, the ability to devote time to "passion projects," opportunities for community engagement and volunteering, the provision of developmental coaching, and the overall warmth and inclusivity of the working environment (Harrell & Barbato, 2018; Project Oxygen, Google). As a manager, and as an organization, what are you doing to become a "destination employer" and/or a unit manager for whom everyone wants to work?

As unemployment rates swing high or low over time, they create generation-wide cohort impacts that become "sticky," meaning they linger even when the employment rate changes. For example, Generation X (people born approximately 1965–1980) came of age during repeated periods of recession. This left them more hesitant to leave a stable employment situation than subsequent generations. It also made them vulnerable to abusive, poor managers. They had less negotiating power when it came to issues like flexible working hours and parental leave. Then their children, the millennial generation (born approximately between 1981 and 1996), came of age during the Great Recession, which technically occurred between 2007 to 2009, but whose impacts lingered for many years. This generation watched their educated, hardworking parents lose their jobs, their savings, their housing, and often their identities. They realized that putting too much of their identities and passions into their work lives made them highly vulnerable, not only economically but also in terms of their mental and relational health. As a result, millennials have pursued greater work-life balance, flexibility, and organizational justice, often to the chagrin and benefit of all other generations in the workplace. Gen Z (born after 1997) has been deeply influenced by the COVID-19 pandemic and the resulting isolation caused by remote study and work. While technologically fluent and flexible, they often prefer face-to-face, collaborative working environments that feel warm, inclusive, and collaborative. They are also the most diverse generation yet. Even individuals from traditionally empowered groups show a preference for inclusive and equitable workplaces in which everyone can express their authentic identities without fear of reprisal or ostracism. They expect gender, racial, and generational equity in which all employees feel empowered to use leave as needed to maintain healthy, happy families. They expect and appreciate regular constructive feedback and developmental coaching that fuels their ability to consistently improve their performance (Birt, Herrity & Esparza, 2022). They expect and embrace the never-ending nature of change and the opportunities for growth inherent therein. They are the least comfortable with authoritarian management styles, which conflicts with their entrepreneurial spirits. Instead, they appreciate facilitative managers who empower them rather than seeking to assert control. Rather than treating employees the same across generations or situations, great managers can use these differences to maximize individual and team performance.

These generational differences are good news for the readers of this text. Conflict comes from unmet expectations. Each generation, and every individual, has unique expectations and needs in respect to their working environments. By getting to know your employees individually and collectively, superior managers can foster the conditions necessary to reduce unproductive conflict while harnessing the positive power of change to reduce turnover and achieve a competitive advantage. Even better, your daily work environment will feel affirming, warm, and engaging.

CALCULATING THE COST OF CONFLICT: KNOWLEDGE IS POWER

A study by Bass and Bass found that "the typical manager may spend 25% of his time dealing with conflicts" (2009, p. 319). It is likely that this number is underestimated because many people do not accurately recognize or label conflict when it occurs. A different study found that conflict takes about 42% of the average manager's day (Watson & Hoffman, 1996) and saw Fortune 500 executives devoting 20% of their time explicitly to litigation. Unfortunately, these statistics are not trending in a positive direction. In actuality, the amount of time a manager spends dealing with conflict depends on the sector, their level within the organization, and the amount of effort they put toward conflict prevention and early resolution. Leaders who discuss and reach shared expectations within their teams simply have less unproductive conflict and the conflicts that inevitably arise are handled in ways that enhance rather than hurt interpersonal relationships and mission achievement. Positive organizational cultures yield fewer destructive conflicts (see Chapter 6). The costs of conflict include the obvious expenses of legal fees and settlements but also include the costs of lost customers, employee turnover, and damage to the reputation of the organization and the brand image.

Alternative dispute resolution (ADR) refers to a host of processes that serve as alternatives to costly adversarial litigation, including mediation, arbitration, peer review, the use of an ombudsman, and others. According to Europe's leading ADR organization, conflicts cost British corporations more than 33 billion pounds per year (US$52 million). To give some perspective, if this sum were a country, it would be the fifty-seventh largest economy in the world. Of this amount, only about 22% comes from legal fees, with 78% stemming from lost business due to customer dissatisfaction (Amble, 2006).

Numerous studies detail the costs of high employee turnover. A survey by Baril (2021) found that 37% of respondents witnessed an employee leave due to unresolved conflict. What's worse is that the average conflict went unresolved for many months, with 16% lasting a year or more. This means organizational leaders had the chance to proactively address the conflict but did not do so. Conflict avoidance is the hallmark of ineffective leaders and dysfunctional teams. According to a study by the Pew Research Center in March of 2022, about one-fifth of employees left one or more jobs voluntarily in 2021 (Parker & Horowitz, 2022). The most common complaints were low pay (63%), no opportunities for advancement (63%), and feeling disrespected at work (57%). While many managers lack the authority to give pay raises, especially in the public sector, they can impact their team's organizational culture to ensure an environment in which people feel welcomed, respected, and connected to the mission. They can also discuss opportunities for employees to gain new skills and advance within their organization. The majority of employees who quit a job in 2021 reported they found a higher-paying job, with more opportunities for advancement, and felt more respected (Parker & Horowitz, 2022). That means some organizations and some managers *are* finding ways to use the labor market to their advantage by being a destination employer, meaning they have become a place where people want to work. Great managers focus on what they can control (e.g., the culture in their teams and their willingness to support and mentor employees) rather than what they cannot control (e.g., the broader economy, supply chain challenges).

Shockingly, four in ten employees stated they quit a job in part because they were forced to work too many hours. Pause to ponder this for a minute: wouldn't it make sense to keep a valued, experienced employee for 30–40 hours per week rather than search for a new employee who will need training while expecting them to work 40+ hours per week? At the heart of it, these are relationships. To make a relationship work for each party, negotiation and communication must occur regularly to ensure that each side is getting its core needs met to the greatest extent possible. It appears that many managers and leaders are using an outdated understanding of the employment landscape in which all the power resides with the employer, who can dictate the terms of the relationship. The first step to reducing turnover is to change this outdated perspective from a one-way relationship to a two-way partnership. People need organizations and organizations need people.

The costs of hiring and training a new employee generally fall between 75% and 150% of the employee's annual salary. The higher the specialty (e.g., surgeon versus fast food worker), then the higher the costs to hire and train new employees. Let's do the math for a moment: for an organization with 100 employees with a relatively low turnover rate of 15% per year and an average salary of $50,000, this turnover rate means costs of $562,000 to $1,125,000 every year! If that much money could be saved by mechanizing or changing a manufacturing process, most managers would jump at the chance to reap this much in savings. Unlike changes to the assembly line or cutting back on technology purchases, many managers feel helpless to reduce employee turnover, improve morale, or change company culture. The good news is these can be changed and at relatively low cost. The higher the turnover rate, the greater the opportunity to make visible, impactful changes.

Prior to 2020, many managers viewed employee turnover as inevitable, like the weather—something that had to be endured because it could not be changed. Since the supply of workers was relatively plentiful for many fields, it seemed to be simply a cost of doing business. Since 2020, managers have realized that employee disengagement and turnover is an epidemic that threatens mission achievement, reflects poorly upon managers, and can even lead to business closures. **Employee engagement** reflects the extent to which employees are fully committed to furthering the organization and its mission. Disengaged employees may be present at work (remotely or in person) without contributing much or worse yet, they may be sowing the seeds of discontent among their coworkers or actively sabotaging the work of the organization or its reputation. Organiza-

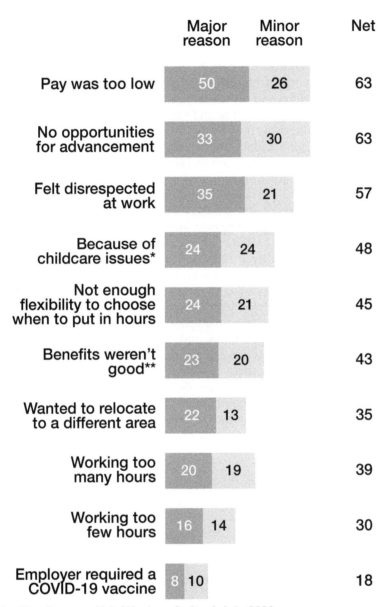

	Major reason	Minor reason	Net
Pay was too low	50	26	63
No opportunities for advancement	33	30	63
Felt disrespected at work	35	21	57
Because of childcare issues*	24	24	48
Not enough flexibility to choose when to put in hours	24	21	45
Benefits weren't good**	23	20	43
Wanted to relocate to a different area	22	13	35
Working too many hours	20	19	39
Working too few hours	16	14	30
Employer required a COVID-19 vaccine	8	10	18

Figure 1.1. Top Reasons U.S. Workers Left a Job in 2021

Note: Figures may not add to subtotals due to rounding.
*Among those with children younger than 18 living in the household.
**Question provided health insurance and paid time off as examples.
Survey of U.S. adults conducted Feb. 7–13, 2022. Data from "Majority of workers who quit a job in 2021 cite low pay, no opportunities for advancement, feeling disrespected," by K. Parker & J. M. Horowitz, 2022, Pew Research Center (https://www.pewresearch.org/fact-tank/2022/03/09/majority-of-workers-who-quit-a-job-in-2021-cite-low-pay-no-opportunities-for-advancement-feeling-disrespected/). Copyright 2021 by Pew Research Center.

tions that have high rates of employee turnover also have related problems with absenteeism, low employee commitment to the organization and its mission, employee tardiness, and overall low worker productivity (Allen, 2008). What's worse is that turnover is like a virus: once key employees or managers leave or announce their intent to leave, others begin searching for new opportunities in more stable environments, often resulting in a wave of resignations.

Yet some organizations and some managers have realized that managing conflict is crucial to retaining employees and thriving as an organization. A growing body of research links high turnover rates to shortfalls in organizational performance and low customer satisfaction. Interestingly, workers under 30 years old are much more likely to quit their job in favor of another one. For 2021, 37% of those under 30 years old quit their job compared to 9% for workers in their 50s (Parker & Horowitz, 2022). In a tight labor market, this means employers are competing for scarce workers and proactively addressing conflict will be key to their ability to attract and retain the best workers.

In a tight budget climate, when raises are hard to dole out, conflict-savvy managers can increase employee retention and productivity gains. This book will examine thoroughly the ways in which managers, owners, and employees can create the kind of workplace where people feel valued, they enjoy their work, and conflicts that inevitably arise from time to time are handled smoothly, collaboratively, and result in strengthened rather than weakened relationships.

You can't have happy customers and high mission achievement unless you have happy employees. It isn't possible. Companies with high levels of employee satisfaction consistently produce high levels of customer or client satisfaction (Zondiros, Konstantopoulos & Tomaras, 2007). In addition to lost productivity at work and high employee turnover, an organization's reputation and brand name suffer due to litigation over unresolved conflicts. A study in the *Journal of Financial Economics* (Baghat, Brickley & Coles, 1994) showed

BOX I.1. SPOTLIGHT: TURNOVER IS TOUGHER ON SMALL ORGANIZATIONS

The loss of key employees can have a particularly damaging impact on small organizations:

Departing workers are more likely to be the only ones possessing a particular skill or knowledge set.

A small company's culture suffers a more serious blow when an essential person leaves.

There is a smaller internal pool of workers to cover the lost employee's work and provide a replacement.

The organization may have fewer resources available to cover replacement costs.

Source: Allen (2008, p. 5).

that the stock value of large firms drops an average of 1% on the announcement of a lawsuit against the company whereas the stock of the plaintiff's company does not increase at all. Stock prices tend to rebound when an out-of-court settlement is announced. One percent may seem small but for the companies analyzed in this study the overall drop in stock value was equal to $21 million. From Facebook's (Meta's) data breach, to Uber's handsy CEO, to Nike's sweatshops and child labor, corporate scandals that could have been avoided have resulted in millions of dollars of losses in stock value, brand image, and employee commitment with long-lasting reductions in consumer trust. This is a failure to manage conflict productively.

According to the Centre for Effective Dispute Resolution (CEDR), Europe's largest dispute resolution organization, most managers state they have not been adequately trained to handle the conflicts they encounter. In CEDR's survey of conflict among managers, more than one-third of managers claimed they would rather jump from a plane in a parachute for the first time than address a problem at work! The desire to avoid confronting problems results in wasted opportunities for improved performance on the part of employees and the entire company, but apparently it bodes well for the parachute business. Managers who are conflict avoidant rarely rise above low-to-midlevel positions. By definition, it is the job of managers to solve problems, rather than pretend they do not exist.

Gerzon (2006), a leadership researcher, emphasizes that "leading through conflict involves facing differences honestly and creatively, understanding their full complexity and scope, and enabling those involved to move beyond the powerful, primordial responses to difference that result in an 'us versus them' mentality. It requires capacities that many leaders have never developed, bringing to bear both personal and professional skills that turn serious conflicts into rewarding opportunities for collaboration and innovation" (p. 4). Conflict can be positive or negative, depending on how it is handled. By handling conflict efficiently, you can harness its creative power for positive change and avoid the negative elements that give it a bad reputation.

Collaboration and collaborative management are evolving as the dominant forms of leadership, but we are not there yet. With an educated, creative, and capable workforce, dictatorial, oppressive leaders are increasingly seen as dinosaurs from the era of factory-style production. With an economy focused on knowledge-creation and service industries, management styles must change to reflect the evolving nature of work itself. Barbara Gray (1989) has been studying methods for superior collaboration for decades and distills it down to four distinct parts:

- Interdependent stakeholders (i.e., those affected by a decision)
- The ability to constructively address differences
- Joint ownership of decisions
- Collective responsibility for the future of the partnership

Collaboration is different from cooperation or coordination because these "two terms do not capture the dynamic, evolutionary nature of collaboration. **Collaboration** from this perspective is best examined as a dynamic or emergent process rather than as a static condition" (O'Leary & Blomgren Bingham, 2009, p. 5).

Conflict management (CM) refers to the systematic prevention of unproductive conflict while proactively addressing those conflicts that cannot be prevented. Every workplace has existing conflict management methods, but these methods may have developed in an ad hoc fashion without explicit discussion. As a result, the existing procedures or habits may need to be examined and (re)designed for maximal utility and user satisfaction. According to Adler and Fisher (2007), two visionaries in the field of conflict management, "By necessity, leaders must be many things: strategists, warriors, moralists, peacemakers, artisans, technicians, managers, and more. Sometimes a leader becomes an 'undercover mediator' within his organization or at the negotiating table" (p. 21).

Nonprofit organizations and government agencies are not immune from the high costs of conflict mentioned already, including costs related to employee turnover problems and dissatisfied clients, customers, and citizens.

Unproductive conflicts can result in costly and unpleasant relationships between companies and regulatory agencies such as the Department of Labor, the Occupational Safety and Health Administration (OSHA), and so on. But you do not have to take my word for it. There are nearly as many useful examples of organizations that have turned things around by making changes to their management of conflict and corporate cultures. Sadly, there are also nearly limitless cautionary tales arising from organizations that failed to act to prevent scandalous behavior from managers and leaders or to hold them fully accountable once those problems become undeniable: from Uber to Papa John's, Wells Fargo, and more. For better or for worse, specialists in collaboration and conflict, and managers versed in these skills and processes, are finding themselves incredibly in demand. This is especially true in the rapidly changing corporate landscape since 2020.

Through the systematic analysis of the sources and types of disputes, organizations can engage in a process called **dispute system design (DSD)**. DSD is a process for assisting an organization to develop a structure for handling a series of similar, recurring, or anticipated disputes more effectively. These can be internal employment disputes or disputes with external conflicts with clients, customers, or regulators (e.g., EEOC complaints within a federal agency or environmental enforcement cases with polluters). Chapter 9 will help you with the process of assessing the disputes facing your organization and then designing processes to prevent and limit the costs from those disputes.

CONCLUSION

The first step to solving any problem is admitting it exists. The "good" news is that every company and every team can improve in the ability to proactively identify and solve problems if they are willing to be introspective and take stock of what is working and what isn't. In fact, that is what often separates the leaders of the pack from the laggards. After reading and practicing the skills and processes contained herein, you can become an expert conflict manager. This will maximize collaboration and mission achievement. The next step is the hardest one: turning knowledge into action. Managers skilled in the art and science of collaborative problem-solving bring the specific skills of mediation, facilitation, process design, and visionary leadership to their work teams and organizations. They become more adept at spotting bias and rationalization, which promotes negative corporate cultures and behaviors. Dynamic, successful leader-managers of today and tomorrow will act as catalysts for positive change and adaptation to the rapidly evolving human and natural environments that require intentional collaboration more than ever before. Competent, inspiring managers draw on the individual strengths of team members and foster firm commitment to a shared mission, accomplished through supportive, humane, energizing work environments. I look forward to leading you through this journey to reshape your team, organization, career, and world.

While this quote has often been attributed to Ghandi, many famous leaders have encouraged us to "Be the change you wish to see in the world."

KEY TERMS

alternative dispute resolution (ADR)   employee engagement
collaboration   Great Resignation
conflict management (CM)   public good
dispute system design (DSD)   regulatory agencies

DISCUSSION QUESTIONS

1. What are the sources of employee turnover in your organization? What difference can a manager make in reducing turnover and increasing employee engagement?
2. What are the current methods for addressing conflicts with customers and employees in an organization with which you are familiar? How satisfied are the users of those processes from what you can tell?
3. How collaborative is your organization? Why? How might it benefit from a more collaborative approach?
4. Describe and discuss the mindset, habits, traits, or behaviors of someone most likely to benefit from the contents of this book. What might make someone resistant to this approach to management and leadership? What can be done to foster openness to trying new approaches to old problems (or to new problems, for that matter)?

EXERCISES

1. Analyze the conflict management system(s) within your current or past work environment. How are workplace disputes prevented, tracked, and managed? What about disputes with clients or customers? Does the current system of tracking and analyzing disputes provide the information needed

to identify the root causes of problems? Is the information about recurring problems getting to the people who are able to offer solutions? How could the mechanisms or culture of introspection and analysis of disputes be improved in an organization with which you interact. Remember, that could be a civic or religious group, your workplace, your health-care provider or insurance company, your family, your homeowners' association, or any other organization.

2. How much of your day is spent dealing with disputes with employees or customers? Review the past 2–3 days in your life. What conflicts or problems arose and how much time, money, relationship credit or emotional energy did they take from you or give back to you? Remember, conflict can make us grow stronger if we handle it correctly. Can you estimate the costs of unproductive disputing for your organization or your team?

NOTES

1. These narratives are based on an amalgamation of actual managers at real organizations and are not based on any one individual or organization.

2. Adapted from Wikipedia, December 23, 2022. https://en.wikipedia.org/wiki/Great_Resignation

PART I

BASIC CONFLICT MANAGEMENT KNOWLEDGE AND SKILLS

I

Manager Know Thyself

The Traits and Behaviors of Great Conflict Managers

Knowing yourself is the beginning of all wisdom.

—Aristotle

Introspection is required for personal and professional growth, as Aristotle aptly points out. Great leaders and managers are constantly learning new skills, inviting feedback, and setting goals for improvement. Using the tools and information in this chapter, you will assess your current managerial approach and skills, set goals for growth, and learn better ways to manage and lead others to achieve their peak performance. After completing the chapter, revisit these learning objectives to ensure you met them.

Learning Objectives

- List and describe the behaviors and personality traits most associated with managerial excellence.
- Identify and describe five common responses to conflict and the pros and cons of each response.
- Analyze the costs and benefits of your own habits when responding to conflict.
- Apply your knowledge of conflict styles to better communicate at work with those whose conflict styles differ from yours.
- Demonstrate active listening skills and know when to employ them.
- Identify your management style on the continuum from permissive to authoritarian and set goals for improvement.
- Analyze and demonstrate your emotional intelligence skills to avoid burnout and improve the performance of yourself and your team.

RESPONDING TO CONFLICT AT THE BUREAU OF RECLAMATION

John is not happy with his administrative assistant, Maria. On the days when John needs her most, she calls in "sick." Today, John is scheduled to begin holding one-one-one meetings required for staff performance reviews. This week, he is supposed to meet with each of his 20 employees to share his ratings of their performance over the past year, while still getting his other work done. Any deficiencies in performance must be discussed, and, unfortunately, there are plenty of deficiencies. Although John has not administered performance reviews at this agency before, he knows that everyone dreads this experience. Because Maria is not here, John will have to find all the files himself, answer calls during the meetings with staff members, and try to keep on schedule without the benefit of his assistant who should strategically "buzz" him to let him know when his next appointment has arrived. Maria left a message on John's answering machine saying that she feels that helping him manage the review process is "above her pay grade." She said that she is happy to work on other tasks but won't participate in the review-management process. While her performance is unacceptable, she has not used more sick leave than she has available and firing her would be an uphill battle for two reasons: first, in this labor market state salaries have not kept pace with the private sector and replacing her would be quite difficult; second, while John plans to document this behavior, Maria's previous supervisor did not document any performance issues so there is no "paper trail" that shows a pattern of documented underperformance. John is wondering what he should do about this problem, and then it hits him: he will send out an email to his staff, including Maria, telling them that the performance reviews are being postponed until Maria is feeling better. Sending out this email will buy him at least another day or two to get his own work done (e.g., creating schedules, ordering supplies, and publishing ads for new positions) before getting sidetracked with the drama that will likely result from the performance reviews and from dealing with Maria. Hopefully she will take the hint and "get over herself."

TRAITS AND BEHAVIORS OF HIGH-PERFORMING MANAGERS

Managers are not great at knowing their own strengths and weaknesses. In fact, the least effective managers are likely to vastly overrate their own performance due to something called the **Dunning-Kruger effect**, which is a cognitive bias that leads people to wrongly overrate their competence in a specific area (Psychology Today, 2022). Researchers from Cornell University, David Dunning and Justin Kruger, found that "Those who performed in the bottom quartile rated their skills far above average. For example, those in the 12th percentile self-rated their expertise to be, on average, in the 62nd percentile" (Psychology Today, 2022). Our psychological self-defense mechanisms make it difficult for us to accurately gauge our skills, especially as leaders or managers.

As Robert Hughes notes: "The greater the artist, the greater the doubt. Perfect confidence is granted to the less talented as a consolation prize" (1996). Introspection is a key trait of great managers. Introspection leads us to be open to the idea that we always have room to grow and improve. It keeps us humble and spurs us to invite feedback from those around us. Overconfidence results in less openness to feedback. Why would you need feedback when you already know everything? Knowing about the Dunning-Kruger effect is important in your quest to learn and grow as a manager. As a positive side note, people will also like you better. While it isn't the job of a manager to make friends at work, people who like you are more willing to follow your direction because they will rate your character and competence higher.

What is the cure or work-around to ensure you do not fall prey to the Dunning-Kruger effect? Be your own "devil's advocate" by questioning what you know and how you know it. Seek out the expertise of others and invite them to point out your blind spots. Have you heard the same criticism or feedback multiple times from different people? Analyze that feedback to determine how you might use it to grow, even when it is painful. These are growing pains and your best strategy is to reframe them as opportunities for improvement. Remember, in most cases, overconfidence is a hallmark of poor managers. Humility, openness to feedback, introspection, and a willingness to tackle bad habits or hard challenges will result in your ultimate success as a manager and as a human being. Stanford psychologist Dr. Carol Dweck calls this a "growth mindset."

> Why waste time proving over and over how great you are, when you could be getting better? Why hide deficiencies instead of overcoming them? Why look for friends or partners who will just shore up your self-esteem instead of ones who will also challenge you to grow? And why seek out the tried and true, instead of experiences that will stretch you? The passion for stretching yourself and sticking to it, even (or especially) when it's not going well, is the hallmark of the growth mindset. This is the mindset that allows people to thrive during some of the most challenging times in their lives. (Dweck, 2007)

A **growth mindset** is the belief that all people can learn and grow, rather than having static potential. This sounds simple enough, but there are key factors that predict one's likeliness of continued growth and skill mastery: persistence, viewing failures as learning opportunities, the habit of giving and requesting constructive criticism, a positive attitude, and setting specific goals for growth that allow one to track progress (Dweck, 2007). In some ways, promoting one's own growth mindset is itself a method of counteracting the Dunning-Kruger effect.

The past few years have taught us that we must be open, even thirsty, to acquire new knowledge, skills, and even new conceptualizations of the problems that face us as leaders and managers because the challenges keep changing. It makes me chuckle, internally of course, when I work with a manager who says, "But that is how we have always done it" or "That is not the way we do things here." The theme for this edition revolves around the need to adapt to rapidly changing environments. That means we must be open to the idea that we must constantly learn, grow, and adapt in order to thrive in times of rapid change. That is what will separate leaders and managers who lead high-performing teams while maintaining their own sanity, health, and work-life balance.

MANAGERS AND LEADERS

This is a good time to introduce the difference between **leaders** and **managers**. **Leaders** set the strategic direction, curate the culture, fill key positions on the executive team, forge and attend to the relationships necessary for current and future success, and spot opportunities for innovative change. Managers implement the decisions made by leaders and attend to the day-to-day running of the organization. Both leaders and managers need to set goals and measure progress toward them in their own careers, teams, and organizations, yet leaders focus more time on crafting and communicating their vision for the organization. Both need to motivate others to achieve their highest performance and inspire them by connecting each employee's contribution to the accomplishment of the mission. Many academics differentiate the role of leaders and managers by defining leaders as agents of change while managers maintain the status quo (Arruda, 2016). That is outdated thinking. Nimble, culturally competent, innovative organizations require managers to implement strategic decisions made by leaders and to measure the performance of individuals and teams. Yet modern managers are increasingly expected to take on leadership roles in their team: to motivate and coach employees, to originate and share product and process innovations, to manage conflict and solve problems effectively, and to build relationships across the organization as needed to maximize both unit and organizational success, and to enhance employee engagement. The best managers inspire and develop employees. They share ideas and concerns up the chain of command, with the understanding that leaders may see things differently. Managers with leadership skills create warm, joyful, innovative, stable, and productive teams. Managers with leadership skills stand out and move up. Therefore, this text seeks to reenvision the role of managers. While leaders create and communicate the strategic direction of the organization, they cannot do it without the input received from their managers. While managers implement the directives and directions received from their leaders, they act as leaders *in* their teams. They often decide *how* to implement and achieve the leader's vision. Therefore, this text will examine both management and leadership skills that prevent and resolve unproductive conflict to improve collaboration and maximize mission achievement.

WHAT MAKES A GREAT MANAGER?

Reflect on the best manager you have ever had. It could be your Little League coach, the supervisor at your first job, or if you are lucky, it could be your current manager. What *traits* made him or her an excellent manager? Traits include patience, kindness, and flexibility. What specific *behaviors* led you to think of him or her as your best boss? For example, some managers respond promptly to email, sponsor social events, recognize the birthdays of their employees, provide needed resources to employees, advocate up the chain of command, or listen empathetically. While personality traits may seem hard to acquire, each of us can engage in more of the behaviors exhibited by effective managers. By making a list of the behaviors of effective managers, you can set your own goals as a manager (or manager in training). Which behaviors would you like to increase or decrease?

When asked to create lists of effective managerial behaviors, employees frequently respond with the following inventory. Great managers show they care; get to know employees as individuals; lead from the front; communicate what they need from each employee (and why) and what they will give back (and why); listen with empathy; nurture, train, support, coach, and hold accountable; are open to new ideas and ways of operating; advocate for the needs of their team; are proactive problem solvers; invite input; share rewards and recognition; and engage in strategic thinking and planning.

A body of management theory known as **leader-member exchange theory** has become popular since the 1980s. This research examines the types of relationships that form between leaders and organizational members and the benefits that accrue because of these relationships. This approach posits that the best managers develop positive relationships with organizational members based on "trust, respect, loyalty, liking, intimacy, support, openness and honesty" (Wilson, Sin & Conlon, 2010, p. 358). Leaders provide members with goods such as access to information, assignment to interesting projects, and recommendations to higher managers, whereas members supply commitment, engagement, and loyalty. Both accrue benefits from the nurturing of close, effective relationships that include recognition of their interdependence.

In early 2009 Google began "Project Oxygen," an internal study aimed at identifying the characteristics of the company's most successful managers. Luckily, what they found applies not only to Google managers, but also to management generally. They mined performance reviews, employee feedback surveys, and nominations for top manager awards to find out what makes the best managers (Bryant, 2011). The Project Oxygen team asked employees to rank the qualities that made for the best managers. The research team predicted that technical expertise would be high on the list of attributes found among the best managers—after all, when employees get stumped on a technical matter they are supposed to turn to their managers for assistance. Yet technical abilities ranked last out of eight attributes of great managers. "What employees valued the most were even-keeled bosses who made time for one-on-one meetings, who helped people puzzle through problems by asking questions, not dictating answers, and who took an interest in employees' lives and careers" (Bryant, 2011, p. 2). Making a connection to employees and being accessible were key qualities of great managers. A study by Watson and Hoffman (1996) found that the most successful and powerful managers engaged in cooperative behaviors with their colleagues and employees whereas lower-power managers attempted to make gains by resorting to authoritarian and competitive practices.

Originally, Project Oxygen yielded eight habits associated with superior managers. Later analysis and additional study yielded two more habits for a total of 10. Box 1.1 examines the findings from Project Oxygen, showing the habits and behaviors of effective managers. This data was collected using past performance appraisals, employee engagement surveys, interviews, and other sources of employee feedback (Miles, 2022).

As you can see from this list, these activities blur the lines between traditional management and leadership activities because great managers are great

BOX 1.1. TEN HABITS OF EFFECTIVE MANAGERS

1. Being good coaches: Get every employee working in their "sweet-spot-role" and engage with them to solve problems together (Schwantes, 2022).
2. Empowering and not micromanaging.
3. Showing interest in employee well-being, including creating an inclusive environment.
4. Being productive and results oriented.
5. Being a good communicator: Listening and sharing information freely.
6. Helping employees with career development.
7. Having a clear vision and strategy for the team.
8. Having key technical skills that help him/her to advise the team.
9. Collaborating across the organization.
10. Being a strong decision-maker.

leaders of their teams. According to Miles (2022), "Instead of simply measuring how much output a manager achieves, the surveys now focus on how much time they spend coaching their team, whether or not they communicate a clear vision, etc. They also developed new management training programs centered around these skills." Measuring managers' performance against these ten habits or behaviors is an effective way to encourage more of these positive actions.

The two additional habits correlate to positive impacts for team members:

> The two new behaviors were highly correlated with manager effectiveness and the updated list of ten Oxygen behaviors was even more predictive of team outcomes like turnover, satisfaction, and performance than our original list of eight. The higher the scores a manager received on the two new behaviors, the better those three outcomes were for their teams over the next year; their team members were more likely to stay at Google, gave higher subsequent satisfaction scores on our employee survey, and were better performers. (Harrell & Barbato, 2018)

Let's elaborate a little more on some of the insights found by Project Oxygen. Many of these behaviors rely on the ability to provide constructive, developmental feedback. Avoid comments about personality and instead focus on actionable behaviors such as not interrupting others during meetings or meeting deadlines, etc. Avoiding negative comments about the employee's personality is particularly important for two reasons: first, personality characteristics are much harder to change than specific behaviors and second, a 2019 analysis of performance review data found that negative personality feedback showed up 76% of the time in reviews of women, while only in 2% of men's reviews (in Bastian, 2019). Unconscious biases likely result in important differences in how feedback is given to men versus women, and awareness of this tendency is the first step to improving both the fairness and efficacy of performance reviews as a feedback tool.

Feedback needs to go both ways. Managers need to invite feedback to improve their own performance as well as providing feedback to subordinates. This signals that you are a team player and models the growth mindset you want others to adopt. Millennials especially do not like hierarchical barriers to giving and receiving feedback that could improve performance and career development. It is important to provide positive feedback when an employee performs well or accomplishes a goal. Feedback is a key coaching and motivational strategy when done well (for specific strategies for giving effective feedback see Chapter 10). Unfortunately, many managers never receive specific training in listening, framing, and feedback skills.

A recent study published in the *New York Times* (Hughes, 2022) found that talking out problems and reaching collaborative solutions literally syncs neurons within the brain across individual team members, not only making them work more harmoniously on their current challenge, but also enhancing their ability to work together collectively in the future. The study used brain scans to track the growth of neural networks during collaborative problem-solving conversations within small teams. In short, humans are made to talk out their problems together and seek communal responses to common problems. Doing so successfully "snowballs" and makes future success more likely. One key finding in the study was that individuals needed to signal their willingness to change their minds based on information shared by others, also known as open-mindedness. Extrapolating from this, we can be relatively certain that managers who are open to feedback themselves are more likely to have employees who are also receptive to receiving feedback.

The avoidance of micromanaging is high on the list because creative, empowered problem solvers wilt under the withering, constant gaze of their supervisors. "When micromanagers don't let go and trust their team members to perform their work, as a result, the employee experience can be downright demoralizing" (Schwantes, 2022). Once employees have been successfully onboarded, acculturated, and trained to do their basic tasks, managers are wise to step back and allow the employee to accomplish the work in their own way. Be sure to signal that you are open for input, mentoring, and skill development, but that you trust the employee to get the job done. They will make mistakes as they learn their job duties, but micromanaging is akin to being a snowplow parent—it leads to a lack of competence and high levels of anxiety. Instead, set the example and the expectation that mistakes are a natural part of the learning process, they should not be covered up or hidden, and all employees at any level should feel free to reach out with questions or ask for help as needed. Build trust and competence so that your employee can learn and grow.

Beyond the avoidance of micromanaging, companies that rely on innovation and the development of new products or services do well to consider providing time for employees to work on **passion projects** individually or in small groups. These are creative projects of interest to the employees even if they are not directly related to their regular duties. The ability to bring their creativity to work can deepen employees' commitment and engagement to the company as well as yielding profitable products. For Google, both Gmail and AdSense came from employees' passion projects (Miles, 2022).

The fifth behavior involves listening and communicating effectively, but listening skills are closely related to many of the behaviors on the list. "Unfortunately, active listening is one of the least taught skills in leadership. Studies confirm that most of us are poor and inefficient listeners. When you talk to your boss, co-workers, or customers for 10 minutes, studies indicate you pay attention to less than half of the conversation. As managers, building up your active listening skills is crucial for solving problems, developing trust, and winning the hearts and minds of people" (Miles, 2022).

When asked what makes a great manager, one of the most common responses is, "Someone who takes the time to get to know me and supports my career goals." Was something like this on your list? Getting to know employees as individuals is indispensable for coaching, creating a warm and inclusive environment, and in providing career support. The Gallup organization lists six elements of employee well-being to which managers may wish to attend: emotional, financial, career, social, physical, and community. For example, at a minimum it is the role of a manager to ensure the basic physical needs of employees are met: do they have access to food and drinks or are they advised in advance to bring their own? Is their working environment as safe as possible? Can they walk to and from their cars in the parking lot safely? Do they feel a sense of belonging and acceptance at work? Are their skills being put to their best use? Great managers work to ensure their employees' needs are met.

While it has improved in the past few years, employees with the U.S. Federal Emergency Management Agency (FEMA) used to joke that the U.S. Cavalry treats its horses better than FEMA treats its employees. Due to the nature of its work in emergency response and recovery, FEMA must move large groups of people on short notice into areas often lacking adequate infrastructure such as electricity, housing, and fresh food. Hurricanes, wildfires, or other disasters require employees to be flexible, adaptable, and prepared to be away from their families for long periods. FEMA managers must attend to the mission and to the human needs of their employees under difficult circumstances. Every organization must meet the reasonable needs of their employees in order for them to get their jobs done each day, then come back and do it again. Employees' needs vary by the individual, the generation, and over time. Great managers ask and listen to their employees to meet those needs whenever possible.

> As a workforce, we've evolved from wanting ping pong tables and nap pods to a workforce craving connection, autonomy, and flexibility. We've pivoted from chasing efficiency and sticking to business to showing up as our whole selves at work and putting belonging and inclusion at the forefront of the employee experience. Through COVID-19 and the Great Resignation, we learned that employees want to find purpose in their work. They also want flexibility, health, and meaning. Employees want to choose when and where they work while still maintain-

ing meaningful connections with others. We've learned that, for many, working remotely actually unlocked creativity, opened up new opportunities, and helped galvanize a workforce to reach more of its potential. (Miles, 2022)

In addition to yielding these ten habits of successful managers, the Google studies also found three pitfalls common to their worst managers. The first pitfall is that great workers do not always make great managers. Rather than promoting an employee into management due to their technical skills, companies should instead seek out employees with superior communication and leadership skills. Once placed into a management role, most of their time will be spent directing, coaching, and supervising employees rather than applying their technical skills. Organizations can ameliorate these deficits through training programs designed to help employees transition successfully to managerial roles or through tests of these skills as part of the promotion process. When organizations choose to hire managers from outside rather than promoting from within, it is crucial that new hires take the time to learn the organization's processes, policies, and culture during their transition phase.

The second and third pitfalls deal with managers who do not communicate consistently, proactively, and effectively. Ineffective managers tend to have fewer and less effective meetings. They don't follow up to ensure their employees' career development needs are being met and they don't listen well.

Great managers are rarely born; they are made. They seek continuous improvement in their skill set no matter how well they already manage. Great managers have less unproductive conflict in their teams because they discuss and reach shared expectations about how the work will be done, how rewards will be shared, how decisions will get made, and other critical expectations between team members. We will discuss this in depth in later chapters. Conflict comes from unmet expectations, so reaching shared expectations is critical to reducing conflict in teams.

Great managers reduce unproductive conflict by identifying and acting on problems early, rather than sticking their heads in the sand and hoping the problems with individual employees, teams, vendors, suppliers, customers, or regulators will resolve on their own. Conflict-avoidant managers rarely rise to the top or reach their career aspirations. Every manager can evolve and adapt their management style to become a great manager for their current team. Different teams need different things from their manager. A manager who excels in one organization or with one team can find herself struggling or failing when leading another team or working in another organization. Great managers adapt their approach to the situations and people with whom they work. This reduces unproductive conflict and enhances effectiveness. As a consultant and executive performance coach, I have seen many managers and even CEOs utterly fail because they applied lessons learned in another environment to the one in which they now find themselves. Doesn't it drive you crazy when your new manager or leader says. "When I worked for _____ (company X), we did it this way and it worked great!" Many lessons learned in our past organizations simply will not transfer effectively into a different organizational culture or they do not fit the current set of circumstances or personalities. While we can learn from our experiences, we must be willing to ask questions, listen effectively, and build a coalition of support for the changes we seek. We must be willing to change everything, starting with our own habitual responses to conflict.

MANAGEMENT STYLES: PERMISSIVE, AUTHORITATIVE, AND AUTHORITARIAN

In addition to the ten managerial habits correlated to the best managers by Project Oxygen is the broader question about which approach, or style of management, is best. While it is possible that managerial styles need to vary based on the organization's culture and mission, it is also the case that some styles are more likely to result in turnover, disengagement, lax discipline, lower mission achievement, and higher litigation costs.

Whether we like to acknowledge it or not, there are significant parallels to good management and good parenting. Both often involve interdependent relationships that are simultaneously collaborative yet hierarchical. Mission achievement requires everyone to pull in the same direction, to communicate empathetically and effectively, and to create a positive team culture. The literature on leadership and parenting styles indicates that permissive managers produce working environments that are characterized by lax discipline, low individual and group achievement, and codependent relationships in which one or more team members takes up the slack for underperforming others. Permissive leaders tend to display the accommodating conflict style in which they give in to their subordinates out of the false view that this will preserve or enhance their relationships. Morale is low, even for the low-performing team members who are shirking their full duties. On the other end of the continuum are authoritarian leaders who bark orders, show low levels of empathy, criticize without skills coaching for better performance, and have teams with low morale, infighting, and levels of disengagement and turnover. Interestingly, the children of permissive and authoritarian parenting styles, and employees with permissive and authoritarian management styles, have higher levels of anxiety and depression as well as lower levels of self-confidence and competence (see Duckworth, 2016; Timpano et al., 2010; Smith & Garza, 2021).

In the middle, authoritative managers and parents act as facilitators of individual and team success. They teach, coach, and encourage continual growth and learning from team members while holding them accountable. These leaders do not berate team members who make mistakes. They see mistakes as learning opportunities. Yet they do not rescue them from the opportunity to do the work of fixing their mistakes because that is how we learn best. They share expertise and engage in collaborative brainstorming with questions like "What would you like to do about that?" and "How can I help?" Authoritative parents and managers have healthier relationships with their team members and greater success at mission achievement. Their team members are not afraid to take reasonable risks and to innovate.

> Permissive parents allow their children to do as they wish with little discipline, whereas authoritative parents implement reasonable guidelines while still providing a warm and nurturing environment. The third style, authoritarian, represents parenting that is rigid and values strict adherence to rules with lower levels of nurturing. (Timpano et al, 2010)

Different generations respond slightly differently to these management styles, with millennials being least likely to accept authoritarian management practices (Miles, 2022).

Which style best describes your approach to management and team leadership? How is that working for you? Can you identify one change to your management style that you can implement to model an authoritative style?

RESPONDING TO CONFLICT: FIVE COMMON APPROACHES

Conflict isn't positive or negative. It is our reaction to conflict that determines whether the consequence will be constructive or *de*structive. Conflict presents an opportunity for positive change, deepening relationships, and problem-solving. How you treat the other party or parties in conflict is highly predictive of the strength and duration of the relationship in the future (Gottman, 2014). In fact, the way in which two people communicate with each other when problem-solving can predict whether they are able to work together productively with over 90% accuracy (Gottman, 2014). Therefore, it is not conflict that hurts our relationships—it is the way we approach it, manage it, and communicate it. As Mary Parker Follett wrote nearly 100 years ago, "All polishing is done through friction." (in Bednarek & Smith, 2023). Tjosvold's (2008) work shows that organizations that encourage constructive debate and the open expression of disagreement among team members can greatly improve their effectiveness, creativity, and efficiency. Nevertheless, when most people use the term *conflict*, there is an implied negative connotation. Is your reaction to conflict generally constructive or destructive? How do you feel after you address a problem with employees, your boss, or your clients? The post-conflict feeling can tell us a lot. Does conflict make you want to "fight" or "take flight"? Or do you feel even closer, more connected, and warmer toward your colleagues than before the conflict?

Before reading further, please complete the conflict styles inventory in Box 1.2 and scoring in Table 1.1. This test uses a "forced-choice" methodology. This means you are forced to choose between response A or B for each question. There may be some questions where you wish you could answer "none of the above," but please select the answer that best corresponds to your preferred methods for addressing conflict, either A or B.

BOX 1.2. CONFLICT STYLES INVENTORY

Think of *two* different contexts (A and B) where you have conflict, disagreement, argument, or disappointment with someone. An example might be a work associate or someone you live with. Then, according to the following scale, fill in your scores for situation A and situation B. For each question, you will have two scores. For example, on question 1, the scoring might look like this: **1. 2 / 4**

Write the name of each person for the two contexts here:

Person A_____/Person B_____

1 = Never   2 = Seldom   3 = Sometimes   4 = Often   5 = Always

<u>Person A/Person B</u>

1. _____/_____I avoid being "put on the spot"; I keep conflicts to myself.
2. _____/_____I use my influence to get my ideas accepted.
3. _____/_____I usually try to "split the difference" in order to resolve an issue.
4. _____/_____I generally try to satisfy the other's needs.
5. _____/_____I try to investigate an issue to find a solution acceptable to us.
6. _____/_____I usually avoid open discussion of my differences with the other.
7. _____/_____I use my authority to make decisions in my favor.
8. _____/_____I try to find a middle course to resolve an impasse.
9. _____/_____I usually accommodate the other's wishes.
10. _____/_____I try to integrate my ideas with the other's to come up with a decision jointly.
11. _____/_____I try to stay away from disagreement with the other.
12. _____/_____I use my expertise to make a decision that favors me.
13. _____/_____I propose a middle ground for breaking deadlocks.
14. _____/_____I give in to the other's wishes.
15. _____/_____I try to work with the other to try to find solutions that satisfy both our expectations.
16. _____/_____I try to keep my disagreement to myself to avoid hard feelings.
17. _____/_____I generally pursue my side of an issue.
18. _____/_____I negotiate with the other to reach a compromise.
19. _____/_____I often go with the other's suggestions.
20. _____/_____I exchange accurate information with the other so we can solve a problem together.
21. _____/_____I try to avoid unpleasant exchanges with the other.
22. _____/_____I sometimes use my power to win.
23. _____/_____I use "give and take" so that a compromise can be made.
24. _____/_____I try to satisfy the other's expectations.
25. _____/_____I try to bring all our concerns out in the open so that the issues can be resolved.

Source: Adapted from Wilmot and Hocker (2001). Reprinted with permission.

Table 1.1   Scoring the Conflict Styles Inventory

Scoring: Add up your scores on the following questions:				
A/B	A/B	A/B	A/B	A/B
1. ____/____	2. ____/____	3. ____/____	4. ____/____	5. ____/____
6. ____/____	7. ____/____	8. ____/____	9. ____/____	10. ____/____
11. ____/____	12. ____/____	13. ____/____	14. ____/____	15. ____/____
16. ____/____	17. ____/____	18. ____/____	19. ____/____	20. ____/____
21. ____/____	22. ____/____	23. ____/____	24. ____/____	25. ____/____
____/____	____/____	____/____	____/____	____/____
A/B Avoidance Total	A/B Competition Total	A/B Compromise Total	A/B Accommodation Total	A/B Collaboration Total

Source: Adapted from Wilmot and Hocker (2001). Reprinted with permission.

The **conflict styles inventory (CSI)** is a questionnaire used to assess an individual's habits in response to conflict. As the CSI indicates, there are five primary responses to conflict: avoidance, accommodation, collaboration, compromising, and competing. Each of these responses is appropriate in some circumstances and ineffective in others. You might have assumed that the collaborative style is the best since this is a book about collaboration. Surprisingly, that is not the case. This text argues that competent conflict managers are adept at analyzing problems and consciously choosing the style most likely to produce the desired results. Sometimes accommodation is called for, while other situations call for compromise, and so on. Each conflict presents an opportunity for the parties to consciously articulate their goals in the interaction and identify the best response to achieve those goals. Sometimes preserving or enhancing the relationship is the goal, while in other cases you seek to make a quick and fair decision. Matching the conflict style to the dispute or decision-making opportunity is an important skill both at work and in our civic and personal lives.

It can be problematic that most of us predominantly utilize only one or two of these conflict styles as we unconsciously respond to problems as opposed to analyzing situations and choosing the style that best matches the problem at hand. Some should be avoided, in some cases you should meet in the middle, etc. At work, even the most stressful conflicts provide you with an opportunity to showcase your conflict management skills. Superior negotiation and conflict management skills convey the importance you place on treating others fairly and respectfully, even when you disagree with the outcome of a dispute. Remember, it is not conflict itself that harms relationships; it is how we handle it that determines whether we emerge from it with stronger or weaker relationships. As Rita Callahan (2023), expert mediator, likes to say, "Ah, conflict . . . an opportunity to improve a relationship."

Your choice of preferred styles likely depends on the culture in which you were raised and the way your family of origin dealt with conflict. Knowing your own habits will help you improve your response to conflict, while deepening your understanding of others—especially if their preferred style is different. Rather than vilifying those who seem to "fight every fight" or those who behave with passive aggression, you will come to understand why others exhibit different responses to conflict and how to work successfully with those who do not share your preferred approach.

Conflict Avoidance

Avoidance becomes the preferred conflict management style for individuals with negative past experiences of failed conflict engagement. If avoidance is your preferred approach, then you probably view conflict as a win-lose situation, with you likely to be on the losing end. Conflict avoiders tend to be people in low-power positions, from cultures that prioritize "social harmony," traumatized by childhood conflict, introverts, and/or people with lower verbal and social skills. Remember—conflict avoiders rarely rise to upper management because leaders must manage conflict every day. While it is important to avoid "no-win situations," by improving your skills or helping others to improve theirs, you can improve the ability to choose among all five styles rather than defaulting to avoidance.

Conflict avoidance is not always a bad or irrational response when faced with a daunting problem. In fact, avoidance is the right approach if a problem is small and likely to go away on its own. When we fight every fight, we expend energy that might be better used to address the most important problems. It is important to pick your battles. If this was your lowest score, you might want to be more judicious at picking your battles so that you can save your energy for problems that are more central to the mission of your work unit or to your career goals. If this was your highest score, then you might want to work on your framing and problem-solving skills (covered in Chapter 2) so you feel confident in your ability to proactively address problems.

For many problems, avoidance works temporarily but makes matters worse in the long run. Avoiders tend to repeatedly let things go until they cannot ignore them anymore and then they explode—sometimes over a relatively small infraction. In other words, "the volcano effect" occurs (see below for more information on volcanoes at work). Large organizations are better at conflict avoidance than smaller organizations. In large organizations, if one person procrastinates about addressing a problem, then maybe someone else will take charge and deal with the issue. In smaller organizations, there are fewer people onto whom we can push our problems.

Do not confuse *conflict prevention* with *conflict avoidance*. **Conflict prevention** occurs when an individual or group examines the sources of predictable and recurring problems, and then takes reasonable steps to address the root causes so they do not occur or recur. Examples of conflict prevention within organizations may include changing overlapping job descriptions to have greater role clarity and accountability. On the other hand, **conflict avoidance** or the **avoiding style** occurs when an individual or group has evidence that a problem currently exists or will soon exist, but no steps are taken to address the problem. Conflict avoiders refuse to acknowledge the problem exists, hoping it will just go away. This may work for small, nonrecurring problems, or when you lack the authority or power to bring change. However, do not underestimate your power to bring organizational change (see Chapter 6). Avoidance is unlikely to work for systemic, recurring, or large problems.

There is a clear connection between some conflict-avoidance behaviors and the psychological phenomenon of *denial*. Like avoidance, **denial** occurs when an individual or group refuses to acknowledge a reality that is highly unpleasant. Denial is a protective mechanism that comes into force when reality is so overwhelming that to acknowledge its truth could result in a psychological or physical breakdown.

If you are conflict avoidant, how did this pattern develop? Perhaps you had traumatic experiences with conflict in your family or in your work environment. Perhaps you feel a sense of hopelessness or powerlessness to positively impact decisions and fix problems. This is called "high external locus of control" and will be covered in Chapter 5. Perhaps you have a shy personality and prefer not to engage in the long conversations often needed to solve problems productively. The first step to becoming a more proactive and successful conflict manager is to understand why you tend to prefer avoiding conflict. The next step is to work on your framing skills so you can feel confident in your ability to proactively impact conflicts and solve problems without risking escalation or outbursts. The third step is to develop a plan and timeline for improving your ability to proactively address problems as they arise (see the goal-setting section at the end of this chapter).

As you push yourself away from the default style of conflict avoidance, you may fear that you are being too confrontational with others or taking on too many problems. This is rarely the case with someone who scored high on avoidance (or, coincidentally, on accommodating). So long as you are not acting out of anger when you address problems with other people, and you use tactful and constructive language, then you are much more likely to see positive results and be viewed as a problem solver.

Accommodation

Accommodation occurs when an individual has a preferred outcome but is willing to sacrifice his preference so the other negotiator can realize her own preference, thereby ensuring no harm comes to the relationship. Those who use the **accommodating style** care deeply about the feelings of others and seek to maintain harmony in their relationships and work environments. If this was your highest score, then you may believe it is often necessary to place your own wishes as secondary to others'. While this belief is certainly true in some situations, a high score here indicates you are probably "too nice." You may seem indecisive when difficult decisions need to be made at the managerial level. Your desire to please others and to be liked by those you manage may mean that some people take you for granted or take advantage of you, with suggestions like, "Ask Barbara to work late, she never says no." Or "Try to get Jose to work that holiday since you have plans. He's such a nice guy." While everyone needs to "take one for the team" now and then, accommodating people tend to sacrifice more than their fair share.

But why not, since it does not seem to bother them? Constant accommodation *does* bother them, yet they have learned to keep their opinions to themselves. Accommodators sometimes experience negative health or psychological effects from holding in their frustration and bottling up their emotions. They often feel like metaphorical doormats. They expect or at least hope that others will read their faint, indirect, signals and put their needs first occasionally. While seeking to preserve or enhance relationships, when accommodation is taken too far it actually does the opposite. Why? Because accommodators end up being resentful, which poisons their relationships. So, if you cannot fulfill someone's request without feeling resentful, consider respectfully setting a boundary with the other person so they understand that you are unable to meet their request.

Conflict accommodators struggle with openly sharing their ideas, feedback, and concerns so as not to offend others. As a result, the team often misses out on the full contribution accommodators and avoiders could make, and so their ideas do not surface. Accommodators have difficulty delegating work to subordinates because they worry that assigning others tasks will upset them. The ability to delegate reasonable tasks to others by using clear direction and adequate oversight is crucial for maintaining efficient workflow and for reserving the manager's time for truly management-level decisions.

In contrast, if this was your lowest score, you may want to consider being a bit more flexible, accommodating, and occasionally making concessions to others so that you are viewed as more of a team player. This shows you care about others and are willing to engage in the give-and-take necessary for healthy relationships. Those who seldom act in an accommodating manner are viewed as pushy, selfish, and not as team players.

Accommodation can be the best approach to conflict when an individual is in a low-power position, with little hope of achieving the preferred outcome; when an issue is of relatively little importance to you but of higher importance to others; and when you seek to demonstrate you are reasonable and build goodwill. However, if you find yourself repeatedly accommodating others, and it is becoming frustrating, then you may not be adequately communicating or asserting your own needs. When accommodators learn how to identify situations calling for a more collaborative, competitive, or compromising approach, they can then use their assertion skills to frame their comments in a way that allows them to share their concerns or ideas without alienating or angering others (framing skills will be covered in greater depth in chapter 2).

Collaboration

A high score in the collaboration category indicates a preference to work together with others to achieve outcomes that meet the needs of all. **Collaboration** occurs when two or more individuals work together to share information and make joint decisions or take shared actions. If you scored lowest on this measure, then you may have trouble delegating and/or sharing decision-making authority with others, even when their buy-in is crucial to the implementation of decisions. If you scored highest on the **collaborative style**, you likely view conflict as an opportunity to solve problems by working positively with others. Some have called this the "**win-win**" viewpoint, meaning that for one person to win in a negotiation or conflict, the other person's needs must also be met (meaning they must also win). You are not willing to win at the cost of the relationship, but you believe that by putting your heads together, you can generally find mutually acceptable solutions to the problems at hand.

Collaboration is important in workplace teams. Workplace teams with cooperative approaches to conflict management, as opposed to competitive approaches, exhibited higher levels of trust between team members (Hempel, Zhang & Tjosvold, 2009). Chan, Huang, and Ng (2008) found that managers with a cooperative style showed more concern for their employees as people, and this concern fostered more trust.

So why isn't collaboration the "best" style of conflict management? Not all problems call for collaboration. Imagine the captain of the *Titanic* realizes there is an iceberg off the starboard bow. He quickly assembles all the officers on the bridge of the ship and asks each one, "What is the best response to this problem?" Just then, the ship hits the iceberg, and the rest is history. Collaboration takes time. When time is short, leaders must act swiftly and decisively. In other situations, the decision is not important enough to justify bringing together everyone to jointly reach a decision. If you have laid the groundwork by building strong relationships with others in your organization, then they will typically trust your judgment when decisions must be made quickly or do not warrant the time it takes to engage in collaborative decision-making.

The larger the group, the harder it will be to obtain 100% consensus on any issue. Imagine trying to get 100 people to agree on whether to order Chinese or Mexican food for lunch. This would not be a good use of time and may create conflict, and a competent leader could make an executive decision on this matter without much pushback. Requiring 100% consensus gives extraordinary power to potential "spoilers" who enter a process with the intention of derailing any agreement or stalling if possible. If the decision is made to use a collaborative style, it will be helpful to clarify the decision-making parameters at the outset. For example, will the manager seek input and brainstorming from the group, but then retain final decision-making authority, or will the manager defer to the expressed preferences of the group? If the latter route is adopted, decisions will require 100% consensus or something less, such as a simple majority vote, a supermajority vote, or consensus minus one or two. Voting is a process that matches the competitive style of decision-making, yet it can be combined with participant input, dialogue, and collaboration to create a process deemed fair, participatory, and efficient.

Sometimes, a collaborative manager should seek input from one or more employees by asking whether a specific issue justifies input from the team. Sometimes they will say, "No thanks. I trust your judgment on this one." In that case, your inquiry has signaled that you value their feelings and that you understand the decision will likely impact them and their work. Reserve the use of collaborative decision-making for the following instances: when others have the information needed to make a good decision; when buy-in will be needed to effectively implement the decision; when there is likely to be pushback if input is not sought; when there is adequate time for input and discussion; and when you seek to build or repair relationships with others.

Compromise

The **compromising style** indicates a preference for "splitting the difference" between the negotiators' positions. Compromise can be a quick, efficient way to reach a solution. For example, in hiring negotiations an employer offered the prospective employee a salary of $80,000 and she countered with a request for $90,000. The two quickly decided the most efficient and fair outcome would be to settle at $85,000. Both got part of what they wanted and left the negotiation feeling that the process was fair. The negotiation was relatively short and painless.

The compromising style is appropriate when a decision is not highly important, the time for negotiation and discussion is relatively short, and the process needs to be viewed as fair to all parties. One risk of using compromise is that value might be left "on the table," so to speak. For example, what if the employee offered to take on additional duties that would have otherwise required the hiring of a part-time employee in exchange for the previously requested $90,000 salary? By engaging in discussions to learn more about each negotiator's needs, it may be possible to reach a solution that is better for everyone. Compromise often misses these opportunities.

The largest flaw in the compromising style is that it focuses on creating a fair process (you each get equal amounts) but can ignore even better solutions that lie unexplored. The compromising style encourages parties to "start high" instead of telling each other what is truly desired and why. To return to the earlier salary negotiation example, the employer may have been willing to go as high as $95,000 but she started small to make it look like she was "being nice" by agreeing to a higher salary. While the salary of $85,000 was appreciated, what if the job applicant really wanted a flexible work schedule and was willing to sacrifice some pay to obtain that type of schedule? Perhaps this would have been acceptable to both sides in the negotiation, yet the needs beneath the monetary amounts were not fully discussed. They walked away with an agreement, but not one that met all of their needs as fully as a collaborative negotiation could have accomplished.

If you scored high on compromising and on accommodating, then you may leave negotiations feeling a bit disrespected or taken advantage of. You generally start off your negotiations using the compromising style because you see it as fair, but if the other individual is a tough negotiator, you give in rather than risk the chance of hurting the other person's feelings or damaging the relationship. You can improve this by choosing carefully among the different conflict styles to utilize the one that best matches your needs in any particular situation. Be sure you have a number (or other result) in your head that is your "bottom line" before you enter the negotiation, and only change that bottom line if new information comes to light during the negotiation that justifies reconsideration.

Competition

The **competitive style** indicates a preference to "win as much as you can," even at the expense of the other side or damage to the relationship between negotiators.

You have probably heard that individuals tend to have either a "fight-or-flight" response to conflict. It is apparent that the responses we are examining here are much more nuanced and varied. However, if the avoidant style represents "flight," then the competitive style represents "fight." If you scored highest on the competitive category, then you tend to hold strong opinions and make decisive unilateral decisions. Competitors tend to communicate directly and are more concerned about the outcome of a decision than they are about the feelings of others. We call this a focus on "task over relationship." They may err in believing that many interactions are competitions with zero-sum outcomes, when the situations are actually more amenable to negotiations that yield joint gains, also known as "win-win" outcomes. Individuals scoring high on the competitive style are often viewed by others as overly assertive, abrasive, or insensitive. Individuals who scored lowest on this conflict style tend to score high in the accommodating and/or avoiding conflict styles. As a result, these individuals are often seen as "pushovers" who will not adequately advocate for themselves or their teams.

When done correctly, competition among coworkers can result in increased productivity and healthy camaraderie. When done poorly, competition pits team members against each other, leading to hard feelings and negative outcomes. When team members or whole teams are interdependent, then collaborative games and rewards will enhance their ability to work together while competitive games will be counterproductive.

A competitive style of decision-making is called for when a unilateral, swift decision is needed because time is short and you, as a manager, believe that your preferred outcome is the only one that is acceptable or in the best interests of the company. It is better to be transparent about this assessment than to pretend to engage in collaboration or compromise, knowing that in the end, your decision will be final.

CHOOSING BETWEEN THE CONFLICT STYLES

As a child, you began learning about conflict management by watching your family members. You may have adopted the conflict techniques exhibited by one or more of your family members, or you may have developed a style that is the opposite because you decided theirs was dysfunctional. Whichever style(s) you tend toward, it took many years to develop your current conflict habits. Changing habits feels awkward at first, and mistakes or backtracking are to be expected. Eventually, with practice and reflection, choosing the best style or approach will become habitual. Until then, it helps to ask yourself some explicit questions about the problem, decision, or conflict in question.

Begin by asking these questions: What will likely happen if no action is taken or if action is delayed? How soon is a decision needed? Is this my problem to solve? If not, who might be the right person and how do I gently set healthy boundaries around what I can or cannot do on this problem? Who will be impacted by the decision, and who will be tasked with implementing the decision? Would a decision that had the input and expertise of other stakeholders likely be

BOX 1.3. CHOOSING THE BEST RESPONSE TO CONFLICT

1. Is this a "no-win" situation due to a power asymmetry that is working against you? If so, consider choosing the avoidant style.
2. Do you need "buy-in" from those impacted by a decision in order to get it implemented? If so, consider using the collaborative style.
3. Does a quick, authoritative decision need to be made? If so, consider the competitive style.
4. Does your colleague care passionately about this issue even if it is of minor or moderate importance to you? If so, consider the accommodating style.
5. Is time short? Do you need a fair process that allows you and the other negotiator to both get something out of the deal? If so, then consider the compromising style.

a better, more implementable decision for addressing the problem? Do I have the information I need to make a good decision? How much buy-in will be necessary for the decision to be implemented smoothly? Do I have the power or authority necessary to make a unilateral decision? Do others in my organization trust that I will make the best decision possible, even if they are not particularly happy with the outcome of the decision? How are my preexisting conflict management habits biasing my answers to these questions?

As you strive to be more analytical and proactive in your approach to dealing with conflict, do not be too hard on yourself. You are developing a deeper cognitive framework for understanding conflict and its management, but changing patterns of behavior takes time and practice. Allow yourself a "do-over" when you catch yourself falling back into old, destructive patterns of communication or decision-making. If you are explicit with others about your desire to improve these skills, you are likely to find that your colleagues and employees are not only open to working *with* you, but they will also appreciate that you are trying to develop your abilities in these areas. At the end of this chapter, review the goal-setting section to get started on making improvements in your conflict management habits.

THE LANGUAGE OF CONFLICT

We learned how to manage conflict the same way we learned language—by watching and listening to those around us. The way in which we communicate our approach to conflict includes both verbal and nonverbal signals we give to others, either purposefully or subconsciously. Just as every spoken language has rules of grammar and punctuation, so does the language of conflict. However, for most people, the unspoken rules, or norms of conflict management, also known as the language of conflict, have never been explicitly discussed except at the most obvious level, with statements such as, "Tommy, we don't hit," or "We have a zero-tolerance policy for bullying." The rules vary within each family or organization and within each of the five conflict styles discussed in this chapter. In other words, organizations tend to exhibit one of these styles more than the others. When an individual exhibits a conflict style that is different from that of the group's style (such as with one's coworkers or with one's in-laws), it seems as if he is breaking unwritten and unspoken rules. Because we learned our language of conflict through the osmosis of watching the world around us, we implicitly believe that everyone saw the same world that we saw, and therefore they should have learned the same lessons. When someone's communication mode or approach to problem-solving irritates you, ask yourself, "What approach to conflict is she using, and how different is it from my preferred approach?" You may find that it is the difference in styles that is the obstacle to smoother interactions rather than the preferred outcomes voiced by each party about the conflict. Once you understand where these differences originate, you will be less likely to take offense or to take it personally. This helps to prevent conflict escalation.

Let's revisit the scenario at the beginning of this chapter with John and Maria. At the Bureau of Reclamation, Maria has previously called in "sick" when she was dreading her work more than usual. She has even told John why she is calling in sick: "I hate performance review season." Her direct, rather competitive approach is at odds with that of her boss. John has not addressed this issue through a problem-solving conversation with Maria. His approach is avoidant. Maria has concluded that it must not bother him too much when she calls in sick, otherwise he would say something, right? For them to communicate more proactively, they would need to sit down together and explicitly discuss what is or is not working. Ideally, they would use 3-step problem-solving to share their individual expectations, find the disconnect, and then reach shared understandings about how these issues will be addressed in the future. In other words, a collaborative conversation is called for because they have an interdependent relationship and John cannot unilaterally change her behavior. John could use his authority to instruct Maria *not* to miss any more work, which would be a competitive approach. However, she could quit or simply ignore him, so long as she has enough sick leave to use. Since he cannot force compliance, collaboration would be the best option. Clearly, a conflict-avoidant or accommodating approach has not worked so far.

BOX 1.4. COMMUNICATION RULES IN COMPETITIVE ORGANIZATIONS

1. Survival of the fittest.
2. Be blunt and to the point, regardless of whether it hurts someone's feelings.
3. Stake out your positions early and don't compromise.
4. Have an audience when you engage someone in conflict.
5. People who don't engage this way are weak.

BOX 1.5. COMMUNICATION RULES IN CONFLICT-AVOIDANT ORGANIZATIONS/INDIVIDUALS

1. Walk away from conflict whenever possible.
2. Don't express strong feelings.
3. Sulking, snide comments, and the "silent treatment" are acceptable means of expressing dissatisfaction.
4. Others should be able to tell when something is bothering you.

John comes from an avoidant and accommodating conflict culture in which emotion is typically conveyed indirectly. Rather than verbally expressing a problem, in John's family they might slam doors, pout, give the silent treatment, or avoid each other until the problem "blows over." John believes Maria should be able to pick up on his anger through the indirect signs he sends her such as how he tries to avoid her when she returns to work. John is conflict avoidant, so he has not said anything to Maria before about this problem, but he has had all he can take. He has put up with this behavior for too long, and this is the proverbial straw that broke the camel's back. In a fit of frustration, John calls Maria and yells into the receiver, "If you value your job, you will be back here tomorrow morning at 8:00 a.m. sharp and ready to do your part with the performance reviews! Good-bye!" This is the "volcano effect." Like volcanoes, John's anger and frustration have been bubbling below the surface for a long time, yet on the outside, he has appeared placid and calm. When something bothers him, he tries to ignore it for as long as possible. Then, something seemingly small triggers a reaction, or an overreaction, and his anger can no longer be contained. Sometimes when his temper erupts, his anger spills out to hurt innocent bystanders or even follows him home. His temper is not helping his health either, as he keeps increasing his dose of antacids and blood pressure medication.

John and Maria communicate in very different ways. In Maria's family, if someone is angry, upset, or hurt, he or she directly tells the other person what is on his or her mind. For example, Maria's husband recently asked her what she wanted for her birthday, and she said, "Nothing really. Just let me go 24 hours without cooking or doing laundry," and she meant it. There was no gift she was secretly wanting, no surprise party in the back of her mind. John's wife communicates indirectly, like her husband. If she says she does not want something for her birthday, what she really means is that he should know what she wants without her having to tell him. Because John knows his wife so well, he knows that she will be offended if he does not get her a nice gift for her birthday, so the goal is to surmise what it is she really wants. By spending time with her and investing in their relationship, he can pick up on her subtle cues. Alternatively, perhaps he will call one of her friends to see if she might have a gift idea to share.

In collaborative organizations and families, individuals share their concerns and preferences tactfully and openly. They listen to one another, convey empa-

**BOX 1.6. RULES IN COLLABORATIVE ORGANIZATIONS/
INDIVIDUALS**

1. Have regular meetings to discuss challenges and make decisions together.
2. The expression of strong feelings is allowed, but sulking and passive aggression is not.
3. Good listening and framing skills are used by all.
4. Strong relationships are built through shared activities and time spent together.

thy, and seek out mutually acceptable solutions to problems. They do not yell or throw temper tantrums. They do not avoid one another, sulk, or use the silent treatment. They express confidence that the problem can be solved through respectful and considerate dialogue, taking turns, and sharing in the costs and benefits of any eventual decisions.

LISTENING SKILLS: THE FOUNDATION OF CONFLICT MANAGEMENT

Few managerial skills are as neglected as listening skills. Listening skills are the foundation for most forms of collaboration, problem-solving, and dispute resolution. They are foundational to the habits of effective managers found in the Project Oxygen study cited earlier. Everyone can improve their listening skills, and when you work on these, people notice. Most managers believe they already have good listening skills, but would their employees agree?

In a typical conversation in English-speaking countries, there is an overlap of one to two syllables that occurs when the speaker slows down and the listener jumps into the conversation, thereby becoming the next speaker (see Figure 1.1). Culture influences speech patterns; therefore, not all English speakers will conform to this pattern, although it will apply to the majority of English speakers. Two problems arise when this listening pattern is used. First, there is an overlap during which the person who is supposed to be listening starts to speak before the speaker has completed her statement. Second, instead of listening to understand, the listener listens to respond, especially in situations of conflict. By **listening to respond**, people generally listen to figure out when they can jump into the conversation and get out their view, opinions, and thoughts.

Speaker A ------------   ---------------   -----------------

Speaker B   ----------------   ----------------

Figure 1.1   Common English Speaking-Listening Pattern

Instead of listening to respond, the first step in a problem-solving conversation is **listening to understand**. Listening to understand requires listeners to suspend judgment and their own need to drive the conversation. Instead of listening to jump into the conversation, the goal of listening to understand is to allow the speaker to completely share his or her thoughts, concerns, or emotions with the listener, uninterrupted. This calls for active listening. It is kind and builds, rather than undermines the relationship—even if you think you know what they were going to say.

Before you can know how best to respond to a concern or problem, you must seek to fully understand it.

Listening to understand is the first step to becoming a better manager, spouse, parent, or friend. Through the application of active listening skills, you can gain the ability to understand the concerns at hand while conveying that the other person's needs are important to you. **Active listening** refers to a set of techniques often used by counselors and conflict resolution specialists intended to help the listener focus on the speaker, elicit detailed stories related to conflicts or problems, build rapport between the listener and speaker, and form the foundation for later problem-solving efforts.

Step 1: Determine the purpose of the conversation.

Not all conversations require active listening. When the speaker has high emotional energy because they are excited, upset, or frustrated, then you (the listener) have an opportunity to increase your understanding and show you care about this relationship by engaging in active listening. Sometimes they seek your help to solve a problem, but equally often, they simply seek someone to listen empathetically. A general rule to follow is to refrain from offering problem-solving advice unless the speaker requests it or you have ascertained that they genuinely seek your input. Some conversations serve a solely recreational purpose. For example, two or more people can discuss a recent sporting event or complain about the bad food in the cafeteria. Rather than seeking to solve a problem, they seek camaraderie as an end in itself. Identifying the purpose of the conversation helps you determine when to apply active listening skills.

Step 2: Give the speaker your undivided attention.

When someone is upset or excited, we need to set aside all distractions and give the speaker our full attention. Even if we think we know what he is about to say, by allowing him the space to say it and listening without distraction, we send the signal that he is important to us. We build rapport. Close the door to make a quiet environment. Silence your cell phone. What if you cannot drop everything when they need to speak to you? Let them know you want to make time to listen to them uninterrupted. Tell them you will circle back to them when you are finished with your conference call (or whatever task is monopolizing your attention), but make sure to follow through.

Step 3: Your body language, eye contact,
and nonverbal signals should convey "I'm listening."

Turn your chair toward the speaker, look them in the eye, and clearly convey this time is theirs to share their concerns.

Step 4: Use door openers, check-ins, and summaries
to encourage them to tell their story fully.

Start with an open-ended question that allows the speaker to tell their story fully such as "What is going on?" or "How do you feel about that?," or "What's happened?" Then, as they speak, if they pause to see if you are still listening, then you can offer a check-in. The form these check-ins take can vary by listener and culture. It could be as simple as a head nod or a short phrase such as, "uh-huh." A longer check-in can summarize the emotion you hear the speaker conveying: "You sound frustrated." The listener's goal is to refrain from saying anything that could take the speaker in a different direction or take the focus off the speaker and onto the listener. Be sure to avoid the temptation to build rapport through shared experiences by stating, "That happened to me once. Let me tell you all about it." Also avoid making comments that indicate approval or disproval. Your goal is to listen to understand before deciding if problem-solving is the appropriate next step. If the speaker is an employee, remember that you are only hearing one side of the matter, so avoid reaching conclusions until you can gather more information, if appropriate.

When the speaker is finished, summarize what you heard so he or she feels understood. Be sure to include a reference to not only the speaker's perceived facts of what happened but also the emotional importance of the event to them. For example, you can say, "It sounds like you are really angry and frustrated because you feel you were passed over for that promotion." As a manager, you may need to respond with your own perception or facts, but not before ensuring the speaker feels heard. This sets a positive tone and reduces escalation.

Step 5: Develop a response to the concerns
raised by the speaker, if appropriate.

After using steps one through four, if the speaker is seeking a response or resolution from the listener (the manager, for our purposes), then the listener should convey a desire to respond to the legitimate needs of the speaker, even if that response requires time for reflection and information gathering. For example, you can say, "I would like to speak to the human resources representative to learn more about this hiring concern and then get back to you in a few days." If the goal of the conversation is joint problem-solving, then each person should leave the meeting with an understanding of the next steps in the process, any action items to be accomplished and by whom, and a timeline for decision or action. However, do not shorten the first four steps to get to step five. Remember, it is often worth asking the speaker to share his or her ideas for problem-solving as well. Not every problem is the manager's to solve. People tend to like their own ideas the best, even if they are the same as the suggestions you would have shared or recommended.

You will be tempted to interrupt by asking clarifying questions. Hold these until the end if possible. When you summarize what you heard, you can ask for clarification then. You will find that some people cognitively process difficult decisions through the act of speaking. For these individuals, all they need is a good listener, and they can solve the problem themselves. In fact, they will often thank you for being a good listener rather than asking you what to do. Avoid interrupting—even when you believe you know what they are going to say—because the act of listening is to understand the speaker, but also show respect and build rapport. Plus, you will be surprised at how often you did *not accurately* predict what they were going to say. Remain open to hearing them and being surprised.

Why would a book on conflict management suggest that listeners avoid trying to solve problems? Good conflict managers have one main tendency in common. We tend to be fixers. We want to help others with their problems by imposing our solutions on them. Sometimes, this is necessary and appropriate for managers or even parents. Fixing the speaker's problem is rarely, if ever, appropriate at the active listening stage. The time to worry about problem-solving is after all parties have had an opportunity to listen actively to each other and to their manager. Opportunities for active listening occur regularly, but we tend to miss them.

Look for signs of high emotional energy on the part of the speaker: excitement, frustration, anger, weariness, or anxiety. Try to identify these opportunities, and you will see noticeable improvements in your relationships and problem-solving abilities.

Listening, when done correctly, can be exhausting. A colleague once told me that he earned money as a lumberjack during his summers in college while he was studying to be a therapist. He claimed that he was significantly more tired at the end of the day as a therapist than as a lumberjack.

In summary, look for opportunities to apply active listening skills and see how it improves your relationships, deepens your understandings, and makes you a better manager.

BOX 1.7. KEYS TO ACTIVE LISTENING

Avoid distractions.
Make eye contact (when culturally appropriate). Use open body language.
Listen to understand.
Use conversation starters and openings.
Summarize what you've heard.
Avoid judging what you hear (positively or negatively).
Avoid trying to solve problems.
Avoid statements that take the focus away from the speaker.

Questioning

Whether you are acting as a meeting facilitator, an informal mediator between dueling employees, or simply trying to better understand a problem or person, questioning skills are critical for many managerial tasks. The first step in selecting the appropriate question is to consider the question's purpose. Questions may be used to elicit information, to promote reflection or analysis, or to challenge the speaker. The next step is to select a question type: "general (open-ended), opinion seeking, fact-finding, direct-forced choice, or leading questions" (Hughes & Bennett, 2005, p. 95).

To elicit the most comprehensive information, open-ended questions may be most useful. Open-ended questions ask speakers to share any information they deem useful to answer the question. For example, "Please tell me how this problem started and evolved?" An example of an opinion-seeking, open-ended question might be, "What kind of solutions would you like to see?"

When more specific information is needed, questioners may turn to fact-finding (slightly more general) for forced-choice (more specific) questions. For example, a fact-finding question would be, "What kind of employment information did you include in your application?" A similar question posed as a forced choice would be, "Did you tell us of your previous termination on your employment application?" These questions provide precise information needed to better understand the problem. These tend to be relatively low-risk, but expect defensiveness to decrease as openness of the question increases. Therefore, you will usually begin with more general questions and then get more specific as your understanding deepens.

Questions designed to promote reflection or analysis are used to get speakers to think through the consequences of potential solutions or to better understand their own role in the problem or solution. These are often phrased as opinion-seeking questions, such as, "If we moved Bob to another team, would your team be short-handed?" or "Can you think of any options or changes that you can make that would lead to a better outcome?" Depending on how they are phrased, questions demanding reflection and analysis can be incredibly useful during a problem-solving or decision-making process. It is important for questioners to have developed rapport and trust with the speaker first, so that they do not become defensive.

Questions that challenge the speaker are the riskiest. They are not part of a problem-solving or decision-making process but are instead used to express frustration or judgment by the questioner. These are often leading questions that are an indirect way for the questioner to make a statement rather than ask a question. Such a question might be, "Don't you think you overreacted?" or the famous standby, "When did you stop beating your wife?" A leading question can be difficult to answer without sounding defensive or guilty. In general, leading questions are not commonly used during active listening or problem-solving processes.

Leading questions lead us to the important issue of framing and reframing. **Framing** refers to the language used to put one's thoughts and conceptualizations into words. As Chapter 2 describes, the **framing effect** is a cognitive bias that occurs when the same option is presented in different formats or with different phrasing (it is framed differently), and the choice of format or phrasing influences one's opinions or preferences on the matter (Druckman, 2001). During conflicts or tense decision-making processes, it is important to choose your words carefully. The wrong word choice can lead parties to question the neutrality or fairness of the questioner. The words used to describe a thought or situation can reveal implicit judgments or biases that influence the course of a conversation or conflict. Additionally, individuals generally seek to avoid losses more than they endeavor to seek out equivalent gains. People tend to avoid risk when a negative frame is presented but seek risks when a positive frame is presented (Kahneman & Tversky, 1972). For instance, if the organization's leaders are seeking to solidify employee support for a proposed merger, they might focus on the risks to the company's survival if they remain small and less competitive in an increasingly globalized world. Framing also speaks to the procedural justice issues raised in chapter 2. For example, a facilitator at a contentious zoning meeting might avoid this framing: "Where will the big-box stores be built?" and instead ask participants, "What is your vision for the economic future of our town?"

Reframing refers to the language used to summarize, paraphrase, and reflect on what a party has said but using different words or conceptualizations than originally intended with the goal of altering the course of the communication and interaction between two or more parties. To illustrate, if two employees come to their manager with complaints about how the other is not doing her fair share of work, the manager might begin to reframe the discussion to refocus on the importance of teamwork by saying, "I can tell that getting the work done well and on time is important to you both. What ideas do you have for improving your teamwork?" The manager is beginning her interaction by reframing the dispute as an opportunity for collaboration rather than competition. If taken to extremes, this technique runs the risk of being seen as manipulative or putting words into the mouths of others, so use caution and be strategic when reframing the words of others.

Facilitators, mediators, and conflict managers often use reframing techniques when creating an agenda based on the expressed positions or concerns of the parties. To exemplify, if a party says, "I'll agree to her demands over my dead body!" a neutral reframing might be, "I can tell you have strong feelings about this. Please tell me more about why you feel this way." Reframing can be used to move parties from a past to a future focus, to depersonalize comments away from a personal attack to an attack on the problem, or to redirect parties from an adversarial to a collaborative focus. There are ethical implications of reframing because it can be used to manipulate a party's statements or to put words in their mouths. When used correctly, reframing helps refocus a conversation from destructive, blame-focused, escalatory language to constructive, joint problem-solving.

EMOTIONAL INTELLIGENCE AND EXCEPTIONAL MANAGERS

Emotional intelligence (EI) refers to the ability to perceive, control, and evaluate emotions in oneself and others (Cherry, 2012; Salovey & Mayer, 1990). Emotional intelligence can be further broken down into self-awareness, self-regulation, motivation, empathy, and social skills. By setting goals for growth in your EI and related behaviors, you can improve your ability to collaborate and lead others while keeping your blood pressure and sanity intact. Great managers tend to have high EI scores. Individuals vary in their ability to correctly perceive the emotional states of others through the interpretation of body language, tone, and facial expressions. Emotion plays an important role in the prioritization of tasks, determining the importance of different events or activities, and motivating our responses to these events. Some individuals are better at using emotion for these purposes. Individuals differ greatly in their ability to manage their emotional states or react to the emotional states of others. This is particularly important in the field of management since supervisors and managers are asked to respond to crises, make decisions that impact others, and communicate the reasons behind decisions to the impacted populations. Employees who are upset with customers, coworkers, or company decisions come to managers to vent their frustrations and seek redress or coaching. The best managers convey empathy and compassion while maintaining healthy boundaries with employees. This requires well-developed EI. Employees or managers who struggle with emotional outbursts or insensitivity to the emotions of others can create difficult working environments, resulting in more formal and informal complaints, higher turnover, disengagement, and even workplace violence.

Using Box 1.8, take a few minutes to assess the areas in which your EI skills are strong and those areas in which you seek to improve. There are many free self-assessments available online to help you better understand your strengths and opportunities for growth related to EI.[1] Once you better understand your baseline, consider setting specific goals for improvement and asking for feedback from trusted family members, friends, or colleagues. In terms of your self-awareness and empathy, how comfortable are you with identifying and labeling feelings,

BOX 1.8. ELEMENTS OF EMOTIONAL INTELLIGENCE

1. Self-awareness: The ability to understand your own emotional state and the impact of your emotional state on others and the ability to have, convey, and build self-confidence.
2. Self-regulation: The ability to regulate rather than overreact to your own emotions while conveying self-control, adaptability, trustworthiness, openness to new ideas/innovation, and conscientiousness or accountability for your choices.
3. Motivation: The sense of drive, commitment, initiative, and optimism.
4. Empathy: The ability to recognize and respond effectively to the emotions of others including your service orientation, awareness of political dynamics at work, desire to develop others, and your willingness to cultivate diversity as a positive team attribute.
5. Social Skills: The ability to influence others, manage conflict, collaborate, lead, inspire, send clear messages, and initiate and manage change.

paying particular attention to somatic signals? Are you tense and breathing shallowly? Or are you relaxed and reflective? Do you recognize your emotional triggers or signals that something is bothering you or others? Are you able to convey empathy and support for colleagues exhibiting anxiety or high levels of stress? Are you aware of the impact that your behavior or attitude has on others? Are you able to request and receive feedback without defensiveness? Can you coach others to do this? To grow in this area, check out Chapters 8 and 10.

As for self-regulation, managers with high EI can take in unpleasant or distressing information and pause to reflect and process that information, before deciding how to feel about it and then develop a course of action or gather more information. Do you pause and reflect before you act or are you more reactive than reflective? Emotional flooding is the term used to describe how it feels when we get overwhelmed by our own emotions while emotional contagion is the term used to describe how it feels when the emotions of others spread to us. Have you ever seen someone cry and it made you feel like crying? That is emotional contagion, and it is a healthy sign that you are not a sociopath. Later chapters will discuss personality disorders, but one sign of antisocial personality disorders (including sociopathy) is the inability to feel empathy for others. Humans are neurologically wired for connection to others, especially those in their community. Yet managers often encounter people in emotional distress (e.g., disgruntled customers or patients, angry employees, etc.). We must be able to register their emotion and empathize, while setting healthy boundaries that allow us to be effective in our work environments. Do you experience emotional flooding or contagion in ways that negatively impact your work? If so, this is a skill to work on that can involve pausing to register the emotion and event, taking some deep breaths or even a walk to calm down before deciding upon a course of action. Great managers remain or attain calmness even amid the chaos and crises they encounter at work and at home.

During daunting challenges like the Great Resignation or supply-chain backlogs, loss of motivation is a key symptom of burnout in ourselves and others. This is linked to EI because motivating ourselves and others is both a key facet of EI but also a key management task. **Burnout** is based on

> three key stress responses: an overwhelming sense of exhaustion, feelings of cynicism and detachment, and a sense of professional ineffectiveness and lack of accomplishment. . . . Burnout results when the balance of deadlines, demands, working hours, and other stressors outstrips rewards, recognition, and relaxation. It's a mistake to assume that burnout is merely an emotional response to long hours or a challenging job. Rather, mounting scientific evidence shows that burnout takes a profound physical toll that cascades well beyond our professional lives. Just as the impact of burnout stifles healthy professional growth, emerging research shows that the chronic psychosocial stress that characterizes burnout not only impairs people's personal and social functioning, it also can overwhelm their cognitive skills and neuroendocrine systems—eventually leading to distinctive changes in the anatomy and functioning of the brain. (Michel, 2016)

Once managers exhibit burnout, it is much harder to motivate those around us. Workers experiencing burnout often report feeling profound emotional exhaustion, negativity, and a crisis in feelings of professional competence. "Much like symptoms of depression, burnout was asphyxiating people's ambitions, idealism, and sense of worth" (Michel, 2016). Therefore, managers must be on the lookout for symptoms of burnout in themselves and others. These are symptoms that the working environment likely needs to change to sustain productivity and retain engaged employees over the long run. Managers can dialogue with employees individually and collectively to ensure that workload expectations are reasonable, that employees have the tools and training they need to achieve performance goals, that sufficient stress relief opportunities are built into the workday, and managers can cultivate a sense of belonging and warmth between team members.

The past few years have made clear that the presence of overwhelming stress at work, at home, and in our communities must be managed productively rather than ignored or viewed as a non-workplace problem. People bring their whole selves to work. That includes their stresses over a lack of childcare, physical and mental health concerns, and their motivation to tackle difficult tasks. Managers must use EI skills such as empathy, self-awareness, self-regulation, motivation, and social skills to deeply understand and proactively address the needs of their workforce.

CONCLUSION

The first step to improving your managerial skills is to take stock of them: understand how you communicate and respond to conflict. Improve your listening skills while identifying managerial behaviors you seek to improve in your own performance. Know your own level of emotional intelligence and find strategies to compensate for areas of weakness (using listening skills more purposefully, framing comments constructively, and regulating your own emotional responses to others). Understanding your own managerial approach and conflict style will assist you to improve your ability to solve problems in a nimble and effective manner.

Look around your organization or at your competitors. Describe the skill sets of the best managers—those with low turnover, high productivity, and high employee/client satisfaction levels. How do they communicate with their employees, peers, and superiors? How do they respond to inevitable problems? Managers who understand themselves will be able to better understand and respond to others.

JOHN AT THE BUREAU OF RECLAMATION

What can John do? Can he control whether Maria calls in sick? No, but he can communicate his needs in a way Maria will understand as well as create and enforce incentives for productive workplace behaviors. John needs to "push the reset button" in his relationship with Maria so that they reach shared expectations about what they both need to succeed at work.

To address this problem as a proactive conflict manager, John called Maria and said, "I know that some days are harder than others around here. I was dreading these reviews myself, but without your help, I don't think I can get them done. What can we do together to make the hard days easier for the both of us? How can we work together as a team to handle problems or challenges that might be too much for either of us individually? Can you recommend any changes for me to consider so that this process (or others) can be improved? In the future, when you feel that sense of dread coming on, can you discuss it with me so we can try to get to the root of the problem? While I can't fix everything, there may be ways we can make improvements so that we both look forward to working here." In essence, he is seeking to create shared expectations with Maria in order to reduce unproductive conflict.

John's goal is to see Maria's behavior as a symptom of the underlying problem: a performance review process that is unempowering and destructive rather than constructive. What can be done to make this process better so that no one feels the need to evade difficult, but important tasks? Chapter 7 examines ways to restructure the performance review process to make it more collaborative, collegial, and even fun. Using this one-on-one time with employees to learn more about their needs and concerns so that it is a two-way communication process will make it more impactful and pleasant for everyone.

While John retains the final decision-making authority as the manager, he has made it clear that he is open to Maria's ideas and that he cares about her as an employee and as a person.

KEY TERMS

accommodating style	Dunning-Kruger effect
accommodation	emotional intelligence (EI)
active listening	framing
avoiding style	framing effect
burnout	growth mindset
collaboration	leader-member exchange theory
collaborative style	leaders
competitive style	listening to respond
compromising style	listening to understand
conflict avoidance	managers
conflict prevention	passion projects
conflict styles inventory (CSI)	reframing
denial	"win-win"

DISCUSSION QUESTIONS

1. While the CSI was developed as an individual-level tool, we often see analogous behaviors within work teams (e.g., departments or units) as well as entire organizations. Which style best describes the unit in which you work or manage? Why? Which style best describes your organization as a whole? How does your individual style fit in with or clash with those in your work environment? Discuss this as a team if possible.

2. Think about a current or previous problem or conflict in your work environment. Which of the five conflict styles best describes your approach

to that conflict? Which style best describes the style(s) used by others in conflict? Was the conflict or problem successfully resolved? Why or why not? In groups of two to five people, share your stories. What might have happened if you used one of the other conflict styles? Analyze these questions collectively and/or individually.

3. Who is the best listener you know? What makes them such a good listener? How does it feel when someone really listens to you?

4. When you are acting in a managerial role (or as a parent), are you permissive, authoritative, or authoritarian? In what ways is your approach working or not working as well as you would like? What specific behaviors would you like to change to exhibit more of the authoritative (facilitative) approach? Discuss this with your team members and let them know that you are working to alter your approach. This way, when your habitual responses change, they understand why the changes are occurring and they will likely receive them with more openness and less confusion.

EXERCISES

1. Either individually or in small groups, develop a list of interview questions for potential new hires. These questions should give you a sense of this person's conflict style and how well they will fit into your team's culture and work environment. In addition to designing appropriate interview questions, what other sources of information will provide clues as to how this person deals with problem-solving and teamwork? Do they communicate directly or indirectly? Are they constructive problem solvers?

2. Choose the best style of decision-making for this scenario: In the last month, three out of ten of your employees have come to you to complain that one of their coworkers is shirking by coming in late, leaving early, and leaving his work for others to finish. You were hoping this employee would "take the hint" from his coworkers and start to do his fair share of the work, but this has not happened. What would it look like if you addressed this situation using each of the five conflict styles discussed in this chapter?

3. In groups of three, practice being the speaker, the listener, and the observer. Have the speaker tell a short story about some problem or concern he or she has had in a past or present work environment. The listener should use the skills described in this chapter, including the use of a summary statement at the end. The observer will provide feedback about the listener's eye contact, body language, use of door openers, ability to refrain from judging or evaluating, and the summarization at the end. Rotate roles every three to six minutes. Discuss these debriefing questions: How did it feel to be the listener? How did it feel to be the speaker? Which skills do you need to practice more?

4. *Exercise: Habits of Effective Managers:* From the earlier list, which of these 10 habits are you doing and which could you start or improve? Which could you request from your own manager (e.g., more coaching, etc.)?

5. Check in with your team to better understand their expectations and views about what makes a great manager (or team member, if you are not a manager). Different people seek to be managed differently. Getting to know their expectations, and then negotiating shared expectations, will assist you as you seek to be the best manager and/or teammate possible.

GOAL SETTING

1. You now have a better understanding of your own conflict management habits and tendencies. How are these working for you? Is there room for improvement? Are you able to consciously choose the best style for each problem encountered? If not, ask yourself this question: "On a scale of zero to ten, where zero equals a conflict management train wreck and ten equals masterful conflict management, where do I fall?" Now, imagine what behaviors you would need to change in order to move your score up by only one or two points. Write down those behavioral changes as goals to pursue this week. Revisit this question next week and see if you have made any progress and whether new goals are appropriate. Sample questions may include the following:

   a. Do I take time to reflect before responding to conflict?
   b. How well do I make room for others to share ideas and concerns?
   c. How efficiently do I deal with problems that arise rather than put off addressing them as long as possible?
   d. How well do I communicate to my employees that I care about them as people?
   e. How well do I create opportunities for my employees to get to know each other and develop strong interpersonal relationships?
   f. How well do I analyze the extent to which a decision should be reached unilaterally versus through a collaborative process?
   g. How well do I listen to others?
   h. How well do I invite feedback?
   i. How well do I communicate my vision to my employees?
   j. How well do I model the behaviors I seek for others to follow?
   k. How well do I regulate my emotions to create a positive, consistent work environment?

2. Use the list of 10 Habits of Effective Managers, stemming from Project Oxygen at Google. Catalog how much time you spend on each of these habits in an average day or week. Which of these habits needs more of your attention? Seek feedback from your colleagues as to how you are doing on each of these habits and how you can improve. Choose 1–2 of these habits to devote more energy to this week.

SUGGESTED SUPPLEMENTAL READINGS

Barthel, T., & Fortson-Harwell, M. (2016). Practice note: Asking better questions. *Conflict Resolution Quarterly, 34,* 43–56. https://doi.org/10.1002/crq.21170

Bastian, R. (2019, March 8). Personality-based performance reviews are fine to give women—As long as men get them too. *Forbes.* https://www.forbes.com/sites/rebekah bastian/2019/03/08/personality-based-performance-reviews-are-fine-to-give-women-as -long-as-men-get-them-too/?sh=642746e31667

Brackett, M. A., Rivers, S. E., & Salovey, P. (2011). Emotional intelligence: Implications for personal, social, academic, and workplace success. *Social and Personality Psychology Compass, 5,* 88–103.

Harrell, M., and Barbato, L. (2018, February 28). *Great managers still matter: The evolution of Google's Project Oxygen.* re:Work. https://rework.withgoogle.com/blog/the -evolution-of-project-oxygen/

Hughes, V. (2022, September 16). How to change minds? A study makes the case for talking it out. *New York Times.* https://www.nytimes.com/2022/09/16/science/group-consensus-persuasion-brain-alignment.html?smid=url-share

Katz, N. H., & Sosa, A. (2015). The emotional advantage: The added value of the emotionally intelligent negotiator. *Conflict Resolution Quarterly, 33,* 57–74. https://doi .org/10.1002/crq.21127

NOTE

1. https://www.workplacestrategiesformentalhealth.com/resources/emotional-intelli gence-self-assessment

2

Theory to Practice

The Root Causes and Cures of Conflict

There is nothing so practical as a good theory.

—Kurt Lewin

Why do they do that? The theories in this chapter are wildly practical for conflict managers and leaders because they provide insights into why people behave as they do, how conflict escalates, and which interventions are most likely to succeed. As Kurt Lewin notes above, theories are practical because they enable us to make sense of what we are seeing. Only then can we design an effective intervention.

After reading this chapter, revisit these learning objectives. All future chapters refer to material on conflict theory contained herein, so it is important to have clearly understood the material reflected in these learning objectives before reading subsequent chapters.

Learning Objectives

- Demonstrate an understanding of the root causes of unproductive conflict.
- Diagnose the causes of unproductive conflict within an organization.
- Engage in self-analysis to better understand ways in which your own perceptions, identity, and viewpoint are likely to influence your analyses.
- Explain the differences among key conflict theories such as attribution theory, procedural justice theory, conflict ripeness, and others.
- Describe the differences between structural and nonstructural sources of conflict.
- Identify common psychological sources of conflict that give rise to interpersonal disputes and miscommunication.

ELISE AND UNPRODUCTIVE CONFLICT
AT MAIN STREET BAKERIES

This morning Elise got a call from Ben, her director for human resources (HR). Ben told her he was asked to find yet another assistant manager for store number 75 because the one they had just resigned. This makes four assistant managers in less than two years. The turnover level for employees at store number 75 is 65% higher than for the rest of the company. In general, Main Street Bakeries holds onto its employees for many years, so it is surprising to see this level of turnover. Ben wanted to bring this issue to Elise's attention, and he recommends that either he or Elise should visit this store (more than 1,000 miles away from the corporate office) to find out what is happening. Elise agrees and decides that Ben should do the initial digging and make recommendations to her about possible next steps.

★   ★   ★

Why did they (or I) do that?! Why are they acting that way? Why don't they get along with their colleagues or customers? Why is this team's work product better than other teams? Why is turnover higher at this store than other, assumedly similar stores? Conflict theories help us diagnose the causes of conflict. By way of example, if a patient comes to their physician with a fever, the doctor can prescribe medication to reduce the fever. But without addressing the root cause of the fever, it is likely to come back in four to six hours when the medication wears off. Is it a virus that will go away on its own? Is it an infection, which needs antibiotics? Is it cancer, which may need more long-term treatment? Physicians strive to uncover the causes of illness rather than solely treating the symptoms. Conflict is like a fever. For example, workplace bullying or sexual harassment at work will certainly cause conflict, yet they may also point to a dysfunctional organizational culture that ignores or even perpetuates unacceptable behaviors. If the bully or harasser is fired, but abusive behaviors continue elsewhere in the organization or in the same team, then we know the ultimate source of the conflict is a dysfunctional organizational culture or ineffective incentives to shape behaviors. The intervention for a culture problem is different in many ways from the intervention that is appropriate when one bully is mistreating people. Analyzing the source of negative behaviors and outcomes is the foundation upon which superior managerial skills are built.

Skilled conflict managers see the signs of conflict, such as turnover, litigation, low customer satisfaction, or poor morale as symptoms rather than causes of conflict. They think like detectives or physicians before selecting the appropriate intervention or approach. Of course, if left untreated, the symptoms become their own problems that worsen the downward spiral facing a leader, a team, or an organization. For example, trauma can lead people to self-medicate through excessive alcohol consumption. While the unhealed, unaddressed trauma is the root cause of excessive drinking and related behaviors such as drinking and driving or absenteeism from work, the drinking itself can also become the cause of conflict and a symptom of deeper causes (e.g., trauma).

In this chapter you will learn how to engage in conflict analysis with the goal of uncovering the root causes of conflicts commonly encountered in the workplace. Only then can we discuss possible processes and skills for resolution or better yet, the prevention of destructive conflict.

ISSUES AND TYPOLOGIES OF WORKPLACE CONFLICT

Some scholars of organizational development divide workplace conflicts into three types: Relational conflicts, task conflicts, and value conflicts (Shonk, 2022) With the use of subcategories, this can be a helpful cognitive framework.

1. Task-based conflicts include disputes about how the work gets done, the assignment of work tasks, the allocation of resources, and the organization's strategic direction.

Resource-based conflict occurs when two or more people, units, organizations, or even nations compete over perceived limited resources. To reduce resource-based organizational conflict, it is imperative to make decisions about the distribution of international resources in ways viewed as transparent, fair, and mission driven.

Role-based conflict occurs when someone behaves in a way that is different from what one would anticipate based on their role. For example, if a peer begins issuing directions to colleagues, it could cause conflict out of a belief that it is not their role to issue orders or directions since they are not a superior in the chain of command. Another common role-based conflict occurs when an employee is promoted to the level of supervisor or manager, but her former peers struggle to accept her decisions since she has always been viewed as a peer rather than a boss. Overlapping or unclear lines of authority also create conflicts based on unclear roles and authority. Our organizational and broader national cultures tell us what behaviors to expect based on the role someone holds as a parent, neighbor, religious leader, elder, judge, teacher, human resources specialist, ombudsman, etc. This is particularly common when a new leader or manager takes over and wants to "shake things up," by using a different leadership style than their organization is accustomed to. While this can be healthy change, it can create conflict, some of which may be necessary and transformative. These conflicts are often mitigated through strategic planning.

2. Relationship-based conflicts include differences in personality, conflict styles (see Chapter 1), communication habits, tastes, and preferences that lead to interpersonal conflict. These could include the challenges posed by personality disorders, past traumas, irrational (and rational) fears, and perceptions of mutually exclusive needs, and other bases for interpersonal conflict.

Based on this history of the relationship, the parties may have low trust or harbor grudges for past problems. Relationship-based conflicts can be mitigated through 3-step problem-solving (see Chapter 7) and coaching from a higher-level manager, mentor, or ombudsman (see Chapter 10).

3. Values conflicts occur when two or more people have differing views about what is right and wrong, sacred or profane, important or unimportant based on different perspectives, viewpoints, identity categories, and/or religious upbringing. While religion and politics are often subjects to avoid at work, these value differences can underlie proposals on everything from dress codes to the provision of family leave, to the selection of projects or clients. Value conflicts are an underestimated reason employees quit. When one feels one must compromise on core values to maintain a job, then the outcome is always bad: resignation, sabotage, depression, or even workplace violence.

UNCOVERING THE CAUSES OF CONFLICT

Imagine an internationally known financial institution in which three of their last four CEOs were publicly disgraced and fired in the wake of scandals involving the misuse of funds and the mistreatment of employees. What about a company in which all managers can take unlimited vacation, yet no one takes any time off. Instead, they quit and work elsewhere. Or a large law firm in which a senior partner has been frequently sued for sexual harassment, but the firm continues to pay to settle these cases rather than to address his predatory behaviors—until a class action suit by more than twenty current and former employees and a few clients leads to humiliating headlines and a cascading loss of clients seeking to distance themselves from the scandal and any potential contagious brand damage. It is not difficult to imagine these stories because they happen nearly every week. They keep organizational conflict management specialists in high demand. These conflicts could have been prevented, but if the causes continue to be misdiagnosed, then they will recur repeatedly.

Incentive structures shape human (and animal) behavior. Behavior continues as long as it is working. While individual personalities matter and screening out narcissists and sociopaths is always a great idea, even selfish, greedy people will change their behavior when faced with organizations that require transparency, monitoring, and sanctioning. The correct amount of transparency and sanctions will prevent most illegal or unethical behaviors. Try to avoid the tendency to blame an individual for wrongdoing without first analyzing the *systemic* factors that allowed the behavior to go on unabated for so long. While individuals must be held accountable for their choices, if you fire an individual without determining the need for changes to incentive structures such as a lack of monitoring and enforcement of rules or policies, then the next person hired may copy the behaviors of their predecessor.

In the second case, an "unlimited vacation" policy sounds like the height of employee empowerment: if you can meet your productivity goals, project deadlines, and still take a long vacation, then do it! Yet this type of policy often comes with unreasonably high workload expectations or upper managers who unofficially penalize employees who dare to take vacation. Additionally, employees may be expected to work while on vacation, which undermines their ability to recharge and reconnect with their loved ones, their health needs, and their hobbies. In other words, the unlimited vacation policy must be backed up with a culture that values and prioritizes work-life balance. Otherwise, it may exist in the employee handbook but not in reality.

Lastly, the harassing lawyer case must be addressed on the individual level but also on the level of the organizational culture. Employees rarely benefit from bringing forward a complaint of harassment. They typically do so out of a desire to make abusive behavior stop and to protect others in the environment from the same threat. A lawsuit typically occurs only when efforts to resolve the matter less formally have failed or been ignored. While firing the lawyer is the logical step, conflict competent leaders will also want to know why this problem was not resolved the first time it came to the attention of the human resources department or upper management. It is common for organizational clients to hire experts to offer training in workplace civility (e.g., how to prevent harassment, discrimination, and bullying) because they have one serially abusive manager or leader. This is a conflict-avoidant response to the problem. Instead of or in addition to organization-wide training, organizations need to clearly communicate expected behaviors and back those up with appropriate monitoring and sanctioning of culpable individuals. Predators who cannot prey at work will either change their behaviors or leave the organization for more fertile hunting grounds. Refusing to take action to stop predators results in devastating impacts, often including brand damage, turnover, litigation, and low morale. Chapter 7 will examine useful ways to bully-proof your organization so that every employee knows how to redirect, dissuade, and report abuses of power including harassment, bullying, and discrimination.

What do all three examples have in common? Without a proper diagnosis of the sources of the conflict, the problems will continue to occur. Theories about the origins, escalations, and interventions for conflict are foundational to your ability to diagnose and solve organizational problems.

Levels of Analysis for Organizational Conflicts

This chapter examines theories at various levels of analysis: intrapersonal, interpersonal, intergroup, and systemic. Corresponding interventions occur at each level.

Intrapersonal conflicts, also known as intrapsychic conflicts, are those we fight in our own minds as we struggle to accurately make meaning out of facts, in the presence of common cognitive biases such as denial, rationalization, defensiveness, unconscious bias, projection, psychiatric conditions, personality types, the effects of addictions, the impact of past traumas, or conflicting sociocultural norms and expectations. The way in which our brains make meaning out of available information can lead to incomplete or even inaccurate or unhelpful responses. Successful interventions for intrapersonal conflicts often involve coaching or mental health therapy designed to improve self-awareness, coping skills, and the ability to identify and remediate cognitive biases.

Interpersonal conflicts occur between two or more people. Successful interventions may include facilitated conversations by a third party, such as a manager or mediator. The goal of these conversations is to reach shared expectations designed to address current problem(s) and prevent their recurrence (see 3-step problem-solving in Chapter 7).

Intergroup conflicts occur between members of distinct groups such as units, teams, identity or ethnic groups, organizations, or even nation-states. These occur when the members of one group believe their interests or values are at odds with those of another group.

System-level conflicts occur when policies, procedures, institutions, or systems such as economic or justice systems work to the benefit of one or more groups at the expense of one or more other groups. The tendency is to blame individuals for behaviors that are encouraged or required by a broader system. By blaming individuals for systemic problems, the system can continue to function unchanged. For example, when Wells Fargo created unreachable sales goals for employees, the employees responded by opening accounts without the permission of the impacted customers. While individually unethical, it was an open secret that thousands of employees were engaging in this fraudulent activity to keep their jobs (Kelly, 2020). Firing employees would not be sufficient to prevent the recurrence of this problem. Instead, the company's culture and systems must change to ensure the problem is fully resolved.

Using the three earlier examples, in the matter of the misbehaving lawyer, common interventions would include termination (individual level); apologies and efforts to redress the harm done to individual victims such as reemployment, raises, the provision of restorative services or other compensation (individual and group levels); steps to empower employees with ethics hotlines and bystander training to prevent and resolve future instances more effectively (systemic levels). When you are trying to get to the root causes of conflict, consider looking through the lens of all four levels to reduce the likelihood that you miss an important source of conflict.

BIOLOGICAL, PHYSIOLOGICAL, AND EVOLUTIONARY THEORIES OF CONFLICT AND RESOLUTION

Recent research has yielded great insights into the biological, physiological, neurological, and evolutionary sources of human behavior. Scientists are learning more every day about what makes us tick, including common sources of and responses to conflict and cooperation.

The Evolution of Cooperation and Conflict

Good managers understand how to motivate their employees and how to behave cooperatively. By understanding the mechanisms through which cooperative behavior has evolved, managers are better able to harness motivating forces in the service of conflict prevention and early resolution. For human beings to live and work successfully in groups, our species has developed the ability to differentiate those who will cooperate for mutual gain from individuals who will seek individual gain at the group's expense. Game theorists label this latter group *defectors*. Game theory uses a combination of mathematics and economics to predict human behavior in circumstances with varying incentive structures (see von Neumann, 1944). For example, how can managers discourage shirking in group environments? One lazy worker can drive a small office crazy as the sense of unfairness rises among those who must pick up the slack.

It is important that leaders and managers align the individual good with the good of the group (or organization). **Perverse incentives** occur when a policy, procedure, or system misaligns the individual's interests against the interests of the organization. Perverse incentives are a pervasive source of conflict within organizations and society. These situations are sometimes unavoidable, such as the need for physicians to take turns staffing the on-call line on weekends and evenings. Yet the goal is to minimize those situations in which an individual must sacrifice his or her own best interest for the interests of the group. Paying taxes is another example. Individuals have an incentive to avoid paying taxes if they think they can get away with it, but if no one paid taxes then we would not have fire departments, roads, or public schools. For this reason, the penalties for tax evasion are meant to realign the incentives facing individuals so they do indeed pay taxes.

> Being nice made evolutionary sense when we lived in small bands surrounded by relatives because helping them helped our genes survive. And we had a direct incentive to be fair to people who would later reciprocate kindness or punish selfishness. But why even consider returning a stranger's wallet you find in a taxicab? Why leave a tip in a restaurant you will never visit again? (Tierney, 2010)

Most people are honest and try hard to be good citizens, neighbors, and co-workers even when there is little overt incentive to do so. However, how do we explain and deal with the occasional individual who claims the work of others as his own or repeatedly fails to deliver on deadlines and promises, leaving others to hold the bag?

Game theorists have learned that cooperative individuals are better off if they can find other cooperative people with whom to trade, unite for mutual defense, reproduce, and otherwise work with for mutual gain (Vogel, 2004). The work of biologist William Hamilton (1964) shows us that humans and other animals cooperate with family members, even at their own individual expense, to ensure that their gene pool is passed on to future generations. Robert Trivers (1971) took this research to the next step by showing how cooperation with unrelated individuals can benefit the altruist as long as one's cooperative or altruistic acts can be expected to be reciprocated in the future. In common terms, this is akin to "what goes around comes around."

Yet an unscrupulous individual could take advantage of a group of collaborators by feigning cooperation, only to dupe them in the end and abscond with benefits beyond their due. Human societies have established social rules that reward cooperators and punish defectors through ostracism, justice systems, or by other means. Once defectors are identified, they are typically punished and often banished from the group. Ostracized or banished individuals are less likely to survive and reproduce. Therefore, individuals with tendencies toward cooperation and collaboration reproduce and form social majorities better than defectors. As cooperators pass on their genes, and defectors do so less frequently, our world is evolving in a more peaceful direction. For this reason behaviors tolerated or normalized a generation ago, such as schoolyard bullying, spanking a child with a belt and leaving marks, and workplace sexual harassment are increasingly less tolerated. These changing norms become codified into law, which reflects their status as widely shared societal expectations.

Believe it or not, deaths from violent crime and war have decreased over the past two centuries. Due to modern media, the fear of violence is likely higher, but the objective threat from violence has gone down over time.

Intrapersonal (and Intrapsychic) Causes of Conflict

Two individuals may interpret the same set of facts quite differently based not only on their experiences and cultural knowledge (see Chapter 5), but also based on their neurological differences. Some people are literally wired to be more or less trusting, impulsive, and/or fearful (Minson & Chen, 2022; Jacobs Hendel, 2020). These differences can be seen in responses to opinion polls as well as in brain scans conducted to map human responses to statements like, "The world is getting more dangerous every day." People with higher levels of fear and who perceive threats where others do not are more likely to be defensively aggressive and less empathetic, which spawns more destructive conflict. While our upbringing and socialization matters too (Jacobs Hendel, 2020; Van der Kolk, 2015), this section will examine biological and neurological differences that explain, at least in part, why some individuals approach the world with suspicion, fear, or even anger while others are open, willing to take risks, and exhibit interpersonal warmth.

Neuropsychologists are doing pathbreaking work on the connection between biochemistry and aggression versus altruism in humans and nonhuman animals. When individuals act altruistically, the parts of the brain responsible for human bonding and positive feelings are stimulated. In sum, altruistic acts *feel good* at a biological level in biologically normal people, but some people feel this more than others (Vedantam, 2007). Humans are communal creatures, so it makes sense that we have developed neural networks to support reciprocity and collaboration. On the other end, multiple studies (Gunnar & Fisher, 2006) have concluded that levels of cortisol, a hormone in the brain, rise when animals are under stressful conditions to help them cope. Chronically low levels of cortisol are correlated with aggressive and antisocial behaviors, meaning that some people cope more poorly with stress and are prone to act on violent impulses in reaction to stress, particularly children (*Science Daily*, 2008).

Cortisol levels vary based on genetics and the environment, being especially prone to variation due to chronic stress during pregnancy, infancy, and childhood, when the brain is rapidly developing (Gunnar & Fisher, 2006). Abused or neglected children have a higher likelihood of experiencing chronically low levels of cortisol, resulting in antisocial and aggressive tendencies (Gunnar & Fisher, 2006). Some forms of autism have been correlated with unusual levels of cortisol (Brosnan et al., 2009).

Biologists have uncovered valuable information about the role that oxytocin plays in increasing empathy and trust between individuals or, by contrast, the role it plays in the absence of empathy and trust.

Researchers found that genetic differences in people's responsiveness to the effects of oxytocin were linked to their ability to read faces, infer the emotions of others, feel distress at others' hardship and even to identify with characters in a role-play exercise. (Angier, 2009, p. D2)

And

Exposure to nurturing and loving parents can contribute to the normal development of this [oxytocin] system. Exposure to adversity, such as stress or illness, can detrimentally affect the development and functioning of oxytocin and the oxytocin receptor. . . . A well-regulated oxytocin system can support greater resilience against excessive drug use and addiction. Animal studies show oxytocin can boost the reward of social connection, lower the effect of drugs, reduce anxiety, and improve management of stressors. (Baracz & Buisman-Pijlman, 2017)

At a very basic level, some individuals are hormonally predisposed to be more trusting, empathetic, and able to connect than others. This does not explain trust and empathy in all situations, of course. Chapter 3 will examine trust at a deeper level, including how to build and repair it during or after negotiations.

Similarly, research on introversion versus extroversion indicates that some employees may be better at working collaboratively with others in high-stress environments, whereas other employees need solitary, less stimulating work environments to be fully productive (Cain, 2012). When managers take the time to get to know their employees, they are better able to ascertain the conditions under which an employee will thrive: Some want more social connection and stimulation at work while others seek calmer, solo workspaces. Some trust others easily and prefer to work in teams, while others take more time to warm up or might benefit from teambuilding efforts.

There are physical and biological differences that explain why two people react differently to the same situation. This may help us to depersonalize conflict when it occurs, meaning that we need not attribute aggressive or antisocial behaviors as signs of personal affronts but instead understand myriad reasons why an individual may struggle to behave constructively in challenging situations.

Although science is just scratching the surface of the nature-nurture debate, this information helps us to better understand that some individuals have an advantage over others when it comes to dealing with stress and social interactions. Regardless of an individual's natural endowment in these areas, these skills can grow through a variety of interventions discussed in this book.

The good news is that human beings are significantly more likely to cooperate with others than to take advantage and that cooperation feels "right" to most humans. Cooperation and helping others are the norms, not the exceptions. For individuals with abnormally poor social skills or maladaptive behaviors traceable to a medical condition or the impact of past trauma, treatments are available that will improve their ability to interact and cope successfully with stressful situations, particularly when combined with training designed to enhance these skills and abilities. Hiring managers may wish to develop and use scenario-response questions designed to determine how well potential applicants work with others, deal with stress, trust, are trustworthy, and so on. This information can help ensure an appropriate match among employees, job duties, and team members.

Rupture and Repair: The Bonding Power of Conflict

The last few years have yielded significant scientific breakthroughs in our understanding of the impact of collaboration and conflict on our brains and relationships, including teamwork (Hughes, 2022). Using magnetic resonance imaging (MRI) across multiple research participants simultaneously, scientist have created a new form of research technology termed *hyperscanning*. This allows neuropsychologists to see how a group of individuals responds at a neurological level when undertaking a joint task. For example, small groups watched a video clip of an emotional interaction between an adult and child. Then they were asked to discuss what was happening in the video, which was taken out of context. As they shared their various ideas, researchers could see the neurological response to conflict in the group and compare individuals and groups in which a consensus emerged versus those in which unresolved conflict erupted (Hughes, 2022). They saw the positive impacts of mediative or facilitative leaders who emerged and the negative impacts of bullies or blowhards. They found that groups that reached harmonious consensus through collaborative conversations performed better on future unrelated tasks. The hyperscans showed synchronicity across the brains of subjects as they resolved conflict productively. They literally formed neural connections that enhanced their ability to work together. Similar experiments yielded similar responses: Our brains develop neural harmony with others after collaboratively solving problems together. Therefore, it is not conflict that is "bad" for relationships or teamwork; rather it is how we engage collaboratively or adversarially that determines whether the "rupture" stemming from conflict gets "repaired" (Gottman and Schwartz Gottman, 2022; Jacobs Hendel, 2022). Like a broken bone that ends up stronger, relationships that display rupture and repair cycles are stronger than those in which participants avoid engaging in difficult conversations ("rupture") out of a fear that conflict will inherently cause harm.

Studies of mothers and their infants have solidified the idea that in all relationships, we accidentally hurt each other or cause distress, such as when one person want the attention of the other, but the other withholds it for various reasons (e.g., too busy, distracted, angry, etc.). That rupture can be repaired in these relationships through apologies, kind words, small acts of physical affection (such as a pat on the back), and soothing verbal tones. These behaviors help to "repair" the rupture (Jacobs Hendel, 2020). All close relationships experience rupture and repair to varying degrees. Understanding this as a normal part of human relationships helps us pay more attention to the little ways in which our behaviors impact others and lead us to focus on repairing ruptures quickly and kindly whenever possible.

How can we use this pathbreaking research to improve our relationships at work, at home, and in all teamwork? When a problem arises, engage in constructive prosocial conflict resolution efforts using the tools contained in the following chapters to discuss the problem(s), seek joint solutions, and avoid harmful communication patterns such as defensiveness, contempt, stonewalling, etc. By doing so, your relationships and your teamwork will thrive through change. Lean into conflict, not away from it. Harness the power of constructive, collaborative problem-solving to enhance your teamwork and managerial performance.

Trauma Healing and the Role of Managers

As a result of trauma or childhood neglect, some employees and customers will be harder to deal with than others. Trauma survivors may be more aggressive, impulsive, antisocial, or untrusting. Rather than taking this behavior as a personal affront it can be helpful to remember that each person has a different biological endowment that may result in varied coping abilities. Understanding the likely roots of these behaviors may help us to be more empathetic and effective as their managers. While it is important to make our expectations clear about the behavior our teams and organizations require, and to hold employees accountable for any inappropriate behavior, this deeper understanding of the root causes provides us with more effective options for successfully leading employees who are survivors of trauma. Since this number is estimated to be between 1 in 3 and 1 in 5 (van der Kolk, 2015), understanding and supporting the recovery of trauma-impacted employees is a critical management skill. This means that many managers are also survivors of trauma. Understanding the impact of trauma on our own reactivity, our triggers, and our interactions with others is key to our ability to set a good example and continue to heal. Humans heal best in community (Winfrey & Perry, 2021). Therefore, it may be best to communicate empathy and openness while continuing to set healthy boundaries about workplace expectations. In other words, you can create a happy, supportive team environment while referring employees to resources that may help them heal (e.g., employee assistance program; health and mental health benefits, support groups, etc. as appropriate).

Infants and children who are neglected or abused are more likely to become adults who are hypersensitive to stress and prone to react more aggressively when faced with unpleasant or confusing situations (van der Kolk, 2015). In part, this is because their brains' early development was influenced by the stress hormones present in utero and in early infancy. The presence of stressful environments and stressed-out caregivers, especially in early life, is associated with a host of lifelong neurological, hormonal, and behavioral differences: impulsivity, attention-deficit disorder, addiction disorders (due to self-medication and numbing behaviors), low self-esteem, depression, problems forming and maintaining healthy relationships, higher rates of unemployment, risk-taking behaviors, eating disorders, impaired cognitive skills, and health problems including hypertension (van der Kolk, 2015; Winfrey & Perry, 2021;). Interestingly, adults who were neglected as infants tend to have less sensitivity to physical pain (van der Kolk, 2015). Humans develop "core regulatory networks" (CRNs) that tell us how to respond, even how to calm ourselves, when faced with unpleasant, dangerous, or uncertain circumstances. (Winfrey & Perry, 2021). Infants and children exposed to abuse, neglect, or chaotic environments often develop dysregulated networks that struggle with the tasks of self-regulation, self-soothing, and the reestablishment of a sense of calm and safety after negative stimulus.

How will you know if an employee is a victim or survivor of trauma? Traumatized people often cling to their secrets and isolation as if they were a life raft when instead they are an anchor, dragging them to the bottom of the sea. Managers (and others) can identify the signs of past trauma in current behaviors such as addictions, anger management challenges, defensiveness, overreaction, discomfort with interpersonal closeness, a lack of empathy, and others listed above. You do not need a definitive diagnosis for the techniques listed herein to make a positive impact. Stressed-out employees may benefit from activities that soothe their central nervous systems and make them less reactive, for example.

Managerial interventions to improve prosocial behaviors often begin with a need to calm the individual's central nervous system so the brain sends signals that the individual is safe and not threatened (van der Kolk, 2015; Winfrey & Perry, 2021). Only then will they return to full productivity and better health in the short and long term. Over time, it is possible to rewire our brains for greater connection, empathy, and rational decision-making. Activities that increase the number and strength of neural connections required for healthy CRNs include those in which individuals coordinate their movements and actions in a cooperative manner such as singing together (such as choral, choir, or karaoke), yoga or tai chi classes, playing catch, etc. (ibid.). The key is that the movement or actions must be collaborative rather than competitive. Walking in nature, massages, meditation, dancing, kicking a ball back and forth, and other activities can also have significant positive impacts on core regulatory networks (Winfrey & Perry, 2021). Rhythmic motion helps form and expand CRNs. "Moderate, controllable and predictable" environments feel best for traumatized people, especially those with multiple therapeutic activities throughout the day, such as those mentioned above.

Managers can use their knowledge of the biological and trauma-related sources of conflict to create workplaces that maximize human productivity and reduce stress: encourage appropriate breaks and vacations; incorporate fun and camaraderie into the workday; allow employees to move between quiet, reflective workspaces and more interactive ones; engage in altruistic collaborative efforts such as volunteer events; and set a good work-life balance example. While foosball tables are not required, finding time for bonding and fun can go a long way to making people look forward to time spent with their colleagues and while they achieve their organization's mission.

PERSONALITY-BASED CONFLICT THEORIES

Individual personalities and previous life experiences may create fertile ground for misunderstandings and conflict. When managers equip themselves with an understanding of the interplay between personality characteristics and conflict behaviors, they can depersonalize the behaviors of others, gain a deeper understanding of the motivations underlying those behaviors, and develop customized approaches for working successfully with individuals displaying a variety of personality traits. We started this discussion in Chapter 1 with an examination of the conflict styles inventory. In this chapter we will extend this understanding of individual-level responses to conflict including need theories, psychodynamic theories, personality disorders, and more.

Need theories refer to those explanations for human behavior, including conflict, based on the unmet needs of individuals. More than fifty years ago Abraham Maslow articulated a theory of human motivation that remains crucial to our understanding of conflict today (see Figure 2.1). According to Maslow (1954) people seek to meet their needs but some needs take precedence over others. To be more specific, physiological needs must be met first, meaning food, water, air, reproduction, sleep, and so on. Safety needs come next, meaning freedom from violence, access to employment, security of property and one's family's needs, and so on. Third, humans need to feel loved and a sense of belonging with family and friends. Fourth, people are motivated to have a sense of positive esteem about themselves and to hold others in esteem. The fifth motivational factor is the desire to be "self-actualized," meaning that people wish to fulfill their potential as creative, moral, intelligent beings.

Some scholars have criticized **Maslow's hierarchy of needs** out of a belief that it is less accurate when applied to collectivist rather than individualist societies (Cianci & Gambrel, 2003). In **collectivist societies**, the needs of the group generally come before the needs of any individual. These cultural differences are reflected in laws and social norms that give priority to the best interests of the group over those of individuals. "Among collectivists, social behavior is guided by the group. Along with group membership come prescribed duties and obligations. Among individualists, one's behavior is guided by one's personal attitudes, motivations, and internal processes" (Neuliep, 2009, p. 46). Therefore, in collectivist societies, Cianci and Gambrel (2003) and others have argued that Maslow's hierarchy would reflect greater emphasis on group belonging, gaining the respect of others, and meeting group needs than meet-

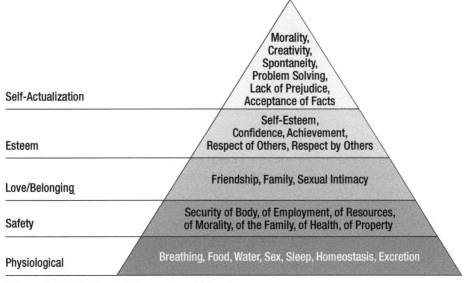

Figure 2.1   Maslow's Hierarchy of Needs

ing individual needs. Conflicts in collectivist societies are likely to occur more often at the group level than between individuals. When individuals experience conflicts in collectivist societies they are more likely to express them more indirectly and collectively through a web of social alliances and ties designed to enforce norms of expected behaviors and reduce overt conflicts that threaten intergroup and intragroup harmony. We will continue to use the original figure and ideas developed by Maslow and note that outside a Western cultural context or when applied to individuals from subcultural groups within Western societies, this hierarchy might need to be amended.

How does Maslow's hierarchy of needs help us understand the origins and escalation of conflict for managers? The lower an issue falls on this hierarchy, the more fiercely people and groups will fight for their preferred outcome. For example, union members might enjoy professional development courses as part of their benefits package, but they will fight much harder for wages and guarantees of employment because these fall on the lowest rung of the hierarchy. Voters may be for or against nuclear power but when the power company tries to locate a new reactor in their neighborhood, they become motivated to organize and lobby for their preference, generally along the lines of "not in my back yard" (also known as the *NIMBY problem* because residents fear for their physical safety as well as economic security related to falling property values). When an employee or customer is fighting for a preferred outcome, ask yourself, "What need is motivating this behavior?" Is this a matter of survival (e.g., a job is on the line)? Has someone's pride been hurt or is there a potential loss of face at issue? Once you understand the unmet need, then it is possible to better understand the range of potential solutions to meet that need. Understanding the underlying needs of any party in conflict is the first step to resolution.

PSYCHODYNAMIC THEORIES OF BEHAVIOR AND CONFLICT

This bundle of theories deals with the intrapsychic processes used by individuals to make sense of reality. Originally developed by Sigmund Freud, these theories and concepts have been amended by his followers, including Carl Jung and Erich Fromm, among others (Sandy, Boardman & Deutsch, 2000). For example, people have control and defense mechanisms designed to "control their impulses, thoughts, actions, and realities so that they won't feel anxious, guilty, or ashamed. If their controls are ineffective, they develop defensive mechanisms to keep from feeling these disturbing emotions" (Sandy, Boardman & Deutsch, 2000, p. 290). When a conflict feels overwhelming, individuals may rely on one or more control and defense mechanisms to control their own potentially negative behavior and to cope with feelings of anxiety that occur when involved in conflicts.

Denial occurs when the reality of a situation is so overwhelming that acknowledging it could provoke a psychological breakdown. Denial allows the unpleasant reality to sink in slowly, rather than all at once. As a mediator and manager, I think of this as "chipping away rather than ripping away." For example, if it is my unfortunate duty to inform a coaching client that feedback from nearly all their subordinates indicates her performance is significantly below average, yet this manager believes her performance is superior, I use two specific strategies to address the denial: first, I endeavor to ensure she is aware of the many ways in which even great managers can benefit from feedback to improve performance; and second, I give some time for the data and feedback to sink in while normalizing the difficulty of receiving negative feedback (see Chapter 10 for more on coaching strategies).

Those scoring high on avoidance as a preferred response to conflict (see Chapter 1) *may* be prone to more frequent bouts of denial than others. One chooses what one sees by ignoring unpleasant facts. By improving one's conflict management skills, it is possible to become more conflict competent, thereby making denial and avoidance less common or less severe. **Projection** is related to denial and involves misinterpreting undesirable feelings or behaviors as coming from someone else rather than acknowledging or dealing with them in oneself. By focusing oneself on the faults of others, one does not need to address them in oneself. **Displacement** involves changing the topic to avoid dealing directly with a problem or acting upset about one issue when it is really a different issue that has caused one's upset (Sandy, Boardman & Deutsch, 2000). Another way to avoid dealing directly with a problem is to minimize its importance and downplay its significance. **Disassociation** occurs when individuals are emotionally overwhelmed by a situation and therefore have difficulty focusing on that situation. Their minds may wander to more attractive thoughts, such as where to go on vacation, or even drift toward making a mental grocery list—anything seen as safe or pleasant. In common terms, they daydream. Overall, people have developed myriad ways to procrastinate in dealing with overwhelming problems. If you or your negotiation partners are becoming defensive, it is helpful to determine the true source of the anxiety and work together to address any perceived threats. Defensiveness makes problem-solving quite difficult. As discussed later in this chapter, it can be helpful to step back and focus on finding an appropriate process to address the problem to learn more about the needs of each party and meet those needs through a fair, respectful process.

Why do managers need to be aware of various forms of denial? There are common scenarios addressed by managers that are likely to evoke some level of denial, such as layoffs, mergers, poor performance reviews, or any source of large-scale change. Managers themselves may fall victim to denial when confronted with proof that a trusted employee has violated a deeply held norm. When a valued employee, peer manager, or supervisor has engaged in embezzlement, sexual harassment, or other inappropriate behavior, the first impulse is to think, "That can't be possible," even in the face of incontrovertible proof. No one is immune to the pitfall of denial when faced with devastating news.

PERSONALITY DISORDERS AND CONFLICT

A **personality disorder** "is a way of thinking, feeling and behaving that deviates from the expectations of the culture, causes distress or problems functioning, and lasts over time" (National Institutes of Health [NIH], 2018). The symptoms of a personality disorder usually present by adolescence or early adulthood and are resistant to change, even once the dysfunctionality of these behaviors is clear. People with personality disorders are responsible for a disproportionate percentage of intractable conflicts (Eddy, 2016). They tend to perceive conflict differently, create or exacerbate problems, and are usually oblivious to their role in the conflicts surrounding them. They externalize blame for their problems, meaning they are basically incapable of taking responsibility for their bad relationships, their difficulty keeping a job or moving up at work, and their generalized unhappiness. They may accuse others of bullying, dishonesty, lying, and unfair behavior, when it is they themselves who have engaged in these behaviors. Theories related to personality disorders can help you understand the impact of personality disordered individuals on conflict as well as indicating a few unusual strategies to respond effectively. Unless you are a psychologist hired to work with a specific client, I advise against applying the diagnosis or label of "personality disorder." Instead, knowing what to look for can help you better understand why the common conflict resolution strategies seem not to work with some individuals, and different techniques might be worth trying (see Chapter 7 for tips on dealing with difficult people).

About 9% of Americans have some form of personality disorder, although most studies indicate the rate of personality disorders to be on the rise among younger people (National Institutes of Mental Health, 2022). Why? Older people are less likely to receive mental health care and diagnosis; people with personality disorders do not live as long; and some young people outgrow behavioral manifestations of narcissism, for example, as they age. Other potential explanations exist, with no clear agreement between experts. For example, some observers point to the increase in one-child families and online interactions between younger people, which reduce the frequency of interpersonal skill-building opportunities. Smaller families may lead parents to overly accommodate the preferences of their only child (or small family), thereby leading them to believe they are truly more special than others (e.g., narcissists). Table 2.1 shows the prevalence of personality disorders among those living in the United States.

A brief description of each personality disorder will help you to better understand the roots of some of the workplace conflicts managers face, especially since personality disordered individuals are disproportionately involved in litigation and embezzlement, and are more common at the highest levels of corporate leadership.

Table 2.1   Personality Disorders by Type and Age-Group (percentage of U.S. population)

Personality Disorder	Overall Average	Age			
		18–29	30–44	45–64	65+
Narcissism	6.2	9.4	7.1	5.6	3.2
Borderline	5.9	9.3	7.0	5.5	2.0
Paranoid	4.4	6.8	5.0	3.6	1.8
Antisocial	3.6	6.2	4.2	2.8	0.6
Histrionic	1.8	3.8	1.8	1.2	0.6

Narcissists believe they are more important, special, smarter, and more deserving than everyone else. Policies or rules that others must follow do not apply to them because they believe they are special. **Narcissistic personality disorder** is characterized by a "pattern of need for admiration and lack of empathy for others. A person with narcissistic personality disorder may have a grandiose sense of self-importance, a sense of entitlement, take advantage of others, and lack empathy" (Psychiatry.org, 2018). Narcissists see others as tools to accomplish their own goals rather than having inherent value. They often view their children, subordinates, and family members as valuable because they can make the narcissist look good. For example, the narcissist may want their children to go to Ivy League schools or achieve high-profile jobs solely because it makes the parent look good.

Narcissists are overrepresented at the highest levels of corporate and political leadership. Why? Their confidence may lead others to follow them in error, while also making them take risks that sometimes pay off. These individuals can be off-putting, or they can be relatively charismatic. They are often, but not always, good at manipulating others into believing their own narrative of superiority. Try asking a suspected narcissist to engage in perspective taking (see Chapter 10). If they are unable to consider the perspectives of others or to experience actual empathy for the needs of others, then your strategies for working with them will need to include explanations about how good behavior is in their own best interests and will make them look like the hero or the "bigger" person. You can identify narcissists by their desire to always look good and their difficulty in taking responsibility for mistakes. Leaders must be able to apologize when they err and set good examples by how they treat others. They are also more likely to falsify reports or their résumé.

Borderline personalities are characterized by behaviors that are the opposite of what one would expect in a healthy relationship. I call this "I hate you, don't leave me" syndrome.

> **Borderline personality disorder** is a serious mental disorder marked by a pattern of instability in moods, behavior, self-image, and functioning. These experiences often result in impulsive actions and unstable relationships. A person with borderline personality disorder may experience intense episodes of anger, depression, and anxiety that may last from only a few hours to days. (NIH, 2018)

To clarify, this does not mean the individual is on the border of having a personality disorder. This is a disorder that may include some of the other personality disorders combined into one toxic cocktail of narcissism, histrionics, antisocial behavior, etc. The key indicator is the individual's tendency to act opposite of the expected actions in any situation. For example, the nicer you are to them, the meaner they are to you. The meaner you are to them, the nicer they are to you. They may tell you how much they dislike working with you but when you ask to be put into a different team, they will act quite surprised and hurt—like you have illogically rejected them.

Paranoid personality disorder "is characterized by a pattern of distrust and suspiciousness where others' motives are seen as mean or spiteful. People with paranoid personality disorder often assume people will harm or deceive them and are reluctant to confide in others or become close to them" (psychiatry.org, 2018). Any disgruntled employee could seem paranoid, so you will need to gather enough information to establish whether this is a pattern (hints at a personality disorder) or whether there is support for their suspicion.

Antisocial personality disorder is characterized by an inability or unwillingness to follow or conform to common social norms, policies, and laws. It is characterized by impulsive behavior, lying, and the violation of others' rights. Often, these individuals are viewed as criminals or con artists. They lack the ability to feel emotional empathy. They have a higher risk of incarceration, violence, and fraud. If they make it into the highest levels of a corporation, they tend to falsify reports and treat those above them quite well while treating those less powerful quite badly. In the common vernacular, sociopaths and psychopaths fall under this category.

Histrionic personality disorder is characterized by a need for excessive attention and excessive displays of emotion. These individuals often dress in ways designed to draw attention to themselves. They often create conflict to draw attention to themselves. They see themselves as the victims in situations they usually create or worsen.

All five of these disorders include an increased propensity for addictive disorders, depression, and anxiety. All personality disordered individuals tend to have an externalization of blame and responsibility, meaning they blame others for their conflicts and problems. They tend to lack self-awareness of the roots of their problems and of their ability to bring change to their behaviors. Because they (inaccurately) externalize blame for their unhappiness to others, they are rarely able to solve the problems they face. They set up others for failure because their managers, friends, and even their attorneys cannot fix the problem by changing others' behaviors. They lack self-awareness, they do not adapt well to change, and they often adopt an attitude of "You either believe me or you are against me." This makes it hard to coach them for self-improvement. In fact, sociopaths do not do well with therapy because they often manipulate their therapists into enabling their behavior. In group therapy, they often turn the group against the therapist.

How can you manage people who have personality disorders? You can avoid arguing, getting stuck in the past, or blaming others. For example, if you ask a narcissist or a histrionic personality to "tell me all about it," they may never stop. They won't voluntarily surrender the role of speaker to others. Instead, after you have heard their concern (which they will try to tell you many times), you may need to redirect them to more helpful behaviors such as crafting proposals for improvement, setting goals, and responding to proposals made by others. For narcissists you can frame proposals in ways that allow them to perceive a victory or to frame any compromise as a sign of their willingness to "be the bigger person here." When working with paranoid individuals, managers should consider assigning them to tasks at which they will excel, such as troubleshooting, auditing, and editing. They tend to be detail oriented and prone to finding fault—put it to work!

Lastly, if you believe your subordinate, colleague, or boss has a serious personality disorder, remember to keep your expectations realistic. You cannot make them fully happy or completely solve their problems. You can refrain from taking their unhappiness personally while setting boundaries and strategies to use the skills they do have while minimizing the damage caused by those they lack. Document all negative behaviors in case you must build a case for discipline or termination. Check the facts they cite or their performance markers if they are self-reported. If you believe that you might have a personality disorder, seek professional help to learn how to minimize the negative impacts of this condition on yourself and those who care about you. Progress is possible in most cases, especially if you recognize that you have room to grow.

In-Group/Out-Group Theory

According to Tajfel and Turner (2001 and earlier editions) there is an important qualifier to the evolution of conflict and cooperation. **In-group/out-group theory** states that individuals and groups tend to define themselves by stating who they are in reference to who they are not. When a person perceives themselves as part of a group, this is termed their "in-group." Humans and many other mammals afford more trust, empathy, and compassion to those in their "in-group" compared to the "out-group." Each of us has multiple identities. For example, you may be a father, son, brother, engineer, manager, vegetarian, runner, amateur painter, dog owner, Indiana University graduate, fraternity member, and so on. Conflict is more likely to occur when we view others as part of our out-group rather than in-group.

When genocide or terrorism occur, they are nearly always framed as in-group/out-group conflicts. We tend to "dehumanize" those from our out-group with whom we have conflict. This means we are more likely to dehumanize them, thereby rationalizing violence or negative treatment. This is also called "othering" and is used to create the psychological distance needed to engage in violence against members of the other group or to justify disparate treatment. This theory has three parts: social categorization, social identification, and social comparison.

Social categorization refers to the human tendency to apply labels or categories to individuals to better understand them and predict their behavior. For example: Republican/Democrat, black/white, professor/student.

Social identification refers to our tendency to model our behaviors and values upon those in our in-group. Meeting the expectations of our in-group is central to positive self-esteem.

Social comparison is when, once we categorize ourselves as a group member and identify with that group, then we compare our group to other groups. To protect or increase our self-esteem, humans tend to seek out information that confirms the superiority or positivity of their in-group compared to out-groups. This is the root cause of prejudice, discrimination, and even genocide.

In summary, while humans are becoming less violent as a species, conflict is more likely between out-groups. Our brains categorize our own identity in opposition to the identities of others. This tendency makes it easier to predict the behavior of others and unite with our kin (and other in-groups) against outside threats. While this aids in identity formation and in-group unity, it tends to bias us against others, thereby creating or increasing conflict.

An amazing study from the University of Chicago has revealed a possible cure or preventative measure for in-group/out-group bias (Garrett, 2018). In their study, a white rat raised in a community of other white rats would not leave a piece of food to rescue a black rat and vice versa. A white rat raised in a community of black rats would rescue a black rat but not a white rat, and vice versa. Interestingly, when a rat was raised in a community with both black and white rats, then a rat of any color would rescue a rat of any color (ibid.). This experiment teaches us a priceless lesson: in-group/out-group bias is not biologically innate, but instead has sociological roots. How we define our community depends on the diversity of the community in which we were raised or currently live. Expanding our social circle to include different types of people quite literally leads to greater compassion and empathy for others.

As a manager, when you hear employees speaking negatively about other groups (e.g., human resources professionals versus production employees in the same company; people of a different race, gender, sexual orientation, or national origin, etc.) remind them that we are all "in it together." Remind them that dividing us against one another works against the mission. Share with them how in-group/out-group theory works as a specific form of psychological bias. "Othering" people may feel natural, but it creates and perpetuates social hierarchies with negative consequences in our workplaces and communities. Harmonious, diverse workplaces require that we do better at identifying negative cognitive and behavioral habits in ourselves and our team members and use them as opportunities to learn, grow, and do better.

Cognitive Biases

When trying to determine a fair outcome, individuals are generally unaware of the many forms of cognitive bias that hamper information processing and objectivity. **Cognitive bias** is a pattern of deviation in judgment that leads to inaccurate conclusions, distorted perceptions of reality, illogical interpretation of facts or events, and often irrational behaviors or thought patterns (Kahneman & Tversky, 1972). Cognitive biases often serve as shortcuts to reaching the conclusions necessary to make decisions, but the shortcuts may lead to poorer decision-making. The first step in conflict management is to heighten your awareness of the existence of common cognitive biases.

We must first understand how we attribute motivations to behaviors. When we give someone the benefit of the doubt, we assume good intentions or reasons for observed behaviors, thereby making us less likely to become confrontational and more likely to work collaboratively. Sometimes the opposite occurs. **Attribution theory** explains the ways in which cognitive biases hinder our ability to accurately understand the motivations behind others' behaviors. There are a host of specific cognitive biases falling under the headings of *attribution theory* or *attribution errors*. **Fundamental attribution errors** occur when we incorrectly attribute someone's behavior to their dispositional or personality characteristics rather than attributing it to a situational factor. For example, imagine that your least favorite coworker arrives late for a Monday-morning meeting. In your mind you think, "Apparently she isn't willing to make an effort to be here on time because she is an inconsiderate person." Later in the day you find out that her car was rear-ended on the way to work. This form of fundamental attribution error is called **accuser bias**, which is "the tendency for an observer negatively affected by an actor's behavior to attribute the behavior to causes under control of the actor" (Allred, 2000, p. 244). You attributed her lateness to her disposition (an inconsiderate personality) rather than to a situation beyond her control (the auto accident). Research shows individuals are more likely to make a negative attribution error when they have had a negative relationship with the other party, when they are total strangers, or when they perceive the person as a member of an out-group. Attributing behaviors to negative traits is likely to escalate conflict (Allred, 2000).

We are most likely to encounter cognitive biases when we seek to understand or explain our own behaviors. Our tendency to downplay our own poor decisions or actions, while attributing them to circumstances beyond our control, is called **bias of the accused** (Allred, 2000). This is akin to what psychologists label **rationalization** or denial, meaning that individuals find rational reasons why their own behaviors make sense under circumstances beyond their control. "I had to eat that cookie despite my diet. I was starving!" If you were the one coming in late to the meeting, you would most likely blame it on bad traffic or other causes beyond your control—even if you hit the snooze button on your alarm twice that morning.

In other words, every fact that we see (for example, someone is late for the meeting) gets filtered through our preexisting cognitive biases. Sometimes our preexisting biases drive us to interpret facts incorrectly or jump to conclusions prematurely. A negative attribution of a fact is likely to result in an angry response that will make escalation more likely and successful resolution less likely. Awareness of the existence and functions of cognitive biases can help managers prevent, explain, and defuse conflict situations when they occur.

BOX 2.1. THE SEVEN DEADLY COGNITIVE BIASES OF NEGOTIATORS

Irrational stubbornness
Zero-sum thinking
Unduly influenced by an anchoring number
Framing bias
Satisficing
It's all about me
Overconfidence

The Seven Deadly Cognitive Biases of Negotiation

You will read more about negotiation theory in Chapter 3, but for now it is helpful to give a brief overview of Bazerman and Neale's (1992) list of seven common decision-making biases that interfere with one's ability to correctly calculate one's own best interests in negotiation or decision-making.

The first mistake is to irrationally stick to an initial course of action, even once it becomes clear this course is no longer the optimal position. This is a classic mistake made in labor-management negotiations. For example, the union makes a public statement proclaiming that nothing short of a 6% raise will be accepted and then has difficulty backing down once managers provide data showing their competitors are paying their workers less or that the profit margins simply cannot sustain a 6% raise. Related to this error is the human tendency to seek out information that confirms our preexisting beliefs and to filter out information that runs contrary to those beliefs (closely related to attribution bias previously discussed). In our labor-management example, this means that union negotiators will tend to discount or disbelieve facts presented by management that bode poorly for their hopes for a 6% raise whereas they seek out data and information that substantiates the need for the requested raise. We'll label this mistake *irrational stubbornness*. It is also known as *irrational escalation of commitment*. This bias also explains why individuals tend to read, watch, or listen to news sources that reflect their own political leanings, thereby reaffirming their existing worldviews and filter out contrary ideas or interpretations of events. This tendency leads to further polarization and poor decision-making.

The second common mistake is zero-sum thinking; it occurs when one assumes that any gain made by the other party in a negotiation must come at your expense, thereby missing opportunities for joint gains that could come from working together. A great example of this comes from the holy grail of conflict management literature, *Getting to Yes: Negotiating Agreement without Giving In.*

> In 1964 an American father and his twelve-year-old son were enjoying a beautiful Saturday in Hyde Park, London, playing catch with a Frisbee. Few in England had seen a Frisbee at that time and a small group of strollers gathered to watch the sport. Finally . . . one Britisher came over to the father: "Sorry to bother you. We have been watching you a quarter of an hour. Who's winning?" (Fisher & Ury, 1981, p. 148).

The third error is to anchor one's judgments of a "good" or "bad" offer based on the initial offer made instead of linking one's judgment to some objective criteria.

More specifically, the first number rendered in a negotiation is called an **anchoring number** and it tends to become the reference point for all future offers. For example, if I offered to sell you my used car for $20,000 but later came down in my demand to $8,000 you might think you were getting a good deal because you are mentally comparing $8,000 to $20,000. But what if the true value of the car was only $6,000? Clearly, it is unwise to anchor one's judgment of an outcome to arbitrary figures solely because those figures were used at the early stages of bargaining or decision-making. Getting unduly influenced by an anchoring number is a common cognitive bias.

The fourth common mistake is to be positively or negatively influenced by the framing or language used by the other party. The **framing effect** is a cognitive bias that occurs when the same option is presented in different formats or with different phrasing (i.e., it is framed differently) and the choice of format or phrasing unduly influences one's opinions or preferences on the matter (Druckman, 2001). This bias is difficult to avoid because a nice person with a bad offer remains harder to refuse than a rude person with a good offer. The framing of an offer may be akin to "putting lipstick on a pig," but sometimes our minds focus more on the lipstick than the pig—making this a particularly humbling cognitive bias. We'll call this the *framing bias*.

The fifth bias is the overreliance on information that is readily available, even first impressions, rather than doing the digging necessary to get the best data possible. Accepting readily available information saves time and makes sense when a decision is relatively unimportant. However, for important decisions, such as whom to hire or promote or which production method is best, gathering and analyzing information becomes quite important. There are no perfect shortcuts to sound decision-making. This tendency was labeled *satisficing* by Herbert Simon many years ago. This means people tend to take the first acceptable option that comes along rather than do the homework necessary to find the best option. This is a perfectly rational choice when faced with an overwhelming amount of data or information—taking the first good option alleviates the need to sift through a large amount of information. Yet it is important to note that satisficing may not always lead to the most efficient outcome possible.

The sixth bias occurs when the decision-maker fails to take into consideration the other's needs and viewpoints. This leads to suboptimal decisions based on false assumptions about the other's motivations. In a negotiation, you cannot get what you want unless the other side agrees to it. Unless your proposal meets his needs, your negotiation partner won't agree to anything. Failing to acknowledge the interdependence of negotiators is a cognitive bias that results frequently in **impasse** (also known as *stalemate*). As a result, no agreement is reached. We'll call this bias *it's all about me*.

The seventh and final cognitive error made by decision-makers is simply overconfidence. Study after study has shown that attorneys generally overestimate their chances of winning at trial, for example. It is difficult to be objective about our own behaviors or chance of winning. Overconfidence leads to a lack of preparation and effort, including a reduced willingness to seek out new information that contradicts our views or to try to understand the other side's views or needs. Most likely, this bias is related to the psychological concept of denial, mentioned previously. Focusing on the possibility of losing is unpleasant, so individuals overestimate their odds of winning an argument, a legal case, or a negotiation.

SOCIAL LEARNING THEORY

Social learning theory posits that humans are not innately aggressive but they learn to behave aggressively or peacefully based on observing others in their social environment. People respond to the expected consequences of their behavior, which are learned from experience or observation (Sandy, Boardman & Deutsch, 2000). For example, if managers in company x speak rudely to their subordinates yet they experience no negative repercussions, then others may learn from their example. If an employee sees her colleague coming in late and leaving early with no negative consequences, then she will learn that punctuality is not rewarded or even expected in this organization. Positive behaviors also prove instructive. If managers are rewarded for keeping morale high by developing positive relationships with their employees, then others will mimic this behavior if they have the intellectual and practical ability to do so.

Using this approach to understanding organizational conflict management, one would observe the behaviors occurring in the workplace, track the consequences of those behavioral choices, then make changes as necessary to ensure that desired behaviors lead to positive reinforcement and undesirable behaviors lead to negative consequences. This alignment of behaviors and outcomes should occur in ways that allow others in the organization to learn through observation and official policy rather than trial and error. Never reward bad behavior. If you do so, do not be surprised that it continues.

The theory of social learning means that we must address negative behaviors in the workplace because they have an infectious tendency that can lead to real changes in workplace culture. Yet managers are often hesitant to confront unproductive or non-collaborative workers. "If we want to have an honest conversation with someone about a problem," Kenneth Cloke and Joan Goldsmith (2003) write,

> We need to confront it. If we want to stimulate a significant personal, organizational, societal, or political change, we need to create a minimal level of impoliteness, discourtesy, and unpleasantness. No one learns to confront someone else unless they are willing to try and face the consequences. By not trying, we allow inappropriate behavior to negatively impact everyone within its reach. (p. 196)

Managers need to learn the skills necessary to successfully address these problems: coaching skills, and the authority to create incentives for improvements and negative sanctions for continued poor performance or negative behaviors. Managers may need to terminate or demote an employee who has clearly crossed a line into inappropriate behaviors or after repeated attempts to improve their performance have failed. When managers work proactively to address negative workplace behaviors or attitudes, they need to feel rewarded for that proactive intervention. Unfortunately, many organizations reward conflict avoidance—allowing an employee to continue to violate norms or policies rather than take affirmative action for change. When this happens, other employees realize the "smart guy" is the one who comes in late, leaves early, and misappropriates organizational resources (e.g., uses the work vehicle for personal errands or takes office supplies home). Because honest employees are not rewarded and dishonest employees are not punished, the organization's culture may begin a downward spiral.

In social learning models, "realistic encouragement to achieve ambitious but attainable goals promotes successful experience, which in turn, aids the sense of self-efficacy. Social prodding to achieve unattainable goals often produces a sense of failure and undermines self-efficacy" (Sandy, Boardman & Deutsch, 2000, p. 300).

FRAMING TOWARD A COLLABORATIVE PROCESS

Framing error was discussed previously. **Framing** refers to the ways in which facts or perceptions are defined, constructed, or labeled.

> Framing is a process whereby communicators, consciously or unconsciously, act to construct a point of view that encourages the facts of a given situation to be interpreted by others in a particular manner. Frames operate in four ways: they define problems, diagnose causes, make moral judgments, and suggest remedies. Frames are often found within a narrative account of an issue or event and are generally the central organizing idea (Kuypers, 2006, p. 7).

How a situation is framed has a great influence on how people behave. For example, if individuals perceive that a situation calls for competition rather than cooperation, then they are likely to behave in ways that are more egocentric, even selfish.

As individuals, we can frame a challenge as an opportunity for growth and a chance to prove ourselves. Or we can frame it as an insurmountable difficulty that makes us want to quit or make excuses for failure. Framing matters. For example, Brian Chesky, the CEO of Airbnb, was interviewed in April of 2020 about the impact of the COVID-19 pandemic on the travel industry. In spring of 2020, Airbnb lost 80% of its business in eight weeks (Thorbecke, 2022). They had to lay off thousands of employees and rethink their business strategy completely. Chesky tells the story of being called by the CEO of American Express, who helped him reframe this disastrous downturn for Airbnb. He said, "Your legacy, your reputation, will be determined *not* by how fast you grew your company or created something new in the travel industry, but by the way you respond to this crisis. This will make your career or break it." In essence, when faced with difficult circumstances, hard choices, and new obstacles to our success as leaders, it is critical that we frame this as an opportunity to show our true colors as an innovative, ethical, resilient leader. Framing matters.

Whether a situation is framed as one of competition versus collaboration is important in any negotiation—and most conflicts or problem-solving sessions involve negotiation at some level. By framing the situation as calling for joint problem-solving (collaboration) rather than a winner-take-all situation (competition), negotiators are often able to think creatively, build and enhance relationships, and work together to reach a more optimal outcome.

Process orientations tend to result in greater collaboration whereas a focus on outcomes over process tends to produce competitive orientations. Let's use the process of performance reviews to illustrate this difference. Feedback from one's boss can focus either on the employee's performance relative to others in the organization (a competitive orientation) or it can examine changes or improvements in the employee's own performance. Framing this feedback as a learning opportunity rather than as competition with other employees is likely to result in greater improvement. This principle also applies to goal setting. When employees are given process-related goals, their performance improves more than when they are assigned task-related goals. As Katz and Block (2000) note, "People who are oriented toward an outcome goal mainly concentrate on the final result or outcome; as a consequence they are preoccupied with their position [or their demand]" (p. 283). The more individuals feel a need to clarify, reiterate, or reassert their own positions, the less time they spend trying to meet the underlying concerns of the other party. When people focus instead on a process goal, they devote their energy to developing a mastery of that process, which usually leads to a more successful resolution of the conflict or problem (Fisher & Ury, 1981; Katz & Block, 2000). Think of Google's instructions to its employees: "Take risks, make mistakes." Rather than telling employees that they must generate a specific level of profit or develop new products at a certain rate, they are given a process goal that encourages them to experiment and think creatively. Framing and processing goals are important to understand the origins, escalation, and cures for unproductive conflict.

FAIRNESS AND PROCEDURAL JUSTICE

When customers, clients, or employees experience conflicts they often claim the status quo isn't fair or that they aren't being treated fairly. **Fairness** can be defined as the quality of being just, equitable, impartial, or evenhanded. Fairness can refer to the process through which decisions were made and the outcome of those decisions. There may be many contradictory viewpoints about what comprises a "fair" outcome depending on one's preference for equity, equality, or need-based outcomes. Concepts of justice and fairness are central to our understanding of conflict and are keys to its resolution. Humans and other primates have an innate sense of fairness and react negatively when they feel they are being treated unfairly (Markey, 2003). An interesting example of the deep roots of our need for fairness comes from a study of capuchin monkeys by the Yerkes Primate Research Center at Emory University (2003). Capuchin monkeys were trained to give a researcher a pebble in return for a small piece of food, usually a slice of cucumber. However, capuchin monkeys prefer grapes to cucumbers. Researchers placed pairs of capuchins next to each other so they could watch the exchanges taking place between their neighbor and the researchers. The first monkey was given a grape as the reward for handing over a pebble. The next monkey was given a piece of cucumber as the reward for handing over the pebble. This equates to equal work (giving a pebble) for unequal pay (grape versus cucumber). The capuchins receiving cucumbers instead of grapes reacted by either throwing their cucumbers back at the researchers or simply refusing to eat the cucumbers. Capuchin pairs who saw only cucumbers exchanged for pebbles ate their cucumbers happily (Markey, 2003). This research demonstrates that humans and other animals have developed understandings of fairness that have enabled them to work together successfully in groups. Fairness matters. A perceived lack of fairness leads to anger, resentment, and conflict within human and primate groups.

The **theory of relative deprivation** explains the fairness concerns held by the capuchin monkeys in our previous example. The capuchins were perfectly satisfied with exchanging the pebbles for cucumbers until they saw another capuchin receive a grape for the same service. The theory of relative deprivation states that a sense of injustice can arise when one compares one's distribution to others in a competitive environment and sees that others are receiving more. In modern society this has led to competitive materialistic pursuits often called the need to "keep up with the Joneses."

Yet fairness can mean different things to different people and is influenced by situational factors. Would the capuchins react differently if the grapes were given to mothers with small offspring and the cucumbers were reserved for those without dependents to feed? To better understand what we mean by fairness we must examine the concepts of procedural and distributive justice.

Procedural justice refers to the fairness of the process used for reaching a decision or resolving a conflict. Individuals tend to perceive that a process is fair when it is transparent, respectful, and allows them to be heard during decision-making:

> One wants procedures that generate relevant, unbiased, accurate, consistent, reliable, competent, and valid information and decisions as well as polite, dignified, and respectful behavior in carrying out the procedures. Also, voice and representation in the processes and decisions related to the evaluation are considered desirable by those directly affected by the decisions. (Deutsch, 2000, p. 45)

Think of this example: your boss issues a memo to all employees that details a new dress code that he has devised for the entire organization. This new dress code will require some minor changes and a slight expense to you personally. How do you feel about this decision? What if the memo stated the new dress code was created by a committee composed of five employees and three managers from different parts of the organization? What if the memo reminded you that those delegates were chosen by a vote from each employee group? Does this change how you feel about the decision? Typically individuals can accept, abide by, and even help implement a policy decision they do not like as long as they feel the process used to reach it was fair and transparent, and they had a reasonable opportunity to participate. Therefore, between the two types of justice, attention to procedural justice typically increases the likelihood that parties will accept and support decisions.

Distributive justice refers to the criteria that lead people to feel that they have received a fair outcome (Deutsch, 2000). Perceptions of distributive justice generally hinge on one of three criteria for determining the fairness of an outcome: equity, equality, or need. The **equity principle** denotes that benefits should be distributed based on each person or group's contribution; those who worked harder or contributed greater expertise to a project should receive disproportionate amounts of the payout. The **equality principle** states that all group members should receive equal amounts of any good or benefit that comes from the labors of the group. Under this version of fairness, all employees would receive the same pay. The **need principle** asserts that more of the goods or benefits should go to those who need more. Therefore, a parent with three young children might receive greater pay or fewer taxes than someone with no children. These principles can be seen as the organizing principles underlying the capitalist, socialist, and communist economic and political systems, respectively. In practice, capitalist societies still pay some attention to need-based distributive principles through the provision of social welfare policies, such as food aid or housing assistance, but they do so to a smaller extent than in socialist or communist societies. According to Deutsch (2000) the equity principle is most often called on when the goal is economic productivity. Workers have greater incentive to work hard when hard workers receive more pay than shirkers and when they know there are few government services to guarantee their livelihoods otherwise. The equality principle is used in situations in which social harmony and positive social relationships are the highest goal. The need principle is followed when the most important goal is ensuring human welfare.

In any situation, individuals rely on one of these definitions of fairness to support their argument for a different outcome distribution than they are slated to receive. "Officer, it is not fair that I get the speeding ticket! That car ahead of me was going much faster" (appealing to the equality principle). "Officer, I should not have to pay such a huge speeding fine. I won't be able to make my rent payment" (appealing to the need principle).

When examining competing claims of fairness, it is helpful to dig more deeply into the underlying definition of fairness employed by each party by asking, "What makes you say it is fair or unfair? What criteria are you using to determine fairness in this situation? What would a fair outcome look like and how could it be attained?" It can be helpful to be metacognitive with the parties, meaning that you take the time to explain to them the various types of fairness and ask them to analyze their own claims to see which type of fairness undergirds them. This allows space to build an understanding that people can hold differing preferences for an outcome but both outcomes can be defended as fair under the equity, equality, or need principle. This lays the groundwork for a respectful discussion of possible outcomes that does not privilege one viewpoint over another or dehumanize one negotiator as patently unconcerned with fairness. Therefore, when you hear employees complaining about fairness, be sure to dig deeper to learn how they define fairness so you can effectively discuss and address their concerns.

CONCEPTS OF FAIRNESS ACROSS CULTURES

When distributing benefits such as bonuses, preferred work tasks, the corner office space, etc. there are culturally based preferences as to whether these should be distributed based on need, effort, or merit. **Individualistic societies** tend to prefer merit-based outcomes while collectivist cultures often prefer a combination of merit, need, and equality. For example, in Sweden and Ireland, there are minimum incomes or standards of living that are guaranteed to all residents, even though higher tax rates are required to reduce large wealth gaps within the society and ensure basic needs are covered for everyone. Social norms support these decisions, overall. Due to ethnocentrism, we tend to believe "our way is the right way." Americans may look down upon the Swedish preference for greater income equality while Swedes may find distasteful the American viewpoint that individual wealth (or lack thereof) is the responsibility of the individual. These are cultural tendencies that hide individual-level variation as well as variation within cultural subgroups. Yet, when our colleagues come from cultural groups different from our own, these differences often lead us to believe their values are "less than" our own. It is important for us to be able to discern the cultural roots of our preferences so we can find ways to work together successfully with the understanding that other approaches are not "wrong" or "unfair," but instead, they are grounded in different yet valid approaches to making sense of our world.

How do theories of distributive and procedural justice affect conflict and its resolution for managers? Clearly, feelings of injustice and unfairness give rise to unproductive conflict. Decision-making procedures that lack transparency and do not allow participatory input from stakeholders or fail to uphold procedural rules often result in a backlash. When managers are acting as mediators between two employees in conflict or when they facilitate a decision-making meeting, it can be helpful to use a process-focused approach, similar to that used by mediators: The mediator can encourage the sides to focus on such processes as finding common ground, developing mutual understandings, empowering one another, and understanding each other's needs and emotions. Doing so encourages using fair tactics and constructive strategies to resolve the conflict (Katz & Block, 2000, p. 285).

Although it is counterintuitive, it can be helpful to remind employees that they are more likely to reach their preferred outcome if they focus instead on walking through a thoughtful and fair process of discussion and information sharing. This process focus, rather than an outcome focus, is most likely to build and enhance working relationships and achieve outcomes that meet their needs.

For information on culture's impact on perceptions of fairness, see Chapter 5.

BOX 2.2. DISTRIBUTING RAISES FAIRLY

Recently, a high school principal at a private school asked a conflict management consultant to conduct an assessment to determine the reasons that her staff seemed frequently disgruntled. That assessment revealed, in part, that teachers were dissatisfied because the merit bonuses were distributed in ways that seemed unfair. Teachers with seniority wanted their loyalty rewarded. Teachers who worked a lot of overtime to improve and update their lectures and materials wanted their efforts recognized. Teachers whose students scored highest on standardized tests wanted recognition for this achievement. Young teachers who had student loans to repay stated a greater need for the merit pay increases. With so many competing criteria, the principal had been distributing raises without any clear criteria to define *merit* or *fair*. Each teacher defined a "fair distribution" in ways that privileged his or her own situation, giving rise to a no-win situation for the principal. How should the principal proceed?

POWER IN THEORY AND PRACTICE

Traditionally, power has been defined as the ability to accomplish one's goals over the objections of others if necessary. Powerful people were those who had the ability to force their will on others. In a modern managerial setting, *power* can be defined as the ability to act effectively (Folger, Poole & Stutman, 2000). This definition can communicate your vision for the organization or your unit, solicit buy-in for that vision, and empower your employees and teams to work effectively toward a shared goal. Power in organizations typically includes influence over force, but both are included in the term's meaning. A host of resources come together to determine one's power: access to resources, knowledge, special skills, access to professional contacts and networks, control over rewards or sanctions, communication skills including persuasiveness, empathy, and even one's personality can contribute to one's power. This list reminds us that sometimes the most powerful person in the organization is the executive assistant to the president or CEO.

Power structures in most organizations are evolving from strict hierarchical designs into systems with disbursed power centers, delegated decision-making authority, and collaborative work products. Bill Ury, in an introduction to Mark Gerzon's book *Leading Through Conflict*, writes,

> A generation or two ago, it is fair to say, most decisions were made hierarchically. The people on the top gave the orders and the people on the bottom simply followed them. That is changing. Nowadays, leaders increasingly cannot simply give orders and expect them to be carried out. (Gerzon, 2006, p. xi)

More than any previous generation, Gen Z seeks leaders who show care for the mental and physical well-being of their team members (Miles, 2022). Leaders or managers who treat people solely to greater profit or mission achievement will find themselves working alone or with a severely understaffed crew. Real power lies in the ability to persuade others to follow your lead or share your vision.

Force is increasingly a sign of weakness more than strength. "Social power stems from relationships among people" (Folger, Poole & Stutman, 2000, p. 120). Managers can exercise their power and authority when others view their exercise of power as legitimate and useful. Even dictators can be toppled by a coup. The best managers have power because others in the organization want to please them, employees want to help them enact their vision for the organization, and they have built a reputation for fairness, collegiality, and effectiveness. Not only is power *with* others more successful than power *over* others; it feels better.

Building positive relationships with one's subordinates, peers, and supervisors is crucial to building and maintaining power as a manager. Positive relationships mean that others are likely to give you the benefit of the doubt when difficult decisions need to be made. Managers who abuse their power or authority by treating people disrespectfully or by repeatedly making decisions that are contrary to group expectations and preferences are likely to lose power, especially their ability to convince others to support and implement their decisions. If you are a manager who is struggling to get your employees to "fall in line" or "follow orders," then it is time to reframe your goals. Instead, focus on ways in which

---

BOX 2.3. DON'T UNDERESTIMATE YOUR POWER TO BRING CHANGE

Individuals and small groups often underestimate their ability to bring change in their workplaces and communities. When corporations or government entities violate environmental, safety, or employment laws, it tends to be the work of one more whistleblower who brings these bad acts to light. There are many ways to bring change and seek justice from within or outside organizations. For example, protests by cheerleaders at Kennesaw State University brought to light unsavory behaviors on behalf of the university's embattled president, resulting in his forced resignation (Adelson, 2017). Where hundreds of tenured professors had failed, a group of five cheerleaders using peaceful, silent protest brought needed change to their organization. Do not underestimate the power you *do* have to bring change. Think about a vexing problem in your community or workplace. Instead of focusing on what hasn't worked or why you cannot fix it, make a list of the actions you *can* take and the power you *do* have.

---

you can build relationships, build trust, request input, and convey a vision that motivates people to follow your leadership. Show me a great leader-manager and I will show you a team willing to follow him or her into metaphorical battle.

When deciding which battles to fight and which to let go, it is helpful to engage in a brief analysis of the contextual power dynamics of the situation. Who has the most power? How important is this issue to him or her? How much power do you have to affect the outcome? This assessment includes the power of your connections with others and your access to resources, including knowledge. What are the costs versus the benefits of your preferred outcome compared to other outcomes? Finally, what process can decision-makers follow to allow them to arrive at the optimal outcome? Would it be helpful to have the decision-making group brainstorm all actions and weigh the costs and benefits? Should stakeholders be involved in the decision-making process? You might be surprised and find that you change your own mind about the preferred outcome once you engage in a clear problem-solving process that includes an analysis of power.

THE TIMING OF CONFLICT INTERVENTIONS

When should managers or neutral conflict resolvers (for example, mediators, facilitators, or ombudsmen) intervene in conflicts to seek a resolution? Timing may not be everything, but it certainly is important. Intervene too early and there may be insufficient information to identify the parties and understand the issue. Intervene too late and tempers have flared, making resolution difficult. Conflict managers call this the problem of *ripeness*.

Box 2.4 displays the spiral of unmanaged conflict. Although originally developed to explain public policy disputes, the concepts are also well applied in the workplace.

BOX 2.4. THE SPIRAL OF UNMANAGED CONFLICT

Once sides have formed, positions begin to harden. Cognitive biases, including attribution bias, work to filter out information that runs contrary to one's own views. Eventually, the disputant(s) refuses to communicate with the other side(s). Then, parties expend resources to hire attorneys or build their case against the other side. They take the conflict outside the immediate parties by telling their story to others, looking for allies elsewhere in the organization or the broader community, or by going to the press or reporting their complaints through a hotline. Perceptions of the dispute and of the other parties become distorted by the lack of information flowing. At this point, a sense of crisis emerges, and one or more parties comes to believe that a resolution is needed right away. They want to be proved right, make the other side pay, and so on. This need for revenge, justice, and resolution means they are willing to pay whatever it takes, or whatever they can pay, to get it resolved. Ironically, intervention at this stage is likely to be less successful than intervention at an earlier stage. The trick for interventionists, including managers, is to allow the dispute to ripen enough to increase the chance of successful intervention, but not wait until the dispute has gotten highly escalated.

In a managerial setting, it can be helpful to allow employees some time to attempt to resolve their own interpersonal conflicts. When employees reach their own resolution, it can (re)build relationships and increase their conflict resolution skills. Yet, conflicts between two employees can quickly become a conflict among ten employees when others take sides or the problem morphs from an interpersonal conflict to an intergroup conflict. Between customers, clients, and employees, it is best to allow employees some specific remedies they can offer to resolve the dispute at the lowest level possible. This means the unsatisfied customer needs only to speak with one employee rather than awaiting transfer to a manager. Both customers and employees tend to be happier when small problems are resolved at the lowest levels. Managers can start by coaching and developing the dispute resolution skill set of their subordinates. When that isn't enough, managers can facilitate a problem-solving conversation (see 3-step problem-solving in Chapter 7).

SYSTEMIC VERSUS NONSTRUCTURAL SOURCES OF CONFLICT

When people experience conflict at work or with clients, they tend to blame it on the other's personality flaws or chalk it up to causes beyond their own control (review denial and attribution bias covered previously). Often the conflict is attributed to a personality conflict. To become adept at managing collaboration and conflict you must develop the ability to diagnose the sources of conflict in much the same way that a physician diagnoses the cause of an illness. Information about the root cause of a dispute can be indispensable to crafting an effective response. The first step in the diagnostic process is to determine whether the source is structural, also known as systemic, or nonstructural. **Structural/ systemic sources of conflict** include unfair, unclear, or inefficient policies, procedures, organizational cultures, or ingrained practices that repeatedly give rise to disputes irrespective of personnel changes. High levels of employee and customer dissatisfaction are nearly always indicators of structural sources of conflict within an organization. A few examples will help to illustrate the most common structural sources of conflict:

- Overlapping job descriptions that create turf battles or conflict between employees who are left unclear as to which tasks are to be accomplished by themselves or others
- Organizational cultures that encourage or fail to punish racism, sexism, harassment, bullying, or other recurring negative workplace behaviors
- Rewards for individual achievement that encourage no-holds-barred competition between members of the same team such as stealing clients from one another or sabotaging the work of one's colleague in order to increase one's chance of winning the monthly sales competition
- Failures to recognize and reward desired behaviors among individual employees and teams
- Incentives to use or lose one's sick time or vacation time resulting in mass absenteeism near the end of the year
- Unrealistically high goals or objectives
- Performance goals or policy changes that are poorly communicated across the chain of command
- Any policy, procedure, or cultural norm that misaligns the needs of the individual and the needs of the whole organization
- An absence of mechanisms for informal employee or customer dispute resolution, thereby incentivizing formal actions, such as litigation, as the only venue for redress

Understanding systemic conflicts requires attention to incentive structures. Sometimes organizations create policies or procedures that have unintended consequences. To elaborate, let's look at an entire subset of conflict based on poor procedures, policies, and practices: those that misalign the good of the individual and the good of the organization. We call these "perverse incentives" because they run contrary to the overall goal. For example, to save money, an organization may create a policy stating that all sick leave or vacation time must be used by the end of the year and will not roll over to the following year. This gives employees the incentive to "use it or lose it," even if this means the organization is understaffed near the end of the year and employees call in sick when they aren't ill. This is particularly problematic for seasonally busy companies, such as toy stores. Another unfortunate example occurs when a manager cannot terminate an underperforming employee, so the only way to move the shirker out of their unit is to suggest the employee for promotion elsewhere. This is called "failing up" and is a consistent marker of dysfunctional organizations. This solves her problem but makes a larger one for the organization. Does your employer have any perverse incentives that create rather than solve problems? The fact that perverse incentives create system-level, repetitive conflicts points to the structural nature of these issues.

A second example: imagine a company that installs and services burglar alarm systems for corporations and government offices. To respond quickly to customers, the technicians are told they must reply to emails or voicemails within ten minutes. To avoid reprimands from their managers, technicians are taking calls and answering emails while driving between customer sites. Abiding by the new policy means they must violate the state's driving laws and common sense. This results in increased car accidents, workers' compensation claims, and overall liability for the entire company. Even if the company terminates the employment of those with two or more accidents or traffic citations, the policy provides negative incentives for all the technicians to continue these conflict-causing behaviors.

In nearly all cases, high employee or client turnover can be traced to systemic sources of conflict. If your organization has terminated the "bad apples" and the problem remains, then the source of the conflict is systemic. For example, if sabotage, theft, and apathy are widespread within a company, there is a need for cultural change rather than simply terminating individual employees. Structural sources of conflict mean the conflict will recur repeatedly until the source of the conflict is addressed. Often, culture change within the organization is required (see Chapter 6).

Nonstructural sources of conflict happen one time or rarely, occurring as isolated events that could not have been predicted or avoided. These are usually resolved by taking action to address the individual problem rather than creating or changing policies across the organization: the employee who is repeatedly late to work or does not treat his coworkers appropriately even after retraining or coaching; the two team members who simply cannot get along with each other but who seem to work well with others. In these instances, retraining, discipline, or termination may be in order. Sometimes an important delivery gets lost in the mail or a product does not live up to expectations. Sometimes these are isolated problems that will not recur. In other instances, they are indicators of a pervasive, unresolved, systemic problem that will require a systems-level change. For example, Boeing's 787 passenger jets remained grounded as of 2022, and this occurred after fatal flaws in the 737 Max led to the deaths of hundreds of passengers and a massive drop in the company's value. Addressing these recurring problems will require changes to processes and organizational culture at a minimum.

Organizations and managers tend to miss the systemic causes of conflict and instead seek to hold one or more specific individuals accountable for behavior that was shaped by policies, procedures, and organizational cultures. For example, imagine a large government organization in which only 20% of the employees are women and 15% are people of color. Yet the organization claims to care about diversity and inclusion. The organization requires all potential employees to travel at their own expense to Washington, DC, for their in-person interview. How might their employee pool be more diverse if they held these interviews in Atlanta, Los Angeles, Hawaii, or Chicago? To make matters worse, those hired are disproportionately graduates of a small number of Ivy League universities because their alumni networks know how to prepare their graduates to successfully get through the hiring process, and many Ivy League applicants find themselves being interviewed by people who are more likely to share their academic and identity backgrounds. Instead of addressing these sources of systemic bias, the organization offered a brief training on diversity to their hiring team in the hope that would solve the problem. It did not. Try to avoid the trap of making individuals responsible for systemic problems. Systemic problems require systemic solutions.

When dealing with nonstructural (i.e., individual) sources of conflict, don't fall into the *elementary school discipline* trap. For example, when one child misbehaves or lollygags in the halls during a trip to the restroom, the principal responds by changing the rules so that individuals can no longer make these trips on their own. Instead, each classroom is assigned two times during the day when they are allowed to use the restroom together as a group. Everyone is punished for the misbehavior of one or a few members rather than dealing directly with those who misbehave. Large organizations tend to do this rather than respond as needed to misbehaving individuals. Ironically, this stems from a desire for conflict avoidance. Rather than dealing directly with the wrongdoer, the organization creates a new policy for the whole organization.

Predicting and Preventing Workplace Violence: Theories and Practice

Workplace violence is often predictable and preventable, yet persistently remains a vexing, dangerous problem. Managers can proactively reduce the likelihood of workplace violence by remaining vigilant for common risk factors, intervening to address disgruntled workers, ensuring that behavioral expectations are clear and codified into policy, referring emotionally troubled employees to resources, and documenting their concerns with the human resources department and any appropriate authorities.

The U.S. Occupational Safety and Health Administration (OSHA, 2023) has defined workplace violence:

> Workplace violence is any act or threat of physical violence, harassment, intimidation, or other threatening disruptive behavior that occurs at the work site. It ranges from threats and verbal abuse to physical assaults and even homicide. It can affect and involve employees, clients, customers and visitors. Acts of violence and other injuries is currently the third-leading cause of fatal occupational injuries in the United States.

According to the Bureau of Labor Statistics Census of Fatal Occupational Injuries (CFOI), of the 5,333 fatal workplace injuries that occurred in the United States in 2019, 761 were cases of intentional injury by another person. However, it manifests itself, workplace violence is a major concern for employers and employees nationwide.

Certain industries and workers are at higher risk for workplace violence: night shift workers, taxi drivers, restaurant workers, law enforcement officers, health-care personnel, construction workers, delivery drivers, and social service employees (ibid.). Some incidences of workplace violence begin as domestic violence that then spills into the workplace when an abusive romantic partner comes to their target's place of employment to harass, intimidate, or harm them. In these cases, it is appropriate to document the situation, involve the authorities and encourage the victim to consider requesting a protective or restraining order from the courts, and involve law enforcement authorities. Some organizations offer relocation services, additional paid leave, counseling services, and other forms of assistance to employees who are victims/survivors of domestic violence.

Managers and employers can take the following 12 strategies to reduce and respond to workplace violence (TechFunnel, 2019):

1. Create clear policies and guidelines.

    Be sure employees and customers are clear about expected behaviors and the consequences of unacceptable behaviors. Conflict comes from unmet and unclear expectations.

2. Communicate policies effectively.

    Using training, posters, and onboarding conversations, ensure employees know which behaviors are expected, the consequences for violating behavioral expectations, and how to report violations they see or experience. Have them sign to acknowledge they understand.

3. Conduct bystander training.

    Everyone in your organization should know how to intervene to stop bad behavior, from using humor and redirection for small or accidental infractions to intervening effectively to de-escalate difficult situations and report violations.

4. Introduce activities to improve company culture.

    Dysfunctional organizational cultures are the primary reason that some organizations or teams have higher rates of violence, discrimination, and harassment than others (see Chapter 10).

5. Make changes in the office design.

    Minimize spaces where bad behavior can go unseen. For example, ensure break rooms have two or more points of ingress and egress; use glass walls for transparency, and ensure cameras are posted and visible in areas like elevators.

6. Install security cameras and access control systems.

    Place cameras in parking structures, elevators, stairwells, and places where bullies or harassers might otherwise feel emboldened. Restrooms cannot have cameras inside, but cameras show people as they enter and exit. Cameras can have a preventative purpose and gather evidence of bad behavior, if need be.

7. Make personal data confidential.

   Bullying and harassment often follow employees outside the workplace. Maintaining data privacy makes this more difficult.

8. Minimize incidents where employees could be vulnerable.

   If a client has a reputation for inappropriate behavior, be sure to send employees in small groups rather than alone. Consider firing a client when they disrespect your employees. If your office is in a high-crime neighborhood, do not expect people to walk solo to their cars after working late. Take proactive steps to keep your people safe.

9. Make the complaint process accessible, prompt, and fair.

   If the process takes too long, yields no clear consequences, or treats powerful employees differently, then employees will quit and/or file formal complaints in the court system or through other mechanisms. In worst-case scenarios, disgruntled employees who feel they were not treated fairly are at higher risk of engaging in workplace violence. Hopelessness and helplessness are red flags for future violence, media leaks, or litigation.

10. Be consistent when handing out penalties.

   No one is above the law or policies designed to prevent and/or punish abusive behavior. As the scandal at Uber taught us, when CEOS and others in the C-suite downplay repeated allegations of sexual harassment, or worse, are implicated, brand damage and regulatory investigations can tarnish the company's name and profits for many years to come (Carson & Gould, 2017). Managers and leaders need to set a positive example, rather than acting like the rules do not apply to them. Hubris predicts leadership failure.

11. Be wary of repeat offenders.

   There is rarely just one victim, one incidence of theft, one incident of discrimination or bias. Each victim may believe they are alone, but proactive companies will dig deep enough into each complaint to determine if there are more victims and if this is a pattern of behavior. In most cases, there is nothing to be personally gained by the victim(s) for coming forward. Taking complaints seriously, investigating them, and assuring appropriate penalties means that predators will stop preying or they will leave for other hunting grounds. Remember, it is human nature to experience denial when the reality is too painful to fully acknowledge, but organizations have learned the hard way that denial is not an optimal strategy for success.

12. Provide protection to complainants.

   Seventy-five percent of employees who file complaints of harassment, discrimination, or bullying claim they experienced retaliation. This means fewer employees will be willing to file a complaint or seek to make positive changes in their workplace (TechFunnel, 2019).

CONCLUSION

This brief introduction to the theories and the terminology of conflict management presents the conceptual frameworks and ideas that make sense of the chapters to come. These theories are organized from those existing within one's own mind, then expanding to the interpersonal realm, and finally, intergroup and systemic conflict. Before managers can prevent or resolve unproductive conflict, they first need to understand how it arises, evolves, and dissipates. When managers understand the biological and evolutionary sources of conflict and cooperation, they see the root causes of human behaviors and learn to depersonalize challenging behaviors from employees or customers. When they understand procedural justice, they gain critical insights into the processes for obtaining buy-in for important decisions that will require employee cooperation across the organization for successful implementation. When managers understand differing worldviews and definitions related to fairness, they learn there are ways to distribute resources or solve problems and that communicating these perspectives can lead to deeper understandings between employees and better relationships. Through an examination of the evolving nature of power relations between managers and employees, collaborative managers may motivate people through cooperation, mutual respect, and genuine understanding—the ultimate source of power for leaders. When managers act as diagnosticians who see conflict as a symptom of a deeper problem, then they become able to diagnose and change the underlying structures or systems that give rise to unproductive and recurring conflicts.

ELISE AND MAIN STREET BAKERIES: BEN'S TRIP TO STORE NUMBER 75

As Ben boarded the flight to deal with the problem at store number 75, he was already building a list of likely causes in his head: Janice, the manager of that store, may be driving other employees away. The last two times Ben called Janice, he left voicemail messages because she was too busy to talk to him and she did not bother calling him back. She is probably avoiding him. Ben hates it when others treat him disrespectfully. No matter how busy she is, she could call him back. Store number 75 is taking up more of his time than the other stores. That is not fair to those managers who are seeking more training, advice, or other resources from HR.

When Ben arrived, he contacted the last two assistant managers who quit and arranged to meet them for coffee. He asked them, "What would make store number 75 a better place to work? What would make it a place where people like you would want to build your careers?" Both assistant managers told the same story. Janice, the store manager, works herself to death. She is so afraid the assistant managers won't make the right decisions that she refuses to delegate anything. The assistant managers are treated like glorified cashiers. The assistant managers are told what to do and how to do it, but their input is never sought. Janice won't listen to their ideas for improvement. When changes are made, the assistant managers are not informed about the reasons for the changes, nor are they informed about policy changes coming from corporate headquarters. There is a lack of communication from the top down and certainly from the bottom up. Assistant managers want to be problem solvers, but their scope of authority is so limited they end up frustrated—always needing to go to the manager to get approval for every little thing. The assistant managers are unclear about their full job descriptions or the ways in which their performance would be evaluated.

When it comes time for the manager to distribute merit bonuses, the assistant managers claimed that Janice does this in an unfair manner that lacks transparency. No one knows why some employees earn more than others, and they suspect favoritism. Some employees wonder if it is because the manager seems to get along better with those employees who are most like her (e.g., gender, race, religion). Additionally, the store lacks a friendly, collegial atmosphere. Employees come to work and leave eight hours later. They do not build relationships or support each other. The environment is lonely and frustrating, so most assistant managers do not stay long.

KEY TERMS

accuser bias
anchoring number
antisocial personality disorder
attribution theory
bias of the accused
borderline personality disorder
cognitive bias
collectivist societies
denial
disassociation
displacement
distributive justice
equality principle
equity principle
fairness
framing effect
fundamental attribution error
histrionic personality disorder
impasse
individualistic societies
in-group/out-group theory
intergroup conflicts
interpersonal conflicts

intrapersonal conflicts
Maslow's hierarchy of needs
narcissistic personality disorder
need principle
need theories
nonstructural sources of conflict
paranoid personality disorder
personality disorder
perverse incentives
procedural justice
projection
rationalization
relationship-based conflicts
resource-based conflict
role-based conflict
social categorization
social comparison
social identification
structural/systemic sources of conflict
system-level conflicts
task-based conflicts
theory of relative deprivation
values conflicts

DISCUSSION QUESTIONS

1. How useful (or not useful) is a knowledge of conflict theory for managers? What is the connection between these theories and your practical management decisions?

2. Think of a conflict that has been in the news recently. Which of these theories best explains why the conflict arose or the choices made by parties to the conflict? Discuss the pros and cons of different theories as explanations for these events.

3. Complete this sentence five times: "I am (a)_____." You might select words like mother/father, wife/husband, daughter/son, engineer, manager, Catholic, Canadian, hiker, runner, vegetarian, Cuban American, etc. What do these words tell others about your in-groups or out-groups? How do you identify yourself compared to others? How does your identity influence the conflicts you decide to engage in or how you interact with others?

EXERCISES

1. First, go to "Elise and Main Street Bakeries: Ben's Trip to Store Number 75" at the end of this chapter. Go through each paragraph and identify every form of cognitive bias or conflict theory you can find. Then develop a list of remedies that Ben can recommend to Elise that will reduce the sources of unproductive conflict. Remember—getting rid of the manager is not the first or only option on this list. In fact, changing the manager may not solve all the problems at store 75.

2. Think of a past performance-review process in which you participated as the reviewer or as the employee. How would it have been different if it took a collaborative and procedural orientation? Brainstorm questions for a performance review that encourages employees to compare their current performance to past performance and set future goals for improvement tied to current and past performance rather than being tied to a comparison of other employees in the company. You can do this individually or in small groups.

3. You are a manager and you just learned that you must lay off one of your 10 employees. Your workplace is not unionized and you have full discretion to decide whom to let go. Which standard of fairness will you use and why? Which factors will you include in your decision-making process, and which will you exclude? Discuss this among others to see how many decision-making criteria you can produce. What kind of fairness does each criterion speak to? Would different managers use different criteria? How is that fair?

4. Alex, Pat, and Sandy own a consulting business together. They just completed a job that brought in $2,400 to their company (after expenses). Alex is a semiretired former executive. Alex's contacts brought the business to the company but Alex only worked six hours on the project. Pat is single and has no kids. Pat worked twelve hours on the project, but with less experience so Pat's work is likely less efficient than Alex's work. Sandy is a single parent with three kids and student loans. Sandy's hectic schedule means that Sandy could only work six hours on the project. Like Pat, Sandy has much less experience than Alex. How much money should each

person receive from this project? Once completed, analyze your answers to see which definition of fairness your distribution uses. (Exercise created by T. K. Hedeen, Kennesaw State University, 2011).

GOAL SETTING

1. For the next week, make notes about the conflicts you experience. Which conflict style did you use to address the conflict and which theories explain how the conflict arose and progressed? Then, set one goal for the upcoming week that you believe will help you more efficiently match your conflict response to the conflict you face. Try to address the conflict before it gets too high on the spiral of unmanaged conflict and see what earlier resolutions can achieve. Set goals that specifically incorporate your new knowledge of conflict styles and conflict theories.
2. Take an inventory of your sources of power within any specific context (e.g., work, your community). How can you leverage your power to be a force for positive change? Set a goal to work on positive change to reduce or prevent conflict at home, work, or in your community using the power you have.
3. What are the recurring sources of conflict in your workplace? What are the sources of conflict at the intrapersonal, interpersonal, intergroup, and systemic levels? Choose one or more recurring conflicts and set a goal for improvement. What can *you* do to improve the conflict?
4. Grow your empathy muscles: Increase the diversity in your wisdom circle by reaching out to form or deepen friendships or professional networking relationships with people different from you in terms of race, gender, generation, national origin, sexual orientation, etc. Having a diverse group of friends and colleagues will improve your ability to gather feedback and advice from different perspectives and influence your implicit understanding of who is part of your "in-group."

SUGGESTED SUPPLEMENTAL READINGS

Axelrod, R. (1984). *The evolution of cooperation*. Basic Books.
Birke, R. (2010). Neuroscience and settlement: An examination of scientific innovations and practical applications. *Ohio State Journal on Dispute Resolution, 25*(2), 477–529.
Eddy, B. (2016). *High conflict people in legal disputes*. Unhooked Books.
Minson, J. A., & Chen, F. S. (2022). Receptiveness to opposing views: Conceptualization and integrative review. *Personality and Social Psychology Review, 26*(2), 93–111.

3

The Power of Negotiation

Essential Concepts and Skills

The most critical thing in a negotiation is to get inside your opponent's head and figure out what he really wants.

—Jacob Lew

Effective problem-solving requires superior negotiation skills. Nearly every interaction with colleagues and customers is a negotiation, whether you recognize it or not. Figuring out what they want, what you are able or willing to give, and then framing everything strategically, will get you pretty far. As the quote from Jacob Lew indicates, we need to deeply understand what our negotiation partner (note: not adversary) needs or wants *and why*. Only then can we decide whether to make a deal with them. A common error made by negotiators occurs when they assume they know what their partner wants and why instead of asking the tough questions required develop deeper understanding. Secondarily, negotiators often refrain from fully sharing their own needs out of a mistaken belief that withholding information will help them in some way. It usually hurts more than helps. This chapter is designed to help you negotiate like a pro, whether you are asking for a raise, brokering a billion-dollar trade deal, or getting your kid to clean their room.

After reading this chapter, revisit these learning objectives to ensure you have understood the basics of negotiation theory and practice.

Learning Objectives

- Demonstrate an understanding of the role of negotiation in managerial life.
- List, describe, and apply common negotiation concepts and skills.
- Analyze and describe the ways in which your gender and other identity characteristics impact negotiation outcomes.
- Demonstrate an understanding of the differences between distributive and integrative (also known as interest-based) bargaining.
- Analyze and identify the interests that underlie positions.

- Demonstrate an understanding of the ethical implications of negotiation decisions.
- Apply negotiation concepts to prepare effectively for negotiations.
- Explain the role of trust building and repair in negotiations and workplace relationships.

ELISE AND MAIN STREET BAKERIES

In recent years, the price of flour has risen dramatically. At the same time, increased bargain hunting by consumers and increased competition has led to reduced profits for many boutique food outlets such as Main Street Bakeries. Elise and her company have weathered the storm relatively well by negotiating long-term, fixed-price contracts with organic farmers and mills around the country. These contracts mean Elise and her team do a lot of negotiating. Elise has a meeting this afternoon with a young farmer named Jacob who wants to sell his organic crops to Main Street Bakeries. She hopes she can strike a good deal because she is trying hard to avoid raising her prices. If she does not reach a deal with Jacob, then her only alternative would be to continue looking for additional suppliers. Because prices are going up quickly, the longer she waits to conclude a deal, the higher the price she will likely pay. If she simply cannot afford to buy local wheat, then she could buy wheat from outside the United States. This is not ideal because her shop has little notes on its products, stating where the ingredients came from; her customers want locally grown, organic food whenever possible.

MANAGERS AS NEGOTIATORS

When was your most recent negotiation? I bet you negotiated today with your coworkers, family members, or your dog as he begged for food under the table. If you cannot remember your last negotiation, then your view of negotiation may be too narrow. You began negotiating as a small child, wheedling your way into a later bedtime, a cookie before dinner, or more screen time. Today, you may have negotiated with a roommate or spouse about household chores, negotiated with the police officer who pulled you over for speeding, negotiated with your colleagues about the division of labor on a project, negotiated with your supervisor to let you leave early so you could get to class on time, or negotiated with your professor to grant an extension on your paper's due date. In the news, we see attorneys negotiating plea bargains, members of Congress negotiating trade bills, government agencies negotiating with the businesses they regulate, large corporations negotiating tax incentives for relocation, and public employee unions negotiating new contract terms. Nearly all collaboration or teamwork requires negotiation. Whether negotiations are formal or informal, they are all around us.

The first step to improving your negotiations is to recognize when it is happening. **Negotiation** occurs between two or more interdependent parties who have a perceived conflict between their needs and desires yet believe a negotiated outcome is superior to what they could achieve unilaterally. The parties are interdependent or they would not be negotiating with one another; neither person can achieve his or her goals without the other's cooperation. If any party to the negotiation can accomplish their goals unilaterally, then they can do so without negotiation. Parties to a negotiation may not be equally dependent on one another; meaning-dependence may be asymmetric. Specific workplace examples of negotiation include performance appraisals, workload distribution, determination of deadlines, salaries and working conditions, time off, preferred office space, flextime schedules, and interpersonal interactions.

Ninja Negotiation Skills

Mastering negotiation skills is like having a secret superpower. You understand the other party's needs, often better than they do. Using your knowledge of conflict theory (Chapter 2), personality disorders and psychology (Chapter 2), conflict styles (Chapter 1), problem-solving processes (Chapters 4, 8, and 10), and differing cultural approaches to negotiation (Chapter 5), you can nimbly work through the stages of the negotiation process to reach a positive outcome.

Before examining core negotiation concepts, it is important to conceptualize the negotiation as an exercise in discernment and framing. Through discernment you seek to grasp the other party's (or parties') motivations, needs, and potential points of leverage or mutual gain. You ask useful, open-ended questions designed to elicit their concerns and show respect for their needs. You frame your questions, comments, and proposals toward constructive, collaborative problem-solving rather than arguing for your position. In your mind and with the other party, you frame this as "me and you against the problem" versus "me against you."

Box 3.1 covers the basics of what I call "Ninja Negotiation." Why "ninja" negotiation? Because if you use all the skills and strategies listed, the other side might not even realize they just engaged in a negotiation. If they knew it was a negotiation, they would hopefully walk away feeling victorious because the outcome was better than they thought possible. They may even believe they "won" when the reality is that you both won: the relationship is stronger than before the negotiation and the core needs of all the parties were addressed. When you negotiate well, everyone leaves the interaction feeling heard, respected, and satisfied with both the process and outcome. But how?

Step 1: Prepare in Advance.

If you know you are about to engage in a negotiation, take time to reflect on your true needs and aspirations. Use the information in this chapter to label your asking price, settlement range, or other helpful concepts. You can revise these

---

BOX 3.1. NINJA NEGOTIATION: ESSENTIAL ELEMENTS

1. Prepare in advance.
2. Build rapport.
3. Listen and ask good questions.
4. Reverse engineer their behavior.
5. Framing matters.
6. Never reward bad behavior.

as more information becomes available. Similarly, try to anticipate the other's needs and concerns, knowing that until you ask good questions, your understanding will be incomplete and more likely fall prey to cognitive biases covered in Chapter 2. Lastly, be sure to do your research to prepare appropriately. For example, Elise needs to know the current price of organic wheat and factors that may lead it to rise or decline. There is more on mediation preparedness below.

Step 2: Build Rapport.

In most cultures, people spend time getting to know one another, building trust, and deepening their rapport before engaging in negotiations. As Chapter 5 demonstrates, there is a trade-off between attending first to the task or to the relationship. Overall, U.S. culture tends to focus on the task before building relationships, using detailed contracts to ensure enforceability of agreements with the assumption of a fair and accessible court system for enforcement. The United States is an individualistic culture in which people change organizations with relative frequency, so building relationships with one negotiation counterpart may make less sense. Collectivist cultures build relationships first, using less-detailed contracts, with the understanding that if a problem arises in the implementation of any agreements, then each negotiator can reach out to the other to solve problems collaboratively. The strength of the relationship and mutual connections in the community are used as a guarantor of promised behavior rather than resorting to courts, which are slow, expensive, and even corrupt in much of the world. Both approaches are necessary and need not require trade-offs: we can build relationships and trust while also using clear and enforceable contracts to secure negotiated agreements. However, U.S. negotiators tend to overlook the benefits of investing in relationship building as part of the negotiation process.

Step 3: Listen and Ask Good Questions.

Chapter 1 included information and exercises designed to enhance your ability to listen to understand rather than listening to respond. To increase the odds of a positive outcome, engage in active listening, open-ended questions, and a deep investigation into the "why." What do they need and why? How would that feel or what need would that meet? How can you help? What would success look like? What are their expectations and what are yours? Why? Before responding to what they tell you, be sure to summarize what you heard them say. If you hear something that triggers an emotional or defensive response, take time to reflect before responding. Ask for a break or for some time to process what you have learned before moving forward. When people feel heard, they are often willing to compromise or even accommodate the other's needs to a greater extent.

Step 4: Reverse Engineer Their Behavior.

Why are they acting like that? Why do they need that? Why do they communicate (or fail to) that way? Observe their behavior, ask questions to gather information, then develop a working hypothesis about their motivations. One of my favorite mantras: *behavior continues as long as it is working*. Based on their observable behavior, what needs are they seeking to meet and why? Using the concepts in Chapter 1, you might start by discerning which conflict mode or style they tend to favor: avoiding, accommodating, collaborative, compromising, or competitive. Knowing their style and your own will help you avoid miscommunication caused by differing preferences around indirectness versus directness. You will understand how to approach them, reassure them, disarm defensiveness, stand up to bullying, etc. Using information in Chapter 2, you might assess which needs they are seeking to meet: basic needs like food and shelter; a sense of belonging; or even self-actualization. You might notice they seem to lack empathy, show open grandiosity, and disregard the needs of others, like narcissists tend to do. If so, then you will alter your negotiation strategy by arguing why an agreement is good for them or makes them look like the hero or victor. In essence, every behavior tells us something about what this person needs, or think they need, in this negotiation. For example, if you have an employee who seems to respond well to words of affirmation, you can be sure to praise their efforts and work products as you enter a negotiation about changing their work assignments. If there is a behavior that needs to change, such as interrupting others during meetings, then you might spend a few minutes thinking about the causes for this behavior: is this related to culture difference (Chapter 5), a fear of being overlooked, a need for control? If you correctly reverse engineer the behavior to determine the motivation behind it, then you can decide how best to meet their needs or address the issue effectively.

Here is an illustrative example with which most of us can identify: Imagine you have an uncle with a difficult personality who comes to Thanksgiving dinner and insists on talking about divisive political issues with full knowledge that he will offend some of those present. Reverse engineer that behavior. Why is "Uncle Perry" doing that? One hypothesis is that Uncle Perry is a middle child in a big family who tends to seek attention, even if he has to be provocative to get it. Test this hypothesis by redirecting the conversation to another topic that still gives him the attention he seeks. "Uncle Perry, you drove across three states to join us. What did you see? What was your favorite part of the trip? When I visit you, should I take that same route or is there a better one if I want to do some sightseeing on the way?" This way, his underlying need for attention is met, but in a less negative way for everyone present. Reverse engineering helps you negotiate like a ninja: Uncle Perry won't even realize what just happened. Everyone wins.

Step 5: Framing Matters.

Frame your comments carefully, constructively, collaboratively. Avoid framing the problem as "their problem." If you are in an interdependent relationship, then any problem is an "us" problem. Remember that people tend to like helping others while they dislike being told what to do. Therefore, "Can you help me ensure the reports get filed on time?" may work better than "You never get your data to me on time!" Framing matters. Good framing will reduce the chances of defensiveness and escalation. It focuses on solving a shared problem together rather than on winning arguments. It is "me and you against this problem" rather than "me versus you." When you reframe your own thoughts toward joint problem-solving, it will change your world for the better.

Step 6: Never Reward Bad Behavior.

We teach people how to treat us. If we reward negative behavior or treatment, then we implicitly teach our negotiation partner that their behavior should continue. People who scored high on avoidant and accommodating may fall prey to this temptation more often than others. Yet, we all fall prey to this negotiation no-no when we aren't paying enough attention to the consequence of behavior: our own and theirs. Common workplace examples:

- Asking an accommodating employee to consistently do more overtime or take on unpleasant tasks because other employees are more likely to balk. By doing this we simultaneously punish good behavior (e.g., being a team player) while rewarding bad behavior (e.g., failure to do one's share of the work).
- Failing up: When it is difficult to fire an underperformer, some managers recommend them for promotion to another unit or otherwise move them around rather than addressing the root behavior. At the same time, highly productive workers are not promoted because their supervisors may be receiving larger bonuses based on their productivity. This is an example of perverse incentives (see Chapter 2).
- Bullies who get their way or get promoted because conflict-avoidant managers do not put a stop to the behavior, thereby suffering higher turnover or formal complaints because good people leave or file lawsuits.

If you do not want people to interrupt, you must stop the interruptions. If you want people to come to meetings on time, then you must start meetings on time even if you are the only one there. They will get the message and show up on time in the future. Be thoughtful about implicit messages your behavior sends: what behaviors are you rewarding? Behavior continues as long as it is working. Don't let bad behavior work.

Understanding the dynamics of negotiation will help you navigate performance reviews; advocate for your department or organization as it competes for limited resources; resolve conflicts that arise with customers, employees, and regulatory matters; and more.

DISTRIBUTIVE VERSUS INTEGRATIVE BARGAINING

Negotiations can be zero-sum or non-zero-sum. In **zero-sum** situations, also called *distributive negotiation* situations, each gain made by one negotiator comes at the expense of another negotiator. In **distributive bargaining** situations, resources are fixed and cannot be increased. Distributive bargaining typically involves only one issue in the negotiation (e.g., price) rather than multiple issues under negotiation. In contrast, non-zero-sum negotiations, also called **integrative bargaining**, are those in which negotiators can achieve their goals without necessarily leaving the others worse off and in which multiple issues are at stake (Lewicki, Barry & Saunders, 2010). We know that negotiators often assume a situation is distributive and therefore competitive when indeed it is not necessarily so (Deutsch, 2000).

In many bargaining situations, it is possible to expand the pie, meaning to find ways to create value rather than compete over an existing fixed pie, or a non-expandable resource. In **creating value**, the negotiators work together to ensure that their needs are met by expanding existing value through collaboration, increased efficiency, or creativity. In distributive bargaining situations, negotiators are focused on **claiming value** for themselves. This means they are competing to claim something they both value. The more one claims, the less remains for the other. Identifying the nature of the negotiation as integrative versus distributive is key to choosing the best negotiation strategies.

Steps in Distributive Bargaining

At its core, distributive bargaining involves either the seller or the buyer proposing the first number (or offer), called the anchoring number, as a proposal and the other side responding with a counterproposal or acceptance of the offer. The negotiators may then share information about why their number is supported by the "facts" as the negotiators' initial offerings move closer together. If a deal is to be reached, they typically reach agreement on a number that is somewhere between the buyer's and the seller's initial proposals. This is an appropriate process for negotiating in some circumstances: when the time for negotiating is short, when the outcome is not crucial to either party, when the relationship between the negotiators is not harmed by this process, and when the deal leaves no value unclaimed. This is not an exact science, but the more of these conditions that apply, the more likely distributive bargaining does no harm. It can be inefficient since the negotiators rarely state their bottom line or true needs early in the process. In other words, distributive bargaining encourages game playing: negotiators may start with ridiculously high initial offers to overstate their resistance to compromise.

Although distributive bargaining has become the default approach used by many negotiators, it is not usually the best choice. Imagine you ask your boss for a raise of $4.00 an hour. He counters with a proposal for $2.00 an hour and you both eventually settle on $3.00. No harm was done but value might have been left unclaimed. Why were you seeking the raise? Was it to help pay the costs of tuition for graduate school so you can move up in your career? What if there were a tuition remission policy at the company about which you were unaware? You both might have been better off by sharing more information during the negotiation and trying to create value rather than to claim value. What if your motivation was fairness, because you learned that a colleague hired after you makes more for the same job? Sharing this concern could lead to a more equitable organization, or you could find out that the colleague has duties or a degree of which you were unaware. In any event, distributive bargaining would not meet the interest in fairness under these circumstances.

The biggest downside to distributive bargaining is that bargainers may get exactly what they have asked for, yet still not have what they need. This happens because the negotiator makes a demand, also known as *stating a position*, and this demand may not contain information about why the demand is sought. A joke to illustrate:

Wife: You need to stop working so many nights and weekends. You are going to work yourself to death if you aren't careful.

Husband: You have been saying this for a while and I have good news to announce. I told my boss that I won't work weekends anymore. Instead, I joined a traveling golf league that plays in a different city each weekend. I can't wait to get started! Why do you look so upset? You are getting exactly what you asked for: I am working less. Golf will be great for my health!

Steps in Integrative Bargaining

In 1981 Roger Fisher and William Ury wrote a book entitled *Getting to Yes: Negotiating Agreement without Giving In.* This book spent years on the *New York Times* best-seller list. It has been called negotiation's holy book because it has been around a long time, sold millions of copies, and given us rules and a common language to guide our negotiations. Fisher and Ury promoted a new way to think about and carry out negotiations. Using their prescriptions, one could be a world-class negotiator and still go to bed each night with a clear conscience. The steps in their model have been adapted into many decision-making and problem-solving processes, including most formal mediation programs in Western societies. By understanding the basic steps in the integrative negotiation process you can greatly improve your outcomes and your relationships with your negotiation partners.

Integrative bargaining combines the needs of both parties into any agreement. The first step to accomplishing this goal is to "separate the people from the problem" (Fisher & Ury, 1981, p. 16). Every negotiation can be broken down into two main categories: substance and relationships. Negotiators are people first—people with egos, the desire to save face, and the need to be treated fairly and respectfully. Negotiators often mistake substantive comments by the other negotiator as personal affronts. A manager may observe, "We are behind on this project." Although it is a factual statement, some employees may take it as an attack on their work ethic or efficiency. Once someone feels they have been treated rudely or unfairly, then the problem grows instead of getting settled. Defensiveness is unhelpful and escalates conflict.

Fisher and Ury recommend dealing with the "people problem" explicitly and separately from the substantive problem.

Negotiators need to keep three categories in mind: "perceptions, emotion, and communication" (Fisher & Ury, 1981, p. 22). It is important to understand how negotiators frame the problem and any potential solutions. Often, it is the way one views or perceives a problem that causes obstacles to settlement more than any possible objective reading of the facts. "Facts, even when well established, do nothing to solve the problem" (Fisher & Ury, 1981, p. 22). It may be helpful during the negotiation to have each negotiator summarize the other's perspective. This reflection does not mean the two sides have reached one shared understanding of the problem or possible solution, only that they have both heard and registered each other's viewpoints. This perspective-taking can be an important step in putting together the pieces of the negotiation puzzle and in building the rapport necessary to reach agreements.

For example, in a dispute between two employees who share an office space, one might consider the other rude for never inquiring into her health or her family's well-being. The other employee might consider herself polite for not prying into the personal life of her workmate. Learning about the other's perspective is often a prerequisite for problem-solving.

If you believe the other negotiator has a negative impression of you, then it may be worth trying to behave in a way contrary to expectations. For example, if you are perceived as stubborn, you could offer an unexpected concession. If you are considered too loud or domineering, you might let them speak first and without interruption. Ask for their ideas, thoughts, and input. Behaving in ways contrary to their perceptions may help them realize their perceptions could be inaccurate.

Difficult negotiations make us feel worried, fearful, anxious, angry, or even guilty. Don't ignore these emotional reactions. Acknowledge the difficulty of the situation and explain how you're feeling. Inquire about how others feel. Normalize and legitimate these feelings—if these negotiations were easy, they would have been resolved already, right? Allow negotiators to let off steam using breaks and by allowing people to talk about their concerns. If a negotiator yells or gets angry, consider sitting patiently and quietly—urge her to say all she needs to say. Escalation usually requires both parties to engage. Do not get defensive or shut down the expression of emotions. If you take part in an ongoing or long-term negotiation, develop rituals and social exchanges that help keep the group bonded over time, such as by celebrating birthdays and milestones together. These experiences remind negotiators they have a lot in common, even if they disagree or struggle with the negotiations. They build the trust and rapport necessary for agreement.

Communication problems can make the negotiations turn personal and lead to attacks on the people instead of the problem. Be sure to avoid statements that indicate the other side is to blame for the problem. Instead of me versus you, change your thinking to me and you versus the problem.

Even if you feel the other person is 100% to blame for the problem, you might consider using a future-focused statement designed to invite the other person to work with you toward a solution, such as "regardless of how we got here, let's talk about how we can fix it going forward."

The next step in the integrative negotiation process focuses on "interests, not positions" (Fisher & Ury, 1981, p. 40). The concept of interests versus positions is the core contribution of *Getting to Yes*. Whereas distributive bargaining focuses almost exclusively on the trading and amending of bargaining positions, integrative bargaining looks at the interests that underlie positions. Think of **positions** as demands: *I demand a raise! Not in my backyard! Turn down your*

Table 3.1   Positions versus Interests

	Positions	Interests
What the statement type communicates	Demands	Needs
Options for resolution	Only one way to meet a position	Many ways to meet an interest
Statement's effect on negotiation	Positions often terminate negotiations	Interests usually open up discussion
Examples:	"I demand a raise!"	"I want to feel that my contribution to this business is fully recognized."
	"Not in my backyard!"	"I am concerned for the safety of my children if the dump is built too close to our subdivision."
	"Turn down your music!"	"I need to be at work very early and cannot sleep with the noise."

music! Instead, **interests** tell us of the needs that underlie the positions: "I want to feel that my contribution is fully recognized," "I am concerned for the safety of my children if the dump is built too close to our subdivision," and "I need to be at work early and cannot sleep with the noise" (see Table 3.1). Positions, by definition, have only one way to be met: you can grant the raise, avoid placing the dump in her backyard, and turn down the music. Positions lead to win-lose outcomes. By contrast, interests can be met in multiple ways that leave both parties better off. There are many ways to help our negotiation partner to meet their need to feel respected, safe, or rested.

Planning for Your Negotiation

Although interests give negotiators much more to work with, people generally begin their negotiations with positional statements, out of habit if not for another reason. Before you enter a planned negotiation, take some time to outline your own positions and interests as well as those you might predict for the other negotiators. Once the negotiation starts, be sure to get a fuller understanding of the other negotiators' interests by asking open-ended questions: How did they arrive at their position? What need does that position meet for them? Tell them you want to better understand their needs and goals in order to reach an agreement that makes everyone better off. The best managers inquire about the interests of their employees, customers, and negotiation partners. Seeking to meet those needs may make it possible to get one's own needs met as well. Interests focus the negotiators on working together to solve problems rather than assuming an adversarial stance.

The third step is to "generate options for mutual gain" (Fisher & Ury, 1981, p. 56). This can be done through the process of brainstorming. When faced with conflicts or problems, people tend to leap to a diagnosis of the causes and solution for a problem before they have fully heard the other perspectives and ideas. We also tend to search for a single solution or assume a competitive rather than creative problem-solving posture. After thoroughly brainstorming as many solutions as possible to a problem, there are multiple paths forward. Sometimes the best solution will be clear to everyone at the end of the brainstorming session. If not, it may be time to create a package of trade-offs or work together to expand available resources.

The last step is to generate and use objective criteria by which to evaluate settlement terms. For example, if you are engaged in salary negotiations, benchmark salaries for similar positions within and outside your organization. If you are selling a house or business, the appraisal will be the objective criteria. If you are determining the correct child support amount, most U.S. states have a formal or general guidance. Your objective criteria may include reference to precedent, professional standards, market values, past practice, equity, or other criteria deemed appropriate by the negotiators (Fisher & Ury, 1981). The goal is to ensure that agreements are not arbitrary but are fair to all parties.

In modern organizations, the way you treat people matters. Your choice of negotiation strategy will affect your reputation as a manager, as a neighbor, as a citizen, and as a person. Although integrative bargaining may be overkill at the local farmers market, it will likely be the most useful strategy to use in negotiations where relationships matter. In cases where you are unlikely to see your counterpart again, integrative negotiation may achieve agreements when distributive bargaining often fails. Even when a colleague, supervisor, or family member approaches you with anger or hostility, you can turn the interaction around quickly by avoiding defensiveness, normalizing the need to work through problems together, encouraging feedback, and uncovering the needs of each party. Your relationships and career will be stronger due to your ability to uncover and address the interests of others.

NEGOTIATION TERMS AND CONCEPTS

Whether you are entering into a distributive or integrative negotiation, understanding the following terms and concepts will improve your negotiation process and outcomes.

Anchoring Number

The **anchoring number** is the first proposal made during a negotiation. It tends to create a cognitive anchor against which all subsequent offers are judged. If there is enough information upon which to create an anchoring number, the negotiator who makes the first offer has the advantage of creating the frame or boundary in which the negotiation will occur. For example, if I am the seller, I may make a wildly high initial offer. By doing so, any later reduction will seem like a concession. However, if I am negotiating in an unfamiliar environment or have little information on which to make an initial offer, it may be best to allow the other side to throw out the anchoring number. If the other side gives the anchoring number, it may be helpful to remind all parties this number need not become the focus around which the negotiations occur, especially once information is shared that makes it possible to evaluate the fairness or feasibility of that first proposal.

When negotiators share an anchoring number that is purposefully overstated, they are using a distributive bargaining technique. Spotting this strategy will enable the integrative bargainer to label it as such and then engage in a dis-cussion about the merits of integrative bargaining over distributive bar-gaining in most situations.

Asking Price

The **asking price**, also called **initial offer**, is the first proposal shared by each party in the negotiation. Each negotiator has an initial offer or asking price, but the negotiation has one anchoring number. Deciding on one's asking price can be tricky. Start too high and you may offend or alienate the other negotiator. If your initial offer is too high, then he or she may walk away prematurely. Start too low and you end up a "sucker," having received less value than you might have won with a higher initial offer. Whenever possible, do your homework in advance of the negotiation to craft an initial offer that is benchmarked appropriately. For example, perhaps you can deliver the item faster for a higher price. It is difficult to choose an appropriate initial offer or asking price without this kind of informa-tion. In the absence of this information, you run the risk that your initial offer will be inefficiently high or low, resulting in an increased chance of **impasse**, meaning failure to reach an agreement, or you may simply strike a poor bargain.

Target Point

A **target point** is the negotiator's end goal or preferred outcome for the nego-tiation. Depending on the strategies used by negotiators, they may or may not directly share this information. One's target point may consider many factors: the cost of the item plus some reasonable profit margin; elements of supply and demand, such as the relative scarcity of the item; the desire to continue a long and profitable relationship with one's bargaining partner so as to maximize long-term, rather than only short-term, profits; and so on. As information is shared during the negotiation, one's target point may change. Occasionally a negotia-tion will exceed negotiators' expectations and they are able to reach a settlement point that surpasses their target. This outcome generally means that the original target point was based on incomplete information about the other side's circum-stances or the nature of the good or service at stake.

Resistance Point

If the target point is the goal, the **resistance point** is the bottom line. For ex-ample, if a merchant purchases his stock wholesale at a cost of $5.00 per unit, his resistance point will be somewhere above $5.00. The resistance point is the smallest amount he will settle for and is sometimes referred to as the *reservation price* (Lewicki et al., 2010).

The **settlement range**, or the zone of agreement, is the space between the two resistance points. For example, the buyer's initial offer is $5,000 and her resis-tance point is $8,000; the seller's initial offer is $9,000 but his resistance point is $6,000, so the settlement range will be between $6,000 and $8,000. Barring communication problems or emotionally based obstacles to settlement, these negotiators can be predicted to strike a deal between the settlement range of

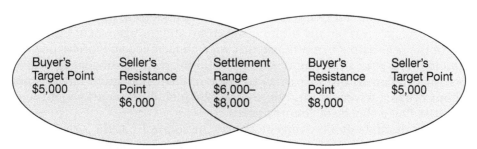

Buyer's Target Point $5,000   Seller's Resistance Point $6,000   Settlement Range $6,000–$8,000   Buyer's Resistance Point $8,000   Seller's Target Point $5,000

Figure 3.1   Key Negotiation Concepts

$6,000 to $8,000. This zone may change during the negotiation itself, especially if the parties engage in integrative bargaining, which may result in the creation of value or sharing of information that allows for a more efficient solution to become apparent to all (see Figure 3.1).

A **negative settlement range** is one in which there is no overlap between the lowest amount the seller is willing to take and the highest amount the buyer is willing to pay. Unless something changes the mind of the buyer or seller, then no agreement will be reached. A **positive settlement range** indicates overlap between the acceptable outcomes for the buyer and the seller. Although one likely comes into a negotiation with target and resistance points in mind, in most negotiations these are somewhat fluid as information is shared and a greater understanding is reached by all parties as to the nature of what is possible and mutually advantageous. The **settlement point** is the number within the settlement range at which the negotiators reach agreement or settle. The goal in distributive bargaining is to reach an agreement that is as close to the other side's resistance point as possible.

Every negotiation entails **transaction costs**, which include the time, energy, and money necessary to facilitate the negotiation and the deal itself. For example, every hour that a union negotiation team is tied up in contract discussions is an hour off the factory floor, per person. In fact, the transaction costs may exceed the value of the resource under discussion in many cases, especially when parties are emotionally piqued. It is therefore important to minimize transaction costs when possible and correctly identify those situations in which the transaction costs make negotiation a losing proposition.

Hiring attorneys, financial advisors, or other experts increases the negotiation's transaction costs. When hiring experts to assist a negotiation, each party must decide whether the added transaction costs of doing so will be outweighed by the better outcome assumed to occur because of this expert help. This decision is a bit of a gamble, because one cannot know the outcome of the negotiation until it is over. Yet engaging in complicated negotiations without legal or financial expertise can also be costly. Divorce is the most common example of this dilemma: hiring attorneys and a forensic accountant may yield the most accurate and fair division of a retirement account, yet if the account holds $50,000 and the experts cost $25,000, then this would be a highly inefficient, yet disturbingly common, method for dividing the assets.

Sometimes each negotiator has a different view of what will happen in the future. For example, Elise thought the price of flour is unlikely to rise beyond a certain price ($11.50, for example) but the farmer disagreed. It can be difficult to reach an agreement when the future is uncertain and the agreement binds one or more of the negotiators to a promise that may, in fact, become impossible to execute. In this type of situation, it can be helpful to create **contingent agreements**. These agreements allow all parties to react to changing future circumstances without needing to renegotiate the contract by including variations in the outcome based on a change of circumstances.

A good example of a contingent agreement comes from the nonprofit field. Humanitarian relief organizations and governments must plan for possible natural disasters such as floods, droughts, earthquakes, tornadoes, wildfires, and so on. Yet, with luck, these disasters may not materialize. Disaster relief organizations often hire and train local employees and volunteers on a contingency basis. For example, an employee's contract might state something like this: "Mary Jones agrees to be available to work up to 60 consecutive days per year with two days of notice. If called on to work, Mary Jones will receive $500/day. If not called on to work within any calendar year, Mary Jones will receive $3,000." Contingent agreements such as this, are helpful when the future is uncertain and the transaction costs make frequent renegotiation undesirable.

BATNA is an acronym that stands for *best alternative to a negotiated agreement* (Fisher & Ury, 1981). Sometimes one or more negotiators realize they can better meet their goals by entering negotiations with a different business partner or by pursuing their end goal without the benefit of the negotiation. A BATNA is not a fallback offer. A **fallback offer** is made once the initial offer is rejected. It is somewhere between the initial offer and the resistance point. Instead, a BATNA is something negotiators can do unilaterally to accomplish their goals if the negotiation fails to reach agreement. A strong BATNA gives the negotiator a strong bargaining position and a weak BATNA leads to a weaker bargaining position. For example, imagine you want to ask your boss for a raise. You already have a job offer from a competing organization. If your boss is unable or unwilling to come close to the other offer, then your BATNA is to change organizations. The chances of achieving your target point are now higher than if you went into these salary negotiations with a weak or nonexistent BATNA.

When negotiations concern specific disputes, the BATNA may be to go public with the dispute or to go to court. These are actions that any side can do on its own, without the other's permission. A BATNA can be strong or weak. Prior to entering a planned negotiation, take some time to think through your alternatives to an agreement. What can or will you do if the negotiations result in impasse or the other side refuses to negotiate? You will likely have a list of alternatives, including doing nothing. The key is to be clear in your mind about your *best* alternative to reaching agreement so you can achieve your best outcome (Magee, Galinsky & Gruenfeld, 2007).

Impasse and Obstacles to Settlement

Impasse is reached when the parties are unable to reach an agreement that is superior to their BATNAs so they terminate the negotiations without agreement. Sometimes an impasse is temporary and lasts only until the obstacles to settlement are removed. Impasses occur for various reasons, including those cases in which there is a negative settlement range (see above) Sometimes an impasse results from communication problems, insufficient time to negotiate, or counterproductive psychological barriers such as anger or frustration. In these cases, it is important to go back to the steps of the integrative bargaining process to ensure that all the interests have been examined and all possible solutions have been brainstormed. When you get stuck, go back to these two earlier phases to see if a step or if some important information was missed. If the barriers to settlement seem to arise from differences in communication style, aggressive behaviors, or personality differences, consider bringing in a mediator (i.e., a neutral third party to assist with the negotiations). When dealing with a hard-nosed bargainer or a difficult personality, the important thing to remember is to focus on what *you* do and say in the negotiation rather than trying to control the other person.

Reactive devaluation occurs when an offer in a negotiation is discounted or disregarded due to a lack of trust in the person making the offer, even though the same offer might be accepted or seriously considered if it came from a neutral or trusted source, such as a mediator. Reactive devaluation is a form of attribution bias (see Chapter 2) specific to negotiation, and can lead to higher rates of impasse than would be objectively predicted based on the interests of the parties to the negotiation.

Personal Attacks or Offensive Behavior

What if the other negotiator uses language you find offensive or speaks to you in a disrespectful way? This happens most frequently in dysfunctional workplace cultures, but it can happen even in a relatively positive workplace climate. The first step to addressing inappropriate expressions of anger, frustration, hostility, contempt, and so on is to try to diagnose the root cause (see Chapter 2). If it seems like a large amount of anger in a small situation, then it is possible the negotiator is angry about something else but the outlet for this anger has become the present negotiation. Alternatively, the negotiator's view of the problem may be quite different, resulting in a belief that the problem is serious. Use your active listening skills (see Chapter 1) to better understand how the other negotiator perceives the problem, its origins, and any possible solutions. Let him or her know you are there to really listen and understand concerns, even if the negotiator perceives that you are the root of the problem (that is to say, he or she received bad customer service or a poor performance review and so on). The key is to avoid letting the other negotiator's anger or outburst trigger a fight-or-flight response in you. If someone yells at you, do not yell back. If they use bad language, do not respond in kind. Remember, you control only what *you* think, say, and do. When someone verbally attacks you, a counterattack may be understandable, but it is indeed not helpful. If the goal is to solve the problem, invite him or her to share feedback or criticism and make specific suggestions for improvement. The goal is to reorient the conflict from a "me versus you" mindset to one of "me and you versus the problem."

If the negotiator is unable to think about constructive solutions due to anger or emotional arousal, consider suggesting a short cooling-off period. The following are examples of some verbal exchanges you might hear in an organizational setting.

With Customers or Clients

Customer: This is the worst rip-off ever! I paid good money and the item I received is worthless. I want my money back!

Manager: I am so sorry to hear of the problems with our product. Can you tell me more specifically what the problem was? I will do all I can to fix this with you.

In Work Teams

Manager: I told you I needed that report last week! Was I unclear?! What do I need to do around here to see that the work gets done on time?!

Employee: I agree, this situation can't continue. I want to meet deadlines and do good work. Can we talk through some changes that might help?

In a more formal negotiation, it can be helpful to agree on ground rules in advance. If ground rules cannot be made in advance, it is still possible to discuss and agree on ground rules once the discussion has begun. This can seem awkward or preachy. It may help to normalize this by stating that ground rules are often helpful to guide productive problem-solving discussions. Ask for all parties to contribute ideas to the ground rules. Post them on the wall or on a piece of paper in the center of the table for everyone to see. Acknowledge that these decisions and negotiations can be difficult and that everyone's patience may be strained. Normalizing these feelings can help parties to understand what to expect and what is expected of them.

Hard-nosed Negotiator

Public employees' union representative: We won't settle for less than a 4% raise and one additional vacation day!

Agency negotiator: Can you tell me more about how you arrived at that proposal? Or could you tell me what need that proposal will meet for you?

Public employees' union representative: It will meet my need for a 4% raise!

What if you are attempting to hold an interest-based negotiation but your counterpart insists on reiterating positions rather than addressing the needs and interests that underlie his position? In *Getting to Yes*, Fisher and Ury (1981) discuss the concept of "negotiation jujitsu" (p. 108). Like the martial art, negotiation jujitsu does not meet an attack with a counterattack. Using power against power may not be as successful as stepping back or aside. When hard-nosed positional negotiators reiterate their position, take it as one possible option. Let the other side know that their position is indeed one possible outcome but that you would also like to examine all other possible options before reaching an agreement. Ask questions to better understand how their position meets their needs. "Could you tell me how this amount will be used?" or "Would $25,000 completely solve the problem or would an amount higher or lower perhaps be appropriate?" Rather than defending your position against theirs, take some time to invite criticism and feedback about your position: "I understand that our offer of a 1% raise is not satisfactory for your group. Please tell me more about why this doesn't meet your needs." By inviting criticism, you avoid triggering the fight-or-flight response and signal that you truly want to understand the other side's needs. Sometimes the *why* question can trigger defensive responses. If this seems likely, consider using other open-ended questions, such as "*What raise* were you seeking and *how* does that number meet your needs?"

Be sure to frame your comments as questions rather than statements. "If we agreed to the 4% raise and added a vacation day, would that be more like what our competitors pay? Can you tell me your thoughts about how it would affect our competitiveness as a company?" It is easier to attack a statement than a question. Questions invite analysis and discussion, whereas statements can seem more adversarial. Do not be afraid of silence. If you ask a difficult question, the other side may pause or seem unwilling to answer. Silence can be a useful tool when posing difficult questions (Fisher & Ury, 1981). Try to use questions to turn hard-nosed bargainers away from their positional tactics.

The Spotlight Is Too Bright

When a negotiation occurs in a public space, especially when the media is present, negotiators tend to resort to more confrontational behaviors, including posturing and positional statements. These are intended more for the audience than for their negotiation partners. Therefore, most diplomatic negotiations have formal sessions in which all parties state their positions and ask general questions in the presence of the press or other observers. The real work of diplomats occurs behind closed doors, away from the prying eyes of the public. Keep this in mind when planning public meetings and decision-making processes. Although some sunshine laws (see Chapter 12) require meetings to occur in public, and for good reason, it is important to understand that the behaviors of negotiators, as well as their willingness to speak frankly, differ with the presence of an audience.

Emotional Investment

When someone sells a used car, the seller typically overestimates its value. The buyer will typically underestimate its value. Cognitive biases stand in the way of an objective assessment of the car's value on both sides. To make matters worse, suppose the buyer and seller had a long-standing grudge against one another. They may decide to call off the deal altogether. Then, each would be worse off, not because a deal was against their best interests but because their emotions worked to sabotage a deal that could have benefited them both.

That is why Fisher and Ury (1981) strongly recommend "separating the people from the problem" (p. 17) whenever possible. Be careful when negotiating with someone who raises an emotional response in you, whether positive or negative. Strong emotions will cloud judgment, making it difficult to objectively evaluate the other side's proposals. Pay attention to your somatic response during a negotiation and act accordingly: take a break; get something to eat, take a few deep breaths, or even walk away if the deal is not worth the emotional or physical toll it is taking on you.

Related to this issue is the way in which we as negotiators show or hide our desire to reach an agreement with the other party. Even if you are desperate to get the job, acting desperate at the interview may result in a lower rate of pay once the job is secured. When selling a used car, the seller need not come down in price by much if the buyer makes it clear he or she loves the car and has had difficulty finding one like it. Lesson: when negotiating in a distributive bargaining situation, it is important to know when to keep your "poker face."

Time Pressure

"Act fast, only two left at this price!" Creating the appearance of a crisis is one of the oldest tricks in the book. When your negotiation partner pressures you to commit and threatens to revoke the offer soon, try to pause for a moment. Evaluate the situation to determine if there is indeed the need for a quick decision. "The higher the other party's estimate of his or her own cost of delay or impasse, the weaker the other party's resistance point will be" (Lewicki et al., 2010, p. 41). If there is no urgent need to close the deal, then slow down. Let your negotiation partner know that you will take whatever time you need to evaluate the costs and benefits of the proposal. However, you may be tempted to use this strategy yourself—create a false sense of urgency to close the deal. Before pursuing this strategy, think about any possible ethical implications, including the impact on any future relationship. This strategy is unlikely to work repeatedly with the same partner.

Absent Decision-Maker

Sometimes the people who participate in the negotiation are not the ones with the authority to reach a deal. This situation is particularly likely in the case of negotiations involving government agencies or large businesses. In these cases, a mid- or higher-level employee may arrive to represent the organization, but in the end, the only person with the authority to sign off on a deal is the agency's director. It is unrealistic to believe that the director will attend every negotiation, mediation, or settlement conference. Therefore, the person representing the agency must have the authority to settle. Typically, organizational leaders will authorize a specific settlement range within which their representative can strike a deal. This works best for distributive bargaining situations. What happens in integrative bargaining situations, during which the participants can come up with creative, unanticipated settlement terms? In these situations, it is important for the negotiators to be able to reach the ultimate decision-maker by phone to gain new settlement authority. If you are attending a negotiation on behalf of your organization, be sure to clarify the limits of your settlement authority in advance of the session. Ensure that your superior(s) will be available by phone during the negotiation in case you need to request a different or additional settlement authority. If your negotiating partner sends a representative to negotiate on his behalf, be sure to inquire about the representative's settlement authority and procedures to secure additional or different settlement authority as needed. Otherwise, you may spend hours in a tough negotiation only to discover the person with whom you have been negotiating lacks the ability to commit to any agreements.

Situations wherein parties send a representative to negotiate on their behalf tend to cause increased use of two particular negotiation strategies: "stalling" and "good cop–bad cop." First, the negotiator may have sent the delegate purely as a stalling tactic—as a last resort the representative can claim to need more time to check with his or her boss. If you believe the other side has incentives to stall for time, insist that the decision-maker participate directly. Second, the representative can play good cop–bad cop to secure concessions. The representative might say, "I think your offer is reasonable, but I have to sell it to my boss, and he already told me that I would not have the authority to settle at that amount." Be cautious when negotiating with representatives in the absence of the authoritative decision-maker to ensure the absence is not used strategically.

Bring in a Third Party

If the negotiations are not making progress or have become too heated to carry on a productive and civil negotiation, it may be time to bring in a third party. This third party can be a neutral person, such as a mediator, facilitator, ombudsman, or arbitrator. If the negotiation is internal to the organization, rather than with a customer or client, then the neutral party may be a higher-up manager, someone from HR, or someone from elsewhere in the organization. This person needs to be someone whom each negotiator trusts as well as someone who can maintain their temper, listen well, and promote productive problem-solving. As Chapter 4 shows, there are many types of processes on which you may wish to draw when the negotiators are unable to reach agreements on their own.

Negotiations to Avoid

There are numerous reasons why today may not be the right time to negotiate. First, have you had time to prepare? Sometimes you may wish to put off a negotiation because stalling for time only improves your strength in the situation by raising the value of what you bring to the table or creating an urgent need on the other's side. If you are feeling apathetic to the potential outcome of an issue, then the level of impact may simply be too small to warrant the time and energy you would spend. When you are rushed, take a step back from the abyss. Don't forget that one common strategy in the negotiation playbook is to create an artificial deadline or perceived state of urgency: "If you don't scoop up this deal right now, somebody else will," says the used car salesman.

Additionally, some situations are no-win situations that should be avoided. For example, when the power dynamics between the parties are highly asymmetric and you are on the low end, your chances of achieving your goals may be too low to make negotiation worthwhile.

Ethical concerns may be the best reason to avoid negotiations or end them without an agreement. A manager's reputation takes years to build and only minutes to be destroyed. If a negotiation's outcome could harm parties who are not present or if your negotiation partner is someone you cannot trust to fulfill her end of the bargain, then forgoing the negotiation may be your best bet. If working with the other side to reach an agreement repeatedly violates your personal boundaries in terms of how you need to be treated, then consider sharing your perceptions and needs as diplomatically as possible. We teach people how to treat us and behavior continues as long as it is working. If your negotiation partner is disrespectful or offensive and refuses to change their behavior after your explicit request, then it is time to walk away. Treating others badly is a move used by bullies. Reaching agreement in mediation may result in reinforcing the use of that behavior in the future.

TRUST BUILDING AND TRUST REPAIR IN NEGOTIATIONS

Friedlander (1970) determined initial group trust is more predictive of later group success than is initial group effectiveness, showing that trust has important implications for predicting successful teamwork. The same applies to negotiations. Building trust is important.

Hempel, Zhang, and Tjosvold (2009) argue that conflicting viewpoints are inevitably present in work teams and certainly in negotiations. However, as with conflict itself, differing views need not lead to reduced levels of trust. The management of those differences results in either higher or lower levels of trust among teams and negotiators.

One thing negotiators can do to build trust is to share information. Sharing information is a sign of trust and works to build additional trust between negotiators. Moye and Langfred (2004) investigated the role information sharing has in group conflict and success. Sharing information works to build trust and relationships, which help negotiators reach and implement sound agreements.

There are three types of trust used commonly in negotiations: identity-based trust, relationship-based trust, and calculus-based trust. The best manager understands how and when to use each type of trust and related trust-building measures (Lewicki, 2006).

Identity-based trust (IBT) comes from the human tendency to trust those with whom they share common traits or characteristics such as religion, race, gender, social class, national origin, and field of work. There is an often-wrong assumption here: that I can predict and therefore trust the behavior of someone from my "in-group" more than someone outside my group(s). Negotiators use this form of trust by pointing out similarities between themselves and the other parties to the negotiation. This can build rapport or even make the other side feel obliged to compromise. Sometimes it works.

Relationship-based trust (RBT) is built upon the parties' history from past interactions or negotiations. If one's negotiating partner has behaved honorably in past negotiations, then there is "positive relationship-based trust," while a disappointing history leads to distrust. Based on the history of the relationship, parties can predict whether they should trust each other. In fact, when negotiators know they will see each other in the future they tend to behave more honestly in negotiations and fulfill agreements. Negotiators can increase the chance of cooperative behaviors by structuring future contact with their counterparts.

In work teams, it is crucial not only to build rapport through shared social experiences during the early phases of the collaboration but also intermittently throughout the partnership (for more on this see Lencioni, 2002). Some organizational leaders may balk that this is nonwork time, but if you begin to see it as an essential part of the negotiation process, your negotiations will achieve better results. Additionally, if you run into problems during the implementation of the agreement, you will have developed a relationship on which you can draw to address these unexpected problems. Once you get to know the other person well, you are less likely to fall prey to negative cognitive biases that make negotiations difficult.

Chapter 5 examines cultural differences in negotiation styles, but it is worth mentioning here that collectivist cultures put more focus on building relationships before addressing a shared task, such as negotiation, while individualistic societies such as the United States tend to focus first on the task and then build or enjoy relationships that may grow through the negotiation process.

What if there has been a breach of trust and the relationship has been harmed by the breach? In these cases, you have two options: rely on **calculus-based trust (CBT)** or take steps to rebuild the relationship. Repairing a breach of trust will require frank discussions between the parties so that each is aware of the other's concerns and perceptions. If one of the negotiators admits intentionally breaching trust, apologizes, and is willing to take affirmative steps to regain trust, then there is a chance of restoring RBT. If the negotiators view the situation quite differently or fail to understand why the other feels harmed by the behavior, it can be helpful to ask a neutral third party to assist with these discussions. This assistance can come from an ombudsman, a higher-level manager, a professional coach, or even a counselor. In the end, if the RBT is not restored, it is likely that any agreements between the parties will need to rely on CBT.

With CBT the parties are more likely to abide by their agreements because it is in each party's rational self-interest to do so. Often, the penalties for failing to uphold the agreement are detailed in the contract or agreement itself, giving each side incentives to uphold their end of the bargain. For example, imagine a business-to-business dispute between a hospital and a vendor of medical supplies. In the past, the vendor has not met contracted delivery dates, causing significant shortages for the hospital. The hospital did not trust the vendor to meet future delivery dates based on their deficient performance record (negative RBT). As part of their contract renegotiations, the vendor agreed that late delivery of any supplies would mean that the supplies would be free. After six months of on-time performance, the sanction for late delivery would become a 25% penalty rather than free supplies. Now, the hospital is confident the supplies will arrive on time and is therefore willing to continue to collaborate with this vendor. For CBT to work, the penalty has to be high enough to motivate each negotiator and the certainty of the penalty's enforcement must be clear to all.

How to Negotiate a Salary Increase

Always know what you want before beginning the negotiation. If new information becomes known, you can change your request, but you certainly won't get what you want if you do not know what you want. Do you seek an increase in salary only, or are you willing to discuss non-salary options like flextime, additional vacation, preferred work tasks, office space, or other options?

Know your value within and outside your organization. Benchmark market rates for your level of experience and job duties within your organization and its competitors. If you are below this amount, then chances are good you can earn more by going on the job market. If you are already on the high end, come prepared with information that sets you apart from the pack. When choosing your anchoring number, be careful to choose an amount that is significant but avoids sticker shock if possible. Salary negotiations should occur with enough frequency that there is no need to ask for a 50% raise, for example, unless you have drastically changed your job duties. Be careful about being offered status instead of more pay. It may cost nothing to the company to change your title without giving you a raise. This is only useful if you are in the job market, and you will use the new titles to leverage a better job elsewhere. Be sure to share information about your current and *future* value to the organization (Perhach, 2023). If you receive the requested raise, how will the company and your boss benefit?

Check your current job duties with your actual job description. If your tasks and responsibilities have grown and evolved, then you have a great argument to increase your salary to match your actual duties. If your salary has not kept pace with inflation, then again, it is worth requesting a raise. Many state or federal government employees cannot negotiate for a salary increase unless increases are granted across the board, but you can suggest a change of job duties, job title, or transfer into a higher-paying position within the organization.

Plan for the negotiation. Benchmark your salary internally in the organization and compare it to external competitors. If you get a higher salary, how will your company benefit? Is it enough that you will stay, or are you prepared to take on additional tasks, train others, or bring other benefits to the organization? Remember, this is a normal part of professional life. Do not take it personally or make it personal.

Know your BATNA. Strengthen your BATNA. If your boss says, "No," what will you do? Are you willing and able to get a job offer for more money from a competitor? Will you leave if your boss cannot match a competitive offer? If your BATNA is to grumble to your coworkers but stay in your current role, consider ways you can improve your leverage and negotiating position.

Ask questions to better understand the needs and positions of your supervisor and the broader organization. Find out their career goals and any limitations on their authority. This raise needs to meet your interests and the interests of your negotiation partner. What are they?

UNCONSCIOUS BIAS IN SALARY NEGOTIATIONS

Currently and historically, power has been influenced by social hierarchies based on race, gender, age, social class (usually wealth as self-made or intergenerational), marital status, and connections to powerful individuals and groups, as well as merit-based achievements such as work experience and educational attainment. These biases may be unrelated to the value an employee or leader brings to their organization, yet they continue to create disparities in pay and working conditions.

Data from the U.S. Department of Labor catalogs pay differences between women and men, with race compounding salary and wage differences: Hispanic women earn 58.4% of what Caucasian men earn; Black women 63.1%; and white women 79.6% (in Shonk 2022). In fact, in 2018, the case of the *EEOC v. University of Denver* (No. 1:16-cv-02471) revealed that female law professors were paid an average of nearly $20,000 less than male law professors. That seems patently unwise, from the perspective of an organization full of professional negotiators and litigators. The fact that the case did not settle prior to making national news is surprising and reveals the extent to which some organizations undervalue their brand image's ties to their internal justice measures.

There are many reasons for these differences, some of which have been tied to differences in the way women and minorities negotiate, yet the Equal Employment Opportunity Commission has explicitly disallowed alleged differences in negotiation styles based on gender as a justification for organizations that pay women less than men.

> Research on competitive business negotiation has found that women are generally less assertive and less successful than men. These findings are especially true in salary negotiations, where women agree to lower outcomes, widening the gender wage gap. Past studies suggests that women and men may come to the table with differing levels of entitlement or self-interest, or that women may be discouraged by social cues that signal assertiveness and do not align with female gender roles. (Amanatullah & Morris, 2010)

In most cultures, women are taught to value relationships and collective outcomes more than seeking individual gain. Women who negotiate assertively for equal pay, or for pay that is commensurate with their value to the organization, are often viewed as pushy or unfeminine (Shonk, 2022). A study of 253 companies revealed that women are 22% more likely to receive feedback on their personalities than men and are 11 times more likely to be called "abrasive" (Peck, 2022). Asian males are more likely to be called "brilliant" or "genius" than Latinx employees. Performance reviews are important examples of negotiations that clearly impact the career trajectory and salaries of employees at all levels, yet data clearly indicates they are commonly influenced by biases based on race, gender, and culture. To remedy this, organizational leaders should avoid comments related to personality and instead focus on behaviors that are impacting performance in a positive or negative manner. It is important to assess the criteria by which employees are measured to root out bias and patterns of difference across identity characteristics like race, gender, national origin, age, etc.

Research indicates that women who negotiate on behalf of someone else, such as a subordinate, are more successful than when they negotiate for themselves (Shonk, 2022). This is consistent with the idea that women are more concerned about being seen as pushing their self-interest within a team environment. One "hack" or tip is to negotiate as if you are bargaining for someone else, such as your colleague or subordinate. Additionally, be sure to engage in benchmarking pay or other differences within your organization that vary based on identity characteristics. Tie these differences to the organization's values and mission. Are these differences consistent with those values? Are they violations of law? Do they interfere with the organization's ability to recruit, retain, and promote a diverse workforce? In the end, moral persuasion rarely carries the day. Tie the impact of these differences back to the bottom line, the brand image, and your own engagement.

For change to come it is important that we refrain from blaming individuals for systemic problems. When gender, race, or cultural differences translate into lower pay, it is unacceptable and unhelpful to state that any individual or group simply did not negotiate hard enough or in a masculine, dominant culture mode. True inclusivity requires organizations to take stock of biases in their organization that result in individual and collective differences in pay, working conditions, workload, and the availability of advancement or professional development opportunities. Only through a regular examination of these differences and corrective action can organizations ensure their values around diversity and equality are operationalized by their policies and outcomes at work.

CONCLUSION

Managers negotiate every day, either formally or informally. Mastering the concepts and skills of negotiation will ensure the most fruitful outcome possible. Skilled, interest-based negotiation not only leads to better outcomes, but it also generally feels better because the process respects the needs of all participants and does not require misleading others to achieve one's preferred outcome. Understanding the key terms and concepts in distributive bargaining remains important because this type of negotiation remains common, like it or not. Negotiation skills will serve you well at work and also in your civic and personal lives. Whether you are planning your wedding, buying produce at your local farmers market, or deciding where to go on your next family vacation, there is no shortage of opportunities to practice these skills. Every negotiation presents you with an opportunity to enhance your relationships with others and achieve your substantive objectives.

ELISE AND MAIN STREET BAKERIES

Elise met with Jacob, the organic wheat farmer. They began their meeting over breakfast and a walking tour of his farm. It turns out that Jacob knows other farmers who supply goods to Elise's company and that is how he heard about this opportunity. Last year the price for a bushel of organic wheat was about $9.00 but this year it has jumped to almost $11.00 per bushel. With such huge fluctuations it has become difficult to maintain stability in the prices charged to customers. Elise prepared for this meeting by thinking about the maximum amount she would pay for a one-year contract ($10.75) but she hoped to strike a deal closer to $9.75. She decided to make an initial offer of $9.00. Although she would prefer a contract period of three to five years, most small farmers are unable or unwilling to do that considering the recent volatility in the commodity price for wheat. She hates to renegotiate contracts each year because of the time and expense. She works with more than 100 farmers around the country, so if she is not careful, she could spend all her time doing nothing but negotiating contracts. She likes to meet personally with each supplier during the initial contract negotiations. If all goes well, other members of her staff will negotiate contract updates or changes as needed.

When she met Jacob, he had some surprising news. He was willing to enter a five-year contract, but it would not involve his farm alone. He has banded with five other organic farms in his region. Each of the farms grows wheat and at least one other crop. They would agree to a multiyear contract at a fixed price but with some special agreements to help address the risk of unknown future conditions. His initial offer was for 50,000 bushels per year at $10.25 per bushel if the average price of wheat on the market does not rise above $11.00 per bushel. If it rises above that price, then Jacob and his farmers would receive $10.75 per bushel. Additionally, they would supply bell peppers, onions, and broccoli through a separate contract. In the end, they settled on a price of $10.00 per bushel in a regular market and $10.50 in an inflated market. By agreeing to a longer-term contract, considering some future uncertainty, and adding additional products for sale, they both came out ahead. Now Elise has fewer individual contracts to negotiate: a win-win outcome.

KEY TERMS

anchoring number
asking price
BATNA
calculus-based trust (CBT)
claiming value
contingent agreements
creating value
distributive bargaining
fallback offer
identity-based trust (IBT)
impasse
initial offer
integrative bargaining

interests
negative settlement range
negotiation
positions
positive settlement range
relationship-based trust (RBT)
reactive devaluation
resistance point
settlement point
settlement range
target point
transaction costs
zero-sum

DISCUSSION QUESTIONS

1. What was your most difficult negotiation and why? What went well and what did not? Which concepts from this chapter explain the outcome?
2. Do you look forward to negotiations or avoid them? How does this align with your conflict styles inventory exercise from Chapter 1?
3. Who is the best negotiator you know and what techniques do they use? How are salaries negotiated in your organization? Is it free from bias? Is it done professionally? What could be done to improve results?

EXERCISES

1. Think, pair, share: Think back to a negotiation in which you participated or witnessed. Was it a distributive or integrative negotiation? How could you tell? Apply the following terms to an analysis of that negotiation. Was value created, claimed, or both? What were the interests, positions, and BATNAs of each party?
2. Review the scenario between Elise and Jacob and label their position, interests, BATNAs, settlement zone, and resistance points.
3. Using a story from the newspaper to analyze a contemporary negotiation, label the positions, interests, and BATNAs, and apply other course concepts. Was the negotiation interest-based or distributive in nature?
4. Negotiation practice: Bureaucrats and Budgets: Imagine you and three co-workers are diplomats working at the U.S. Embassy in _____ (fill in the blank with any country). Each of you has a "pet project" that you want to see implemented, yet the US$4 million budget was recently cut in half. Negotiate with your colleagues to decide which projects get funded and at what level. Remember, the total spending cannot exceed $2 million. Your primary goals for spending are to promote U.S. interests abroad.

    Role 1: Embassy Security Officer: You sought $1.4 million to increase the number and strength of the barricades and gates surrounding the embassy and to hire more guards. After incidents like Benghazi and elsewhere, your analysis indicates more security is needed.

    Role 2: Economic Development Officer: You originally asked for $1.5 million to fund the construction of a new road from the capital to the main regions for mining and agriculture. Currently the existing road is not paved and often impassable when rain strikes, thereby making it difficult for local businesses to get their goods to market or to the port for export. More U.S. investment would come to this country if only there were better roads to promote commerce.

    Role 3: Health and Human Security: You originally asked for $700,000 to vaccinate locals against Ebola and dengue fever. These diseases have resulted in an outflow of foreign investment, dropped tourism to almost zero, and endangered your staff. This amount would allow you to vaccinate all health workers, public servants, and schoolchildren. The vaccine has a 97% ability to prevent these diseases with few side effects.

Role 4: Education: You asked for $400,000 to create and distribute new social studies textbooks to the country's high school students that contain a pro-U.S. version of world history. This is a long-term effort to create a positive view of the United States by locals in this country.

Debrief: Which negotiation techniques did you use and why? Which projects came out ahead and why? How did the personalities of negotiators play a role here? What conflict theories explain the path of your negotiation or differences in outcomes across multiple negotiation teams, if you did this exercise in class?

GOAL SETTING

Think of an upcoming negotiation in which you will participate. Prepare for the negotiation by determining your target point and resistance points. What are your interests and what is your BATNA? How will you react to positional bargaining by your counterpart? What can you do to ensure an interest-based negotiation? Conduct your negotiation, then engage in reflective practice. What worked well? What can be improved for future negotiations?

SUGGESTED SUPPLEMENTAL READINGS

Fisher, R., Ury, W., & Patton, B. (2011). *Getting to yes*. Penguin. (Originally published in 1981.)

Shilton. A. C. (2018, August 10). How to be an ace salary negotiator (even if you hate conflict). *New York Times*. https://www.nytimes.com/2018/08/10/smarter-living/how-to-negotiate-salary.html

4

The Alternative Dispute Resolution (ADR) Continuum

The obstacle is the way.

—Marcus Aurelius

Obstacles present opportunities for growth every time. We do not control what happens to us, but we control our reaction to it. This is a key lesson from the Roman emperor Marcus Aurelius. He turned criticism into feedback and used setbacks to point out the ways in which he needs to learn and grow. Obstacles are the stone that sharpens our steel. Great leaders and managers lead by example: they demonstrate how to use setbacks or conflicts to learn, grow, and become even better. This chapter describes processes for preventing and resolving disputes, which can yield deeper understandings of the root causes of recurring conflict, enabling you to prevent future similar problems, or at least to manage unavoidable conflict effectively and fairly.

A variety of processes can be used to prevent formal complaints or to resolve disputes before they escalate. After reading this chapter, revisit these learning objectives to ensure you have a clear understanding of the differences between these processes and the types of problems for which each process is best suited. The goal is to "fit the forum to the fuss" (Sander & Goldberg, 1994).

Learning Objectives

- Demonstrate an understanding of the differences among alternative dispute resolution (ADR) processes such as facilitation, mediation, arbitration, and others.
- Analyze dispute characteristics to match the dispute with the appropriate ADR process.
- Describe the costs and benefits of various ADR processes.

JOHN AT THE BUREAU OF RECLAMATION

Today has been frustrating. John spent much of last week interviewing internal applicants for an open position in mid-level management. He feels he chose the best person for the position but there were at least three other applicants who were also well qualified. Now one of those applicants (Dorys) has filed a complaint with the Equal Employment Opportunity Commission (EEOC) claiming discrimination based on race and gender. The organizational ombudsman has approached John to see if it is possible to resolve the dispute through a less costly, less adversarial process. John is open to all ideas because he has learned that these EEOC complaints can take years to reach resolution. the ombudsman recommends a process called_____. (You will be able to fill in the blank after you read this chapter.)

* * *

Often, we miss the chance to recognize and solve problems because we just want them to go away. Employees who bring forward allegations of bullying, harassment, or other misdeeds are often labeled as troublemakers. While it is accurate to say that some individuals are indeed difficult to work with, by engaging in denial and minimizing the veracity of their concerns, managers do themselves, their teams, and their organizations a disservice. Only through a serious examination of the root causes of complaints can organizational leaders use them for improved organizational justice and mission achievement. In other words, we often misinterpret our obstacles as barriers to success rather than viewing them as portals to change. The ADR processes discussed herein offer various ways to turn obstacles into insights. What are the obstacles facing your organization and how can you use those obstacles to be better?

The purpose of this chapter is to introduce a variety of processes used to solve problems without resorting to the courts or other formal, adversarial, and expensive processes.

These processes have the potential to reduce costs, time, and the emotional energy required to resolve disputes. They also have the potential to address legal and nonlegal issues while improving rather than worsening relationships. Listening skills were covered in Chapter 1 and are the foundational skill for processes such as negotiation (Chapter 3), mediation (this chapter) and many problem-solving processes (Chapter 8).

THE ADR CONTINUUM

Figure 4.1 shows the ADR processes used to resolve internal workplace disputes. Typically, these are conflicts between employees holding different positions within the hierarchical structure of an organization, such as between a supervisor and a frontline employee. However, they could also occur between peers. On the continuum pictured in Figure 4.1, the amount of control that a third party has in the outcome increases as the dispute moves up the steps. The first step, direct negotiation, leaves all the control over the outcome of the dispute with the parties themselves. The last step on the continuum, arbitration, takes control of

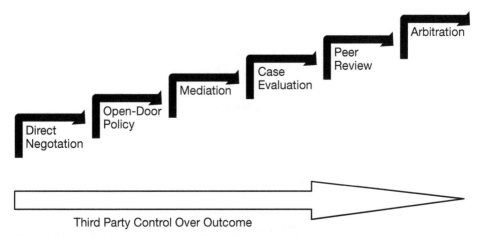

Figure 4.1   ADR Continuum for Workplace Disputes

the outcome away from the parties and places it entirely with the arbitrator, who is essentially a private judge. Adjudication is not included on this continuum because ADR is meant to be the alternative to going to court. The lower the step on the ADR continuum, the fewer expenses will be incurred during the dispute resolution process for most cases.

Direct Negotiations

The first step in resolving nearly any workplace dispute is to encourage direct discussions between the disputants. If an employee has a complaint with his supervisor, then he should first go to that supervisor and attempt to have a productive discussion about the concerns and explore the possibility of informal resolution. Employee training can be useful to develop the needed framing and communication skills to increase successful interactions when these difficult conversations occur. Consider using 3-step problem-solving as a format for reaching shared expectations to resolve conflicts and prevent their recurrence (see Chapter 7).

Open-Door Policy

An **open-door policy** means that any employee with a problem can go to any manager for help. Although there is usually a preference to start low on the chain of command and work upward as needed, ultimately an open-door policy means the employee may choose any manager to approach for help.

In the process continuum, if direct negotiation failed, the next step is using the open-door policy by speaking to the supervisor of the party involved in the conflict. All supervisory employees should be trained in the basic skills of listening (Chapter 1), framing comments constructively, giving and receiving feedback, and problem-solving (Chapter 7). An open-door policy can mean anything or nothing, depending on the organization's culture. Some organizations claim to have an open-door policy, but when employees come to a supervisor with a problem, the supervisor claims to be too busy to listen to them or clearly displays a conflict-avoidant disposition. For an open-door policy to work, all supervisors and managers must be trained and acculturated. They must be trained in the skills needed to solve conflicts. Employees won't seek help if they fear reprisals.

Mediation

If an employee has tried speaking to his or her boss and used the open-door policy, yet the problem remains unresolved, the next step on the continuum is mediation. **Mediation** is a process of facilitated negotiation in which a neutral third party, the mediator, does not act as a judge but instead assists the parties as they strive to engage in a civil, productive conversation about how to resolve the dispute and rebuild relationships if a continuing relationship is to exist. Mediators typically allow each party to state his or her view of the dispute; they draw out information about the parties' needs and interests, engage parties in brainstorming for resolution options, and work with the parties to enforce ground rules and overcome obstacles to settlement. If the parties reach an agreement, the mediator generally drafts a memo outlining the terms of the agreement. Sometimes, the agreements reached in mediation address nonlegal matters. For example, "the parties agree to speak directly to each other when a problem exists instead of sharing their complaints with others at work." Often, the terms of the agreement form the basis of a binding contract that is enforceable in the courts. If the mediation is related to ongoing litigation, then the agreement will usually be filed with the court to be reviewed by a judge, and once signed by the judge, it becomes an order of the court. For example, if the employer agrees to reinstate the employee immediately and pay $40,000 in back pay no later than November 1, then these terms form the basis of a binding contract.

Mediation is a collaborative problem-solving process rather than an adversarial process. In essence, it is assisted negotiation. In court, also known as **adjudication**, each side argues to the judge about why their side is right. In mediation the parties work *with instead of against* one another to find a solution that is acceptable to both.

There are many approaches to mediation (Moore, 2003). The traditional model of mediation is one in which mediators play a facilitative role—they encourage the parties to come up with their own solutions to the dispute; they do not evaluate the legal arguments or seek to predict the outcome in court. Mediators guide parties through the process, help them create and enforce ground rules related to civility, and assist them with the drafting of the resulting agreement. In this style of mediation, the mediator truly has no impact on the outcome of the case. Facilitative mediators do not pressure the parties to settle, nor do they impose or recommend settlement terms. The parties retain full power over the outcome of their dispute.

Evaluative (or directive) **mediation** is a style more akin to case evaluation or nonbinding arbitration, to be discussed soon. In this approach, mediators tell parties how a judge or jury would likely decide in their case. They evaluate the strengths and weaknesses of each side's arguments and evidence, then render nonbinding decisions. The parties use this information to inform their settlement negotiations. Additionally, mediation works to persuade the parties to step away from unrealistic demands and apply pressure on them to compromise and reach a resolution. Party satisfaction with this style of mediation tends to be lower than for facilitative mediation, but in some types of cases settlement rates may be higher, particularly those cases in which the parties will not have an ongoing relationship. Some research indicates that evaluative or directive mediation settlements are less durable and less likely to be fully implemented than those agreements achieved through the facilitative approach (Charkoudian, Eisenberg, and Walter, 2019).

In the transformative model of mediation, mediators seek to enhance the parties' abilities to maintain or improve their relationship. Mediators seek to capitalize on moments of empowerment and recognition. They work to empower the parties to come up with their own resolution to the dispute while also striving to enhance their dispute resolution skills. Mediators seek to create and highlight opportunities for the parties to recognize the validity of the others' interests and viewpoints, which allows parties to rehumanize each other in the conflict rather than tear each other down. By recognizing the humanity and inherent value of the other person in the conflict, parties can have a genuinely open and productive dialogue, with settlement being only one resulting benefit. In this model, the parties do not meet separately with the mediator (separate meetings are called caucuses), but instead stay in the same room throughout the process, face to face. Because of the emphasis on relationship building and improved communication skills inherent in the transformative mediation model, the United States Postal Service (USPS) and the United States Transportation Safety Administration (USTSA) have adopted the transformative style of mediation for their workplace mediation programs. It is possible to work on relationship building through facilitative mediation strategies as well.

Satisfaction with mediation programs tends to be significantly higher than with other forms of dispute resolution such as arbitration and adjudication. In a study of court-connected general civil case mediation in nine Ohio courts, Wissler (2002) found that "litigants had highly favorable assessments of the mediation session and the mediator" (p. 5). The majority thought that the mediation process was very fair (72%) and would recommend mediation (79%). In the USPS mediation program, 90% of the complainants were either highly or somewhat satisfied with the mediation process, with respondents, usually the supervisors and managers, having a 93% satisfaction rate (Bingham, Kim & Raines, 2002). Similarly, 91% of EEOC complainants say they would participate in mediation again if faced with another complaint and 96% of respondents concurred (McDermott et al., 2000). As an interesting side note, those complainants who brought attorneys with them to USPS mediations were significantly less satisfied than those who brought no representative (Bingham et al., 2002). The strongest explanation is that parties are allowed to speak for themselves and tell their own story when they come to mediation without a representative. This is an important element of procedural justice (see Chapter 2). Being heard during the dispute resolution process is directly tied to participant satisfaction rates in all processes, including arbitration, peer review, and adjudication. In voluntary processes such as mediation, coaching, or working with an ombudsman, when disputants feel their voice is not heard, they are more likely to terminate their participation in the process or to negotiate less productively (Duffy, 2010).

ADR had a positive impact on parties' ability to express themselves and tell their story during the conflict, which is a significant marker of procedural justice (Charkoudian et al., 2017). Disputants using ADR were more likely to shift away from a belief that "the other person needs to learn they are wrong" and were more likely to take responsibility for the dispute than those who did not use ADR, whether the case settled or not (p. 23). Regardless of case outcome, ADR improved the relationship between the parties. Reaching agreement in ADR reduces the chances of repeated litigation between the parties by 21% (p. 36). While the cases in Charkoudian's study were court-connected mediations, the impact on relationships should be the same or higher for workplace matters since coworkers have a strong incentive to improve their working relationships.

Some disputes go through a mediation process with an outside mediator or an inside mediator who is a full-time employee of the organization. For example, many international institutions have full-time internal mediators, such as the United Nations, International Monetary Fund (IMF), World Bank, and more.

It is also common for managers to conduct informal mediation as part of their regular duties. **Informal managerial mediation** occurs when a manager facilitates a problem-solving conversation between two or more parties in conflict. As informal mediators, managers listen to each party and encourage both to listen to each other. They engage the parties in a problem-solving discussion with the goal of reaching an agreement that meets the needs of all parties and is superior to continuing the dispute via more formal channels.

While a manager sometimes has the authority to tell employees to change their behavior or "just get along," it is rare that a manager can actually force employees to work well together. Instead, managers can use processes such as 3-step problem-solving (see Chapter 7) to facilitate warmer, more collaborative relationships.

Case Evaluation

Case evaluation is a process in which a neutral expert is hired to evaluate the strengths and weaknesses of each side's case and predict what would happen in court. A case evaluator is someone with substantive expertise related to the dispute, such as medical malpractice, personal injury, sexual harassment, and so forth. Case evaluators, like arbitrators, usually have a legal background as a lawyer and/or judge, but there may be cases where a non-attorney is also helpful. Case evaluation can be costlier than mediation because the extensive preparation is similar to litigation, and because case evaluators charge more than mediators. Case evaluation is a settlement tool because it gives each side a glimpse of what might happen in court. Sometimes a party is hesitant to take his or her attorney's advice about a settlement offer but getting a second opinion from a neutral expert can help break the impasse.

Peer Review

Peer review is a process commonly used within organizational settings to deal with internal employment disputes such as claims of discrimination, wrongful termination, demotions, favoritism, nepotism, or employee appeals of other disciplinary actions. Peer review processes are generally not used to address decisions made through downsizing, workers' compensation claims, unemployment or Social Security benefit claims, health insurance claims, severance package agreements, or company policies and business decisions related to corporate strategies.

Although many variations exist, at its core the peer review process is designed to allow employees to decide whether their peers are being treated fairly by the organization and its managers or supervisors. One example of the peer review process comes from United Parcel Service (UPS). In this process, the employee chooses two members of the panel from a roster of employees and the company chooses the third member of the panel. Peer reviewers cannot work in the same unit as the employee under review or be part of that employee's chain of command. Peer reviewers are employees from a similar job type but in a different location or department so as to avoid bias. Some organizations may prefer to have a five-member review panel. Any size panel will work if there is an odd number. The larger the panel, the higher the costs because employees are taken away from their primary tasks to sit as panel members.

Peer reviewers are trained to maintain neutrality, to ask good questions, and to review written submissions by the parties. Reviewers ask both sides questions about the issue or behavior that forms the heart of the complaint. After the process, the panel meets to discuss the session and reach a decision. The panel then drafts a written finding that is shared with both sides in the case. In some organizations, the findings of the peer review panel are binding on both the company and the employee. In others, the decisions are advisory. Peer review panels generally offer the same remedies that would occur through other processes such as arbitration or EEOC adjudication: reinstatement, back pay, compensation for harm including pain and suffering, and so forth. Although some companies may hesitate to place this much power in the hands of their employees, it is a sign of confidence that the organization believes it treats its employees fairly and wants to address any potential errors transparently. Organizations use peer review panels to resolve disputes and build positive organizational culture; peer employees are no more likely to reward shirking or negative behaviors than are managers because these behaviors place a heavy toll on their peers.

Arbitration

Arbitration is an ADR process in which the parties hire a neutral, expert third-party decision-maker to act as a private judge in their dispute. Arbitration is commonly used to resolve disputes in unionized workplaces, and arbitration decisions can serve as precedent for future similar cases within a union contract. Arbitration rulings do not set a legal precedent in the courts and cannot generally be appealed there except in cases of arbitrator misconduct. An arbitrator is simply a private judge. So why hire a judge when it costs relatively little to file your case in court? First, the parties can jointly select an arbitrator with subject-matter experience. In court, a judge may hear a divorce case, a commercial dispute, and a probate matter all on the same day. Imagine a case of alleged construction flaws to a roller coaster. An arbitrator with a law and engineering background might be a better choice than a public court judge. Second, parties can get to an arbitrator faster than court. Third, the outcome of arbitration can be private. Many organizations seek to protect their brand name by keeping negative information out of the public record and media spotlight. Fourth, parties have more control over the process itself: They can decide what kind of evidence or testimony will be allowed and how long the process will last (e.g., one day or more). These decisions can affect the cost of the arbitration and the strategies of the attorneys and parties involved. Finally, arbitration rulings are not subject to appeals. If a party wins in court, the other side can appeal to a higher court, thereby lengthening the dispute's lifespan and increasing costs and uncertainty.

The U.S. Supreme Court has been supportive of mandatory arbitration clauses in consumer and employment contracts due to the high volume of these cases, which could overwhelm the court system.

Binding arbitration is standard, meaning all parties agree to be bound to the arbitrator's decision. A less-common form of arbitration is nonbinding arbitration. This process is the same, except the arbitrator's ruling is advisory. Parties use these rulings as a settlement tool to promote further dialogue and negotiation rather than as a final decision. In these ways it is like case evaluation except that the arbitrator's decision may include a specific settlement recommendation, based on the arbitrator's estimation of the case's value.

Adjudication or Court Action

The purpose of ADR is to avoid the costs, delay, uncertainty, adversarial nature, and publicity of going through costly litigation that ends in a trial or hearing before a judge. An added benefit of many ADR processes is that they involve collaborative rather than adversarial methods for resolution. To understand the attractiveness of ADR processes, it is helpful to review the costs and benefits of using the courts to solve problems.

Litigation is the process of filing a court case and taking the necessary procedural steps to prepare that case for adjudication. **Adjudication** is the formal process through which a judge renders a decision in a case before the court. Adjudication is the costliest option but remains the best choice when one seeks to set a legal precedent or to bring media scrutiny to serious injustice that affects a large group or the public at large. Employment cases that reach the level of a civil suit are incredibly costly in terms of money, time, and emotional energy for all involved—especially for the employee. Although the company continues with its mission, the employee in litigation may remain unemployed, may be paying unaffordable sums to an attorney, and is the most harmed by a case that drags on indefinitely. For workers currently employed while they proceed with a discrimination or harassment complaint, tensions can be high, resulting in increased use of sick leave and health benefits, with lower overall productivity.

Most employees cannot navigate the litigation process on their own and need an attorney to represent them in cases of alleged wrongful termination, harassment, bullying, or other matters. They may be unemployed while the case is in litigation. Howard (1995) reports that the results of a survey of 321 National Employment Lawyers Association members indicate that nineteen out of twenty employees (95%) seeking to hire legal counsel cannot get an attorney to take their case. Attorneys know these cases are difficult to prove and they are usually paid a contingency fee—if they do not win, they do not get paid. Therefore, only the most egregious cases, those with lots of evidence, are likely to be represented by counsel.

Formal complaint processes such as litigation or an EEOC filing are usually disappointing for workers filing complaints (usually referred to as complainants). For example, only 17.4% of complainants received a favorable resolution in 2020, the most recent year for which data has been released at the time of this publication (eeoc.gov). In addition to the difficulty in finding and paying for an attorney, if employees hope to get relief through the EEOC process, they had better be patient. Staff shortages have led to long waits for a case to be processed and eventually dismissed, settled, or adjudicated.

In employment discrimination suits that use the court system instead of the EEOC process, the case-processing time (filing to disposition) varies between 11 months and 5 years (Kyckelhahn & Cohen, 2008). It is highly likely that the case will be dismissed. In the federal courts, employment claims of sexual harassment and discrimination fall under the "civil rights" category, where only about 1% of plaintiffs prevail at trial (Captain 2017). Employers win 14% of the time and the parties settle out of court approximately 78% of the time (Captain 2017).

The media highlights cases in which the employees win at trial more frequently than those in which they lose. Large, unusual awards make headlines, thereby skewing public belief that employers are held accountable by the court and EEOC system at higher rates than actually occur. This leads to *jackpot syndrome*, or the false belief that lawsuits are a way to get rich quick or get justice. In their study of adjudicated cases followed by the media and in which a victor was announced, Nielson and Beim (2004) found that plaintiffs prevailed in 85% of the cases, as opposed to the 17.4% of winning complainants cited above. Additionally, the average size of awards covered by the media was 30 times higher than the average actual awards.

Does resorting to an ADR process mean parties are losing their access to justice? Since most employees cannot afford the costs of lengthy litigation, ADR provides access to resolution at a higher rate than litigation. The good news is that satisfaction with most ADR processes is higher than satisfaction with court processes. With adjudication, even the "winner" often leaves feeling dissatisfied, unheard, and frustrated. Of all the possible ADR processes, mediation has been the most studied and we can compare the costs of mediation versus court.

Employees have a better chance of receiving relief in mediation compared to proceeding with litigation. Discrimination and harassment charges are simply difficult to prove with the level of evidence needed to win. For example, in 2020, EEOC cases that went to mediation had an agreement rate of 69.4% with an average time to disposition from the date of case filing to resolution in mediation of 147 days (EEOC.gov, 2022). If the parties decide not to use mediation, most cases result in dismissal or a "right to sue" letter, which notifies the complainant the EEOC has closed the case so they can file a civil case if they wish. It can take 180 or more days to receive the right to sue letter, with few penalties invoked for deadlines missed by the respondent or EEOC.

These statistics regarding the EEOC and civil suit process leave one to wonder why employers settle these cases out of court rather than go to trial. We know employers have a much better likelihood of (1) being represented by attorneys, (2) having the case dismissed with no finding of fault against the organization, and (3) if it goes to trial, employers usually win. So why should managers take part in an ADR process aimed at settling the case? Why aren't employers free to treat employees any way they want because employees will have great difficulty fighting and winning a legal case against their employer?

First and foremost, organizations that treat their employees well are more likely to flourish in the marketplace—happy, satisfied employees are the first step to having happy, satisfied customers and clients. Second, who wants to work in or lead an organization where people are treated poorly? In a tight labor market, employers are competing for a relatively small pool of employees. Attracting and keeping this is critical to mission achievement and brand reputation. Companies that develop a positive, fair organizational culture will have a more productive workforce with fewer complaints and lower employee turnover.

Adjudication is the right process for some disputes. For example, *Brown v. Board of Education* was the case that led to school desegregation in the United States. If that case had gone to mediation, the parents of the children involved might have reached an agreement for their children, but it would not have affected children in other school districts by setting a precedent and drawing needed attention to a public dispute. Additionally, the courts are entrusted with protecting the rights of less-powerful groups in society. Sometimes, individuals or groups need to resort to the courts to have their rights established and protected. It is important to remember, however, that the majority of cases decided by the courts do not set legal precedents. Instead, they involve individuals and organizations that did not solve problems or collaborate successfully, so they seek the services of a third-party neutral judge. The good news is that many ADR services will help parties to meet these needs at a lower cost and allow the limited resources of the courts to be focused on those cases that establish precedents, clarify, or establish legal rights, and bring public scrutiny to bear on issues of public interest.

Negotiated Rulemaking

Negotiated rulemaking (also called "regulatory negotiation" or "reg-neg") is a multiparty consensus process in which a balanced negotiating committee seeks to reach agreement on the substance of a proposed government agency rule, policy, or standard. The negotiating committee is composed of representatives of those interests that will be affected by or have an interest in the rule, including the rulemaking agency itself. Affected interests that are represented in the negotiations are expected to abide by any resulting agreement and implement its terms. This agreement-seeking process usually occurs only after a thorough conflict assessment has been conducted and is generally undertaken with the assistance of a skilled, neutral mediator or facilitator. The term *negotiated rulemaking* is specifically applied only to negotiations with government agencies and impacted stakeholders (see Chapter 12).

The ADR processes just discussed are the most commonly used for employment cases. However, there are other process options that fall off the ADR continuum that merit presentation as well.

Ombudsman (Ombuds)

An **ombudsman (ombuds)** is an organizational conflict management specialist who works to resolve internal disputes with employees or external disputes with customers, clients, vendors, or business partners. The term *ombudsman* is Swedish in origin and is gender neutral in that language. Unfortunately, when used in English it has a masculine connotation, so some English-speaking societies use the shorter term, *ombuds*, but both are correct. The ombuds can provide conflict prevention and resolution training and informal mediation. Ombuds can suggest changes to policies or organizational culture designed to reduce conflict and increase mission achievement. Chapter 10 examines ombuds' tasks and tools in depth.

Facilitation

Facilitation is a group process in which either an inside or outside person leads the discussions in a neutral manner in order to assist in promoting an efficient and civil process that stays on track. "A meeting without a facilitator is about as effective as a team trying to have a game without a referee" (Bens, 2005, p. 7). According to Ingrid Bens (2005), a facilitator is someone "who contributes structure and process to interactions so groups are able to function effectively and make high-quality decisions. A helper and enabler whose goal is to support others as they pursue their objectives" (p. 5). Unlike mediation, the goal of a facilitation process may or may not include reaching a written agreement. Instead, many facilitations are designed solely to increase the group's understanding of a problem or improve intergroup relations. Facilitation may be used simply to lead contentious business meetings within an organization or work unit. Many organizations offer facilitation training, including the International Association of Facilitators.

Facilitation of focus groups is one way to gain feedback from external stakeholders regarding the quality of the organization's products or services. Internal focus group facilitation can be used to brainstorm solutions to problems, manage change, and gather information about newly implemented policies and procedures. Facilitation skills, including framing and questioning, are useful tools for all managers to master. Facilitators believe that people have the power to make good, fair decisions for themselves and that two heads (or more) are better than one when making complex decisions. By helping the parties to create an efficient and fair process, facilitators take leadership of the meeting and leave the parties to determine the content of any decision or discussion.

Frequently, managers will be called on to use their facilitation skills in those situations when group input, buy-in, or information sharing are called for. Facilitation is a way to help ensure a high-quality outcome through a fair process that gives everyone a chance to be heard. "Facilitation is a way to provide leadership without taking the reins" (Bens, 2005, p. 7). Sometimes employees or colleagues come to the manager to ask for advice or a decision. There are times when it makes more sense for the manager to *facilitate a process* through which people reach their own conclusions than to make decisions for them. Manager-facilitators lead organization members when they engage in strategic planning, create goals and objectives, conduct program reviews or assessments, build relationships across or within teams, share feedback for performance improvements, or conduct focus group meetings to gather needed information to improve products or processes.

Facilitators have several tools and skills they use repeatedly: staying neutral, managing time, creating and developing an agenda, skillful questioning, summarizing and paraphrasing, listening actively, convening the right players for each gathering, helping parties to test their assumptions and think creatively, playing devil's advocate when needed, brainstorming, helping parties think analytically, and prioritizing. The best managers and leaders are skilled facilitators.

Summary Jury Trials

Summary jury trials or minitrials (SJTs) are mock trials. Before the SJT begins, the attorneys and parties reach agreements related to the types of evidence to be admitted, the length of the trial (usually one to three days), and whether the verdict will be binding or advisory. If the process is advisory, it is used as a settlement tool to enable both sides to see the strengths and weaknesses in their case while getting the jury's perspective on the matter. SJTs are most useful for complex cases that would take weeks or months to try in court. This process allows both sides to pick the judge and hear how their case plays out with a jury. If both sides had agreed that the verdict would be binding, the jury is thanked (and generally paid) for their service and dismissed. If the process was advisory, after the jury renders its verdict both sides can pose questions to learn more about which elements of their argument were persuasive or unclear. Sometimes a twelve-person jury is divided into two groups. Each group deliberates separately and renders its own verdict. This method can provide useful information, and it is not uncommon for two juries to render opposite verdicts. This mimics the unpredictability of real juries, which can be helpful for intransigent parties or attorneys to witness.

Summary jury trials remain an expensive dispute resolution option, nearly as expensive as a real trial. Attorneys spend significant resources preparing their case, conducting depositions, selecting the judge, and composing the jury. Expert witnesses are sometimes hired and paid for their work on a case and for their testimony. So why would parties choose this process? Parties often want to avoid the publicity of a real trial, shorten the length of the trial, and control the choice of judge.

Public-sector managers and companies facing class action or multimillion-dollar claims might consider the benefits of a summary jury trial but only if less expensive options such as mediation or arbitration have failed or are unacceptable to the parties.

Coaching

Coaches help people to improve their performance, thereby making the whole team better. Executive or performance coaching within a workplace setting is used for two main purposes: to improve the performance of underperforming employees or to maximize the performance of managers and leaders seeking to constantly improve their performance and gain new skills. The field of executive coaching is growing, with some coaching tasks undertaken by ombuds, some by managers, and some by external consultants.

Managers act as coaches nearly every day as they help equip and motivate employees to maximize their performance. **Coaching** is a one-on-one process designed to offer training, skill development, support, goal setting, and progress measurement designed to help each employee/manager reach his or her full potential at work. Because coaching is the first step and most common service offered by ombuds, Chapter 10 examines coaching in-depth and provides sample coaching tools.

ADDITIONAL PROBLEM-SOLVING TECHNIQUES

Timing is critical for good decision-making and problem-solving. **"Ripeness"** is key. When a dispute is ripe, the timing for intervention is ideal because the parties perceive a mutually hurting stalemate and the possibility of an outcome that is superior to continuing the conflict with the status quo (Coleman et al., 2008a). If intervention occurs too late, tempers are high and resources have been committed that make it hard to walk away or agree to small settlements. At the opposite end of the spectrum, before a conflict is ripe for intervention, it may not be viewed as important or the parties and issues may be unclear. The goal is to intervene as early as possible once the parties, issues, and possible options are known, but before the sides become so entrenched in an adversarial posture that settlement becomes less likely.

Brainstorming is an important part of a problem-solving process. During brainstorming all parties agree to think broadly about all possible solutions to the problem. It is critical that the participants agree to separate the process of generating options from the process of evaluating those options. Imagine that one employee proposes a creative solution to the problem and from across the table another person says, "That's the craziest idea I ever heard!" Who would want to go next? Therefore, the manager as process facilitator can gently remind everyone about the importance of separating the process of generating ideas from the process of evaluating them.

Backcasting is a problem-solving technique in which the facilitator, mediator, or manager asks the parties to envision a future in which the problem is solved or the relationship is repaired. The parties are asked to describe what that looks or feels like. Then, the parties are asked to describe the steps that each of them would need to take to reach that ideal future state. The parties are asked to focus on the actions that they can take rather than focusing on the actions they wish the others would take because we only control what we think, do, and say. We cannot control others.

Through the choice of the appropriate ADR process, and problem-solving, most managerial conflicts can be handled early before they grow to threaten the health of the organization.

CONCLUSION

This chapter has served as a brief introduction to the many ADR processes being used to address complaints within and external to organizations. In addition to explaining the differences between processes such as mediation, facilitation, and arbitration, we discussed the role of the organizational ombudsman and other neutrals such as coaches. Additional techniques for problem-solving were examined, such as brainstorming and backcasting. To efficiently resolve disputes, managers need knowledge of these processes and to understand how to fit the dispute to the appropriate process.

JOHN AT THE BUREAU OF RECLAMATION

The last thing John needs is to have to respond to an EEOC complaint. He has heard about the endless paperwork and lengthy delays that are common with this kind of process, plus he resents the accusation that he has discriminated against anyone during the hiring process. After meeting with the organizational ombudsman, John decided to invite Dorys to take part in mediation, using an outside neutral mediator. Dorys agreed to give mediation a try. At the mediation, John explained that he was not allowed to share private personnel information about the other applicants with anyone, but he was able to share with her the criteria on which he based his decision. Dorys met the minimum qualifications for the position and had performed well while at the bureau, but John explained he was looking for someone with more experience in dealing with budgets and overseeing staff. He explained to Dorys the way in which he assigned point values to various elements he was looking for, such as education, specific types of experience, and seniority. He also asked Dorys to share her concerns with him. Why did she believe she had been discriminated against? John learned Dorys was concerned because there were no mid- or upper-level managers within the bureau who were Hispanic and there were very few women at the highest level of the organization. John agreed this was a problem that needed attention. He agreed to bring this concern to his own bosses for discussion at the next leadership meeting with an eye to assessing any barriers to more diverse hiring and promotion.

As a result of the mediation the following agreement was reached: John would recruit a diverse set of employees from different levels within the organization to develop proposals for increasing diversity at the middle- and upper-management levels. Dorys would meet with the human resource manager for one-on-one coaching about how to be more competitive for any future promotions. Dorys would drop the EEOC case.

KEY TERMS

adjudication

arbitration

backcasting

brainstorming

case evaluation

coaching

evaluative mediation

facilitation

informal managerial mediation

litigation

mediation

negotiated rulemaking

ombudsman (ombuds)

open-door policy

peer review

ripeness

summary jury trials (SJTs; also known
   as minitrials)

DISCUSSION QUESTIONS

1. Share any experiences you have had with alternative dispute resolution. What worked or didn't work well?
2. Think of a conflict in your work environment or in the news. Which ADR process would have been best to address this conflict and why?

EXERCISES

1. ADR Process Matching Exercise: Match each term to the process described. See end of chapter.
2. Make a list of the sources of recurring, predictable conflict within your organization or with its customers or clients. Which skills or processes could be applied to reduce the negative effects of those conflicts and resolve them at the lowest possible level?
3. Think of a challenging relationship in your work life or a persistent unresolved problem at work. Now, imagine that two years have passed and this relationship or problem has reached an ideal state. What actions would you need to take now to reach that ideal state in two years? Engage in backcasting.

GOAL SETTING

1. This week, take stock of the conflicts faced by your organization and decide which processes make the most sense for those conflicts.

Match the dispute resolution process to the appropriate definition:

mediation
facilitation
case evaluation
summary jury trial/minitrial
negotiated rulemaking
ombudsman/ombuds
arbitration
no intervention needed
adjudication

You may use any process more than once or not at all.

1. You are the CEO of a large corporation (more than 20,000 employees). Lately your company has lost a lot of money due to some high-profile lawsuits involving sexual harassment and discrimination. You feel that a lot of time and money are used up in fruitless daily conflicts on the workroom floor. Therefore, you have decided to promote one of your long-time employees into a new position called an _____. This person has a good reputation among the other employees and he or she will be available for any employee to come and talk to about on-the-job problems or conflicts. This person will have the authority to recommend new policies and procedures (including training) designed to overcome old patterns of destructive conflict.

2. Your boss gave overtime to an employee who has less seniority than you, and you believe this is a clear violation of the union contract. You are going to file a grievance and go to _____. You like this process because it is binding, you can bring a union representative and/or an attorney, and you feel like you get your day in "court" without actually going to court. (Plus, the union contract requires that you use this process.)

3. An individual was denied a promotion within a large corporation because she didn't drink, smoke, or eat meat (for religious reasons), and when she entertained corporate guests in her home she refused to allow them to smoke, drink, or eat meat. As a high-level executive within the company, entertaining corporate guests was specifically written into her job description. She wants to use a dispute resolution process that will allow her to set a legal precedent to protect the rights of other members of her religion in the future. Therefore, she has decided to use a process called _____.

4. Riots recently broke out in your city between members of two different ethnic groups after a police shooting of an unarmed mentally ill teenager. The police chief and mayor have decided to conduct a large-group _____ to bring residents together to build relationships, increase understanding, and engage in dialogue. Agreements may or may not result from the process, but the goal is to improve relationships while leading an efficient process.

5. The EPA is considering a new rule to regulate fuel efficiency and emissions in diesel-powered vehicles. Since the last attempt was delayed in court for nearly a decade, they have decided to use a _____ process designed to gather input from the main industry and environmental groups impacted by this decision to reach a collaborative agreement.

6. You and your spouse have decided to divorce. Both of you want to avoid the costs, delay, and emotional trauma of a drawn-out court battle, so you have decided to use a process called _____. In this process you will have the assistance of a third-party neutral as you try to work out issues such as debt and asset division, custody and visitation, etc. This person is not empowered to make decisions for you but will try to help you to reach a mutually agreeable settlement while improving your capacity to work together well.

7. Individual A accidentally rear-ended the car of individual B a few days ago. Individual A admits fault, but he wants to pay the least amount possible to get the cars fixed. No one was injured. Individual B was pretty upset, but he has since calmed down and the parties have had some tense, yet reasonably productive discussions together on the phone. Which dispute resolution process should they use? _____

8. You are an attorney for an auto insurance company. An injured individual who was hit by a drunk driver is suing your company because his career as a pro athlete was ruined. You know you want to settle with this individual but you feel they are asking for too much money. Therefore, you have both agreed to use a process called _____. This process will allow you to go through the motions of a trial, using a mock jury, to determine about how much the case would be worth if it went to court. This process will be much shorter and less expensive than a normal trial, and you have both agreed that the results will be binding.

9. There are three gas stations at one intersection in MetroCity. One or more of these leaked, resulting in remediation costs of $5 million. The state environmental agencies have filed a lawsuit against all three gas station owners to recoup these costs but all sides have agreed to submit their data and evidence to participate in a _____ process. This person will evaluate the strengths and weaknesses of each side's case and offer an opinion as to what would happen in court.

SUGGESTED SUPPLEMENTAL READINGS

Barthel, T., & Fortson-Harwell, M. (2016). Practice note: Asking better questions. *Conflict Resolution Quarterly, 34*, 43–56. https://doi.org/10.1002/crq.21170

Brinkert, R. (2016). State of knowledge: Conflict coaching theory, application, and research. *Conflict Resolution Quarterly, 33*, 383–401. https://doi.org/10.1002/crq.21162

Brubaker, D., Noble, C., Fincher, R., Park, S. K., & Press, S. (2014). Conflict resolution in the workplace: What will the future bring? *Conflict Resolution Quarterly, 31*, 357–386. https://doi.org/10.1002/crq.21104

Charkoudian, L., Eisenberg, D. T., & Walter, J. L. (2017). What difference does ADR make? Comparison of ADR and trial outcomes in small claims court. *Conflict Resolution Quarterly, 35*, 7–45.

EEOC.gov. (2021, February 26). *EEOC releases fiscal year 2020 enforcement and litigation data.* https://www.eeoc.gov/newsroom/eeoc-releases-fiscal-year-2020-enforcement-and-litigation-data

Kuttner, R. (2011). Conflict specialists as leaders: Revisiting the role of the conflict specialist from a leadership perspective. *Conflict Resolution Quarterly, 29*, 103–126.

5

Managing across Cultures and Generations

Deeper Understanding for Maximal Performance

If you haven't got the best talent, you're not going to be the best; if you're not representing properly the available pool of talent, then you're missing an opportunity.

—Alex Wilmot-Sitwell

How does it feel to come to work? Do people really "get you" and like your authentic self or do you simply try to stay "under the radar"? Do you strive to fit in by hiding aspects of yourself at work such as your religiosity, sexual orientation, or your status as a first-generation state college graduate surrounded by Ivy Leaguers? The quote by Wilmot-Sitwell points to the importance of creating and re-creating (every day) an organizational culture that attracts, rewards, engages, and retains the best people. Organizations that do not get the best out of each worker, across generations and identities, will simply be outperformed.

It is the job of managers to bring out the best in each employee and in their teams. This is difficult or impossible to do when people are wasting energy trying to hide their true selves or when they fear sharing radical new ideas or pointing out flaws they have found in a process or product. This chapter links the creation of a warm, welcoming workplace to mission achievement and shows you how to maximize both.

For the purposes of this chapter, **diversity** refers to all the ways in which individuals' identity groups differ: gender, race, ethnicity, age, technical or physical abilities, educational or professional backgrounds, sexual orientation, gender identity, religiosity and religious affiliation, national origin, social class, work style, worldview, introversion, extroversion, and so on.

Learning Objectives

- Describe the ways in which diversity, equity, and inclusion are linked to mission achievement, attrition, and brand strength.
- Explain the difference between tolerating diversity and embracing diversity.

- Analyze your organization's approach to diversity and inclusion to identify the strengths and weaknesses in its culture, policies, and approaches.
- Describe the common ways in which cultures differ and how those differences impact collaboration and communication.
- Explain the impact of ethnocentrism on intercultural communication and conflict at work.
- Analyze intercultural interactions to determine the root cause of miscommunications.
- Explain the root causes and cures for generational conflict at work.
- Describe strategies used to identify and overcome barriers to successful management across cultures and generations.

ELISE AT MAIN STREET BAKERIES

Business is going so well that Elise has decided to open a branch in Quebec. She has multiple bakeries in Vermont, New Hampshire, Maine, and New York, so moving across the border seems like the next logical step. Colleagues have warned her that moving fifty miles across the border is not as simple as it sounds. In addition to the need to understand different regulatory requirements and the language barrier, she has been told that the workplace culture is quite different in Quebec. To succeed, she will need to learn more about Quebecois culture to meet the expectations of both her customers and employees.

ANTHROPOLOGICAL HACKS TO UNDERSTAND CULTURAL DIFFERENCE

Why are they doing that? Why is that manager acting like a jerk? It turns out that we all learn how to survive and thrive in the specific environment in which we were raised, but in some ways each of our environments was unique. The term *environment* is broadly defined and includes the physical geography (e.g., weather), economic conditions (e.g., scarcity versus abundance), sociocultural expectations (e.g. manners, shared cultural knowledge, hierarchies based in race, gender, and other differences); political systems (e.g., extent to which our voice matters); and the extent to which we believe we can shape our own destiny, happiness, or success (meaning we have an **internal locus of control**) versus the extent to which our destiny, happiness, and success are shaped by factors beyond our control (i.e., an **external locus of control**), to name just a few. We absorb lessons about how to survive and thrive through observation of the world around us, from our caregivers and teachers, and from the painful process of trial and error.

What is even more painful is that we tend to carry these lessons with us across time and space. When our environment changes, as it always will, we continue to apply outdated lessons that no longer help us thrive. Imagine you are a manager who graduated from college in 1965 and went to work in the marketing industry. Fast-forward to today and that manager will be fired or at least cancelled for "failure to evolve" for using the marketing strategies and the office etiquette from 1965. What if you were born in a country with a vastly different legal system and the way one "wins" there is to bribe the judge or jurors on your case. While illegal, it is widely done and rarely punished. If you apply those cultural lessons to your new life in the United States, you might get a different result.

The painful truth is that each of us is "programmed" with implicit and explicit lessons about how to succeed in our families, workplaces, communities, and cultures. Yet those spaces evolve faster than we do, or we leave those spaces and travel to vastly different ones. Yet, we tend to apply our old lessons to our new environments. The predictable results are . . . dissatisfying to everyone.

To overcome this dynamic, we need to understand the ways in which cultures and generations tend to differ and why. Once we understand "why they do it that way," then we can engage in conversations designed to make our implicit expectations and assumptions more explicit. Only then can we reach the shared understandings necessary for us to work and live successfully together. It goes back to the concept of *root causes* from Chapter 2. Once we understand why we have different preferences about how to do the work, then we can minimize the unpleasant surprises that lead to unproductive conflict in our teams and organizations. Then, we can adapt more quickly to changes in our environment and thrive through change. This will separate great managers from struggling managers.

The goal is to create an environment in which all people can achieve their full potential, free from artificially or socially constructed barriers designed to advantage some while disadvantaging others. This is an environment that frees everyone to focus on achieving individual and team success while valuing each other.

Failing to adapt to changing cultural and economic environments leads to career failure, and it is a learned skill. Twenty percent of American managers sent to work abroad return before their tour of service is over due to performance problems, and 80% are demoted after working abroad (Neuliep, 2017). Only 11% get promoted after working abroad. This means that companies are not doing a good job helping their managers succeed in intercultural environments. The tools in this chapter will prepare you to communicate and collaborate effectively with those who differ from you in important ways.

As a society (or societies), we have moved beyond the concept of "tolerating" diversity. I "tolerate" broccoli. With some cheese, I might like broccoli a little bit. The word *tolerate* leads us astray for a few reasons: it gives power or legitimacy to a false assumption of diversity's opposite—monoculturalism—as the preferred norm; it indicates that nontolerance or nonacceptance of diversity is an option that implies those in power (assumed to be monocultural) are being generous by choosing to tolerate others, and the language of tolerance assumes diversity is negative rather than positive. Let's unpack these assumptions.

Culture is comprised of a set of values, beliefs, and understandings that tell us how to behave and succeed in our environment. These beliefs are often shared by other members of our cultural group. Our cultural beliefs and practices are nearly invisible to us, but noticeable to those who do not share our culture. Only when we step outside our culture, for example when we travel internationally, do we often realize that things we thought were universal were, in fact, specific to our own culture.

Monoculturalism is the belief that one identity group (one gender, race, nation, or ethnicity) is the norm, and all others vary from that norm. It places one group at the center around which all others must revolve and to which others must adjust or accommodate. This worldview sets up organizations for endless power struggles between those in power and those excluded from power. It also reduces the chances that an organization's leaders will mirror the diversity of its customers, patients, or end users. This negatively impacts mission achievement. Monoculturalism operates at the group level in ways like ethnocentrism at the individual level, and it is the opposite of multiculturalism. **Multiculturalism** is the "co-existence of diverse cultures, where culture includes racial, religious, or cultural groups and is manifested in customary behaviors, cultural assumptions and values, patterns of thinking, and communicative styles" (see ifla.org, 2005).

Ethnocentrism is the belief that one's cultural practices are inherently superior and preferred to those from other cultures. Everyone has some degree of preference for the values and habits originating from their own culture—it is only human. In organizations, when cultural habits become engrained into policies without reflection about their differential impact on those who have different cultural preferences or habits, it creates obstacles to equality. For example, in the fall of 2019, FedEx appointed its first Black CEO, Ramona Hood, who changed the FedEx dress code to allow "natural hair" for the first time. Requiring Black employees to straighten, keep short, or otherwise change their natural hair to conform to the white majority definition of beauty is a form of discrimination that carries financial, emotional, and time-as-money costs. Defining beauty based on a majority group norm, then measuring all people against that expectation, is form of ethnocentrism.

Structural violence refers to "systematic ways in which social structures harm or otherwise disadvantage individuals" (Tanous, 2021) or groups, usually based on an identity category such as race, culture, gender, national origin, age, sexual orientation, and/or physical ability. When a policy or law has a disproportionately negative impact on the ability of one group to make a living, exercise political rights, or live as long as more powerful groups, then it can be seen as an example of structural violence. For example, in the 2018 elections in the United States, the Supreme Court ruled that people without a street address could be refused the right to vote. Native Americans living on reservations, often remote and without paved roads, are more likely to use post office boxes because there is no mail delivery to their homes. A lack of infrastructure investment left them without adequate roads, leaving them without addresses and without the right to vote, which reduces their chances to successfully pressure elected officials to improve their roads. A circular problem. This law had a differentially negative impact on Native Americans, which is a form of structural violence. Another example would be unequal access to high-quality public schools. If a child is born into a poor family in a blighted neighborhood with underfunded schools, then there is an unequal chance that child will succeed economically compared to a child born into a neighborhood with higher-quality schools. Unequal access to education is a form of structural violence because it results in structural, systemic barriers to equal outcomes. When difference (race, ethnicity, geographic origin, and so on) is translated into discrimination, then it leads to conflict, which negatively impacts individuals, organizations, and communities. It is a common, yet fallacious, tendency to blame individuals for systemic problems or to hold up the outliers who became successful despite long odds to justify the continuation of structural barriers to success. While individuals need to be held accountable for their behaviors (e.g., committing crimes or violating company policy) it is also important to look for systemic causes that shape behavior, especially when we see disparate demographic outcomes. Do not blame individuals for system problems because it reduces the likelihood that the system incentives shaping behaviors will be examined and remedied.

Tolerance assumes difference (or diversity) is a negative that must be accepted. If only the world were just like "us," whomever that is. This mental construct keeps companies from recognizing the full benefits of creating an inclusive environment in which many distinct types of employees and customers can succeed and contribute. It places monoculturalism at the center and requires those who vary from the assumed cultural norm to fit into the expectations, habits, and values of the more powerful group at the center. Tolerance also makes the center and its associated characteristics invisible while all deviations from that socially constructed norm are visible. It creates obstacles to the success of those whose culture is not at the center. These obstacles are often perceived as positive or neutral by those at the center, but as oppressive or discriminatory by others. For example, a dress code that bans male facial hair means that some minority religious groups are not welcome. Managers' retreats that involve golf, drinking alcohol, and late-night poker games might inadvertently exclude women or those whose upbringing did not prepare them for these pastimes. This is not to imply these practices must end. Instead, leaders at all levels must be attentive to how their decisions impact everyone and find ways to include instead of exclude team members. These choices privilege one gender, social class, etc. over others.

Privilege refers "to a right or immunity granted as a peculiar benefit, advantage, or favor. Within American and other Western societies, these privileged social identities—of people who have historically occupied positions of dominance over others—include whites, males, heterosexuals, Christians, and the wealthy, among others" (Garcia, 2018). Someone who has privilege (often correlated to power) in one situation may not have the same privilege or power in another situation. For example, women tend to run Parent-Teacher Associations (PTAs) in public schools, often leaving male volunteers to feel like interlopers. A professor may have privilege when trying to get their kids into college due to their inside knowledge of the admissions process and helpful connections. A police officer may experience privilege when pulled over for speeding. Privilege is situational, contextual. In a family business, children of the founder or owner may have benefits and advantages.

When one group is in a higher power position in an organization, they tend to create policies, procedures, and organizational cultures based on their own preferences, often without realizing it. When criticized, they may scoff at others for being "too sensitive." When the policy, procedure, or organizational culture takes on the norms, practices, and expectations of one group as "standard" and sees all others as deviations from that center, those at the center often do not see or understand why others find it problematic. This is called "privileged obliviousness." Just because one does not see a bias, that does not mean it is not there. It could mean that one's blind spots are obscuring it. Our cultural conditioning leads us to believe that our way of doing things is right, expected, and normal. Therefore, if others do not like it, they are simply unaware of the right way. For example, a dress code that has everyone wearing blazers and polo shirts is based on assumptions related to gender, ethnicity, and social class that make others conform to a norm that may feel unnatural to them. One of the most obvious examples of this is the wearing of curly white wigs by barristers and judges in the United Kingdom regardless of their gender, race, or ethnicity. Nonverbally, it instructs "others" to conform to the norms and expectations of the historically dominant group.

In the United States, Caucasian, non-Hispanic people account for 57.8% of the population (census.gov, 2021), but are overrepresented on corporate boards, with 16 of the Fortune 500 companies having no ethnic diversity at all (Leech, 2022). "Of 5,403 board members, 69 percent are male, and 78.5 percent are white" (Leech, 2022). The year 2021 saw a significant increase in women on corporate boards, but at the current rate of change it will be twenty years or more before the diversity of boards matches societal diversity (Konigsburg & Thorne, 2022). It is also true that women, people of color, gender-diverse individuals, and people of differing physical abilities have always been part of the workforce and contributed in important, if often under-recognized, ways. The goal is to make everyone's contribution welcomed and visible and to benefit from diverse perspectives. People from varying backgrounds are more likely to notice different things and less likely to fall prey to **groupthink**, which is "a pattern of thought characterized by self-deception, forced manufacture of consent, and conformity to group values and ethics" (Merriam-Webster, 2023).

Diverse teams are better at creative and problem-solving tasks (see Chapter 8). Missing these perspectives hurts the bottom line, as well as being unacceptable for ethical and moral reasons.

Many studies show that increased diversity has a positive return on investment for organizations and improves profitability. A 2019 investigation into the return on investment from diversity found that a 10% increase in board diversity correlated to a 0.8% increase in corporate profitability (Reyes, 2019). As of 2016, the average age of a Fortune 500 board member was 63.1, leading to the conclusion that one of the biggest gaps on boards is generational diversity (Blank, 2016). It is difficult to imagine that companies producing products and services for a target market they know little about will reach their fullest success and avoid unproductive conflict. Humans simply do not know what they do not know. Diverse decision-makers make better decisions.

One of the recurring themes of this edition of *Conflict Management for Managers* (*CMM*) is the need to respond quickly and effectively to rapidly changing environments to ride the waves of change that have occurred and will continue to occur for the foreseeable future. Interestingly, the longer a company has been in existence, the more likely it is to have a non-diverse board and management cadre. Younger, more innovative companies tend to have greater diversity and are better able to respond to the quick pace of market changes and innovate their products and services.

It is not simply having women and minorities represented at all levels of the corporation that results in positive impacts. Boards are increasingly promoting the notion of creating a mixtocracy—which is ensuring that those in the board-room can offer different viewpoints, skills, backgrounds, and experiences to set up organizations for success (Deloitte, 2017).

> Having women or minorities on your board but ignoring their contributions and opinions does not add value to your organization. It might take effort to change people's mindsets but listening to and including the viewpoints of your diverse board in a real way can bring a new perspective and new ideas to help your organization succeed. While there are many ways to bring diverse perspectives to your board, hiring women and minorities, who have inherently had a different experience, is one way to do so. (Hersh, 2017)

Reaping the benefits of diversity requires the creation of a positive organizational culture (see Chapter 6), which is a key management skill.

Embracing diversity changes the mindset and language so that diversity recognizes that no one group is at the center of power or organizational life. It means we all accommodate each other and find shared meanings, rules, and policies that do not work best for one group at the expense of the other groups. Embracing diversity recognizes the benefits and challenges that come from working with and for people who are different than ourselves, and these differences make life rich and rewarding. Inclusivity means we create a work environment that recognizes and valorizes all cultural and identity groups.

DIVERSITY AND CONFLICT

Conflict comes from unclear, unshared, and unmet expectations. When two or more people share a similar cultural upbringing, there is more likely to be shared cultural knowledge that tells them how to act in specific circumstances: when to silence cell phones, who speaks first at a family reunion, when to stand or sit during a religious ceremony, which behaviors indicate respect or disrespect. This means that diverse work teams may need to have explicit conversations about what to expect from each other and how the team will work together effectively. Chapter 7 covers 3-step problem-solving, which is a simple process through which two or more individuals or teams can reach shared expectations to reduce unpleasant surprises and maximize teamwork.

Conflict comes from unmet expectations. When people behave differently than we expect, it often causes conflict. The more similarities we have with others, the more we think we can predict how they will act. In their study of teams called "Project Aristotle," Google found that diversity did not necessarily predict conflict in work teams. Rather, the lack of shared norms and expectations creates conflict. Therefore, the trick is to create shared expectations to reduce conflict in all teams, including diverse teams.

Culture-based issues that may arise include the following: timeliness and deadlines (monochronic versus polychronic orientations to time), the use of email or work on weekends (work-life balance issues), the impact of gender on issues like leave policies or the distribution of work tasks (e.g., are women expected to bring the coffee or is this task shared?), the distribution of rewards such as merit versus equal pay or benefits (e.g., preferences for individualism versus collectivism), how to address each other (e.g., preferences for hierarchy versus equality), gendered or general bathroom facilities, the amount of socializing mixed with work (e.g., some cultures prefer not to socialize with coworkers while others expect it), dress codes and appearance or grooming issues (all cultural), who and how to speak up at meetings, and other task-focused matters. Which holidays will the company recognize? Each person's religion and culture will lead them to a different preference, but we need to coordinate this throughout the company. Otherwise, some will show up on December 25 or January 1, while others will not. Inclusive organizations might address the issue of holidays by observing the dates that are national holidays and then giving each employee a specified number of additional days to allow for the observance of other celebrations. By explicitly discussing and reaching consensus, teams can reduce conflict that leads all to feel respected.

Cognitive conflict stems from disagreements over issues at work including meeting schedules, workload distribution, decision-making processes, or the task itself (Gulati, Mayo & Nohria, 2017). Affective conflict is that "in which individuals attack each other's personalities through criticism, threats, and insults" (Gulati et al., 2017). Cognitive conflict is helpful in organizations to prevent groupthink, increase creativity, challenge the status quo, and increase motivation while affective conflict is detrimental in organizations by leading to anger, frustration, low morale, and decreased satisfaction (Jehn et al., 2008).

POWER, DIVERSITY, AND CONFLICT

Great managers are able to motivate people to follow their lead, to enact their vision or to create a shared vision, and to reach their full potential.

"Power with" is much greater than "power over" (Brown, 2018). A boss (or parent) with power over you may get you to do something you do not want to do (clean your room, eat your vegetables, or work on a Saturday). Nonetheless, that power comes with a risk of sabotage, turnover, and a toxic work environment. "Power with" comes from the knowledge and attitude that none of us succeeds alone. It occurs when we work together to accomplish shared interests. Bosses using "power with" can communicate why a specific course of action will work best; they listen to the views and preferences of others and then seek a path forward together.

It is common for the people at or near the top of a social power hierarchy to lack understanding of those who have less power, while those with less power have a deeper understanding of the motivations and needs of the powerful (see Figure 5.1). Imagine the court of French King Louis XVI and his queen, Marie Antoinette. As the story goes, the queen was so ignorant of the daily lives and circumstances of everyday people that when they complained of having no bread to eat, she famously said, "Let them eat cake!" Without a doubt, those at the lowest ends of the power hierarchy were familiar with the queen's needs, wants, and

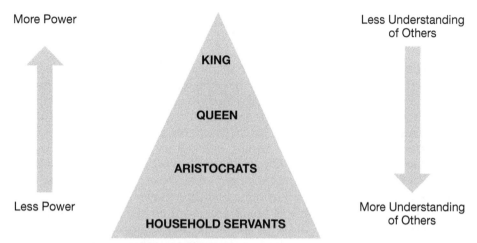

Figure 5.1   Power and Diversity Triangle

daily life. This is a metaphor that rings true across power structures. Those who are low on the power hierarchy must understand those above them to survive, but those at the top do not need to understand those below them because their survival or happiness does not depend upon it. The people lower on the triangle are replaceable. For example, the administrative assistant knows how the boss likes her coffee, but the boss might not know the same about the administrative assistant. If someone cleans your house, they know a lot about you, but you know extraordinarily little about them. But remember, power is not immutable. Today's bartender could be tomorrow's physician, engineer, or president. As a sidenote, it is worth noting that in the United States, only approximately 7% of people born into blue-collar families will rise to white-collar careers and incomes and only 8% of children born in 1980 will outearn their parents due to stagnating wages and greater concentration of wealth (Lu, 2020).

Many company leaders have been shocked by the efforts of their employees to unionize or demand better wages or working conditions. When these efforts take leaders by surprise, it is a reflection of the gap in understanding common to people on top of a social hierarchy and a sign of being out of touch with those less powerful. Think about a group you have struggled to understand. What is their relationship to you and your identity group(s) on the triangle? To prevent such surprises, it is best for managers and organizational leaders to spend time inviting feedback and listening to the concerns of those at all power levels within the organization as well as the customers.

It is also helpful for leaders in the organization to spend some time on the front lines so they can understand the challenges faced by employees at all levels of power. There is no substitute for "walking a mile in their shoes" and spending time observing those you seek to understand. Leaders and managers must create mechanisms through which the concerns, ideas, and innovations of all employees are harnessed for positive change. This increases the ability of leaders and managers to be effective and responsive, while showing concern for all members of the organization. "Power with" beats "power over" every time.

ORGANIZATIONAL CULTURE CHANGE:
ANSWERING THE QUESTION "WHO ARE WE?"

Unfortunately, many leaders do not see the need to change from monoculturalism to multiculturalism because they have benefited from the status quo and, honestly, change may involve growing pains. Recently, one CEO told me, "We know we need to change to make our organization more inclusive, but I am worried about moving too quickly." He said this in a room of diverse leaders gathered to brainstorm methods to address racism and bigotry in their organization. My guess is that some people in the room felt they had waited long enough. What is more, the organization was rapidly losing market share and experiencing diminished mission achievement due to their inability to attract and retain younger employees. The organization was holding on to their outdated, biased culture as if it were a life raft when in fact it was an anchor, dragging them downward.

Your biggest challenge may be to help convince others of the rational need to change the way they think, speak, and create organizational culture through policies, hiring, promotion, dress codes, and other markers of organizational culture. Inclusive companies are stronger and more profitable, have more positive cultures, happier customers, and better brand image. Why wait?

Every organization must decide "Who are we now?" and "Who do we want to be?" Without consciously recognizing it, every organization answers these questions every day based on how they treat each other and the policies and processes they use. The tone is set at the top, but everyone has a role to play in determining "who we are." Why should your organization change? Superficial, yet valid, answers include avoiding litigation, reducing employee turnover, and protecting the reputation of the organization. At a deeper level, these changes create a warmer, more humane, and more welcoming environment for everyone, including those making the policies. Organizational justice—like most movements for justice—liberate everyone. Beyond that, organizations that have made conscious choices to leave behind oppressive, unfair policies and procedures often reap unexpected benefits for employee morale, turnover, customer satisfaction, brand image, profits, and most importantly, a joyful, fulfilling workplace. "Workplace diversity is no longer just a good thing to do—it has become a business necessity." (Sourry, 2018).

How do you change your organization's culture? Change needs to occur not only at the relational level (also known as "interpersonal" level) but also at the organizational and broader societal systems levels. Unfortunately, most lawyers, human resource departments, and even consultants focus on changing only interpersonal relations because biased or discriminatory interpersonal relationships and individual actions lead to litigation (discrimination in hiring and promotion, sexual harassment, and hostile work environments) and bad press. Yet, disturbing behaviors are symptoms of a dysfunctional culture in need of change. Occasionally, there is one bad manager or employee who needs to be fired for inappropriate behavior. More commonly, the behavior has been going on for a long time without any negative consequences. It was tolerated because it was not important enough to warrant change, or the person engaging in these behaviors provided some skill set or benefits the organization was hesitant to risk losing. In other words, at the symbolic and material levels, the organization chose to answer the question "Who are we?" with this answer: "We are not an organization that values kindness, fairness, equality, and social justice." There is no trade-off between people and profits. Organizations that treat people well tend to be more profitable (e.g., less turnover, higher morale, happier customers). There is, instead, an unwillingness to confront injustice and discrimination for many reasons: a preference for conflict avoidance in general (see Chapter 1), powerful people enabling their peers, or a host of other root causes that portend badly for the organization's health.

Change at the relational level encompasses the ways in which we treat each other, speak to each other, and work with each other. In positive organizational cultures, employees and customers are treated with respect, value, and equality irrespective of their various identity groups. Employees and customers are not disposable. Training is useful to bring change, but it will not stick unless it includes changes at all three levels. Change on the relational level should not focus only on the "do's and don'ts" of organizational life (e.g., avoid assuming that your coworkers share your political beliefs and want to talk politics) and should include skills for engaging in difficult conversations designed to build shared expectations. Relational training should include active bystander skills designed to re-norm individuals whose behaviors are not consistent with "who we are" as an organization.

What is an active bystander? An **active bystander** is anyone who sees unacceptable behavior or a person in distress and takes action to help. Active bystanders interrupt "a problematic or potentially harmful situation, stopping action or comments that promote sexual or discriminatory violence, bullying, harassment, intimidation, or threatening behavior."[1] Anyone who witnesses an unacceptable behavior has a choice: pretend not to see it, thereby enabling it at some level, or take a reasonable action to stop the behavior through distraction, delegation, or direction. For example, imagine you are at a coworker's retirement party hosted by your boss. You see a colleague who is flirting with a clearly uncomfortable intern. You could choose to do one of three options: distract your colleague by inserting yourself into the conversation; delegate your efforts to disrupt the negative behavior to someone else who might have better leverage to intervene, such as the boss; or direct your colleague to stop the offensive behavior. Direction is often accomplished with humor, especially when given by someone without power and authority.

Organizational culture is being constantly shaped by the actions or inactions of everyone in the organization. While culture change efforts are best accomplished from the top, everyone has a role to play. Teaching active bystander skills is a way for each employee to take responsibility for the "who are we" conversation. Are we an organization where people in power prey on those lowest in power, such as interns? Or, alternatively, are we an organization that supports the career development of new entrants to the field by creating a safe, harassment-free place to learn and grow? For this to work, leaders must lead by example, set out their expectations of "who we are," and support everyone whose behaviors exemplify rather than denigrate "who we are." Each person is, therefore, allowed to set reasonable boundaries for how he/she/they want to be treated, and these boundaries are to be respected and supported by those at every level of the organization. There must be low-risk mechanisms for those seeking to report violations of these norms as well as a willingness to discipline and reeducate those who violate them. Otherwise, the answer to the "who are we" question becomes, "We are an organization that claims to care about fair, appropriate treatment, but allows powerful people to prey on the less powerful with impunity." No one wants to work at such an organization except for the predators. These organizations are prone to litigation, turnover, and high-profile scandals.

The symbolic level of culture changes examines the ways in which the organization makes meaning of various facts and recognizes "who we are" through symbolic events. To illustrate, someone in a wheelchair may be fully able to fill a specific job description, but if we do not have wide enough doors or ramps instead of stairs, then we have taken the fact that he uses a wheelchair and turned it into a barrier to inclusion; we made meaning out of it, but we could have made a different meaning. We make meaning out of facts, and how we do so reflects our values as individuals and organizations.

Dysfunctional organizations enact their values through symbols that recognize some groups and exclude others. Do we celebrate birthdays for everyone, or only the boss? This conveys our beliefs about power and equality. How do we decorate the walls? Do we celebrate the diverse ethnic heritages of our team members, or do we only recognize the holidays of the majority group? Does our workspace recognize the need for transparency and still allow for appropriate private conversational space? Do we have restrooms that work for everyone including families, transgender individuals, and the differently abled? Do we allow an employee to place a large Confederate flag on the wall of his office, even though other employees may feel intimidated by the symbolism associated with the flag? What nonverbal signals are sent via the ways the organization communicates its values?

At the material level, organizations put policies and practices into place that may explicitly or implicitly benefit some and disadvantage others. This happens through written policies as well as unwritten ones. Examples of this abound: male employees are paid more than female employees with the same job description and qualifications; dress codes are built on majority-group norms but disallow others from expressing their identities at an equal level through their appearance; organizational hierarchies that have members of one or more ethnic or identity groups doing the frontline work while other identity groups hold management and leadership positions; biased distribution of workload; favoritism; nepotism; cronyism; employment tests that result in systematically higher scores from some groups over others; and university admissions policies that prioritize children of alumni or big donors. Does the organization recognize Christmas and Easter as paid days off while refusing to allow a Jewish employee to take leave for High Holy Days, or discourage a new father from taking family leave?

Does the organization create hypocritical policies that allow for employees in the home country to be paid and treated fairly while utilizing child labor, unsafe workspaces, bullying, and harassment in factories they operate abroad? If yes, then "who are we?" These are deep questions for organizations seeking to remain profitable, protect the brand name, and treat all employees humanely and regardless of the geographic location of the plant or the gender, age, or ethnic makeup of the workforce.

THE GLOBALIZED NATURE OF WORK
IN THE TWENTY-FIRST CENTURY

For many of us, work has gone global. Organizations seeking the best, most talented employees hire from places such as universities, tech companies, and so on. Some of us work in virtual teams with colleagues located in other states or countries. Multinational companies (MNCs) founded in one country build plants in their customers' countries to be closer to their markets, to circumnavigate barriers to free trade, or to access low-wage labor (e.g., Volkswagen, Honda, Toyota, YKK, Adidas, Nike, Accenture, Novo Nordisk, Google, Intel, Microsoft, Coca-Cola). In this globalized workforce, a nurse from Nigeria or the Philippines may be hired to work in New Jersey or Alaska. Borders are becoming more permeable with important implications for management best practices and requiring a deeper level of intercultural adaptability.

Typically, companies are founded within one national cultural context and shaped by those laws and norms. They create policies and standard operating procedures (SOPs) that reflect both the host and home environment. When a corporation opens a branch in a foreign country, they take with them many of their assumptions about "the best way to do the work," predicated upon years of experience in their home environment. Then, they learn the hard way that many of those hard-learned lessons do not transfer well to the host culture or legal infrastructure (e.g., Home Depot in China; see Box 5.1). In fact, policies painstakingly developed over time may be illegal in the new context. For example, U.S. companies operating in Europe or parts of Asia find they are required to provide paid family leave to new parents. Job descriptions that would be commonplace in one country include language that is illegal in another.

There are significant differences in preferred management practices across cultures (Globe, 2020). For example, workers in the United States tend to prefer autonomy and eschew micromanaging while workers in hierarchically organized cultures are more comfortable with close supervision (e.g., Germany or Japan). Later in this chapter, we will examine what it is like to work with various cultural groups with the understanding that the study of culture requires us to make broad generalizations that do not apply equally to all members of that culture. For the sake of comparison, we will generalize.

BOX 5.1. HOME DEPOT IN CHINA

Most experts on Chinese culture could have warned Home Depot that its "DIY" (do it yourself) model of home improvement and building supplies would be unlikely to work in China. The Home Depot model originated in Atlanta, Georgia, United States, and was exported to other cities in the United States and Canada. With the high labor cost, many in the United States prefer to engage in their own home repair and improvement projects. Home Depot's model is built on the American cultural assumption of individualism: if you want something done right, you must do it yourself. Contrast this with China's collectivist culture in which labor is cheap and families develop long-lasting ties with carpenters or plumbers that may span generations. A Chinese accountant may easily turn to a plumber or electrician he trusts because his family has relied on the same person or family for many years, or the referral came from a close contact. In fact, installing his own ceiling fan or painting his own living room may feel like a burden when someone with the specialty could do it better. Because these are long-lasting relationships in a culture where reputation and face-saving are important, the work will meet the customer's expectations and the customer will pay well while treating the service provider respectfully. When someone needs building supplies, he does not pay a fixed price for the material. He goes to a retailer from whom he has bought supplies many times. They may haggle over the price, with the final price reflecting any fluctuations in the current market value of the item. In contrast, IKEA has done well because it is appropriate for each person to buy home decor items or furniture to decorate as one sees fit. In large part, Home Depot failed in China due to a failure to recognize key cultural differences and instead assume that "what works here will work anywhere."

Conflict, Communication, and Culture

Management skills are culturally specific (Hofstede, 1984). The way a manager speaks to, directs, and motivates employees varies based on the norms and expectations of the culture in which she works. While this is obvious in multinational corporations, it is increasingly critical for managers with diverse teams and customers within their own borders.

Culture provides a lens or filter through which all information is processed and made into meaning. We acquire culture meaning mostly through observation of our surroundings and the behaviors of those in our in-group (see Chapter 2 for in-group/out-group theory). Culture tells us how to make meaning of sensory input like sounds, sights, and smells. Even the definition of "food" varies across cultures: snails, dog, pork, lobster, and tarantulas. All of these are food in some cultures. Our culture tells us how to behave in workplace environments. Do we speak up at staff meetings or remain silent? Do we share our ideas directly, or give them to our supervisor to share as her own? Are we expected to answer emails over the weekend? Are decisions made collaboratively or unilaterally? The good news is that each of us can shape organizational culture as well as be shaped by it (see Chapter 6).

As Chapter 2 discussed, in-group/out-group theory predicts that we have more empathy for those in our identity groups. **Cultural distance** refers to the extent to which two cultures differ on key factors such as gender role differentiation, the importance of context in verbal communication, views of hierarchy versus equality, etc. The greater the difference between two cultures, the greater the likelihood of intercultural misunderstandings between members of these groups. This chapter will provide you with the tools to identify and redress the roots of culture-based conflict. Figure 5.2 shows a variety of ways in which cultures differ. The more distance there is between two national or ethnic cultures on these preferences, the more they will need to work to develop shared expectations and understandings about how to accomplish their work together successfully. For example, what does "on time" mean in this circumstance, or how will we treat each other (especially considering distinct cultural preferences of gender roles or respect based on hierarchy)?

Managers and employees can maximize their success by learning key differences in communication and conflict behaviors that stem from cultural variation. Once we know *why* someone is communicating in a way that is different or even unpleasant, then we can respond more effectively and refrain from taking offense or misinterpreting their meaning. Diverse teams can bring great benefits to organizations. To reap these benefits, intercultural communication knowledge and skills are indispensable.

High-Context and Low-Context Cultures

In **high-context cultures** most meaning is conveyed via nonverbal means such as eye contact, tone, silence, and scripted conversations. "High context" refers to the degree to which one must understand the context of the conversation to understand the intended meaning. In high-context cultures, the burden of understanding falls on the listener, not the speaker. If the listener understands the context well enough and has nurtured a strong relationship with the speaker, then he will understand the intended meaning. Relationships come first, and tasks or activities second. High-context cultures tend to be more rigidly hierarchical and homogeneous, which allows for the development of shared norms governing communication. Typically, social harmony is highly valued, which means that conflicts are addressed indirectly through informal mediators or emissaries rather than directly. High-context communication cultures developed in isolated and homogenous societies with low levels of immigration (e.g., Japan, Finland, and Hawaii). This isolation facilitated the development of shared norms of behavior. Avoidance and accommodation are more common styles in these cultures than competition and compromise.

The United States is a **low-context culture** in which most of the meaning is conveyed in the explicit verbal conversation as opposed to being implied through

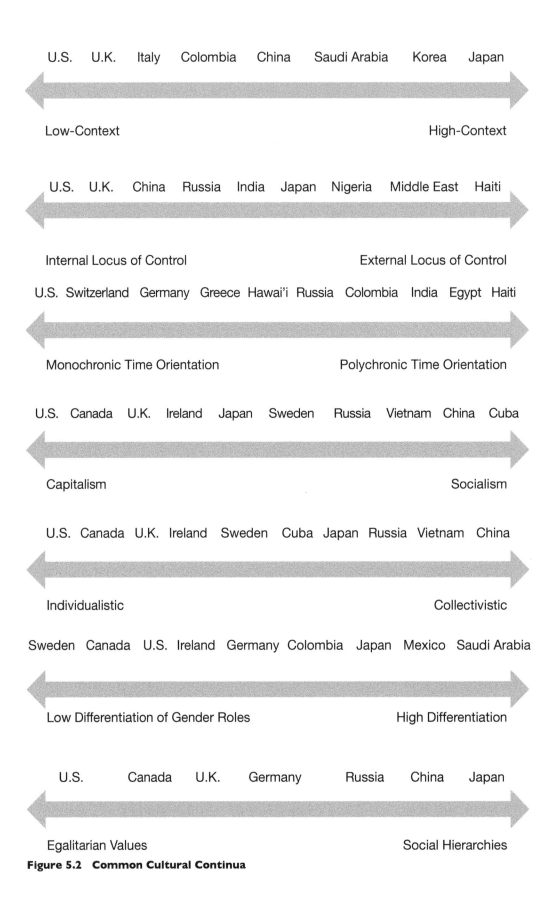

U.S.   U.K.   Italy   Colombia   China   Saudi Arabia   Korea   Japan

Low-Context   High-Context

U.S.   U.K.   China   Russia   India   Japan   Nigeria   Middle East   Haiti

Internal Locus of Control   External Locus of Control

U.S. Switzerland Germany Greece Hawai'i Russia Colombia India Egypt Haiti

Monochronic Time Orientation   Polychronic Time Orientation

U.S. Canada U.K. Ireland Japan Sweden Russia Vietnam China Cuba

Capitalism   Socialism

U.S. Canada U.K. Ireland Sweden Cuba Japan Russia Vietnam China

Individualistic   Collectivistic

Sweden Canada U.S. Ireland Germany Colombia Japan Mexico Saudi Arabia

Low Differentiation of Gender Roles   High Differentiation

U.S.   Canada   U.K.   Germany   Russia   China   Japan

Egalitarian Values   Social Hierarchies

Figure 5.2 Common Cultural Continua

context, nonverbal cues, or scripted conversations. In low-context cultures, the burden for understanding falls on the speaker: if the speaker is clear enough, then the listener will likely understand the intended meaning. Low-context cultures developed at societal crossroads in regions with high levels of immigration or in cultures prone to imperialism, which brought them into frequent contact with foreign cultures (e.g., Great Britain, France, and New York City). Low-context cultures tend to score higher on competitive and compromising styles than high-context cultures. It is important to note that an individual's cultural context and individual personality traits oftentimes determine preferred communication and conflict styles. Be sure to avoid stereotyping individuals from cultures different from your own. Individuals may not always exhibit the communication tendencies of their broader cultural group.

Many cultures prefer nonverbal and indirect communication. Indirect communication works best when communicators build deeper, long-term relationships that provide the context needed to correctly decode nonverbal or scripted communications. **Nonverbal communication** includes contextual cues that convey acknowledgment of power dynamics and emotional ties or the lack thereof between individuals or groups. Nonverbal communication is conveyed through vocal tone, body language, eye contact, and even clothing, hairstyles, and demeanor, which communicate relative social status and dominance or submission within a chain of command.

Like nonverbal communication, all cultures use scripted conversations to varying degrees. A **scripted conversation** is one in which both parties understand what they are expected to say due to prevailing cultural norms that dictate appropriate and inappropriate responses during the conversation. For example, when a U.S. American asks a casual coworker, "How are you?" there is an implicit understanding that this question really means "Hello" and is meant to create a friendly tone of greeting rather than as a sincere inquiry into the health or emotional status of the other person. The responder knows that only a few kinds of responses are considered appropriate to this question, with the best one being something akin to, "Fine, thanks. How are you?" This is an example of one of the few scripted conversations that exist in U.S. culture. However, in some communication cultures, there are many more scripts that cover the acceptable conversations between a supervisor and an employee, between casual acquaintances, between professors and students, and so on. In these cultures, context and power relations are key to understanding the meaning that the speaker wishes to convey. Context can include the known power dynamics between the communicators as well as the place or timing of the communication. Organizations tend to exhibit either direct or indirect conflict communication styles. How does your organization communicate, and what are the implications of those communication tendencies?

Managerial tip: Learn the scripts common to your workplace. When you are frustrated by another person's communication style, think about the reasons that your communication styles are so different. If cultural difference may be part of the reason for your frustration, try communicating with the other's preferred style so they can "hear" you better. Consider having an open discussion with your colleagues to negotiate shared expectations around communication.

Meta-communication occurs when people communicate about how they communicate in order to reduce miscommunication by explaining both the intent and the content of a message. To exemplify, during a performance review, a manager may say, "Jose, the reason I send you memos outlining what we discussed at each of our meetings isn't a lack of trust. It is because I have a poor memory. By sending you a brief memo after each meeting, I decrease the chances that we will leave the meeting with different understandings or forget what was discussed. By doing this, we can succeed together."

Individualism versus Collectivism

Individualistic societies (**individualism**) are those in which the needs, rights, and responsibilities of the individual are prioritized above those of the group or community. In these societies, it is generally considered positive for individuals to stand out from their peers through individual achievements, whereas in **collectivist societies** (**collectivism**), it is less appropriate for individuals to "stand out from the crowd." In individualistic societies, members are encouraged to be independent from others, support themselves financially, make decisions for themselves, and deal with the outcomes of their decisions, whether good or bad. The field of psychology defines this as the locus of control. Individuals with an **internal locus of control** believe they are in control of events that affect themselves rather than being controlled by external forces such as fate.

Individuals with an **external locus of control** believe they are controlled by factors external to themselves such as a higher power, the environment, political forces, and so on. Individualists are more likely to put their faith in individuals' abilities to master their environment and make decisions or take actions that result in positive outcomes for the individual. Therefore, in individualistic societies, distributions based on need are less supported than other definitions of fairness, and the equity principle is typically preferred. Because individuals are thought to be able to control their environments through good decision-making and hard work, an equity distribution makes the most sense. When taken to the extreme, those with a strong internal locus of control are likely to assume people who are poor have failed to work hard or make good decisions. Those with a high external locus of control feel the opposite: that poverty results from factors outside an individual's control. While most individualistic societies exhibit high internal locus of control measures (Mueller & Thomas, 2001, p. 51), this is not uniform across cultures. Interestingly, innovation is correlated to a high internal locus of control and in cultures with a higher tolerance for risk (ibid.).

The locus of control concept also explains cultural differences regarding future planning. Individuals with an external locus of control tend to be uncomfortable making plans far in advance because of a belief that the future is unknowable and out of their control. For example, in many Arabic-speaking, Middle Eastern cultures, the term *inshallah* (as God/Allah wills) is used when making plans for the future: "I will meet you for lunch on Tuesday, inshallah."

In collectivist societies in which individual identities are based on ties to the group or community, it is more common to share resources based on equality or need. For example, in Russia, Liberia, or China, an individual's fate might have more to do with the family one is born into or the political climate (e.g., whether your family is politically powerful or whether there is peace and stability or war). Even getting to work on time might have more to do with luck than individual choice because the public buses might be unreliable or run off schedule. In truth, in developing economies or war-torn regions, it is more true that an individual's fate does indeed lie more heavily with factors beyond his or her own control due to societal inequity, random violence, and corrupt political systems. Collectivist societies tend to believe that it is fair to distribute the costs of education, health care, parenthood, and so on across society rather than to allow persons to shoulder these burdens individually. They may use a web of social relationships to get ahead, but rarely do they believe individuals will succeed or fail solely based on their own efforts.

As a manager in a multicultural workplace, it is important to understand the root causes of employee behaviors. The locus of control helps us understand why employees may have culturally based differences in their concepts of fairness, future planning, and initiative. It also helps to understand preferences for team-based or individually based assignments. Individuals from each perspective tend to get frustrated in dealing with the other. Those with a high internal locus of control find their opposites to be indecisive and slow to act; those with a high external locus of control believe their opposites tend to exhibit a high degree of hubris or consider them egotistical. Understanding these worldviews and views of self can be helpful in finding fair and productive ways to work together. For example, an "employee of the month" recognition program would be inappropriate in a collectivist culture but appropriate in an individualistic one. Collectivists would prefer team-based recognition. In fact, a collectivist would be embarrassed by individual recognition and worry about offending his team since their contribution would undoubtedly have been important in his achievements.

Orientations toward Time

Do you ever wonder where the term *island time* came from? Why are people from Germany or Switzerland so punctual while those from Haiti or Colombia tend to run late? Anthropologists have, thankfully, found an explanation for these cultural differences. Cultures that evolve in climates with four distinct seasons espouse beliefs and habits indicating there are "right" times to do certain tasks: for instance, there is a season to sow and to reap. If European farmers do not plant at the right time of year, they will be hungry all winter long. Even weddings in European societies (and their diaspora colonies) are more likely to happen at a certain time of the year (May through June) because that is the time of year when it is warm enough to take one's annual bath. On the other hand, in cultures that arise in mild and equatorial climates, the timing of farming or other activities is less critical. Things happen when they happen.

There is another complicating factor: economic and societal disruptions. For example, Russians are less punctual than the British, but their climate is harsher. This makes sense when you consider the poor economy during and after the Soviet era. Buses did not run on time, so it was impossible to know exactly when one would arrive at work. On the way to work, if the bakery happened to have bread in stock, you might queue up for three hours to stock up. You would get to work when possible. Under Soviet-era rules, you would receive the same pay whether you worked a full day or not, so there was no rush. This gave rise to a culture with a high external locus of control because so many factors were out of the control of the average person. Similarly, cultures with long histories of war, conflict, or natural disasters will also develop a polychronic orientation toward time.

A **monochronic orientation** toward time indicates that one prefers to adhere to strict schedules and deadlines; time is something tangible that can be saved, spent, or wasted. This orientation toward time is most common in countries such as Great Britain, Germany, Switzerland, the United States, Australia, and other cultures of Western European origin. People with this orientation may be less flexible and more driven by deadlines. They may also prefer to get right down to the task at hand rather than spend time building relationships. A **polychronic orientation** to time means one believes there are many "right" times to complete different activities (e.g., arrive at work anytime between 8:30 a.m. and 10:00 a.m. or take a flexible lunch break). Polychronic cultures tend to arise nearer the equator where seasonal differences are smaller (e.g., many Latino and Island cultures). Individuals from polychronic cultures tend to be more comfortable with flexible deadlines and spend time building relationships before attending to tasks.

Managerial tip: Be careful when pairing monochronic and polychronic team members unless they are able to work relatively autonomously, or you have spent time building shared norms around issues concerning deadlines and work schedules. People with different time orientations may be able to work well together, but it will be helpful for them to discuss their preferred work styles so as to be respectful of differences. Developing shared norms related to the definition of "on time" and the negotiability or flexibility of deadlines is crucial. When corporations from monochronic cultures open branches in countries with polychronic cultures, challenges stemming from these different approaches must be proactively discussed, negotiated, and clarified. It may help to incentivize the behaviors expected for all team members. Another approach is to create project-specific deadlines and let individual team members work at their own pace as long as the project meets the deadline. These matters, however, will cause fewer conflicts if team members and leaders reach shared expectations regarding the management of different work styles and punctuality.

Gender Role Differences across Cultures

Few differences are as daunting in the workplace as those based on gender. In cultures with **low gender role differentiation**, there is a belief that most tasks are not gender specific (e.g., cooking, driving, child rearing, farming, teaching, policing, managing a company, and secretarial work). In these countries, differences in power, income, and decision-making are relatively similar between men and women even though differences tend to exist in all societies. In contrast, cultures with **high gender role differentiation** divide tasks as well as power, income, and decision-making based upon gender. For instance, as a country with relatively low gender role differentiation, men in Norway are more likely to be the primary caregivers for small children than in Saudi Arabia or Mexico. Now, imagine that people from different cultures are working together in a multinational corporation. Top managers rotate between manufacturing plants in France, Mexico, Japan, and the United States. Challenges due to misunderstanding, different preferences about communication styles, and ethnocentric perceptions (a preference for one's own cultural practices) will be common.

Organizational Assessment Exercise: Take stock of how your organization and your unit are doing on measures of equity. Does pay vary based on gender, race, national origin, or other demographic differences within the same job title or level? If so, why? Examine the policies, procedures, decisions, and interpersonal interactions to assess the extent to which biases have influenced the organization's cultures. Are there biases in the dress code that benefit some at the expense of others? What about family leave policies? Is hiring and promotion done in a way that privileges some over others? Are you removing names from résumés to avoid name bias? Are employees expected to pay some of the costs of their own work-related travel? Do employee surveys indicate workers feel they are treated fairly at work? A comprehensive review of your policies and procedures will provide the information needed to decide next steps.

Hierarchy versus Equality

Some cultural groups prefer hierarchy based on social class, gender, race, immigration status, sexual orientation, religion, age, and/or merit. This means some people are not seen as "management material." In many countries, discriminatory hiring practices are common, expected, and viewed as acceptable. Hiring based on family ties or the web of social relationships happens everywhere, but it is more common in some countries than others.

When addressing the owner or leader of your organization, do you use their given name (e.g., Jose, Bob, or Shawnna), or speak more formally (Mr. Smith or Ms. Gomez)? Alternatively, is it inconceivable that you would ever speak directly to someone so high above you in the hierarchy? Can you offer ideas or raise problems, or is that not your job? Can you envision promotion into the highest levels of leadership, or is that out of reach for someone from your identity group(s)? The answers to these questions indicate the extent to which your organization prefers hierarchy or equality in its social relationships.

Some organizations have a rigid hierarchy in which the person at the top gives orders and they are conveyed downward, but communication rarely makes it from the lower levels to the top. There is a clear American preference for informality (an indicator of less preference for hierarchy) than in most other countries, yet not all regions of the United States are the same in this preference. For instance, children in the Southern states are more likely to call their adult neighbors and friends "Mr. Tom" or "Miss Becky" as a sign of respect and familiarity. People of all ages are more likely to respond with "Yes, sir" or "No, ma'am" in the South than in other regions. Any culture that prefers hierarchy will typically frame this as a matter of "respect." When working in a hierarchical culture, it is important to know how to show respect (e.g., make or do not make eye contact, use formal titles, do not speak until spoken to). The more hierarchical the society, the more these displays of respect will be nonverbal, nuanced, and ritualized. These expectations will not be in an employee handbook because they are assumed to be shared cultural knowledge. This makes it harder for those who come from a different culture (even organizational culture) to avoid causing accidental offense. Cultural outsiders or those new to the organization need to watch and learn while also having a trusted bicultural insider who can answer these tough questions. A bicultural insider is familiar with both cultures and can act as a cultural translator by explaining "why we do it this way."

Is hierarchy better than a flat organizational structure? According to the *Harvard Business Review*, hierarchically organized companies struggle to keep up with change and have overall lower performance (Kastelle, 2013). Yet, it is not necessarily the structure that causes conflict. It is the tendency of hierarchy to limit contact and communication between those at various levels of the hierarchy or a failure to lead effectively that causes these inefficiencies (Willink & Babin, 2015). When those at the top are divorced from the actual work of the organization, and those at the bottom cannot easily share their ideas for innovation and improvement up the chain, then conflict increases and innovation declines. This is particularly important in light of the rapid changes impacting companies since 2019.

The key to success lies in communicating shared expectations about how the work will get done, who makes decisions, and who benefits from the work. Clear expectations and active lines of communication result in less conflict. As Chapter 8 discusses, successful managers in the United States and Western cultures may wish to take an authoritative rather than authoritarian approach, taking care to avoid harsh, dictatorial approaches in favor of facilitating employee growth and success through mentorship and development.

Common Causes of Conflict in the Intercultural Workplace

In some countries, employers have an affirmative obligation to create a workplace free from harassment and discrimination. However, the definition of and consequences for harassment and discrimination vary. It is worth examining the common causes of conflict in intercultural workplaces.

- *Hiring and promotion practices:* In some cultures, it is common that children or family members of existing managers will get preferential treatment in hiring. By hiring someone who is already known to the work team, it is possible to predict that the candidate will fit in, or so the logic goes. Similarly, in countries with large gender distance, there are jobs done only or mostly by men and others done by women. Therefore, the first, most common cause of challenges in the intercultural workplace involves hiring and promotion.

  Solution: Discuss the reasons for the company's current practices and the ways in which they comply or fail to comply with the laws governing the organization, which could originate in the home or host country, or both.

- *Direct versus indirect communication*: In hierarchically organized societies with low-context cultures, it is common to reprimand an employee in front of others without attention to face-saving. In contrast, in egalitarian or some high-context societies, treating someone that way would be considered less appropriate or even hostile, rude, or abusive.

  Solution: The work team can avoid this type of conflict by explicitly discussing and reaching agreements about how communication and feedback will occur. To illustrate, in a factory located in the United States, the work team might agree that reprimands or criticism will be given in private. They might agree (or be coached) on the most effective ways to communicate with each other.

- *Personal space, physical contacts, and signs of romantic interest*: For example, when standing in line at a bank or other public space, the correct amount of personal space in the United States is an arm's length or the space of a hula hoop surrounding each of us. In China, the correct amount would be just a few inches. When friends sit next to one another in the United States, they tend to keep this same amount of space, but in many Arabic-speaking countries, friends should sit close enough to smell each other's breath (Neuliep, 2009). It is easy to imagine that an American may misinterpret the closeness in the workplace without understanding that the invasion of personal space is actually a sign of friendship. In some countries, platonic friends of the same sex will hold hands or walk arm in arm down the street. In other countries, this is interpreted as a sign of a romantic relationship. Likewise, inviting a coworker of the opposite sex to lunch could be a sign of collegiality, but in other countries, it would be interpreted as a romantic overture. Eye contact is a sign of respect in most Western countries but is a sign of disrespect in most Asian societies when coming from a subordinate. In many cultures, it is disrespectful for any physical contact to occur outside one's family. This includes simple transactions in which a clerk hands over coins or money in a transaction, being careful to push the coins toward the customer instead of handing them over directly. Out of respect, men in many cultures with high gender distance do not speak to women other than those in their own family. A woman of Western origin may find it disrespectful that a male customer or colleague will not speak to her, but it is generally intended as a sign of respect, rather than disrespect.

  Solution: Being able to read each other's signals comes with time but reading about the cultural habits of other cultures will help you correctly interpret others' behaviors. Then, explaining why your organization chooses this or that cultural habit can be helpful. For instance, ignoring female employees is not acceptable in U.S. workplaces, but it may be helpful to discuss ways to make everyone as comfortable as possible when working across cultural groups.

- *Dress codes and visible expressions of identity:* The way we dress and groom expresses our gender identities, national origin, social class, ethnicity, generational, and even political identities. The desire to stand out as an individual is common in many Western societies, but this individualistic expression can run afoul of a company's desire to present a uniform image across employees or to communicate a brand identity. The desire for uniformity in appearance will be more pronounced in collectivist organizational cultures. Policies against facial hair, head coverings, the wearing of crosses or religious iconography, hairstyles, and even tattoos or piercings can be closely related to one's national or religious culture, which are often protected by laws governing free speech, the free practice of religion, and protection against discrimination based on national origin.

Solution: Dress codes determined through a consensus-based process with representatives from each level or unit within the company often result in less conflict and greater compliance, but they will not necessarily respect diversity unless all impacted identity groups are included in the process. Be sure to weigh the trade-offs between conformity and individuality. Note that generational differences and the tendency to default to majority cultural habits will privilege some over others, making the workplace less welcoming.

- *Sensory preferences*: Even sensory information is filtered through our cultural lenses. The definition of a "good smell" is cultural and linked to our food preferences. Have you ever walked into a fish market? For some cultures, this smells great while for others it is overwhelming. In some cultures, it is expected that natural biological smells will be masked by deodorants or perfumes. In other cultures, those natural smells are considered superior to the smell of chemicals often found in deodorants or perfumes. An American working abroad would expect to conform to local practice on this issue. However, in the U.S. workplace, there is an expectation that body odor, "bad" breath, and other smells should be prevented or masked (Khazan, 2015). In fact, according to Althen and Bennett (2011), Americans believe they are not clean unless they smell as if they came straight out of the shower. Barbara Kingsolver's novel *The Poisonwood Bible* mentions that Congolese residents note a near-absence of smells in the United States compared to the pungency to which they are accustomed. Even different Western countries have different expectations of personal grooming. In the United States, hot water is much less expensive than in France or Italy. Americans expect that everyone will bathe or shower almost daily and use deodorant (Khazan, 2015).

  Solution: Explain the reasoning behind managerial policies and cultural preferences in these matters and try to depersonalize them. Without this intercultural knowledge, there is a tendency to view individuals as "dirty" or "less than." A bicultural translator may be helpful in explaining these cultural preferences in less offensive ways. Clearly, these are difficult subjects on which to seek consensus or share cultural preferences.

- *Challenges unique to multinational corporations (MNCs)*: MNCs are unique because their organizations were born and grew within the legal and cultural context of one country or region and then expanded to create plants or offices in different legal or cultural contexts (e.g., IKEA, VW,

Coca-Cola, Toyota, Siemens, Microsoft, Uber, Samsung, Apple, and Royal Dutch Shell). Many of these companies are iconic examples of the cultures that gave rise to them. Oftentimes, these corporations send top-level managers to run factories or workstations abroad, taking their communication and cultural assumptions with them. Rarely are these managers trained in cross-cultural management skills, with predictably disappointing results. In many cases, the managers sent to work abroad plan to "do their time" and then return home in the hope of a well-deserved promotion. Not only are some of these expansions short lived (see Box 5.1), but even the best examples of success run afoul of unanticipated cultural challenges. Some MNCs explicitly seek to transfer their home culture to the host country by encouraging language lessons on the part of local employees, celebrating home country holidays within the host location, and applying managerial or communications strategies that worked at home.

Solutions: The most successful MNCs can combine the best of the home and host cultures. They train their managers and employees to be nimble cross-cultural communicators. They find a middle path between high- and low-context cultures. They abide by the applicable laws of each country, often going beyond the minimum required in terms of wages, benefits, or environmental policies to find the middle way between practices of their home and host cultures. They find ways to joke about idiosyncratic differences that cause small faux pas or miscommunications. They understand and forgive cross-cultural mistakes while making the effort to learn about home and host culture differences. They acknowledge their own ethnocentric preferences and seek compromises that make everyone comfortable (or make them all equally uncomfortable).

These are simply examples of familiar challenges that occur across cultures. When high-level managers or leaders are transferred from one national cultural context to another, it is advisable to pair them with a coach familiar with intercultural management concepts to avoid faux pas that occur when lessons from one context are applied in an utterly different one.

There are specific suggestions for working with specific home-host culture differences in the following section.

Working Successfully with Multinational Corporations

This section examines the challenges that occur when specific cultures come together at work. These lessons are hard won based on my experiences working with and researching solutions to the problems faced by German, Korean, and Japanese companies that have established factories or divisions in the United States, Canada, and Mexico. To be clear, the location of the facility matters: the challenges faced by a Korean company in Georgia are different from those faced by a German company operating in Mexico or Tennessee. Based on these experiences, this section will provide insights into the problems faced by these MNCs as well as potential solutions.

German Managers Working in the United States

In many U.S.-based plants, the frontline workers include a diverse group of employees from various Latin American countries along with U.S. Americans from various ethnic backgrounds. While many managers come from Germany, some come from other European countries, South America, and Asia. Depending on the nature of the industry (tech versus automobiles), foreign workers at many levels are brought in to fill vacancies, thereby creating a highly diverse workplace. In these corporations, engineers or other technical experts are often promoted into the management ranks with little to no training designed to empower them to manage people. This practice is not limited to MNCs, but is often practiced by U.S. corporations as well, to predictably disappointing results.

Task versus relationship: Germans prefer not to mix business with pleasure. When at work, they prefer to work. They avoid small talk and recreational conversation about their families, sports, and so on. In fact, Germans are less likely than Americans to engage in unimportant conversational topics such as the weather or the outcome of last night's soccer or football game. Since talking will not change the score or the winner, why waste the effort? They prefer to stick to the task at hand and do not necessarily form friendships with coworkers. In contrast, many Americans have "work families" with whom they spend both work and recreational time. They may even spend holidays together and form deep attachments with coworkers. Americans may characterize this preference on task versus relationship as "cold" while Germans may characterize the American preference for relationship building at work as invasive and shallow. Germans are likely to form long-term friendships that outlast their career moves or changes while Americans tend to change friends when they move or encounter a life change (e.g., getting married or divorced, becoming parents). On the other hand, Germans receive approximately eight weeks of paid leave by law in their home country (Lauszat, 2014). Nevertheless, their overall productivity is higher than that of American workers. In 2014, the German company Daimler (later Daimler-Chrysler) created an automatic bounce back email stating that emails received on work holidays would be automatically deleted and would need to be re-sent on a non-holiday (Handelsblatt Global, 2018). Germans work efficiently while at work and enjoy their copious time off while not working. Americans get little paid vacation with zero federal requirement for paid leave. In fact, only 76% of American workers receive any paid vacation (Hess, 2018). Companies offer an average of only ten days paid vacation per worker annually with great variation depending on the rank and length of time with the company (ibid.). Thereby, Americans are much more likely to mix social and recreational time with work. The key to cross-cultural collaboration is to understand the root causes of these differences, to not take them personally, and to acknowledge the "rightness" of each approach in its own way.

Management style: In general, German culture appreciates or accepts hierarchies more than American culture (Expatica, 2018; Neuliep, 2009). As opposed to Americans, Germans typically value clearly articulated, closely followed rules and procedures. Due to their comfort level with hierarchy, Germans do not require their superiors to explain every decision. In contrast, due to the

American preference for equality and no hierarchy, many American workers feel empowered to share their own ideas about how to best do the work or change policies. Germans (along with the British) are likely to find this American tendency a reflection of misplaced hubris. Germans, for example, rarely skip the hierarchy to complain to a higher-level manager (above their own) because they believe it disrespectful to go around one's own supervisor. However, American workers who are not consulted are less likely to exhibit buy-in and fully engage or implement changes with which they disagree. They are likely to complain to the top boss. On the other hand, Germans are likely to be frustrated and annoyed by the American tendency to require explanations, offer their own ideas, or push back against unilateral decision-making. As a result, German culture is better at creating products that consistently meet specifications while American companies tend to be better at innovation and change. An effective cross-cultural manager will recognize that he must lead in a way his employees will understand and appreciate. Otherwise, he will be ineffective. Successful employees will do their best to meet the expectations of their managers while sharing those ideas or concerns they feel only the most important for catching mistakes early or asking questions only as needed to understand how to follow the directions given. They will send the signal of obedience when they can, even if this goes against their cultural tendencies.

Direct communication: Germans will openly criticize each other during meetings without fear that this will damage their working relationships. There is little cultural value placed on face-saving in Germany. Combine this with an emphasis on task over relationship, and you can imagine why Germans are less threatened by public criticism. They are less likely to take it personally. Now, take that approach and transplant it into a U.S. workplace. Without an understanding of the origins of these differences and the willingness to meet in the middle, U.S.-based facilities are likely to experience higher employee turnover or even employment litigation alleging a hostile work environment. Without a cross-cultural lens, these communication patterns could seem like bullying behaviors. The key to less conflict and more collaboration lies in the need to educate German managers to soften their language and give criticism behind closed doors while simultaneously educating Americans and others to understand that these German communication habits are not meant as personal attacks.

Communicating across cultures may be challenging and sometimes uncomfortable, but it gets easier with practice.

Gender distance: Gender roles are more rigid and patriarchal in Germany than in the United States. There are fewer women in management roles in Germany than in the United States. In part, Germans tend to attribute this to the likelihood that many women will use Germany's generous family leave policies to take up to two years of paid leave per child. Therefore, they rack up less experience, and companies may be hesitant to groom them for leadership roles, only to lose them to family leave. German mothers who work are often labeled with derogatory terms (e.g., Rabenmutter, meaning Raven-mother) and socially ostracized (Wecker, 2015). Even though most German corporations have committed to recruiting more women for corporate boards, there are few significant changes to corporate cultures that exclude, silence, or dismiss the contribution of women.

According to Bennhold, "Despite a battery of government measures—some introduced in the past year or so—and ever more passionate debate about gender roles, only about 14 percent of German mothers with one child resume full-time work, and only 6 percent of those with two" (Bennhold, 2011). One particularly challenging obstacle to female workforce participation in Germany stems from the fact that the majority of German primary schools close by lunchtime so that children can eat lunch at home with their mothers (Bennhold, 2010). While this is slowly changing, the cultural assumption against women working remains in place. When women make it into the German workforce, male managers share three reasons they do not rise to managerial roles:

> A 2009 study commissioned by the Ministry of Family illustrated this bias. The Sinus Sociovision institute in Heidelberg surveyed male and female managers in German companies and identified three patterns of thinking among male bosses: Those who simply don't think women are cut out for it; those who think they are, but fear their colleagues don't and worry about cohesion; and those who say that in theory gender does not matter but in practice women who make it "overcompensate" and are not "authentic." (Bennhold, 2011)

These habits of excluding women and minimizing their contributions at work travel with German managers to the U.S. workplace, leaving German corporations with a smaller percentage of women and minorities than some of their U.S. competitors (Warner & Corley, 2017). Women of color are represented in lower numbers in both Germany and the United States. While many corporate boards in Germany are required to include female representation, this hasn't necessarily trickled down to lower levels of management. In a 2018 study of six countries, Germany had by far the fewest women in top leadership roles: United States (24.8%), Sweden (24.1%), United Kingdom (20.1%), Poland (15.5%), France (14.5%), and Germany (12.15%; Sullivan, 2018).

For German managers to succeed in U.S. workplaces, they must pursue active policies to recruit, develop, and promote both the presence and the contribution of women at all levels of the organization. Without consciously working against cultural predispositions, German companies operating in the United States are likely to advertently or inadvertently exclude or minimize the contribution of women in the workplace, leaving them vulnerable to litigation, turnover, and simply lacking the benefit their perspectives provide. Proactive human resource managers will prepare Germans to work successfully in the United States, Canada, and potentially elsewhere by helping them change their view of women in the workplace as necessary.

Time: Germans have a strong monochronic time preference, seeking to stick to schedules and deadlines. Meetings should start and end on time. Americans are punctual compared to many other cultures and most will have few problems conforming to this expectation. However, employees from polychronic countries may struggle at first to adjust (e.g., Mexico, Haiti, Colombia, and India). German factories in Latin America are likely to have greater challenges in reaching shared understandings around punctuality than is the case in the United States and Canada.

Decision-making: In brief, German culture prioritizes in-depth research and planning before implementing decisions. In contrast, U.S. culture prioritizes learning by doing, meaning there is a tendency to experiment with a new process or product, see what works, and make changes based on trial and error. Neither approach is more "right," but these differences can lead to friction if unaddressed.

Japanese Managers Located in the United States

It is common for Japanese managers in MNCs to be required to serve three to five years at an American, Canadian, or Western operation, although there is a widespread belief they do so hesitantly and without much enjoyment. For some who serve too long abroad, their position at home becomes unavailable, and the Japanese colleagues may worry they have taken on too many American habits.

Japanese culture is high context and prefers hierarchy-formality, while U.S. culture is low context and more informal. The dress code involves dark colors and formal attire. Handshakes are reserved for formal business settings while bowing is more common in daily work life (Global Affairs Canada, 2018). Japan's high-context culture means more of the meaning is embedded in non-verbal language, with many culturally known "scripts" determining what is acceptable to say and how to act (Neuliep, 2009). Surnames are used at work, even among longtime coworkers. Japanese culture, more than others, conveys power through many nonverbal mechanisms, public displays of anger from a superior to a subordinate (but not in reverse), and the expectation that those working with the boss stay until the boss leaves each day. Like most German companies, "Every decision, no matter how small it may seem, should go through the chain of command and get the stamp of approval from the boss. Employees should immediately report any problems to their bosses before trying to take care of anything on their own" (Merchant, 2018). This will likely cause friction with American workers who prefer to have their individualism and autonomy recognized through some degree of independence at work. Instead, Japanese companies prioritize work in teams, valuing the team's collective successes and needs above those of the individual.

Since even small decisions are well vetted at all levels in the chain of command, they are generally well thought out and easier to implement because all impacted levels will be familiar with the decisions made. In an effort to assist Canadian employees working with Japanese firms, the Canadian government issued this description of decision-making within Japanese firms:

> Firstly, gather and analyze all related data, examine pros and cons thoroughly while exploring the business case and feasibility of each. Secondly, communicate a new strategy with immediate authorities and solicit their feedback. Sometimes the first two steps are repeated several times while a strategy is further refined and widely communicated within an organization. This process is called "Nemawashi"—and consists of an informal way to gain consensus. Once everyone is well informed and approves the strategy, it reaches the final stage of the decision-making process. During a final formal meeting, the decision is signed-off. (Global Affairs Canada, 2018)

Japanese communication styles between peers include a desire to maintain harmony and avoid open confrontation. Unlike the American habit of filling silence with words, in Japanese culture, silence may be used to give people time to think and process information. It is rude to interrupt someone in Japan, so when in doubt, err on the side of silence. On the positive side, when mistakes are made, Japanese companies search for solutions more than blame while American companies may do the opposite. Similarly, Japanese managers are not afraid of doing the frontline work and pitching in to meet deadlines. This makes them more knowledgeable about the problems and solutions needed for success. Because they are all in it together (collectivism), there is little individual praise or recognition for hard work. This may be frustrating for Americans who feel that individual work should garner individual recognition (Rehfeld, 1990).

Japanese people tend to avoid confrontation with others, and as a result, they often do not explicitly express a negative response. For instance, when they receive a proposal, they say "*Kentoshimasu,*" which means, "I/we will consider it." However, that may just be a polite response, used even if they are not planning to positively consider the proposal. It is therefore important for non-Japanese people to pay close attention to any subtle remarks or slightly negative phrases, and be aware that the remarks or phrases may have stronger meanings than it would appear. Non-Japanese people also need to become sensitive to the nonverbal cues of their Japanese counterparts—these may also indicate discomfort or disagreement. In replying to any of these indirect disagreements, an appropriate response would be to say that you would welcome receiving further considerations and recommended adjustments. Any obstacles to solve or further negotiating points would be raised by the Japanese at a subsequent time, not immediately (Global Affairs Canada, 2018).

In terms of intercultural relationships, unlike Germans, Japanese employees frequently socialize after work to forge strong ties and network for advancement (Merchant, 2018). This is especially true for older men but slightly less common in the United States than Japan due to the lack of public transportation in many U.S. cities. There appear to be generational effects too, as younger workers feel freer to go home to their families after work.

Japanese managers work long hours: six-day workweeks are common. In recent years, the Japanese government has sought to reduce this cultural practice. The term *Karou-shi* refers to dying from overwork. Workdays usually run nine to twelve hours for managers. Of course, hourly employees are less likely to work such long hours, but many employees are salaried. Both Japanese and American managers rarely use all of their vacation days because they have so much work waiting for them. If they use their vacation time, they will not be able to complete the assigned work, which is similar to many American managers, with over 60% of Americans working during their vacations (Merchant, 2018). Contrast this with German workers who receive approximately eight weeks of paid time off and use it all yet have the highest workplace productivity of all three groups. While Japanese firms have the longest working hours, they also have the lowest worker productivity of all developed economies (Lewis, 2015). The next cultural frontier for Japanese companies is to move from measuring input (work hours) to measuring output (productivity and profitability). Americans may be able to help with that effort.

There are key Japanese management principles worthy of understanding. The Kaizen method is comprised of five key elements, all focused on making small, consistent process and product improvements. This idea was borrowed and termed "Total Quality Management," or TQM, in many U.S. companies (12 Manage, 2018). The five key elements to Kaizen include the following: team-work; personal discipline; improved morale; quality circles; and suggestions for improvement that may come from any level but must be vetted at all levels before implementation (12 Manage, 2018). Through quality circles, employees come together regularly to brainstorm improvements and troubleshoot prob-lems. The focus is on continuous improvements. This overcomes the challenge of hierarchically organized workplaces that continues to plague German compa-nies because hierarchy has a tendency to place each person in a narrowly defined role with specific tasks. Employees in hierarchically organized companies tend to myopically focus on their part of the overall endeavor and keep new ideas to themselves to "stay in their lane," as Americans would say. The use of quality circles and team-based work helps Japanese companies to more easily solve prob-lems and make improvements, whereas individualism combined with hierarchy in German workplaces make it harder to implement similar changes.

In terms of social class divisions, there is little poverty and fewer class divisions in Japan than in most Western countries (Brasor & Tsubuko, 2018). There are few racial divisions as well due in large part to the ethnic and racial homogeneity of Japanese society. Japanese people are not particularly religious, yet they may participate in cultural celebrations with religious roots. While the establishment of professional ties between coworkers is important, favoritism is uncommon and viewed as unfair to the group (Global Affairs Canada, 2018). Japanese firms have a cultural practice of reserving the highest management positions for Japanese managers, which has resulted in complaints related to employment discrimination based on national origin, race, and gender (Kilborn, 1991). Additionally, Japanese firms tend to exclude non-Japanese managers from many meetings for two main reasons: First, language barriers make it more laborious for Japanese managers to include Americans and, second, non-Japanese managers are less bound by company loyalty and may leave for a position elsewhere. Japanese managers do not want to invest time and effort in training non-Japanese managers, only to have them leave. While European firms operating in the United States engage in similar practices, these are more pronounced within Japanese companies.

The low birth rate in Japan has led to calls for increased immigration and more women in the workforce; nonetheless, these remain nascent efforts. Women are mostly absent from Japanese corporations, especially in management positions. According to one expert, "The Japanese business system prioritizes the lifelong employment of male workers in order to sustain the male-breadwinner family model and insider-oriented management, and to stabilize industrial rela-tions. Workers are expected to devote themselves to one company, working long hours in exchange for rigid age-based promotions and pay" (Nemoto, 2017). As a result, Japanese women who work outside the home are likely to hold only low-level positions regardless of their higher education out of a belief they may leave the workforce to raise children and for the sake of upholding a cultural preference for male leaders. This tendency for women to appear mostly at the bottom of the organization's power and wealth structure is known as **vertical sex segregation** and is most common in Asian companies, then German and European companies, and less so in Canadian and American firms (Nemoto, 2017).

The gender distance in Japan is quite high due to the Confucian culture, with male and female roles clearly defined and social ostracism for variation from those norms. In Japanese society, male infidelity is common and more socially accepted than female infidelity in romantic relationships (Global Affairs Canada, 2018). Gay men are more accepted than lesbians, and male-to-female transgender individuals are accepted in society (ibid.). These rigid gender roles make it difficult for female managers to succeed in Japanese companies operating in the United States and Canada and therefore result in increased litigation based on allegations of violations of U.S. labor laws.

Lastly, Japanese etiquette is critical. You should never enter a room or sit unless invited to do so. Do not put your hands in your pockets while speaking, sit up straight, do not cross your legs, and leave your hands at your sides while communicating (Lastauskaite, 2015). Smile and be patient while slowly building relationships and creating a positive record of long hours. Attend as many social events as possible and allow others to save face by never saying "no." Instead, say phrases like, "Attending that event will be difficult" (Lastauskaite, 2015). Due to the language barrier, they may avoid you. Do not push against this, but instead, honor it by ensuring Japanese translators are present whenever possible in order to minimize their discomfort. Bring small gifts such as candy or cookies to share with new contacts. While Japanese businessmen working in the United States may try to accommodate local expectations, your willingness to make them comfortable using familiar behaviors will likely be noticed and appreciated.

The greater the cultural distance between two groups, the more effort it will take to bridge the gap in communication styles, power relations, and the values placed on identity group affiliation. Patience and preparation are the keys to success. Additionally, you will need to decide about when compromise is justified versus when it makes sense to stick to your own culture's values and approaches (see Box 5.2). How would you navigate the intercultural ethical issues posed when working as an American abroad or within an MNC based in your home country?

For Japanese managers working with Americans, the advice is to respect the desire of Americans to spend time with their families after work and on weekends. This will increase their loyalty more than spending social time together. Do not confuse long hours with productivity. Actively promote the presence and contribution of women and non-Japanese managers, as they can help you to better communicate with and manage American workers and regulators. Seek out someone familiar with both cultures to act as both a linguistic and a cultural translator. This will help you avoid unpleasant surprises.

BOX 5.2. SWIMMING AT THE U.S. EMBASSY IN INDIA

Imagine you work as a U.S. diplomat stationed at the embassy in New Delhi, India. The mission of the U.S. Embassy is to promote American business interests abroad while assisting American citizens living, working, or traveling in India. The building and grounds of the embassy are considered sovereign U.S. territory and are often used like a country club. Americans and powerful Indian politicians and businesspeople meet there to negotiate deals during parties designed to celebrate U.S. cultural events such as the Fourth of July. Most Indians are Hindu and recognize a rigid caste system in which the generally lighter-skinned Brahmins are at the top, and the darker-skinned Dalits or "untouchables" are so far below that they are considered outside the caste system (BBC News, 2017). Observant Hindus seek to avoid physical contact with Dalits, as touching them (or anything they touch) could taint one's spirit. As such, strict segregation is observed in many venues of public life. When Americans stationed at the embassy bring their kids to swim in the embassy pools, their "untouchable" nannies cannot accompany the children into the pool because a nearby sign clearly states the following: "In deference to local norms, no Dalits may swim in the pool." Some Americans find this a repugnant decision that enables societal bias instead of using the U.S. Embassy to model a different, more American, outlook. Still, if the embassy goes against the preferences of rich Indians, then fewer business deals will be made. If you were promoted to the position of ambassador, would you promote U.S. values of equality or adjust to local norms that support segregation?

South Korean Managers Working in the United States

There are important similarities and differences between South Korean and Japanese management styles. They are both high-context, hierarchically organized cultures with high levels of gender distance. Longevity leads to promotion, and those with greater age and experience receive great deference. Like Japanese companies, in Korean companies each person has a well-defined role, and it is critical to gain a deep understanding of each person's role and their connections to others in the organization. It is the web of relationships and the hierarchical relationships between those relationships that tell you how to act with each person in each situation. Korean managers often put relationships above deadlines, but they also understand the need to remain punctual to meet the expectations of Americans and most Europeans (Commisceo Global, 2018).

South Korea's modern economy was created in the aftermath of the Korean War (1950–1953), yet Korean policies have always limited direct foreign investment; it is an interesting amalgamation of Korean and U.S. cultures. Korean managers tend to be more open to learning with and from U.S. managers, seeking to find a middle path. Korean management styles are

> A combination of Confucianism and western behavior, depending upon the person's education and background. Since this is a hierarchical culture, most decisions are made at the top and then given to the employees to implement. Personal opinions and criticism are suppressed, and the team generally follows the ideas of the more senior members of the team. (Commisceo Global, 2018)

In contrast to German management approaches, disagreements and criticism are voiced privately to allow for face-saving. Like German firms, instructions come from the top down, and there are few mechanisms to allow for bottom-up feedback or innovation (World Business Culture, 2018). Additionally, there is a cultural practice called *inwha*, which focuses on the importance of harmony between those of equal rank and status.

Unlike Japan, Korea has more distinct social classes and a preference for those of a lower class to remain in lower positions within the organization. "Since social class is important to the culture, it is nearly impossible for a lower-class person to supervise a person from a higher class. Intercultural sensitivity is essential as it is a serious breach of etiquette to put a young person in charge of older workers. Employees expect companies, and their managers, to be paternalistic" (Commisceo Global, 2018). Supervisors will often take an interest in the personal lives of their subordinates, seeking to help them manage the challenges of life. This may seem invasive to Americans and Germans but is seen as a way to ensure the reciprocity of favors and loyalty between those of different ranks in Korean companies. It also builds relationships that may assist with team functioning.

Gender distance in Korean firms is relatively similar to that of the Japanese culture. In fact, in Korea, managers often reprimand and fire a female employee for getting married or pregnant, even though laws against this form of discrimination exist. If they do not fire pregnant employees, they must provide them with a year of paid maternity leave, from which only 30% return due to a lack of acceptable childcare (*The Economist*, 2016). As legal protections against these behaviors have grown, firms may pressure women to quit by giving them too much or too little work, unpleasant work tasks, or other moves designed to make their work life unbearable. There are more working women in Korea than Japan, especially those who have (increasingly) chosen not to marry or have children. International companies located in Korea are more likely to hire women than are local Korean companies. Since the culture values education, Korean women tend to be well-educated, underutilized, and accustomed to receiving less pay than men (*The Economist*, 2016). Women are almost completely absent in the highest levels of Korean corporations: "Female representation on corporate boards is just 1 per cent, compared with 2 per cent in Japan and 8 per cent in China. Underscoring the challenges, most female Korean executives are either the children or grandchildren of the founders of their company" (Jung-a, 2013). However, many Korean managers working in the United States are able to work successfully with American female colleagues, so long as their family lives do not interfere with the long work hours expected of all leaders.

Overall, it seems that Korean firms located in the United States maintain many of their cultural preferences yet accommodate to local cultural norms more readily than Japanese companies, while this sentiment is not uniformly shared. To succeed as a non-Korean worker, be sure to familiarize yourself with Korean work ethics and communication practices. Understand that the protections against discrimination are weak in Korea. In return, Korean managers must familiarize themselves with these differences and adjust to U.S. work-life expectations and labor laws.

Working across Generations

As indicated in the beginning of this chapter, our culture prepares us to survive in the environment in which each of us was raised. That "environment" includes rapidly changing factors such as the climate, gender identities, economic conditions, race relations, work-life balance, and so on. Employees who entered the workforce in the 1960s had vastly different expectations than those entering it now. Generational knowledge creates its own form of ethnocentrism in which each generation tends to prefer and prioritize its own way of doing things, leading to inevitably unproductive conflict and even litigation because . . . times change, as they should. Most of us do not want to go back to workplace norms of 1965 in which women, people of color, and LGBTQ people were rarely considered for leadership positions. Bullying, hazing, and sexual harassment are taken more seriously now, new parents may be entitled to paid leave (depending on their state or company), and people who are sick are encouraged to stay home.

Here is a quick "hack" to help you understand and predict generational changes. When you watch children play, you can see generational differences that predict how their lives will be different from yours or from your parents'. For example, a boy born in 1960 might have been criticized for playing with dolls. It was less common for men of that generation to be seen as caregivers of children, so they were encouraged to play with trucks or tanks. Fast-forward 20 years, and boys are less likely to be criticized for playing with dolls or an Easy-Bake Oven. Why? Men are increasingly sharing childcare and homemaking duties with their partners. Remember when millennial children were criticized for spending too much time playing video games indoors instead of outside with friends? Then, when the pandemic happened and work/school went online for many types of occupations, it all made sense. This generation was prepared in a way that older generations were not. The play of children reveals the future of socioeconomic factors. What can you predict based on the play of children today?

The world is facing the biggest generation gap since the 1960s. Boomers (born 1946–1964), Gen Xers (born 1965–1980), millennials (born 1980–1996), and Gen Zers (1996–2020) were raised to inhabit different worlds. Catastrophic events shape each generation's character, habits, and preferences. The Great Depression and World War II left behind a generation of frugal, hardworking people often unwilling to "rock the boat" for fear of the deprivation that accompanies unemployment. Gen Xers were the first generation of "latchkey" kids, left alone at home as divorce rates soared and single parents worked long hours. They became independent, driven, and often in need of control over their environments. They became "helicopter" parents who attended every soccer match and parent-teacher conference as overcompensation. Millennials saw their parents struggle through the Great Recession, when even educated, hardworking parents lost their jobs, houses, and important parts of their identities. They grew up in an era of greater diversity and work well across all types of difference. Gen Z, while new to the workforce, appreciates face-to-face contact, having been deprived of it as young people during the COVID-19 pandemic. They strive to attain a healthy work-life balance while being (perhaps) more independent than millennials, although it may be too early to tell.

Each generation brings its lessons, preferences, and talents to the modern workplace, even if that is comprised of a home office or digital nomads. Stop and think about what you like about your own generation's work habits as well as what you admire about those of other generations. As a manager, the goal is to appreciate everyone, knowing that generational events and trends inform how each person exists in the work world. Can your organization survive without hiring and working successfully across generations? If not, then seek to refrain from criticizing generational differences and focus on the ways in which each employee can contribute to their fullest potential.

Recently, I had the pleasure of coaching a 65-year-old law firm partner who was frustrated by the fact that the lawyers in their 20s weren't "dressing appropriately." The firm represented artists and entertainers. The young lawyers dressed more casually than the older attorneys, but often were better at building rapport with and retaining new clients. As an external collaboration consultant, I was asked to "make them dress right." My response? "If you can figure out how to get a 26-year-old woman to dress like a 65-year-old man, please let me know. I have never seen it work yet." In essence, how important is it for us to all be the same, versus allowing us to reap the benefits of being ourselves? These are important trade-offs, but there are likely more important issues upon which to focus to build a successful team across generations.

Consider implementing a teambuilding program in which employees pair up in groups of two or three to share ideas, experiences, and skills across generations. At its best, this should be two-way mentoring in which each generation shares information and perspectives with the other, with some preparatory coaching focused on the skills of perspective taking (e.g., putting yourself in the other's shoes), asking good questions, and being open to learning from those younger/older/different than us. Encourage relationship building so that when the team members need to work on a shared task, they have developed a deeper appreciation of each other's talents.

When we take the time to understand why a generation tends to behave in a specific way, then it is easier for us not only to appreciate their attributes; we can also show respect and kindness in ways that encourage rather than inhibit teamwork.

Critical Conclusions for the Intercultural Workplace

Working across cultures and generations poses challenges, but there is potential for significant personal, professional, and organizational growth. The key for all managers is to cultivate a disposition of openness to other ways of working. Additionally, we need to help others fight the natural tendency to prefer their own outlook and work habits. Working across cultural and generational groups can be challenging and requires us to stretch and grow in new ways. We will make mistakes, but we must normalize these challenges, allow for the learning curve, and do what we can to prepare ourselves to succeed.

In sum, our cultural affiliations and identities shape how we see the world and view fairness. Managers need to take the time to ask their colleagues and employees about their perceptions and to explain their own. Workplaces develop their own cultural norms over time. Having fair, transparent, and culturally sensitive processes to make joint decisions when appropriate can provide an opportunity to build deeper relationships and understanding among those with whom we share our work lives.

ELISE AT MAIN STREET BAKERIES IN MONTREAL

Before taking any action to expand across the border, Elise spent three weeks visiting various bakeries, coffee shops, and grocery stores in Montreal to observe how people interact and carry out business. She made it a point to speak with managers and employees—making sure to seek out both Anglophones and Francophones—since she had read that significant cultural differences exist between them within Canadian cultures. She also noticed that Montreal is an international city, with immigrants from all around the world added to the mix. She met with regulators from the Departments of Labor, Commerce, and the Environment to better understand the myriad of different regulations that would impact her business. While she has a team of managers and a corporate attorney to help with these matters, she wanted to understand some of these issues firsthand.

Upon returning home, she began the hiring process, looking first for a bilingual and bicultural project manager with experience working on both sides of the border and within Anglophone and Francophone groups. She began studying and reading about the experiences of other U.S. companies that straddled the border in order to learn from their mistakes and victories. With this information, along with the help of experienced Canadian managers hired to roll out the first few branches, Elise was poised for success in her venture.

KEY TERMS

active bystander
collectivist societies (collectivism)
cultural distance
culture
diversity
ethnocentrism
gender role differentiation (high or low)
groupthink
high-context cultures
individualistic societies
   (individualism)

locus of control (internal or external)
low-context cultures
monochronic orientation (to time)
monoculturalism
multiculturalism
nonverbal communication
polychronic orientation (to time)
privilege
scripted conversation
structural violence
vertical sex segregation

DISCUSSION QUESTIONS

1. Analyze and discuss the communication styles prevalent in your workplace. Is there an overall preference for direct or indirect communication? Do the employees generally share a polychronic or monochronic approach to time, or is there an absence of consensus on this issue? What is your organization's approach to gender role differentiation? Do men and women tend to do different types of work, or is the work done interchangeably? Why? Does this work to the advantage of one group over the other? As a manager or employee, what is your role in addressing any concerns regarding the ways in which cultural and generational differences are addressed (or unaddressed)?

2. Using the Power and Diversity Triangle (see Figure 5.1), spend some time developing a list of things that people closer to the bottom know about those at or near the top, but not vice versa. How does this impact the organization? To what extent is this normal and healthy? Are demographic characteristics associated with different levels of the Power and Diversity Triangle at your organization? If so, how can the organization become more reflective of the diversity of its community and/or customers at all levels?

3. Have you ever been an active bystander or seen one intervene? Has there been a time you intervened or wished you had done so? What workplace behaviors are ripe for active bystander interventions? What are your limits or boundaries, meaning, which behaviors would you try to ignore, and which would provoke you to become an active bystander? Knowing your boundaries will prepare you in case an issue arises.

4. Think of an organization with which you are familiar. How well is it doing on all three levels of organizational culture (the relational, the symbolic, and the material)? Are material benefits distributed or earned without any biases related to race, gender, disability, and others? Has a pay equity study been done to look for differences in pay based on race, sex, or national origin? Why or why not?

EXERCISES

1. With your classmates, coworkers, family, or others, create an active bystander response to these scenarios. You can act them out or just discuss options for effective bystander interventions.

   a. You see a parent screaming at her three-year-old in the parking lot of the grocery store. Then, she grabs a hairbrush and starts hitting the child with it.

   b. Your colleagues have a habit of making crude, sexual remarks about the body shapes of other employees when speaking in the break room. You just walked in on yet another of these conversations.

   c. At the bar after work, your coworker says that the new employee probably got his/her/their job only because of their status as a member of group X (e.g., race, gender, age). This comment was made in a group of five coworkers. What if it was made in front of a group of 100 employees?

d. You are on a hiring committee tasked with hiring an upper-level manager. Two of the committee members just said, "I don't think we should even consider Mary Jones for this job. She has three little kids."

e. On the subway, you see a young man slide next to a seemingly shy, attractive young woman who he does not seem to know. After his attempts to speak with her are rebuffed, she gets up and moves a few seats away to get away from him. Then he follows her. She appears scared.

f. You just saw an employee mocking and mimicking another employee who is openly gay.

g. Your new boss is an immigrant, originally from _____ (could be nearly any foreign country). Your coworker tells you, "Sheesh, I don't want to work for that _____ (fill in the blank with an assumed racial/immigrant slur)." How do you respond?

h. You stuck your head outside your office because you heard a supervisor loudly berating an underperforming employee. You heard him use the words "stupid," "lazy," and "destined to fail" in his reprimand so loudly that others are also sticking their heads out of their doors.

i. You came to pick up your son early from football practice for a dentist's appointment. You just heard the coach call a player a "sissy" because the kid said he needed to get some water because he was dizzy and nauseous from the heat. The coach yelled at him, "No water for wimps, sissy. Give me two laps around the track." The assistant coaches are not intervening.

2. Alligator River Exercise

Read the following story to yourself or aloud as a class. Then, rank the characters from most (1) to least (5) honorable on the table provided (see Table 5.1). Then, pair up with a partner and write down their ranking. Share information as to why you ranked them as you did and see if you can reach any agreements on the ranking of the characters. Enter any agreements in Column C. Then, add one or more members to your group and start the process again. At the end of the exercise, re-list your own rankings and take note of any changes that may have occurred because of your discussions. Try it at home as well for a great dinner table conversation.

Alligator River Story

Once upon a time there was a woman named Abigail who was in love with a man named Gregory. Gregory lived on the shore of a river. Abigail lived on the opposite shore of the river. The river that separated the two lovers was teeming with man-/woman-eating alligators. Abigail wanted to cross the river to be with Gregory. Unfortunately, the bridge had been washed away by a heavy storm. Then Abigail went to ask Sinbad,

Table 5.1   Alligator River Exercise

My ranking	My colleague's ranking	Our shared scores after discussion	Shared scores (group of 3+ members)	My final scores
1.				
2.				
3.				
4.				
5.				

a riverboat captain, to take her across. He said he would be glad to if she would consent to go to bed with him before he takes her across. She promptly refused and went to a friend named Vana to explain her plight. Vana did not want to be involved at all in the situation. Abigail felt her only alternative was to accept Sinbad's terms. Sinbad fulfilled his promise to Abigail and delivered her into the arms of Gregory. When she told Gregory about what she did to cross the river, Gregory cast her aside with disdain. Heartsick and dejected, Abigail turned to Slug with her tale of woe. Slug, feeling compassion for Abigail, sought out Gregory and beat him brutally. As the sun sets on the horizon, we hear Abigail laughing.

Characters: Abigail, Gregory, Sinbad, Vana, Slug

Rank them Most Honorable (1) to Least Honorable (5)

Alligator River Debrief

After using this exercise more than 150 times with various groups, a number of key lessons come through, although you are likely to find additional lessons in your group.

a. National cultures, generations, gender, and identity matter. I have run this exercise with groups of Chinese government officials, Peace Studies faculty in India, German managers, Saudi Arabian and Palestinian businessmen, various corporate and governmental organizations in the United States, and mixed groups of graduate and undergraduate students. Some notable patterns emerged:

- Chinese officials (men and women, all between the ages of 28 and 40) consistently ranked Vana the lowest. Why? Confucian cultures place a strong emphasis on the role and duties of a friend, which Vana did not fulfill. No one expected Vana to solve the problem, but she should have been empathetic and loyal.

- In India, Slug rated lowest overall because of a cultural preference for nonviolence.
- With a group of NGO workers focused on refugee issues, one attendee noted that Sinbad meets the definition of a "human trafficker" because he commodified Abigail and used her to an end rather than intrinsically worthwhile.
- The Middle Eastern group of businessmen ranked Sinbad highly because he kept his word and took Abigail across the river. He could have taken advantage of her by refusing to honor the bargain after he got what he wanted. While most ranked Abigail low due to a cultural preference for chastity in women (what Hofstede would rank as high gender role distance), some of these men rated her highly and Gregory the lowest because she sacrificed herself for him while he failed to protect her.
- U.S. Americans, as expected, are quite diverse in their viewpoints on this exercise, which reflects their diversity regarding ethnicity, generation, national origin, sexual orientation, religion, and so on.
- Generational differences: Imagine how your own grandmother might rank these differently than you even though you have some shared (and some different) cultural identities. Answers change across generations.

b. The first step to problem-solving and working together successfully is to rehumanize, not dehumanize those with whom we have conflict. We must be able to successfully engage in dialogue to get to know one another as people rather than solely as a representative member of some identity group (e.g., Black/White/Latino, millennial, LGBTQ). Once we see each other as people with different yet valid worldviews, then we can find a way to work together and overcome shared problems or work through differences in preferences.

c. What else did this exercise teach you?

3. Cross-Cultural Dialogue Scenarios

Read each scenario and try to determine the cultural roots of the misunderstanding. Do not read the debriefs until you have first puzzled through the conflicts. For the purposes of this exercise, you can assume the cultural backgrounds of these individuals based on their names, even though that is a risky assumption in real life.

Scenario: Many Hands Make Light Work

Professor Smith: Hello Professor Wan. I am terribly sorry that I had to report the Chinese students for plagiarism.

Professor Wan: I heard about that. Can you tell me more about the problem?

Professor Smith: There were fourteen Chinese students out of a class of twenty-five. This was an individual assignment, but they turned in nearly identical papers.

Professor Wan: Hmmm . . . fourteen students, all cheaters? That is too bad. Were the papers any good?

Scenario: Job Opening

Mr. Elliott: Have you posted the job announcement yet?
Mrs. Hernandez: Good morning, Mr. Elliott. Not yet. I have the perfect person for that job. My nephew is a really good boy and would be perfect for the job.
Mr. Elliott: Great, tell him to apply.
Mrs. Hernandez: Apply?

Scenario: A Job Well Done

Mr. Jones: Mr. Yoshida has done a wonderful job at the Alabama plant.
Mr. Takeda: Yes, the team has done well.
Mr. Jones: Perhaps we should give him a plaque and thank him at our next plant meeting.
Mr. Takeda: That is possible. Perhaps we could consider it and discuss it again later.

Scenario Debriefs

Many Hands Make Light Work. At the root of this miscommunication are cultural assumptions related to individualism versus collectivism. American students are generally expected to work independently and display their knowledge through tests or research papers. In Chinese culture, students will often work together to study and produce group projects. For one or a few students to stand out above all others would be embarrassing to them and inappropriate. The U.S. cultural assumption is that one must be able to stand on his own while the Confucian assumption is that you will always have your friends and colleagues around to help you as needed. If some students know more, they should share it with others. What good does it do to keep this knowledge to yourself when the goal is for everyone to learn? *Takeaway*: When working with collectivist cultures, stick to group assignments. If an assignment or test must be accomplished individually, explain the reasoning behind this, and separate the team members to avoid the tendency to stick together.

Job Opening. Why would Mrs. Hernandez need to advertise the position if she already knows the perfect candidate? American employment law is built upon the assumption that each person should get a job or promotion based solely on merit and skill set despite a cultural history of racism, sexism, and other "isms." In Mrs. Hernandez's way of thinking, someone may be trained to do the necessary work, but you cannot train someone to be a good person or to fit in with the existing team. Out of filial piety and duty, Mrs. Hernandez's nephew would likely work hard, and she would not have recommended him if he could not do a good job. Mrs. Hernandez and Mr. Elliott both want a good person to fill the position, but the former put the emphasis on personal characteristics and family ties while the latter emphasized previous training and a skill set that is listed on a résumé.

A Job Well Done. Mr. Jones is making a culture-based assumption that an individual who has worked hard will want public acknowledgment of his efforts. On the other hand, Mr. Takeda is likely to believe the work done by Mr. Yoshida reflects the efforts of the whole team rather than the sole efforts of Mr. Yoshida. By recognizing one person above others, it would embarrass Mr. Yoshida and possibly alienate his coworkers. Note how Mr. Takeda does not openly disagree with Mr. Jones out of respect and a desire to maintain harmony. Mr. Jones should read between the lines to understand what is meant rather than what is said due to the high-context/low-context differences.

SUGGESTED SUPPLEMENTAL READINGS

Avruch, K. (2003). Type I and type II errors in culturally sensitive conflict resolution practice. *Conflict Resolution Quarterly, 20,* 351–371.

Brothers, L. M. (2014). Identity and culture in ombudsman practice. *Conflict Resolution Quarterly, 31,* 421–434. https://doi.org/10.1002/crq.21095

Neuliep, J. W. (2017). *Intercultural communications: An intercultural approach* (7th ed.). Sage.

NOTE

1. https://studentaffairs.du.edu/health-counseling-center/promoting-health-wellbeing/active-bystander%5D

PART II

THE PREVENTION AND RESOLUTION OF INTERNAL ORGANIZATIONAL CONFLICTS

6

Building Healthy
Organizational Cultures

The Foundation of Success

Culture eats strategy for breakfast.
—Peter Drucker

Imagine an organization that hires the best people, has a motivating mission, yet turnover is high; effectiveness is hampered. Lawsuits and scandals recently damaged the company's brand name and reputation. Profits are down. This happens when an organization's internal culture is dysfunctional. Bullying, high levels of attrition, quiet quitting, absenteeism, disengagement, sexual harassment, discrimination, embezzlement, sabotage, and other forms of unethical behaviors are all *symptoms* of a poor organizational culture. Until the culture is changed, the symptoms will continue even after "problem" employees have been fired. As Peter Drucker points out, culture problems will stymie attempts to change policies, procedures, and strategies. You simply cannot plant the seed of positive change into the toxic soil of a dysfunctional organizational culture and expect it to thrive. This chapter teaches you how to diagnose culture problems in organizations and design interventions for change at every level. Life is too short to work in an unpleasant environment.

Learning Objectives

- Recognize the symptoms of functional versus dysfunctional organizational cultures.
- Diagnose the root causes of recurring organizational conflict.
- Demonstrate active bystander skills as they specifically relate to changing organizational culture.
- Create assessment tools to measure the health of an organization's culture.
- Identify barriers to organizational change.
- Demonstrate methods for creating positive organizational cultures.

JOHN AT THE BUREAU OF RECLAMATION

John has undertaken a needs assessment to better understand why some units seem to function smoothly and with less turnover than others (see Chapter 9 for more on conducting a needs assessment). He used an anonymous survey instrument to conduct an employee morale survey; tracked turnover and absenteeism by unit; and solicited a list of unresolved and recurring problems from employees. Of the five units he supervises, he found one that has high marks on every score, one that is uniformly underperforming, and then four in the middle. On a scale of one to ten, the overall employee satisfaction was 6.5, with great variation between units. Alarmingly, three separate employees named one specific manager as being a "bully," describing him as "disrespectful" to those who are lower on the power hierarchy. It is no surprise that this unit had the lowest scores and highest turnover.

Yet firing people is quite hard at John's agency, and rarely his first choice anyway. In fact, low performers are often recommended for a promotion or lateral move when their supervisor has had enough. This is called "failing up," and it is common in the most dysfunctional organizations. John needs to develop a plan to improve culture overall, with specific attention to the units with the lowest scores. This chapter will help him accomplish that goal.

DEFINING AND UNDERSTANDING ORGANIZATIONAL CULTURE

Consider this metaphor: Organizational (and team) culture is like a garden. If untended, it will grow weeds. If properly cultivated, it will grow flowers and fruit. Yet it will continue to grow, one way or another. As the opening quote by Peter Drucker indicates, culture is foundational to an organization's success. Implementing a new strategy into a dysfunctional culture is akin to planting seeds into toxic soil. They will not survive. How healthy is the "soil" in your team or organization? In what ways do you or others cultivate positive organizational culture? Keep reading for ideas you can implement today. If you need to practice outside work, remember that each of our families is also an organization with its own cultural "soil." We can intentionally grow positive interpersonal relationships, solve problems productively and respectfully, and make decisions in ways that leave everyone feeling positive about both the process and outcome.

Organizational culture is the proverbial "canary in the coalmine," meaning that if your organization is underperforming compared to its peers or its potential, look first to the organizational culture. If it is troubled, then pursuing other strategies for improvement will be akin to moving the deck chairs around on the *Titanic*. A great strategy won't succeed in a dysfunctional culture because it would be like planting seeds in toxic soil, yet even a mediocre strategy could triumph when implemented by a team with a strong cultural foundation.

The culture of an organization shapes and impacts everything else: How employees are treated; customer satisfaction; litigation, morale, and mission achievement. The *Business Dictionary* definition of organizational culture is instructive. **Organizational culture** is comprised of the

> values and behaviors that contribute to the unique social and psychological environment of an organization. Organizational culture includes an organization's

expectations, experiences, philosophy, and values that hold it together, and is expressed in its self-image, inner workings, interactions with the outside world, and future expectations. It is based on shared attitudes, beliefs, customs, and written and unwritten rules that have been developed over time and are considered valid. Also called corporate culture, it's shown in (1) the ways the organization conducts its business, treats its employees, customers, and the wider community, (2) the extent to which freedom is allowed in decision making, developing new ideas, and personal expression, (3) how power and information flow through its hierarchy, and (4) how committed employees are towards collective objectives; (5) It also extends to production-methods, marketing, and advertising practices, and to new product creation. Organizational culture is unique for every organization and one of the hardest things to change. (Business Dictionary, 2018)

Even though organizational culture impacts mission achievement more than any other singular factor, the majority of organizations fail to cultivate or maintain their desired cultural environment. Worse yet, they often inadvertently foster counterculture policies and interpersonal behaviors.

Much of an organization's culture is learned through osmosis, meaning that it permeates the organization's methods of communication and decision-making but may not be explicitly or accurately stated. It might not be reinforced through meaningful policies and leadership. Every organization has written (e.g., policies) and unwritten ways of doing things.

It is the manager's job to encourage, promote, model, and create opportunities for the creation of a positive, shared culture in each unit and across the entire company.

Employees who are not managers also have a role. They set healthy boundaries, communicate proactively, treat others respectfully, enjoy their colleagues and have fun together, and intervene as active bystanders when a counterculture behavior emerges. This re-norms others to the desired culture of the group.

ASSESSING ORGANIZATIONAL CULTURE

To the neophyte, culture seems invisible. To the expert, it is clear as day. To everyone, it is inescapable. There are many useful questions to determine the health of your organization's culture. The ones you choose may be specific to the concerns you see or goals you wish to set. Consider these sample questions, which could be administered in an anonymous survey, using a 5-point Likert scale (i.e., strongly disagree to strongly agree).

- I am motivated by the mission of our organization.
- I am clear about my role in achieving the organization's mission.
- I like my coworkers.
- I trust my supervisor to make hard decisions when necessary.
- My supervisor treats me fairly.
- My input is valued.
- I would recommend this organization to a friend seeking work.
- I plan to look for another job in the next six months.

- My team members treat me with respect.
- My supervisor treats me with respect.
- My supervisor resolves conflicts productively.
- I am paid fairly for the work I do.
- This organization is fair in its hiring and promotion policies.
- Anyone can succeed here, regardless of race, gender, sexual orientation, national origin or other identity categories.
- Use two words to describe how it feels to work here. (Look for positive or negative trends.)
- What, if anything could be done to make this an even better place to work? (open-ended)
- What is your favorite thing about working here? (open-ended)

Add additional questions specific to your team or organizational needs or change efforts. Once you gather this survey data, you or your leadership team can set specific goals for improvement, tie the goals to change efforts, and then readminister the same questionnaire after some time has passed to measure the impact of culture change initiatives. Culture, like sales or customer satisfaction, can be measured. Happy employees make happy customers.

In addition to assessments through employee or customer surveys, you may wish to measure employee turnover, general customer or business-partner satisfaction, mission achievement, costs of litigation, or other quantifiable outcomes related to culture. Table 6.1 lists various symptoms of unhealthy organizational cultures.

YOU CAN'T HIRE YOUR WAY OUT OF A BAD CULTURE

Recruiting outstanding employees won't be enough to overcome a dysfunctional organizational culture. If a high-performing employee is placed into a poor culture, she will leave or take on the behaviors of low-performing employees to adapt and survive. It is too frustrating to give 100% to a team, boss, or organization that

Table 6.1   Symptoms of Dysfunctional Organizational Cultures

Internal Symptoms	External Symptoms
High employee turnover	Unhappy customers
Low morale	Negative (or reduced) brand image
Lack of trust	Lack of compliance/Regulatory fines
Disengagement	Litigation
Absenteeism/Presenteeism	Errors/Product malfunction
Employee Stress/Health impacts	Media leaks
Bullying/Harassment/Discrimination claims	Reduced market share
Gossip	Scandals
Conflict avoidance	
Domineering communication styles	
Lack of "ownership" or accountability	
Sabotage/embezzlement	

gets in the way of its own success on a regular basis. Therefore, the first rule of culture change is that you cannot hire your way out of a bad culture. You must proactively change culture from the inside out. The only exceptions occur when a predator needs to go and/or when the top leaders are replaced with the clear mission to change a dysfunctional organizational culture. This usually results from a crisis or scandal. Remember, the best employees will leave because they can. Hiring to solve a culture problem is like bailing out a leaking boat. Unless you plug the holes, the boat will eventually be swamped. Therefore, successful conflict managers attend to culture first, hiring second.

Once you have done the work or been lucky enough to benefit from the work of your predecessors, and your organization exhibits healthy responses to conflicts and problem-solving, then ongoing maintenance is required. Small work units or organizations are highly susceptible to small changes, whereas it takes larger changes to impact huge bureaucratic organizations. Even one new employee who exhibits destructive communication patterns can devastate team productivity and morale in a small team environment. Hiring employees who share your team's approach to problem-solving will be helpful to maintaining a positive and productive work environment, and once hired, they must be acculturated purposefully, so they can better understand what is expected and how to fit in.

To integrate new employees into the desired culture, consider appointing one or two employee "ambassadors" to help new employees acculturate and reach top performance more quickly. This is similar to the concept of a "host family" for foreign exchange students. An employee ambassador is a trusted team member who shows the new employee around on day one, introduces them to others, answers their questions, models the behavior they should follow, and allows them to ask lingering questions they might feel embarrassed to ask otherwise. Developing warm interpersonal relationships is one of the biggest predictors of employee longevity. Both the ambassador and the new employee should normalize the difficulty of the cultural learning curve—it is common for missteps to occur. For example, you might tell new employees they are highly encouraged to constructively share their feedback, ideas, and concerns with their colleagues and managers, either in a joint session or privately, as determined by your team's preferences. Each company will vary and this is often unwritten cultural knowledge with significant consequences.

You may decide to use tools like the conflict styles inventory (Chapter 1) or other assessment tools to help you understand the conflict management habits and approaches of applicants before they are hired. Secondly, you will want to have explicit discussions with new (and even with existing) employees to share your organization's expectations regarding the handling of inevitable problems that will arise as well as expectations regarding preferred interaction among team members.

Overcoming the Obstacles to Culture Change

Behavior continues as long as it is working. Remember that gem from Chapter 3? Who is benefiting from the current dysfunctional culture, which may be expressed through unfair or inefficient policies, procedures, or unkind interpersonal relations? If no one gained from this culture, then it is likely that someone would have changed it by now. Corrupt or self-serving leaders are the biggest obstacle to culture change. Sometimes these leaders inadvertently created or worsened the organization's hostile climate, and they are, therefore, loathe to acknowledge their culpability for current problems. For example, in June of 2017, Uber's CEO was forced to resign after a shareholder revolt resulted from unaddressed claims of sexual harassment, discrimination, hostile and aggressive leadership styles, federal investigations for technology used by Uber to skirt traffic laws, and even litigation over intellectual property used for its app (Isaac, 2017a, 2017b). These are classic symptoms of a dysfunctional workplace culture in need of radical revision. Uber's board of directors believed that CEO Travis Kalanick was an obstacle to that culture change, so he was ousted. The competitive, aggressive traits that helped him crowd out initial competitors, build a product and a strong reputation, and subdue internal and external competitors may have been compatible with the early phases of his organization's life, but his ouster indicates the company sought a steadier, more humane leader as it stabilized and institutionalized its place in the marketplace. See Chapter 8 for more on the life cycles of organizations.

Leaders, like all of us, may not understand the ways in which their behaviors contribute to negative cultures and inhibit mission achievement. Executive coaching is indispensable for leaders seeking to lead organizations through change. See Chapter 10 for more information on coaching and the role of organizational ombudsmen in this process.

A quick look at corporate scandals indicates they often involve complacency and/or complicity by leaders and those to whom they answer, such as boards. For example, the CEO of Volkswagen and eight other high-level leaders were charged with "conspiring to mislead regulators about the German car maker's efforts to cheat the emissions tests of its diesel-fueled vehicles" (Sherman, 2018). Patricia Dunn, the chair of the board at Hewlett-Packard, engaged in an illegal effort to spy on board members in an attempt to find a leak. She was eventually charged with four felonies (Kaplan, 2006). Dunn also worked for Wells Fargo and Barclays, which indicates a tendency for unethical leaders to survive within an organization for a while before being driven out, only to land in another organization where they continue to behave in ways that lead to brand damage and scandals (Babiak & Hare, 2006; Sims, 2010). Because organizations seek to protect their image, when they can oust these leaders with a "golden parachute" rather than a public scandal, they are rewarding negative behaviors and increasing the likelihood the negative behavior will continue in a different organization. These self-serving individuals, who often exhibit narcissistic or even sociopathic tendencies, will remain an obstacle to the creation of a positive organizational culture unless they feel it is in their interests to leave. Sometimes it is necessary to pay them to leave or find a way to frame their departure that enhances their reputation, even though that often means they move on to wreak havoc elsewhere.

Sadly, once scandals force out unethical leaders, the blame is cast upon those much lower in the hierarchy. Rank-and-file employees are often required to receive training on ethics or sexual harassment when they were not responsible for the problems. Any effort focused on retraining these employees is generally wasted money used to deflect criticism from its rightful place. Instead, the organization must create new systems and checks to ensure ethical and pro-cultural behaviors at every level.

Aside from the topmost leaders, there are always individuals or units that benefit from the status quo of a negative culture. This could be as innocuous as simply being resistant to change: "We've always done it this way." In more sinister situations, follow the money and other incentives. Who benefits from the negative culture? Negative behaviors will end and culture change will occur only with the alteration of current incentive structures. Rooting out perverse incentive structures is key to removing obstacles to change. **Perverse incentives** occur when a policy, procedure, or system misaligns the individual interests against the interests of the broader organization. In other words, when individuals (or units) pursue individually rational objectives, they hurt the larger community or organization (see Chapter 6).

CHANGING ORGANIZATIONAL CULTURE

The pace of change depends mostly upon the depth of the leader's buy-in for these efforts or the seriousness of the crises facing the organization. Necessity is indeed the mother of invention when it comes to organizational change. If the leadership team is convinced of the importance of these efforts, and they follow the steps outlined in this section, then even large bureaucracies can change fast enough for those within and outside the organization to feel some relief relatively fast enough to win both their patience and backing for these efforts. In the absence of leadership support for culture change initiatives, change will only come when either the customers or employees revolt—or both.

There are a few key steps to increase the pace and success of culture change efforts (see Denning, 2011; Willink & Babin, 2015).

BOX 6.1. CRITICAL LEADERSHIP STEPS FOR CULTURE CHANGE

1. Articulate a clear vision.
2. Be the change you seek: Lead from the front, stay connected with the front lines.
3. Build a coalition of support for change within and outside the organization.
4. Engage in radical transparency and visibility.
5. Align everything with the new culture: practices, products, and brand.
6. Empower customers and employees to participate in this effort.
7. Avoid reorganizing or bringing in all new managers. This may delay culture change.

Step 1: Articulate a Clear Vision.

When you think about the best version of your organization and its people, you must ask yourself one critical question, comprised of two sub-parts: "Who are we?" This should be the driving question, tied to the mission. The two subparts are "Who are we now?" and "Who do we seek to become?" These questions will drive everything. Are we the kind of organization that treats everyone with respect and inclusivity? That innovates and passionately fulfills its critical mission? What behaviors, policies, and practices are we currently engaged in that do not reflect who we really want to be? The first step of any culture change effort is for the leader (and then all unit leaders) to clearly articulate a vision that helps everyone within and outside the organization answer the question: "Who are we?" This is often tied to strategic planning efforts and comes in the form of a mission and vision statements along with a set of values the organization seeks to uphold (see Chapter 8 for more on strategic planning as a leadership function). Ideally, this vision is created through a collaborative, inclusive process. Yet, it is not necessary to put culture change efforts on hold while the mission, vision, and values are crafted. Change cannot wait. The leader can articulate a motivating vision that inspires people to "hang in there" and collectively strive for change. Strategic planning can take place during these efforts or even after the initial phases of culture change have been launched. This vision needs to be announced to the entire workforce and then reinforced through frequent communications within each work unit. This visible pronouncement should acknowledge the leader's understanding that change is needed, ask for the patience of all stakeholders, and affirmatively commit to following up this pronouncement with efforts to align policies, procedures, and behaviors with the newly articulated vision and values. Leaders, managers, and supervisors need to take visible actions to ensure behaviors align with desired changes. If they tolerate bad behavior from "high performers" or well-connected employees, then others will scoff at and ignore culture change efforts.

Step 2: Be the Change You Seek: Lead from the Front,
Stay Connected with the Front Lines.

When leaders seek to improve their organization's culture, they must visibly, repeatedly, and consistently model the behaviors they seek to encourage. Leaders must embody respect, embrace diversity, listen to the concerns of all, show their willingness to learn and grow through humility, and normalize the difficulty inherent in personal and organizational change. As Angela Duckworth discusses in her pathbreaking book, *Grit: The Power of Passion & Perseverance* (2016) parents and leaders must not be afraid to try hard things, make mistakes, admit those mistakes, use them to learn and grow, and model this behavior to other organizational members. No one expects perfection. They expect effort and honesty.

Do the work: Culture change requires a deep understanding of the challenges facing the organization and its people. Leaders at all levels should spend time working on the front lines of the organization in various positions so as to demonstrate their willingness to learn, to gain credibility and the loyalty of the employees, and to remain grounded in the mission of the organization. This can be 10–25% of their time, but it should not be overlooked (see Chapter 8 on leadership). How can leaders enact changes to corporate processes when they are out of touch?

Step 3: Build a Coalition of Support for Change Within and Outside the Organization.

Culture change leaders must identify the key stakeholders who can help or hinder their efforts. These could include union leaders, respected elders or employees within the organization, political appointees, local regulators or officials, and department heads including human resources, legal affairs, and others. By meeting with each of these stakeholders, the change leader can share her vision while making it clear that she is open to hearing theirs as well. What would they like to achieve in their units? What kind of work environment would they find most fulfilling and what is standing in the way? Make no mistake: This is a negotiation. The leader must get each stakeholder onboard by learning more about their individual and collective interests. Some key stakeholders seek only to improve the organization and enhance mission achievement, yet others will seek individual career advancement or other opportunities. By building these relationships and coalitions of support, change becomes possible. You cannot do it alone or against the wishes of key stakeholders. Use of force or power will not work either. Influence, yes. Force, no. You must use your negotiation, persuasion, and leadership skills to win their support. It will take conscious effort, persistence, and resilience to win them over. Revisit and apply your interest-based negotiation skills from Chapter 3.

Step 4: Engage in Radical Transparency and Visibility.

Hiding problems only works to prolong them. **Ostrich syndrome** occurs when individual managers and leaders stick their heads in the metaphorical sand in an attempt to avoid seeing problems. It never works and it leaves your most vulnerable side exposed.

Radical transparency requires full information, repeatedly delivered, with the understanding that we must acknowledge problems before we can fix them. Radical transparency prevents the water-cooler gossip that arises when employees know changes are coming, but they lack specific information about forthcoming changes. Your employees shouldn't have to read the newspaper or watch TV in order to find out what is happening in their own company. Tell them what you know, what you don't know, and when you hope to know. Create mechanisms to allow direct, frequent communication from those at any level to any level in the organization. An intranet site can be used to allow employees to submit questions, concerns, or problems and receive a response, with the option to remain anonymous. These can be used to create "frequently asked questions" with clear and consistent responses. Radical transparency will build trust, which will be necessary for accountability and problem-solving.

What about media leaks? Keeping managers, supervisors, and employees abreast of expected changes may lead to potentially harmful information becoming public. As Benjamin Franklin famously said, "Three can keep a secret if two of them are dead." It would be unrealistic to share information about layoffs, an innovative new product, or a leadership change with dozens of managers or employees and expect that information to remain confidential. That is like trying to hold water in your hands. No matter how hard you try, gravity will do its work. Therefore, leaders must balance the need to inform their chains of command about big changes with the need to make a coordinated press release. At a minimum, organizational managers and supervisors can be notified minutes before the press release and leaders can explain the reasons behind sharing or withholding information that may impact stock prices or other critical factors. Overall, leaders tend to under-share information rather than overshare it. This reduces trust and reflects poorly on the organizational culture.

The organization's leaders must be visible during these change efforts, repeatedly articulating the ongoing efforts to bring needed changes and making himself available to hear ideas and concerns as needed. Leaders should normalize the difficulty of these efforts, their ongoing nature, and that "we're all in it together."

Step 5: Align Everything with the New Culture: Practices, Products, and Brand Image.

What behaviors are tolerated or embraced? How do those behaviors fit with "Who we are"? Facilitative training may help reorient managers to model valued behaviors and develop the skills needed to change old habits. Changes will also be needed in company policies, products, and services to align them with the desired culture change. Set goals for desired culture changes, with measurable indicators of success. Each functional unit, or cross-functional team, should be allowed to weigh in about the extent to which policies and procedures promote or detract from the desired culture and mission achievement.

Alignment includes structured changes to communication patterns designed to increase communications across divisions or silos, to reduce and reframe negative or destructive tone and framing into more positive ones, and to ensure communication up and down the chain of command. Asking people to communicate across silos is ineffective. Instead, structure communication channels through required consultations and routinized interactions.

Step 6: Empower Customers and Employees.

Every member of the organization must be empowered to reinforce the new cultural norms. Use training to teach employees *how* to uphold and enact these values, while holding each other accountable in a respectful way that leaves room for continual improvement. When employees seek to report counterculture behavior, it is important to take their concerns seriously. If reports of sexual harassment, discrimination, unfair treatment, or unethical behaviors are dismissed or ignored because the accused is a powerful or high-performing employee (or manager), then all credibility is lost in the culture change effort. If trust is low, consider the creation of confidential methods for reporting, such as online "tip lines," suggestion boxes in the break room, and the creation of an ombudsman office. Employees need to see transparent, timely responses to concerns or their natural cynicism will grow and negative cultural patterns will be reinforced instead of reduced.

Active bystander training can be used to empower employees to learn methods for gently "checking" or redirecting negative behaviors among peers or even managers.

Step 7: Avoid Reorganizing or Bringing in all New Managers; This May Delay Culture Change.

It is tempting to say, "Off with their heads!" and replace problematic managers with new ones, but remember the **10–80–10 rule**. Ten percent of employees won't steal or behave unethically under any circumstances. Another 10% are unethical and nothing can be done to change their behaviors other than monitoring and sanctioning them. The other 80% will be influenced by the workplace culture and the behaviors of their peers. Therefore, the key to reducing workplace theft, ethics violations, and malfeasance is to create a workplace culture in which employees feel loyalty toward their organizations and where cultural norms mitigate against such behaviors. Therefore, firing employees without specific culture change will not fix the problem. People who behaved unethically in a negative culture may adapt and change their behavior once the new cultural expectations are clear and enforced. One caveat: predators must be fired. Refusing to fire someone who is a known predator in the organization will drive away the ones you want to stay and may result in public scandals.

Reorganizing alone is insufficient to address a dysfunctional culture and may distract from efforts to bring deeper change. Worst-case scenario: reorganization takes up time and resources that distract from the real problems.

What if the organizational leaders are ignoring the concerns of employees and managers? What if they seem more concerned about the next step in their careers than furthering the mission? What if they inherit the family business, but it isn't their passion? How can you change organizational culture when the leaders are either absent or seem determined to run it into the ground? Culture change from the bottom up is your next step. Even better, once it gains momentum and attention, leaders either get on board or they leave, to be replaced by more responsive leaders. Stop waiting for your prince/ss to come. You can rescue yourself from a toxic culture in your daily work team.

BOX 6.2. BOTTOM-UP CULTURE CHANGE

1. Don't wait for someone else to make your work life better.
2. Each of us shapes the organizational culture every day.
3. Set and communicate boundaries respectfully.
4. Negotiate shared expectations.
5. Use the power you *do* have.
6. Invite leaders to join in.
7. Communicate strategically both within and outside the organization.

I. Don't Wait for Someone Else to Make Your Work Life Better

The least risky change effort involves the negotiation of shared expectations in your work unit. These efforts can stay under the radar. Any attempt to connect the changes in your unit to the broader need to change the organization across units or vertically upward could attract attention from the top. That is good and bad. Before taking your efforts outside your units, analyze your job security and risk tolerance. Is it easy or hard for your organization to fire people? If you are a tenured faculty member, you are hard to dismiss. This is actually true in many public and private organizations: Some bureaucracies simply don't fire people except for extreme malfeasance, or sadly, not even in the face of it. In those cases, setting healthy boundaries and shared expectations in the team will likely result in behavior changes or the defector will simply leave since their behavioral strategies are no longer working for them.

As any therapist will attest, you can only change what you think, say, and do. You cannot change others. However, the deep irony is that changing yourself and your unit will have an incremental change on the organizational culture overall. More importantly, it will make your daily life more tolerable or even happy. It is possible to have a solid, tight-knit, effective unit within a generally dysfunctional organization. Don't wait. Leaders come and go. You are taking a gamble by waiting for a new leader to change or for change in the existing leader.

For example, one top manager in a large family construction business once told me, "For fifteen years I have been telling the owner that his brother-in-law is a liability and is repeatedly the cause of lost contracts and missed deadlines. This is driving me crazy and makes my work so frustrating." What was my response? "Sounds like you are trying to change him instead of changing yourself and your situation. After so many years, you have enough data to know that he isn't going to pick you over his family member. What can you do to stop being so frustrated?" He went on the job market immediately and found a job with a 40% pay increase and a role that let him pick his own team members. He was joyful the next time we spoke. His choice was stark: stay put and accept what you cannot change or leave. By focusing on those factors within his control, he made his life better. It only took fifteen years for the light bulb to go off. Let's hope, dear reader, that we can learn from this example.

You do not control what others think, say, or do. Remember the tips from Chapter 3 and refrain from rewarding negative behaviors by setting and holding healthy boundaries.

2. Each of Us Shapes the Organizational Culture Every Day

It is best when leaders articulate the cultural values they seek to foster, but don't wait for them to do so. The culture in your work unit is determined more by the people working in it than by the top leaders. If you are the unit supervisor or manager, you set the tone by articulating the values you hope others will share, while being sure to invite them to add their own values to the mix. *The way you treat others operationalizes your values.* Do you respect their input? Do you invite it, consider it, and sometimes implement it? When someone in your unit behaves counter to its values, do you or other teammates become active bystanders or just look away? (See Chapter 5 for active bystander skills.) Whether you recognize it or not, your choices and behaviors reinforce or change the culture in your unit every day.

3. Set and Communicate Boundaries Respectfully

Boundary setting is a psychological concept referring to a conscious limit between acceptable behaviors that uphold personal dignity versus those behaviors that cause emotional harm. Setting a boundary occurs when one communicates the limits of acceptable behavior. Holding the boundary occurs when there is an appropriate response to a crossed boundary. Possible responses could include a verbal or nonverbal reassertion of the boundary, termination of the relationship either temporarily or permanently, or any other negative consequence deemed to be appropriate by the boundary setter. In a workplace, the most common signs of frequent boundary crossing include formal complaints of sexual harassment, discrimination, hostile work environment, or bullying. Less formal signs of boundary crossing would include low morale, high turnover, gossip, sabotage, or embezzlement. If you work in a unit or organization in which your boundaries are repeatedly crossed, then you need to respectfully negotiate and communicate them to the boundary crossers. If the behavior continues, communicate your BATNA (best alternative to a negotiated agreement, see Chapter 3), which could include reporting the behavior, interfering with the other's clear goals and initiatives, harming their reputation by making their behavior public, asking for a transfer, quitting, filing a complaint, and so on. They may be predators, but you do not have to be their prey. Make sure they know it. Their negative behaviors usually rely upon secrecy. Making their behavior visible to others may be a good first step to ending it.

Be sure to respect the boundaries of others whenever possible or renegotiate them together when the gap is untenable. One common example includes work-life balance. For example, if one team member states they do not work weekends in order to prioritize their family time, but your team members must occasionally cover weekend shifts, then it would be necessary to discuss and reach consensus about how weekend work will be fairly handled. On the other hand, if overtime is optional, it is helpful to respect those who choose to work at every opportunity and those who choose not to do so. This reflects an acceptance of individual difference that must be embraced for the organization to truly "walk the talk" of diversity and inclusion.

4. Negotiate Shared Expectations

Conflict comes from a lack of shared expectations. For example, you expect the report to be submitted Monday at 9:00 a.m., but it doesn't happen. You expect your employee to call you "Sir/Ma'am" or "Doctor," yet he calls you "JoAnn." You expect your boss to speak calmly to you privately when she criticizes your performance, but instead, she yells at you in front of your colleagues. In addition to negotiating work-life balance trade-offs, your work team can enhance its unit culture by building shared expectations through explicit discussions and agreements covering interpersonal communication, workload distribution, sharing of the credit, etc. There are few right or wrong expectations, only those that are unclear.

5. Use the Power You *Do* Have

Unhappy employees and managers tend to focus on the power they don't have instead of what they can accomplish. You may not be able to give yourself a raise, choose your boss, or make high-level strategic decisions for your organization. Yet, you likely have sources of power you have not fully realized: knowledge, connections, access to resources, experience, insight, positive intra-organizational resources, access to decision-makers, moral persuasion, knowledge of company or leaders' secrets, the power to unite with others to bring change (even unionization), and the ability to communicate strategically within or outside the organization (e.g., including speaking to the media). Analyze your sources of power. Use that analysis to decide how to match your acceptable level of risk with your next steps.

Deciding to use your power is important. Secretaries have brought down CEOs when they used their power to expose wrongdoing. Cheerleaders have brought down campus presidents when they asserted their right to free speech in the face of his clear opposition (Adelson, 2017).

How do you weigh the risks versus the options? Try this: Make a list of your values and give each a number between zero and one that corresponds to how much you weigh this value. Then, list each option you are considering, making sure to generate as many options as possible. One of the common failures of human decision-making is to get prematurely attached to the first reasonable option that comes along (Johnson, 2018). Once you have listed your values and weighted them (step 1), then listed the options and scored them (step 2), then you multiply the values' weights by the extent to which each option fulfills each value. By summing the outputs of each calculation, you can see how well each option is likely to meet your underlying values (Johnson, 2018). Conflict between your values and your choices causes unhappiness and stress. This decision-making process helps you be more rational about ensuring the match between your values and the ultimate decision you make. See Table 6.2 for an example of this exercise.

Of course, the numbers we list are subjective and some are relatively unknowable. For example, you might not know how long it will take to find a new

Table 6.2   Decision-Making Matrix

	Option 1: Do Nothing	Option 2: File a Complaint	Option 3: Speak to the Media	Option 4: Quit and Work Elsewhere
Fairness at work (0.75)	25 × 0.75 = 18.75	80 = 60	75 = 56.25	90 = 67.50
Meaningful work (0.60)	50 × 0.60 = 30	60 = 36	60 = 36	80 = 48
Personal financial stability (0.90)	100 × 0.90 = 90	80 = 72	50 = 45	75 = 67.50
Maintaining positive relationships at work (0.80)	65 × 0.80 = 52	50 = 40	60 = 48	65 = 52
Score for each option	190.25	208	185.25	235

job or whether speaking to the press can be done while protecting your identity. Learn as much about your options as possible to increase the accuracy of the decision-making process.

6. Invite Leaders to Join In

If your efforts to improve unit-level organizational culture begin to work, it's likely those higher up in the hierarchy will notice eventually. Mission achievement will go up and attrition will decrease. People are "attracted to the light," as we say. Leaders will want to know what and who is responsible for these improvements. When they start asking these questions, it is possible to get their attention long enough to share your turnaround story. Perhaps they will hear you out and consider implementing similar changes elsewhere in the organization.

What if they do not accept the invitation or even stand in the way? Self-serving, shortsighted leaders may be jealous of positive changes initiated by anyone other than themselves. Most of the time this will not be the case, so avoid getting paranoid and try to give your leader the benefit of the doubt. If, however, the leader is indeed threatened by positive changes in your unit, then you need to forge an alliance with other powerful people in the organization to push back against unfair efforts to hamper your unit's ability to positively shape its culture. An additional strategy is to ensure internal unit cohesion, which allows your group to successfully stall changes from above or to challenge them outright. In the end, higher-level leaders need to get on board, or at least stay out of the way of positive changes. If need be, offer them the ability to claim credit for the improvements. It may be frustrating, but if it gets them on board or out of the way, the price may be worth paying. Refer back to Chapter 3's ninja negotiation lessons. You need to figure out what they want and then sell them on the ways in which positive culture changes further their own goals. Get inside their head.

7. Communicate Strategically Both Within and Outside the Organization

When, how, and to whom you communicate your efforts at culture change is critical. You will want to keep quiet about your unit-level efforts to bring change unless powerful leaders are supportive. If your goal is to bring broader organizational change, against the absence or incompetence of higher leaders, then you will need to build a coalition of support with key stakeholders within and outside the organization. If the changes you seek are related to ending unethical or illegal behaviors, then communicating these externally may be an important step. Investigative reporters could be valuable assets in shining a light upon organizational wrongdoing, thereby forcing the organization to replace unethical leaders or practices. In many situations, the media will allow confidential sources to remain anonymous in the press. This should be negotiated during first contact with the reporter. Unless otherwise agreed upon, all communications will be "on the record," so be careful to clarify your needs and expectations. The media has been key to removing unethical leaders at corporate, government, and nonprofit organizations. Ask permission to view a draft of the story to ensure accuracy before it is published. They may balk, but accuracy protects everyone.

COACHING FOR CULTURE CHANGE

If workplace bullying, sexual harassment, or aggressive communication styles have been tolerated, then longtime employees or managers have acquired habits that may be hard to change. Coaching is a common process used to empower individuals to replace their unproductive behaviors with more productive ones (see Chapter 10 for specific coaching tools and processes).

Conflict coaching is "a process in which a coach and client communicate one-on-one for the purpose of developing the client's conflict-related understanding, interaction strategies, and interaction skills. Coaches help clients to make sense of conflicts they experience, help them learn to positively manage these conflicts, and help them master specific communication skills and behaviors" (from Jones & Brinkert, 2008, p. 4–5). In essence, coaching involves individualized training designed to meet the skill deficits and career goals of individual employees at any level of the organization.

If the assessment yields information indicating that one specific unit (or a few), or one (or a few) individuals are disproportionately responsible for conflict within the organization, then coaching is a useful response designed to empower their change efforts. It is not enough to tell someone to "Stop bullying" or "Stop talking to people like that." It would be equivalent to telling someone to start speaking in a foreign language without teaching them that language. By teaching them new communication and interaction skills, they have a chance of adapting to new cultural expectations. Efforts should be made to help everyone to succeed rather than replace them without first making these efforts.

TRAINING FOR CULTURE CHANGE

Training can't fix everything, but that won't stop organizations from trying. When organizations ask me to train their people, I always ask them, "What problem are you seeking to fix or what do you hope to accomplish" by the training? I get all kinds of answers. For example, "We have one particularly manager who has been accused of sexual harassment by multiple interns and admins, so we want you to provide civility training to all 500 employees." Yikes! This is a conflict-avoidant response (see Chapter 1 for conflict styles). Coaching is a better way to handle individuals with problematic behaviors, along with clearly documented warnings and a written performance improvement plan designed to set boundaries about expected behaviors. Forcing everyone to take training that most of them don't need is a waste of time and resources. Worse, at least some of the attendees will know the roots of the problem and see that the organization is not taking decisive action to address the specific causes of poor behavior.

Training cannot address structural problems either, yet it can be used to explain these changes and prepare people to implement them effectively. Structural problems include unclear or overlapping job descriptions, policies that misalign individual incentives with the best interests of the organization, or discriminatory policies. Before agreeing to provide training, be sure the presenting problem is one that training can ameliorate. Otherwise, the organization will believe the training failed. Lastly, prior to or at the commencement of any training effort, be sure to learn more about the problems facing trainees. Explicitly tie your training to their needs, to develop buy-in and assure attention from trainees. Ask them to create a plan to transfer the skills acquired in training to the work of the organization using goalsetting and an implementation plan.

WHISTLEBLOWERS

Whistleblowers report illegal or unethical behaviors committed by their leaders or colleagues. These reports may be made internally to persons of authority within the organization or they may be made externally to law enforcement agencies, government regulators, or other possible sources of redress. Usually, whistleblowers act in the public or national security interests, at great risk of reprisal or retaliation. While some statutes protect whistleblowers who file claims with the Occupational Safety and Health Administration (OSHA) or U.S. Department of Labor, or other agencies, whistleblowers are generally people in a relatively low-power position seeking to stop the negative actions of those more powerful. As such, they act at great personal or professional risk.

Usually, whistleblowers act when the organization fails to create or implement internal systems that monitor, catch, and report illegal or unethical behaviors without a need to seek the help and protection of external forces. When employees feel safe, they report concerns to their supervisors, human resources departments, or company leaders, knowing the matter will be investigated and appropriate action will be taken. Sometimes, leaders are complicit in the unwanted behaviors. Other times, they simply try to cover up problems to avoid the embarrassment that comes from having allowed these behaviors to occur on their watch. By creating mechanisms for reporting and responding to ethics concerns internally, and by creating a culture that supports ethical behaviors, organizations may avoid the embarrassment and oversight that comes from having their dirty laundry aired in public.

Should I Stay or Should I Go Now?

There are three kinds of organizational trajectories:

A. An organization that is well run, competitive, and staying near the top of its competition.
B. An organization that is struggling, but consistently getting better.
C. An organization that was doing well but is now going downhill.

Employees at types A and B are generally much happier than those at type C. Being #1 or close to the top tends to feel pretty good. On the other hand, being an up-and-coming organization also feels pretty good. But being at an organization that is now being run into the ground feels . . . you get the picture.

One charismatic CEO with whom I worked used to say, "We need to build such a strong company culture that any jerk can run this place, because someday one will." He was right! He made realistic plans for a legacy of cultural strength, where managers come together to negotiate changes and policies that respect everyone while accomplishing the mission.

When the company ship is taking on water, when do you bail faster versus jumping ship? Everyone asks themselves this question at some point in their career. In dysfunctional organizations, employees ask themselves this question every day. Consider using the decision-making matrix listed earlier. Otherwise, consider this: If you are working at an organization that is taking on water, do what you can to make the culture better for as long as you are there. You can "light a match or curse the darkness." When the darkness gets overwhelming, or you see an attractive life raft, you may decide it's time for a move. There are no easy answers to this question. Seek mentorship, keep your options open, and bail smarter, not harder.

JOHN AT THE BUREAU OF RECLAMATION

John met with his management team to collectively brainstorm around the questions of "Who are we?" and "Who do we want to be?" He articulated his vision for the organization, but amended it to include some of the concerns they raised. He worked with them to develop a plan to articulate a vision for culture change designed to acknowledge the organization's problems and chart a positive path forward. Then, he held a town hall meeting of all employees and managers, in which he announced this vision and plan. He listened to their questions and responded non-defensively and transparently. Within the next three days, he took some high-profile steps to show everyone this was not just "lip service" but real change: He had every unit leader engage in brainstorming with their team to determine how they could make changes to put the new cultural values into place and to develop shared expectations designed to promote these values and reduce conflict. This would require changes to policies, procedures, data collection, what is valued and rewarded in performance reviews, and a better system to collect morale feedback both internally (employees) and externally (clients, vendors, etc.).

Within a week or so, it became clear that some managers and employees would need coaching and support to adapt to the new culture. The services of a professional coach were enlisted to assist in this effort. John knows this is a long-term effort, but he already senses a new hopefulness among the agency's employees.

KEY TERMS

boundary setting

conflict coaching

organizational culture

ostrich syndrome

perverse incentives

10–80–10 rule

whistleblowers

EXERCISES

1. Use the decision-making matrix to weigh any important decision facing you in your personal or professional life.
2. List the values your organization espouses officially. Then compare those values to its cultural practices to assess the extent to which there is alignment. What can you do to improve alignment within your unit or your role? If misalignment exists, consider whether or how to raise these concerns to your next-level supervisor.

GOAL SETTING

1. Analyze the policies, practices, and interactions in your unit. Which are promoting positive cultural values and which are hindering them? Set a goal to improve the organizational culture in your unit by changing your interactions with others this week. Don't be afraid to tell others about your plan so they are not surprised when they see these changes. In many cases, they will join in the effort happily.

SUGGESTED SUPPLEMENTAL READINGS

Carter, S. (1999). The importance of party buy-in in designing organizational conflict management systems. *Mediation Quarterly, 17*, 61–66. doi:10.1002/crq.3890170106

Gawerc, M. I. (2013). Research note: Integrative ties as an approach to managing organizational conflict. *Conflict Resolution Quarterly, 31*, 219–225. https://doi.org/10.1002/crq.21083

Gibbons, P. (2015). *The science of successful organizational change: How leaders set strategy, change behavior, and create an agile culture* (1st ed.). Pearson.

7

Interpersonal Dispute Resolution at Work

Enhancing Employee Engagement and Teamwork

Ah conflict . . . an opportunity to improve a relationship.

—Rita Callahan

The last decade has yielded great insights into the positive benefits of engaging in hard conversations early and often (Gottman & Schwartz Gottman, 2022). Ignoring problems in the hope they will resolve on their own is much worse for relationships than collaborative, respectful problem-solving. As conflict resolution expert Rita Callahan notes, conflict is always an opportunity to improve a relationship. How we treat each other during the process will determine the extent to which our relationships improve or are damaged, not the problem itself.

Regardless of the size of your organization, losing employees due to low morale, unresolved conflicts, or other preventable causes wastes resources and interferes with mission achievement. Even worse, it can make you dread coming to work. Demoralizing performance reviews, unclear expectations, and a lack of leadership support inevitably drive away the best workers and managers.

After reading this chapter, revisit these learning objectives to ensure you are prepared to maximize employee engagement, beginning with your own.

Learning Objectives

- Explain the links between employee satisfaction and customer satisfaction.
- List and describe the causes of high employee turnover and low morale.
- Demonstrate the techniques used to diagnose the underlying causes and cures for employee turnover and low morale.
- Demonstrate 3-step problem-solving to reach shared expectations with others.
- Identify the causes and cures for workplace incivility, including bullying and harassment.
- Create a plan for an improved, two-way dialogue for your next performance review experience.
- Demonstrate best practices for successfully managing difficult people.

ELISE AT MAIN STREET BAKERIES

In Chapter 2 Elise had sent Ben, her director of HR, to store number 75 to learn more about the relatively high rates of employee turnover and disgruntlement experienced at the store. In general, turnover in Main Street Bakeries is low, approximately 15% per year for frontline, hourly employees and 6% for salaried employees (i.e., managers and assistant managers). Ben and Elise are concerned because of store number 75's rates of attrition that are more than double this average and slumping sales.

Elise's system for tracking costs charges each store for the costs of hiring and training new employees. These costs come off the store's bottom line so that managers have incentives to keep their employees when possible. Oddly enough, absenteeism is relatively low at the store, which is surprising given the level of turnover and low customer satisfaction.

The underlying causes of the high turnover are negatively affecting the store's ability to deliver high-quality service to its customers: unhappy employees lead to unhappy customers. Ben needs to analyze the situation, interview former employees, and come up with an intervention plan.

★ ★ ★

Stress among workers is at an all-time high (Tugend, 2023). While some factors are beyond the control of individual managers or organizations, such as global economic disruptions caused by war, inflation, or pandemics, managers who proactively resolve and manage their team's ability to collaborate and interact effectively will rise to the top. Workers are reasonable: they understand their managers are not responsible for these global challenges, yet they need help to make the best of difficult situations, to recognize their contributions, and to make work feel as good as possible. In the end, truly dissatisfied employees are a sign of a dysfunctional workplace. Whether the cause is a counterproductive workplace culture, one or more bullies, a misalignment of individual and corporate incentives, out-of-touch leaders, or other systemic factors, employee satisfaction is closely tied to mission achievement and profitability.

Research studies show a clear link between employee satisfaction and customer satisfaction, which goes in a virtuous circle, meaning that happy employees lead to happy customers, which in turn increase employee satisfaction. In short, employee and customer satisfaction are inextricably linked (Barween, Alshurideh & Alnaser, 2020). Perhaps most importantly, life is too short to remain in a dysfunctional, unfulfilling workplace.

While the previous chapter focused on organizational culture cures, which are systemic in their nature, this chapter focuses on interpersonal dispute resolution processes and skills to enhance problem-solving and warmth between team members. This chapter will help you understand the causes, costs, and cures for low morale, high attrition, and disengagement. Great organizations attract, develop, and retain the best workers. This gives them a competitive advantage and makes work enjoyable. The good news is there are many things you can do to change the dynamics in your team and make your organization the kind of place where employees want to stay.

THE BIG QUIT: EMPLOYEE ATTRITION AND THE NEW NORMAL

In December 2019, the number of people who left their jobs through voluntary quitting, layoffs, discharges, and all other reasons was 3.5 million, but it was 5.9 million by July of 2022 (Farrugia, 2022). Times have changed and we are not going back anytime soon: instead of employees competing for a small number of jobs, employers are competing for a too-small pool of workers. There are many reasons for this sea change: a smaller cohort of younger workers, inflation that has outpaced wage growth, reduced immigration since the pandemic, and a significant gap in the needs and expectations of Gen Z and millennial workers versus Gen X and boomer bosses. There are many good things about these changes for organizations, employers, and managers, in spite of the tendency to see the pre-2019 era as the "good ol' days." Let's discuss new ways to succeed in the "new normal."

The costs of poor employee morale are seen in a variety of ways: failure to achieve the mission, absenteeism, "presenteeism," reduced productivity, sabotage, litigation, and the costs of hiring and training new employees. **Employee turnover** (or **attrition**) refers to the rate at which employees leave the organization and should be broken down by rank and location to better isolate the potential causes. Average rates of employee turnover vary by industry and within organizations.

Absenteeism is costly to organizations, especially when it occurs in positions demanding significant training, because it is nearly impossible to have someone seamlessly step into that employee's shoes during his or her absence.

In some ways, absenteeism may be preferable to **presenteeism**, also known as **quiet quitting**, which occurs when an employee wishes to leave the organization but hasn't done so yet. Although remaining in the job, the employee is less committed to the organization, its customers, and other employees. They basically check out, while remaining on the payroll. Rates for presenteeism are estimated to be approximately three times higher than for absenteeism.

> While the term "quiet quitting" might have been recently coined, the phenomenon is not new. According to figures from a Gallup poll, the portion of American workers who are "actively disengaged"—those doing the minimum and who are psychologically detached from work—has hovered between 13 percent and 18 percent between 2000 and 2020. (Kim, 2023)

Yet 36% of Americans state a belief that their lives are less happy than prior to 2019 and 28% are pessimistic for their futures (ibid.). This overall ennui infects employee satisfaction, of course.

It's not all bad news. Some of these changes may be legitimately viewed as growing pains.

> Somehow, over time, our culture has become focused on work as an identity, as the only thing worth devoting our time to. This has led performance standards to become completely out of whack, requiring an unhealthy amount of dedication to one's job to even come close to getting that merit increase or promotion. (Lauren Winans in Kim, 2023)

Gen Z is leading the charge to rebalance the role of work in our broader whole lives. This effort began with millennials, who witnessed their parents' hard work often go unrewarded during the **Great Recession** of 2007–2009 and longer. Workers, especially those under 40, are reconceptualizing the role of work in their lives. They may be less willing to sacrifice family time and physical and mental health in the pursuit of external validation and financial remuneration.

Younger workers have transitioned into workplaces that are fully or partially remote, meaning they need more one-on-one or small group mentoring than previous generations who could learn from their colleagues in the next cubicle. The lack of connection, stressors related to the pandemic, and remote working isolation mean that people need something different to succeed than they needed prior to 2019. The needs of employees, and customers to some extent, have changed, but workplaces and managers have not evolved quickly enough.

According to a global study of employee engagement conducted in the fall of 2022, only 15% of workers around the world feel fully engaged in their workplaces, but this number is 10% for Europeans and 33% for employees in the United States. That gives American companies a big advantage (Jouany & Mäkipää, 2023).

This provides a competitive advantage for companies and managers who can *rehumanize the workplace*. What does this mean? All humans need a sense of belonging, meaning, fun, and growth, as well as the financial resources necessary to provide sustenance for themselves and their families. Managers who create warm, inclusive, affirming, impactful workplaces will attract and retain the talent they need to outperform their competition. Companies with highly engaged employees have 21% higher average profits, according to a study conducted in the fall of 2022 (Jouany & Mäkipää, 2023).

> Having a poor manager leads the list of reasons people are discontented with their jobs. Last year, a survey of 3,000 employees in a variety of fields by GoodHire, a company that provides employee background checks, found that less than half feel their managers are open and honest about salaries, benefits and promotions, and that they truly care about their employees' progression. (Tugend, 2023)

Table 7.1 shows employee behaviors linked to engagement levels, but this research was conducted prior to 2019. An updated version should include questions like, "I have the flexibility I need to succeed at work" and "I have received the mentoring and support needed to succeed at work." Updated research using questions like these has yet to be completed, but one can expect that the pivot to hybrid and online work environments has changed what workers need to feel engaged.

The information in Table 7.1 is helpful because it provides a list of potential survey questions designed to measure your employees' engagement. The numbers in the table are based on a national average across ranks and employee type (e.g., managers, rank-and-file, different sectors). If your scores are higher than the average agreement measures, then your organization beats the U.S. national average. Regardless of the score, this survey will help you determine whether and how deeply employee engagement or disengagement is problematic for your

Table 7.1   Employee Behaviors Linked to Engagement

	Strongly Disagree	Disagree	Neutral	Agree	Strongly Agree	Overall Agreement
I am confident I can reach my work goals.	1%	2%	8%	40%	49%	89%
I am highly motivated by my work goals.	2%	5%	17%	40%	37%	46%
I have a clear understanding of my organization's mission/vision.	2%	4%	17%	46%	31%	77%
While at work, I'm almost always completely focused on my work projects.	1%	8%	20%	44%	27%	71%
I am provided with the resources to do my job well.	2%	11%	19%	24%	44%	68%
I frequently feel that I'm putting all my effort into my work.	2%	6%	24%	39%	29%	68%
I have passion and excitement about my work.	2%	8%	24%	39%	26%	66%
I am often so wrapped up in my work that hours go by like minutes.	3%	10%	24%	33%	31%	64%
I enjoy volunteering for activities beyond my job requirements.	3%	13%	27%	35%	22%	57%
I feel completely plugged in at work, like I'm always on full power.	2%	12%	31%	35%	20%	55%

Source: Adapted from SHRM (2016).

organization. Since it includes averages, this table hides important differences between salaried and hourly workers.

Hiring an external consultant to take periodic employee engagement surveys can cost about $250,000 for large employers (in Tugend, 2023). Yet, many organizations gather this information without using it because the results are not positive. Collecting survey data without taking action "is like pulling a pin on a grenade and not throwing it," says Leigh Branham, who, with his coauthor Mark Hirschfeld, analyzed more than two million employee engagement surveys and exit interviews for their book *Re-Engage* (Tugend, 2023).

Best practices for employee engagement surveys are to ask a small number of questions with relative frequency, such as quarterly or even monthly, and then use that information to provide feedback and incentives for desired managerial behaviors. For example, "How has your relationship been with your manager in the last week? Do you feel like you made a difference last week? Did you receive any positive feedback?" (Tugend 2023). Frequent, short input is helpful to catch problems early and show employees their engagement matters.

An **exit interview (exit survey)** is used to gather information about the reasons employees are leaving the organization, their perceptions about what is going well and what is not, better ways to achieve the mission, and various other points of information deemed vital to constant improvement. Employees who have made the choice to leave the organization may be more honest about their observations than ongoing employees who may fear reprisals or retribution for speaking out. Again, do not bother gathering this information if you do not intend to use it. That leads to deeper apathy.

Employees who feel unappreciated, overworked, and mistreated are more likely to engage in sabotage, embezzlement, and theft at work. "Studies reveal a direct correlation between prevalence of employee conflict and the amount of damage, theft of inventory and equipment. Covert sabotage of work processes and of management's efforts usually occurs when employees are angry at their employer" (Dana, 2001). Experts refer to this as the 10–80–10 rule (see Chapter 6). This means that 10% of employees won't steal under any circumstances; another 10% are dishonest, and nothing can be done but closely monitor resources; and the other 80% will be influenced by the workplace climate and the thoughts of their peers. If the workplace culture indicates it is all right to bring home office supplies or small items, but not large ones, then that is what the average employee will do. In some workplaces, the norm is "just don't get caught," but everyone steals at least a little. Disgruntled employees rationalize their behaviors with the idea that the organization "deserved it" due to low pay, rude managers, etc. The key to avoiding theft, embezzlement, and sabotage is to create a positive workplace culture in which employees agree these behaviors are truly unacceptable and the sources of disgruntlement are proactively addressed. See Chapter 6 for organizational culture cures.

The good news is that organizations that proactively manage conflict have less litigation and less turnover. "Corporations that have developed collaborative conflict management systems report significant litigation cost savings: Brown and Root reported an 80 percent reduction in outside litigation costs, Motorola reported a 75 percent reduction over a period of six years, NCR reported a 50 percent reduction and a drop of pending lawsuits from 263 in 1984 to 28 in 1993" (Ford, 2000). When Haliburton implemented an ombuds office, they estimated a return on investment of approximately 20 dollars for each dollar invested (Yarrington, 2017). Conflict prevention or early resolution is one of the surest ways organizations can improve the bottom line.

Changing jobs isn't all about the money, as 74% of younger employees would accept a pay cut for a chance to work at their ideal job, and 23% of those seeking a job wouldn't need a pay increase to take a new position (Jouany & Mäkipää, 2023)

Let's do the conflict math for a disgruntled employee earning $75,000 per year:

Fourteen sick days: $4,200
Six months working below full capacity: $12,499
Managerial time spent listening to disgruntled employee and others: $10,000
    Hiring and replacement costs: $75,000 to $150,000
Lost productivity while the position is unfilled: $23,000
Total cost: $124,699 to $199,699

Hiring and retraining new employees is costly, with costs rising with the level of education and specialized training needed by the employee. Studies routinely estimate the cost of hiring and training an employee to be approximately 75 to 150% of the employee's annual salary (Phillips, 1990). The cost involved in hiring and training new employees vastly outweighs the cost of additional training, professional development, and support for the employees you already have.

Why Employees Leave or Stay

According to research conducted by Randstad US, in 2019, these were the top five reasons why employees leave: compensation too low, limited career path, work-life balance issues, insufficient challenges, and poor leadership in the organization (Jules, 2019). Fast-forward to the summer of 2022, when the same research group found that 65% of workers who quit stated they did so due to work-life balance (Randstad, 2022). Other reasons include salary and benefits, lack of job security, and the work environment (ibid.). Interestingly, the "work environment" included concerns such as "too many distractions," "too much noise," as well as "hostile work environment" and "lack of socializing with colleagues." After the social isolation of the pandemic and taking into account the physical environment in which work takes place, the overall work environment is key to reducing stress and increasing productivity. Forty percent of employees who quit their jobs did so without having another one secured first and 22% of current employees were planning to quit soon (Randstad, 2022).

What does this mean for you as a current or future manager? One-on-one conversations with each employee are required to ascertain what each person needs to thrive at work. Do they need flexible schedules or a hybrid environment? Do they seek mentoring and coaching (giving or receiving or both)? Often, there are inexpensive things you can do to help each employee reach their full potential. It is the job of managers to remove obstacles to employee success.

Rehumanizing the workplace requires embracing the whole human being. What do humans need? They need food, shelter, and rest (e.g., a comfortable physical space); a sense of belonging (e.g., camaraderie and friendship); the ability to be their authentic selves (e.g., embracing difference as strength); meaningful work, and a little fun. When people enjoy their coworkers, find meaning in their work, and are treated with kindness and respect, they usually stay. We can do that, right?

By way of a negative example, one government employee told me, "The cavalry treats its horses better than my organization treats its people. They expect us to work 12–14-hour shifts without many breaks or healthy food. We are not given time to exercise or connect with our families. If we complain, we are told we are not adequately committed to the important mission of serving our country. I am about to serve it right into the grave . . . so I am quitting." In the end, human beings have human needs. Ignoring these does not achieve the end goals assumed by the leaders making shortsighted decisions. People are not disposable.

A CEO for a large manufacturing plant recently told me,

> Over the next 2–3 years our managers need to know they will be missing family birthdays, anniversaries, kids' soccer games, and Sunday dinners. They need to convey to their families the importance of our mission so they can devote all their time to meeting our production targets. Our organization is growing rapidly, and we need their full commitment to getting these projects implemented.

Think about this: What kind of person agrees to give up family time for years? Would they make good managers? No. They would be stressed out, depressed, unhealthy people who struggle to be empathetic to others because their own needs are unmet. Would they be a diverse group that includes women and people from cultures or generations in which family commitments are taken seriously? No. In the end, if this CEO does not change his outlook, he will be the only one left. His tactics are undermining his ultimate goals. Sometimes it is easy for leaders to focus so intently on the mission, they end up undermining it by dehumanizing their workplaces, with inevitable results.

Successful managers and leaders attend to the human needs of their people, rather than seeing them as working machines, dehumanizing them.

The remainder of this chapter examines specific techniques managers can use to improve interpersonal relationships, team morale, and mission achievement.

Improving Performance Reviews: Building Relationships, Commitment, and Performance

Do you dread receiving and giving performance reviews? If so, let's turn this around. Performance reviews offer the opportunity to build the manager-employee relationship; develop shared understandings of individual and team needs and goals; discuss strategies for achieving maximum success both in one's career, current tasks, and the mission; and allow the manager time to coach the employee (or sometimes vice versa) to enhance the skills necessary for peak performance (see Chapter 10). According to Schultz (2015) a peak performance appraisal system would be about creating a vision for the team, instilling fundamentals, providing help, supporting growth, and fostering teamwork. Jawahar (2012) found that satisfaction with the performance appraisal feedback and rating as well as the satisfaction with the *rater* are positively correlated to continuity in the job, satisfaction, engagement, and commitment. Providing feedback in a supportive manner is crucial in influencing the employee's satisfaction level and their ability to absorb and utilize the feedback (see Chapter 10 for more on giving and receiving feedback).

Consider these questions to learn more about the employee's needs while sharing your own:

- What are your personal and professional goals?
- What are the obstacles to achieving your goals? How can I help?
- How do those goals match your current tasks? What can we do to bring these into maximal alignment?
- What motivates you and makes you want to work here? What, if anything, makes you think about leaving?
- Are there any skills you wish to further develop, mentoring you seek, or other professional development opportunities that would be of interest to you? (The manager could share ideas here too.)
- What ideas do you have about the sources of poor performance and ideas for improvement, if applicable? (Help them to focus on what *they* think,

say, and do rather than externalizing blame for their performance. Doing this increases their odds of improving their performance.)

• How can we work together to achieve our objectives both individually and collectively? (It is fair for the manager to also share with the employee how she can help the manager to achieve his or her own goals as well.)

Make sure each person understands the overall mission of the organization, their unit's mission or role, and the connection between their work and the greater mission. Employees who feel disconnected from the mission have lower levels of engagement. Whether one mops the floors, maintains the computers, or runs the budget, each person contributes in important ways.

When an employee is underperforming, it is important to get to the root cause of low performance and chart a path forward together. Normalize the idea that everyone has room to grow and improve, even yourself. Document any specific requests for change as well as your shared overall expectations related to output expectations for each employee. If the employee has been underperforming, make sure this is clearly detailed in their human resources record, along with the support you will give them to improve their performance (e.g., training or professional development) and clearly articulated, measurable goals. It is important to avoid vague feedback or goals designed to save face. Rather, frame the desire for improvements as consistent with your mutual goal for their success, while offering the support needed for their performance to meet or exceed expectations.

A word of caution: Avoid the tendency to comment on negative personality traits and instead stick to behaviors. "In one study across 28 companies, 76 percent of critical feedback given to women included comments on her personality—e.g., a woman was "abrasive"—while only 2 percent of negative reviews for men included such comments" (Herrera, 2018). Our own cultural biases mean we are more likely to find fault in those who are different from us—different gender, race, sexual orientation, national origin, generation, social class, and so on. To overcome these tendencies, focus on measurable, objective indicators of performance whenever possible. For many managers, this will include their interpersonal and communication skills, but keep the focus on observable behaviors. For example, "Bob, please be sure to offer more positive feedback than negative feedback to your subordinates. This will build rapport and help them better hear you when criticism becomes necessary."

For performance reviews to be fair and objective, all employees and teams need to have clear goals and performance indicators against which their performance can be judged. Second, the organization needs to gather data related to individual and group performance. For example, you may ask customers and clients to complete feedback surveys related to their experiences. In manufacturing settings you can look at output or other readily quantifiable measures, which should include both quality and quantity to avoid trade-offs between the two. All employees can be rated on their punctuality and adherence to deadlines. If employees have engaged in problematic workplace behaviors, such as unfriendly, bullying, harassing interactions, consider providing coaching to change these behaviors with specific, measurable goals and consequences for the continuation of unacceptable behaviors.

Ideally, performance reviews should have a 360-degree feedback mechanism. A 360-degree review takes in anonymous feedback from all people with whom you work: peers, subordinates, supervisors, and managers. This system works best in large organizations but can be done in small organizations, though with less anonymity. Employees should rate their satisfaction with their supervisors' and managers' abilities to resolve problems efficiently and collaboratively. In the same survey, be sure to gather their ideas about how to improve workplace morale, efficiency, and mission fulfillment.

By gaining input from employees and allowing them to have a voice in this process (remember the concepts of procedural justice), they will be more likely to support the outcome of the evaluation and any subsequent employment decisions. Lastly, performance reviews should occur more than once per year. Feedback and guidance can occur as needed, even daily. Frequent performance check-ins and feedback are important for all employees and managers, but especially for those seeking to make changes.

Motivating Employees

Motivating employees is a critical duty for all managers. Motivated employees have less conflict in their teams and lift up the performance of other team members. When it comes to motivation, one size does not fit all. Each employee needs something different from their work, so one-on-one discussions with them are required for managers to build rapport and understand their needs. Motivation usually stems from a mix of pay, praise, professional growth, meaningful work, and belonging (Kreps, 2017).

At the lowest levels of pay, employees will leave for higher wages. Yet, once employees and managers earn enough to live comfortably, they will stay at an organization where they are happy and productive, even if offered more money by a competitor. However, competitive pay is both expected and shows respect for the workforce. Periodic benchmarking can ensure your organization is offering fair pay and benefits to remain competitive and attract the best employees.

There are many ways to motivate employees beyond pay and benefits; Acknowledging a job well done costs nothing and helps some employees feel valued. Hard work is not always its own reward—especially if no one notices. Like the *Five Love Languages* (Chapman, 2010), some individuals are motivated by words of affirmation, gifts, acts of service, and/or quality time spent together. Of course, the fifth love language is usually best avoided at work: physical touch. For some employees, praise seems hollow if unsupported by actions (i.e., acts of service) while others seek support for their ideas, advancement, etc. Bringing someone a cup of coffee when they're nose-deep in a spreadsheet can be a meaningful act of service that helps them feel supported. When managers seek to treat all employees the same, they miss the critical fact that what works for one won't work for them all. Great managers figure out what motivates *each* employee, then seek to provide a customized response to their needs.

Motivating across Generations

Many interpersonal disputes at work arise across generational differences. Motivating, retaining, and successfully managing employees is significantly impacted by generational differences (Gurchiek, 2016). Proviso: Individuals within generational or other cultural groups may not follow the tendencies of their cohort, yet it is worth sharing recent research about motivating workers across generations since the generation gap between older and younger workers is the biggest in many decades. This happens when rapid economic and environmental changes require rapid sociocultural shifts. In other words, younger people will live in a very different world than other people. Therefore, the rules of the game (e.g., cultural programming about how to succeed in one's environment) will also change rapidly.

Conflict comes when a person from one generation expects someone from a different generation to act like them, dress like them, think like them, work like them, parent like them, and share their priorities and values. Different generations *are* different cultural groups. Differences are to be expected and embraced. For example, younger millennials spent much of their teenage years making and playing with friends online instead of outside, much to the chagrin of Gen Xers and boomers, who defined "play" differently. Yet, anthropologically, the purpose of childhood play is to prepare kids for their adult lives. It turns out, younger workers will spend much more of their adult lives living and working online. Their play predicted their work. If you are Gen X or older, what can you learn from observing younger workers or what can you infer about the future of work?

Recent research indicates that older generations are more motivated by pay, benefits, and bonuses, while younger generations seek greater feedback, mentoring, flexibility, and meaningful work (Gurchiek, 2016).

Work-life balance is one of the most fractious topics across generations and one that is likely to give rise to conflict when older managers seek to motivate younger workers (or vice versa!). Gen Xers and older generations came of age at a time when there were not enough "good jobs" to go around. Education was critical to obtaining, retaining, and promotion. This often meant long workdays, sacrificing family time and sometimes even demanded sacrificing one's personal health to long, unremitting work demands. Younger generations observed these behaviors and decided not to make the same choices.

There is a tendency to feel and convey contempt for the work-life trade-offs of others when they are different from ours. Some employees will "live to work" while others will "work only to live." This is a continuum rather than just one or the other. Wherever an employee falls on this spectrum, so long as they meet expectations, it is important to respect their boundaries. For example, if an employee doesn't answer emails over the weekend, but that is not a job requirement, then it needs to be respected. Workaholism leads to burnout and irritability at work; therefore, it should not become a cultural expectation of the organization (Brown, 2018).

When you catch yourself feeling disdainful of other's work-life balance choices, especially across generations, ask yourself these questions: (1) Are they meeting the expectations, deadlines, or requirements of their position? Remember, not everyone can or must perform above average, by definition. If they are meeting expectations, consider letting it go. (2) Are you their supervisor? Does their work-life balance impact you? If the answer to both questions is "no," then consider setting a healthy boundary that focuses on *your* own work-life boundaries and let others do the same. Remember, when your mantra with colleagues is "you can be you and I can be me," then you will have healthier, happier relationships. We tend to engage in the psychological practice of "projection" when we feel insecure or dissatisfied with our own work-life balance. This means we criticize others (at least in our own minds), when in fact, we are unhappy with our own ability to set and keep healthy boundaries around our work-life balance. Engage in introspection to see if this might be happening within your own mind. It is possible that an individual's work-life balance is not consistent with the organizational culture of a specific team or organization. That simply means they do not "fit," and the worker may be a better fit elsewhere. If this frequently arises, then it is time to reassess the organization's expectations of its employees. Are you treating humans "worse than the cavalry treats its horses"? If so, make changes. And by the way—the U.S. Cavalry treats its horses well. We can learn by treating our people at least as well.

In the end, each human being will decide how much work is too much and how to meet the needs of their families, health, and mental health. Trying to convince others to adopt your approach will be a fool's errand.

Consider these tips for creating a successful, motivating intergenerational workplace (Gurchiek, 2016):

- Promote collaboration and celebration. Consider investing in online platforms where employees can share their successes.
- Managers should seek to understand individual work styles and how people like to be recognized for accomplishments.
- Make the customer the mutual priority. This has everyone working together on a common purpose.
- Enable personal growth and work-life balance. This is something all generations appreciate.
- Develop employee strengths through a mentorship program. Start a reverse mentorship program in which each employee is both a mentor and a mentee.
- Define culture in a way that can be explained to everyone, and survey employees at all levels of your organization to get a 360-degree view of the culture.
- Carefully select managers based on experience, aptitude, capacity for growth, leadership style, and understanding of organizational and employee challenges and opportunities.
- Enhance employees' well-being.

DEALING WITH DIFFICULT EMPLOYEES

Let's face it, although employee turnover is expensive, occasionally there are employees you are happy to see go. In fact, one difficult employee or manager can drive away many good ones. It is important to respond effectively to difficult people at work, but firing someone is usually the last option. The most difficult employee is someone with poor communication or people skills or a negative attitude, a shirker, or a bully. Poor performance isn't enough to make someone difficult. An employee who struggles to meet performance goals but is open to feedback and coaching is likely to grow and eventually succeed. Although it may not be easy to admit, some employees just don't fit in with the organization's culture, work well with others, or help the organization achieve its mission. What's worse, some individuals have personality disorders that are severe enough to wreak havoc in their work teams, such as severe narcissism or antisocial personality disorder, or engage in behaviors such as systemically falsifying their résumé or performance indicators. Private companies generally have an easier time firing or laying off an employee for poor performance than do public-sector employers or corporations. The first step in addressing problem employees is to make sure you are doing all you can to hire, train, and acculturate employees to succeed in your team.

How can you deal effectively with difficult coworkers or supervisors? Rafenstein (2000) offers some ideas to help reduce problems with employees, including strategies such as trying to understand the employee's perspective, helping the employee develop the skills necessary to give and receive feedback constructively (see Chapter 10), and making sure expectations are clearly understood by all parties as part of the annual review as well as ongoing communications (see 3-step problem-solving later in this chapter). Many problems with underperforming employees can be attributed to a lack of agreement between the employee and manager with regard to goals, prioritizing resources including employee time, and difficulty in making corrections or changes when problems arise.

Typology of Difficult People at Work

Eeyores

Everyone has had the experience of working with an "Eeyore," meaning someone who sees only dark clouds but never silver linings. They may be suspicious of others, whether due to depression, past negative experiences, or because inadequate attempts have been made to build trust and rapport with them. When placed in the right position, these individuals bring great strengths to their companies. They tend to be detail oriented and good at finding faults (Preston, 2005). Use them as auditors, editors, quality control technicians, and so on. Although it is important for these employees to feel heard and have their opinions valued, it may be a good idea to meet with them privately rather than allowing them to vent or share their negative views in a large-group setting. Complaining can be contagious and certainly reduces group morale. By getting to know difficult employees well, and by gaining their trust, you may be able to turn their annoying habits into strengths for the team.

Westwood (2010) notes that rather than labeling employees as difficult, managers should instead make notes of those behaviors that are helpful or unhelpful in the work environment (see Table 7.2). When providing feedback to employees,

Table 7.2   Helpful and Unhelpful Behaviors in the Work Environment

Helpful Behaviors	Description
Listens actively	Makes eye contact, as possible and appropriate, uses questions, summarizes what has been heard, refrains from interrupting.
Supports	Encourages others' suggestions, recognizes others for ideas and attempts at problem-solving, refrains from shooting down others' ideas prematurely.
Clarifies	Asks clarifying questions to clear up confusion.
Offers ideas	Shares suggestions, ideas, solutions, and proposals; does not make complaints without offering solutions.
Includes others	Asks quiet members for their opinions, making sure no one is left out.
Harmonizes	Reconciles opposing points of view, links similar ideas, points out similarities.
Manages conflict	Listens to the views of all, clarifies issues and key points made by opponents, seeks solutions together, shows non-adversarial attitude.

Unhelpful Behaviors	Description
"Yeah, but . . ."	Discredits the ideas of others.
Blocks	Insists on getting one's way, doesn't compromise, stands in the way of the team's progress.
Grandstands	Draws attention to one's personal skills, boasts.
Goes off topic	Draws attention to other topics, poor time management.
Dominates	Tries to run the group through dictating, bullying.
Withdraws	Doesn't participate or offer help or support to others.
Plays devil's advocate	Takes pride in being contrary.
Uses personal slurs	Hurls insults at others and is disrespectful.
Dictates	Tries to control the agenda, negates others' priorities and concerns.

Source: Based on an earlier version of a chart found in Bens (2005, p. 80).

ask them to work on minimizing the unhelpful behaviors and maximizing the helpful ones. Managers should lead by example and reward positive behaviors and improvements. These behavioral changes can be included as categories in reviews, with incentives for improvements.

Divas at Work

A workplace diva is a high producer, someone the organization cannot or does not want to do without. Unfortunately, divas know it and use it, sometimes contrary to the team's benefit. They may ask for or expect special privileges, higher pay, better office space, and more attention. They may be narcissists, or they may just be quirky. Handling them effectively requires a combination of flattery and boundary setting. Read below for more on working with narcissists. Acknowledge their important role in the organization while reminding them that the rules need to apply to everyone, for the overall good of the organization and to maintain fairness between employees. Do what you can to ensure no one is irreplaceable in the organization through cross-training, mentoring, and recruitment.

Prophets at Work

A prophet is the person who invented (and continues to invent) the key product, services, or concept of the organization. This person is best suited for the lab, as their interpersonal skills are sometimes dwarfed by their inventive genius. Recognizing the prophets in your organization is key to continued innovation. These individuals may want to run the company, but they generally lack the managerial skills to do so. For example, Alexander Graham Bell, Nikola Tesla, Elon Musk.

Racehorse at a Pony Show

This is an employee who is under challenged, overqualified, bored, and disengaged. The trick is to identify the racehorses and find new challenges for them that allow them to grow and stretch in their current roles or move them up in the organization. If no positions are open in your unit, look across the organization for positions that will allow them to grow. If you don't challenge them, they will leave for greener pastures.

Hermit Crabs in Bureaucracies

This is an employee with a lot to offer the organization, but he has given up because of the stultifying nature of the bureaucracy that repeatedly limits his creativity and impact. Occasionally, when a new leader arrives or there appears to be a crack in the wall that has limited the hermit crab, then he will stick out his head and look around a bit, hoping he won't be told again to "stay in your lane." Managers need to identify these underutilized, talented, innovative, yet beaten-down employees to rebuild their trust and reengage their potential. This will likely happen step by step. It is important to keep promises, communicate transparently, and convey that "we are in it together." Normalize the fact that large organizations change slowly, but that you commit to treating them fairly in making the changes you have the power to make.

The Burnout

Burnout is defined by the American Medical Association as "Emotional, mental, and/or physical exhaustion accompanied by lower performance, decreased motivation, and negative attitudes towards oneself and others." It is characterized by a sense of helplessness and hopelessness often arising from overwork, a joyless environment, disconnection from others and from the mission, and a sense of being trapped. Physical symptoms include fatigue, depression, hypertension, headache, anxiety, and digestive problems. Lack of time outdoors and insufficient exposure to sunlight can worsen symptoms. Burnout and disengagement go hand in hand.

According to Michel (2016):

> Three key stress responses: an overwhelming sense of exhaustion, feelings of cynicism and detachment, and a sense of professional ineffectiveness and lack of accomplishment. Burnout results when the balance of deadlines, demands, working hours, and other stressors outstrips rewards, recognition, and relaxation. It's a mistake to assume that burnout   is merely an emotional response to long hours or a challenging job. Rather, mounting scientific evidence shows that

burnout takes a profound physical toll that cascades well beyond our professional lives. Just as the impact of burnout stifles healthy professional growth, emerging research shows that the chronic psychosocial stress that characterizes burnout not only impairs people's personal and social functioning, it also can overwhelm their cognitive skills and neuroendocrine systems—eventually leading to distinctive changes in the anatomy and functioning of the brain.

Burnout can literally change how our brains function. What can managers to do help? Model healthy self-care, including taking breaks and vacations, exercising, and eating well. Make time for collegiality, bonding, and fun in the workday and encourage others to do the same. Help remove "busywork" or routine meetings that interfere with workers' ability to focus on the frontline work. Give positive feedback. Make people feel "seen." Rehumanize even the most stressful work environments by prioritizing the physical and relational needs of employees. Convey reasonable expectations. Look for signs of burnout and speak one-on-one with employees to brainstorm ways forward.

Personality Disordered Individuals

Individuals with personality disorders will be disproportionately associated with conflict at work. They struggle to get along with others, meet expectations, and behave in predictable ways—a true conflict cocktail. A **personality disorder** is a "deeply ingrained and maladaptive pattern of behavior of a specified kind, typically manifest by the time one reaches adolescence and causing long-term difficulties in personal relationships or in functioning in society" (Dictionary.com, 2019). Personality disorders are covered in Chapter 2, so this chapter will briefly point out why these individuals are overrepresented among "difficult people" at work and how best to work with them. Note that all personality disordered individuals will externalize blame for their choices and behaviors. That means they blame others, rationalize, and justify bad actions. Be on the lookout for this behavior as your first clue that you might be working with someone who has a personality disorder.

Narcissists are overrepresented in top corporate leadership roles because they seek promotion frequently, due to a surfeit of confidence and a desire for attention, yet their overall impact on organizations is negative (Braun, 2017). Because narcissistic leaders will always put their individual interests above those of the organization, their self-serving decisions can hurt the bottom line while driving away key players and partners. They also vastly overestimate their importance to the organization and their employees' satisfaction with their leadership (Braun 2017). If they are to remain in the organization, then managers and subordinates must understand how to work with them successfully. First, they will only compromise or make sacrifices for the team when doing so can be framed as a victory for them or make them look better in some way. Consider saying, "You can show yourself to be the bigger person here" or "Be our hero and help us out." While manipulative, it is in the service of both the narcissist and the company, since curbing their behaviors will be key to longevity in the company. The occasional ego massage may help feed their need for attention, while directing their contributions. Borderline personality disordered individuals will be moody, unpredictable, paranoid, antisocial, and selfish, and exhibit tendencies of all the personality disorders combined. They do best when working alone. If this is not possible, be sure to run interference and limit the damage their mood swings do to others. Let others know not to take it personally when these people verbally lash out. Set and maintain boundaries, document expectations, and take action to protect others in the workforce from these negative behaviors.

Antisocial individuals don't like to follow rules. They seek their own best interests, although they do not usually seek attention, unlike narcissists. Some are psychopaths, who may enjoy causing pain, while others are sociopaths, who do not care if they cause pain but do not actively seek it out. Both will lack the ability to empathize with others, which makes them prone to poor social relationships and increases their likelihood of illegal behaviors. Sociopaths can often mimic socially expected behaviors, even if they do not feel genuine connection to other people. "Antisocial personality disorder (ASPD) is characterized by a pattern of socially irresponsible, exploitative, and guiltless behavior" (Black, 2015, p. 309).

Some of the worst corporate scandals involve antisocial personality disordered individuals who are prone to "cook the books" or engage in other illegalities to serve their own desires (e.g., Bernie Madoff, Elizabeth Holmes). The best defense is to keep these individuals out of the organization in the hiring stage. Verify any claims made on their résumés, speak with people who worked with them previously to ascertain how they treat those above and below them on the power chain, and be skeptical of anyone who is "perfect"; they are likely to have forged all or part of their identity to meet your exact needs. While psychopaths make up about 1% of the U.S. population, they comprise about 3% of corporate leaders and make up about 15% of the prison population (Lipman, 2013). If we include psychopaths and sociopaths together, the percentage in the prison population rises to 25% (Braun, 2017).

Since personality disordered individuals breed conflict at work, be on the lookout for these behaviors (Eddy, 2016; Eddy and DiStefano, 2015):

1. Emotions dominate thinking
2. Difficulty accepting and healing from loss (stuck in the grief cycle)
3. Inability to reflect on own behavior
4. Preoccupied with blaming others (blame is an addiction)
5. Impulse control problems
6. Avoiding responsibility for the problem (and, therefore, for the solution)
7. Expecting others to solve problems (e.g., seeking out union representatives, therapist, mediators, lawyers, judges)
8. Lacks empathy (can't easily engage in perspective taking); shows frequent contempt
9. Lacks genuine remorse for bad behavior, but regrets getting caught
10. No respect for boundaries

Try setting a reasonable boundary with a high-conflict personality to see if she can respect your request. For example, "Please call me Mr. Smith, rather than John, because that is the practice of our organization." Or, "Please do not email me on Sundays." If she or he cannot respect a reasonable boundary, it is a clue the root cause may be personality disorder. The other key indicator is a need to blame others for their own failings. Denial is a common behavior when one feels under attack, but high-conflict people take this to new levels and cannot easily identify any area of their life or skill set that is in deficit. A lack of introspection makes it hard for them to change. Articulate your expectations in writing as part of the performance review or other formal feedback, then document negative behaviors and performance before proceeding with formal reprimands or termination. Not all high-conflict individuals need to be terminated. It may be possible to limit their contact with other employees, set them on solitary tasks, and they may respond to appropriate incentives. If they can't, it is important to limit their ability to drive away customers and other employees. If they decide not to change their behaviors, and you maintain boundaries that limit their ability to misbehave (e.g., checking their reports for misrepresentation; ending sexual harassment by ensuring they are never alone with potential prey), then they will move on to more fruitful hunting grounds.

Once you have identified the root cause of the difficult person's performance troubles, it is key to proceed effectively. Pelusi (2006) lists five pieces of advice for dealing effectively with difficult people: (1) uncover their interests, (2) attempt to correct overgeneralizations or perceptual distortions, (3) acknowledge a mistake but do not accept personal labels—that is, separate the people from the problem, (4) summarize what you have heard them say, and (5) use questions instead of statements to get to the bottom of what they want. Tiffan (2009) points out that many managers procrastinate in dealing with difficult employees out of fear of "escalating the situation," uncertainty about how to handle the problem, and "discomfort with conflict" (p. 86). As a result, the problem grows and becomes more unmanageable.

This advice sounds much like that given to negotiators in Chapter 3, and with good reason. Even though managers are in charge, dealing with employees is always a negotiation on some level. The employees' alternatives to an agreement with the manager include leaving the company, filing a complaint, saying negative things about the boss behind her back, calling in sick when not sick, and shirking. The goal is to avoid behaviors that indicate employee alienation by addressing difficult employees proactively. Do not reward or accept bad behavior. It will only increase.

What if you are the "difficult personality" at work? The reality is that each of us can have a bad day or bad patch that leads us to be irritable or selfish. Statistically speaking, some of the people reading this text will have a personality disorder. Reach out for help. Mental health professionals can provide useful tools to reduce the frequency of negative behaviors and minimize the pain caused to yourself and others. Anyone who is willing to be introspective, admit they can do better, set goals, and measure progress can indeed improve their performance and their interactions with others. If you have transgressed, apologize. Admit you failed to meet your own expectations for your behavior, that you take responsibility for it by working to repair the harm done, and you will take affirmative steps to assure the problem does not recur. Apologies are useless unless accompanied by specific acts to remedy the current harm and prevent any recurrence.

In healthy organizational cultures, most employees will be happy. The group norms will not allow disruptive, selfish, or antisocial behaviors to go unconfronted by those who find the behaviors unacceptable (see active bystander skills in Chapter 5). In the most dysfunctional workplaces, where terminating an employee is difficult to accomplish, managers sometimes suggest their most difficult employees for promotion elsewhere in the organization, thereby solving their own problem and passing it off to someone else. I call this "failing up." Never reward negative behavior. Everyone will know and then positive behaviors and culture are undermined.

If none of the strategies discussed herein are working, then it may be time to help the employee "find another dream," as I like to say. If the employee is not a good match for their team and organization, they aren't happy either. Through a coaching conversation (see Chapter 10), try to help them envision the type of organization or work situation that would make them happier. Then, help them take steps to get there. It is best if they leave on their own to pursue another dream, but you may, in fact, have to show them the door. This is why you must document shared expectations, violations of those expectations, and the support and assistance you gave to help them meet realistic expectations.

When a difficult employee leaves to pursue their new dream, or they are terminated, workplace morale will likely surge rather than decline, if you have followed the steps outlined in this section.

Identifying and Eradicating Workplace Bullying and Violence

"**Bullying** can be considered as a form of coercive interpersonal influence. It involves deliberately inflicting injury or discomfort on another person repeatedly through physical contact, verbal abuse, exclusion, or other negative actions" (Forsyth, 2006, p. 206). The key to this definition is that the behavior must be intentional, repeated over time, and have a negative impact on the target. Bullying behaviors include verbal abuse; offensive conduct and behaviors that can be verbal or nonverbal; attempts to threaten, intimidate, or humiliate; and attempts to prevent the victim from accomplishing required tasks at work with the goal of negatively affecting the victim's career (Lutgen-Sandvik, Tracy & Alberts, 2007). Bullies wear down their victims, also known as targets, usually for more than a year in workplace settings (Einarsen & Skogstad, 1996). If actions are not taken to stop them, these behaviors escalate until a crisis is reached, commonly resulting in the target quitting his or her job, the bully getting fired, or violent action of an offensive or defensive nature by one or both parties. A positive workplace culture is the best defense to prevent bullying throughout your company (see Chapter 6), but even in strong workplaces, occasional bullying may occur and must be stopped.

It should be noted here that some forms of bullying constitute harassment or discrimination and others simply constitute rude, inappropriate, or intimidating behaviors. If a victim was singled out for worse treatment due in part to his or her status as a member of a protected class, then the bullying may result in a greater legal liability for the organization. For example, if the bully includes name-calling or disrespectful treatment based on race, national origin, sex, religion, age, or other protected status, then the employee may have stronger grounds for a lawsuit or to file a complaint with the EEOC (in the United States).

The best research indicates that about 13% of employees are bullied in an average year, with 30% having experienced bullying at some point in their careers (Lutgen-Sandvik et al., 2007).

According to a 2021 study, 30% of Americans have suffered abusive conduct at work and another 19% have witnessed it (Namie, 2021). Interestingly, remote workers are more likely to experience bullying (43.2%), often in virtual meetings rather than emails, making it difficult to prove, unless others in the meeting witness it or the meeting is recorded. Workplace bullying reports have increased 57% since 2017 (ibid.), although it is not clear if younger workers are more likely to report bullying and less likely to accept it, or if the actual incidence of bullying is increasing. The targets of bullying include non-managers 52% of the time and managers 40% of the time, with higher-level managers less likely to experience bullying, which makes sense because bullying is about asserting power and dominance over others. Women are more likely to bully other women than they are to bully men (ibid.).

Bullying impacts everyone, not just the bullies and targets, but the witnesses too (Comaford, 2016). Witnesses may act as active bystanders (see Chapter 5) or they may do nothing, but in either event they can suffer secondary trauma, lose loyalty to the organization, and seek to leave if the problem is not addressed. When unaddressed by those in power, bullies create a toxic work culture that ends in turnover, lawsuits, and damaged brand image.

Workers who have experienced bullying are more likely to quit than to file a complaint. It is crucial that managers and organizational leaders take bullying seriously. Failure to act sends a terrible signal organization-wide. It is appropriate to investigate claims and communicate expected behaviors to all members of the organization. By its nature, bullying often occurs out of the sight of witnesses. If concerns about bullying are raised, begin by coaching the alleged offender and victim (separately first) to convey appropriate expectations and encourage more documentation of interactions between both parties. Sometimes mediation or facilitated problem-solving are helpful to reach shared expectations to reduce the recurrence of problems. Bullies rarely recognize their behavior as hostile or inappropriate and targets sometimes miss opportunities to set and enforce boundaries, minimize time alone with the bully, or communicate their own sources of power. Managers, human resource professionals, and ombudsmen may use these instances as coaching opportunities designed to end unwanted behaviors and/or to enhance productive communication between the parties. It may be inadvisable to bring the parties together, especially if either party feels physically unsafe.

Most research, but not all, indicates bullies are more likely to be male and in supervisory or managerial roles, due in part to the need for bullies to be in positions of power to successfully intimidate their victims (Zapf & Einarsen, 2003). When bullies are female, they tend to use psychological warfare tactics such as spreading false rumors, excluding victims from important meetings and information networks, and ostracism (Crothers, 2009). Perpetrators of bullying tend to exhibit higher-than-average levels of aggression, whereas victims tend to exhibit low levels of self-esteem. Victims *and* perpetrators have weak social skills. "Social competency is closely linked with empathy, the capacity to share the emotional state of another and is also associated with altruistic behavior. deficits in social competency, specifically those aspects relevant to close relationships, are clearly linked to engaging in offending or humiliating behavior against others" (Matthiesen & Einarsen, 2007, p. 740). Bullies tend to seek external validation, meaning their ego needs the approval of others to thrive. Bullies who turn to violence at work tend to exhibit an inability to empathize, lack of self-control, type A personalities (on a Myers-Briggs personality assessment), unrealistically high self-esteem, and a history of depression (Lutgen-Sandvik et al., 2007).

For the targets of bullies, low levels of social skills make it difficult for them to identify the behavior as bullying and make it difficult for them to reach out to powerful individuals for help. That is *why* they are targeted. The most common reaction to bullying is withdrawal. Ironically, a subset of victims is also composed of bullies themselves, meaning those who have been bullied are somewhat more likely to be perpetrators in the future (Palmer & Thakordas, 2005). The key to ending the cycle of bad behavior is to build skills and set clear, firm expectations about how team members and leaders will treat each other. In the current employment environment, bullied employees are likely to leave for less hostile environments.

The best prevention against workplace bullying is the creation and maintenance of a positive, collaborative workplace culture that fosters strong social ties among team members and creates clarity about expectations and roles. If bullying does occur in this type of organization, it is likely to be caught sooner and dealt with more swiftly. Highly competitive organizational cultures may have greater difficulty recognizing this behavior as unacceptable because their cultural norms may encourage "survival of the fittest." During the employment applicant-screening process, employers may wish to use scales that measure empathy and other emotional intelligence to screen out those who will be more apt to bully or work poorly in teams.

Even in healthy organizational cultures, occasionally a manager or employee will need to intervene to stop bullying. Workplace policies need to define bullying as well as the potential consequences of such behaviors. Victims need to know where to go for help and that their concerns will be proactively addressed. Even if a manager feels the behaviors do not fully meet the definition of bullying, the fact that an employee has raised these concerns is a sign that some intervention in the relationship between accuser and accused is necessary.

Because bullies often act out of a sense of threat to self, it is important to clarify their roles, set appropriate boundaries, and work with them to develop better coping skills and behaviors. One example is perspective taking—which is to empathize with the target and see how this might have a negative impact on the target and the broader organization. Consider having employees attend counseling through an employee assistance program or other venues to work on improving their social and empathy skills. In the end, it will be important to set clear expectations about the behaviors that must stop and any reparations or apologies due to the victim. Written records of this meeting and any resulting expectations should be kept in case litigation from either party arises. Although it is important not to blame the victim, there may be similar resources made available to help the victim to reduce the chances of future victimization by this or any other bully.

3-STEP PROBLEM-SOLVING
(ALSO CALLED 3-STEP CONFLICT RESOLUTION)

What separates high- and low-performing teams? Google launched Project Aristotle more than a decade ago to answer this pressing question (Duhigg, 2016). Most of Google's work occurs in teams—lots of different types of teams. They decided to begin by measuring team "success" and then looking for correlations based on assertions commonly made in the field of management science. For example, do teams that spend more time socializing outside work function better? Sometimes. Do face-to-face teams produce better results than remote teams? Sometimes. Do hierarchically organized teams have more conflict than teams with an egalitarian structure for decision-making? Sometimes. Do diverse or cross-functional teams have more conflict than homogenous teams? Sometimes. It turns out that none of these factors consistently predict high-producing teams. Project Aristotle found one consistent correlation that predicted high-functioning teams: Teams with more conflict had lower performance. What predicted more or less conflict and therefore higher productivity (aka "success")? Only one factor consistently predicted better team functioning: Shared expectations (ibid.).

Consider making this one of your dispute resolution mantras: "Conflict comes from unmet expectations." Usually, our expectations are implicit and assumed to be shared. This is rarely the case. For example, if I am a soldier in the military, I expect to receive and follow orders unless they are inherently illegal or immoral. Yet, if I am a professor and my boss barks orders at me, my response is likely to be different because my expectation is different. In our daily work and personal lives there are many times we encounter frustrating situations in which someone did not behave as we expected. When this happens, consider using the 3-step problem-solving process to deescalate, normalize, and resolve conflict through the creation of shared expectations (See Box 7.1).

BOX 7.1. 3-STEP PROBLEM-SOLVING

Step 1: Normalize conflict and show optimism:
"It's totally normal that when two people work together on a project they will run into challenges from time to time. I bet if we put our heads together, we can find a solution that works for us both."

Step 2: Conflict comes from unmet expectations:
"Conflict often comes from unmet or unclear expectations. Can you share your expectations with me and then I can do the same? What would success look like to you? What are your expectations about deadlines and the division of labor on this project?"

Step 3: Negotiate shared expectations:
"Ok, now that we have discussed our expectations, I can see why we were both getting frustrated. Let's brainstorm possible shared expectations about the deadlines and how to divide up the project. Sound good?"

CONCLUSION

Satisfied customers and successful organizations are built on the foundation of satisfied employees, who are treated and compensated fairly. High employee turnover results in preventable costs that limit the ability of organizations to achieve their missions and remain competitive in the marketplace. Productive workplaces require thoughtful hiring, training, coaching, feedback, and the alignment of individual incentives with group goals. When problems arise, such as bullying, collaborative managers intervene to create and maintain a positive workplace culture in which all team members can thrive. Processes such as 3-step problem-solving (see Box 7.1) are useful tools for resolving interpersonal disputes and building shared understandings for better teamwork. Whether you manage two employees or two thousand, effective collaboration leads to reduced employee turnover, deeper engagement, and maximal mission achievement.

HIGH EMPLOYEE TURNOVER AT MAIN STREET BAKERIES

Using the company's employment records, Ben contacted the last three assistant managers and three former frontline employees. He met with them personally. He explained that his goal is to improve the workplace climate and make it a place where employees feel valued, satisfied, and empowered to do their jobs well. All were pleased to talk to him—in fact, they talked his ear off! He got a consistent story from everyone: the current manager of store number 75, Jane, is a bully. She pressures hourly employees to work off the clock if they are unable to complete their tasks during their regular eight-hour shifts. She accuses staff of being "lazy," "stupid," or not being willing to "take one for the team." If employees ask for time off for a doctor's appointment or a family commitment, they are punished by being taken off the schedule for a week without pay. She turns employees against one another and promotes only her favorite employees who act like sycophants. She rarely holds staff meetings and then gets angry when employees fail to correctly implement new policies or procedures. She works 75 hours per week and cannot understand why others are not willing to show similar levels of commitment.

What should Ben do? Brainstorm this before you continue reading. Ben sat down with the manager and had a frank discussion. He told her that her own pay and bonuses would now be tied to employee workplace climate surveys, customer satisfaction surveys, and a reduction in employee turnover. Every employee who leaves during the next six months will take part in an exit interview by phone with Ben so he can get more feedback about how to improve the store and its management. He arranged for an executive coach to work with Jane on her people skills and told her she was required to meet with this coach for at least two hours per week for the next six weeks, and then at least one hour per month for twelve months. He made it clear that his goal was to help her reach her potential as a manager. He explained that her own job will be easier once she feels confident in her abilities to delegate to her assistant managers, her own stress level will go down, and her job satisfaction will increase. The manager signed a 90-day probationary contract agreeing to abide by these conditions. She met twice with her coach and then abruptly resigned. In her exit interview she said she did not feel she was a good match for Main Street Bakeries' approach to management. She said she wanted to be fully in charge and hire and fire as she saw fit.

Ben contacted MaryAnn, one of the previous assistant managers he had interviewed on his trip. He asked MaryAnn to sign the same 90-day probationary contract with all the same provisions he had required of Jane. Exit interviews, executive coaching, and employee and customer satisfaction surveys with and turnover will be tied to MaryAnn's bonuses. Within three months, turnover was significantly reduced, customer satisfaction was up, and MaryAnn called Ben to thank him personally for supplying the executive coach—whom she came to deeply appreciate as a valuable resource for ongoing professional development. Ben and Elise can now turn their attention to other matters because store number 75 is clearly back on track.

KEY TERMS

bullying

burnout

employee turnover (attrition)

exit interview (exit survey)

Great Recession

personality disorder

presenteeism (quiet quitting)

DISCUSSION QUESTIONS

1. What does your organization do to minimize employee turnover and increase engagement? What improvements could be made at a reasonable cost?
2. Discuss the *process* of your last performance review. What improved your motivation and what decreased it? What were you able to use to improve your performance? How could it be improved, if at all?
3. What motivates you? How does this compare to one or more of your coworkers?
4. Have you ever seen, experienced, or been the workplace bully? What conditions give rise to this behavior? What can employees at all levels do to prevent or stop bullying behaviors at work? How have these been handled well or not well?

EXERCISES

1. Create a survey that will be used to gain feedback on workplace morale and engagement within individual work units at your organization. What questions would you include? How would you integrate this survey into the annual bonus or merit raise structure of your organization?
2. Develop a list of exit interview questions to ask employees who have left your organization. Use these to analyze the root causes of turnover and develop an improvement plan.
3. Draft a script using the 3-step problem-solving process to reach shared expectations with someone you work or live with. Try it out!

GOAL SETTING

1. Use the information in Table 7.2 to analyze your own workplace behaviors. Choose one to three workplace behaviors to improve over the next week.
2. Develop a plan for effectively working with one or more difficult people at work. What can you do to bring out their best?

SUGGESTED SUPPLEMENTAL READINGS

Dickey, T. (2015). Integrating unions in integrated conflict management systems. *Conflict Resolution Quarterly, 33*, S45–S66. https://doi.org/10.1002/crq.21143

Masters, M. F., Albright, R., & Gibney, R. (2015). Is there a future for labor-management cooperation? *Conflict Resolution Quarterly, 33*, S95–S99. https://doi.org/10.1002/crq.21151

Freeman, R. B., & Hilbrich, K. (2013). Do labor unions have a future in the United States? In R. S. Rycroft (Ed.), *The economics of inequality, poverty, and discrimination in the 21st century*. Praeger.

Fuller, R. P., & Putnam, L. L. (2018). Union framing of conflict-related issues in the entertainment industry. *Conflict Resolution Quarterly, 36*, 53–67. https://doi.org/10.1002/crq.21221

Gottman, J., & Schwartz Gottman, J. (2022). *The love prescription: Seven days to more intimacy, connection, and joy*. Penguin Life.

Rhodes, C., Pullen, A., Vickers, M. H., Clegg, S. R., & Pitsis, A. (2010). Violence and workplace bullying. *Administrative Theory & Praxis, 32*(1), 96–115.

8

Leadership amid Chaotic Change

New Tools for a Transformed World

Anyone can hold the helm when the sea is calm.

—Publilius Syrus

No one knows the name of the ship's captain until it hits the iceberg. As this quote from Syrus points out, your reputation as a leader-manager will be tested and demonstrated by your response to crises. Do you rise to the occasion or sink like the *Titanic*? Framing matters. Will you frame the current or next crisis as an opportunity to learn, grow, and outmaneuver your competition or will you use it as an excuse for poor performance? The good news is that supply chain challenges, labor shortages, inflation, and shocks to the global economy are faced by you *and* your competition. The difference that matters will be your response to the challenges. Leaders are called upon to steer their organizations through rough, uncharted waters. This chapter shares conflict management processes and skills for leaders, which will enable you to create, inspire, and direct teams to reach their highest potential. Today's organization cannot be led using yesterday's tools and strategies. In essence, 2019 might as well be 1919. You can adapt and change or become irrelevant. The application of a strategic approach to management will allow you to grow your career, keep your organization healthy and competitive, and maintain your sanity in the process. Get excited about going to work again. Here's how.

Learning Objectives

- Analyze the challenges facing you and your team to determine what you can take ownership of for improved team performance.
- Identify which of your current leadership behaviors are consistent or inconsistent with the behaviors of superior managers.
- Understand the phases of team formation to get to the "performing" stage faster.
- Describe the common stages of an organization's life cycle and the implications for your leadership approach.

- Demonstrate the key behaviors of a strategic leader, especially before and during crises.
- Identify ways to build trust and psychological safety in your team to empower rapid, effective responses to changing circumstances.

JOHN AT THE BUREAU OF RECLAMATION

John took over as the head of his agency at a time when inflation was rampant and state government salaries were not keeping pace. He needed to keep and develop the employees he currently had, if possible. The first thing he did was meet individually with each member of his inherited team. He wanted to get to know them better, build rapport, and understand their strengths and career goals. He asked each manager about the dynamics within their own work teams: about morale, employee engagement, and perceptions of obstacles to the fullest achievement of the mission. He asked them to describe their team's culture: How does it feel to work in this organization? In this team? In other words, he started by listening and learning.

What he learned did not surprise him. Employees struggled to respond quickly enough to rapidly changing situations such as regulatory changes, long delays caused by inconsistent access to equipment, reliable employees doing the job of 2–3 people as the cover for vacant positions, and signs of impending burnout.

John has five managers, each heading departments of 10 to 25 employees. While resources seem perennially short, some of the teams exhibit camaraderie, low turnover, and success in the accomplishment of their missions. Two of the five departments seem plagued with lower productivity, high turnover, and occasional litigation.

John's first step is to work with his managers on the skills and practices found in Chapter 7 (The Big Quit: Employee Attrition and the New Normal). Visible improvements were seen in all departments after each manager implemented a process to track employee satisfaction and morale, began using exit surveys to learn from mistakes, strengthened their employee recognition program (the previous one was built solely on years of service), and to provide developmental feedback to all employees. Turnover is down and productivity is up. In fact, some of his seasoned employees have decided to stay on after reaching the years of service needed for full retirement—this was unheard of in the past. Yet those two departments continue to perform at lower levels than the others in the organization. John now believes the underlying cause of this problem lies in their teamwork, or lack thereof. He is looking for ideas to improve team functioning within these two departments, but some of what he learns will be helpful for the other departments as well.

APPLYING STRATEGIC LEADERSHIP FOR
CAREER AND ORGANIZATIONAL GOALS

There are no bad teams, only bad leaders (Willink & Babin, 2015). In their compelling book, Willink and Babin share an illustrative story from the training of Navy SEALS during "hell week." This is a week in which SEAL applicants are divided into about seven teams and must carry a rubber raft everywhere as they engage in exhausting, physically demanding races and exercises. The winners get to sit out the next race, earning much-needed rest. In their example, one team consistently comes in first, while another always places last. The underperforming team has a leader who berates them, calling them "lazy." He blames the poor team performance on the weakness of individual members. They appear demoralized. The winning team leader cheers on his team members collectively and individually. When one stumbles, the others help him up and compensate until their fallen comrade has recovered. The winning leader announces short-term goals ("Row to that buoy!"), briefly celebrates the achievements, then encourages the team to focus on the next goal. The winning leader doesn't blame bad weather, bad luck, bad teammates. He focuses on what he *can* control.

As an experiment, the trainers directed the winning team leader to switch teams with the losing leader. Miraculously, the losing team began coming in first and the previously winning team consistently placed second. Lessons? Leaders matter and a team with a cohesive, positive organizational culture can withstand bad leaders to some extent. The poor leader came to the tough realization that he was the cause of the team's poor performance, not the weaknesses of individual or collective team members. Leaders articulate a vision for what the team can accomplish, encourage high performance, take responsibility for team performance, and encourage team members to help and support each other rather than playing the blame game. They take ownership of their team's performance. With this example in mind, let's examine some specific behaviors of strategic, high-performing leaders.

Over the past few years, how many times have you or your boss blamed poor performance on supply chain issues, staffing shortages, pandemic economic disruptions, and other systemic challenges beyond your control? While these disruptions certainly impact performance, they do so for your competition too. Rather than focusing on those factors beyond one's control, great leaders practice "extreme ownership" (ibid.). This concept hearkens back to the idea of an "internal locus of control" rather than an "external locus of control" as discussed in Chapter 5. Those individuals and cultures with a high internal locus of control view their success as largely within their control rather than being controlled by fate or other factors beyond their control. Individuals with a low internal locus of control often feel helpless and powerless to change their circumstances. These feelings are linked to depression, negative health impacts, and even workplace violence. Instead, by owning the performance of themselves and their team, great leaders focus on what they can influence or control. For example, there may be a shortage of electrical engineers, but you can focus on recruiting, retaining, and maximizing the performance of the best possible team. What can you "own"?

The concept of extreme ownership applies to your homelife as well as your work. For example, a few months ago my son complained that he had a poor grade in physics class and this grade could negatively impact his ability to get accepted by the universities to which he was applying. He had many reasonable explanations: the teacher had never previously taught physics; in fact, she was a biologist forced to teach physics due to a teacher shortage. The class average was a 63 (out of 100), while his grade was a 68. While all these facts were true, they were unempowering because they focused attention on matters beyond his control. Instead, I helped him reframe the question to redirect attention to those things within his control: "You seem to be giving your teacher too much power over your future as well as your present. There are many ways to learn physics. Having a good teacher is only one way. What are the other ways you can learn physics?" He brainstormed a list that included private tutoring, watching online videos, forming a study group, and so on. By the end of the semester, he had a 92%. No matter how bad the circumstances in which you find yourself, focusing on what you can control or "own" will lead you to better results while fueling your passion for your work.

Strategic leadership is the ability to articulate a compelling vision, set an example, and balance multiple competing demands in ways that promote the best interests of the organization, its people, and the leader himself or herself. Strategic leaders understand the current state of their organization while predicting future threats or opportunities. They carefully shepherd their teams and their careers. In times of calm, they lay the groundwork to avoid crises. In times of crisis, they call upon the relationships and resources they have built to navigate rough waters.

How can you become a strategic leader? Engage in planning and execute that plan. Whether or not you are a manager, you can implement strategic thinking in your work life to move your performance to the next level. Strategic leaders are more proactive than reactive. They don't spend much time putting out fires because they attend to fire prevention. They care about people and view them as inherently valuable, rather than as fodder for profits. They walk the talk. They speak about the organization and its people, choices and even mistakes using the language of "we/us" rather than "they/them" because they take ownership as a leader or future leader (Young, Stumpf & Arnone, 1995; Willink & Babin, 2015). This means they do not view the decisions made by the organization as being done *to* them, but instead *for* or *with* them. This linguistic shift comes organically when an employee becomes a manager-leader who is involved in making and implementing decisions or when a leader seeks to convey personal accountability for the collective impacts of her decisions.

It's worthwhile to examine the skills and abilities of strategic leaders, the foci that will help them prevent and manage crises, and the common pitfalls that bring down leaders prematurely or hamper their success.

The Skills and Abilities of a Strategic Leader

Strategic leader-managers develop and share their perspectives about "where we are now" and their vision for "where we are going." They lead problem-solving discussions about "how to get there," relying on the wisdom and experience of their team members to influence next steps and the best approach to tackle the presenting challenges. They are facilitative, inspiring, humble, kind, and passionate about the organization's mission and their people.

Review Box 1.1 (Chapter 1) to remind yourself of the tasks associated with the most effective managers based upon Google's Project Oxygen. This chapter will build on those skills, with a deeper focus on the pivotal role of leaders in organizations. As opposed to managers, **leaders** set the strategic direction, curate the culture, fill key positions on the executive team, forge and attend to the relationships necessary for current and future success, and spot opportunities for innovative change. Managers implement the decisions made by leaders and attend to the day-to-day running of the organization. Both leaders and managers need to set goals and measure progress toward them in their own careers, teams, and organizations, yet leaders focus more time on crafting and communicating their vision for the organization. Both need to motivate others to achieve their highest performance and inspire them by connecting each employee's contribution to the accomplishment of the mission.

Great leaders engage in *strategic planning* on a daily, weekly, monthly, and annual basis. With input from others, they set goals and benchmarks to help them evaluate accomplishments. Each action is tied to one or more short-, medium-, or long-term goals. These goals can be organizational as well as professional or career oriented. Strategic managers seek to understand what is working (and why) and what is not. They do not pursue change for change's sake or solely to make their mark on the organization. Each proposed change is tied to the desire to put "Who we want to be" into action. For example, "We want to be the premier/most impactful organization in _____ (location or market niche)."

For example, "We want to be the #1 conflict management graduate program in the United States." Then, we answer the "how to" questions. We will accomplish this goal by engaging in the following activities over the next 3 months, 6 months, 1–3–5 years, and so on. We will define success and measure it by X, Y, Z. We anticipate the obstacles to our goals will include A, B, C. We will work on removing or overcoming those obstacles by engaging in the following activities and building the following networks.

Success comes when you develop your own idea of what success looks like and how to get there, then ask your team(s) to join in that process. While you articulate your definitions of success, you must be open to change, based on what you hear and learn. Collectively, you and your team must forge a path forward.

Individually, you must also chart a path for your career that answers these same questions. If your vision for your career involves a mission or activities that cannot be accommodated in your current organization, then you need to decide whether to change your vision for your career or find an organization that is a better fit for your dreams and goals. See Box 8.1 for the skills and abilities of strategic leaders.

Strategic leaders lead from the front. That means they understand the work of the organization and are not too proud or too important to do that work. The owner of a restaurant chain should occasionally work as a food server, chef, host/hostess, prep cook, etc. and that includes the need to take direction from those frontline supervisors. Only by doing this periodically will leaders retain credibility, build loyalty, and understand the work of the organization they lead. This work should take up 10–20% of your time, depending upon your level within the leadership hierarchy. To do less is to give "lip service" to these tasks, which undermines loyalty and credibility. To give more reduces the time you devote to management decision-making and implementation.

Leading from the front means sharing the pain of difficult decisions: If there is a freeze on raises or cuts to the travel budget, it must impact you too. If everyone

BOX 8.1. TASKS AND ABILITIES OF STRATEGIC LEADERS

- Own the performance of yourself and your team.
- Demonstrate strategic planning, vision, and change management.
- Lead from the front.
- Show resilience (without numbing).
- Build coalitions of support for your initiatives.
- Communicate effectively up and down the chain of command.
- Project creativity, flexibility, adaptability to change.
- Create and re-create positive organizational culture every day (chapter 6).
- Delegate effectively (see chapter 10).
- Model brave leadership skills: work-life balance; humility; reasonable risk taking; fallibility; accountability and trust; loyalty; empathy.

must take mandatory training on sexual harassment, workplace civility, or defensive driving, then you need to sit through it with your people. If it is a waste of your time, then it is a waste of their time too. Lead from the front.

Resilience is an under-discussed trait of strong leaders. No one gets to the top (or even the middle) without resilience. There will be setbacks to your career, your team, and your organization. Your ideas will get shot down sometimes, even when they are "right." You may get passed over for a promotion or special projects. You may have a supervisor who is a jerk, with poor people skills or a self-serving agenda. Worst-case scenario: you might uncover corruption or ethics violations only to be told, "Shhhh . . . look away" by those with the power to right the wrong.

The trick is to normalize the occasional defeat (actually, losses tend to come in waves rather than one-offs), allow yourself some time to grieve the setback, avoid negative numbing behaviors such as overuse of alcohol, stress eating, or sending angry midnight emails, and then make a new plan to move forward. This is so much harder to do than to say. By anticipating and normalizing setbacks and finding healthy ways to deal with the stress that accompanies them (e.g., exercise, talking to a trusted mentor), you will be better able to absorb them when they come without becoming defeated. Remember, organizational change is a war, not a battle. You can lose some battles but still win the war. You want to survive to keep forging ahead, while allowing yourself the space to heal and recover along the way.

Leaders cannot implement changes on their own. Therefore, they must *build coalitions of support* for their initiatives. Begin by meeting with anyone whose approval or resources will be needed for success. Explain your plans and use your ninja negotiation skills (Chapter 3) to ensure their needs are met too. Meet with those who may act as obstacles to your goals and seek to win them over. Help them see why your plans are in the organization's best interest as well as their own.

Communicating up and down the chain of command is a key leadership behavior. Gossip fills an information vacuum in organizations. Let people know what changes and support they can expect. Leaders must model transparency, which includes making their pay, benefits, and motives clear to others. They should have nothing to hide. Information is powerful when it is shared more often than it is withheld. To get team members rowing in the same direction you must communicate the "why" behind your decisions.

Creative adaptability to change has never been more important for leaders than it is today. Personnel changes, swings in the budget due to rapidly changing economic conditions, and cultural shifts that require rebranding or changing outdated language and approaches—all have become the "new normal." Great leaders take a moment to mentally process bad or surprising news, develop a plan in response with input from others, then move forward. People leave teams, regulatory fines or recalls happen. The question is, "What are you going to do about that?" There is no need to pretend these changes don't hurt. Normalize that crises will occur and it is our response that defines us.

Modeling *brave leadership* empowers everyone in the organization to make their fullest contribution, feel respected, and sustain their effort over the long haul (Brown, 2018). Leaders are brave when they do not hide their humanity, vulnerability, and fallibility. This includes modeling respect for work-life boundaries by refraining from sending midnight or Sunday emails (depending on the culture and schedule of the organization); supporting health habits at work (e.g., no one is expected to skip lunch or stay late without advance notice); and admitting mistakes or fears rather than pretending they don't exist. Brave leaders open the door for frank conversations built on trust, which underlies all positive change. Remember the concept of "rupture and repair" from Chapter 2? It is not conflict that harms our working relationships. It is our unwillingness to collaboratively discuss it and brainstorm solutions together that interferes with our team bonds. Modeling respectful problem-solving builds intimacy and commitment in teams. Great teams really "see" and appreciate each member, striving to deepen their mutual understanding through important, problem-solving conversations (see 3-step problem-solving in Chapter 7).

The Achilles' Heels of Doomed Leaders

Sadly, the headlines are full of leaders brought low by their own poor choices. Whether these behaviors include midnight calls to escort services, getting caught with their hands in the corporate cookie jar, or general mistreatment of subordinates, leaders expose their Achilles' heels when they fail to hold themselves to the same standards as their subordinates. Avoiding these downfalls seems easy, yet the headlines would indicate otherwise. To avoid allegations of hubris or misbehavior, ensure that your budget, salary and benefits, and other actions have as much transparency as possible.

One of the pitfalls of leaders is boredom and a desire to leave their unique mark on the organization. Sadly, this leads to efforts to bring change for change's sake. They often embark on efforts to reorganize internally or engage in unwise mergers or acquisitions to leave their mark on the company or agency. When undertaken for the wrong reasons, these changes are costly to your own reputation and to mission achievement. Be sure that any changes you undertake are clearly tied to the mission and arise through a collaborative planning process.

Leadership Models and Conflict

There are many models of leadership, and while most leaders tend to follow one more than others, they also borrow from the different approaches based on the best approach for the problem they face. This brief examination of a few leadership models is not meant to be comprehensive, but instead ties various models to their implications for unproductive conflict. Before reading further, consider reviewing the implications of permissive, authoritative, and authoritarian styles of management (and parenting) covered in Chapter 1. The authoritative approach (also known as facilitative) is consistent with both relational and transformational leadership, but likely incompatible with positional or transactional leadership models.

Relational leadership is a "model of leadership that suggests the effectiveness of a leader and relates their ability to develop positive relationships within an organization. It also relates to the process of people working together to achieve the greater good or accomplish a positive change in the workplace. Relational leaders use empathy skills to empower their teams to build strength in their current skills and develop new skills" (Indeed Editorial Team, 2022). Relational leaders strive to embody the highest level of ethical behavior, empowering employees through developing them, a focus on inclusivity, and focusing on creating and following good processes to result in positive outcomes. Teams led by relational leaders are correlated with higher employee morale, lower attrition, deeper engagement, and higher mission achievement than transactional or positional leadership. Relational leadership focuses on creating and sustaining humane, effective workplaces that lead everyone to reach their full potential. Relational leaders show an interest in others, they build rapport with people within and outside the organization, and they build coalitions of support for change rather than imposing it unilaterally or through dominance. Often, relational leaders have power and influence because of their example rather than any official position or title, although they may have both.

> Relational leadership can be incredibly successful, particularly when it is authentic, empathetic, reinforced through gestures of friendship and embedded in the culture of a team. It's not the only style of leadership but can be powerful and personally fulfilling. (Coleman, 1992)

Relational leaders influence others by their example and through the relationships they have built. Younger workers respond well to relational leaders due to greater expectations for an individualized approach to management, which requires leaders and managers to get to know their team members at a deeper level.

Transactional leadership is "a managerial style that relies on attaining goals through structure, supervision and a system of rewards and punishments. This results-oriented approach works well with self-motivated employees. Transactional leadership doesn't focus on changing or improving the organization, but instead, aims to hit short-term goals while establishing unity and conformity with the company. The rewards or punishments are, therefore, referred to as the 'transaction'" (Indeed Editorial Team, 2022). Examples of transactional leadership include bonuses or quotas for sales or other performance indicators, with the transaction being financial gain for performance. This works best in the short term or in certain types of positions but can lead to unethical behavior such as the misrepresentation of one's performance, so close monitoring is required. Reliance on transactional leadership does not generally lead to a commitment to the mission or vision of the organization, but instead maintains the focus on individual rewards.

Transformational leadership is a theory of leadership in which the leader works with followers to go beyond their self-interest to adopt a collective identity as a team and organization to identify needed change, create a vision to guide the change through influence, inspiration, and executing the change in tandem with committed members of a group. Transformational leadership enhances motivation, morale, and the performance of employees by connecting their sense of identity to the organization; being a role model who inspires them and raises their interest in the mission; challenging employees to take greater ownership for their work; and understanding the strengths and weaknesses of team members, which allows the leader to align employees with tasks that enhance their performance. Transformational leaders are strong in the abilities to adapt to different situations, share a collective consciousness, self-manage, and be inspirational while leading a group.

Positional leadership occurs when a leader's power stems from their specific position, a formal title, and derives their influence and authority solely from this position. Conversely, relational leaders are those who act without the formality of a title. This style is often authoritarian, and therefore, likely to increase unproductive conflict in the workplace.

Which leadership model is best? The best leaders likely combine elements of relational and transformational leadership by getting to know their team members, building trust and rapport while encouraging them to develop an identity as an integral team member who is passionate about their role in the mission. In a perfect world, great leaders would borrow elements of the various approaches as appropriate to the problem at hand. Overall, transactional and positional leadership models are waning in popularity as they tend to reduce employee commitment and morale.

UNDERSTANDING CORPORATE LIFE CYCLES

What is the best type of leader? It depends on the organization's current needs. Miller (1990) argues that organizations are similar to organisms in that they have a generally predictable life cycle, which begins with birth (e.g., the creation of the product or service that gives rise to the organization) and ends when the

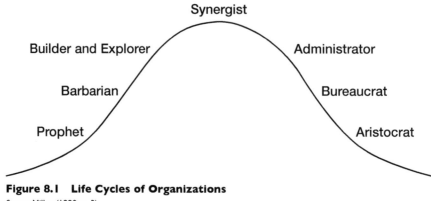

Figure 8.1   Life Cycles of Organizations
Source: Miller (1990, p. 3)

company (or nonprofit, agency, etc.) collapses from the weight of its own bureaucracy and internal strife. As you strive to be a great leader, you must understand the phase your organization is currently experiencing and respond accordingly. "Creative response is the essential function of leaders. The moment leaders rely on yesterday's response to today's challenges, the decline begins" (Miller, 1990, 2–3). Figure 8.1 (from Miller 1990) illustrates the stages organizations frequently exhibit during their life cycles. As an organization is created, grows, and evolves, the key challenge is to manage that growth in ways that serve and enhance the mission rather than interfering with it. Large, bureaucratic organizations that lose focus on the mission generally decline and eventually fail.

In its inception phase, the organization was created by a *prophet* or inventor, such as Nikola Tesla, Thomas Edison, Alexander Graham Bell, Elon Musk, or Mark Zuckerberg. This is the creative genius who got their start in the lab, creating, experimenting, coding, and testing new products or services. These individuals have great ideas, but they often lack the management skills to bring their ideas to market. They often pair up with a *barbarian*. This is the person who overcomes all initial obstacles to bring the product to the market. This person must deal with patenting, hiring, securing customers, and getting the company launched. They have passion, a competitive spirit, and are resilient when faced by setbacks. They may also be abrasive, short sighted, and willing to cut corners to carve out a niche for the new organization: Think Alexander the Great, an aggressive and decisive leader.

Next, we get to the *builder* and *explorer* phase. Builders focus on developing internal expertise as the company grows. For example, they may grow big enough to require a human resource specialist, shipping, engineering, marketing manager, etc. The explorer is the salesperson, focused on expanding market share and getting feedback from end users to improve the product or service. This phase requires more collaboration and delegation because one leader cannot do it all alone. For these first three phases, the focus of the organization is external, meeting the needs of the customer. In the last three phases, the focus shifts to the internal operations of the organization at the expense of the mission.

We will skip the *synergist* for now and explain the role of the *administrator*. Once the organization has secured a relatively stable position in the market, this person builds the internal capacity of the organization to meet the steady demand. This is the person who creates standard operating procedures, audits spending, and ensures the company is running smoothly. Yet, this remains balanced against the need to meet the customers' expectations. It is here the organization faces a critical point in its evolution: It has now grown large enough that many employees and leaders are disconnected from the frontline work of the company and they may begin to create policies and procedures that do not serve the mission but serve to keep bureaucrats busy. For the administrator, the focus shifts from expansion of the company to its long-term security. Potential examples of this phase include Amazon, Apple, and Airbnb. The challenge for this leader is to remain fluent in the actual work of the organization and the needs of the customers, while systematizing the company's workflow and procedures. To do this, he needs to keep one foot in the world of practice, while spending most of his time managing and leading. For example, a restaurant chain's owner needs to spend 10–20% of his time cooking, waiting tables, washing dishes, ordering supplies, and so on. Otherwise, he loses his empathy for people in those roles and his understanding of how best to do the work. It also shows he can "lead from the front," thereby building loyalty among employees (Miller, 1990).

When an organization slides into the bureaucratic phase, it is the beginning of its undoing. In this phase the leaders become disconnected from the daily work of the organization, its mission, and the needs of both customers and employees. This phase is characterized by a willingness to put the bureaucratic process and rules above the mission: Excess administration and tight control over employees drives away and punishes innovative prophets, barbarians, builders/explorers, and rational administrators. The organization loses its creativity, innovation, competitiveness, and mission focus. It stops growing and starts shrinking. A need for senseless uniformity and control from above displaces consensus and passion. Overspecialization means that the different silos in the organization find themselves at odds instead of working together to achieve the mission. Divides erupt between workers and management, as the latter becomes increasingly disconnected from the frontline work and mission, often giving rise to unionization movements. Bureaucratic organizations avoid new ideas and positive change. They reward people who keep their mouths shut, cash their check, and put their passions elsewhere.

The last phase is rather short and plagued by scandals and turmoil. The *aristocratic* phase is characterized by leaders who did not come up through the ranks, never worked on the frontlines, and view the workers (and sometimes the customers) with disdain. The organization becomes divided in an "us versus them" mentality that pits managers against workers with the assumption that they do not share common interests (Miller, 1990). Aristocratic leaders line their pockets or put their career goals above the mission and are utterly unable to understand or empathize with most customers or employees of the organization. Sometimes these are leaders who inherited the family business, or they received degrees they never used because their job is to be the face of the company or to manage the external, political relationships rather than the day-to-day work. Aristocrats tend to freeze wages, but not their own, of course. They seek to cut costs to wring the last bit of profitability out of the company since innovation and market expansion have stopped. They blame those on the bottom for not working hard enough, while those same workers are constantly stymied in their attempts to innovate and change the organization. The gaps between the workers and leaders grow, leading to rebellion such as strikes, lawsuits, shareholder revolts, and the eventual collapse of the organization.

While decline is common, it is not inevitable. A *synergistic* leader can identify the strengths and weaknesses of each team member and assign tasks based on their strengths. Prophets should remain in the lab, creating innovations, for example. They can push back against the tendency to create policies and training for their own sake, disconnected from any real impact on the mission. They allow reasonable specialization, but with cross training and institutionalized mechanisms for communication across units, to avoid the negative impacts of silos. Each policy or procedure change is evaluated as to its true need and costs in terms of employee time, frustration, and mission relevance, with a preference for rational flexibility with accountability. Synergists engage in the work of the organization on a regular basis, so they meet frontline workers, hear their ideas and problems, and fully understand what it takes to deliver the company's products or services. They require their mid- and upper-level managers to do the same.

In a company that has been around for a long time, the goal will be to push back against the negative impacts of bureaucracy and aristocracy, to allow for continued innovation, impact, and growth. What kind of leader does your organization need right now, in its current phase?

STRATEGIC LEADERSHIP FOR CRISIS PREVENTION AND MANAGEMENT

The literature on leadership is full of fads, with pop-culture authors pitching specific ideas, only to be displaced in a year or two when the next fad hits. Bolman and Deal (2017) have spent 25 years analyzing the scholarly and popular literature on leadership and management. They found this literature falls into four categories or "frames" through which the work of leaders can be understood. Each of these frames contains a set of activities or foci to which all leaders must attend, or be hampered in their efforts: Human resources, political, structural, and symbolic frames. Unfortunately, most of us have strengths and preferences for the tasks in two or three areas, while neglecting one or two others. At the end of this chapter, there is a link you can use to take an online survey to measure your strengths regarding these four areas or frames.

- *Human resource frame*: How can you hire, train, promote, and motivate the best people? What can you do to attend to morale, reduce turnover, and prepare your people to succeed?
- *Political Frame*: How can you build networks up, down, and laterally across your organization so you have supporters upon whom you can call when things get tough? How can you build and use these networks within and outside the organization to promote its mission, including building relationships and ties with regulators, vendors, business partners, union leaders, and

different divisions within your organization? When you need a favor, will the people with the power to grant it already know who you are and want to help, because of the networks you took time to build and maintain?

- *Structural Frame*: What do you measure and track to ensure constant improvement? This includes strategic planning and the implementation of that plan. This frame relies on data and rational decision-making.
- *Symbolic Frame*: The activities in this frame deal with the leader's charisma and her ability to articulate a motivating vision both within and outside the organization. "Who we are" is expressed through our decision to celebrate milestones and successes, make meaning of our actions, and provide hope and inspiration that our mission is important and achievable (Bolman and Deal, 2017).

By regularly attending to the activities in all four areas, managers can maximize their success at preventing or reacting effectively to crises.

Strategic Planning

The term *strategic planning* is sometimes met with groans by people who have experienced a weak, ineffectual version of this task. For conflict managers, strong strategic planning is indispensable and must be undertaken by a representative group of the organization's members. Strategic planning answers these questions at a minimum: Who are we? Who do we want to be? How can we get from here (where we are now) to there (where we want to be)? What are our shared expectations about how we will accomplish our goals (see 3-step problem-solving in Chapter 7)? and What short- and medium-term objectives will we need to meet to chunk our long-term goals into manageable, measurable pieces?

While there is a role for charismatic leaders who articulate their own vision on these questions, they must be open to hearing about the visions and preferences of others, and then seek to reach consensus. This can only be done collaboratively but need not take inordinate amounts of time. In most cases, even in very large organizations, it can be done in two to six hours by beginning in small groups, looking for common themes across groups, and then using a facilitated dialogue to craft a final version.

A **mission statement** is a formal summary of the purpose, goals, and vision of an organization, unit, and/or individual. As a manager, be sure you have one for yourself, your team, and the organization. Each member of the organization should be able to recite the organization's mission and describe their unique contribution to that mission. Whether they mop the floors or build the rockets, each person is critical to mission achievement, and they need to feel it in their bones. In part, it is the manager's job to help tie each person's tasks to the mission in a way that motivates them to do their best each day. Here are some sample mission statements:

Public Broadcasting System (PBS): To create content that educates, informs, and inspires.
USO lifts the spirits of America's troops and their families.

National Wildlife Federation: Inspiring Americans to protect wildlife for our children's future.

Oxfam: To create lasting solutions to poverty, hunger, and social injustice.

Coca-Cola Company: To refresh the world in mind, body, and spirit. To inspire moments of optimism and happiness through our brands and actions.

A statement of the organization's values should be a guiding document against which specific policies and business decisions can be measured to ask, "Does the proposed decision X reflect our values?" If not, then either the values or choices need to change to ensure alignment. Goals should be SMART: Specific, measurable, achievable, realistic, and timely, meaning there is a clear timeline for their achievement (Doran, 1981).

For example, a restaurant chain might create values like these:

- Nourish: To fulfill and satisfy what is necessary for life and growth; to nurture the whole self.
- Empower: To strengthen and equip our team members to reach their full potential.
- Community: To grow and sustain an environment that fosters a sense of belonging.
- Diversity: To celebrate the unique variations of influences within our community.
- Sustainability: To responsibly manage our social, environmental, and financial impacts.
- Integrity: To foster a commitment to quality, transparency, and trust.

The next step in the strategic planning process is to create a list of specific actions to achieve the mission and enact its values. These could be related to human resource matters (e.g., we will provide training to ensure all employees are familiar with our ethics policies) or they could relate to improvements in the products/services offered. These actions should be tied to timelines that cover the short-, medium-, and long-term planning cycle. This task should be revisited, perhaps in an abbreviated format, periodically as objectives and goals are reached and new ones are needed.

BEST PRACTICES FOR TEAM BUILDING

Rajagopal (2006) states that well-developed teams "include clear identification of goals, clarity of roles, common feeling, motivation, commitment and collaborative attitude" (p. 5). Do these words describe your team? If not, this chapter will help you learn how to bring needed change to your group's functioning.

Chapter 6 describes ways to create and sustain a healthy organizational culture. Building on those tasks, great leaders carefully select team members, train and develop them directly or through well-prepared managers, and create an environment that supports their success. Experts on teambuilding usually focus on several key areas, including methods for creating and building a team; how teams think and communicate; the role of trust building and repair in teams; team conflict; and dysfunction.

Consider the Team's Purpose

When creating teams, consider their main tasks and raison d'être. Teams tasked with creative duties need maximum diversity in every sense, including demographics such as gender and gender identity, race, age, national origin, educational background, and life experiences. Teams tasked with implementing policies or changes will need good communication, flexibility, empathy, stamina, and social-emotional skills. A team's composition should be well matched to its purpose.

Teams need a little shaking up now and then. For example, a study by Skilton and Dooley (2010) provided evidence that teams who have worked together on previous projects may find it difficult to match their success on subsequent projects. The researchers suggest that a solution for this is to integrate a new person into the team on projects where the production of highly creative ideas is important.

While managers may not always be able to build teams from scratch for each project, it will be helpful for managers and team members to take the time to learn how each member tends to communicate and how the team prefers to work. This meta-communication enables teams to gain shared understandings of one another's personality types and how their communication styles impact the team (Gevers & Peeters, 2009, p. 396). **Meta-communication** occurs when people communicate about how they communicate. This information can prevent misunderstandings and attribution biases that often occur when one communicates with someone whose preferred patterns or methods of communication differ from their own. Personality and communication assessment tools can be helpful in this effort: which team member is an auditory learner, and which is more visual? Knowing how your team members scored on the conflict styles inventory (Chapter 1) helps you to know how best to approach them when a problem arises. Learning each other's modalities and preferences will help minimize miscommunication and maximize synergy, and meta-communication will help speed up this learning curve.

Enhancing Communication and Decision-Making in Teams: Keeping Pace with Rapid Change

The pace of change, often chaotic change, seems to be increasing in our work lives. Teams form, reform, and disband quickly as needed or as turnover dictates. Great leaders and managers must help teams proceed efficiently through the first few phases of team formation so they can reach peak performance quickly while pivoting as needed when situations dictate needed changes.

According to Cooke and colleagues (2007), one of the most important factors in team functioning is the ability to think like a team, called **team cognition**. In their meta-study of the literature on team cognition, DeChurch and Mesmer-Magnus (2010) state that "team cognition has strong positive relationships to team behavioral process, motivational states, and team performance . . . team cognition explains significant incremental variance in team performance after the effects of behavioral and motivational dynamics have been controlled" (p. 32). The ability to think as a group may in fact be a prerequisite to the team's ability to act as a group. Viewing each other as an "in-group" means team members are more likely to sacrifice individual interests to accomplish shared goals or to help each other out as needed (see Chapter 2 for in-group/out-group theory).

There are two key concepts relating to team cognition: **team mental models**, or **TMM**, and **transactive memory systems**, or **TMS** (Kozlowski & Ilgen, 2006). According to Austin (2003), a TMM is a set of jointly held information within a group, and the TMS is like a mental map disseminating the information held by individual members. Those aspects of knowledge known by each team member are collectively known as the **shared mental model**, or **SMM** (Kozlowski & Ilgen, 2006). The TMM is a broad construct representing a wide variety of what the team knows collectively, the SMM is a construct representing the knowledge that all the team members share, and the TMS is an intricate web of who knows what in the team (Kozlowski & Ilgen, 2006). This information helps us understand what has long been called *institutional memory* as well as the role of individually held knowledge within teams. According to Beng-Chong and Klein (2006), the overall key to having a team mental model likely to increase performance is to focus on team members having similar, shared, accurate concepts of who knows what in the team (p. 403). For new teams it is helpful to spend time sharing information about each member's strengths, interests, or experience to ensure the smooth development of TMS.

Good, clear, planned communication is the key to having both institutionally held information and to having individually held information or expertise. Gillespie and colleagues (2010) write that "in surgery, up to 70% of adverse events are attributable to failures in communication" (p. 642). Most organizations do not measure the impact of poor communication as well as the healthcare industry, but we can assume that poor communication is to blame for many lost customers, contract disputes, and general inefficiencies. "Disagreements thrive from ambiguity: around the boundaries of job roles or functional teams, the relative importance of organizational priorities, or the ownership of resources" (Haynes 2009, p. 10). When employee turnover is high, finding a way to share information about "who knows what" is critical to maximize efficient task distribution and problem-solving and to avoid redundancy.

Research by Langan-Fox (2004) shows that teams with well-developed and functional TMM share information more quickly and efficiently as well as synchronize their efforts more effectively. The improved efficiency is due to being in sync, rather than spending lots of time debating the assignment of tasks out of a lack of knowledge of each other's strengths. This can only happen when team members know each other well.

As Covey (2008) writes, when team members trust in the character and competence of their leader, they are more willing to quickly implement directions as opposed to questioning or challenging them. Leaders who engage in transparent, honest communications, admit their mistakes, elicit expertise when needed, and take the time to understand the work of team members are likely to be viewed as having high character and competence. This leads to trust, which makes rapid decision-making and implementation possible. Do you rush to implement the decisions of a boss you do not trust? Few of us do.

Decentralized decision-making speeds problem-solving and response to crises. To succeed in rapidly changing environments, leaders must take the time to develop trust in themselves and team members. They must be willing to delegate decision-making appropriately, which shows their trust of subordinates. If all decisions must be made at the top, rapid change, innovation, and response to crises are not possible.

Teams and Trust

The work of Klimoski and Karol (1976) provided early evidence that teams displaying higher trust perform better than teams lower in trust (p. 630). While many researchers (Friedlander, 1970; Hempel, Zhang & Tjosvold, 2009; Lencioni, 2002) have shown that trust has important implications for teamwork, it is helpful to get more specific in terms of understanding links between trust and teamwork as well as methods for building trust in teams. Individual characteristics can play an important role in determining whether one individual trusts another or whether one team trusts another team. Dirks (1999) found that "perceptions of risk and vulnerability" cause trust to vary (p. 449). When an individual or team feels vulnerable, then feelings of caution are likely to lead to either less trusting behaviors or trust that grows only slowly. According to Dirks, "liking, cohesion, familiarity, and reciprocating behaviors" are all copresent with trust, so it is sometimes difficult to discern a difference between one of these variables and trust itself (p. 450). While this makes research difficult, it helps us better understand that by working on these factors we also increase trust. In his study of trust in teams, Dirks found that decreased trust on the part of team members reduced individual members' motivation and reduced productivity.

Trust leads to specific behaviors that improve group outcomes. Moye and Langfred (2004) investigated the role that information sharing has in group conflict and team efficiency. The authors indicate that information sharing leads to better group outcomes, but more specifically, they predicted that information sharing in existing groups will prevent two kinds of conflict: "task conflict and relationship conflict" (p. 384). Similarly, Lencioni (2002) lists trust building as a precursor to successful team functioning. Teams without trust do not fully share their ideas, feedback, and criticisms with one another. Due to the presence of attribution bias (Chapter 2) they misinterpret one another's intentions and are more likely to take adversarial, rather than collaborative, positions when problems arise. Managers can play a key role in building trust and repairing damaged trust within and between teams. For more on trust building and repair, see Chapter 3 on negotiation.

Similarly, in *The Five Dysfunctions of a Team* (2002), Lencioni writes that well-functioning groups have five common characteristics: they trust one another, they engage in unfiltered positive conflict about ideas and strategic directions, they commit to decisions and action plans even if some members disagree with them, they hold one another accountable for delivering their commitments, and they focus on the achievement of collective results (i.e., they are team players). Under Lencioni's model, it is the primary duty of organizational leaders to hire individuals who will fit in well with the organization's cultural norms, support its mission, and engage in these five practices.

Phases of Teambuilding

It is helpful to understand the evolutionary phases that most groups experience as they form, get to know one another, and seek to accomplish shared tasks. These phases have been termed forming, storming, norming and performing (Tuchman & Jensen, 1977). During *forming*, the group comes together either spontaneously or by design. The group members hardly know one another and are in the "honeymoon" phase of the relationship. Individually, they strive to hide any flaws and behave more formally as they slowly get to know one another. In this phase, there is little structure to group interactions and the group is not working at maximum efficiency, if at all. Next, the group goes through a *storming* phase. In this phase hostility arises between members and subgroups often form. Lack of clarity between roles, differences in communication structure, and personality conflicts can worsen this difficult period. This phase is characterized by negativity, aggression, and rivalry (p. 423). Some members may leave the group if this phase lasts too long. The third phase, *norming*, occurs as the groups develop shared behavioral norms and expectations. They exhibit higher levels of trust and affection than in the previous two stages and the group membership stabilizes. During the fourth stage, *performing*, the group reaches its peak performance levels. Group members are clear about their roles, shared expectations exist, and group members collaborate effectively. Because they know one another well, they can communicate effectively, distribute tasks based on team member strengths (see TMM above), and solve problems proactively. Eventually, most groups go through a fifth stage, *adjourning*. In this stage, the task has been finished or the group disbands for other reasons. This phase can be quick, with all the members disbanding at once, or they can leave slowly, one at a time. This phase is often accompanied by some form of grieving, either collectively or separately, depending upon the way the group disbanded. Remember, if one or more new members join the team, they may get temporarily thrown back into an earlier phase as they strive to incorporate this member into their midst. The smaller the team, the more likely it is that one new member will result in the need to go through all phases again, rather than simply expecting the new person to acculturate to the existing team.

As a manager, your goal is to help the group get to the "performing" stage as quickly as possible and stay there. Three-step problem-solving can be used to create and re-create shared norms in an ongoing manner. As a leader, your job is to hire the best team members possible, place them in the tasks that match their skill sets, and ensure they are effectively acculturated to organizational norms, thereby fostering rapid adjustment toward the "performing" stage.

ASSURING HIGH PERFORMANCE IN TEAMS

How can you get your teams past the trial-and-error required to get past the storming and norming phases, into the "performing" phase? Google has been studying teams to better understand what makes great teams. They tested whether diversity really matters, socializing outside work, virtual versus face-to-face teams, and many other variables. While some variables matter sometimes, what they learned is that teams with shared expectations succeed. Conflict comes from a lack of shared expectations. Specifically, Google found four needs to which managers must attend to create and lead great teams:

In order of importance:

- *Psychological safety:* Psychological safety refers to an individual's perception of the consequences of taking an interpersonal risk or a belief that a team is safe for risk taking in the face of being seen as ignorant, incompetent, negative, or disruptive. In a team with high psychological safety, teammates feel safe to take risks around their team members. They feel confident that no one on the team will embarrass or punish anyone else for admitting a mistake, asking a question, or offering a new idea (*note*: Brown, 2018 echoes this finding).
- *Dependability:* On dependable teams, members reliably complete quality work on time (versus the opposite—shirking responsibilities).
- *Structure and clarity:* An individual's understanding of job expectations, the process for fulfilling these expectations, and the consequences of one's performance are important for team effectiveness. Goals can be set at the individual or group level and must be specific, challenging, and attainable. Google often uses objectives and key results (OKRs) to help set and communicate short- and long-term goals.
- *Meaning:* Finding a sense of purpose in either the work itself or the output is important for team effectiveness. The meaning of work is personal and can vary: financial security, supporting family, helping the team succeed, or self-expression for everyone, for example.
- *Impact:* The results of one's work—the subjective judgment that your work is making a difference—is important for teams. Seeing that one's work is contributing to the organization's goals can help reveal impact (Duhigg, 2016).

Managers should explicitly discuss these elements of teamwork, to see where areas of consensus or division may exist. Groups should work to create shared expectations, such as ground rules, which increase perceptions of psychological safety, shared visions of their desired impacts, why the work matters, how to depend on each other (and boundary setting), and the tasks and duties for which each team member is taking ownership.

These ground rules or norms need to be revisited periodically. Are they working or do they need to be changed? Help the group to clarify roles and responsibilities. If necessary, mediate agreements between individuals or groups and check to ensure these agreements are being followed. When problems arise in teams, proactivity can prevent small problems from becoming large ones. Remember, conflict is an opportunity to improve a relationship. Lean into difficult discussions to improve team performance and relationships. Refusing to talk about problems never solved them.

Conflict versus Dysfunction in Teams

Conflicting viewpoints are inevitably present in teams. Conflict itself need not result in reduced trust or decreased group efficiency. Instead, it is the way conflict is handled, rather than its mere existence, which determines the impact on trust and team outputs (Hempel et al., 2009). A study by Farh, Lee, and Farh (2010) found that moderate levels of conflict within teams are correlated with maximum levels of team creativity.

It seems almost a cliché that in groups you frequently see an unequal division of labor that can result in feelings of resentment by some team members against others and, eventually, against those managers who allow this to go on too long. One way to address this problem is using rewards for *both* individual and group productivity. When organizations wish to encourage more teamwork, they often switch to team-based incentives and reward programs. Yet, this can lead to **social loafing**, **shirking**, or presenteeism as mentioned in Chapter 7. Social loafing, also known as shirking, occurs when an employee chooses not to do their share of the collective workload. Shirkers lead others in the organization to feel disgruntled, overworked, and taken advantage of. In their study of teams and workload distribution, Pearsall, Christian, and Ellis (2010) note the importance of rewarding both individual and group achievement to reduce the incidence of this problem. Explicitly discussing workload sharing expectations is also key to reducing conflict in teams. This must be done periodically, rather than only once.

Tjosvold (2008) argues that positive conflict is important for the health of teams and organizations. **Positive conflict**, also called cooperative conflict, is the healthy sharing of differences of opinion and negotiation necessary to make tough decisions. In conflict-positive organizations, team members do not hold back their ideas or concerns out of a worry that to share them will cause conflict or disharmony. Team members will frequently debate and discuss different solutions, approaches, or ways forward for the organization, without fearing this will be taken personally or harm relationships. Through this discussion and debate, either a consensus will emerge, or it will become clear that the team members see pros and cons to the multiple options under discussion. In these situations, it will be necessary for the leader to make an executive decision and ask all members to stand behind that decision. Lencioni (2002) calls this strategy *disagree and commit*.

While positive conflict is crucial to optimal team performance, conflict avoidance can result in costly failures. When team members find problems, or have ideas they are reluctant to share, the mission suffers (Tjosvold, 2008). A study by DeChurch and Marks (2001) found that groups who actively used conflict management techniques to manage conflict had more positive outcomes than those who passively managed conflict. It seems worthwhile to spend some time at the beginning of a group endeavor to normalize conflict (conflict will occur in any group project) and share tools for positive conflict management.

There are two primary sources of conflict in work teams: task conflict and relationship conflict. **Relationship-based conflict** occurs when two or more people experience nonstructural conflict stemming from a lack of rapport or personality conflicts between team members. Relationship conflict is associated with negative impacts on the team's ability to accomplish its tasks (Farh et al., 2010). **Task-based conflict** occurs when the group disagrees about the best ways to accomplish its tasks. Moderate levels of task conflict are associated with greater creativity and better outcomes, while relationship conflicts are associated with reduced productivity and morale. Interestingly, teams with high levels of gender and ethnic diversity exhibit more conflict, but the impact of that conflict can be good or bad, based on the way those conflicts are managed (King, Hebl & Beal, 2009). Some authors convincingly argue that task **integration** should only begin once relationship integration has been well addressed (Birkinshaw, Bresman & Hakanson, 2000), otherwise, the tasks will not be done well and damage may result to the organization's brand or customer relationships.

Taken together, these findings indicate that managers should be quicker to intervene in relationship conflicts by seeking to mediate solutions between the parties and by taking affirmative steps to improve rapport among team members (Jehn et al., 2008).

How do you know when conflict has become dysfunctional for the group? Cole, Walter, and Bruch (2008) state that conflict becomes dysfunctional when *team dysfunction* is pervasive and disrupts the work environment (p. 947). The most important implications about team dysfunction are that a single disruptive member can ultimately cause a downward spiral of overall team dysfunction (p. 947). This happens because the behavior of team members can be negatively influenced by observing dysfunctional behaviors of one or more members (Bandura, 1973; Cole et al., 2008, p. 947). When Bandura's (1973) social learning theory is applied to team settings, it is sometimes termed *"the spillover effect"* (Cole et al., 2008, p. 947; Keyton, 1999).

Leading Virtual Teams and Hybrid Work Environments

Many core leadership tasks may be harder or at least different when leading virtual or hybrid teams. Great leaders need to articulate a compelling vision, build trust in their character and competence, facilitate collaborative problem-solving, and quickly adapt to changing environments. Charismatic leaders may be better at doing this in person, but since 2020 we have learned there is usually a way to get work done online, with the obvious exception of work that must be done face-to-face (F2F) such as childcare, food service, etc. Creative leaders can find ways to engage in these behaviors in virtual environments, but the increased level of distraction or lower levels of engagement can indeed pose significant challenges.

Good news: Recent research indicates that "employees with a strong sense of social belonging experience less work-family conflict and, in turn, report lower levels of burnout" when working in virtual environments (Allgood, Jensen & Stritch, 2022). This means that effective leaders of employees working virtually will endeavor to increase their sense of belonging as an integral member of a team.

One challenge is that leaders and managers of virtual teams tend to compensate by holding more meetings, which can interfere with other work. Consider ways to build team spirit and engagement without overly increasing the burden of more meeting time. Consider creating mentoring teams of 2–4 employees who support each other in various ways at their own convenience. Or include some social time during regularly scheduled meetings, focused especially on collaborative games, which has been shown to improve team function on later work tasks (Hughes, 2022). Research on neuroscience indicates that individuals who work together to solve problems as simple as a crossword puzzle or as complicated as crafting a joint budget, then work better together on future, unrelated tasks (ibid.). Brain scans (MRIs) show the syncing of neurons between individuals who work successfully to solve problems together. This primes them for better future collaboration. There are many ways that innovative leaders and managers can use this knowledge to improve team performance and a sense of belonging.

Leader's Role in Hiring, Layoffs, and Conflict Management

Economic changes have revolutionized the world of work since 2020: increased virtual work, demands for flexible work schedules, greater use of temporary workers, swings in demands away from and then back to industries like hospitality and retail shopping, can lead to the need to restructure operations, including rapid increases or reductions in the number of people employed. Rapidly changing environments understandably lead to anxiety, stress, and (sometimes) the search for more stable, secure jobs. Great leaders assess current organizational needs, forecast the short- and long-term future, effectively frame and communicate these to team members, and prioritize the needs of their people whenever possible. "Conflicts arise when people are downsized from a crisis" (Haynes, 2009, p. 9), especially when rapid changes then require a quick about-face, causing metaphorical whiplash among employees, customers, and for connotations around brand image.

The most common mistake made during organizational downsizing occurs when leaders settle upon a predetermined headcount targeted for layoffs. Employees and managers at all levels of the organization should provide suggestions and input to answer this question. In nearly all cases, the simple elimination of positions will not achieve the positive change leaders seek.

Instead, a deeper restructuring of job duties, processes, and policies is more likely to result in productivity and profitability gains. The question is, "How can we best achieve our mission while remaining profitable (or efficient, for nonprofits or government agencies)?" The answer could include changing products or services offered; increasing, reducing, or changing the ways in which technology is used; short-term pay cuts to all employees and/or voluntary attrition rather than large-scale layoffs (with employee input); or other changes designed to increase profitability of efficiency. Layoffs are only one way to save money and are

BOX 8.2. TEAM-BUILDING LESSONS

1. Attack the problem, not the person (Fisher & Ury, 1981). Remember, we all work toward the same mission, even if we disagree about the best way to get there.
2. Focus on relationship building prior to working on shared tasks.
3. Define roles and responsibilities clearly.
4. Make sure team members collectively have the skills to get the job done.
5. Meta-communicate: Share information among team members about how to communicate. Develop norms.
6. Reward both individual and team efforts.
7. "Disagree and commit" (from Lencioni, 2002). Sometimes difficult decisions need to be made. When the team cannot agree on the best path forward, management will make an executive decision and all will agree to its implementation.
8. Managers should facilitate early resolution of intra-team conflicts.
9. Pay attention to organizational culture; communicate transparently and frequently.

often not the wisest, especially if this decision was based on temporary shocks to the supply chain, sales, economy, or labor pool.

Remember, when remaining employees are asked to do the work of those who have been fired, laid off, or quit, they may look for work elsewhere or "quietly quit" out of frustration. Poorly managed restructuring leads to increased litigation, claims of unfair or discriminatory treatment, and high levels of resentment and anxiety in those employees who remain. Although a great deal is heard about organizations being "lean and mean," the importance of fair treatment cannot be overemphasized as a means of gaining employee commitment (Fedor & Herold, 2008). If restructuring will indeed result in job losses, organizational leaders need to determine what kind of services, if any, will be provided to employees including résumé preparation, severance, career coaching sessions, assistance with job placement, and so forth. Employees who have been consulted during the restructuring phase, and are treated humanely during their exit phase, leave with less ill will and those employees who remain will not suffer as much damage to their loyalty and commitment.

Leader-Led Facilitated Problem-Solving

Times of rapid change require the repeated use of nimble, effective, collaborative processes for assessing available information, inviting input, leadership decision-making, and group buy-in. Sound impossible? It isn't. That is what happens in the huddle of nearly every American football team (or rugby, if you prefer). Here is an illustrative example:

Manufacturing setting: Today, 500 vehicles were supposed to be collected from the plant by their shipping company and distributed to dealerships in four states. Unfortunately, a nearby train derailment has resulted in an unplanned delay: The cars cannot be picked up today and it is unclear when the railway will be operational again. This means that as cars come off the assembly line, there is nowhere to put them. Production has stopped while the leaders decide how best to proceed. This is untenable. The plant's CEO gathered his team and asked, "What do we know about the situation, how long it might last, and our options?" The team came together briefly, shared what they knew (which wasn't much because no one knew how long the problem would last, not even the railroad company). They brainstormed ideas and decided that they would need to ask employees to park off-site, carpool back to the facility, and free up parking spaces. The only other option was to shut down until the railway was cleared again, most likely without pay. Each division manager gathered their frontline supervisors, explained the situation, asked for their input in case other options might have been overlooked, and shared the idea that "we are in this together." All managers and C-suite leaders led the way by parking off-site, with some shuttling employees back and forth personally. This continued for three days until the problem was resolved. In the end, while everyone was inconvenienced, they found ways to laugh about it and come together as a team.

The last few years have taught us to expect the unexpected. When a crisis emerges, great leaders rise to the occasion. They practice *extreme ownership* by focusing on those factors they *can* control, rather than blaming poor performance on those beyond their control. They articulate a clear vision while remaining open to the ideas of others. They build relationships with key stakeholders in the good times so that when crises arise, they can reach out for advice and support. They inspire trust and stay connected to the frontline work of the organization. They recognize the importance of agile, effective decision-making. They prioritize their people and their mission, understanding that the former cannot be sacrificed for the latter because they are truly interdependent. As a result, people want to play on their team and they bring their best game.

Organizations need people and people need organizations. Great leaders understand this interdependence to the benefit of both.

JOHN AT THE BUREAU OF RECLAMATION

John asked employees in the under-functioning teams to complete a team assessment questionnaire (listed at the end of this chapter). This questionnaire asked about levels of trust, collegiality, rapport, and willingness to collaborate. From this questionnaire he realized that these team members had little trust between them. Team members exhibited a desire to claim accomplishments individually rather than the result of team efforts, partially due to the existing reward structures that failed to acknowledge team results. Team members noted overlapping and unclear roles and responsibilities. Some tasks weren't addressed at all. When they noticed problems or had ideas for improvement, they didn't share them easily, out of fear of being shot down. The team frequently missed deadlines, and no one took ownership of their work.

Based on this information, John decided to work on rebuilding these teams. He asked each employee to complete some assessments to learn more about their communication preferences and conflict styles. He used two full workdays to hold mini-retreats that included activities designed to help the employees get to know one another, share their strengths, and analyze ways to make the team function more smoothly. The groups used 3-step problem-solving to create shared expectations about how they would work best together. They engaged in strategic planning to set measurable goals for their projects and deliverables. They clarified overlapping job duties and responsibilities so there were fewer "turf" battles. They agreed that when problems arise, they will try to work them out through direct, problem-solving discussions. If these discussions fail, they agreed to seek John's help to facilitate a fair resolution to these problems. They talked about the kind of workplace culture they wanted to create in their units and how to go about achieving it. John created institutional rewards that recognized teamwork and team accomplishments. This latter change required collaboration with union leaders, who feared that individual employees might suffer harm if their individual annual reviews were unfairly influenced by the poor work of other team members. He also had to persuade his own bosses that time spent in teambuilding would yield cost savings down the line, rather than being viewed as a waste of taxpayer money.

Over the next two months, John checked in to see how these agreements were being implemented. He offered some coaching to a couple of employees who were struggling with their ability to frame concerns constructively and address them proactively. The number of formal complaints decreased, and productivity improved. Morale has increased and these departments are now on par with the others in his bureau. Best of all, people feel hopeful.

KEY TERMS

integration
leaders
meta-communication
mission statement
positional leadership
positive conflict
psychological safety
relational leadership
relationship-based conflict

shared mental model (SMM)
shirking (social loafing)
strategic leadership
task-based conflict
team cognition
team mental model (TMM)
transactional leadership
transactive memory system (TMS)
transformational leadership

EXERCISES

1. What kind of leader does your organization need right now, in its current phase? Using the information provided in this chapter, ascertain the current phase of your organization and list specific actions needed by its leader to maximize success.
2. What model of leadership does your manager and/or organizational leader use and how is it working? What model of leadership do you prefer and why? Analyze your current leadership behaviors to determine which you seek to increase and which to decrease.

3. Take the Four Frames survey by Bolman and Deal to ascertain your own strengths and weaknesses in each area: http://www.leebolman.com/re framing_teaching_resources.htm. Then, use this scenario, either alone or as a group exercise, to determine which activities you would undertake in each area in response to a crisis management issue.

CASE STUDY: THE MANUFACTURING MESS

You work for a manufacturing business located in Alabama. Your corporation has branches in two U.S. states and five countries. You are the senior leader at your plant.

Unfortunately, three employees recently suffered serious burns at work. The Occupational Health and Safety Administration (OSHA) conducted a thorough investigation into the incident and issued a fine of $200,000 for failure to comply with federal regulations governing worker safety. OSHA has given you 30 days to make big changes to your equipment, manufacturing processes, and employee training or they will shut down production at your plant. The required changes are estimated to cost approximately $2 million. Unfortunately, the accident and resulting OSHA actions have attracted unwanted media attention and you are now facing reduced stock values along with public hostility on social media. Employees have heard that the plant might be shut down and some are beginning to look for other jobs. In this tight labor market, you might have difficulty replacing them. Your corporation has given you $1 million to begin to address these problems, with a promise of more to come, but not within the 30 days required by OSHA.

Using the Four Frames model, what actions will you take under each of the four areas of activity? What do you do first in each category?

1. Use the Four Frames to plan some new activities for your work life over the next two weeks. What will you do to build strengths in each of the areas: human resources, political, structural, and symbolic?
2. Think, pair, share: Think back to the most successful team of which you have been a member. This can be a sports team, a work team, or a team in your civic life. Why was that team so successful and enjoyable? Which factors from this chapter can explain its success? Now do the opposite—think of a dysfunctional team. What was it lacking? Why was it unsuccessful? How does this analysis match up to the material covered in this chapter?
3. Work in teams or singly to create a list of interview questions you might use to help ascertain how well an applicant will fit into your ideal work team. What traits or behaviors are you looking for and how would you measure them? What questions would you ask of their references?
4. Analyze your current organization to ascertain its current life cycle phase. How can you lead your unit to avoid the pitfalls associated with its current phase?
5. Team Assessment Tool
   Instructions: Use the scale below to indicate how each statement applies to your team. It is important to evaluate the statements honestly and without overthinking your answers. Then, choose 2–3 areas in which you and your team scored lowest to set goals and chart a path for improvement.

3 = Usually, 2 = Sometimes, 1 = Rarely

___Team members are passionate and unguarded in their discussion of issues.

___Team members call out one another's deficiencies or unproductive behaviors.

___Team members know what their peers are working on and how they contribute to the collective good of the team.

___Team members quickly and genuinely apologize to one another when they say or do something inappropriate or possibly damaging to the team.

___Team members willingly make sacrifices (such as budget, turf, head count) in their departments or areas of expertise for the good of the team.

___Team members openly admit their weaknesses and mistakes.

___Team meetings are compelling and not boring.

___Team members leave meetings confident that their peers are completely committed to the decisions that were agreed on, even if there was initial disagreement.

___Morale is significantly affected by the failure to achieve team goals.

___During team meetings, the most important—and difficult—issues are put on the table to be resolved.

___Team members are deeply concerned about the prospect of letting down their peers.

___Team members know about one another's personal lives and are comfortable discussing them.

___Team members end discussions with clear and specific resolutions and calls to action.

___Team members challenge one another about their plans and approaches.

___Team members are slow to seek credit for their own contributions, but quick to point out those of others.

SUGGESTED SUPPLEMENTAL READINGS

Allgood, M., Jensen, U. T., & Stritch, J. M. (2022). Work-family conflict and burnout amid COVID-19: Exploring the mitigating effects of instrumental leadership and social belonging. *Review of Public Personnel Administration, 0*(0). https://doi.org/10.1177/0734371X221101308

Kuttner, R. (2011). Conflict specialists as leaders: Revisiting the role of the conflict specialist from a leadership perspective. *Conflict Resolution Quarterly, 29*, 103–126. https://doi.org/10.1002/crq.20042

Scannell, M., & Scannell, E. (2010). The bucket list. In *Big Book of Team Motivating Games* (pp. 57). McGraw-Hill Education. (*Note*: Based on the motivation research of Pearsall, Christian, and Ellis (2010). I suggest that managers have individuals complete their own collages as well as have them all complete a team collage together.)

9

Dispute System Design and Working with Unions

Truth never damages a cause that is just.

—Mahatma Gandhi

Ideally, systems for tracking and managing disputes should help organizations understand the root causes of problems, discern preventative solutions, and constantly improve their products, processes, and employee performance. Instead, dysfunctional organizations or teams tend to engage in denial by ignoring problems that are obvious to outsiders, or worse, they engage in victim blaming. As the quote from Gandhi indicates, we must be open to learning the truth, no matter how hard it may be, to *be better*. For example, if customers are leaving your team or organization at a faster rate than the industry or organizational average, you need to ask "why?" If your hospital has high reinfection or readmission rates or customers are increasingly dissatisfied with the products or service provided by your organization, seeking out the causes will yield better results than ignoring the problems. In the short term, however, it can require courage and the willingness to ruffle the feathers of those who prefer to remain in denial (see Chapter 2). The truth may set you free, but it might not win you friends in the short term. That is why leaders matter: they challenge us to gain new insights and reorient our vision.

What type of disputes recur in the life of your organization, such as product malfunctions, allegations of discrimination in hiring or promotion, medical errors, etc.? It makes sense to create systems for managing those conflicts that cannot be avoided and to gather feedback from disputants to prevent future unproductive conflict. Designing trustworthy, effective systems for resolving disputes is critical to protecting employees, customers, brand image, and your career trajectory. How is your workplace doing in its resolution of disputes?

Learning Objectives

- Explain the steps and principles key to conducting a needs assessment (i.e., conflict assessment) in organizations.
- Describe the role of internal and external stakeholders during dispute system design (DSD) processes.
- Describe the role of power, rights, and interests in DSD.
- List and describe various process options to consider when creating dispute systems.
- Analyze the costs and benefits of systematizing processes for dispute management.
- List and describe the best practices for engaging in dispute system design.
- Familiarize yourself with common dispute resolution mechanisms used in unionized workplaces.

ELISE AT MAIN STREET BAKERIES

Elise does everything she can to keep her employees happy. Despite her efforts, her company occasionally encounters a disgruntled employee or someone claiming to have suffered from sexual harassment or discrimination. This is expected in a company with thousands of employees, yet she knows she must be proactive to reduce both the incidents of these behaviors and spurious allegations that may occasionally arise. Elise's goal is to constantly improve her company as a place to work and shop. Therefore, she has hired a consulting firm to conduct a needs assessment and make recommendations to further reduce the costs of unproductive conflict within her organization.

DISPUTE SYSTEM DESIGN

The term **dispute system design** (DSD) is the applied art and science of designing the means to prevent, manage, and resolve streams of disputes or conflict (Blomgren Amsler, Martinez & Smith, 2020, p. 7). Disputing systems are commonly defined for internal employment disputes or disputes with external stakeholders such as clients, customers, or regulators (e.g., Equal Employment Opportunity [EEO] complaints within a federal agency or environmental enforcement cases with "polluters"). The term *integrated conflict management system (ICMS)* is used synonymously with DSD. Instead of treating each dispute as a unique, one-time event, a DSD approach seeks to identify the sources of recurring disputes, take preventative steps to avoid such disputes when possible, and take a problem-solving approach to efficiently resolve those disputes that cannot be avoided. All organizations have disputing systems, either by design or by accident (Nabatchi & Bingham, 2010). By working to prevent and efficiently resolve disputes, organizations can enhance their reputations, improve their products and services, and reduce the costs of conflict.

This chapter will focus primarily on internal workplace applications, but also will lay the conceptual framework for the discussion of dispute systems for external stakeholders in Chapter 11, such as vendors, customers, and regulators.

Well-designed, fair, efficient, and transparent systems for resolving disputes are critical to mission achievement: without tracking and systematically resolving problems, how can your organization learn, grow, and harness the positive power inherent in conflict to do better in the future? No one expects a perfect workplace, products, or services. They expect that when problems arise, they will be handled professionally, fairly, and with an eye to justice. Poorly designed and executed dispute resolution systems undermine trust, protect predators and other repeated offenders, and drive good people away. Let's look at three examples of dispute resolution systems so you can better understand what DSD is and why it matters.

1. Sexual Assault Investigations in the U.S. Military

For many years, all branches of the U.S. military have faced criticisms that their system for investigating and punishing sexual assault is ineffectual and under-resourced and fails to hold most offenders accountable. For example, in the U.S. Air Force (O'Donnell et al., 2021), 94% of survivors were represented by prosecutors not trained to handle sexual assault and domestic violence cases. The army and navy both failed to provide prosecutors who were adequately trained in 59% of cases; the Marine Corps fell short of the requirement 30% of the time. This led U.S. Congresswoman Jackie Speier to state, "The system is rigged against these victims. It almost appears that they want to make sure these cases don't see the light of day" (ibid). In 2016, only 4% of filed allegations resulted in some form of disciplinary action (Tilghman, 2016). By 2021, the percentage increased to 30% (Department of Defense, 2021). Changes to this DSD remain in process, with the goal of reducing sexual assaults, holding offenders accountable, and increasing workplace safety for all who serve. Clearly, dispute resolution systems matter and can further the mission of the organization or fail to do so.

2. Equal Employment Opportunity Commission (EEOC)

The EEOC investigates discrimination complaints based on an individual's race, color, national origin, religion, sex (including sexual orientation, pregnancy, and gender identity), age, disability, genetic information, and retaliation for participating in a discrimination complaint proceeding and/or opposing a discriminatory practice (EEOC.gov, 2018c). By their nature, many discrimination complaints will be difficult to prove, since discriminatory comments or actions may not be witnessed or documented via emails, company policies, or other evidentiary standards. In 2021, the EEOC found "reasonable cause" in only 2.76% of cases, which means the EEOC believes discrimination did occur, but does not necessarily result in any payment or other redress for the specific complainant. The average complaint investigation takes ten months, which may be an awkward time for the complainant, their bosses, and coworkers, in the event they remain working together during the investigation. In fact, retaliation charges are by far the most common complaint filed with the EEOC (EEOC.gov, 2022). In essence, very few allegations of discrimination, harassment, or retaliation result in a positive finding for the employee; the process can be long, emotionally draining, and procedurally difficult to navigate without legal help. For both the employer and employee, the process can be expensive and frustrating.

3. Grade Appeals, Common University Processes

Ever receive a grade you felt was unfair? Of course, we are not objective arbiters of our own work products or performance (see Chapter 2 for a review of psychological biases). It is not surprising that most universities have some process in place by which students may challenge their grade. In most circumstances, the student is asked to explain to the department chair the reasons for their concern and to show how, if at all, the faculty member did not follow the requirements of their own syllabus or was otherwise arbitrary or unfair. The department chairperson then has the unenviable task of weighing the evidence and reaching a decision. Of course, the chairperson can also facilitate a problem-solving conversation between the student and teacher if the underlying problem appears to be a miscommunication or misunderstanding. Most universities do not keep data to indicate how many grade appeals were filed, against which faculty members, and the result of these appeals. There are pros and cons to this system: it recognizes the subjective nature of the grading process for many types of assignments, it prioritizes the evaluation of the faculty member (the assumed "expert") over the student (the assumed "novice"), and since all grade appeals go through the chairperson, he or she can look for trends or repeated allegations against any single professor. Yet in most instances, all parties leave the process with hurt feelings and frustration. Some universities have mediation or ombudsman services designed to improve communication and mentoring with the hope of turning these cases into learning opportunities for both sides.

As these examples illustrate, dispute resolution systems are all around us. From the process used to return online purchases, to appeals to your health insurance company to cover a new drug or medical procedure, to fighting a traffic ticket—all require dispute resolution systems of one kind or another. In the workplace, we have processes for redress when we believe we were unfairly discriminated against in the hiring and promotion process or when we feel our performance review was too harsh. Creating effective systems for dispute resolution is important for employee engagement, customer satisfaction, and organizational justice.

Begin with the End in Mind

What is the ultimate, often underlying, purpose of the dispute resolution system? To resolve customer complaints in a way that builds customer loyalty? To protect members of the armed services from crime, which ultimately undermines our military's readiness and recruitment? To discourage formal employment complaints by creating a process that takes 2–5 years and rarely ends in a finding for the employee and against the manager? To prevent claims of discrimination through better training and the creation of an ombuds office or maybe an arbitration program? When you are tasked with designing a dispute resolution system, be sure to think deeply about the underlying goals of the system and what it says about your company's values. If you already have a dispute resolution system (or more than one), how do employees perceive it? Is it seen as fair, adequately transparent, and efficient? Or is it seen as a tool to suppress conflict within the organization? If you are not sure, conduct a survey of potential users of the DSD as well as those who have used it. This could include employees, supervisors, managers, employment lawyers hired by employees, and human resource team members as well as members of the organization's legal department.

PROCEDURAL JUSTICE AND DISPUTE SYSTEM DESIGN

When considering the creation of systems, policies, and procedures for managing conflict it is crucial to focus on procedural justice (see Chapter 2). As these systems are forged, transparency and stakeholder participation will be key to gaining buy-in and gleaning the information needed to create robust, effective systems. If employees or other stakeholders feel these changes are forced on them from above or perceive the disputing system to be biased, unfair, or confusing, then it will serve to increase rather than reduce unproductive conflicts.

It is common for employees to be skeptical about new dispute resolution procedures. They may wonder why the organization would assist them with the pursuit of a complaint, or they may doubt that it will be done impartially. Workplace alternative dispute resolution (ADR) programs live or die by their reputations. A dispute resolution system may be perfect on paper, but if trust in it is low, or if it is cumbersome or biased, then it will not do the organization much good.

Power, Rights, and Interests

Disputes can be resolved in three ways: through a resort to power, rights, and interests (Ury, Brett & Goldberg, 1988). Power is the ability to assert one's preferred outcome onto others. In workplace settings power is used to resolve disputes through mechanisms such as strikes—in which the organization and the union seek to show they are more powerful than the other. Workplace violence, or the threat of violence, is also a way that individuals in dispute try to assert and display their power over others. Rights are established through law, union contracts, or official policies. Contests over rights are often determined by the courts, the Equal Employment Opportunity Commission (EEOC), or through union grievance arbitration. **Grievance arbitration** is a process in which a neutral third party is hired by the disputants to render a binding decision to a dispute between the union and employer, typically determining whether one or both sides failed to abide by the terms of their shared contract. Basically, grievance arbitrators act as private judges to resolve disputes in unionized workplaces. Interests are addressed through negotiation, mediation, and other processes in which all parties seek to reach agreements that meet each other's needs without resorting to the coercion of power-based approaches or the use of an external decision-maker as with rights-based approaches (see Chapter 4 for a description of each type of ADR process). In terms of costs, power-based approaches tend to be the most expensive, then rights-based approaches, and finally, interest-based approaches. Interest-based approaches also hold the possibility of addressing the underlying causes of the dispute more thoroughly than the other two since they seek to meet the underlying needs of the parties (Constantino & Merchant, 1996; Ury et al., 1988). Parties' needs could include psychological needs such as face-saving, relational needs such as apologies and the restoration of interpersonal harmony, procedural needs for a process that is a good fit for the dispute and feels fair, and substantive needs for things like a pay raise, promotion, etc. Research has shown that interest-based approaches are more cost effective, satisfying, long lasting, and sustainable for recurring problems in ongoing relationships, such as those in workplace settings (Blomgren Amsler et al., 2020; Colquitt et al., 2001).

Values Underlie the Design

What motivates your organization to consider redesigning its systems for disputing? Usually, a crisis provokes change. Leaders realize their current system is inefficient due to expensive litigation, high turnover, loss of business or reputation, and/or new efforts by the employees to unionize. If the organization's leaders are sincere about making changes that prevent and efficiently resolve disputes, there is a good chance that long-lasting improvements can be made. On the other hand, sometimes leaders bring in DSD experts to *appear* willing to make changes, rather than having a sincere desire to change (Blomgren Amsler at al., 2020; Greenberg, 1990). This "lip service" usually comes back to haunt organizations through increased cynicism, media leaks, and brand damage.

Stakeholders are those who are directly or indirectly impacted by a proposed change—they have a stake in the outcome. Within organizations **internal stakeholders** include employees at all levels and the legal and human resources departments. **External stakeholders** could include customers, vendors, shareholders, patients or the affected public, and regulators. For public policy facilitation, **primary stakeholders** are those most impacted by the policy outcomes. **Secondary stakeholders** are individuals or groups who are indirectly impacted by decisions or actions of an organization. For example, when the U.S. Environmental Protection Agency creates a new regulation regarding fuel efficiency in cars, the primary stakeholders are the members of the automobile industry and the secondary stakeholders are all people who drive cars and breathe air; literally everyone is impacted at some level by these policies. Some secondary stakeholders will be impacted more than others, such as children with asthma.

For efforts at DSD to be taken seriously, leaders must "walk the talk" and avoid meddling in dispute processes, such as mediation programs or an ombuds office. They must be open to feedback and changes in company policies and procedures, so long as those changes are designed to improve dispute prevention and resolution.

What values are at the heart of efficient disputing systems? Efficient systems are equally accessible to all. They allow parties to feel heard. They address root causes as well as the symptoms of conflict.

Better dispute systems foster and reinforce norms of reciprocity, which aids in creating shared confidence and trust among disputants and increases cooperation. The extent to which dispute systems achieve reciprocity, confidence, trust, and cooperation determines, in part, the likelihood of reaching satisfying and sustainable solutions to conflicts. Moreover, the better the dispute system is at resolving conflicts in terms of satisfaction and sustainability, the greater the likelihood of employee retention and the possibilities for future cooperation, as opposed to more conflict. (Nabatchi & Bingham, 2010, p. 215)

The values that underlie the creation of a disputing system should be tied to the purposeful evolution of the organization's culture. If leaders seek to nurture a spirit of cooperation, self-determination, understanding, and fairness, where people feel valued, then they will craft a dispute system that mirrors and upholds those values. Perhaps they will choose to emphasize mediation and an ombuds office to maximize the opportunities for parties to share perspectives about their problems and craft their own solutions in a confidential atmosphere. If they see employees as somewhat disposable, then the DSD model may instead focus on quick resolutions through binding arbitration. Whether the leadership team explicitly imbues their system with their values, or does this accidentally, *the disputing systems within organizations always reflect the priorities of organizational leaders.*

DSD CONCEPTS AND PRACTICES

In their seminal work, Constantino and Merchant (1996) discuss six key principles of dispute system design.

Focus on Interests

While it may be possible to get a final, relatively quick decision through arbitration, the use of adversarial processes such as arbitration make it difficult for the parties to continue working productively together. It is difficult to attack the other party in an adjudicatory forum and then work next to him or her in a collaborative manner. Additionally, many disputes deal with interpersonal differences or differences in communication styles. These are not able to be resolved through adjudication, although they may indeed lead individuals to file claims of discrimination or inappropriate treatment. When an employee feels mistreated or senses that "the manager just doesn't like me," they may feel subject to unequal treatment. Often, there is no litigation or internal recourse mechanism to deal with true personality conflicts—only illegal behaviors, such as discrimination, are grounds for formal action. This means some parties to conflicts have little recourse within most organizations. Therefore, it is crucial to create informal mechanisms through which these day-to-day problems can be resolved early and efficiently. Interest-based processes such as negotiation, coaching, mediation, and facilitation are often best to address the root causes of workplace conflicts.

Provide Low-Cost Processes to Secure Rights

If interest-based processes fail to resolve the dispute and an authoritative decision is needed, such an option should be provided within the DSD. Whether this process is peer review, arbitration, or some other process, parties in dispute should have a quicker, less costly, and more final route for reaching a decision than going to civil courts or the EEOC. Individuals who believe their rights have been infringed should have a forum where they can feel heard, seek restitution, and bring change to the company. Creating an internal rights-based option will achieve savings and shorten the pain of such a process while preserving the organization's external reputation.

In general, it is best to start with an interest-based process, such as an ombudsman's services or mediation, prior to the use of a rights-based process such as arbitration. While rights-based processes are necessary, it is best to consider less adversarial and less formal means of dispute resolution first.

Provide Loopbacks to Interest-Based Procedures

If the parties initially try to negotiate a resolution to their problem and the effort fails, they may choose to move to another process such as a nonbinding peer review. If the employee is dissatisfied with the outcome of that process, then he or she should be able to "loop back" to an early process such as negotiation or mediation. Sometimes a case takes time to "ripen." An employee may not be willing to settle at first, but after trying one or more settlement processes, he or she may be inclined to reopen the settlement negotiations. Providing loopbacks means that disputes need not always move toward more costly and adversarial dispute resolution processes.

Learn from Each Dispute

It is important to gather feedback from the parties in dispute to avoid future similar disputes, not only by these parties but by others facing similar circumstances. This can be done through an ombudsman's office, an alternative dispute resolution administrator, or an employee relations specialist. The goal is to gain specific feedback about the perceived causes of the conflict, as well as satisfaction with the dispute resolution processes available for handling the dispute. Companies that treat each dispute as a unique event lose the opportunity to constantly improve the efficiency with which disputes are prevented and managed.

Try Low-Cost Processes First

The process options should be arranged in a stepwise fashion with the lowest-cost options tried first and the highest-cost options reserved for use only when processes such as negotiation mediation and the help of an ombudsman have not succeeded (see Figure 9.1). When, if ever, should the lower-cost options be skipped? Most DSD experts agree that there is little to be lost in attempting direct negotiation or mediation before going to peer review, arbitration, or other

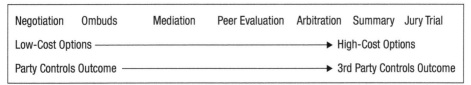

Figure 9.1   Continuum of Workplace ADR Processes

rights-based processes. Parties, their attorneys, and even mediators are bad at predicting which cases will benefit from interest-based processes like mediation. Unless it is unsafe to bring the parties together (even virtually), or one side seeks to create a legal precedent for similar cases, then these processes are worth a try. Workplace mediation programs in the United States commonly have full settlement rates of between 60 and 85% (Raines et al., 2023).

Additionally, each organization will need to decide what kinds of cases can use the internal ADR process. Table 9.1 lists complaints that are often included or excluded from internal ADR processes. In addition to ADR processes that may be created during the design phase, other interventions may be recommended, such as training in communication or conflict management skills, meeting facilitations, and changes in the frequency or methods for communications.

Ensure Organizational Members Have the Skills, Knowledge, and Resources Necessary for Success

If you build it, will they come? Nothing is as frustrating as a brand-new disputing system that no one knows about or wants to use. If you create a complaint hotline and no one calls, does that mean there are no complaints, that employees are too afraid of retaliation to make a call, or they do not know about the option? The system needs to be advertised to employees so they know it exists, why it exists, and under what conditions they may wish to use it.

To build employee confidence in the fairness of the internal disputing system, some companies make the offer to pay the employee's lawyer for a consultation or a specified amount of fees. This consultation may help the employee to choose the best ADR options, help prepare them to successfully participate in one or more of these processes, and give the employee an unbiased view about the strength or weakness of their case. We know from materials

Table 9.1   Disputes Commonly Included or Excluded from Internal ADR Processes

Complaints/Disputes Excluded	Complaints/Disputes Included
• Workers' Compensation claims • Social Security Benefits claims • Individual complaints regarding health/ dental/ vision benefits • Unemployment compensation • Severance packages that have already been accepted by the employee	• Wrongful termination • Favoritism • Discrimination in promotion, raises, or treatment based on race, religion, sex, age, national origin, physical disability, and accessibility complaints, etc. • Interpersonal disputes (e.g., "My boss and I don't get along.") • Sexual harassment • Bullying complaints

presented in Chapter 4 that only a small percentage of EEOC cases are decided in favor of the complainant. Often, when an employee receives a legal opinion from an employment attorney, they learn their case will be much harder to win in court than they anticipated.

FOUR STAGES OF DISPUTE SYSTEM DESIGN

The process of dispute system design happens in four stages: (a) organizational diagnosis, (b) system design, (c) implementation, and (d) exit, evaluation, and diffusion (Constantino & Merchant, 1996).

A **needs assessment** (also known as organizational or conflict assessment), is an evaluation of the conflict, issue, or organization to understand the history, identify the stakeholders, and calculate the costs related to the status quo to determine the likely success of changes, including the use of a collaborative process(es) to address dispute(s). During the assessment of current disputing systems, the design team examines the history of disputing at the organization. What are the sources of recurring disputes? How much has been and is being spent on the current system of disputing, including lost time and productivity for those employees involved and any damage to the brand or reputation? How many disputes? Who handles them and how? What is working well? What isn't? Who are the disputants and what are their needs? What role does the organization's culture play in the management of disputing within the organization or with external disputants? The analysis needs to examine the "goals, processes, structure, stakeholders, resources, success, and accountability of the dispute system. For example, it is important to know whether the disputes involve factual, technical, legal, procedural, or interpersonal issues" (Nabatchi & Bingham 2010, p. 216–217). Begin with a macro focus, looking at issues of culture, communication methods, organizational structure, and decision-making methods across the organization (see also Blomgren Amsler et al., 2020). Map the flow of current conflicts through existing processes to get a clear understanding of the baseline. Decide whether to focus on internal or external disputes. These systems should be designed separately because the conflicts are likely to be distinct. Then examine the micro level by analyzing the number, source, and costs of complaints. Be sure to benchmark the company's current DSD compared to its competitors or peer organizations. How do they manage disputing? What costs or benefits have they realized?

The individual or team that conducts the assessment should interview and/ or survey individuals from across the spectrum of the organization to gather all possible perspectives on these questions, perhaps even including former employees and/or customers. Key stakeholders should not be overlooked, such as the leaders in the legal and human resources departments, union leaders, as well as managers and employees from different parts of the company. These interviews provide an opportunity for the designer(s) to build rapport and gain the trust of the organization's stakeholders. You will need their buy-in for the needs assessment to be accurate, but also for any eventual changes in the system to work. During the needs assessment ask tough questions about what is working and what is not. Particularly in the legal and HR departments, there may be some fear that the assessment will cast their work in a negative light or that the proposed changes may encroach on their turf. For these reasons, it is important to communicate the values that underlie this effort and the ways it supports the organization's overall mission and people. The needs assessment should share aggregate information only—avoid revealing the names of the participants if possible and do not identify problem employees by name. Tell participants there will be no retaliation for their participation, after first securing this promise from upper- and mid-level managers. Will employees have access to read the report? These are issues to be negotiated with the company during the contracting stage. If the designer communicates these values and takes the time to build rapport and trust with key stakeholders, it is usually possible to gain access to needed information as well as building buy-in for the DSD.

Who is the best person to conduct the needs assessment? While an existing employee knows the organization, its culture, and key players, he or she may be viewed with skepticism by colleagues. If one or more existing employees are chosen for this role, they should have a positive reputation within the organization, with widespread approval at their selection. This designer will create a **design team (DT)** comprised of employees from different parts and levels of the organization who will assist in the development, implementation, and evaluation of the dispute system design. The DT will need to be trained in the basic concepts and practices of DSD. This training can last one day or up to a week, depending on the size of the task at hand. The DT is critical in ensuring that the outcome of this process will be workable and will not encounter unanticipated obstacles during the implementation phase. The DT will discuss design options and understand how they might fit within the organization's culture. Most importantly, the DT will become internal supporters of the eventual design and promote its use and acceptance among the rest of the employee population. For these reasons, it is important to be sure this is a representative group, using a transparent process.

If there is a union representative or a member of the legal or HR team who seems highly skeptical of the DSD effort, be sure to include him or her on the DT. As they see the process unfold and learn more about how and why it will benefit the organization and its employees, their reticence will nearly always decrease. These individuals will be helpful in pointing out the obstacles to the creation and implementation of a new disputing system. Winning them over can be key to successful implementation and uptake of the new system.

During the needs assessment, the organization's leadership needs to clarify the goals of the potential DSD process. Common goals include reducing litigation costs, reducing employee turnover, improving the company's public image, improving morale, and preserving relationships, etc. During the evaluation phase, it will be necessary to find methods to evaluate progress toward these goals. With that information, organizational leaders can decide whether the new system is worth maintaining or expanding.

At the end of the needs assessment phase, a written report is issued to the organization's leadership. If the organization already has a positive culture and system for disputing, the assessment may indicate that only small changes are needed. In cases like these the leaders may decide to create a stand-alone process such as mediation to add to their existing disputing system. Or the assessment may indicate a need for the implementation of broader changes designed to re-vamp current practices and create an integrated conflict management system with multiple steps to address many types of disputes. This report will include an analysis of the costs and benefits of the current system, potential gains from a new system, resources needed to implement a new system (including time), and benchmarking information on the best practices in DSD used by similar organizations. Then, the leadership team will discuss whether, when, and how to move on to the next phase.

System Design Phase

An analysis of multiple dispute system design efforts reveals a pattern of about 14 different decisions that must be made during the design phase (Bingham, 2008, pp. 12–15):

1. The sector or setting for the program (public, private, or nonprofit).
2. The overall dispute system design (integrated conflict management system, standalone program, ombuds program, outside contractor).
3. The subject matter of the conflicts, disputes, or cases over which the system has jurisdiction.
4. The participants eligible or required to use the system.
5. The timing of the intervention (before the complaint is filed, immediately thereafter, after discovery or information gathering is complete, and on the eve of an administrative hearing or trial).
6. Whether the intervention is voluntary, opt out, or mandatory.
7. The nature of the intervention (training, facilitation, consensus building, negotiated rulemaking, mediation, early neutral assessment or evaluation, summary jury trial, nonbinding arbitration, binding arbitration) and its possible outcomes.
8. The sequence of interventions, if more than one.
9. Within intervention, the model of practice (if mediation, evaluative, facilitative, or transformative; if arbitration, binding, or nonbinding, etc.).
10. Who pays for the neutrals and the nature of their financial or professional incentive structure?
11. Who pays for the costs of administration, filing fees, hearing fees, hearing space?
12. The nature of any due process protections (right to counsel, discovery, location of process, availability of class actions, availability of written opinion or decision).
13. Structural support and institutionalization with respect to conflict management programs or efforts to implement.
14. Level of self-determination or control that disputants have as to process, outcome, and dispute system design. Qualifications of neutrals and stakeholder input therein.

Additionally, or perhaps more explicitly, it is important to think about how this DSD will fit in with other services offered to employees through the employee assistance program (EAP), human resources (HR), unions, or other resources within the organization. Consider creating some sample decision trees that walk employees through the various choice points of a problem-solving or dispute process so they can better understand which venue or process is best for different kinds of problems.

Decisions made at the design stage are influenced by the information gathered during the needs assessment. "For example, an organization with a flat structure, a cooperative culture, and disputes that center on factual or technical matters may likely want or need a system different than that of an organization with a hierarchical structure, a competitive culture, and disputes about interpersonal or relational issues" (Nabatchi & Bingham, 2010, p. 218).

To get as much buy-in as possible from the potential users of the system, it is important to maximize self-determination both at the systems level and at the case level. This means that employees have input into the decisions made during the system design process. Consider using focus group discussions, suggestion boxes, online boards, or other mechanisms through which all employees are invited to share their concerns, ideas, and questions during the design phase. Make this a completely transparent and participatory process to maximize its perceived legitimacy among future users.

During this phase it is necessary to deal with the administrative questions that arise during implementation: Who will administer these programs or processes? Will it be an ombudsman or some other type of administrator? How big should this staff be and to whom will they answer within the organizational structure? What kind of budget will be required? There are no right or wrong answers to these questions since all will depend upon the context of the organization.

Implementation Phase

In some ways, the first two phases are the most difficult and they are the most determinative of success. If the planning is done thoughtfully, then it makes the implementation easier and provides a blueprint for those tasked with implementation. Those tasked with implementation need to be excellent communicators, even diplomats. They will be called upon to repeatedly explain why the system was created, how it works, and why parties should use it. The new dispute system will need staff to administer it. In small organizations, this can be existing staff who have other duties, but who receive some reduction in duties in order to assist with the administration of the dispute resolution system. In small organizations, these individuals will usually be called on only intermittently to assist with the processing of disputes through the system as well as any annual evaluation reports. In larger organizations where a higher volume of complaints is expected, it is better to hire either internally or externally for one or more full-time positions. The design team may be included in some of these hiring decisions, where appropriate. The DT should also be called upon to help educate and acculturate these employees into their new role: who better to explain the system than those who had a hand in creating it?

Once the decisions listed under the design phase have been made and the system is ready to launch, it will be crucial to undertake an employee awareness campaign. Large organizations often do this through intranet postings, emails and inclusions in organizational newsletters, looping videos on break-room televisions, regular staff meeting updates, brochures, flyers, and so on. In some organizations, participation in the internal system will be mandatory for disputes as part of an employment contract. In these cases, there needs to be a mechanism created that will steer employees to the process administrator, who will then assist them with using the process steps.

Do not be surprised if the number of disputes initially increases when the system is launched. If there was pent-up demand for a dispute resolution mechanism, and if these processes are deemed relatively low cost to try, then we would expect an initial surge in the number of complaints. This is positive—it means that previously unaddressed problems are now surfacing and being managed proactively.

Aligning Incentives for Effective Dispute Resolution

Before we leave the design phase, it is useful to draw your attention to the work of Craig McEwen (1994) on the use of ADR in corporations. In this work, McEwen persuasively argues that the creation of mediation, arbitration, and other ADR processes can certainly be useful and result in cost savings in organizations. However, the biggest cost savings and improvements are to be found when organizations imbue their corporate cultures and organizations with positive problem-solving methods rather than merely creating some new programs. He argues that the costs of disputing need to be measured and tracked over time. Employees at all levels within the organization need to have incentives for proactively managing problems with customers as well as with fellow employees. Conflict management skills need to be taught and performance reviews need to include measures of these behaviors, as well as rewards for improvement and for high performance.

McEwen gives the example of managers within an anonymous company, which we will call Company A. When managers at Company A have complaints or disputes, they simply hand them over to the legal department. That way any cost of resolution comes out of the legal department's budget and the manager's time is freed up for other tasks. As a result of the handoff, the legal department must fulfill its due-diligence requirements, investigating each claim fully before determining how to proceed or respond. This process often involves costly discovery of evidence, including depositions and thumbing through records, etc. Eventually, the case may end up in mediation, arbitration, or court. This method of resolution does NOT encourage early resolution at the lowest possible levels within the organization. Compare this to Company B, which gives managers some authority to settle complaints directly, within specified limits. Company B tracks both the number of complaints and the time to settlement, time spent by in-house attorneys on each case, and the cost of eventual settlements. In Company B, all of the costs of disputing are billed to the department from which the dispute originated, and managers are rewarded for their efficient handling of disputes. In the end, organizations that weave ADR principles throughout the incentive structures and workflows will see the greatest benefits.

Evaluation and Diffusion Phase

Evaluation is often the last thing on the minds of organizational leaders as they implement new programs and policies—it gets too little attention and resources and is often forgotten until its absence creates problems. When employees receive training, for example, they often receive an exit survey that indicates whether they liked the trainer, rather than an evaluation of the impact of that training on employee performance or customer satisfaction. Without thoughtful evaluation, how will you know if the goals of the ADR system were achieved partially, fully, or not at all? How will you argue to the organizational leaders that money spent on these preventative measures will result in less money spent on litigation, less employee turnover, a better reputation, etc.?

It can be a struggle to implement a disputing system in a manner that remains true to the initial values and goals. During the implementation phase, shortages of time, money, or administrative staff may result in some drift away from the initial concept proposed in the design phase. Basically, the ideal and the real collide. One way to minimize this drift is to think about evaluation early, during the design phase. For each value established and goal that is set, ask yourselves, "How will we measure attainment of this value or this goal?" If you create your evaluation framework early in the design phase, well before implementation begins, you will be able to use that framework as objective criteria to determine whether changes to the initial design are justifiable and not overly injurious to the likely outcome of the evaluation. Another benefit of planning ahead for evaluation is that it allows for the gathering of baseline data (pre- and post-implementation comparisons). This leads us to the number one rule of evaluation: start early, not late.

The most obvious goals are also the easiest to measure: reduced employee turnover, higher morale, reduced litigation costs, fewer EEO case filings, and so on. Satisfaction with the process, the neutral, and the outcome need to be measured and evaluated. Additionally, designers may seek to change the organization's culture. They may seek to improve labor-management relations and see improvements in the workplace climate.

Some DSD evaluation experts argue that greater focus should be placed on measuring changes in perceptions of *organizational justice*, which in turn impacts behavior within organizations. **Organizational justice**, according to Moorman (1991) is comprised of four components: **distributive justice** (whether outcomes and payouts are fairly distributed); **procedural justice** (fairness in processes); **informational justice** (the quality of explanations about issues, outcomes, and procedures for decision-making); and **interpersonal justice** (whether one is treated with dignity, respect, kindness, honesty, and so on). Perceptions of organizational justice are related to a host of behaviors within organizations that are crucial to mission achievement, including employee turnover, sabotage or embezzlement by employees, shirking, absenteeism, presenteeism, and the commitment to caring for customers/clients. Measures of organizational justice may be closely tied to the values chosen early in the needs assessment and design phase. For example, self-determination is closely related to procedural justice, and therefore positively related to perceptions of organizational justice. It turns out that caring for employees is good business.

Make sure your evaluation process examines the impacts on organizational justice and culture that may have long-term impacts on organizational health, even if they are slightly harder to measure. Culture change and perceptions of organizational justice can be measured via the use of surveys or interviews, so long as participants come from a randomly selected group of employees from all parts of the organization, and enough surveys are taken to generalize throughout the organization.

Diffusion occurs when the pilot program is expanded to the rest of the organization or grows to handle a broader array of disputes. Growth and diffusion of the program requires training employees who will take part in its administration; maintaining quality control as the program grows; and engaging in periodic evaluation to check for continual improvement, high levels of user satisfaction, and broader impacts throughout the company.

SAMPLE PRIVATE-SECTOR DISPUTE SYSTEM DESIGN

Private-sector businesses, whether large or small, may find their dispute resolution needs to be somewhat different than organizations in the public and nonprofit sector. Private-sector companies may pursue DSD out of a desire to reduce turnover, prevent and/or settle lawsuits early, or improve the bottom line through the maintenance of a collegial and productive workplace. Some companies seek to address employee concerns proactively rather than face unionization efforts. Whatever the reason, many corporations have experienced the benefits of a well-designed and executed conflict management system.

SAMPLE PUBLIC-SECTOR DISPUTE SYSTEM DESIGN

Public-sector employers generally have some common characteristics that will influence the type of disputing system they select. Government agencies tend to have lower employee turnover than the private sector, so a DSD must consider the need to nurture and sustain relationships over long periods of time. In some public-sector organizations, it is difficult to terminate an employee who is underperforming or who creates strife within his work team. Therefore, a system that includes skills coaching and relationship building may be more useful than one in which a neutral renders decisions about particular disputes. Due to the public nature of these organizations, there may be some limits on confidentiality that are less likely to be present within the private sector. For example, public-sector ombudsmen or mediators may be required to report fraud or waste, whereas their counterparts in the private sector have more leeway. The heads of many government agencies change with each election. As a result, employees have grown weary of fads in leadership or new initiatives that last only as long as the organization's director remains in favor with his or her party leader. As a result, agency employees tend to find ways to resist change, with the knowledge that the impetus for the change itself may be gone if they can hold out long enough. For these reasons, DSD in public-sector organizations needs not only the buy-in from the highest leaders, but from individuals and groups agency-wide. In all, the characteristics of public-sector employers lead to a unique culture and political environment in which DSD is both necessary and challenging.

The United States Postal Service (USPS) REDRESS® Mediation Program

Few government organizations have reputations for being as dysfunctional as the U.S. Postal Service. During the early 1990s an outbreak of workplace violence involving postal workers led to the coining of the phrase "going postal," to indicate that one is so frustrated, the resort to violence may be imminent. In 1997, the postmaster general was called to testify before the U.S. Congress to share any plans he had for addressing the problem. Coincidentally, some members of the USPS legal staff had recently returned from mediation training and urged him to adopt a workplace mediation program. The timing was perfect: Postmaster Runyon assured Congress that he was taking steps to resolve employee disputes and disgruntlement more proactively, and their employment mediation program called REDRESS was born!

REDRESS stands for "redress employment disputes, reach equitable solutions swiftly." It is an example of a stand-alone ADR process rather than an integrated conflict management system. It is used exclusively for the resolution of claims of discrimination that have been filed as EEO complaints, or in which an employee is threatening to file such a claim. As such, this program addresses claims of discrimination but does not address other disputes, including those in which an employee feels he or she has been treated unfairly but cannot trace that treatment to a protected status such as race, national origin, sex, religion, and age. While this sounds like a relatively small category of disputes, the USPS generates a disproportionate number of EEOC claims each year, with the average claim taking nearly two years to be investigated at a cost of more than $50,000 per claim. By 1996, there were nearly 90,000 union grievances filed by USPS employees at a cost of over $200 million per year (U.S. GAO, 1997). Nearly 30,000 EEOC claims were filed annually in the mid-1990s, making up nearly 40% of all such claims from federal workers (ibid.). With more than 800,000 employees, REDRESS quickly became the world's largest mediation program.

The disproportionate number of complaints and disputes occurring in the USPS can be traced back to its organizational culture. The USPS was modeled along military lines with a clear hierarchy, strict discipline, and a leader who is given the title of "postmaster general." Job applicants must take the U.S. Civil Service exam, which gives extra points to those who have served in the military. Managers are nearly always promoted from within, and while they know the technical side of the job, they have little in the way of management skills training. Supervisors and managers often use techniques that can be commonly found in the military: superiors barking orders at the rank-and-file employees, even occasionally using name-calling or other intimidation tactics to clarify the pecking order and urgency of the tasks at hand. This may work in the military, but the USPS is also populated by civilians, who are unaccustomed to being treated so roughly. The workplace culture showed little concern for face-saving and interpersonal rapport. In 1997, the U.S. Governmental Accountability Office castigated the USPS, citing "autocratic management styles . . . adversarial relationships between postal management and union leadership . . . and an inappropriate and inadequate performance management system" as evidence of "the persistent labor-management problems in the Postal Service." (U.S. GAO, 1997, pp. 1–4)

The work itself is similar to a factory setting, with increased mechanization and reduced mail volume resulting in frequent downsizing efforts. In this highly unionized setting, there are clear "us-them" divisions between employees, supervisors, and managers. Everything from the distribution of overtime to the number of bathroom breaks is governed by highly detailed labor-management contracts. The union grievance process is used to address alleged violations of the contract, but that doesn't address the overall hostility, heated verbal exchanges, and bullying that can be seen in some postal facilities.

With great insight, the developers of the REDRESS program sought not only to solve EEO cases quickly, but also to address the underlying causes of complaints between workers, supervisors, and managers. Supervisors and managers had almost no incentive to use the mediation process: EEO complaints could take as long as 10 years to work their way through to a hearing before an administrative law judge and nearly 95% of complaints are either dropped by the complainant or they lose at the hearing stage (Bingham & Novac, 2001). To get supervisors and managers to the mediation table, the USPS leadership decided to make mediation optional for employees but mandatory for supervisors and managers. But why should the organization mediate when it wins 95% of the time? Because these claims cost tens of thousands of dollars to investigate and the parties involved often remain hostile and ripe for further conflict as they work together for years during the investigation and litigation of these claims.

The underlying goal of the REDRESS program is not only to settle cases, but to improve working relationships between managers and employees. The program seeks to empower both sides by improving their communication and dispute resolution skills so they can resolve the current disputes as well as future problems more productively. For this reason, the USPS chose the transformative model of mediation (see Chapter 4), which focuses on relationship building rather than merely settlement. USPS mediators are trained to empower the parties to find their own settlement to the dispute and to maximize *recognition* between the parties. Recognition occurs when parties "voluntarily choose to become more open, attentive, sympathetic, and responsive to the situation of the other party, thereby expanding their perspective to include an appreciation for another's situation" (Bush & Folger, 1994, p. 89).

Additionally, the program guaranteed mediation would occur swiftly upon request. Research indicates that early mediation results in higher satisfaction levels with the dispute resolution process and fewer costs for all parties (Charkoudian & Wilson, 2006). Mediations are scheduled during work hours and the parties can bring any support person they desire: an attorney, a union representative, or a friend/spouse, etc. Interestingly, parties are happiest when they come without any support person, probably because they can tell their story themselves (Bingham, Kim & Raines, 2002).

The REDRESS program was piloted in three Florida cities in 1994. It was so popular that it was expanded to the rest of the country within five years. The evaluation effort was highly detailed and included mediation exit surveys to gauge satisfaction with the mediator, the outcome, and the administration of the process. Interviews were conducted with about 200 randomly selected employees at all levels to better understand the workplace climate before and after the rollout of the REDRESS program.

How well has it worked? One way to judge success is the percentage of complainants opting to use the mediation process. By 2004, 89.1% of those offered mediation agreed to use it (Bingham et al., 2009). The USPS has worked to provide as much information as possible to employees considering the use of mediation in order to aid transparency and build a willingness to try it (see https://about.usps.com/what-we-are-doing/redress/prepare.htm). Nearly all (92%) of the parties to these mediations agree or strongly agree that the process is fair; 96.5% are satisfied or strongly satisfied with the mediators; and 64% of complainants and 70% of respondents (i.e., supervisors) said they were satisfied with the outcome of mediation (Bingham, 2004). Although settlement is not the key indicator of "success," 54.4% of complaints are resolved at the mediation table. Another 15–25% of complaints are dropped by the complainant within 30 days of the mediation (Hallberlin, 2001). This means a total case closure rate of 70–80%, saving millions of dollars per year and shortening the life cycle of disputes.

There is also evidence of a broader positive impact on the workplace climate and a reduction in the overall number of disputes being filed. An interview study of USPS employees before and after the rollout of REDRESS indicates the presence of more "open doors" from managers and less use of yelling, arguing, disciplining, and intimidating by supervisors and managers (Bingham et al., 2003). In fact, one supervisor stated that "Since I'm going to have to listen to their problems in mediation anyway, I just go ahead and listen to it when they come to me so we can get it resolved without any need for a complaint." Discrimination complaints have lowered by 30% since their height before the USPS implemented REDRESS, and complaints are now coming from 40% fewer people (Bingham et al., 2009).

The REDRESS program is widely viewed as a success by both internal and external observers: It saves money, reduces the life cycle of most disputes, and is viewed as fair and efficient by the majority of its users. In addition, there is evidence of some positive spillover impacts on the broader workplace climate and labor-management relations. Workplace climate studies at USPS indicate incremental improvements in the relationships between supervisors and employees, including increased positive communication and reduced use of authoritarian management practices. In addition to the creation of the REDRESS program, concurrent efforts to provide managerial training and reward managers for positive conflict management have been instituted, although there remains work to be done in these areas.

Disputing Systems in the Nonprofit Sector

Nonprofits generally attract employees who deeply share a belief in the organization's mission and are committed to its work. Yet they may disagree about how best to accomplish that mission. DSD within nonprofits should include a focus on the disputes common to other organizations but may also wish to consider conflict management techniques for creating or changing its mission, goals, and objectives. These can be highly stressful environments in which to work, with resources stretched thinly. Additionally, some nonprofits have missions that require employees to be in high stress environments (e.g., humanitarian or disaster relief, homelessness assistance) with limited time frames for action or service provision. Many of these organizations operate in a near constant state of crisis, which takes a physical and emotional toll on employees, leading to increased conflicts. The often-precarious state of revenues in nonprofits can mean that employment seems constantly tenuous. In these environments, one often hears: "there is no time to focus on fire prevention because we're too busy putting out fires." The nature of nonprofits creates a unique employment environment as well a unique need for DSD experts with an understanding of the challenges facing managers and employees in nonprofits.

The World Bank

The World Bank (WB) was established in 1944 to aid in the reconstruction of Europe after World War II. Its current mission is to fight poverty through the funding of development projects worldwide, but particularly in poorer countries. The WB is headquartered in Washington, DC, but has offices worldwide with a total of more than 10,000 employees. The bank brings employees together from 160 countries, with predictable culture clashes and interpersonal conflicts.

The WB offers a host of conflict resolution services, starting with the ombuds office. Communications with the ombuds is confidential, except for "imminent harm" to the employee or others. The role of the World Bank ombudsman is to help staff and managers resolve problems in the workplace; inform management about trends and potential problems that require changes to enhance the working environment; and to administer the "Respectful Workplace Advisors (RWA) Program" (World Bank, 2011). Box 9.1 describes the functions of the ombuds at the World Bank. In addition to the ombuds office, the World Bank's dispute system offers a plethora of options, tailored to various types of concerns. These services include Respectful Workplace Advisors (RWA), mediation services, peer review, administrative tribunals, and a vice president for integrity.

The RWA program is overseen by the ombuds office and consists of trained volunteer peer advisors stationed throughout the World Bank offices globally. These volunteers are nominated by their peers and serve four-year terms. The RWAs listen and provide guidance to employees facing harassment or inappropriate treatment at work. The RWAs do not get directly involved in the conflict. Instead, they serve as a sounding board for employee concerns, advise their peers as to the services available through the WB system, and report trends to their

BOX 9.1. SERVICES OF THE WORLD BANK OMBUDS

- Hold confidential discussions to listen to your concerns or inquiry.
- Analyze the facts of a given situation.
- Complete an impartial review of the matter.
- Help identify and evaluate your options.
- Help decide which option makes the most sense for you.
- Coach you on how to deal with the problem directly.
- Facilitate resolutions to disputes.
- Assist in achieving outcomes consistent with fairness and respectful treatment.
- If requested by staff, may become actively involved in trying to resolve problems and may speak with anyone in the organization in order to do so.
- Provide information on policies and procedures.
- Help you raise issues you are reluctant to raise within regular channels.
- Explain other available resources and refer you to other units in the World Bank that may help.
- Provide information and advice about the Bank Group's formal grievance system.
- Alert management to systemic trends and issues.
- Make recommendations for a change in policy or practice.

managers or the ombuds office. Like the ombuds office, RWAs provide informal and informational services rather than a formal dispute resolution process.

Mediation services are available to WB staff and managers faced with a workplace conflict. Both internal and external mediators are available at no cost to the employee. Mediation satisfaction rates are about 95%, with settlement rates of 80% (World Bank, 2011). Mediation at the WB is seen as a method for improving communication and enhancing relationships, as well as settling disputes.

The Peer Review Service (PRS) is available to employees who believe a WB decision, action, or inaction was inconsistent with their terms or conditions of employment (World Bank, 2011). This is important because many employees are hired under temporary or fixed-term contracts, or as consultants. Contracts spell out expected work duties and the rubrics by which performance reviews will be evaluated. An employee can request a peer review at any time, even after termination. The panel can refer the case to the vice president for human resources if they feel the bank's decision was inappropriate. Alternatively, the panel can dismiss the case or suspend it for a specific period of time. The results of this process, as well as the evidence presented, are confidential. No one apart from the peer reviewers, PRS chief (administrator) and the human resources department will be aware of the proceedings. Before the PRS is used, informal methods such as mediation should be attempted. WB employees may request a PRS process within 120 days of the event giving rise to the complaint. The PRS process is considered a formal process.

The administrative tribunal process hears similar complaints to the PRS process but is heard by a seven-member judicial panel and its outcome is binding. Each of the judges comes from a different nation and must be of "high moral character." Judges are chosen by the bank's executive directors from a list drawn up by the bank's president. Complaints come from employees "alleging nonobservance of their contracts of employment or terms of appointment. Depending on the nature of the case, recourse to the Appeals Committee, the Pension Benefits Administration Committee or the Workers' Compensation Administrative Review Panel is a requirement before you submit your application to the Tribunal. As an exception, the parties may agree that the application be submitted directly to the Tribunal" (World Bank Administrative Tribunal, 2023). Judgments and orders are available on the WB Tribunal website and can serve as guidance for future similar cases. The tribunal is the most formal of all employment dispute resolution processes at the World Bank.

The vice president for integrity is tasked with preventing and punishing fraud and corruption within World Bank–financed projects. This office trains employees to spot fraud, operates a fraud reporting hotline, and investigates fraud. Companies found guilty of fraud or corruption can be banned from all future work with the WB, but the WB also encourages national governments to debar these companies from any other government contracts. This office is included within the scope of the employee conflict resolution system because it works both at the preventative level and it has the power to sanction and terminate employees accused of misconduct.

Lastly, the office of Ethics and Business Conduct trains employees on ethics rules and appropriate business conduct in the hope of minimizing problems with fraud, corruption, coercive practices, etc. This group has many duties beyond those related to employee issues but is involved in investigations of certain types of staff misconduct, specifically those that violate the WB's ethics rules. This office also reports trends and concerns related to ethics practices in the workplace to the senior management.

A large, multicultural organization such as the WB demonstrates that a robust ADR system will have multiple points of entry, including both formal and informal dispute resolution processes. This menu of ADR services makes sense for a large organization, but what about smaller organizations that can ill afford so many options? Are dispute systems only made for large organizations?

Dispute System Design in Small Organizations

The examples given so far come from organizations with tens or even hundreds of thousands of employees. What about designing dispute systems for small and midsize organizations? There is a clear economy of scale with any kind of system design. That means the costs associated with creating a disputing system are relatively lower when there is a high number of disputes to process each year. In organizations with fewer than 15–30 employees, a formal dispute design endeavor may be overkill.

If your organization is so small that disputes are relatively rare events, then it may make more sense to focus on creating and sustaining a positive organizational culture with warm interpersonal relationships and problem-solving attitudes. This will go a long way to preventing unnecessary disputes and resolving those disputes that cannot be avoided. Additionally, it is helpful to create a dispute resolution menu in preparation for any serious disputes that arise. This menu should include a description of all of the processes the company would like to encourage, the cost to the employee (if any) for using these services, and whether there is a binding ADR clause in the employment agreement that requires employees to use these processes before they can turn to the courts. It doesn't cost much to train supervisors and managers in the skills necessary to make an "open-door" policy meaningful, and organizations of all sizes could benefit from this type of training. Lastly, some entrepreneurial ombudsmen are available to assist small businesses to access their services on an hourly basis rather than asking small companies to hire a permanent ombuds who may not be fully utilized in small organizations.

As companies grow, they might find it useful to send a trusted employee for ombuds training. This employee could be the "go-to" person for coaching and problem-solving assistance in addition to holding other duties within the organization. This is not uncommon in midsize organizations and even in universities and colleges. If your organization generates some reasonably predictable, recurring disputes that are costing time, money, energy, and damage to the organization's reputation, then it is worthwhile to engage in a needs assessment. The needs assessment will indicate whether a full-blown DSD effort is in order or if smaller tweaks to existing systems will do the job.

DSD UNIONIZED WORKPLACES

Unionization efforts are most common in dysfunctional organizational environments, where employees are disgruntled, and their concerns have not spurred corrective action by organizational leaders. At the University of Missouri–Kansas City's Institute for Labor Studies, director Judy Ancel argues that efforts to unionize and the success of those efforts is proportional to the strength and efficacy of hospital management: "There's the old saying that bad managers get unions. The desire to unionize is directly related to working conditions" (Stafford, 2011). Unions can be a great way for companies and agencies to learn about the needs of their people, but proactive organizations should do this with or without unions. As Chapter 8 indicated, unions are more likely to arise later in the life cycle of organizations, when the leaders have become distant from the frontline work and an "us versus them" mentality has taken over the culture of the organization in terms of divisions between workers and leaders. There are many cures for these cultural ills, and unionization is one response to these challenges.

Unionized workplaces include organized and highly ritualized forms of negotiations between labor unions and company leaders, called **collective bargaining**, which is a process of negotiation between employers and the employees' representatives aimed at reaching agreements that regulate working conditions and pay. A **collective bargaining agreement** is the contract reached between an employees' union and the company outlining the terms of employment. This agreement covers the initial contract between a group of employees and company leaders as well as periodic renegotiation of that contract. In each of these separate arenas, various forms of ADR have been used successfully to reduce antagonism and improve collaborative outcomes. As we examine the history of unionization in the United States and current trends in unionization, we will present and define terms used commonly in unionized workplaces.

Labor-Management Conflict in the United States

In the early 20th century, the U.S. economy was transitioning from a heavy reliance on agriculture to a greater reliance on industrial productivity. This meant large population shifts from rural to urban areas, whereas today we are seeing shifts to exurbs and rural environments due to remote work options. During the Great Depression, the slowing U.S. economy generated a surplus of skilled and unskilled labor. Until 1938 the United States had no federal minimum wage law or laws governing the use of child labor. As public sentiments shifted in favor of such laws in the northern and New England states, factories moved into the southern United States, where historically higher unemployment led to less political opposition (University of Iowa, 2011).

Unions began forming in the United States as early as the 1830s but became stronger during the Great Depression of the 1930s. In the United States the National Labor Relations Act of 1935 was passed by Congress, covering most private nonagricultural employees and employers engaged in interstate commerce. The act made it illegal for companies to spy on, harass, or retaliate against employees who attempt to form unions for collective bargaining. Companies cannot refuse to negotiate with the representative appointed by union members, nor can unions require employees to join as a condition of employment.

In 1947, in response to labor unrest and repeated strikes, Congress moved the mediation function from the Department of Labor to the Federal Mediation and Conciliation Service (FMCS; Barrett, 2007). The FMCS provides mediation services to industry and government organizations, including mediation services to end the 2011 strike in the National Football League.

Unions began in sectors such as mining and manufacturing, where they remain the strongest even today. Unions have traditionally represented **blue-collar** workers. Employees who are blue-collar work at jobs that are based on hourly pay and usually include manual labor. They may be considered skilled laborers or unskilled laborers. **Skilled labor** is used in jobs that require special training, knowledge, and often an apprenticeship, such as plumbers, electricians, or carpenters. **Unskilled labor** is used in those jobs that require little training and education, making workers easily replaced at a lower cost to employers. Traditionally, the labor market has had a larger surplus of unskilled than skilled laborers, making the former more vulnerable to poverty and at a bargaining disadvantage in terms of their ability to press employers for higher wages or better working conditions. However, recently tight labor markets have included a shortage of unskilled workers, which has allowed for increased unionization efforts in companies such as Starbucks and Amazon. Unionization efforts are easier when labor shortages exist.

White collar is a term used to describe skilled workers who do not usually wear uniforms; undertake intellectual, rather than physical, work; and usually have pursued education beyond secondary school (meaning they have attended college or university). These employees generally include supervisors and managers. The labels of white versus blue collar are loosely defined, with many jobs meeting one or more of these conditions but not all. For example, teachers and others who work for local, state, and federal government entities are often part of unions regardless of their specific job duties. Nurses wear uniforms and sometimes have physically demanding work yet are considered white collar due to the level of education and commensurate salaries associated with their jobs. White-collar workers have historically been the slowest to unionize for various reasons: they have been harder to train and replace, thereby increasing their capacity to bargain individually for higher wages and better working conditions, and they often see their interests as more aligned with organizational managers and fear that alienation of those leaders will stifle their ability to move up within the organization.

Unions are commonplace for workers employed by the U.S. federal government. In fact, multiple unions often compete for members among the same pool of government workers, thereby reducing the power of these workers to bargain as a collective. Unions have provided a voice for the needs and interests of workers within specific organizations as well as within the broader society and political system. Unions successfully pushed for laws governing child labor, workplace safety, minimum wages, and antidiscrimination.

Trends in Unionization

Unionization has gone through various phases of formation and reformation in the United States and Canada. The U.S. Department of Labor states that 10.3% of U.S. employees were covered by collective bargaining contracts in 2021 (U.S. Bureau of Labor Statistics, 2022). Yet a Gallup Poll indicates that in 2022, 12% of U.S. workers employed full- or part-time indicated they were union members (McCarthy, 2022). These are slight differences, which are likely accounted for due to differences in study methodology and a slight uptick in recent efforts to unionize workers in service industries like Starbucks and Amazon. About 37% of government workers are part of a union, with older workers being more likely to be part of a union than younger workers (ibid).

"The more educated a worker is, the more likely they are to be a member of a labor union. The rate is highest, at 18%, among workers with a postgraduate degree. Workers with a high school degree or less (8%) are the least likely to be union members" (McCarthy, 2022).

The Great Recession refers to the period of negative and slow economic growth and high unemployment and underemployment that began in approximately 2007 and continued until at least the fall of 2009, yet with lingering workforce impacts well into 2012. When unemployment is high, unions tend to be weaker. Large numbers of unemployed workers make it harder to fight for higher wages and better working conditions. Employers may decide to hire strikebreakers if unions engage in work stoppages in their quest for improvements. In tight labor markets, wages typically increase, and unions are better able to organize and gain concessions from employers who know it will be hard to replace large numbers of workers. According to Bernstein (2017), "Union workers typically earn about 13 percent more in wages than peers with similar credentials, and the decline in unionization since 1979 depressed wages for non-union men in the private sector by 5 percent in 2013."

Tight labor markets in 2022–2023 saw an increase unionization effort in sales, food service, and management jobs, and an increase in the use of strikes to bring organizational change. "Over the last two years [2021–2023], employees went on strike over security, pay, racial justice, discrimination, schedules, staffing levels, union recognition, a demand to rehire a terminated employee, paid time off, demand for the removal of a manager, healthcare, first collective bargaining contract, job security, and on the list goes" (Projections, 2023).

In the United States, state laws regulating unions vary, with barriers to union formation and maintenance higher in some states, in part resulting in significantly lower unionization rates in Southern U.S. states of about 6% (U.S. Department of Labor Statistics, 2022). Some states, such as Georgia, are considered right-to-work states, meaning that union membership cannot be required in order to obtain or maintain a job and state employees can be fired for participating in or advocating a work stoppage or collective action. This creates a challenging political environment for unions.

While unionization efforts have been successful among unskilled laborers, government employees, and blue-collar workers, recent efforts to unionize many professional workers, such as professors and nurses, have been gaining ground. An emerging trend is for these employees to join a hybrid professional association union, such as the American Association of University Professors (AAUP). These organizations give employees greater influence on workplace policies and governance without actually negotiating collective contracts (Overman, 2011). In these hybrid organizations employees can join and pay dues if they wish and the organization takes up whatever agenda items its members deem appropriate—without negotiating collective contracts for members. For example, these organizations can be a conduit to share employee concerns, desires, or ideas regarding benefits, working conditions, and workplace policies. They can also lobby for governmental laws or policies that favor their industry, from the point of view of employees rather than from that of shareholders or CEOs.

Interestingly, as the gap between high and low wage earners has grown, recent trends reflect a more positive view of unions, especially by younger workers. "Their favorability hit 60 percent in a January 2017 survey from Pew, with only 35 percent of Americans viewing them unfavorably. Unions are most popular among young people; even most millennial Republicans support them" (Bernstein, 2017). Then, an updated Gallup poll in 2022 showed that 71 percent of Americans now approve of labor unions—up from 68% in 2021. "Union support is also up from 64%, before the COVID-19 pandemic, and is the highest the polling firm has recorded since 1965" (Diaz, 2022). Pandemic health concerns and global economic shocks have brought greater attention to and empathy for the needs of workers at all levels.

In keeping with the lessons of this text, the goal for unions and organizations is to seek to collaborate for mutual interests. Unions that make irrationally high demands will undermine the organization's profitability and long-term success. Companies and agencies that fail to meet the economic and other needs of their employees will struggle to hire and retain an adequate labor pool. Those organizations that retain adversarial relations between labor and management are likely to become less competitive over time, with predictable reductions in profitability and longevity.

Union DSD: Common Steps in the Union Grievance Process

The earliest ADR systems in the United States evolved in highly unionized workplace settings. Collective bargaining agreements between employers and unions frequently include an arbitration clause or a broader dispute resolution clause. These clauses lay out the steps that each side will go through when either one believes a breach of the contract has occurred. Generally, allegations of contract breaches are made against the company by the employee, represented by a union delegate. It is not impossible for the company to argue that the union has not upheld its commitments as laid out in the collective bargaining agreement, but it is much less common. A **union grievance** is an alleged violation of the "contract, past practice, employer rules, previous grievance or arbitration settlements [which set precedence for the contract's interpretation], or any violation of laws such as Occupational Health and Safety, Americans with Disabilities Act, Family Medical Leave Act, or EEOC regulations on race, age or sex discrimination" (UE Information for Workers, 2011).

For example, provisions for overtime pay are commonly addressed in collective bargaining agreements such that optional overtime is offered to the employee with the highest seniority first. If that employee chooses to decline the opportunity for overtime, then the opportunity would go to the next most senior employee until a worker is found who agrees to accept the added hours or additional shift(s). Supervisors may find this onerous for a few reasons: perhaps the employee with the right skills is not the one with the most seniority, the most senior employee historically has turned down opportunities for overtime yet the offer must be made to him or her before the offer can be made to a less senior employee, or the supervisor may simply believe that another worker is more enjoyable to work with or works harder than the most senior employee. If supervisors do not follow the terms of the contract in offering optional overtime work and pay to the most senior employee, then they may be seen as playing favorites, bypassing senior employees to instead benefit their friends or preferred employees. If the supervisor offers the overtime to someone other than the most senior employee, then she has breached the terms of the collective bargaining agreement and the senior employee who was bypassed can pursue a claim through the union grievance process.

The collective bargaining agreement lays out each step in the grievance process and requires all parties to use each step in chronological order, without skipping or bypassing a step unless both sides agree to do so. There are some variations among the grievance process steps in many collective bargaining agreements, but it is common to expect the employee to first engage in some form of direct negotiation before taking the first formal step in the grievance process. This means the employee should speak directly with his or her supervisor or manager, share information related to the complaint—which must be an allegation that the collective bargaining agreement has been violated in some manner.

Most organizations have something akin to an open-door policy, meaning that employees can go to any supervisor or member of management to share their concerns and seek redress or assistance with problem-solving. Most organizations prefer employees to use the chain of command, starting first with their frontline supervisor and moving up the chain as necessary to solve the problem. In the United States, the National Labor Relations Board gives employees the right to talk with their supervisor with or without the union representative's presence. Employees who are covered under a collective bargaining agreement cannot craft agreements affecting wages, benefits, or working conditions without the approval of the union. This means that if a supervisor and employee strike a bargain to solve a problem, they will need to seek the blessing of the union's representatives before the agreement is finalized.

A **union steward** is the first point of contact for union members when a grievance arises. The union members elect the union steward, someone who is generally liked and trusted by the employees. A union representative may accompany employees to any grievance process such as mediation or arbitration. The steward can provide information about the contents of the collective bargaining agreement and those issues that may or may not fall under its terms. For example, employees may be disgruntled at the way in which their supervisor treats them, or their crabby demeanor, but this issue is not covered under the collective bargaining agreement. Working hours, safety conditions, overtime pay, breaks and vacation days, benefits, the process of promotion and merit pay raises, and non-retaliation for the filing of grievances are the types of issues typically covered in the collective bargaining agreement.

Step 1

First, the employee contacts the union steward to share his or her concern. The steward will try to find out if there are any witnesses who can support the employee's statements of fact. Then the steward must decide if this problem is covered under the collective bargaining agreement. At this step, the steward may discuss the matter with the chief steward to better understand past practice on the issue and whether any similar grievances have been filed and resolved that set a precedent that the company and the union need to follow. The steward may develop a list of information requested from the company, which would provide their answers to these questions (what, when, where, how, who, and why). Once this information has been received, the steward will usually set up a meeting with the organization's representative, such as the employee's supervisor, to speak to him or her about why the problem occurred and to get his or her perspective. Any act of discipline against an employee would follow this process. It is the supervisor's duty to tell the steward why the action was taken.

At this point, the steward would tell the company what happened from the employee's perspective, state which part of the contract was violated, state which specific action or remedy the union is seeking, and request any further information needed by the union. In the overtime case, the union would want to know which employee received the overtime, his or her seniority status, and reasons that the company chose to overlook the most senior employee (assuming the contract awarded overtime based on seniority). The most requested remedy would be for the senior employee to receive pay for these hours that were not worked because of being overlooked. The supervisor may agree with the union that a contract violation occurred, whether it was accidental or not. She may agree to grant the union's requested remedy. At this point, the agreement should be put into writing and any necessary department or division, in this case payroll, should be notified so the agreement can be implemented. Most violations of the union contract are resolved at this level. Step 1 is so informal that many employees don't even realize this is an actual step in the resolution process. They may instead think of more formal steps such as arbitration when they think of grievance steps.

Step 2

If the steward and the company's manager are unable to resolve the issue in step 1, then the steward puts the complaint into writing and it becomes a formal grievance. If the union believes the employee was in the wrong or if the union's leaders believe the complaint is not covered in the union contract, then the union may decide not to proceed with the complaint and to drop it at the end of step 1. Each union contract spells out the time limits for the union to file a written grievance on behalf of the employee. If these time limits are missed, the grievance dies. At this point, some unions will attempt to show the employer that the other workers are supportive of their coworker against whom the violation has occurred. They may do this by wearing buttons or stickers, signing petitions, and holding meetings to keep the membership informed of the progress of the dispute. At this point the upper management of the organization gets involved and may grant the requested remedy or see the dispute progress to step 3.

Step 3

The third step will vary among organizations. In some, the third step is mediation. Grievance mediation tends to be "faster, cheaper, and unused" according to Camille Monahan's (2008) research (see also Blomgren Amsler et al., 2020). For those organizations who have implemented either mandatory or voluntary mediation, union members and managers have found it more satisfying than arbitration. Yet arbitration has been the default dispute resolution process used in collective bargaining agreements for so long that many contracts are simply renewed without much thought as to updating these procedures based on newer trends. In grievance mediation, the parties come together with the assistance of a jointly chosen mediator. They talk about the issues in dispute and see if there is a solution that they both feel is preferable to going to arbitration, where they could win it all or lose it all. If the union seeks to create a precedent for future similar disputes, then they will not want to use mediation. However, they may use mediation for exactly that reason—because they do not want one case to determine future outcomes. In mediation the union and management could agree to negotiate to amend the contract in order to accomplish the same goals as an arbitral settlement, but with both sides having more control over the language and specifics of that amendment than would occur through an arbitrator's decision. In grievance mediation, if the parties are unable to reach an agreement, they can still proceed to arbitration. Because arbitration is an adversarial rather than a collaborative process, it can further erode working relationships.

If mediation has failed or if the organization does not have a mediation option, then the next step of the process will likely be **grievance arbitration**. Union contracts carefully detail the process by which arbitrators are chosen, with each side having some power to veto or recommend one or more arbitrators. In some cases, a single arbitrator is the norm and in others the contract calls for a panel of three arbitrators. During the hearing, witnesses may be called or asked to submit written statements. The rules of evidence and procedure will either be written out explicitly in the union contract or they will use the standard procedures of the organization supplying the arbitrator, such as the American Arbitration Association. Arbitration is generally binding for both the union and the company or agency unless they agree in advance to advisory (nonbinding) mediation. If the ruling covers an issue that was vague or unclear in the union contract, then the arbitrator's ruling will set a precedent for all future similar cases within the organization. Some unions have developed encyclopedic rulings that continue to grow as the contract is interpreted and reinterpreted, much like the constitution and common law, forming dozens of printed volumes going back decades.

The Evolution of Collaboration in Labor-Management Relations

On both sides of the labor-management divide, it is clear that teamwork and positive, collaborative relationships are conducive to long-term organizational health as well as to fostering high levels of workplace morale. When labor and management work against one another, they both lose. This is likely to be increasingly true in the fast-paced globalized marketplace in which a work stoppage creates an opening for one's competitors to move in and usurp market share. For labor-management relations to become more collaborative, both sides must understand the benefits of this change, build trust through reciprocity and transparency, and work creatively together to solve problems that arise, keeping the focus on shared interests. Companies have made these changes in multiple ways: "Various names have been given to these innovations, including mutual gains, bargaining, principled negotiations, employee-centered management, employee involvement, quality of working life, innovative work practices, the high-performance workplace and learning organizations" (Alexander, 1999, p. 1). Transitioning to collaborative relationships will bring tangible benefits of reduced sick time and turnover as well as employee engagement that brings forward innovative ideas and high morale.

Leaders within the organization must make some visible changes to the way they treat employees so that it is clearly more than lip service (see culture change in Chapter 6). An easy first step is to create reward structures for employee ideas that are shared upward and adopted for the improvement of customer service or product quality or efficiency. The next step could be a formal invitation to employees to participate in focus groups, surveys, or other information-gathering methods that gauge morale as well as the points of opportunity for positive change. Work with union leaders and all levels of supervisors and managers from across the organization to create some overarching goals for change and specific actions and timelines necessary to enact those goals. This sounds like strategic planning, and it certainly can be a full-fledged strategic planning initiative designed to redefine labor-management relations. Or it can be smaller, more focused on specific changes to the organizational culture and top-down policies.

Becoming a Collaborative Leader in a Non-Collaborative Environment

What if the senior leaders in your organization are unwilling to make the deep cultural and policy changes necessary to reverse the ingrained habits of distrust and opposition between themselves and their unionized employees? Then you must become the change you seek by creating a microculture of collaboration and mutual respect. Change in an organization's culture or patterns of behavior must come from the executive level to have the most impact, but managers and employees at all levels can affect the outlook and behaviors of those in their units (see Chapter 6). Be transparent about what you are doing and why you are doing it. Let employees know that you value their ideas and want everyone to be as happy as possible in their working lives. Get to know them as individuals—an important step toward building the trust necessary for reciprocal relationships and mutual support. Work with them to create benchmarks or goals to work toward within your unit and discuss any rewards or recognition that you or the group will provide for realization of those goals. Be clear about what is within your control and what is not. Communicate to the union steward or other union officials that you see them as partners in change and success rather than as obstacles. In fact, the union's structure and close communication with its members can serve as a conduit for information and ideas upward in the organization as well as communicating problems early on. Linden (2003) describes collaborative leadership as the "art of pulling people together from different units or organizations to accomplish a task that none of them could accomplish—at all or as well—individually" (p. 42). Managers seeking to change the culture and adversarial nature of relationships between themselves and unionized workers must model the trust, transparency, empathy, and respect with which they hope to be treated.

ADR in the Creation of Collective Bargaining Agreements

For more than 100 years, arbitration has been used to settle disputes over wages, working conditions, and benefits between collective bargaining employees and their employers. As opposed to the arbitration of union grievances, also called rights arbitration, the arbitration of the terms of the actual union contract has come to be known as interest arbitration. Historically, when unions and management cannot reach agreements about wages and working conditions, they have resorted to a contest of power to see who will prevail through strikes and lockouts. Whichever group can last the longest wins. Yet both groups also lose, and this has been demonstrated repeatedly throughout labor-management history. This fact has been acknowledged most explicitly in the public sector, in which the general public suffers when police, firefighters, and other public employees strike. Although some union contracts for the private sector resort to binding interest arbitration, others retain the right to strike when the two sides cannot find mutually agreeable terms for contract renewal.

In light of U.S. Executive Order 10988, passed in 1962, public employees may risk jail for striking. Disgruntled public employees have found many ways to display their dissatisfaction with proposed contract terms that work around this ban on the use of strikes, such as the "blue flu" or massive **sick-outs**, in which employees call in sick or do the minimum amount of work necessary to avoid the penalties of officially violating the order. In 1981, U.S. president Ronald Reagan fired ten thousand air traffic controllers for striking after being warned that a strike would not be met with a compromise from the Federal Aviation Administration. To avoid these negative outcomes, interest arbitration has been used either by mandate or by mutual agreement between labor and management. There are various forms of interest arbitration. For example, "last, best offer" arbitration is famously used by professional baseball players, but it is also used by many public employees as well. In this kind of arbitration, the arbitrator examines the last offer made by each side to determine which was the fairest and the most generous. Then, the arbitrator chooses the best offer in its entirety without picking and choosing the best elements of each proposal or deciding to compromise between the two offers. The goal of last, best offer arbitration is to avoid arbitration. Both sides have incentives to be as generous as possible or risk having to accept the other side's proposal.

How do contracts created by arbitrators compare to those reached through mutual negotiation? "Interest arbitration tracked the downward path in wage growth; there is no evidence that interest arbitration 'pulls up' or 'pushes down' wages. We do find that wage settlement patterns through arbitration have less variation as compared with bargained settlements" (Zullo, 2011, p. 1). On the whole, there appears to be relatively few differences in the outcome of arbitrated versus negotiated agreements, except that agreements reached through negotiation allow union and company negotiators to claim more agency in the outcome as well as use the negotiations as a forum to share information and build better relationships.

Nothing in this chapter should be interpreted as an attack on the importance of unions. In fact, unions have an important role to play in enhancing employee engagement and collaborative workplaces and ensuring fair wages and safe working conditions. Union workers tend to earn more than nonunionized workers in the same profession. Union workers also have fewer wage differences based on gender or race (Bernstein, 2017). These are important accomplishments that should not be overlooked.

Both unions and management need to acknowledge they have shared interests in maintaining positive working relationships, an efficient and economically competitive organization, high morale, and low employee turnover. When employers and employees fully recognize their shared interests in the success of the organization and adopt a worldview that sees the other's success as key to their own, then unions can fulfill the role of being a communications conduit and organizing structure to realize jointly planned initiatives. As the saying goes, "We all succeed together."

For those organizations and leaders stuck in the adversarial patterns that have tended to characterize labor-management relationships in large public and private organizations, it is time to rethink and restructure this relationship. "To refuse to change while the universe changes around us, is ultimately to choose a slow death" (Quinn, 2012, p. 111).

CONCLUSION

All organizations have dispute management systems, but they may not know it. Problems that arise are addressed one way or another: perhaps through informal discussions with managers, perhaps with litigation, perhaps with complaints to the Better Business Bureau. Organizations of every size stand to benefit from taking stock of the types of recurring complaints or problems encountered, the existing methods for dealing with those complaints, the direct and indirect costs of the current methods, and an analysis of the costs and benefits stemming from designing new dispute management systems. Existing employees may be trained to engage in this endeavor, or an outside consultant may be brought in to help. Either way, it is important to engage all stakeholder groups in a collaborative effort to understand and improve disputing within the organization. Whether this is a first effort or a periodic "tune-up," it is helpful to take stock of the costs and benefits of the current methods.

For dispute system designers this work brings with it a host of ethical considerations to be addressed explicitly: Why is DSD being considered now? Who benefits from the status quo and will they object to changes to the disputing system? Will all voices be heard in this process? If written recommendations are issued as a result of a needs assessment, who will have access to that document? What, if any, risks of retaliation are there to employees who share their disputing experiences or problems during this process? Will the outcome of this process increase or decrease the efficiency and fairness of dispute resolution for all involved?

Throughout the phases of dispute system design, it is critical to ensure transparency and procedural justice if the system is to be trusted and used by those facing conflicts in the workplace. Well-designed disputing systems save resources, improve the organization's image internally and externally, and assist in creating a positive culture in which the company and its stakeholders work together for mutual success.

By thinking critically and speaking explicitly about the disputing methods within your organization, you can reduce the incidence and expenses of negative conflicts at work while creating a culture of respect and collaborative problem-solving.

ELISE AT MAIN STREET BAKERIES

Collaboration Consultants Inc. (CCI) conducted a thorough needs assessment. They analyzed data from the legal department to determine the average number and type of employee complaints as well as the costs associated with those complaints. To calculate costs they included not only settlements but also legal and court fees, managerial time away from work, and damage to the "brand." CCI spoke with former employees and current employees at all levels to learn more about the potential sources of complaints. Once the needs assessment was complete, CCI made the following recommendations:

- *Open-Door Policy and Related Trainings*: Managers at all levels will be trained in "open-door" skills, meaning they will learn listening, framing, and problem-solving skills. Elise will attend this training too and communicate her expectation that any employee can come to any manager for help in solving problems. If any manager feels unsure about the appropriate methods for dispute resolution with an employee, then he can contact Ben in human resources for assistance.
- *ADR Programs*: Main Street Bakeries will create an internal ADR program that includes mediation using outside neutrals for all claims of harassment or discrimination; a peer review process for disputes arising from disciplinary actions; and binding arbitration for any complaints that did not get resolved through either of these processes or as the preferred process for those employees who seek a quicker and binding resolution.
- *Data-Gathering*: Human Resources will implement a quarterly employee satisfaction survey that will query randomly sampled employees on a host of questions regarding morale, perceptions of organizational justice, satisfaction levels about supervisors' conflict management skills, and their ideas for improving the company.
- *Ombuds?* At this time, the relatively low volume of complaints may not warrant the creation of an ombuds office. CCI and Elise have decided to pilot the changes listed above and revisit the issue in six months.

KEY TERMS

blue collar	organizational justice
collective bargaining	primary stakeholder
collective bargaining agreement	procedural justice
design team (DT)	secondary stakeholder
dispute system design (DSD)	sick-outs
distributive justice	skilled labor
external stakeholder	stakeholders
grievance arbitration	union grievance
informational justice	union steward
internal stakeholder	unskilled labor
interpersonal justice	white collar
needs assessment phase	

EXERCISES

1. Analyze the current system of disputing in your organization. In that system, what is working well and what isn't? What are the costs, benefits, and consequences of the current disputing system? Who are the stakeholders in that system?
2. Think, pair, share. Think about the values that your organization's current dispute system embodies. What does the current system say about your organization's culture or leaders' vision for the organization? Pair up with a colleague or classmate and discuss the role of organizational culture and values in your organization's disputing system past, present, and future. Share your key insights with the class or your colleagues.
3. Make a list of interview questions that you would include as part of a needs assessment for an organization with which you are familiar. Whom would you interview or survey for your needs assessment? Would there be any obstacles to conducting a needs assessment in your organization? How might those be overcome?
4. Have you worked in a unionized setting? If so, how was it similar to or different from nonunionized settings? In what ways did the union work to improve the way in which employees were treated or make their work life better?

SUGGESTED SUPPLEMENTAL READINGS

Amsler, L. B., Martinez, J. K., & Smith, S. E. (2015). Christina Merchant and the state of dispute system design. *Conflict Resolution Quarterly, 33,* S7–S26. https://doi.org/10.1002/crq.21149

Blomgren Amsler, L., Martinez, J. K., & Smith S. E. (2020). *Dispute system design: Preventing, managing, & resolving conflict.* Stanford University Press.

Edwards, B. (2013). Renovating the multi-door courthouse: Designing trial court dispute resolutions systems to improve results and control costs. *Harvard Law Review, 18,* 281.

10

The Ombudsman at Work

Coaching, Facilitating, Training, and Shaping Organizations

A good coach will make his players see what they can be rather than what they are.

—Ara Parseghian

This quote from Notre Dame coach Ara Parseghian points to a recurring theme in modern leadership literature: There are no bad teams, only bad leaders (see also Willink and Babin, 2015). Great leader-managers identify latent talent rather than seeking out only star players. A team comprised of stars is often less successful than a team comprised of unknown players who are eager to learn, grow, and perform at their highest level. Great leader-managers engage in coaching, training, and shaping organizational members and culture so they can reach their highest potential. Ombudsmen do the same, while seeking to prevent and resolve organizational conflict effectively.

After reading this chapter, revisit these learning objectives. The work of an organizational ombudsman builds on concepts and tools from earlier chapters, especially Chapter 5 (organizational culture change) and Chapter 7 (leadership strategies and processes). An organizational ombuds is an ally of every organizational member because of their specialized perspectives, experiences, skills, and wisdom.

Learning Objectives

- Describe the history and evolution of the ombudsman role.
- Identity the different types of ombudsmen.
- Demonstrate commonly used coaching techniques and tools.
- Describe the methods for institutionalizing the ombuds role.
- Explain the costs and benefits of hiring an outside ombudsman versus promoting from within.
- Describe the importance and common expectations surrounding the ethics of organizational ombuds including independence and confidentiality.

JOHN AT THE BUREAU OF RECLAMATION

As part of his culture change initiative, John instituted 360-degree reviews whereby each employee performs and receives reviews of those with whom they work: supervisor, subordinate, and peer feedback. Based on his analysis of this feedback and other metrics, he has identified the top 10% and lowest 10% of performers. Unfortunately, there are some pernicious problems, some of which he can identify and some that remain quite confusing. Clearly, some employees would benefit from coaching, but John feels ill-equipped to do this himself. In fact, he would love to get the help of a performance coach to improve his own management and people skills, if possible. He also remains convinced that the agency may have policies and practices that cause conflict by advantaging some groups over others in the organizations. He could use some help in getting to the underlying cause of conflict at work and supporting better performance from some team members and managers.

THE WORK OF THE OMBUDSMAN

Ombudsman (or ombuds) is an organizational conflict management specialist working to resolve internal disputes with employees or external disputes with customers, vendors, or business partners. Ombudsmen seek to reduce the sources of recurring conflict by recommending changes to policies, procedures, training, and culture to top organizational leaders and by increasing the capacity of organizational members to resolve their own disputes through the provision of coaching services. The term *ombudsman* is a Swedish word and is gender neutral in that language. When transferring this term into English, it appears gendered, therefore the term is often shortened to "ombuds" in English-speaking organizations, yet either term is accurate as is the term **"ombudsperson,"** although it is a mouthful. The International Ombudsman Association (IOA) defaults to the term *ombudsman* and this chapter will vary use of the term. Additionally, some sources capitalize "ombuds" in every use, but this chapter argues that proactive managers may engage in many similar tasks as the ombudsman; therefore, we shall use the lowercase as we do with "manager." Regardless of the terminology, ombuds are available to consult with employees (often referred to as "visitors"), or customers, patients, or vendors who are experiencing a problem or complaint. They do not supplant or replace other dispute resolution options such as grievance arbitration, the filing of a complaint with the Equal Employment Opportunity Commission (EEOC), or even litigation in court. The ombudsman provides information to assist complainants to solve their own problems, when appropriate. This could include information on the organization's policies, procedures, and even its habits or preferred practices in the workplace. The ombudsman often coaches individuals to develop and practice negotiation, communication, and problem-solving skills to address their concerns and empower them to prevent or resolve problems. The ombudsman may facilitate conversations or informally mediate between conflicting individuals, units, or groups so long as the individuals agree to have the ombudsman do so. The tasks on the first two tiers of Figure 10.1 may also be undertaken by proactive managers or organizational leaders. The ombuds

Figure 10.1   Common Tasks of the Organizational Ombuds

can refer parties to external mediators, arbitrators, or other dispute resolution processes that may be useful and appropriate. Ombudsmen can provide training in conflict management or any other specific skill that they deem helpful to the prevention of future disputes. They can design new ADR procedures and policies in conjunction with key stakeholders within and possibly outside the organization. And crucially, ombuds can advise the organization's leadership regarding needed changes to better prevent or manage conflicts. Those changes may include training, standard operating procedures or policies, performance coaching, organizational culture change initiatives, navigating the challenges of mergers and acquisitions, and more. Basically, the ombudsman is the in-house specialist for collaboration and conflict management in an appropriate, informal, constructive, and cost-effective manner.

There is an inherent trade-off between the time spent on the lower-level tasks of coaching visitors and facilitating problem-solving conversations versus focusing on culture change efforts or capacity building through training. If an ombuds doesn't work on the underlying structural causes of conflict, such as a dysfunctional organizational culture, then she or he will need to spend a lot of time working on individual disputes with disgruntled visitors. While listening and coaching visitors is critical to the work of all ombuds and it can make a huge impact on the work lives of individual employees, it is also true that spending too much time at the bottom of the pyramid and too little time working on the higher-level tasks is equivalent to bailing water out of a boat rather than plugging the holes that are making the vessel take on water.

As Figure 10.1 shows, the more basic tasks of coaching and referral incur few risks because they are less visible to those higher in the organization, while the higher-level activities are associated with both greater risks and greater rewards in the form of deeper impacts on the organization. For example, efforts to overturn ineffective policies create new systems for feedback and management of disputes or change a dysfunctional organizational culture could invoke the ire of powerful leaders. There are always individuals and groups that benefit from the status quo, even when the overall impact is negative for the organization. Change is hard. Big changes attract attention, either positive or negative. Bringing bad news to leaders comes with risks. To minimize these risks, ombuds need to engage in interest-based negotiation strategies, especially framing, so that leaders see great challenges like culture change as great opportunities to leave their mark and enhance their personal leadership reputation while maximizing mission achievement.

Ironically, ombuds who spend too little time on the lower ends of the pyramid in Figure 10.1 may inadvertently be making their office vulnerable to budget cuts or elimination. Why keep an office and an employee when the leaders are not sure what they do or what value they bring? Efforts higher on the pyramid raise visibility and have impacts that are felt by a wider swath of employees, managers, and leaders (Raines & Harrison, 2019). As stated by the IOA (2023), "An ombudsman should not be risk-averse and should understand that this position may, on occasion, challenge even the highest levels of leadership in an effort to foster fair and just practices."

To help insulate the ombuds office from retribution by managers or others in the organization, ombudsmen do not report to the human resources or legal departments. Ombudsmen report directly to the organization's leadership, whether this means a board of directors, president, or chief executive officer, etc. This independence allows the ombuds to maintain confidentiality and avoid the potential biasing effect of hearing complaints raised against his or her own supervisor. Of course, complaints against the highest leaders are not unheard of and there is simply no way to fully insulate the ombuds office from those pressures. The ombudsman maintains confidentiality by revealing neither the names of visitors nor any information about the substance of the problems he or she hears unless the visitor allows the sharing of the information or complaint with others. Ombuds are not subject to reporting requirements of others in the organization. For example, U.S. federal government employees must report allegations of "fraud, waste, and abuse" and all public university faculty and staff must report certain crimes occurring on campus under the Clery Act, yet the ombuds is exempt from these reporting requirements.

TYPOLOGY OF OMBUDS ROLES

There are variations among ombuds offices in terms of their mission and the extent or limitations of their powers, although users of their services are often unaware of the nuances of the roles, who they serve, and the type of power they have or lack. While more variations exist, this section examines the most common type of ombudsman services. After this brief overview, our focus will be on the organizational ombudsman role.

Classical ombudsmen: The use of ombudsmen in Sweden began in the federal sector about 200 years ago in order to help balance power between citizens seeking redress from inappropriate exertion of governmental authority and their elected or appointed leaders and institutions, and this continues to be the case for classical ombudsmen. These ombudsmen receive and investigate complaints and concerns regarding governmental policies and processes. The mandate of these ombuds is generally articulated through statutes; they may be either elected or appointed. For example, the Queensland ombudsman in Australia reviews government actions by federal sector agencies and reports to Parliament if his review of agency action results in the conclusion that the agency took "unlawful, unreasonable or wrong" action (Queensland Ombudsman, 2022). These ombuds work solely in the public sector.

Advocate ombudsmen: These ombuds may work in either the private or public sector. Their primary task is to advocate on behalf of aggrieved individuals or groups who are typically vulnerable such as elders in long-term-care facilities or juveniles in detention. Many U.S. states have long-term-care ombudsmen who investigate allegations of code violations or wrongdoing in nursing homes and corrections facilities to help those who have suffered because of these violations and to bring the facilities into compliance with applicable laws, rules, and regulations. In Michigan, for example, there is an ombuds who investigates claims of abuse brought by prisoners and parolees (Michigan Legislative Council, n.d.). Consumers are often offered the assistance of an ombuds; for example, the Consumer Financial Protection Bureau has an ombuds service.

Executive or organizational ombudsman: This is the most common form of ombuds, commonly used in universities and private-sector companies to receive complaints or queries concerning the actions (or failures to act) of organizational managers, leaders, contractors, or coworkers. The executive (aka organizational) ombuds may work with organizational leaders to improve the performance of the organization by improving organizational culture; assuring fairness in hiring and promotion; bringing allegations of wrongdoing to the attention of organizational leaders (when appropriate); training managers and others on conflict management and communication skills; and addressing the root causes of problems like employee turnover, low morale, sabotage, harassment, bullying, disengagement, or other organizational challenges that negatively impact mission achievement. Executive ombuds generally have an internal employment/workplace focus, but some also address conflicts with investors, regulators, or others. Organizations with executive ombuds include Coca-Cola Enterprises, all fourteen of the UN agencies, the U.S. Marshal Service, the International Monetary Fund, Mars Inc. (the candy company), Pfizer pharmaceuticals, Chevron, U.S. Federal Emergency Management Agency, and many more.

Legislative ombudsman: The legislative ombudsman works to address concerns about potential ethics violations or breaches of trust levied against an elected leader or group of leaders. For example, Arizona and Hawaii both have legislative ombudsmen.

Media ombudsman: The purpose of the media ombudsman is to promote transparency, accuracy, and neutrality in the reporting of news. This type of ombuds is familiar with journalistic ethics and standards of practice that are meant to ensure fairness, accuracy, and ethical reporting for the public's benefit. For example, National Public Radio (in the United States) has an ombudsman who helps to explain the journalistic process to listeners and help them understand the decisions that go into deciding what stories get reported, which don't, and how the reporting is carried out. The ombuds can ask questions of the newsroom but cannot interfere with the reporting process. She is a bridge between listeners who are often concerned with perceived bias and reporting ethics, and those conducting the news investigations and reporting (NPR, 2016).

Who Becomes an Ombuds?

Ombudsmen can be promoted from within the organization and then trained in the processes and skills of conflict prevention and resolution or they may be hired from outside the organization to bring in both objectivity and expertise. Internally hired ombudsmen have the benefit of understanding the organization's culture, norms, policies, and mission. An internally hired ombuds needs to be someone admired and respected by her peers, deemed likely to keep confidences and deal fairly with others. Externally hired ombudsmen lack the organizational knowledge held by insiders, but they may be seen as more objective, with fewer preexisting alliances, and they likely have more conflict resolution experience and education. Externally hired ombudsmen are more common when an organization has a history of systematic discrimination or trust violations. In these cases, an outsider is likely to be a more acceptable choice to all involved. Inside hires will need to receive specialized training and mentoring by experienced ombuds to get up to speed in their new role.

The skills and characteristics common to ombuds include a reputation for integrity, trustworthiness, and empathy. Ombuds must be sensitive to issues of diversity, since visitors may have concerns regarding discrimination in hiring, promotion, or treatment at work. To attend to issues of organizational culture and justice, ombuds must understand the ways in which discrimination is deeply enmeshed in organizational culture, hiring, promotion, and the treatment of employees across all identity areas (e.g., gender, race, ethnicity, religion, disability, national origin, sexual orientation, age, social class, educational background). Ombuds must be able to maintain a calm, nonjudgmental demeanor when hearing allegations of individual or organizational wrongdoing. Ombuds generally have strong emotional intelligence, including well-developed social and networking skills. This improves their ability to build coalitions for change initiatives as well as to seek redress for individual visitors as needed. Ombudsmen tend to be competent public speakers with above-average communication skills, which helps them engage in training and conflict resolution efforts with those at all levels of the organization's hierarchy. Lastly, whether they are promoted internally or brought into their organizations specifically for the ombuds role, they must attain a deep understanding of the written and unwritten rules, norms, and practices of their organizations and its leaders.

Table 10.1   Ombuds Salary Averages across Sectors

Sector	Mean
Academic (n = 55)	$107,800
Corporate (n = 11)	$164,384
Government (n = 15)	$130,986
All respondents (n = 96)	$130,664

Ombuds typically hold the minimum of a bachelor's degree, but graduate degrees and additional training are common. Salaries vary depending upon the sector and organization but tend to range from $107,000 to $160,000 per year.

Table 10.1 summarizes the findings of a salary survey of mediators in 2017 undertaken by Hedeen, Rowe, and Schneider (2018). Ombudsmen tend to be experienced career professionals who need to earn the same as or more than they would have been earning in their regular position within the organization (e.g., engineer, manager) in addition to the fact that only a minority of people are suited to the potentially stressful work of listening to and working through conflicts every day.

Assessing and Sharing the Organizational Benefits of the Ombuds Office

Ombudsmen promote mission achievement and reduce the costs of unproductive conflict in an organization by reducing employee turnover, increasing engagement, avoiding employment or other litigation costs, protecting the "brand" or image for the organization, improving morale, and enabling the creation and re-creation of healthy, collegial workplace cultures. Organizational ombudsmen "Build a reputation for being safe, fair, accessible and credible" (Rowe, Hedeen & Schneider, 2020). An ombuds' contribution to mission achievement is to prevent those conflicts that can be prevented, resolve the remaining conflicts early, and create systems to identify and address organizational problems proactively. Ironically, the confidential nature of ombuds' services makes it difficult to fully account for and report quantifiable benefits such as cost savings. What is the benefit to avoiding litigation, union grievances, or having to replace a valuable employee? While these are hard to pin down, it is common practice for ombudsmen to keep track of the number of visitors received each year and the types of issues brought by visitors, record demographic information on visitors, and seek to determine which issues or cases reached full, partial, or no resolution. Many ombuds provide satisfaction surveys for visitors designed to track trends in the satisfaction of users of ombuds services. Ombuds may also wish to track the list of concerns they raise to leaders, since the early identification of problems may have significant benefits, even though these may be difficult to quantify. The ombuds should track and report the number of hours spent on training provided to the organization's members. According to Rowe (2018), only 10% of ombuds reported no systematic efforts to evaluate the costs/benefits of their offices. Table 10.2 shows the different types of benefits commonly resulting at universities from the implementation of an ombuds program (Schenck & Zinsser, 2014, p. 34).

Table 10.2   Potential Benefits of an Ombuds Office

Economic	Organizational	Humanistic
• Expanded productivity	• Supplemented programs	• Increased engagement
• Increased retention	• Navigated systems	• Strengthened organizational
• Preserved management time	• Heightened transparency	trust
• Enhanced operational efficiency	• Enhanced accountability	• Expanded fairness
• Advanced individual and team development	• Protected and maximized personal responsibility	• Enhanced creativity and risk taking
• Reduced disputing process and outcome costs	• Increased ethical and compliant behavior	• Augmented individualized career development
• Improved reputation/brand protection	• Advanced preventative conflict-posture	• Heightened respect
• Reduced incivility (sabotage/theft)	• Advantaged under the federal sentencing guidelines if wrongdoing is proven	• Improved and preserved working relationships
• Lowered or eliminated insurance costs		• Reduced incivility (bullying, mobbing, isolating)

In its study of the effectiveness of the Office of the Organizational Ombudsman, Baker Hughes found that 39% of visitors raised concerns regarding supervisor-employee relations, 15% raised concerns or questions about career advancement, 9% had concerns about pay or benefits, 9% raised concerns about their relationships with coworkers, 8% involved concerns about ethics or policies, 5% raised general organizational issues, 4% raised the issue of violations of law, with miscellaneous concerns making up the remainder (Bonnivier, Brooke-Lander & Lewis, 2015). Visitors represented all levels and job types within the organization, with mid-level professionals and employees with two to nine years of service raising more concerns than others.

A report by the Oregon State University Ombudsman (Sulzmann, 2018) office reveals that approximately 32% of their visitors come from faculty-to-faculty disputes, 17% are faculty-to-administration, 17% are faculty-to-student complaints, 8% are staff-to-faculty disputes, 5% include group issues, and the remainder include student complaints with each of these groups (i.e., staff, administrators, and other students). If only 25–50% of these problems were successfully resolved, the potential benefits to the organization would be enormous.

Anecdotal reports from individual organizations and the rapid growth of the creation of ombuds offices indicate a general belief in their overall benefits even in the absence of clear data. According to the International Ombudsman Association (IOA), organizations with an ombudsman office commonly cite the following benefits of the service (International Ombuds Association, n.d.):

- Offers a safe place for members of the workforce to discuss concerns and understand their options without fear of retaliation or fear that formal action will be taken simply by raising concerns.
- Helps identify undetected and/or unreported criminal or unethical behavior, policy violations, or ineffective leadership.
- Helps employees become empowered and take responsibility for creating a better workplace.
- Facilitates two-way, informal communication and dispute resolution to resolve allegations of harassment, discrimination, and other workplace

issues that could otherwise escalate into time-consuming and expensive formal complaints or lawsuits.

- Provides the ability to address subtle forms of insensitivity and unfairness that do not rise to the level of a formal complaint but nonetheless create a disempowering work environment.
- Aids compliance with the Sarbanes-Oxley Act and the U.S. federal sentencing guidelines.
- Provides an early warning diagnosis system that identifies and alerts institutions about new negative trends.
- Helps employee satisfaction, morale, and retention by humanizing the institution through the establishment of a resource that provides safe and informal opportunities to be heard.
- Provides conflict resolution skills training.
- Provides upward feedback to management about organizational trends.
- Helps avoid negative press by addressing issues at the lowest and most direct level possible.
- Provides the organization with an independent and impartial voice, which fosters consistency between organizational values and actions.
- Serves as a central information and referral resource for policies, processes, and resources within the organization.

Standards of Practice for Ombudsmen

Ombuds adhere to standards of practice articulated by their professional associations, such as the International Ombudsman's Association (IOA), which include a commitment to procedural fairness, integrity, and respect for all members of the organizations.

Independence—The ombudsman is independent in structure and function as much as possible. This means he or she is independent of the regular chain of command and does not report to anyone except the leader of the organization. Some organizations have bent this rule and allow the ombudsman to report to the risk management, human resources, or legal departments. Some critics claim this means they should surrender the ombudsman title in favor of "patient care advocate" or other alternative title.

Neutrality and impartiality—For the ombudsman to remain neutral, she avoids circumstances that could present a real or perceived conflict of interest.

Confidentiality—The ombudsman does not breach confidentiality except to prevent imminent, serious harm. In nearly all circumstances, the ombuds does not disclose the identity of visitors, the matters they raise, or any information that could put them at risk of retaliation or other negative repercussions. However, the ombudsman may draft periodic reports indicating the number of visitors served and the aggregated sources of complaints, and make suggestions about needed changes within the organization to leaders.

Avoidance of formal processes—The ombudsman doesn't participate in any formal adjudicatory or administrative proceedings brought against any member of the organization. The ombuds may suggest, but do not require, the use of mediation, arbitration, or other processes of potential benefit to visitors and the organization.

Processes Utilized by Ombudsmen

Using Figure 10.1, this section will examine the processes and skills commonly utilized by ombudsmen and proactive managers to prevent and resolve conflict at the lowest level possible.

Conflict and Performance Coaching

As Figure 10.1 would predict, the first and foundational process is conflict coaching. Conflict coaching may be effectively applied when an employee comes to a manager or ombuds to voice concerns or seek help to solve a problem between himself and others in the organization. Jones and Brinkert (2008) define **conflict coaching** as "a process in which a coach and visitor communicate one-on-one for the purpose of developing the visitor's conflict-related understanding, interaction strategies, and interaction skills. Coaches help visitors to make sense of conflicts they experience, help them learn to positively manage these conflicts, and help them master specific communication skills and behaviors" (pp. 4–5). Coaching is a common part of the performance review process, in that it is the primary duty of managers to provide feedback, information, skill development, and new perspectives designed to help employees maximize their performance at work. Coaching can be offered to employees at all levels of an organization and is increasingly used by high-level executives to continually improve their performance.

When coaching executives, ombuds often seek to "modify an executive's style, assist executives in adjusting to change, help in developmental efforts, and provide assistance to derailed executives" (Jones & Brinkert, 2008, p. 6). Coaches may also be asked for career advice and mentoring during coaching sessions.

Coaches generally begin the first coaching session by asking the visitor about his or her goals for growth and improvement, and then administering some assessment tools to better understand the visitor's baseline skills and habits in terms of conflict management. For example, the Conflict Styles Inventory from Chapter 1 can be a useful predictor of the visitor's approach to conflict, communication styles, and challenges related to working in teams or delegating. For example, people who score high on the "competing" mode tend to struggle with delegation because they prefer to retain control over projects and outcomes. They also tend to communicate quite directly, even if that makes them seem abrasive or rude. For strong competitors, one of the key skills to work on is softening their language, inviting input from others, taking turns, and allowing others to receive their preferred outcomes at an increased rate. People scoring high on accommodating or avoiding tend not to delegate well for fear of provoking conflict in their subordinate or damaging the relationship. They tend to communicate nonverbally and indirectly, which is easily misunderstood or seen as passive-aggressive because when they are upset, they often avoid the person with whom they have conflict or speak about them to others rather than constructively addressing the problem directly. By working on their framing skills, those who score high on accommodating and avoiding can feel more confident when engaging in difficult conversations because they will learn how to voice ideas or concerns without fear of provoking defensiveness in others. Knowing how someone scored on the conflict mode assessment can help the coach to determine which skills to work on with the visitor.

In his 1997 article, Alan Tidwell promoted a stepwise process for coaching called "problem solving for one." Tidwell recommends the following steps in the conflict coaching process:

> *Preamble and introduction*: The coach introduces the process, including rules around confidentiality and shared expectations between the coach and participant (or visitor).
>
> *Storytelling*: The visitor tells the coach why he is seeking assistance and describes the conflict or problems encountered at work.
>
> *Conflict analysis*: The coach encourages the visitor to deeply examine the problem(s) through an examination of its "origins, parties, issues, dynamics, and possibilities for resolution" (Tidwell, 1997).
>
> *Alternative generation and costing*: The visitor is encouraged to brainstorm all possible options for resolving the problem and determining the potential costs and benefits of each option.
>
> *Communication strategy development*: The coach and visitor work together to develop or improve any specific skills necessary to implement the chosen strategy. These often include listening, asserting, questioning, framing skills, stress-reduction strategies, giving or asking for feedback, or any other appropriate skills.
>
> *Restatement of the conflict-handling plan*: The coach and visitor make an implementation plan and develop mechanisms for determining improvement or success. "How will we know if this is working?" Then, after implementation of the plan, the visitor comes back to the coach for follow-up, as needed.

Sometimes managers make decisions or instruct employees as to how to resolve a particular problem or conflict. However, the benefit of coaching and developing employees' problem-solving skills is that it empowers them to prevent and manage their own disputes in the future, while deepening their commitment to decisions that result from processes they lead or initiate.

In addition to coaching visitors through specific conflicts, when ombuds and managers act as coaches they often engage in specific skill building with their clients on issues such as delegation, giving and receiving feedback, techniques for team building and conflict prevention, strategic planning, managing workload distribution, etc. In general, coaches engage in one-on-one training and skill building designed to meet the individual needs of clients.

In addition to coaching, ombuds may refer visitors for services like mental health counseling, external mediation or arbitration, legal advice, professional development, or other services.

Mediating or Facilitating Conversations between Two or More in Conflict

When two or more people or units are in conflict, the ombuds (or a proactive conflict manager) may be asked to informally mediate between them by facilitating a problem-solving conversation. The ombudsman will only do so when all parties voluntarily agree to participate and the conversation remains confidential. If agreements are reached, they often include provisions related to interpersonal relations (e.g., "We will not argue in front of other employees") but may also include changes to work duties, salary, or other terms of employment so long as the parties to the mediation have the authority to reach such decisions.

Similarly, it is relatively common for the ombuds (or a proactive manager) to facilitate problem-solving conversations between two or more units within an organization that are experiencing conflict or seek to improve their ability to work together productively (e.g., sales and engineering; human resources and payroll). Because conflict usually stems from unmet expectations, in most cases the critical questions to ask include:

- What do you need and expect of each other? (Try to reach agreement on shared expectations.)
- What is the source of any unmet expectations?
- How can you work together more productively in the future? What agreements, ground rules, or practices will help you achieve your desired results?
- When problems arise, how can you solve them together?
- Are your individual and group incentives aligned? If not, how can you change that alignment?

For example, if an organization states that two units within its organization seem to be working as silos, refraining from sharing information needed for each unit to reach its highest potential, then at least part of the solution is to create mechanisms to increase the amount of communication occurring between these units (e.g., shared message boards, regular meetings, an occasional lunch or breakfast gathering).

Training for Conflict Prevention and Skill Development

There is a missing step on the pyramid pictured in Figure 10.1 because most ombuds develop at least an anecdotal understanding of the primary sources of complaints or conflict within their organization through the course of their work. Based on the concerns brought to them by employees at all levels, they become aware of "hot spots" or sources of conflict that can be geographic (e.g., in unit X or those who must work with manager Y), or it is topical (e.g., unfair hiring and promotion practices or aggressive communication patterns embedded in the organizational culture). But some managers go beyond this anecdotal understanding of the sources of conflict in the organization by engaging in a conflict assessment or needs analysis (covered in Chapter 9). Using surveys, focus groups, and/or the examination of statistics related to employee turnover or customer satisfaction (or other data), the ombuds may develop an understanding of the root causes of conflict at work. Only then can she decide whether to engage in training and what training to include.

Organizational leaders and human resource managers often seek training as a panacea for widespread problems. Yet training everyone, or even a large subset of employees, is not going to fix the problems caused by overlapping lines of authority and job duties, a misalignment of individual and group incentives, or one predatory manager who is driving employees away or leading to litigation for sexual harassment. Training, especially facilitative training, can help employees reach shared expectations that help prevent future conflict.

Facilitative training is a mix of problem identification, targeted training to address those problems, and follow-up to measure any impact of the training on those problems. If those problems include a lack of shared expectations, norms, or understanding of the mission or shared values (the "who are we" questions), then the trainer uses the training period to lead a problem-solving discussion designed to build consensus on the issues at hand. Essentially, this is a mix of facilitation and customized, responsive training. Prior to the training or near the beginning of the session, the trainer solicits input from the trainees as to the repetitive sources of conflict they face on the job. This can be done through a pre-training survey or by passing out 3 × 5 cards at the beginning of the training and asking each participant to list one recurring problem at work per card, using as many cards as they wish. Then, the trainer groups the cards into themes that emerge from the cards, such as "communication problems," "workload distribution," "management issues," etc. She then takes this input, lists the themes and some of the specific comments (keeping the sources confidential) on the board or flipchart. She then uses this information to create a customized training experience to meet the specific needs of the trainees. This way, those present realize from the beginning of the session that their concerns will be addressed rather than sitting through a generic conflict management training (or other training) that won't help them with their challenges.

Training can improve employees' skills related to communication, delegation, collaboration, problem-solving, culture change efforts, policy implementation, specific management skills, and their ability to embrace diversity. Therefore, before any training occurs, the ombuds should ask this question:

What problem are we seeking to solve through this training OR what are we hoping to make better through this training?

Once the ombuds has a clear understanding of the repetitive sources of unproductive conflict in the organization, then he can design and provide training to bring needed change. Training may be geared at one individual (through the coaching role), one unit or group, or the entire company. Before recommending training, it is important to build a coalition of support for such an effort by clearly demonstrating both the need and the return on investment (ROI) to the company's decision-makers. Even if the training is done in-house by the ombudsman, the cost may be high in terms of time away from the primary work of the organization. Therefore, the training should be specifically tailored to the root causes of conflict in the organization, it should be precisely targeted to develop the skills or knowledge lacking in the status quo, and its impact should be measurable in terms of changed behaviors or reduced costs of conflict. If done correctly, employees will immediately see the value of the training and ask for more. If not, they will come only when ordered and remain disengaged throughout the session, with few resulting benefits.

What is the risk posed by suggesting training targeted at the root causes of organizational conflict? Usually someone or some unit is benefiting from the conflictual status quo and raising the often "unspoken" issues in the organization can cause **growing pains**. This is the pain that comes from the hard work of resolving conflict, which often results in personal growth and development for the parties involved and results in positive change. Both can be painful, yet necessary and productive. To gain support for any training initiative designed to bring real change, the ombuds (or proactive managers) must begin by building coalitions of support along the chain of command by explaining the need for the training as well as the expected ROI. Conflict-avoidant personalities may prefer not to engage in training that may bring to the surface underlying sources of conflict, even though doing so is a necessary part of future conflict prevention and resolution.

Why is training risky for ombuds or other proactive organizational leaders? For example, if a university has experienced repeated conflicts over its failure to follow the Family and Medical Leave Act (FMLA), then the ombuds might suggest that all department chairs receive training about how FMLA is applied in university settings and the importance of refraining from retributory actions against a faculty or staff member who decides to take family leave. The ombuds might initially believe that department chairs simply lack an understanding about how to accommodate faculty members who need to leave mid-semester for the birth of a child, for example. Upon further investigation, he might learn that most of the department chairs are clear about how the law works in university settings but have decided to discourage employees from taking leave mid-semester, since it is difficult to find faculty replacements to teach half of a course, under the previous faculty member's syllabus. The lack of compliance with FMLA was not due to ignorance of the policy but was a response to the inconvenience and cost associated with following the law and university policies. By addressing this issue directly, the ombuds may be perceived as pressuring the department chairs to change behaviors that have been successful at deterring faculty from taking leave, even if those behaviors result in occasional lawsuits and ill will among faculty toward their chairpersons. What seemed like a simple training issue morphed into a need for culture change to make the university more family friendly and legally compliant. In cases such as this, it is important to work with other relevant department heads such as the human resources and legal teams to send a united message about the importance of living up to our values, which includes following relevant laws and policies. Remember, tenure-track faculty are likely to stay with the organization for many years. Showing them kindness and support will be a good investment and is "the right thing" to do. Framing needed changes constructively is critical.

Policy Change and Implementation

If the ombudsman realizes that an existing policy (or the absence of one) is creating confusion or outright conflict, then he might decide to bring the issue to the organization's leadership with a request for change. To increase his chance of success, the ombuds should come prepared with specific information that reveals the need for the change as well as the expected benefits of the new or revised policy and suggestions for its smooth implementation.

The best process for achieving buy-in and compliance with any change is to gather input from those impacted and be sure to meet their interests if possible. This is simply the process of interest-based negotiation in a large-group setting as discussed in Chapter 3. When a new policy is imposed on stakeholders without their input, it is likely to cause pushback or outright refusal to uphold the new policy.

Think about this example: You work at a midsize company with 200 employees, organized into some units that interact with customers and some that do not (such as IT or accounting). After one particularly embarrassing event in which a customer entered the office and saw a small group of employees from the IT team, wearing low-rise jeans (with exposed underwear), tank tops, and flip-flops, the boss issued a memo banning blue jeans, open-toed shoes, bare shoulders, visible tattoos, and "general dishevelment." The employee response was predictably negative, even passive-aggressive. Some employees left for other organizations. Now, imagine a different process: The boss sends a memo sharing her desire for a new dress code. She asks each of the six units to appoint a delegate to serve on a committee that will draft a new dress code. This committee will include individuals from both management and hourly employees across the organization. After sharing concerns and ideas from their units, the dress code committee issued new dress codes: (1) for those employees interacting with customers and (2) for those who do not interact with customers. Each dress code ensured at least a minimally acceptable level of appearance. These dress codes were generally well received and followed, as we would predict from procedural justice theory (Chapter 2).

Changing policies that impact the daily work experience of employees must be done carefully, inclusively, and with buy-in up and down the chain of command. Otherwise, it is common to have unanticipated negative outcomes that cost more to the organization than the status quo. The ombudsman may take the lead in suggesting policy changes designed to reduce unproductive conflict at work. Additionally, the ombuds' skill at designing collaborative processes makes him an ideal candidate to design and facilitate stakeholder-driven processes used to gather stakeholder input and increase buy-in.

Dispute System Design

Chapter 9 explores the recommended steps and processes for designing disputing systems to manage those disputes that cannot be avoided. When engaging in a DSD effort, it is critical to ensure the new system is not a perceived or real attempt to limit the legitimate expression of employee concerns. The system should provide an outlet and voice for those seeking to resolve conflicts early, at the lowest cost, and with an eye toward preventing the recurrence of future similar conflicts. These efforts take time because the ombuds must first clearly understand the types of recurring conflicts in the organization and the costs and benefits of the company culture along with the likely level of receptiveness to a new disputing system, and the ombuds needs to have built up trust among all levels of the organization.

A participatory process that includes stakeholder input is likely to increase the chance of successful implementation and positive impacts on the mission. Evaluation procedures must be built in for every step in the process as well, to gauge satisfaction with and the efficiency of the overall process and outcomes. Gathering this data will make it possible to tweak the design during the pilot phase to ensure the best fit possible with the needs of the organization and its stakeholders.

What are the risks for the ombuds? Any new disputing system displaces the previous methods for disputing, even if those were informal and implicit. Some will see this as a positive change and some may not, in part, depending on their comfort level with the acknowledgment that conflict is a normal part of the organizational (and human) experience. Getting buy-in from those threatened by the new system will require ninja negotiation skills (see Chapter 3). Creating a pilot or trial period can be a helpful step in securing the willingness to try the new system without any commitment to making it permanent.

Culture Change Efforts

The past few years has been a watershed period of culture change for U.S. corporations generally, and for some large corporations and industries more specifically. Big name brands have ditched their CEOs or other top leaders amid scandals indicative of a desire to move from dysfunctional cultures that cover up and protect predatory behaviors, to more transparent and equitable organizations that hold all employees accountable for their behavioral choices, even the topmost leaders. Uber, Papa Johns, and the Weinstein Company all had their leaders removed for sexual harassment after years of paying off or otherwise silencing victims; Volkswagen's Martin Winterkorn knowingly allowed technology to be installed into VW vehicles with the sole purpose of outsmarting pollution regulations; Martin Shkreli's unapologetic decision to corner the market on needed pharmaceuticals and then sell them at astronomical prices damaged the company's image; and Wells Fargo's use of draconian incentives for new accounts led to illegal and fraudulent behavior across the corporation, and this is just a sampling. Scandal and brand damage are symptoms of dysfunctional cultures within organizations. As Chapter 6 discussed, it is nearly impossible for a company to succeed at its mission while allowing a negative culture to take root and grow. Organizational culture is created and re-created every day from every level, but the "buck stops at the top" in terms of accountability. Leaders set the cultural tone and behavioral expectations explicitly through policies and clear statements of the company's values. Or they set the tone implicitly, without fully understanding that culture will grow and evolve organically due in large part to the example they embody. Most dysfunctional cultures arise out of neglect and oblivious leadership. Most positive cultures arise and grow due to conscious and conscientious efforts that can be positively shaped and influenced by the ombudsmen and by leaders at all levels.

What if you aren't an organizational leader yet? Every employee shapes the culture of his unit every day. How? By setting an example that shows "How we treat each other" and "How we treat customers." Through respectful listening, openness to ideas from everyone, collegial efforts to make decisions and solve problems, respectful disagreement, efforts to enhance and build relationships, and setting reasonable boundaries, employees not only shape culture in their units; they can drive away organizational predators who might otherwise engage in counterculture behaviors such as sexual harassment, discriminatory language or behaviors, bullying, or just a lack of kindness and respect. Peer-to-peer norming is key (see Chapter 6) and occurs when any employee gently corrects or re-directs another employee when that person exhibits negative behaviors at work. Often statements like, "Hey Mike, that's not how we do it here. Could you try X instead of Y?" For example, "Hey Mike, our company discourages flirtatious behavior from supervisors toward subordinates. You might want to dial it back a notch so Chloe doesn't feel uncomfortable."

What are the risks for ombuds and managers who seek to bring culture change? If the highest leaders in the organization agree there is a need for culture change, then the risks are relatively low. Yet the change agent will need to build a coalition in support of these changes across the organization at all levels. Then she will need to include training, policy change, coaching, and program design/evaluation to succeed. However, if the organization's leaders are the source of the problem, meaning they benefit from and re-create the dysfunctional cultures every day through their actions or failure to act, then the ombuds or change agent is better off working at lower levels on the pyramid of tasks shown in Figure 10.1. Of course, the sad reality is that individual complaints from employees and low morale are symptoms of a negative culture that cannot be remediated without culture change. Treating the symptoms without the ability to treat the root cause of the illness gets tiring, frustrating, and repetitive for everyone.

Case Study of Dysfunctional Corporate Culture: Wells Fargo

From 2015 to 2018, the corporate malfeasance of Wells Fargo Bank became public knowledge as scandal after scandal came to light. After first seeking to deflect blame onto the frontline customer service personnel by firing 5,300 employees (Egan, 2016), Wells Fargo admitted that ill-conceived and implemented policies had resulted in the creation of fake accounts for which existing customers were charged millions of dollars illegally. Other scandals included the repossession of cars belonging to active-duty service members, unapproved fees for services like pet insurance, the mistaken foreclosure of thousands of homes, and the sale of faulty mortgage-based securities in the period just before the collapse of the U.S. housing market. A culture of corporate greed, obfuscation, and inconsideration for the needs of both clients and employees pervaded the executive suite, with negative reverberations across all aspects of the corporate culture. CEO John Stumpf was forced to retire as a result of these scandals and the culture that allowed them to occur. He was replaced by Tim Sloan, a company veteran with more than 30 years of experience at Wells Fargo. Then, they did it all again and again (Morrow, 2022). In December of 2022, the Consumer Financial Protection Bureau (CFPB) issued $3.7 billion in fines for continued wrongdoing, which speaks to the lack of real culture change at the bank. Rohit Chopra, director of

CFPB, stated, "Wells Fargo's rinse-repeat cycle of violating the law has harmed millions of American families" (ibid).

Due to a widespread lack of consumer trust in the brand, Wells Fargo claimed to have embarked on a culture change initiative after the scandals of 2016 and 2018. Their ad campaign from summer 2018 states: "Wells Fargo: Established 1852. Re-established 2018, with a recommitment to you." Yet as of November 2018, Wells Fargo's misdeeds were still coming to light, resulting in fines of more than $1 billion. In 2018, CEO/President Tim Sloan earned bonuses and salary of $17.4 million. "CEO Tim Sloan enabled the bank's massive fake accounts scam, got rich off it, and helped cover it up. He should have been fired—instead, he just got a big, fat raise" (Roberts, 2018). Sloan was eventually forced out in 2019 after continued scandals came to light, replaced by an outsider, Charles Scharf.

One sign of a sincere desire to change the corporate culture of greed and misadventure is to hire an outside expert with a stellar reputation for ethics. Once hired, the new leader must sweep all metaphorical "dirt from under the rug" or otherwise expose any fraud, waste, or abuse that is found, or risk being associated with ongoing wrongdoing. Since Wells Fargo was sanctioned again in 2022 for widespread wrongdoing, efforts to address the cultural roots of dysfunction remain unfinished and will require a thorough analysis of policies, procedures, incentives, and interpersonal norms required to bring change if change is sincerely sought.

Coaching Tools for the Most Common Workplace Complaints

When engaging in corporate training, I commonly ask attendees to anonymously share the sources of repetitive conflict or problems in their organizations. Logistically, I do this by passing out notecards and asking each person attending to write down one problem per card, using as many cards as they wish. Over the past three years, I have gathered more than 600 of these cards, from companies engaged in auto manufacturing, hospitality, technology innovation, and knowledge creation. The trainees included engineers, accountants, chefs, assembly line workers, sales managers, human resource professionals, insurance agents, and more. Most were managers at some level, but about 20% were non-managers. About 75% were Americans, while 25% included people from Germany, Poland, Japan, Brazil, Mexico, Russia, England, Czech Republic, Portugal, Japan, and elsewhere. About 70% were male and 30% were female. What surprised me is that in spite of this great diversity of participants, the types of conflicts they detail are strikingly similar:

1. Inadequate communication within and across levels of the organization.
2. Lack of shared expectations, which causes conflict between people and units.
3. Micromanagement or general unhappiness with managerial style or behaviors (includes favoritism, disrespect, discrimination).
4. Change management: changing courses too often; inadequate mechanisms for evaluating the success of change efforts; new policies made

without input needed for success; no involvement of lower-level employees in change.

5. Team building/maintenance problems: lack of trust, disengagement, unfair workload distribution; lack of collaboration.
6. Miscellaneous: perceived lack of physical or psychological safety; pay inequity or inadequacy; issues of shared or a shortage of space; working with difficult personalities.

When individuals come to the ombuds or other managers with these complaints, it is important to coach visitors to improve their abilities to solve conflict independently, so that when appropriate, they are empowered to prevent and resolve conflict constructively now and in the future. Remember the adage, attributed to Albert Einstein: "The definition of insanity is doing the same thing repeatedly and expecting a different outcome." The goal is to better understand the underlying cause of the problem, find out what strategies have *not* worked, and help the team or individuals design new responses.

Communication problems: Ombuds often train visitors on communication skills including listening (Chapter 1), questioning, assertion, framing, and giving and receiving feedback. One recurring comment I receive is that "gossip" and speculation are sources of conflict at work. What cures gossip and speculation? Transparency. If employees know that leaders are making decisions that will impact them, but the process and outcome of these decisions are not widely shared, then employees will gossip and speculate to fill in the gaps. Organizational leaders need to be as transparent as possible to avoid the negative cultures that arise in the absence of shared information. By sharing "frequently asked questions" on an intranet bulletin board, widely distributed memos, or by holding "town hall" meetings where leaders receive and answer questions in a non-defensive posture, then employees do not need to guess at what is happening in the halls of organizational power.

Silos: At a deeper level, many conflicts arise from communication problems with structural roots, such as a lack of mechanisms for sharing needed data across units, overlapping job descriptions, insufficient collaboration across departments, or a failure to solve joint problems. These problems require a change to the flow of information through the creation of new procedures for communication that could include the creation of periodic joint meetings, checklists, shared e-bulletin boards, or other mechanisms.

Unshared expectations: Conflict comes from a lack of shared expectations. It often falls for managers and/or ombuds to facilitate conversations designed to bring these challenges to the surface and then seek consensus toward shared expectations. Here is a sampling of specific problems raised by managers and employees around which shared expectations should be created: workload distribution within the team; respect for work-life balance differences; prioritization of projects or tasks; understandings of shared values and missions; work hours and deadlines; job duties or boundaries of each role within the team; preferences around taking work home and emails over the weekend, and so on. When a team leader needs assistance to facilitate these discussions, an ombuds or manager from another unit might be helpful to lead these discussions while demonstrating facilitation skills so the manager can lead similar future meetings.

Management styles: Another recurring source of conflict comes from different preferences for management style and skills deficits among some managers. Did you know that different national cultures tend to prefer different management styles (House et al., 2004)? For example, Germans are more comfortable with authoritative decision-makers as managers while Americans more frequently expect collaborative approaches to management. When companies founded in one nation (e.g., Japan, Germany, or the United States) open manufacturing plants or offices in a foreign land, the managers they send often fall short of meeting local expectations due to a misapplication of managerial approaches that worked at home but don't transfer well to a foreign environment (see Chapter 5 for more information on intercultural conflict and management). Some cultures expect and even appreciate a manager who is "hands on" and closely supervises her employees, while workers from other cultures prefer less "micromanaging." Ombuds are often asked to coach managers to succeed across cultural divides.

Unequal treatment: Managers are sometimes criticized for unequal treatment of employees, yet the "secret" to being a great manager is to get to know your employees as individuals. Only then can you learn how to support them to succeed in their work. Some employees need managers who remove obstacles from their path, but otherwise work well independently. Others need frequent check-ins, pep talks, or motivation to perform at their highest potential. By getting to know each employee, managers can ensure the tasks they are assigned meet their skill sets and give them the type of manager *they* need, within the limits of policy and law to avoid any accidental or purposefully discriminatory behaviors. Ombuds can help by ensuring that managers and supervisors know where the line is between supporting individual employees and engaging in discriminatory practices, favoritism, or cronyism. Ombuds can avoid providing legal advice by asking the legal and/or HR teams to create brochures, websites, trainings, or other resources to increase knowledge on these issues.

Requesting feedback: Managers need to request feedback from their employees so as to improve their own performance: "How can I help you succeed?" and "What actions could I take to make your work environment more productive and pleasant?" While the manager is not a concierge, being open to feedback and creating an environment that makes employees comfortable and productive will reduce complaints that identify the manager as a recurring source of conflict. Ombuds and managers can help all employees from the bottom to the top learn how to request, analyze, and use feedback for continual improvement.

Change management: The pace of change since 2020 has been astounding. It's no wonder that organizations are struggling to keep up. However, some managers make the mistake of creating new policies, procedures, or priorities to address an organizational need and then change them before they have had a chance to reap results. This leads to "employee whiplash," meaning they cannot keep up with the frequent changes and redirection. By the time they understand what is expected of them and how to deliver it, the rules and instructions change. Sometimes new leaders or managers make the mistake of creating "change for change's sake." This means they want to make their mark on the company, so they introduce big changes without fully understanding their costs and benefits or the problem they seek to solve. In organizations with frequent leadership turnover, the requests or instructions to change come so frequently that employees start to tune it out and actively avoid change implementation. An ombudsman should work with new leaders of the organization to help them understand what is working and what isn't, so that changes are well conceived and thoroughly communicated, and unproductive conflicts are avoided. Ombuds can teach and model processes such as 3-step problem-solving to help all team members quickly get to the root of problems and find shared solutions in a respectful, efficient manner.

Trust building: Lastly, ombudsmen frequently hear complaints that indicate a lack of trust between employees as well as between employees and management. Trust, like respect, is earned. It cannot be demanded or forced. In fact, attempts to do so only undermine it. When someone behaves in a way that is different than we expect, predict, or desire, then the disconnect between our expectations and their behavior often becomes a source of conflict and distrust. Lack of trust in teams signals dysfunction that can often be addressed through the facilitation of difficult-yet-critical conversations around shared norms and expectations. Previous chapters examine the importance of trust and how to build it. Ombuds are often the ones called upon when there is a breach or absence of trust between individuals or groups at work. The ombuds or other organizational leaders can work to build the foundations of trust, which can grow over time to create resilient, mutually supportive, collaborative, and tight-knit teams.

COACHING TOOLS: A QUICK DOWNLOAD
FOR MANAGERS AND OMBUDS

Because coaching is the most practiced process across all types of ombudsman roles and by managers, this section will provide an overview of coaching tools you may find useful at work. The skills used include listening (Chapter 1), questioning, framing, summarizing, perspective taking, brainstorming, one-on-one training, problem-solving, and impact evaluation. Most coaches also acquire an understanding of basic psychological concepts, such as personality disorders (see Chapter 2), addiction disorders, and psychopathy, since individuals with these challenges are overrepresented among those experiencing repeated, unresolved conflict at work (Eddy & DiStefano, 2015).

There is a clear link between the visitor's conflict style and the source of recurring conflicts at work. For example, people scoring high on competitiveness struggle to delegate effectively because they tend to believe "if you want something right you must do it yourself." While accommodators often avoid delegation out of fear that it will harm their relationship. There are many ways coaches may use this information in helping to teach key skills as well as choosing their words and approach carefully so as to maximize the likelihood that the visitor will be able to receive the information without defensiveness.

As a manager or ombuds to whom people come with complaints, it is helpful to "normalize" the existence of conflict at work. Ask visitors if they see these solely as "the" problems or whether they are also symptoms of underlying issues. People often define the conflict as the problem, when it is usually a symptom of an underlying problem such as a dysfunctional team culture, an unclear policy, the misalignment of individual and group incentives, or a skill deficit in one or more team members that leads to interpersonal strife. Only when you understand the underlying cause can you work with others to discern next steps.

Tools for Intake

When a visitor arrives, the coach (either an ombuds or manager) needs to assess the reason for the visit. If the coach or manager is seeking to help the visitor improve her skill set so that she can better manage conflict in the future, then the ombuds wants to get a better picture of those skills that are most in need of development. Managers who seek help to develop their conflict management and communication skills often ask for help to deal with a specific unresolved conflict, seek to work more effectively with difficult employees or customers, prioritize their time, delegate effectively, motivate employees, communicate up and down the chain of command, manage their work-life balance, and think/act/ plan strategically. Whether they use an intake questionnaire or interview, ombuds need to get to the root of the problem in an efficient and sensitive manner (see Table 10.3). Once the ombuds or manager has a better understanding of the needs identified by the visitor, then it may be helpful to use additional assessments before determining next steps.

Conflict Styles Coaching Tool

For example, the conflict styles assessment from Chapter 1 may be administered to better understand the visitor's habits and tendencies when faced with conflict:

Table 10.3   Common Coaching Intake Questions

Question	Goal
1. What brings you in today?	Encourage information sharing.
2. Describe the recurring conflicts or problems you are experiencing.	Look for patterns and ability to engage in introspection versus externalization of blame.
3. What skills would you like to improve in order to manage conflict more effectively at work?	This helps the ombuds understand the visitor's baseline of knowledge about their own skill set and priorities.
4. What feedback have you received from those around you that might lead you to work on one or more specific skills?	Look for defensiveness versus openness to feedback and content.
5. What have you tried already in your attempt to resolve this/these problems?	Understand what has worked/not worked and ascertain the level of conflict avoidance (if any) in the visitor.
6. How might I help?	This helps the ombuds or manager understand the expectations of the visitor in order to begin the process of reaching an agreed-upon agenda for your time together as well as the limits to the ombuds' role/power.

avoidance, accommodation, collaboration, compromise, or competition. These tendencies tend to correspond to the visitor's communication style preferences as well. Avoiders and accommodators prefer indirect, even nonverbal, communication when seeking to convey displeasure with another person. Competitors prefer direct, even blunt, communication styles. Understanding the preferred approach to conflict will help the coach interact more effectively with the visitor as well as indicate, at least in part, the root causes of conflict. For example, conflict avoiders and accommodators tend to ignore conflict as long as possible and then "blow up" when they can't take it anymore. This leads their coworkers or subordinates to minimize their contact and view them as unpredictable or untrustworthy. Avoiders tend to withhold needed information out of fear that sharing bad news will lead to conflict, which becomes a self-fulfilling prophecy. Avoiders rarely rise to mid-level management or higher. On the flip side, competitive, authoritative decision-makers often rise into upper management, but their communication style is considered pushy or abrasive to many. Once the coach understands the visitor's tendencies, then he can provide feedback to help the visitor understand and change those elements of communication style that may be unproductive.

Once the visitor has completed the conflict styles assessment, it can be used to help them develop a plan to try a different approach than their "fallback" or default style. When a visitor has experienced a recent or recurring conflict that has not reached a satisfactory resolution, the coach may ask: "Which of the five approaches to conflict did you use? How did that go? Now, let's walk through the conflict story, but retell it as if you had used each of the other four approaches. For example, you say you used the competitive approach (e.g., you yelled at your subordinate and ordered her to change her ways). What would that interaction have looked like if you had used the avoidant approach, accommodating approach, compromising approach, or collaborative approach? Are there any of these styles that might have been a better fit for the problem at hand? This week, would you like to try to reengage this problem, using one or more of the other approaches? Then, when we meet again, you can tell me how things went."

The ombuds may use the information shared in the conflict story to indicate that some work on emotional intelligence skills would be helpful. For example, "emotional flooding" occurs when one is overwhelmed by emotion. If the visitor can learn to pay attention to the somatic signs of emotional flooding (e.g., rapid breathing, rising tension, frustration, even increased blood pressure or body temperature), then they can be encouraged to take a break to engaging in "reflecting before reacting." The conflict story can provide many insights for savvy conflict managers and ombuds seeking to help others improve their performance at work, or to improve their own performance.

Perspective Taking

When people tell their conflict stories, they tend to portray themselves as either the victim, hero, or witness. They rarely tell a story in which they are the bully, harasser, domineering boss, or general "jerk at work." After the visitor tells her conflict story, it can be helpful, and a little risky, to ask the visitor to tell the story from another vantage point. "Pretend you are your boss. Can you tell the story again, from his perspective?" or "If you were a witness to this interaction, what did you physically observe or hear?" If the visitor is unable to try to view the interaction from another's perspective, then the key task is to work on his ability to engage in empathy. A lack of empathy makes a poor manager, unpleasant coworker, and a generally difficult human being. If she is able to engage in perspective taking, this is a good first step to reimagining new ways to engage in difficult conversations or build the skills needed to successfully give feedback or resolve problems. It also brings to the surface the need to better understand the interests and motivations that underlie behaviors of ourselves and those around us. This exercise provides the coach with many points of data that she can use to decide the next steps of the coaching process.

Conflict Stories and Difficult Personalities

Recall that we discussed difficult personalities at work in Chapter 7. Imagine you are coaching an "Eeyore," meaning a person who only tells their conflict story with the perspective of the victim. Nothing and no one is fair, in their mind. They are generally unhappy, and it is always the fault of someone else. Try this: "I hear you saying that you have been mistreated by your last two supervisors and you feel your coworkers are not doing their share of the work. Your daily experience at work sounds unpleasant. Imagine a better future, two years from now, in which you like your coworkers and get along well with your boss. Your workday includes frequent laughter, camaraderie, and a sense of accomplishment. What could *you* do today to work toward that ideal future?" This technique is called **backcasting**, and it encourages people to think about how to create a different story for their future. It must focus on what they think, say, and do, since no one controls the behaviors of others. Ask them what skills, attitudes, or behaviors they might try out to see what, if anything, helps.

Delegation

If a visitor is feeling overwhelmed with work or struggling with time management (e.g., meeting deadlines) and they need to work on prioritization and delegation skills, it is helpful for the coach to know how the visitor scored on the conflict styles assessment, as mentioned above. For example, accommodators avoid delegation for fear of harming relationships. By working on their framing skills (e.g., how to say what they need to say in a way that won't provoke defensiveness or anger), they will feel more comfortable negotiating the delegation of tasks. Every instance of delegation is a negotiation at some level, even if the delegate is in a lower power position. Those who score high on compromise may tend to delegate quickly, with an eye toward a fair distribution of tasks, but they might not provide enough support, oversight, or guidance to ensure the success of the delegated tasks. Those who score high on "competing" tend to avoid delegating out of a belief that only they can do the task correctly. They prefer to control both process and outcome, which makes it hard for them to mentor or develop their subordinates—a key leadership task. In fact, when forced to delegate, they often create self-fulfilling prophecies by supplying inadequate information or skill building to the delegate, thereby ensuring that the task won't be done satisfactorily. For competitors, the coach will work to help them understand that (1) others will indeed do the task differently or less well at first, depending upon how much time is spent up front in training and preparing the delegate to succeed—the key here is to manage one's expectations; (2) nearly all repetitive, relatively simple tasks should be delegated in order to free up time for higher-level tasks by the manager/leader; and (3) the higher one rises in the organization, the more one needs to delegate, so you might as well work on mastering it now.

The Boy Scouts of America have long used the **EDGE model**, which stands for "explain, demonstrate, guide, and empower." This is a leadership model used to develop subordinates and others by teaching them how to accomplish a task, then setting them free to do so, providing positive encouragement, alongside realistic expectations.

> **E**xplain: Tell your subordinate what to do, why and (if appropriate) how.
> **D**emonstrate: Show the subordinate how to do the task while they watch.
> **G**uide: Have your subordinate do the task while you watch and verbally guide them.
> **E**mpower: Have your subordinate do the task without you there, knowing they can come to you with questions as needed. You provide feedback and encouragement, normalizing the fact that it will take practice before they can do it perfectly.

This is the opposite of helicopter or snowplow parenting and management practices. Helicopter leaders hover indefinitely, seeking to control and cajole others into doing tasks exactly as they would have done, which shows a lack of trust in the competency of your subordinates. Snowplow managers remove every obstacle to "make it easy" for others to succeed. Guess what? It is not the job of leaders, managers, or parents to make life easy for our subordinates or children. It is our job to prepare them with the skills and grit to overcome the inevitable obstacles that will arise. We can do hard things, both together and individually. Ombuds can help by normalizing the learning curve and conveying the importance of developing the experience and skill set of others. I assure you the head of Ford Motor Company does not make every car by himself. Successful delegation is a key managerial and leadership skill.

What if you are not a manager yet or if your own boss is delegating tasks to you that you are not prepared to do? Negotiating healthy boundaries at work means that each of us must determine what we can reasonably achieve with the time, resources, and skill sets at our disposal. Using the information in Figure 10.2, determine if the task being assigned to you is a logical next step in your development. If it is, then ask for direction to learn more about how this new task or responsibility will be reflected in your performance review and what, if anything, needs to come off your plate to make space for the new activity. Rather than proclaiming, "I can't (or won't) do it!" instead try, "Thank you for trusting me with this important task or opportunity. To ensure that we have shared

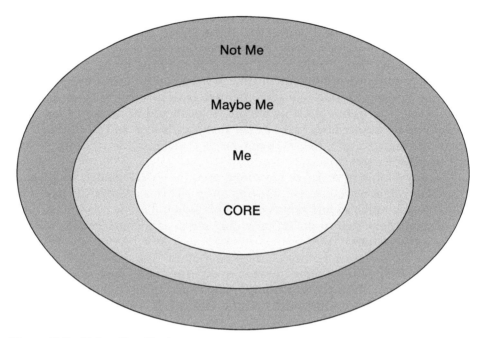

Figure 10.2   Delegation Tool

priorities and expectations, can you tell me which activities you would like me to do first, second, etc., knowing there might not be time to do them all?"

Figure 10.2 contains some helpful ways to visualize or prioritize those tasks that can or can't be delegated effectively. Some tasks can only be done by the manager or visitor because they have the unique skills set or authority to accomplish them. Other tasks might be done by the visitor but could also be shared by others through either delegation or specific assignment by a higher-level manager. Still other tasks might be enjoyable or interesting to the visitor, but simply aren't part of the visitor's performance review or job description and should therefore be the purview of someone else in the organization. The coach can help the visitor to draw onto this figure the tasks they have been doing in order to better understand where they fall and what might be either delegated or simply aren't the duty of the employee. For example, no one else could write this book and put my name on it; therefore, it could not be delegated. To free up time for this core duty, I was able to delegate copy editing to a professional copy editor (the "maybe me" tasks).

Effective delegation combines with healthy boundary setting, and negotiation will help avoid burnout and increase both performance and individual skill development. The ombuds has a legitimate role to play in coaching or training on these processes and skills to empower employees at all levels.

Life-Balance Wheel Coaching Tool

Just like a car that is out of alignment, when our life gets too far out of balance, we run the risk of crashing. During the human life cycle, there are periods when balance will be quite hard to achieve, at least temporarily. For example, most new parents know their own sleep, health, work, and romantic lives suffered at least temporarily when each new baby joined the family. Striving for balance between our physical health, relationships, work/money, and other demands requires significant effort and conscious choices. When visitors complain of stress, fatigue, and a sense of being overwhelmed, then the life-balance wheel may be a useful tool to help begin a discussion aimed at helping the visitor reclaim control over their out-of-balance lives. Using Figure 10.3 or some similar version (the internet is replete with many free versions), the coach asks the visitor to use a pencil to trace a line in a circle that corresponds to how well they are attending to each of the areas on the balance wheel. For example, if they are fully satisfied with their career and money, then the line would follow the outside boundary of that section of the circle, but if they are disappointed with their relationships, health, etc., then those lines might be drawn in the middle of the space or closer to the center. Once this is complete, the coach and the client can discuss specific strategies designed

Figure 10.3   Sample of a Life-Balance Wheel

to regain balance: "It sounds like you are happy with your career and money, but your relationships have suffered due to the time spent working on the weekends. What could you try to change over the next few weeks in order to rebalance your wheel? Would it help to discuss ways to prioritize your time or discuss work hours with your supervisor? I could brainstorm that with you."

All people can benefit from periodically measuring their satisfaction with various elements of their life balance. The best resource I have found to engage in the process of creating and re-creating one's happiest life is *Designing Your Life: How to Live a Well-Built, Joyful Life* (Burnett & Evans, 2016). This text contains specific, guided exercises to help readers analyze the tasks and activities that lead to feeling engaged and energized versus those that drain them, and how to deal effectively with both. Ombuds may wish to familiarize themselves with tools to help visitors analyze sources of disgruntlement that may include but go beyond work-related causes to refer them to helpful resources.

It does the organization no good for employees to work so hard they burn out, get sick, or leave for another company. Finding a reasonable balance between life's competing and endless demands is a struggle for everyone. Normalizing this task and brainstorming specific ways to bring change can be an important role for the coach, whether that coach is a manager or ombuds. Focus on what the visitor can control. Then find a need to build related skills such as how to build and maintain healthy relationships at work (or in general). Again, these are skills and knowledge that an ombuds may choose to work with visitors on or they may refer them to specific assistance on skills that go beyond their view of the ombuds role.

Framing Feedback Coaching Tool

Great leaders are brave enough to admit their weaknesses and develop a plan for improvement. The EPM and AAAA models (keep reading) are great tools for coaches to help visitors gain the confidence needed to give feedback or criticism effectively and to benefit from it.

Ratio of Positive to Negative Feedback

Remember, positive feedback or compliments must outweigh negative feedback or criticism about four or five to one in the relationship overall. Otherwise, employees will just tune you out. Their natural tendencies to engage in denial and rationalization will kick into overdrive if all they hear from you is negative. This is critical for coaches, managers, and ombuds to remember. Coaches must build up their visitors with positive feedback that acknowledges the strengths and inherent value of each visitor, build trust and rapport, and only then provide critical feedback. Similarly, when coaches train visitors to give feedback effectively, they need to remind them to build a positive relationship history with employees so that when criticism is needed, the employee believes it comes from a place of concern and fairness.

EPM Feedback Model

The **EPM feedback model** is a feedback model that begins with an empathetic statement, then pinpoints the problem with specific information, then asks how best to move forward together. Consider sharing your intent before any content to reduce defensiveness and reduce the odds of incorrect attribution bias on the part of the person receiving feedback. Once the person receiving feedback feels attacked, they stop listening and begin to think about how to get out of the situation (flight) or argue as to why the provider of the feedback is wrong (fight). By making an empathetic statement that conveys a positive intent to help, the recipient of the feedback can really "hear" what is being said.

Pretend you are coaching a manager who needs to give feedback to an employee struggling to get to work on time. Intent before content: "My goal is to make you succeed here and get your day off to a great start." Then, make an empathetic statement, "I know morning traffic around here is terrible." Next, pinpoint the problem by providing fact-based specific feedback, "The problem is that when any team members are missing, we cannot start the meeting on time." Then ask them to help brainstorm solutions for moving forward, "What can we do to fix this problem?"

E (empathize), P (pinpoint the problem) and M (move forward).

E: I know the work has been piled on lately, with this merger going on.
P: The problem is that your reports were late, so we weren't able to make timely decisions.
M: What can we do to ensure the information gets to us in time?

When coaching someone about how to invite and receive feedback, the key is to get them to be open to really listening without becoming defensive. A defensive response creates a conflict spiral that reduces the chance of improving performance and the relationship. One model for receiving feedback is called the 4 A model:

A1: Anticipate a learning experience (be open to feedback).
A2: Agree with something.
A3: Ask for specifics.
A4: Analyze the feedback to determine what you can or can't use to enhance your performance.

The second A (agree with something) is also designed to avert a conflict escalation spiral. The criticizer may anticipate that the recipient of feedback will be defensive. By agreeing with something, the recipient of feedback sends a positive signal that she is open to feedback and will not react defensively. For example, if the criticizer says, "You aren't a team player," the recipient can say, "I agree that team play is important (A2) . . . can you help me understand what, specifically, I have done to have this concern (A3)?" And lastly, by analyzing the feedback we can determine what to use and what to let go. Most of the time, we can benefit from criticism or feedback, even when the person giving it needs our help to be an effective critic.

Listening Tools for Ombudsmen and Managers

When listening to visitors and/or leaders in the organization, there are a few common problems or themes for which the ombuds should be prepared. They include listening for indicators of bullying or sexual harassment, the existence of perverse incentive structures in the organization, the tendency for organizations to reward negative behaviors, and what I call the "rule of three times."

Bullying or Sexual Harassment

Chapter 7 examines the challenges posed by workplace harassment and bullying. One bad manager or employee can drive away many good ones while simultaneously creating or growing a negative culture that interferes with mission achievement. Bullying behaviors are intentional, repeated over time, and designed to influence coercive control over others. Similarly, **sexual harassment** can include unwelcome sexual advances, requests for sexual favors, and other verbal or physical harassment of a sexual nature. Harassment does not have to be of a sexual nature, however, and can include offensive remarks about a person's sex. For example, it is illegal to harass a woman by making offensive comments about women in general. Both victim and harasser can be either a woman or a man, and the victim and harasser can be the same sex.

Although the law doesn't prohibit simple teasing, offhand comments, or isolated incidents that are not very serious, harassment is illegal when it is so frequent or severe that it creates a hostile or offensive work environment or when it results in an adverse employment decision (such as the victim being fired or demoted; EEOC, 2018c).

Victims of both bullying and sexual harassment tend to believe they are the sole target of the abuser, yet this is rarely the case. The ombuds may hear multiple complaints against the same harasser, even though it is common for each target to believe they are the only target. When this happens, the ombudsman should ask permission from the visitor to share this concern with the organizational leaders or HR department to stop the behaviors immediately. If the visitor refuses to allow the ombuds to reveal his or her name, then the ombuds must hold it in confidence, even if this makes it difficult to stop the abuse. In most cases, bullies and harassers are predators who can only prey on others when the organizational climate allows them free rein to do so. Remember the mantra from Chapter 3: "Behavior continues as long as it is working." If the company's leaders, managers, and HR department take proactive steps to inoculate the organization against this behavior by making it easy to report this behavior confidentially, by investigating reports thoroughly, and by taking transparent action to sanction inappropriate behaviors, they convey the message that "This is not how we treat each other here." That message will drive predators to change their behavior or leave the organization. The first step to identifying predatory behaviors as well as individual instances of aggressive and inappropriate interpersonal treatment may come from the ombuds since these incidents are often raised to them in confidence by visitors seeking advice about how to address the situation. In the era of #MeToo, organizations are learning that sweeping these incidents under the rug, firing the victims, or paying them off may seem like a short-term solution, but long-term costs are generally quite high.

Perverse Incentive Structures

To illustrate, imagine an organization in which each manager receives a hefty bonus each quarter based on the performance of her unit. Imagine that "Mary the Manager" has five employees to supervise and one of these is chronically late, absent, and simply shirks work whenever possible. As a result, her bonuses have gone down since "Mike" began working in her unit. She works for a large, very bureaucratic organization and firing someone is nearly impossible. So, she recommends Mike for a promotion to another unit. **"Failing up"** occurs when a 'bad' employee is promoted or transferred by their current supervisor to free themselves from the negative impacts of this worker in their unit, thus avoiding the opportunity to directly address problematic behaviors or performance. This happens when it is easier to move than terminate an employee. In this example, not only does Mary have a perverse incentive to promote the unproductive worker, but the hardworking employees are passed over systematically. Mary is not alone in this practice. Other managers are doing the same thing, so you can predict how this will go over time. **Perverse incentives** occur when a policy, procedure, or system either knowingly or accidentally misaligns the individual interests against the interests of the organization. In other words, when individuals (or units) pursue individually rational objectives, they hurt the larger community or organization. A common example involves sick leave or vacation time that does not "roll over" from year to year but must be used by year's end. What happens? Everyone takes vacation or sick leave in December. If you are a toy company, this could be a big problem. Think about the policies and procedures of your organization. Which have perverse incentives?

Rewarding Negative Behaviors

In most organizations, what is the reward for being a competent, hard worker? More work. And the opposite is also true: Incompetent workers and shirkers are given less work, usually for the same pay. This is an example of a positive reward for negative behavior (shirkers) and a negative consequence for positive behavior (hard workers). Any organization that continues on this path will create a negative culture of disengagement where the best people leave for more rational organizations, leaving the rest to simmer in disgruntlement and disengagement. Ombudsmen and proactive managers need to look for these patterns and offer ideas for new policies, procedures, and managerial training to counteract these tendencies in order to preserve the organization. The hardest workers must be recognized and rewarded and those at the opposite end must receive the feedback and professional development necessary to improve their performance and if that does not happen, they may need help to "find another dream." Think about the policies and habits in your organization. Can you identify anything your workplace and individual managers are doing to reward negative behaviors? What would it take to stop? Usually, the answer involves greater monitoring or measuring of individual performance and then rewarding those behaviors that should be encouraged and creating negative consequences for negative behaviors. Never reward negative behaviors.

"The Rule of Three Times"

Whether negative performance comes from tardiness, low productivity, unwelcome workplace behaviors, or other sources, do not wait for a problem to solve itself. If you have heard of a problem three or more times, or you have given instructions three or more times, then it is time to try something different. The change needed tends to fall into three categories: (A) change yourself (as a manager or giver of instructions)—mostly, this means stop rewarding negative behaviors and back up your words with consequences; (B) change the incentives that shape the behaviors; and (C) teach them another way. It is possible for a needed change to cover more than one of these categories.

A. *Change yourself*: When coaching or training, I give an example close to home, literally. This needs to be an example in which one has repeatedly given instruction, direction, or voiced a need, which has not had the desired impact. For example, "I've told my son 100 times, 'Don't leave your dirty clothes on the bathroom floor. Put them in the hamper'" Shame on me—not on my kid. If I have told him anything more than three times, then each additional time was a waste of *my* energy and effort. All I did was teach him that he didn't have to listen to me. A better technique would be to simply stop washing his clothes unless they are in the hamper. Or have him wash all the clothes on the bathroom floor. This takes no additional words or actions. He will figure it out all by himself. The trick was to change *me*. By picking up clothes on the floor and washing them, I was teaching him that he did not need to put his clothes in the hamper. Lesson: Actions speak louder than words. When I want to change someone else's behavior, I must first examine my own. This is a great lesson for managers—and parents.

   Now, apply this to the workplace: Think of something you have asked for or given instructions on three times or more. One manager told me that he asked two administrative assistants to stagger their lunch periods so there would always be someone present to answer the phones. When this did not happen, he then scheduled their lunch periods so that there would always be coverage. He told them they could switch by mutual agreement, and they would need to send him an email (copied to the person they are switching with) to confirm the switch. Any absence during a scheduled work time would be treated as an unauthorized absence. Problem solved. He did not need to change them. He needed to change his approach *and* the incentives surrounding their behaviors.

B. *Change the incentives that shape behavior*: This example comes from the challenges posed by group projects. Managers often hear reports of a shirking employee who drags down the team's ability to meet its goals or achieve its mission. If you, as a manager or ombuds, have heard negative reports about the same employee three or more times, then change is needed. It is important to monitor the behaviors you wish to change (e.g., gather data or otherwise learn what the actual performance levels are). In addition to receiving a performance review from one's supervisor, each peer team member should assess each other group member on various rubrics of performance such as meeting deadlines, quality of work product, ability to receive feedback openly, overall contribution to the end result, and "I would volunteer to work with this person again." Then, those employees who routinely fall short of the mark are placed in a group and required to work together. This group may be given different or less preferable tasks. If an individual's performance improves, then she may be placed into another group. Through performance coaching, any of these underperforming team members may work on gaining the skills or behaviors needed to improve performance. Therefore, this need not be seen as a punishment, but as a workshop for skill improvement and a path to higher performance reviews. Employees unwilling to improve their skill set or use the proffered coaching or professional development may indeed decide to "find another dream." This helps protect high-performing, collaborative team members from the toxic grind of repeatedly working with someone who does not "pull their weight." It connects performance with consequences and improves mission achievement overall.

C. *Teach them another way*: One of the most frustrating experiences as a coach occurs when a manager says, "I told him to stop doing X or start doing Y, but he hasn't done it!" If I told you to come to work tomorrow and only speak French, would you be able to do so? Someone would have to teach you French if they want you to speak it. You simply don't know how, right? Your failure to speak French might not reveal an unwillingness to change, but instead, it indicates a sincere lack of knowledge about how to do so. As a coach, manager, or ombuds, you will be called upon to teach visitors/employees *how* to communicate differently, collaborate differently, interact and work differently. The first step is to identify the skill deficit, teach and develop the skill, get them to go into their world to practice and apply the skill, then come back with data about how it went. Telling someone to change usually has frustrating results. You must teach them how to do it differently.

For example, imagine you have been asked to help an underperforming manager. His subordinates have repeatedly complained that he is not a good listener, unsympathetic, cold, inflexible, and harsh in his tone or delivery. After administering the Conflict Styles Inventory, you explain why people with his management style tend to be perceived as somewhat difficult, then coach him on the skills needed to elicit input more often, be accommodating when appropriate, get to know employees as people and show concern for them as people, etc. People can change. To do so, the coach must teach them the behaviors that indicate change.

Systemic Tools for Ombudsman and Manager

In addition to the many useful coaching tools, only some of which are highlighted here, ombuds and others seeking to prevent and address organizational conflict must seek out data to help identify the areas of highest need. For example, most proactive organizations of more than 15 employees should engage in an annual (or more often) workplace climate survey to better understand what is going well and what can be improved. It is important to ensure anonymity in these surveys, but midsize to large organizations can break this data down to the different geographic locations and work functions or units within the organization to identify a "**conflict hot spot**." A conflict hot spot is a unit within an organization that has a disproportionate amount of unproductive conflict that is revealed through lower-than-average morale, higher turnover, employee disengagement, and rates of litigation. The hot spot may be due to the presence of one or more dysfunctional managers, the presence of disincentives for positive performance, or a negative unit-level culture that breeds negative behaviors and disgruntlement.

Other sources of data may be used to indicate trends toward improved or worsened conflict management within the organization as a whole or specific units of the organization. For example, exit surveys and interviews are critical to ascertaining why people leave the organization. They must be done by someone the former employee trusts so he will confide openly the reasons for leaving. Proactive organizations will also interview those who were offered jobs, but declined them, to better understand the source of the decision: "Were the salaries and benefits not competitive? Was there something about the atmosphere or climate that dissuaded you from joining us? Did this seem like a workplace you would recommend to others? Why or why not?" This information will allow the ombuds, HR, and proactive managers to address the root causes of conflict. If the company cannot attract and retain the best employees, it can't fully achieve its mission. Similarly, the ombuds can gather data from clients, customers, and vendors to understand the source of unresolved conflict and enhance collaboration.

CONCLUSION

An ombuds can bring enormous benefits to employers of all sizes. Medium and large organizations are increasingly hiring ombudsmen or promoting them from within and providing them with needed conflict resolution and ombudsman training. Small organizations may reap the same benefits, even though they cannot afford a full-time ombuds. To do so, they can either send one of their existing employees for training and then assign ombuds duties in addition to their other tasks or hire an "on-call" ombudsman to work as needed. Managers can use many of the same strategies and tools employed by ombuds, to improve the performance of their organizations. All great managers are coaches: How will you use these tools and strategies to improve the performance of your team members?

JOHN AT THE BUREAU OF RECLAMATION

John lacks both the time and expertise to uncover some persistent sources of conflict and poor productivity in his unit and in the broader organization. He has requested and received funds to hire an ombudsman who will work to prevent and resolve conflict at work. He chose to hire someone external to the team because he seeks someone with documented experience in the field of conflict resolution and organizational development. He also hopes an outsider will have "fresh eyes" and notice problems that have become invisible to current staff, himself included.

After three months, the ombudsman has been able to point to significant problems in the alignment of incentives for individual and group performance as well as some biased policies that made it easier for some groups to succeed than others. The ombuds has begun to meet with employees to build their capacity to resolve conflict productively and have healthier, happier workplace relationships. Overall, this has been money well spent.

KEY TERMS

advocate ombudsmen
backcasting
classical ombudsmen
conflict coaching
conflict hot spot
EDGE model
EPM feedback model
executive or organizational
   ombudsmen

facilitative training
failing up
growing pains
healthy boundaries at work
legislative ombudsman
media ombudsman
ombuds/ombudsman/ombudsperson
perverse incentive
sexual harassment

DISCUSSION QUESTIONS

1. How might your current organization benefit from the work of an ombudsman?
2. Which of the coaching tools can you apply in your work? Which seem less applicable and why?
3. Identify one or more perverse incentives in your workplace, your homeowner's association, or civic group with which you are familiar. What would it take to change it?

EXERCISES

1. Whose opinion can improve your performance? Write down the names of four to six people who know you, care about you, and want you to succeed. The more diverse their identities and experience, the better. These are the people whose opinions matter most. This week, tell them you value their opinion and seek their advice to improve your performance.

Ask them to provide specific feedback, focused on behaviors you can change or improve, to improve your performance as an employee, manager, spouse, parent, friend, etc.

2. Use Figure 10.2 to map out your recurring work tasks. Which must be done only by you, which could be shared, and which should go to someone else?

GOAL SETTING

1. Which instructions or directions have you given three or more times without the desired result? Now, try something different. Have you been ignoring or rewarding negative behavior? How can you change your strategy? What incentives can you change to ensure their behavior receives natural consequences (either positive or negative)? How can you teach them to master the new behaviors you seek? Make a plan for change. Write it down, implement it, and analyze what worked or did not.

2. Use Figure 10.3 to map out your current level of balance or imbalance in your life. Set a goal to spend more time on at least one area that has been neglected.

3. Delegating Skills: Choose at least one task you can delegate this month. Use the EDGE model to teach the delegate how to accomplish the task successfully. Make it clear you are available for any questions.

SUGGESTED SUPPLEMENTAL READINGS

Brinkert, R. (2016). State of knowledge: Conflict coaching theory, application, and research. *Conflict Resolution Quarterly, 33*, 383–401. https://doi.org/10.1002/crq.21162

Brubaker, D., Noble, C., Fincher, R., Park, S. K., & Press, S. (2014). Conflict resolution in the workplace: What will the future bring? *Conflict Resolution Quarterly, 31*, 357–386. https://doi.org/1002/crq.21104

Burnett, B., & Evans. D. (2016) *Designing your life: How to lead a well-built, joyful life.* Knopf.

Gadlin, H. (2014). Toward the activist ombudsman: An introduction. *Conflict Resolution Quarterly, 31*, 387–402. https://doi.org/10.1002/crq.21099

International Ombuds Association. (n.d.). *Ombuds benefits to organizations.* https://www.ombudsassociation.org/Ombuds-Benefits-to-Organizations

Levine-Finley, S. (2014). Stretching the coaching model. *Conflict Resolution Quarterly, 31*, 435–446. https://doi.org/10.1002/crq.21097

Michigan Legislative Council. (n.d.). *What we do.* http://council.legislature.mi.gov/Ombudsman/about

Noble, C. (2011). *Conflict management coaching: The Cinergy model.* Cinergy Publishing.

NPR. (2016, December 14). *About the public editor.* https://www.npr.org/sections/publiceditor/2016/12/14/505405614/about-the-public-editor

Queensland Ombudsman. (2022, May 20). *How an agency responds to an ombudsman investigation.* https://www.ombudsman.qld.gov.au/what-we-do/investigations/how-an-agency-responds-to-an-ombudsman-investigation

Tidwell, A. (1997). Problem solving for one. *Mediation Quarterly, 14*, 309–317. https://doi.org/10.1002/crq.3900140405

PART III

THE PREVENTION AND RESOLUTION OF EXTERNAL ORGANIZATIONAL CONFLICTS

11

Principles and Systems for Superior Customer Service and Customer Recapture

Your most unhappy customers are your greatest source of learning.

—Bill Gates

As the quote from Bill Gates illustrates, customers who take the time to complain are doing the company a favor: they share insights about products and services that only fresh, outside, eyes can see. They usually do not know how a product is made, but they certainly know if it meets their needs and expectations. Harnessing their feedback is crucial to continuous innovation and quality control. Companies and nonprofits that ignore feedback from their customers and supporters won't last long. Public agencies that repeatedly annoy citizens through subpar service or poor mission fulfillment will find their themselves subject to increased legislative oversight and turnover at the top of the agency. They will struggle to attract and retain quality employees.

Before delving into customer and client disputes, we first addressed internal organizational issues because companies must have their internal house in order if they seek to provide great customer service. Now we turn our attention to the ways in which innovative, courageous leader-managers can systematically gather, analyze, and benefit from external feedback as they seek to prevent and resolve disputes effectively.

Learning Objectives

- Identify the causes of common customer service complaints.
- Explain the linkages between satisfied employees and satisfied customers.
- Compare and contrast the relative benefits of seeking out new customers versus increasing customer satisfaction with existing ones.
- Develop monitoring tools to gather data on customer/client satisfaction and use that information to make improvements to products and services.
- Explain methods for creating employee incentives for superior customer service.
- Describe the benefits of a *relationship management* approach to reducing and managing conflicts with repeat customers and vendors.

ELISE AT MAIN STREET BAKERIES

Main Street Bakeries is doing well. The trend toward locally grown and organic foods has helped the company grow quickly and establish a stable niche in the marketplace. But for the last twelve months, growth and profits have flattened out. Additionally, Elise can't help but wonder if she is reaching her full market potential; her customers are generally upper-middle-class, educated urbanites and suburbanites. She believes that healthy, local, organic foods should be available and attainable for everyone, but she is not sure how to reach out to new customers while keeping her existing ones.

★ ★ ★

Whether you work in the private, public, or nonprofit sector, you must pay attention to the needs of the end users of your products or services. You may call them clients, customers, patients, guests, constituents, the community, or "the public." For the purposes of simplicity, in this chapter we will call the end users of our services *customers*. "**Customer satisfaction** is defined as a measure of how a firm's product or service performs compared to the customer's expectation" (Zondiros, Konstantopoulos & Tomaras, 2007, p. 1086). This chapter examines the prevention and resolution of customer conflicts. While some of the content overlaps with general management literature, the perspective will focus on conflict prevention and customer recovery. **Customer recovery** refers to the policies and practices put into place to address disgruntled customers with the goal of winning back their loyalty and business. "Research shows that customers who have never had a problem with a company are less loyal than those who have had a problem satisfactorily resolved" (Solovic, 2018).

Consulting firm Bain & Company surveyed managers across U.S. industries to find that 80% of managers believe their organizations provide excellent customer service but only 8% of their customers agree (Greengard, 2003, p. 32). We simply aren't good at judging our own performance. "Horror stories abound. Callers get trapped in seemingly endless Interactive Voice Response (IVR) loops; they can't find phone numbers at Web sites; no one responds to their e-mail messages; and, if they manage to get through to a representative, they cannot get the problem resolved promptly" (ibid.). These horror stories have been increasing since the Great Resignation and labor shortages experience in the past few years and are not expected to abate anytime soon.

In the public sector, complaints about poor service or inefficiencies may lead to ousted leadership or reform demands from legislators or courts. When it happens, the managers and leaders may suffer preventable career damage.

Each conflict is an opportunity to enhance a relationship. By working with customers to fix problems, it is possible to recapture and transform them into loyal, happy, return customers. Box 11.1 introduces some key rules for delivering superb customer service. Each deserves further elaboration.

BOX 11.1. RULES FOR STELLAR CUSTOMER SERVICE

Rule #1: A House Divided Will Not Stand.
Rule #2: Deliver What You Promise: Quality Products/Services.
Rule #3: Improvements Require Monitoring.
Rule #4: Create Incentives for Desired Behaviors.
Rule #5: Empower Employees to Resolve Disputes at the Lowest Level Possible.
Rule #6: Avoid a Myopic Focus on New Customers over Existing Ones.
Rule #7: Devise, Evaluate, and Revise Systems.

RULE #1: A HOUSE DIVIDED WILL NOT STAND

It is impossible to have happy customers while having unhappy employees (Klinger, 2021). Proactive conflict managers strive to create a culture where employees at all levels feel valued, they buy into the organizational mission, and they treat each other and customers respectfully. Happy employees are foundational to satisfied customers. According to Zondiros and colleagues (2007), "Employee satisfaction is one of the most important factors leading to customer satisfaction, the others being expectations and disconfirmation of expectations" (p. 1086). In other words, customer expectations are important for satisfaction—if your marketing efforts set up unrealistic expectations, and those expectations are disappointed, then satisfaction will decline.

Increasingly, disgruntled employees are the cause of bad press; they use blogs, Twitter, Facebook, and other social networking mechanisms to communicate their disgruntlement. Employees who have been mistreated, just like customers who have bad experiences, are likely to share their stories with literally a dozen or more others, further damaging the organization's reputation and brand. In the worst cases, employers accused of discrimination or blatant disregard for their employees' welfare have been on the receiving end of customer boycotts—remember the accusations of "sweatshop" conditions against Nike (Hunt, 2018)? To rebound from these instances of brand damage, Nike chose a marketing campaign backing the social justice activist Colin Kaepernick. For this campaign to increase rather than decrease sales, Nike recognized that it needed to attend to internal organizational justice efforts as well or face especially bad press. In short, Rule #1 is to get your internal house in order (see Chapter 7). Treat your employees well so that they have the energy and the will to pass on that same treatment to your customers.

RULE #2: DELIVER WHAT YOU PROMISE: QUALITY PRODUCTS/SERVICES

The best customer service in the world cannot make up for defective or underperforming products. Be sure your products meet the needs of your current customers and are innovative enough to attract new ones. For many organizations, their "product" is a service. For example, universities offer educational services; marketing companies, law firms, health-care practitioners, all offer a service as their product. For these industries, the quality of the service and the service experience will be central to building a reputation that keeps and attracts clients. Whether you make widgets or conduct market research, "If the quality of your products is great and your service is mediocre, a customer might return, but you won't gain any repeat customers if you have subpar products, even if your service is outstanding," (McGown, 2009, p. 66). There is no substitute for doing your homework: What do your competitors charge for the same products or services and how does their quality compare to yours? If your products are equivalent to others on the market then you have only two routes to success: (1) Find ways to improve your products or pricing to gain a competitive advantage, or (2) Beat them by offering a superior service experience.

Be sure to avoid a common pitfall—overpromising. Sometimes an organization's marketers are better than their engineers. If your marketing efforts create unrealistic expectations among consumers and your products/services do not fulfill those expectations, then costly conflict is likely to result. It is easier to meet low expectations and nearly impossible to meet overly high expectations. Make sure your advertising is in sync with your customers' expectations.

Rolex makes great-quality watches and Harvard trains great lawyers. The quality of their products/services does not substitute for good customer service, but they could not have built solid reputations spanning generations without building and maintaining high quality control standards that have become synonymous with their brands.

RULE #3: IMPROVEMENTS REQUIRE MONITORING

As this text has indicated repeatedly, feedback is the lifeblood of a successful collaborative manager. This is equally true for the organization as a whole: Feedback on the product itself, on the sales experience, on the payment and delivery processes, about the organization's internet or telephonic resources, on the cleanliness or attractiveness of the facilities, on any dispute resolution processes used, about ways to improve the customer's experience, and overall feedback as to whether the customer would recommend the organization's products or services to a friend. This information forms a vast reservoir of ideas for constant improvement. If time and money are short, ask the "temperature-taking" question: "Would you recommend X to a friend? Why/why not?" In order for these instruments to be useful, and worth the time and money it takes to administer them, the organizational leaders must be open to whatever results they find.

Customer satisfaction surveys frequently create a skewed picture. Many companies use self-serving questions—or fail to address key issues such as whether the resolution process was handled efficiently. So, while the rep may have performed admirably and received the highest rating, the caller may remain frustrated by the length of time or effort it took to reach a rep or because the incident wasn't resolved in a satisfactory way (Greengard, 2003, p. 35).

The American Consumer Satisfaction Index (ACSI) offers a comprehensive overview of customer sentiment over time. One of the most important questions in the ASCI is how likely a customer is to recommend your business to family or friends (Klinger, 2021).

Customers' perceptions are just that—their perceptions. It makes no sense to argue about why the customer should not have felt the way they did; their perception of their experience is inherently valid. Don't argue with customers. While the occasional curmudgeon may be impossible to please, trends in the data cannot be ignored. While you are likely to aggregate this data to look for trends or repeated sources of problems, be sure you do not leave your customers with the impression they are just a "number" or "case." Anything you can do to personalize the customer's experience and meet their individualized preferences is likely to serve you well (Rigge, 1997).

RULE #4: CREATE INCENTIVES FOR DESIRED BEHAVIORS

People respond to incentives. Want to see customer service improve? Tie raises and promotions to consistent improvements and high levels of customer satisfaction at the individual and team-unit levels. For example, when a car dealership from Company X performs well on measures of customer service in both the sales and mechanical service departments, they qualify to receive in-demand new models and parts faster than those with lower ratings. So, if Main Street Motors wants to stock the newest hybrid vehicle that is "all the rage," they had better keep their customers satisfied. Otherwise, they get put on a waiting list behind those with better service records. Or when merit raises are handed out each year, Bob from accounting may get passed up because the internal managers and employees he supports have consistently said he does not meet his deadlines. The information gained from monitoring performance must be tied to employee incentives; otherwise, there is a missing link between knowledge and action. Incentives can include merit raises, promotions, public recognition (such as "employee of the month"), preferred parking, preferred job duties, or other benefits.

It is important to create challenging yet attainable goals and objectives for customer service. If deadlines or goals are repeatedly missed, regardless of the personnel tasked with meeting them, then they are clearly too high. Unrealistically high goals lead to cynicism and apathy on the part of employees: "Why should I even try? I'll never be able to reach that goal." If you want to set realistic goals, make the first few months or quarters a "pilot" phase that allows you to experiment with an offer of carrots (positive incentives) rather than sticks (negative sanctions for missing the mark). Consider offering financial incentives, recognition, and rewards for employees who come up with improvements to products, processes, or services. Frontline employees are likely to know both the products and customers better than those at higher levels.

RULE #5: EMPOWER EMPLOYEES TO RESOLVE
DISPUTES AT THE LOWEST LEVEL POSSIBLE

Nothing is more frustrating than explaining your complaint to the salesclerk at the store or the representative on the phone only to be transferred to someone else, requiring you to start over from the beginning. Once this has happened three or more times, what might have been a relatively small complaint has now become a big one. Many frontline employees have zero authority to address customer complaints. This frustrates both the employee and the customer, resulting in wasted time and lost customers.

Instead, consider the following plan: Use the data gathered from Rule #3 to determine the most common types of customer complaints; after taking steps to reduce or eliminate the root causes of as many of these complaints as possible, organizational leaders should determine which complaints warrant the attention of supervisors and managers, versus those that can be handled by the frontline employees. If your leaders decide none of the recurring complaints can be handled by employees, it may be the case that (a) your leaders are uncomfortable with delegation as a managerial skill (if so, see Chapter 10); (b) you have not properly hired, trained, and acculturated your employees so as to entrust them with these tasks; or (c) your organization has so few complaints that each one needs to be handled as a unique event by mid to upper management. If explanation *c* is the case, yours is indeed rare among organizations and you may wish to reconsider *a* and *b* as possible options.

Employees need to be trained to handle complaints efficiently, fairly, and in a way that makes the customer more, rather than less, likely to return. Nearly all frontline employees can benefit from training in listening, framing, and problem-solving skills. This training will help them convey empathy to the customer, deeply listen in order to understand the needs of the customer, and work with the customer to find a solution that meets their needs. Scott (2008) advises individuals in conflict situations to avoid the tendency to vent anger or frustration, understand the reasons behind the conflict, and then use intuition to solve the problem. However, employees should also be prepared to deal with customers who voice their anger or disappointment in hostile ways. The trick is to remind employees not to take it personally—any employee could have answered that call or waited on that customer. By remaining calm and reassuring the customer that the issue will be fairly and efficiently rectified, the organization can seize an opportunity to improve a relationship with a client. Remember, it is not conflict that harms relationships. Instead, it is the way in which conflict is handled. In fact, good customer service in response to a complaint is one way to solidify a customer's loyalty.

Each employee should know where her settlement authority begins and ends. For example, when a customer is unhappy with your product, the employee can offer a full refund or an exchange (in addition to a sincere apology, if warranted). But be wary of template solutions that do not allow employees to use their own judgment to come up with more creative solutions to meet the occasional customer whose complaint or needs are unusual. This flexibility respects the employee's intelligence while ensuring the customer is not passed around like a "hot potato," seeking someone who can be of assistance. Frontline employees and each layer of management above them need to be clear about their settlement authority, as well as providing feedback upward about what is working well and what is not.

Sometimes a customer will be satisfied with a sincere apology and an effort to fix the problem through a refund or replacement of the item or service. A study by Robbennolt (2003) indicated that recipients of full apologies are more likely to accept a settlement, while settlement offers with no apologies are less likely to be accepted. The results for partial apologies were mixed. The "I'm sorry for your harm" type of apologies did not result in settlement rates as high as full apologies (Robbennolt, 2003). Other research has found that approximately 8% of the disputes stemming from eBay transactions involved a request or demand for an apology as a condition of settlement (Raines, 2005). In fact, a significant percentage of disputants rejected monetary offers of equal or greater amounts than the value of their purchase if no apology was forthcoming. Giving your employees permission to offer a sincere apology and to work to fix the problem can go a long way to reducing the number of disputes that escalate and become formal complaints or litigation.

Another customer service pitfall is to create a punitive policy based on the bad behavior of a small number of customers who try to game the system. "What pains many organizations . . . is that they apply a general template to all customers or penalize 99 percent of their customer base because of the bad behavior of 1 percent" (Greengard, 2003, p. 35). For example, when a customer buys an airplane ticket online with Delta Airlines, using their self-service portal, it is predictable that an occasional user error will occur. For example, "I accidentally booked the ticket for March 5, but I meant to select April 5." So long as the customer calls soon after the sale, and this is not a repeated problem for this customer, then the Delta Airlines employee can assist the customer to change the ticket without paying a "change fee." Another example comes from retail stores: Some require a store receipt for a return, and only allow the return within a specified period after the purchase (30 days, for example). They may do this to avoid customers who buy clothes for a special occasion only to wear them and return them. Other retailers convey they trust their customers, but track returns to spot those customers who abuse the organization's policies.

Should there be scripts for employees? Generally, no. Each customer (or vendor, etc.) will have different expectations about the resolution they seek and

BOX 11.2. EFFECTIVE APOLOGIES INCLUDE . . .

- Expression of regret
- Explanation of what went wrong (summarizing for the customer if appropriate)
- Acknowledgment of responsibility
- Offer of repair (asking for suggestions or making offers)
- Taking steps to ensure no similar future occurrence

their preferred communication style. By way of example, American Express has instructed its call center employees to take their cues from the customer's tone, pace, and demeanor. If the customer is in a hurry and communicates directly, then so should the employee. If the customer wants to chat and take time to be friendly, then so should the employee. Train your employees to take their communication cues from the customer.

If you are unsure as to the best methods for addressing customer complaints, consider tapping the collective wisdom of your employees, as well as asking for feedback from complaining customers. Use this information to pilot various approaches and tweak the system until the desired results are achieved. The Ritz-Carlton provides a perfect example of what happens when employees at all levels are empowered to make customers happy and resolve problems.

Ritz-Carlton: Employee Empowerment for "Delighted" Customers

The Ritz-Carlton hotel chain seeks to "delight" its customers. This means they seek to exceed customer expectations every time, not just meet them. Customer satisfaction is "a measure of how a firm's product or service performs compared to customer's expectations" (Zondiros et al., 2007, p. 1086). So part of the goal is not to overinflate customer expectations by overpromising. The second part of the equation is to overdeliver. By exceeding customer expectations, organizations are likely to win new customers and gain market share or improve their organization's reputation.

At the Ritz-Carlton Hotels, all personnel in direct contact with customers are empowered to drop what they are doing to help a customer or take action to exceed their expectations. This means the front-desk staff, the concierge, housekeepers, food servers, everyone can tap into their own creativity and kindness to help out a customer who has had a bad day by sending them flowers or running an errand for them. In fact, a budget is set aside for these activities. If a customer is feeling sick, the staff might send them flowers or bring a special treat from the kitchen—whatever it takes to show they want the customer's experience to be memorable and unique. The Ritz-Carlton has realized that by empowering the staff to make the customers happy, they have made the employees happier, too. It turns out that random acts of kindness equate to stellar customer service, repeat business, and low employee turnover.

RULE #6: AVOID A MYOPIC FOCUS ON NEW CUSTOMERS OVER EXISTING ONES

This rule is the perennial downfall of credit card companies and cable television services across the United States. These companies often attract new customers by offering extremely low prices or interest rates for the first six or twelve months only to have them jump up thereafter. This reflects a strategy designed to attract new customers while disregarding current ones. It is likely that the internal incentive structures in these companies also reward the acquisition of new clients over the retention of existing ones. See the Wells Fargo example in Chapter 10 as an example of the pitfalls of this approach.

Why are existing customers more important (or at least as important) as new ones? The first reason is that some customers who have had a particularly bad customer experience may make it their mission in life to destroy the reputation of a business. A second, more obvious, reason for customer retention is that customers cost money to win in the first place. To survive, businesses must attract return business—ongoing revenue not offset by the cost of acquiring a new customer for every sale. At first glance, customer retention is a simple concept—happy customers who feel important and are regularly communicated with in the right way will keep coming back (Bland 2004, p. 16).

An increasing refrain heard in the literature on business management is the need to view **customers as business partners**. This means organizations should evolve their mindset from a worldview that sees each transaction as a one-time event to instead seeing each transaction as a chance to build a long-term, mutually beneficial relationship (Witschger, 2011). Business literature often refers to the specific techniques used to court and retain valued customers and partners over a long period of time as **relationship management**. This can be as benign as assigning one consistent employee to large customers or business partners with the goal of assuring smooth communications and institutional memory that will assist in ensuring these partners' needs are consistently met. In other cases, it can include rather obvious or obnoxious attempts to bribe organizational leaders by providing free theater tickets and rounds of golf. When done right, relationship management allows two individuals (or a small team) from one organization to develop strong relationships with their business partners or repeat customers, in the service of an ongoing mutually beneficial business relationship.

In some ways, this is where small and midsize companies have a comparative advantage. In small businesses, the owner or manager often has more direct contact with the customers or clients. This access provides the venue for a customized, personable, responsive experience that large corporations or the federal government cannot as easily provide.

Coleman (1992) provides advice about how business partners can build healthy relationships. He gives nine dimensions of business relationships that should be explored during the formation of **business-to-business** partnerships (also known as **B2B**): autonomy, goals, compensation, decision-making, cost sharing, entrance and exit of partners, equity, firm management, and type of partnership (p. 114). He recommends that partners rank these items from most to least important and share their rankings to make sure they are in agreement about the prioritization of each element in their business relationship. The same is true for a valued and repeat customer—if any one customer is critical to the life of your business or organization, then it behooves you to sit down face to face to better understand their needs, share yours, and develop methods for working together.

What about **customer loyalty programs** that encourage customers to come back again rather than merely seeking out the best price or most convenient vendor? For example, many hotel chains, airlines, and even coffee shops offer something akin to a "baker's dozen" reward system. This is a method for rewarding return customers by giving them their "13th night free" or a free domestic airline ticket once they accumulate 50,000 frequent flyer miles, and so on. These programs may help lure customers back to your business when there are others offering basically the same products and services at similar prices. However, "They provide a discount because points are easily converted to dollars. But you cannot buy loyalty" (Greengard, 2003, p. 35). These incentives will not be enough to overcome persistently bad service experiences. Increasingly, as nearly all airlines and hotel chains offer similar customer loyalty programs, they are becoming less valuable in retaining customers or differentiating your company from others.

What about public-sector or nonprofit organizations that do *not* seek repeat customers? If you work for Child Protective Services, a drug rehabilitation center, or the unemployment office, you are not seeking out repeat customers. In fact, one indicator of a job well done is that these customers or clients do not come back at all. In these cases, there are two critical questions: (1) Who are my organization's customers? and (2) How should my organization (or my unit within the broader organization) define and measure customer/client service?

For public- and nonprofit-sector organizations, customers may include the public, or a narrower segment of the public (such as children in state custody, addicts and their families, unemployed people, and potential employers). Regulatory agencies have at least two sets of customers: the businesses they regulate, which seek an efficient and fair regulatory process, and the public. One could argue that regulatory agencies must also be responsive to informational requests posed by the legislature and to demands from the leader of the executive branch of government. From the length of the wait times at the Department of Motor Vehicles to the rate of tax collection for the IRS, every organization can come up with metrics by which to gauge service delivery and mission accomplishment.

RULE #7: DEVISE, EVALUATE, AND REVISE SYSTEMS

Your internal house is in order. Your product and/or services are competitive and attractive to customers. You are monitoring, incentivizing positive employee conduct, and empowering employees to resolve problems at the lowest level. You are focusing on retaining current customers while attracting new ones. Now that your system is designed and in place, be sure to analyze the data, take stock, and make any needed changes to processes, products, or personnel so as to maximize the achievement of your organizational mission while maintaining a positive workplace environment. Reassess and make needed changes periodically to ensure consistent improvements. For some organizations, this will be every quarter, for others it will be every six months or annually. The key is to make sure you are mining the data necessary to make appropriate management decisions. Additionally, you can ask end users for ideas to improve or innovate your products or services for consistent growth.

Technology and Customer Service

Advances in technology are resulting in the increased automation of interactions between organizations and their customers: Robo-calls confirm doctor's appointments, internet surveys are used to gain customer feedback, internet platforms are used to log complaints and await a response. There is no doubt that technology can save money for organizations seeking to reduce personnel expenses associated with customer services. Yet there are costs to automating customer service functions, especially customer complaints. When a customer is upset or disappointed with a product or service, an automated system cannot listen, show empathy, or look for creative solutions to the problem. They also annoy people who are seeking to speak to a human being—yet they are inevitably likely to see increased use during labor shortages. While automation may indeed be a good idea in some circumstances, be wary of the rush to technology purely as a cost-saving mechanism. In the long run, it may be costlier than anticipated.

Alternative Dispute Resolution for External Stakeholder (Customers/Clients) Disputes

What happens when conflict prevention and early resolution have failed? What if the customer threatens litigation, goes to the media to complain, or files a complaint with the Better Business Bureau or a similar organization? At this point, you and your organization may wish to consider the menu of alternative dispute resolution (ADR) options covered in Chapter 4. If direct negotiation with the customer has failed to resolve the matter, then perhaps mediation should be tried. The parties can jointly select a mediator and seek his or her assistance in the resolution of the complaint. What happens in mediation, and many mediated agreements, is covered by confidentiality provisions, thereby making this a good process for the protection of your organization's public image and reputation. Mediation settlement rates for most types of commercial cases range between 55% and 90%. Remember, mediation is a non-adversarial process in which both parties seek to explore the possibility of reaching an agreement that leaves them both better off than going to court. Since parties work together to find a resolution in mediation, this process is advisable if there is any desire to maintain an ongoing business relationship between the parties. This may apply more often in B2B disputes.

Citing statistics gathered from a survey of 1,000 U.S. corporations, Mallick (2007) argues for the use of mediation as an effective means for disputes with consumers. The author shares results from ADR programs used by many U.S. corporations (Toro, Wells Fargo, U.S. Postal Service, Air Products and Chemicals, Inc., American Express). Even though Toro had successfully litigated cases in the past, the implementation of a mediation program saved the company money overall and enabled it to reduce costs spent on legal fees. Wells Fargo implemented a multistep process for consumers with disputes of $25,000 or more, believing that this alternative to litigation would create a less negative experience for customers and improve its reputation. American Express took an interest-based approach, employing experienced mediators as their attorneys with a focus on settlement.

If mediation fails to resolve the matter, or if you instead prefer to receive a binding decision from a third-party expert, you can enlist the services of an arbitrator. The benefit of arbitration is that it guarantees a binding, generally unappealable outcome that is private rather than public knowledge. When swift closure is necessary and both sides are willing to abide by the arbitrator's ruling, this may be the best choice. Arbitration is most common when there is a disagreement over the meaning of contract terms, allegations of breach of contract, or other failure to perform as expected. Chapter 4 goes into additional processes and greater detail on their relative costs and benefits.

ADR CLAUSES IN CUSTOMER AGREEMENTS

Increasingly, businesses are utilizing mandatory ADR clauses in their customer and "user" agreements. The best-known type of mandatory ADR clause is the **mandatory arbitration clause**, which is a binding pre-dispute contract committing both parties to use arbitration for dispute settlement in the event of a future dispute. By signing a mandatory arbitration clause, both parties give up their right to resort to resolution through the court systems. In January of 2012, in *Compucredit v. Greenwood*, the U.S. Supreme Court upheld the use of mandatory arbitration clauses in employment and consumer contracts over the outcry of many consumer groups who claim these processes deny citizens their due process rights.

These clauses have proliferated and are generally unavoidable if you want to rent a car, open a bank account, use a credit card, carry health insurance or insurance of nearly any kind; they are even a condition of admission to many movie theaters and theme parks. Arbitration clauses usually run only a sentence or two, such as this one from the International Court of Arbitration: "All disputes arising out of or in connection with the present contract shall be finally settled under the Rules of Arbitration of the International Chamber of Commerce by one or more arbitrators appointed in accordance with the said Rules" (International Court of Arbitration, n.d.).

These contracts often require the plaintiff (usually the consumer) to pay a steep filing fee as well as split the arbitrator's hourly fees. Therefore, the cost of arbitration may be hundreds or even thousands of dollars to each party when the case's value is itself much smaller (such as the cost of a mistaken charge by a car rental company or a movie rental). While small claims court fees might be reasonable given the value of the case, arbitration fees may put justice out of reach for many consumers while benefiting businesses with deeper pockets. Yet arbitration remains an adversarial process that bodes poorly for continuing the relationship between the parties after the arbitrator's decision is made.

In their work on mandatory arbitration clauses, Devasagayam and DeMars (2004) advise that ADR processes will only be the most pleasing choice to consumers when they perceive these methods as fairer and less risky than litigation. However, they also argue that the use of ADR processes will likely increase as consumers become familiar with these options, thereby becoming more comfortable and less distrustful of them. Unfortunately, these clauses have sometimes been used in ways contrary to a desire to foster genuinely fair dispute resolution mechanisms. For example, Drahozal and Ware (2010) reviewed multiple studies regarding business contracts and the use of arbitration clauses. They conclude that some businesses use arbitration clauses in order to avoid class action lawsuits (p. 467). On the whole, ADR clauses have the potential to be beneficial to both consumers and businesses—it is all in the way the programs are designed and funded, which goes to the underlying motivations of the businesses using these clauses. These are merely tools that can be used for good or ill, depending on how they are wielded.

When engaging in B2B contracts internationally, mandatory arbitration becomes much more attractive for both parties than litigation. When it comes to international business, questions of jurisdiction may complicate resolution through the courts, as well as the added difficulty of collecting on a court settlement that might have originated in a different country than the one in which the defendant resides. The costs of international travel to attend court proceedings make resolution for relatively small matters unaffordable. Most companies that conduct business internationally have developed a level of comfort with the use of binding arbitration or mediation-then-arbitration for dispute resolution. In some cases, these processes may be conducted virtually, using video or teleconferencing services to further reduce the time and expense associated with resolution.

Patient Care Advocates: Reducing Formal Complaints in Hospital Settings

Hospitals are unique among organizations in that they can be private-sector, for-profit endeavors or they can be run as nonprofit organizations. Either way, addressing patient complaints early is crucial to providing high-quality health care and avoiding future litigation. Toward those ends, many hospitals have created positions for conflict management experts who are on staff to intervene as soon as a conflict comes to light. These individuals are most commonly called *patient care advocates*, but they can hold other titles depending on whether they work under the auspices of the risk management or patient care departments.

A **patient care advocate (PCA)** works either in the emergency department or in other parts of the hospital and is on call to manage patient complaints, to deescalate conflict when it arises, and to solve problems whenever possible. For example:

A patient in the emergency room becomes irate because he feels he is waiting longer than is fair and that other patients who arrived later than he did have already been seen. He is getting increasingly agitated and begins yelling at the staff. The PCA intervenes, takes him aside or to a private space for conversation. She listens to him and assures him that his needs will be met. She seeks out information from the other staff members to share with him regarding his expected wait time and the reasons for the delay. She seeks to calm him down through listening and tells him she will be his point of contact in case other problems arise during his stay.

At a teaching hospital, a patient was recovering from surgery and under the influence of pain medication. The patient was about to receive a blood transfusion from a nursing student when she panicked and yelled to the staff that her blood type was O positive rather than A positive, as the label on the bag indicated. The nurse assured her that her blood had been drawn and the type had been checked twice. The nurse told her she was "woozy" from pain medication, and she needed to trust the staff to do their jobs right. The patient picked up the phone and dialed 911. She verbally withdrew her consent for care and told them to stop treating her immediately. The nurse called the PCA, who arrived at the same time as the police. The PCA offered to have the patient's blood type checked one more time to reassure the patient. She convinced the nurses this was a small price to pay to calm the patient and get on with her care. The patient said, "I'm forty-two years old and I donate blood every three months. I know what my blood type is, but go ahead and check it!" As it turned out, the patient was right, and the protocols for administering a blood transfusion were not being correctly followed in this hospital. A potential health-care disaster and a lawsuit were averted.

Sometimes the PCA accompanies doctors as they deliver the news of a death to family members or checks in on patients to make sure all their questions have been answered clearly. The PCA is there to ensure that all patients receive the best service possible and address complaints and problems before they become formal complaints. There is an increased use of PCAs within hospital settings, a trend that indicates recognition of the benefits of early resolution for complaint prevention and customer recovery.

CONCLUSION

As successful managers know, great service does not imply that mistakes are never made. It implies that employees at all levels of an organization are committed to proactively addressing problems that arise, without defensiveness, and with an eye toward problem-solving and consistent improvement. Proactive customer dispute prevention and early resolution involves planning. It requires monitoring customer feedback for nuggets of knowledge that hold the key to improved goods and services. Yet some organizations fail to gather input from their customers or clients, or they gather it but disregard its implications. Gathering feedback during the design of dispute management systems will be important to ensure perceptions that the system is fair and designed with an eye toward fairness rather than simply for the convenience of the institution in the more powerful position (Bingham, 2008).

The ostrich approach to conflict management serves as an invitation to one's competitors. By resolving problems at the lowest levels, using well-trained and empowered employees, organizations can maximize the accomplishment of their missions while making their workplaces more harmonious and profitable.

ELISE AT MAIN STREET BAKERIES

Upon the advice of her marketing team, Elise and her team decided to hold focus group discussions with a diverse group of her existing customers as well as inviting some noncustomers. Each participant was paid for their time, given a tour of a store, and sampled various products during the introductory period and breaks. The team asked the participants to describe Main Street Bakeries in three words; to discuss why they did or did not shop there; and to share ideas about ways in which the company could appeal to a broader clientele without alienating its current base. In addition to these focus groups, customers were asked to take a survey via a link printed on their receipts in exchange for discounts on products at their next visit.

The information received identified some important areas of improvement for the company. People with household incomes of less than $75,000 per year perceived Main Street Bakeries as being a luxury food boutique where specialty items were found, rather than as their routine grocery store. Even existing customers voiced a desire to see more "everyday" items at the store in addition to a greater variety of sales or bargains. To address this perception, Main Street Bakeries initiated a marketing campaign using the slogan "Seasonal means reasonable," through which they promoted a rotation of seasonal vegetables and food items at low prices while stocking a wider price range of items such as pasta, dairy, and canned goods.

The feedback they received from existing customers was used to identify the things customers liked the best about the store (things like the cleanliness, friendliness, and free cooking lessons) as well as the things they liked the least (shortages of fresh baked goods during afternoon hours and long checkout lines). Each individual store used the data collected to develop goals for improvement, with guidance from upper management. Different survey questions were designed to ensure data would be available to assess progress toward goals. Employees at all levels of the organization received feedback about their customer service performance and incentives were developed to encourage superior efforts on the part of employees.

As a result, satisfaction among existing customers started to rise while new customers started coming in. The stores seemed reinvigorated.

KEY TERMS

business-to-business (B2B)
customer loyalty programs
customer recovery
customer satisfaction

customers as business partners
mandatory arbitration clause
patient care advocate (PCA)
relationship management

EXERCISES

1. Think, pair, share: What type of customer service information does your organization gather and analyze? How could that data-gathering and analysis be improved?
2. What customer loyalty programs do you participate in? Are they effective tools for attracting or retaining your business? Why or why not?
3. Does your organization use a mandatory arbitration clause in its employment or consumer contracts? How is this perceived? What are the costs and benefits implicit in your organization's decision to use or not to use such clauses?

SUGGESTED SUPPLEMENTAL READINGS

Cheng, L. Y., Yang, C. C., & Teng, H. M. (2012). An integrated model for customer relationship management: An analysis and empirical study. *Human Factors and Ergonomics in Manufacturing & Service Industries.* https://doi.org/10.1002/hfm.20343

Coleman, D. (1992). How to achieve a productive partnership. *Journal of Accountancy, 173*(5), 113–118.

12

Public Policy Decision-Making and Collaboration with Regulators

There is no reason to believe that bureaucrats and politicians, no matter how well meaning, are better at solving problems than the people on the spot, who have the strongest incentive to get the solution right.

—Elinor Ostrom

As noted in the introduction to this text, people need organizations and organizations need people. Organizations also need other organizations. Think about how many organizations partner with yours to accomplish your mission: from the company supplying maintenance staff, to vendors and distributors who get your product to market, to the Departments of Labor, Environment, Trade, and others. These organizations need to communicate well to solve problems, while inviting and incorporating feedback from those impacted by their work because those on the receiving end of decisions are often "the experts," as the quote from Ostrom leads us to consider (quoted in Surowiecki, 2004, p. 158).

Whether you work for a regulatory agency or struggle to meet their requirements, the relationship between regulators and the regulated is a crucial nexus for conflict and savvy management. Positive, collaborative relationships between organizational leaders, regulators, and policymakers increase the odds that an organization will remain compliant with regulations. When unforeseen problems arise, those relationships lend themselves to problem-solving and early resolution rather than the blame game.

Learning Objectives

- Describe the common characteristics of public disputes compared to other disputes covered in this text, such as employment complaints.
- Match common types of public disputes with the best process for dispute resolution.
- Describe the evolution toward collaborative decision-making for public policies as well as the pros and cons of this trend.
- List and describe the common steps in the process of making administrative rules and regulations.

ELISE AT MAIN STREET BAKERIES

Elise wants to ensure her business is as accessible as possible, yet the rapid growth of "service" animals has made this difficult for food companies like her chain of bakeries. While she loves pets, they sometimes have accidents requiring time-consuming and unpleasant clean-ups by her staff. Unruly pets have eaten or damaged food displays. There have been more than a few dogfights in her stores, which has led to litigation from employees and customers. Customers have brought "emotional comfort" animals that are unsanitary and frightening, such as a boa constrictor, a chicken, multiple rabbits, parrots, cats on leashes, and many dogs. Elise wants to ensure accessibility for all people with disabilities while ensuring a clean, safe, and pleasant shopping experience. It is a difficult conundrum.

Then Elise heard a rumor that a joint effort of the U.S. Food and Drug Administration (FDA) is crafting new rules about service animals in food service and production areas. Rather than waiting and worrying, Elise has called the FDA to find out more about the process for decision-making. She learned the FDA is convening a group of stakeholders to discuss this new initiative, share information with the agency, and engage in negotiated rulemaking. Elise has never heard of this before but has agreed to participate in a teleconference call with other potential stakeholders to learn more about this process.

★ ★ ★

Managers from public, private, and nonprofit sectors often interact in ways that indicate adversarial rather than collaborative relationships. Adversarial relationships are not necessary to protect the public good or to keep businesses profitable. In fact, adversarial relationships between regulators and those they regulate frequently reduce efficiency for both sides. There are many shared interests that can mitigate these previously hostile relationships. Corporations seek to protect their brand name and government agencies do not want to get the reputation for stifling job creation or encouraging companies to relocate to "pollution havens" or other low-regulatory environments. Civic and nonprofit groups may accomplish more change by nurturing collaborative partnerships with regulators than by being thorns in their sides. Managers from the private, public, and nonprofit sectors are increasingly coming together through the use of collaborative processes to create or change policies in ways that further the missions. The ability of regulators and regulated communities to proactively address policy issues are core managerial skills that are central to mission achievement. The application of ADR methods to public policy issues is referred to as **environmental and public policy conflict resolution (E/PP)** or environmental conflict resolution (ECR).

From negotiated rulemaking to policy dialogues or case evaluations, this chapter will examine innovative efforts to transform regulatory relationships with the goal of creating policy that is more effective, implementable, and subject to fewer legal challenges. From zoning disputes to new health-care regulations, case studies demonstrate how leaders in regulatory and regulated communities have successfully reached out to one another in order to protect and promote public and private interests. These two need not be mutually exclusive.

If you work for a nonprofit or a corporation, do not jump to the false conclusion that this chapter and the one that follows do not involve you or your organization. Nothing could be further from the truth. Many civic and nonprofit groups are involved with and seek to influence the creation and implementation of public policies, rules, and regulations. Therefore, nonprofits are usually included as key stakeholders in E/PP efforts. This chapter will introduce the menu of processes related to managing public disputes as well as other stakeholder gatherings, such as shareholder meetings and other forms of large-group decision-making processes.

CHARACTERISTICS OF PUBLIC DISPUTES

Imagine these three common public policy conflicts:

- Your state government wants to build a juvenile detention facility near a middle-class suburban neighborhood. Local residents have staged protests and moved to block the rezoning effort, and groups have lined up on both sides of the facility.
- Video footage was released that appears to show an unarmed Hispanic man being shot by police as he fled a traffic stop. Immediately afterward, riots ensued at the state capitol with hundreds of thousands of dollars in damage to vehicles, shops, and buildings. More than one hundred arrests have been made and the city's simmering ethnic tensions have boiled over.
- The EPA was sued by a civic group claiming it has not adequately protected the safety of America's drinking water by failing to create standards for many common forms of prescription drugs that find their way into the water supply. The judge agreed with the civic group and now the EPA is tasked with creating a host of new water-quality regulations. Local governments, the U.S. Association of Mayors, pharmaceutical companies, and hundreds of water utilities across the country are concerned about the costs of any proposed new regulations. The EPA is entangled in its mission, a court mandate, and with stakeholders on all sides of the issue.
- A multinational car manufacturer recently received the largest fine in U.S. history (both EPA and Consumer Product Safety Commission) because they misled regulators and consumers by claiming their cars had much higher gas mileage than was accurate. The CEO was replaced due to his complicity in the scheme and public outrage. The new leader seeks to rebuild trust with regulators and the public by complying with all regulations in a transparent manner.

Each of these scenarios depicts a dispute, or more broadly, a decision-making process that involves managers of public, private, and nonprofit organizations. Increasingly, managers are called on to use their skills and the visibility of their positions to speak as representatives for their organizations at public meetings or within some type of decision-making processes that affect their products, services, or missions. By working together to find solutions to complex problems, both public and private interests can be protected. This means prolonged, unproductive conflicts may be avoided or at least shortened.

Public disputes are different from the labor-management and employment conflicts discussed in earlier chapters. We must begin with a broad definition of **public disputes** as complex, multiparty decision-making or consensus-building processes on issues affecting the public interest or policy that involve complicated networks of interests, unequal accountability among stakeholders and strongly held values, and are highly influenced by governmental rules and regulations.

Diversity of Stakeholder Interests: In the drinking water scenario above, stakeholder groups include the EPA, U.S. Fish and Wildlife Service, the U.S. Department of Agriculture, state and local government representatives, local water utilities (some publicly operated and some privately), potentially dozens of pharmaceutical manufacturers, drug retailers such as CVS, civic groups representing public health or the environment such as the Sierra Club, and technology manufacturers that wish to sell water-quality equipment or services involved in the purification of drinking water or the detection of impurities.

Access and Influence: Each of these stakeholder groups would want one or more representatives at the negotiating table if talks were to occur related to new regulations. These negotiations would likely occur over a period amounting to months or even years. Each stakeholder would need to commit to keeping his or her constituency updated on the status of the negotiations and any proposals under discussion. The stakeholder representative (we'll call this person an *advocate*) will need to funnel the concerns of his constituency back to the larger group and serve as an intragroup negotiator to help his own constituents gain a realistic understanding of the nature of the compromises likely to be necessary to reach an agreement that is superior to litigation.

Participation: To complicate matters, it is not uncommon for new groups to emerge even late in the negotiation process. Perhaps a local or national environmental nonprofit learned about the negotiations months after they began. Or once the group has crafted a specific proposal and this proposal was released to the press, a group that was not previously interested now believes their interests are threatened. Because of the nature of public meetings and public policy processes, it is usually difficult, unwise, or even impossible to exclude individuals or groups who wish to be included in these negotiations, even if they come late in the game.

Accountability: Some of these advocates are bureaucrats working for governmental agencies. As such, they can be officially reprimanded or even fired as a way of holding them accountable. Sometimes elected officials take part in these efforts, and they are held accountable at election time. Still others, citizens who represent themselves or a civic group, may have no accountability at all. The same goes for corporate advocates, who are not necessarily expected to uphold the public good. These varying levels of accountability make collaborative processes more complex than the other processes discussed in this book.

Duration of Process & Relationships: In some public disputes the parties will come together for a few meetings and never see each other again, as may be the case with the juvenile detention facility vignette. More commonly, in cases such as the race riots or water-quality issues, the stakeholders will have repeated contact with each other either as neighbors or colleagues. Whether they come together in the future on the same issue or on other issues of mutual concern, these groups are interdependent, with their paths crossing repeatedly over many years. Therefore, these collaborative processes represent an important opportunity for building social capital and networks that will enhance current and future communications and problem-solving abilities. By getting to know one another as people, neighbors, and colleagues, these collaborative processes can serve as springboards for other joint efforts and as mechanisms that can be called on throughout the process of decision implementation. When problems arise during the implementation phase, which they often do, parties can call on one another to again work together collaboratively in order to efficiently and fairly discuss and solve those problems. They have built relationships as people, not just as representatives of their particular interests. The multiple meetings required to engage in these processes may make participation expensive or unrealistic for some civic groups that rely on volunteers. Consider ways to maximize the participation of all stakeholder groups or risk missing out on needed perspectives that may result in biased outcomes.

Statutory procedural requirements: Each governmental agency has developed different protocols for decision-making that must be followed. In many federal government agencies, this means that a draft rule or regulation is created and published in the *Federal Register*, a daily publication of the U.S. government. Public comments are accepted for a specified period, after which the final rule or regulation is issued. In some cases, especially at the state and local level, public meetings must be held to gather comments or announce planned changes before they can take effect. Yet the specifics of these processes are unique to each government agency and sometimes one issue crosscuts the jurisdictional boundaries of multiple federal, state, and local governmental agencies. In the public sector, corporations have clear hierarchies through which decisions are made and implemented. Civic groups may have less hierarchical and more consensus-based or democratic decision-making processes. When a decision must be made quickly, and the decision affects government, industry, and civic groups, these varying processes for decision-making can lead to delay and confusion. The complexity of these decision-making structures and the necessity of getting them to converge means that public disputes are much more complex than intraorganizational disputes. These disputes occur at the nexus between organizations rather than within them. As you will see from the variety of collaborative processes described in this chapter, most governmental agencies and corporations do not have formal guidelines for participating in collaborative processes. This means that each opportunity for collaborative decision-making or problem-solving is handled differently by each agency and even dispute by dispute. This is not necessarily a negative, considering that each dispute may be unique enough to justify an individualized approach. But it also means that some agencies are leaders in the use of dispute resolution processes and others are laggards who rarely entertain collaborative processes.

Media Presence: The public nature of these negotiations can be a complicating factor. In 1976, in the wake of the Watergate scandal and heightened levels of public distrust of government leaders, the Government in the Sunshine Act was passed. This act requires all agencies of the federal government, except the Executive Office of the President, to conduct meetings publicly and allow citizens to testify and present concerns about past, present, and future agency actions (Harrison, Harris & Tolchin, 2009). State and local governments have generally followed this example. The term **sunshine laws** refers to federal, state, and local laws that require regulatory meetings, decisions, and records to be open to the public. This means that the media are often present during the negotiations and mediations that occur on public issues, making frank discussions difficult. Elected or appointed leaders may be afraid to engage in creative brainstorming, knowing that any idea they suggest or anything they say may end up on YouTube or the five o'clock news. Advocates know they can often use the media to pressure fellow negotiators or to sabotage proposals before they are fully discussed. The open nature of public disputes makes them more complex and difficult to navigate. Dealing with the media and turning them into a process ally rather than a process scuttler is a skill we will cover later.

Public decision-making processes involve deeply held values tied closely to personal and community identities. The choices we make about methods to care for our sick or elderly, provide education for our children, punish or deter wrongdoing, protect our environmental resources, or regulate economic activity reveal our underlying values as people. When something appears to threaten these values, people react strongly, sometimes even violently. Discussions on these issues bring out passionate pleas to do "the right thing" from the advocates involved. Yet, the dilemma is that we are often faced with the need to prioritize or choose between these values and therefore different people will weigh them differently (see Alligator River Exercise in Chapter 5). Do we take away the right to drive from elderly people who may pose a risk to public safety? Do we save an endangered species at a cost of millions of tax dollars? The moral and often personal implications of public decisions make these negotiations quite difficult and exhausting yet terribly important to society.

Managing these complex issues increasingly calls for the skills of **collaborative public management**, "the process of facilitating and operating in multiorganizational arrangements to solve problems that cannot be solved or easily solved by single organizations. Collaborative means to co-labor, to achieve common goals, often working across boundaries and in multi-sector-actor relationships. Collaborative public management may include participatory governance: the active involvement of citizens in government decision-making" (O'Leary & Blomgren Bingham, 2009, p. 3).

THE SPIRAL OF UNMANAGED CONFLICT

In the field of conflict management, experts frequently refer to a concept called **ripeness** (Coleman et al., 2008a). A conflict is ripe for intervention once it is clear who the major players or stakeholders are, once the issue is of significant urgency to demand action but has not yet reached crisis style, and before the relationships between stakeholders are characterized by demonization and disrespect and the dispute becomes intractable. Yet, intervene too early and it is difficult to sustain energetic participation by stakeholders or there may be a lack of data on which to base ideas for resolution. Although it is never too late to attempt collaboration, the odds of success are greatest if the intervention occurs when the dispute is ripe for intervention.

Carpenter and Kennedy (2001, p. 12) have outlined the common phases that public disputes experience on their way to becoming intractable, what they call "the spiral of unmanaged conflict." Each individual dispute may go through these phases faster or slower or may skip a step only to circle back to an earlier one. Progress through the phases may be linear for some disputes and circular for others.

In the first phase, the problem emerges. Generally, a private or public organization announces some planned change—a new building, a widened road, a new regulation, a change to products or services, and so forth. There is mild concern that grows slowly at first, starting with those most directly affected by the planned changes. Stakeholders seek to get more information about the planned changes and are often frustrated by the response they receive. Organizations do not like to share information about plans until that information is relatively finalized. This lack of information and uncertainty feeds fear among stakeholders, who begin to contact their elected officials or others in power to help them get the information they need.

The apparent unwillingness or inability to share information leads to negative attributions by stakeholders, who may say things like "What are they hiding?!" Groups of stakeholders form on all sides of the issue; rarely do these issues have only two sides, even though the media often find it simpler to portray issues in this manner. These groups start to get organized, gather resources to support their future activities, and make their game plans. As the sides form, the media begin to cover the issue, thereby increasing the rate at which the sides harden. Individuals begin to talk only about the issue with those who have similar views. They tune out the opinions of those who disagree with them, and as a result their positions harden. They may develop ideas about the dispute that favor their position as the morally right, prudent, or obvious course of action. As a result, communication and negotiation between the groups comes to a standstill. The less communication occurs, the less the likelihood of a collaborative resolution.

Because it has become clear to the stakeholders that the other side(s) is unwilling to capitulate, they commit resources to promote adversarial paths to resolution. They may spend money to hire lawyers and file a lawsuit or injunction. They may seek the services of a media consultant to make their case in the press and garner further support for their cause. They may hire expert witnesses or consultants to gather data that supports their side. Once these resources are committed, no one in the group will settle for less than what has been spent so far, including an outcome that is worthy of the time and energy they have committed.

As the conflict grows, it leaves the confines of the original parties and comes to the attention of regional, national, or international groups who may join the fray. At some point along this path, perceptions of the other get distorted as attribution biases and other forms of cognitive bias take hold. Nothing they say can be trusted, even proposals for resolution or new data that could undermine your group's position. As time passes and the problem grows unchecked, a sense of crisis emerges. Clearly something needs to be done. As the crisis grows to fever pitch, actions that would have initially been seen as over the top are now on the table. Each side is willing to spend more than originally planned and compromise becomes unthinkable.

The goal of effective conflict management is to increase and improve communication across opposing groups, seek data jointly to avoid a battle of the experts, and bring in a facilitator or other process neutral early on, to disrupt the cycle of escalation common to public disputes.

PUBLIC POLICY PROCESS AND CONCEPTS

Before we examine public dispute resolution processes in greater detail, it is important to develop a shared understanding of the traditional process for public decision-making, since collaboration is the alternative. The first set of key concepts deals with laws, statutes, ordinances, rules, and regulations. Laws, statutes, and ordinances are passed by the legislative branches of government at the federal, state, and local levels that assign rights and responsibilities to various members and groups in society. The legislative branch creates these laws, but it is up to the executive branch to see to the details of their implementation, which is accomplished via the bureaucracy through their administrative law powers. "**Administrative law** is the name given to agencies' rulemaking and resolution of conflicts regarding their rules" (Harrison et al., 2009, p. 479). **Administrative rule-making** is the "process by which upper-level bureaucrats use their administrative discretion and their expertise in the policy area to create rules, regulations, and standards that the bureaucracy will then enforce" (p. 480). In the United States, federal administrative law is codified as the Code of Federal Regulations. In essence, Congress passes laws and administrative agencies pass rules that allow them to put the laws into practice. For example, Congress may pass a law that requires workers to be safe from known and avoidable hazards in the workplace. But this is too vague for practical enforcement. Therefore, it would be the duty of the Occupational Safety and Health Administration (OSHA) to determine the specific actions needed by employers to ensure a safe workplace. OSHA would need to make specific regulations as necessary to meet the requirements of the law as set out by Congress. Additionally, agencies involved in administrative rulemaking have the authority to impose fines or criminal penalties on those individuals or groups who violate administrative rules.

Administrative adjudication refers to the process through which agencies determine whether an individual or group is guilty of violating administrative rules (Harrison et al., 2009). Citizens who believe an agency has not acted correctly in its application of the laws passed by Congress can file suits to force the agency to change its behavior and enforce its rules more or less stringently, depending on the court's ruling. For example, in 2007 several states successfully sued the EPA for its failure to fully implement the Clean Air Act.

The process for drafting new rules for executive agencies is laid out in various federal statutes, including the Administrative Procedure Act of 1946. This act requires nearly all federal agencies to publicize proposed rules in the *Federal Register*. State and local governments have generally adopted this practice as well, with more regional or local newspapers serving the same function as the *Federal Register*. This is the first official step to creating a new rule. Although variations among agencies exist, it is most common for the agency's staff to study the issue and issue a draft rule. Interested citizens, corporations, and civic groups have a specified period in which to respond with their comments, objections, or preferred alternatives. The agency is required to consider these comments and then issue a final rule that reflects the public interest. In general, there tends to be little change in the rule between the first issuance of the draft and the final rule. The most important time to influence the content of a rule is before the first draft is issued. Once a rule is finalized, the stakeholders who are negatively affected by the rule may seek to halt its implementation through the courts. For example, when the EPA considers regulating greenhouse gases or requiring increased fuel efficiency in cars, agency leaders know that powerful industries and civic groups on all sides of the issue are ready to challenge their action in the courts to argue they are overreaching the authority granted by Congress or they are not doing enough to protect the environment and public health. Proposed rule changes that affect the strongest interests may spend literally a decade or more in the courts, costing the parties tens or even hundreds of millions of dollars to fight. In the meantime, the public interest waits.

This expensive, slow, adversarial process of regulation is complicated by a couple of other important challenges that often work against the public interest. First, there is a revolving door between government agencies and many of the industries they regulate. The **revolving door** refers to the fact that government bureaucrats often leave their government careers behind and go to work for the agencies they used to regulate. Similarly, members of Congress often become lobbyists when they leave office. The powerful ties among industry, Congress, and government regulatory agencies mean that a relatively small, tight-knit group of powerful decision-makers are usually involved in rulemaking within each agency's issue area. This reduces the number and variety of voices heard when important decisions are being made and increases the public's distrust of many decision-making processes. The revolving door can also lead to a concept called **agency capture**, which occurs when governmental regulatory agencies begin to advocate for the industries they are supposed to regulate rather than objectively ensuring they adhere to all applicable laws and rules.

HISTORY OF ANTAGONISTIC RELATIONSHIPS BETWEEN REGULATORY AND REGULATED COMMUNITIES

The history of relationships between regulatory agencies and regulated communities swings wildly from periods of agency capture in which working relationships are too close and clear conflicts of interest are not publicly acknowledged to the other end of the spectrum, in which there is an absence of trust and antagonistic relationships between both groups. Most commonly, members of industry view regulators warily, worried they are there to impede progress and profits by heavy-handed enforcement. Regulators are often viewed as traffic cops waiting to impose fines for everyday behaviors. Civic groups representing workers, the environment, immigrants' rights, and other issues view agencies as unsympathetic and largely captured by the powerful interests they regulate. Among regulators and the regulated, there is often a cultural norm that assumes a distributive bargaining, zero-sum situation in which gains for one side can only come at the expense of the other. Don't corporations and the EPA have a shared interest in avoiding unnecessary pollution and cleaning up any accidental spills quickly? To a large extent, regulators and those they regulate have many legitimately shared interests on which they can focus as a starting point for collaboration.

The beginning of public policy collaboration can be traced to various sources, with an interesting example coming from the Quincy Library Group. For fifteen years local environmentalists and loggers engaged in heated, often violent actions designed to thwart each other, which came to be known as the *timber wars*. When tree spiking, blockades, and other tactics led to a mutually hurting stalemate, a group of diverse stakeholders began meeting at the library in Quincy, California. The library proved to be a good place for these meetings because the parties could not raise their voices without facing ejection. In the early 1990s this group created a joint plan for logging the Lassen, Plumas, and parts of the Tahoe National Forests. Unfortunately, government officials had not been involved in the negotiations and decided not to abide by the group's agreement. In a show of unity, none of the timber companies put in bids to log the forests until the Department of the Interior agreed to implement the plan created by the Quincy Library Group (Varettoni, 2005). Although the negotiations among the environmentalists, logging companies, and local and federal government agencies are an ongoing effort, with the expected ups and downs, this group is seen as one of the most notable early efforts to reach collaborative decisions that address the interests of all major stakeholders.

President Clinton passed the Administrative Dispute Resolution Act of 1996, which required each federal agency to create some sort of ADR program and track progress in the encouragement of ADR over litigation. This act allowed agencies to hire external neutrals such as mediators, arbitrators, and facilitators as well as train employees to conduct these services internally or in a shared neutrals program between agencies. Most agencies chose to implement workplace mediation programs and hire ombudsmen to deal with internal workplace disputes. The EPA created a variety of ADR programs to address disputes against potentially responsible parties (also known as *polluters*) who have been accused of violating agency regulations. A few other agencies also began experimenting with the use of ADR processes internally with employees, externally with regulated communities, or both.

For example, the Federal Emergency Management Agency (FEMA) responds to disasters involving multiple levels of governmental agencies with overlapping authority as well as exhausted, distraught survivors of disaster. FEMA employees leave their homes and families on short notice and temporarily live in disaster zones where housing, food, and modern conveniences may be lacking in quantity or quality. Disputes are inevitable. In response, FEMA created a cadre of alternative dispute resolution specialists who assist with employment and other disputes on site, to improve team functioning and intergroup communication in literally dire circumstances. Normalizing and responding to conflict effectively promotes better public service and employee well-being.

The state of ADR in U.S. federal agencies continues to evolve. On November 28, 2005, Joshua Bolten, director of the Office of Management and Budget, and James Connaughton, chairman of the president's Council on Environmental Quality, issued a policy memorandum on environmental conflict resolution. "This joint policy statement directs agencies to increase the effective use of ECR and their institutional capacity for collaborative problem solving. It includes a definition of ECR and sets forth 'basic principles for agency engagement in environmental conflict resolution and collaborative problem solving'" (EPA, 2000). It also includes a compilation of mechanisms and strategies that may be used to achieve the stated policy objectives.

ENVIRONMENTAL CONFLICT RESOLUTION AND PUBLIC POLICY

Environmental conflict resolution (ECR) refers to people with differing views and interests working together in a systematic and organized way to find workable solutions to shared problems about environmental issues, usually with the assistance of a neutral third party (EPA, 2000). These same procedures and processes can be used for environmental and non-environmental cases of decision-making, but environmental agencies have led the way in designing, evaluating, and promoting the use of these processes so the most common term used to describe them has become *environment and public policy conflict resolution (E/PP)*. A government agency was created to promote the use of these processes, housed at the University of Arizona's Udall Center in Tucson, Arizona (ADR. gov, 2023). Their website includes a host of examples for which ECR processes have been used:

- Managing public lands for people to use and enjoy in different ways, such as planning how a national forest can serve future needs for watershed protection, timber harvesting, and recreation
- Natural resources disputes, for instance, fairly allocating rights to use water, timber, or mineral resources
- Conflicts over facilities siting, such as where to locate highways, dams, power lines, or wind farms
- Protected area disagreements, for example, managing recreational uses and still protect a sensitive natural area in a park
- Endangered species issues, for instance, how to implement protective actions that are required to prevent the extinction of a species
- Federal and tribal government relations, such as how to respect tribal sovereignty and protect sacred sites when planning or implementing projects

In addition to these examples from the environmental arena, similar processes have been used to draft new statewide policies: for dealing with mentally ill people who come into contact with the criminal justice system, to make decisions about the allocation of tax dollars on educational infrastructure spending, for the design and construction of megaprojects such as bridges and airports, to design a new rule related to interstate highway access management (such as where to place on- and off-ramps), and to make decisions about which schools to close because of a shrinking youth population.

When decisions must be made on scientifically and economically complicated matters, having more experts at the table can increase the quality of the outcome—especially when viewpoints from the public, private, and nonprofit sectors are all represented. Decisions made through consensus and collaboration are also likely to encounter fewer snags on implementation (Raines, 2002). When problems occur during the implementation stage, which they nearly always do, the relationships built between the parties make it easier for them to work together to solve problems rather than focusing on accusations and blame (Anderson & Polkinghorn, 2008). In fact, research has shown that parties have increased their negotiation and collaboration skills as a result of participation in these collaborative processes as well as building trust among private stakeholders, government regulators, and civic groups (Raines & Kubala, 2011).

E/PP processes are a good choice when no single stakeholder group can resolve the problem on its own, when the outcome is genuinely in doubt, when all major parties are willing and able to participate, and when the issue is considered important to all major stakeholders. ECR processes are not likely to work when one or more parties believe they have a quicker, more surefire method for accomplishing their goals, such as a public relations campaign in the media or a court case. It also is unlikely to work if one or more of the major stakeholders will not acknowledge the existence of the problem or participate in the process. It is crucial for all major stakeholders to be represented at the negotiating table because the absence of any major group means that one or more types of interest will not be heard or considered during the discussions. For example, what if new regulations were made to address pollution and safety concerns on offshore oil rigs but only the oil companies and the EPA were present? In the absence of input from environmental groups or worker safety organizations, it might appear as if the oil company interests had exerted an inappropriate amount of influence. Such a decision would be more likely to be challenged in court and might not adequately reflect the needs of all the groups affected by the regulations.

Politicians are some of the most enthusiastic supporters of collaborative processes for complicated public decisions for this reason: When groups are aligned on all sides of an issue, then politicians risk alienating a significant proportion of their constituency no matter what decision they make. By delegating decision-making authority to a group of representative stakeholders, including government agencies, politicians can claim that the outcome was reached democratically and transparently. In fact, decisions reached through collaborative processes nearly always produce more support from the participating stakeholders than decisions reached unilaterally by regulatory agencies, thereby being a politically safer route.

Other stakeholders, including government agencies and civic groups, typically voice more satisfaction with decisions made through collaboration (Raines

& Kubala, 2011). Studies of more than 48 environmental conflict resolution efforts in the western United States found that 87% would recommend a collaborative process to others and only 7% would not; 77% indicated the collaborative process resulted in more effective and durable outcomes compared with a traditional decision-making process; 96% of participants understood the terms of the agreement reached; 100% felt the agreements addressed parties' interests more than the traditional process; 100% felt all legal requirements were addressed in the agreement; and 100% felt that the agreement took advantage of all available information relevant to the issues under discussion (Raines & Kubala, 2011).

In a study of water collaboration efforts in metro Atlanta and north Georgia, 100% of participants agreed that their knowledge of the water resource was increased through the collaborative process. About 71% of the participants agreed that relationships between regulators and regulated organizations had improved as a result of collaboration. Beierle and Cayford (2002) examined 239 cases of environmental decision-making, considering the five goals typically exhibited by these processes: (1) addressing public values, (2) improving decision quality, (3) incorporating conflict resolution tools, (4) building trust between institutions and groups, and (5) addressing public education on the issues under negotiation. The authors found that these five goals were better addressed through collaborative processes but that more progress could be achieved by spreading the outreach and trust building beyond the core group of participants. Getting all stakeholder groups involved is key. Even more, it is critical to help stakeholder groups to inform and educate their individual members across the community. Only then will these processes fully achieve their potential to transform public consciousness on policy matters as well as increasingly empower members of a democratic society.

Yet these processes are not universally popular. They are time-consuming and occasionally frustrating. Sipe and Stiftel (1995) found that the median cost savings for mediation compared to court action for the respondents (the parties accused of polluting) was approximately $150,000 per case. Multiple studies show that collaboration may take more time up front than traditional decision-making processes. Collaborative processes require parties to listen to the ideas and opinions of those with whom they disagree, and to seek out common ground. In the study by Raines and Kubala (2011), only 12% of the water managers studied felt that they were not fully heard during the process. Although further study is required, initial findings indicate that those with more extreme views on either side of the issue are given less attention in collaborative processes out of a desire to find common ground and the evolution of shared norms and values that tend to emerge over time. In some ways, this is an understudied and underacknowledged benefit of these processes; they force parties to become more moderate and those who refuse to "play nice" cannot grandstand the way they can during traditional public meetings.

Sponsoring an ECR or other public policy collaborative process takes time and resources for the sponsoring agency. Even if these resources may be less than the regular process, they tend to be more up front and require one person to take a lead role to manage the agency's participation. When no one comes forward to take the lead on these initiatives, they often founder.

Characteristics of Public Disputes

Number of parties: There are some important ways in which environmental and public policy conflict resolution differ from employment disputes or customer conflicts previously discussed in this book. First, these processes involve more people than a typical workplace mediation or resolution process. There can be anywhere from five to literally hundreds of stakeholders who seek to participate in meetings and negotiations. Second, because of the numbers of stakeholders affected by the issue, most stakeholder groups appoint one or more representatives to attend meetings and funnel back the issues raised and generate or review proposals. In other words, the negotiators are representatives of much larger constituencies.

Multilevel negotiations: This means negotiations are occurring on at least two levels: within each stakeholder group the individual parties must seek to reach consensus as to the positions and interests of the group itself and then the representative of that group will negotiate with the other representatives within the E/PP process itself. It is not uncommon for stakeholder groups to bicker internally or even fracture into multiple groups when they cannot reach an internal consensus. Stakeholder representatives must work hard throughout the process to keep their constituencies informed of the ongoing negotiations. They must clarify the limits of their settlement authority so as not to commit their group to a position that the membership will not support. Facilitators, mediators, or other neutral third parties may need to visit with these stakeholder groups to assist them with their intragroup negotiations before convening the broader group of stakeholders for negotiations. Because some of the participants will be volunteers, it may be a struggle to find the resources necessary to secure their full participation. The EPA has recognized this as a challenge and developed some funds to assist civic and tribal groups to participate in collaborative processes.

Longevity: Third, these negotiations can literally last years. For some of these initiatives, the goal is to negotiate an agreement and then disband. For others, the mission involves permanent ongoing negotiations and decision-making surrounding a shared resource, such as shared waters from a common river. A representative for a governmental agency may retire only to go to work for one of the agencies that she previously regulated or join a civic group working on the same issue. Because relationships between stakeholders may span years or entire careers, it is helpful to build in time for relationship building, recognition of individual and shared milestones, and other traditions that help to bond the group together and build camaraderie.

Complexity of technical issues: Fourth, unlike most types of disputes, public decisions typically involve highly complex and technical matters, yet the stakeholders vary widely in their educational backgrounds and levels of knowledge. In a meeting on climate change you might see a citizen with a high school education sitting next to a PhD in meteorology, who sits next to someone from the Department of Defense. Each organization has its own jargon and subject-matter-specific knowledge. It is the role of the neutral to help create a shared level of knowledge in the room and ask all participants to define terms, avoid jargon, and share information.

Accountability Varies: Fifth, the diversity in stakeholder roles means that some representatives are accountable to voters directly through election (the politicians) or indirectly as employees of a government agency who can be dismissed for overstepping their authority or inadequately safeguarding the public interest. However, some stakeholders represent small civic groups or their own interests as farmers, business owners, parents, residents, and so on. Corporations send lawyers, managers, scientists, or professional negotiators to the collaborative process to further their organization's interests. Many of the advocates are experts on the issue at hand, having advanced degrees in science, policymaking, or other related specialized knowledge. However, you will encounter regular citizens with no specialized expertise who participate as representatives of a neighborhood or nonprofit group. The use of jargon, acronyms, and incorrect assumptions about shared knowledge makes these meetings unwieldy. Discussions on technical matters may engage only 20% of the attendees and others are baffled and unable to follow the discussions. Sometimes this happens even to the facilitator! Therefore, it becomes important to consider the utility of beginning this kind of collaborative process with some sharing of basic information that will be foundational to the productivity of subsequent discussions. Some of this presentation will focus on the technical terms and issues under debate, and basic skills or concepts related to collaborative decision-making may also be covered.

The facilitator or lead government agencies may decide to create a list of definitions and acronyms that parties can refer to throughout the process as well as an organizational chart or other tool that clarifies the roles for each public organization represented at the table. Unequal levels of accountability raise thorny issues about the democratic nature of these processes. Some believe them to be more democratic because citizens can participate and directly represent their interests, whereas others find the lack of accountability counter to the goals of representative democracy. For these reasons, environmental and public policy decision-making processes are significantly different and likely more complex than the conflicts experienced by managers within their own organizations or between their organizations and customers or vendors.

PROCESS MENU OPTIONS

Since the 1980s a plethora of processes have sprung up to meet the demand for greater stakeholder participation in public policy decision-making. Ideally, the process chosen should be tailored to the needs of the parties and the issue under discussion. Indeed, some governmental agencies have become adept at matching the process to the dispute. In others, one or two processes have become the default methods for managing collaboration out of a belief that these processes are well suited to the types of decisions made by a particular agency and the desire to avoid the transaction costs inherent in designing new processes with each dispute. Reinventing the wheel is not something agencies have time for, so they rely on practices and procedures previously used by their agency or similar agencies. It is helpful to provide the general outline of some of the most commonly used processes for environmental and public policy decision-making. When these processes are applied to individual cases, they are likely to vary a bit in the details of their application. In some E/PP cases, the process of collaboration is broken down into phases, with the first phase consisting of an assessment of the conflict to determine which process, if any, is best suited to the dispute as well as to better understand who the parties are, learn more about their interests, and gauge their willingness to take part in a collaborative process.

Conflict assessment helps to identify the issues in controversy in a given situation, the affected interests, and the appropriate form(s) of conflict resolution. The assessment process typically involves conferring with potentially interested persons regarding a situation involving conflict in order to assess the causes of the conflict; identify the entities and individuals who would be substantively affected by the conflict's outcome; assess those persons' interests and identify a preliminary set of issues that they believe are relevant; evaluate the feasibility of using a consensus-building or other collaborative process to address these issues; educate interested parties on consensus and collaborative processes to help them think through whether they would wish to participate; and design the structure and membership of a negotiating committee or other collaborative process (if any) to address the conflict (USIECR, n.d. b).

Case evaluation and neutral evaluation is a process in which a neutral expert is hired to evaluate the strengths and weaknesses of each side's case and predict for the parties what would happen in court. If the parties are unable to reach agreement during the evaluation session, the neutral evaluator may offer an impartial nonbinding opinion as to the settlement value of the case. If both parties agree, the evaluator's opinion may become binding.

Collaborative monitoring seeks to engage interested and affected stakeholders, public agencies, and scientific and technical experts in a more direct fashion to jointly gather data and information in an ongoing manner. This helps avoid the tendency for each group to gather information on its own that supports its own preferred outcomes. Participants in collaborative monitoring may play a variety of roles: determining target outcomes, defining criteria and indicators to monitor those outcomes, determining the appropriate system for monitoring, participating in the data-gathering and analysis, and interpreting the data over time. Collaborative monitoring is being implemented in a variety of program contexts and it has been conducted within many different structural settings.

Consensus building describes a number of collaborative decision-making techniques in which a facilitator or mediator is used to assist diverse or competing interest groups to reach agreement on policy matters, environmental conflicts, or other issues of controversy affecting a large number of people. Consensus building processes are typically used to foster dialogue, clarify areas of agreement and disagreement, improve the information on which a decision may be based, and resolve controversial issues in ways that all interests find acceptable. Consensus building typically involves structured (yet relatively informal), face-to-face interaction among representatives of stakeholder groups with a goal of gaining early participation from affected interests with differing viewpoints, producing sound policies with a wide range of support, and reducing the likelihood of subsequent disagreements or legal challenges.

Dispute system design (DSD) is a process for assisting an organization to develop a structure for handling a series of similar recurring or anticipated disputes (such as environmental enforcement cases or EEOC complaints within a federal agency) more effectively. A dispute system designer typically proceeds by interviewing representatives of interested or affected groups (including people in the agency) about their perceptions and interests; analyzing the organization's existing system for handling these conflicts; designing and implementing conflict management or dispute resolution procedures that encourage early, informal resolution of conflicts; and perhaps evaluating the impact of these new dispute resolution procedures to ensure their effectiveness.

In public policy decision-making processes, facilitation is a collaborative process in which a neutral seeks to assist a group of individuals or other parties to constructively discuss a number of complex, potentially controversial issues. The facilitator typically works with participants before and during these discussions to ensure that appropriate persons are at the table, help the parties set ground rules and agendas, enforce both, assist parties to communicate effectively, and help the participants keep on track in working toward their goals. Although facilitation bears many similarities to mediation, the neutral in a facilitation process (the facilitator) usually plays a less active role than a mediator and, unlike a mediator, often does not see resolution as a goal of his or her work. Facilitation may be used in any number of situations where parties of diverse interests or experience participate in discussions ranging from scientific seminars, board meetings, and management meetings to public forums.

Joint fact-finding is a process by which interested parties commit to build a mutual understanding of disputed scientific or technical information. Interested parties can select their own experts who presumably reflect differing interpretations of available information. Alternatively, they can also jointly decide on an unassociated third-party expert or a panel of experts. This process is similar to case evaluation yet different in that the fact finder does not make recommendations as to how the facts should be used as a settlement tool by the parties. A facilitator or mediator works to clarify and define areas of agreement, disagreement, and uncertainty. The facilitator or mediator can coach the experts to translate technical information into a form that is understandable to all interested parties. The goal is to avoid adversarial or partisan science in which competing experts magnify small differences rather than focusing on points of agreement and creating a strategy to provide for a joint conclusion.

Mediation has been defined and discussed at length previously. When applied to environmental and public policy processes, mediation refers to facilitated negotiation in which a skilled, impartial third party seeks to enhance negotiations between parties in a conflict or their representatives by improving communication, identifying interests, and exploring possibilities for a mutually agreeable resolution. The disputants remain responsible for negotiating a settlement and the mediator lacks power to impose any solution; the mediator's role is to assist the process in ways acceptable to the parties.

Negotiated rulemaking (also called *regulatory negotiation* or *reg-neg*) is a multiparty consensus process in which a balanced negotiating committee seeks to reach agreement on the substance of a proposed agency rule, policy, or standard. The negotiating committee is composed of representatives of those groups that will be affected by or have an interest in the rule, including the rule-making agency itself. Affected interests that are represented in the negotiations are expected to abide by any resulting agreement and implement its terms. This agreement-seeking process usually occurs only after a thorough conflict assessment has been conducted and is generally undertaken with the assistance of a skilled, neutral mediator or facilitator.

Policy dialogues are processes that bring together representatives of groups with divergent views or interests to tap the collective views of participants in the process. The goals include opening discussion, improving communication and mutual understanding, exploring the issues of controversy to see if participants' different viewpoints can be distilled into general recommendations, and trying to reach agreement on a proposed policy standard or guidelines to be recommended by government. They are often used to address complex environmental conflicts or public policy disputes constructively. Unlike processes that explicitly seek to obtain consensus (such as negotiated rulemaking or mediation), policy dialogues usually do not seek to achieve a full, specific agreement that would bind all participating interests. Rather, participants in a policy dialogue may seek to assess the potential for developing a full consensus resolution at some later time or may put forward general, nonbinding recommendations or broad policy preferences for an agency (or other governmental entity) to consider in its subsequent decision-making. Policy dialogues can take the form of town hall meetings or many other forms and can include relatively small groups of five to ten key stakeholders or can grow to include hundreds of participants.

Advances in technology have led to new efforts to reinvigorate public debate on complex policy issues through the use of deliberative democracy and related processes. Public deliberation is central to legitimate lawmaking in democracies. Deliberative democracy refers to a process of public decision-making that uses consensus decision-making as well as elements of majority rule, particularly when a full consensus cannot be achieved. Although deliberative democracy processes vary, they generally include groups of citizens coming together to learn more about a particular public policy issue or problem and to discuss or create options for addressing the problem at hand. Through the use of instant voting via iPads, laptops, and handheld devices, small discussion groups can share their ideas or votes with larger groups as they work toward consensus.

PUBLIC-PRIVATE PARTNERING: BEST PRACTICES

Multimillion- or billion-dollar construction projects have historically been a cash cow for litigators. When one subcontractor makes a mistake or runs behind, it causes challenges for all the other subcontractors whose own work was dependent on the successful completion of the phase coming before their own. In 1987, the Construction Industry Institute at Texas A&M University created a task force focused on finding new ways to prevent and effectively manage construction disputes in the hope of breaking the increasing cycle of litigation and counter litigation that was plaguing the industry and driving up the costs of construction. The process created by the task force came to be known as **partnering**, which is defined as a long-term commitment between two or more organizations for the purpose of achieving specific business objectives by maximizing the effectiveness of each participant's resources (Anderson & Polkinghorn, 2008). Partnering relationships must be based on trust, a focus on common goals, and an understanding of each party's expectations and values. The task force subsequently issued guidelines for the implementation of partnering in construction projects, which included provisions for the management of disputes. Successful partnering requires frequent communication, relationship building between individuals and organizations, a focus on problem-solving rather than blame casting, and proactive collaborative processes that involve stakeholders at every step of the process, from planning to construction and evaluation. Box 12.1 lists the key leadership insights that help to ensure successful partnering projects. Nearly all of these insights apply to collaboration between large stakeholder groups outside as well as within the construction industry.

These insights warrant further elaboration. Although insight 1 may appear obvious, it is a relatively common industry practice to lowball bids on public contracts. Once the contract is awarded, contractors may come up with a host of reasons for asking for increases in the original bid price (bad weather, price increases for needed commodities, etc.). They typically also provide reasons for failures to meet targeted completion dates. Therefore, to build and keep trust, partners need to create reasonable expectations and be honest in the original contracted promises so as to avoid later losses of trust. Transparency is key to building and maintaining trust. The lowest bid should not always be awarded the contract. Firm reputation and realism within the bid must be taken into consideration. With the public, those who will be affected by a decision need to have their concerns heard early and often. When possible, accommodations should make the construction process less inconvenient to neighbors.

BOX 12.1. KEY LEADERSHIP INSIGHTS FOR PARTNERING

1. Establish and maintain public trust.
2. Prevent counterproductive behaviors.
3. Keep senior management informed.
4. Make decisions to increase bid competition.
5. Make friends with key stakeholders.
6. Acknowledge that the manager is not the smartest about everything.
7. Recognize showstoppers early and take action.
8. Step outside the box.
9. Realize that there will be technical problems.
10. We all succeed together.

Source: Anderson and Polkinghorn (2008, p. 176).

Insight 2 refers to problematic behaviors sometimes exhibited by individuals that make the team's success harder to achieve: insisting on having the last word, inability to admit mistakes and seek help, desires to settle scores or seek retaliation when another stakeholder makes a mistake, and taking things personally rather than remembering that this is business. This would be close to the principle espoused in *Getting to Yes* (Fisher & Ury, 1981), which advises parties to attack the problem, not the person.

Insight 3 requires that all parties be clear as to which decisions can be made at the lowest level and which require input and authority from higher up the chain of command. When peers in collaboration cannot reach agreement on a decision, then the decision quickly gets elevated to the next highest level of decision-making. They agree to abide by any decision made higher up the chain, with no hard feelings. When decisions are made higher up the chain, it is crucial that those decisions be communicated and explained to those lower on the chain, thereby closing the loop. Anderson and Polkinghorn's (2008) work shows that a common failure in partnering lies in the communication up and down the chain of command, with distrust resulting.

Insight 4 applies to nearly all government agencies and corporations that put projects out to bid. By breaking huge projects into manageable pieces, bid competition is increased as well as the ability to choose contractors with specialized abilities. When enormous, multipart projects are put out as one bid, the contracting agency loses control over who does the work because much of the work will be accomplished through the subcontracting process. By purposefully creating interdependence among successful bidders, the sponsor can build in collaboration, enhance creativity, and produce better outcomes. It also means more eyes on the work being done at each phase of the project to catch mistakes early on, when it is still possible to address them at a reduced cost.

Insight 5 is not as intuitive as it seems. Rather than cultivate superficial relationships through cocktail parties and meet and greets, the goal is to build strong relationships between key stakeholders before any problems or crises emerge. The rapport built between parties provides a deep well of support when problems invariably arise so that parties can focus on joint problem-solving rather than blame casting and seeking cover for themselves. During multiyear collaborations, as is common in the public policy arena, it is important to recognize milestones in the project and in individual careers. Celebrating retirements, project anniversaries, and other ceremonial occasions allows parties to know each other as people rather than only as functionaries; such celebrations and milestones should not be underacknowledged. When technical problems arise, as they surely will at some stage (insight 9), it is easier to normalize them and proactively work together once trust and rapport between parties has been built.

Insight 6 addresses a key assumption underlying this entire book: Managers who seek out employees' knowledge, expertise, and ideas will be more effective, respected, and responsive. In addition to reaping the knowledge of one's employee base, it is important to include the abilities of outside experts as needed: technical experts to give occasional advice, public relations specialists to help publicize success and gather public opinion, and coaches or mediators to help solve problems that arise. Asking for input and assistance when needed models the behaviors we seek in our employees as well and should be acknowledged. Otherwise, employees may act in the absence of correct information and make costly mistakes.

Insight 7 has important implications for all large-group conflict resolution processes. "One essential characteristic of megaproject leadership is the combination of vigilance for trouble and propensity for action. Paying attention to potential problems by encouraging everyone to focus on 'surprises as opportunities to learn' is a hallmark of early warning systems that has been honed to a fine art through this project" (Anderson & Polkinghorn, 2008, p. 185). When problems arise, rather than taking defensive action to build a case against the others, the goal in partnering is to engage in creative problem-solving to minimize the cost and disruption caused by the inevitable problems and rely on strong relationships and trust to avoid counterproductive behaviors. This is closely related to insight 8 (step outside the box). When problems arise or are anticipated, decision-makers need to engage in joint brainstorming to consider all possible venues for proactive conflict resolution and problem-solving. This may include going to influential community members in advance to discuss potential disruptions or hear their concerns. It may include experimenting with new methods or materials as makes sense to all involved. Many large organizations, whether public or private, get hamstrung by the idea that "we have never done that before." Leaders blaze new trails.

Insight 8 involves sharing recognition for successes throughout the partnering organizations during the project rather than only at the end. It also requires an acknowledgment that one stakeholder's loss or gain affects all the others. What if one of the contractors suffers a loss? Suppose the price of steel drops, leading to significantly increased profits for one of the partners. That partner may choose to share some of that unexpected gain with others whose commodity prices increased, thereby threatening their ability to continue in the project. Through collaborating in innovative ways, partners can take the long view and act in ways that will keep their organization's reputation and prospects strong. Finally, partnering and collaboration have been shown to improve the communication and conflict resolution skills of managers involved, thereby empowering them to succeed in other future endeavors (Anderson & Polkinghorn, 2008; Raines & Kubala, 2011). "Without much fanfare, conflict intervention practice has moved into highly specialized public and private arenas as industry insiders incorporate basic conflict resolution skills into their occupational skill sets" (Anderson & Polkinghorn, 2008, p. 167). The increased use of conflict management skills and processes by managers within public and private organizations is a testament to their utility in saving time, money, and angst for those seeking to simply get their jobs done. Lastly, we all succeed together. We are a team. As a manager, if my employee performs highly, it reflects well on me. It is not a competition.

COMMON ERRORS IN COLLABORATION: A CAUTIONARY TALE

When done well, the techniques of environmental and public policy conflict resolution can result in superior outcomes to complex problems. However, there are some key pitfalls to avoid in order to ensure that ECR techniques result in positive rather than negative outcomes.

Mistake One: Asking for Collaboration When You've Already Made a Decision

One of the most frequent mistakes made by organizations occurs when they invite stakeholder input on pending decisions and then disregard it when it's "bad news." Sometimes organizational leaders want to appear open to participation when they really are not. Decision-making processes must be transparent and adhere to the principles of procedural justice. If stakeholders are asked for their opinion, the extent to which that opinion will influence the outcome of policy should be clarified in advance. If the public's opinion will be advisory only, then those in power need to clarify their intent to retain decision-making power. To ask for the public's input and then disregard it comes at significant political risk.

Mistake Two: Not Allowing Enough Time, Space, and Money to Support Collaboration

When collaboration fails, it is often because the sponsors did not adequately prepare participants for the length of time and depth of participation necessary. Unilateral administrative decisions are generally quicker than those achieved through collaborative processes, but they often take longer than expected if challenged in court or when stakeholders drag their feet on implementation. When stakeholders gather to share information and perspectives on a policy issue, it takes time to hear from all the affected interests, to gather the high-quality information needed for a comprehensive solution, and to engage in negotiations with the help of a facilitator or other neutral. The meetings necessary to accomplish these tasks may take weeks, months, or even years. These efforts usually kick off with much fanfare but can run out of funds to support collaboration, pay the neutrals, gather and assess data, and write reports (Raines & Kubala, 2011). Collaboration fatigue occurs when stakeholders drop out of a process because it is taking too long to show results. Often, participants drop out in the middle of the process when the hardest work occurs, only to reappear near the end to voice disapproval for the consensus reached by those who stuck around for the hard work! To counteract this tendency, collaboration efforts should include clear milestones within the project to recognize and assess progress toward deadlines. An open-ended process without timelines encourages lots of talk and little progress. Timelines and deliverables should be one of the first issues discussed and agreed on by the stakeholders and sponsors. Gathering and keeping stakeholders involved in an efficient and effectual process is key, as is cultivating reasonable expectations from the outset.

Mistake Three: Proceeding in the Absence of Key Stakeholders

In any collaborative process the stakeholders most likely to participate are those who can do so as part of their regular job duties—city planners, water treatment plant managers, and paid staff of civic or environmental groups. Local citizens, small business owners, and volunteers for civic groups are least likely to attend because they are forgoing income in order to take time off of work to attend. In these cases, meetings may need to occur in the evenings or on weekends. Sponsoring agencies may need to find grant money to help subsidize the participation of key stakeholders or pay the costs of their travel. In some cases, collaboration is simply not possible due to the absence of key groups. Continuing with a process that is clearly not representative of all major interests may be worse than having no collaboration at all. Absent parties can legitimately challenge any agreements with the claim that they are biased toward the wealthy interests that participated in the collaborative process. A needs assessment should be done near the beginning of the process so that these issues can be fleshed out before any decisions are made about whether to proceed with collaboration.

ADR in the U.S. Federal Sector: Leaders, Laggards, and Trends

Each agency has pursued ADR to varying degrees, often depending upon the existence of a "keeper of the flame," meaning someone with a passionate belief in the power of conflict resolution principles and processes to bring positive change to their organization and its constituents. The type of ADR process that thrives within each agency is often quite unique to each mission and organizational culture.

U.S. Environmental Protection Agency

The U.S. Environmental Protection Agency (EPA) has long been a leader and trendsetter in the use of ADR and environmental collaboration and conflict resolution (ECCR). Its Conflict Resolution & Prevention Center (CRPC) serves as a clearinghouse for information of use to local, state, and federal agencies; tribes; and nonprofit organizations seeking to improve the environment while minimizing conflict. The CRPC provides training and support for collaborative decision-making and negotiation processes. The EPA has studied the impact of its ADR programs with an eye toward continuous improvement. They found that

- mediated cases were resolved in ⅓ less time in litigated cases;
- mediated cases required 30% fewer staff members to support than litigation;
- mediated cases required 79% fewer staff hours than litigation (https://www.epa.gov/eccr/learn-about-environmental-collaboration-and-conflict-resolution); and
- in addition to these benefits, ADR at the EPA has resulted in better relationships between stakeholders and a better public image for the agency.

The EPA is divided into ten administrative regions, each having one or more ADR specialists tasked with promoting the use of collaborative dispute resolution with external stakeholders. When needed, the EPA can assist civic volunteers or others with the resources needed to participate in ECCR processes in order to ensure balanced stakeholder participation.

Additionally, the EPA frequently uses ADR for internal workplace disputes. In 2017, the CPRC trained over 520 people in the use of collaboration and conflict resolution. Harvard's Ash Center for Democratic Governance and Innovation recognized the CPRC as one of the top 25 programs for innovation in American government. However, within the EPA, some regions are leaders and others engage in little to no ADR, so the depth of impact varies significantly.

Department of Justice

The U.S. Department of Justice (DOJ) is a natural fit for ADR, since it prosecutes criminal cases. According to the DOJ, in 2017, 75% of voluntary mediations resulted in settlements, with a 55% settlement rate for court-ordered ADR (usually mediation). Even in those cases that did not settle, attorneys and parties reported benefits from the use of ADR (DOJ, 2018). The DOJ has quantified the financial savings of ADR, with more than $15 million saved for 2017, with 13,886 days of reduced staff and 1967 months of reduced litigation (ibid.). Unfortunately, since 2016, the number of cases approved to use ADR has been slightly declining, but it is too soon to know if this is a long-term trend. Some of the cases settled using ADR have been quite high profile, including a 2018 settlement with Lance Armstrong, former cyclist, who agreed to pay $5 million to settle a suit related to false claims.

More recently, the DOJ is investigating the increased use of restorative justice approaches to some crimes. **Restorative justice** is a process that defines crime as doing harm to victims, the community, and the wrongdoer, so all of these individuals and groups must be included in efforts to put things right by creating opportunities to encounter each other and really listen. Then, with the help of the mediator, they negotiate amends while seeking to support the offender during and after the process to avoid recidivism and reintegrate him or her back into the community. Restorative practices often use victim-offender dialogues, circle processes, or other practices designed to bring healing to the victim, the community, and the offender rather than seeing crime as solely an act against "the state." While these efforts are more recent, the use of ADR and restorative justice has marked the DOJ as an innovator among government agencies using ADR processes.

U.S. Department of Education

The Department of Education (ED for short, so as not to be confused with the Department of Energy), has a broad-ranging mandate and equally broad ADR offerings. For example, there is a student aid/student loan ombudsman, an Office for Civil Rights (OCR) to investigate claims of discriminatory practices that were unresolved by lower-level educational agencies, and the Consortium for Appropriate Dispute Resolution in Education (CADRE). This last program likely has the largest footprint for ADR nationwide, with parents of special-needs children receiving facilitation and/or mediation assistance to resolve disputes over the placement and services provided for children qualified through an individualized education plan (IEP) covered under the Individuals with Disabilities in Education

Act (IDEA). The goal of these programs is to avoid both expensive and complicated litigation, but more importantly, to ensure that each student's needs are met to assure them a "free and appropriate public education." As the percentage of special-needs students is quickly increasing in the U.S. population, these programs are likely to grow.

Technology in ADR

The COVID-19 pandemic taught us to incorporate technology and virtual work in ways that will be far reaching. The use of online meeting platforms and public comment gathering has decreased the cost of participation for many individuals and groups. While face-to-face (F2F) meetings may be best for building rapport and relationships, when they require expensive and time-consuming travel, then they reduce participation. Collaborative processes are regularly carried out via virtual meetings, phone calls, web surveys, and other technologies in ways that have made direct democracy more manageable, especially for rural areas so long as internet access is available.

The use of technology to provide ADR services or solve disputes is often referred to as **online dispute resolution** (ODR). The research on ODR indicates that it can convey many of the same benefits of face-to-face processes including relatively high settlement rates, improved relationships (if the parties had a relationship or hope to have one in the future), and overall high satisfaction levels from the parties involved (Raines 2005, 2006).

CONCLUSION

The good news is that the use of collaborative processes is becoming more common in the public policy arena. Traditional ADR processes such as mediation and facilitation are supplemented by policy dialogues, negotiated rulemaking, partnering, and many others. These processes typically bring stakeholders, including regular citizens, together to share their ideas, concerns, and knowledge in the hope of reaching sound, implementable, and sustainable decisions. Governmental and nongovernmental organizations are springing up to provide support for these efforts in the hope that our increasingly complex world will be better managed through these collaborations.

ELISE AT MAIN STREET BAKERIES

During the teleconference, Elise learned that the FDA wanted to gather opinions as to the creation of a new rule related to service animals in restaurants, grocery stores, and food processing facilities. The sponsoring administrator at the FDA said his agency needed more information on the financial and other impacts of any new rules on businesses of various sizes and types and the need to be compliant with the Americans with Disabilities Act (ADA). The agency's goal is to balance the needs of disabled Americans while maintaining health and safety standards. In the end, the agency will issue a draft rule based on the input it receives from this stakeholder group, but it wants to see whether some consensus is possible between affected stakeholders about what the rule should include or exclude. They may even test proposed rule options with willing businesses to gather data before making final decisions. After learning more about this process, Elise agreed to participate in meetings with other stakeholders that would be held online for four hours each month for six months. Each participant agreed to study the financial, employee, and customer service impacts of various different rule proposals and funnel that information back to the larger group. Professional facilitators would be meeting with individual stakeholders throughout the process to gather and prepare information for presentation and discussion at the monthly meetings.

At the end of the six months, the group agreed on language for the new rule as well as a twelve-month implementation timeline so signage could be posted, and customers and staff could be educated about the new rules. The group presented its recommendations to the FDA and the FDA agreed to issue these recommendations as the draft rule. Although these negotiations took Elise away from other activities, she now feels comfortable with these changes and sees them as a potential marketing advantage for her business. Of course, she was at times frustrated to listen to the views of other stakeholders whose motives were in some ways antithetical to her own, such as pet industry representatives who wanted no limits on the type or number of animals in restaurants and grocery stores. Elise also made some important networking contacts with other businesses and regulators. She feels more in control and less at the mercy of government dictates. If given the opportunity, she would definitely participate in this kind of process again.

KEY TERMS

administrative adjudication
administrative law
administrative rulemaking
agency capture
collaborative monitoring
collaborative public management
conflict assessment
consensus building
environmental and public policy
   conflict resolution (E/PP)
environmental conflict resolution
   (ECR)

joint fact-finding
negotiated rulemaking
online dispute resolution (ODR)
partnering
policy dialogues
public disputes
restorative justice
revolving door
ripeness
sunshine laws

DISCUSSION QUESTIONS

1. Which governmental agencies regulate your company or organization? What does your organization do to work smoothly with them?
2. If you work for a regulatory agency, what steps are taken to encourage collaborative and mutually beneficial relationships with the organizations you regulate and other stakeholders?

3. How does high turnover in governmental agencies and the companies they regulate impact the ability to build collaborative relationships? What, if anything, can be done to mitigate this challenge?

EXERCISES

Public Policy Dispute Resolution Process Matching

Match each process name to its description below:
negotiated rulemaking
conflict assessment
joint fact-finding
case evaluation
policy dialogues
collaborative monitoring

Mediation

1. Jacob McGuire owns a gas station. The state's environmental protection agency has discovered that his underground gas tanks have been leaking and threatening the safety of an underground aquifer. The state intervened and spent $500,000 to clean up the mess and protect the water supply. They are now seeking repayment from Mr. McGuire, who claims he cannot and will not pay that much. The two have decided to enter into a process of _____ in which a neutral third party will help them carry out a productive dialogue with the goal of reaching an agreement that all can live with.
2. In the preceding scenario, the two sides have decided to enter a process called _____. Mr. McGuire was not convinced the pollution was coming from his gas station because there are two other stations located at that same intersection. He wanted a neutral third-party expert to look at the evidence, gather more evidence if necessary, and then share the facts of the case with both sides in a neutral manner.
3. After the process listed in number 2 was completed, it was clear that Mr. McGuire's station was indeed responsible for 90% of the pollution. However, Mr. McGuire contends the amount charged for cleanup is excessive. Therefore, they have hired a neutral expert to conduct a _____. This person will tell them what will likely happen if they go to court and spell out the strengths and weaknesses of each case.
4. The Department of Public Health is considering changing the rules regarding restaurant health inspections. Budget cuts have reduced staff levels, necessitating fewer inspections. As a result, the department has proposed using only random, surprise inspections with tougher standards so as to allow for fewer reinspections. Stakeholders are deeply concerned about the changes and include restaurant owners, local hospitals (since they request inspections after incidents of food poisoning), a local consumer

advocate group, and county inspectors. The director has decided to engage a facilitator to lead a _____ process. The director has agreed to abide by the decision reached by the group, so long as his deputy director participates in the negotiations.

5. You were hired to be the facilitator in the process mentioned in number 4. Before you begin the process, you will conduct a _____ to learn more about the parties, their positions, their interests, their willingness to participate, etc.

6. Six counties, the U.S. Fish and Wildlife Service, and the state's environmental protection agencies are all concerned about the quality and quantity of water in a specific watershed that crosses all six county lines. All counties are currently under restrictions related to new water withdrawals out of concern for an endangered fish species. Each county is pointing the finger at the other counties as the major source of river pollution. In order to learn more about the sources of poor water quality, the counties have decided to engage in a process called _____. They will share the costs incurred to measure water quality at various points throughout the watershed and determine the sources of pollution.

7. Three months ago, riots occurred after a confessed child murderer was released from custody due to a clerical error at the County Jail. The jail was supposed to release a different inmate with a similar name (Mark Johnson). While on the loose, Mr. Johnson killed two more people before being shot and killed by police. Now, local politicians, local residents, local businesses, and homeowner associations are calling for the jail to be closed and relocated to a less-populated area. The governor has decided to hold a series of _____. These are designed to share information between groups, build understandings, and discuss potential policy changes.

GOAL SETTING

1. If you work for a private company or nonprofit, make a list of those regulatory agencies that have the most impact on your organization. If your organization depends on these agencies for funding or licensing, or has other repeated interactions, make a point of getting to know at least one point of contact within that (those) agencies. These connections can be useful when any problems or questions arise and will allow you to be proactive in the management of this relationship.

SUGGESTED SUPPLEMENTAL READINGS

Bingham, L. B., Nabatchi, T., & O'Leary, R. (2005). The new governance: Practices and processes for stakeholder and citizen participation in the work of government. *Public Administration Review, 65,* 547–558. https://doi.org/10.1111/j.1540-6210.2005.00482.x

Fisher, M., & Sablan, T. (2018). Evaluating environmental conflict resolution: Practitioners, projects, and the movement. *Conflict Resolution Quarterly, 36,* 7–19. https://doi.org/10.1002/crq.21222

Moore, L. (2013). *Common ground on hostile turf: Stories from an environmental mediator.* Island Press.

Podziba, S. L. (2018). Mediating conflicts over sacred lands. *Conflict Resolution Quarterly, 35,* 383–391. https://doi.org/10.1002/crq.21217

Quinn, C. (2012, February 21). Changes to licensing proposed for half-million Georgians. *Atlanta Journal-Constitution.*

Raines, S., & Kubala, D. (2011). Environmental conflict resolution and water utilities: Applications and lessons learned. *Journal of the American Water Works Association, 103*(6).

Surowiecki, J. (2004). *The wisdom of crowds: Why the many are smarter than the few and how collective wisdom shapes business, economies, societies, and nations.* Doubleday.

U.S. Interagency Alternative Dispute Resolution Working Group. *Environmental Conflict Resolution.* https://adr.gov/about-adr/environmental-conflict-resolution/

13

Facilitating Meetings
and Large-Group
Decision-Making Processes

This meeting should have been an email.

—Everyone

This chapter will convey methods for holding effective, efficient, useful meetings of all sizes with minimal drama. Why, how, and when should people come together to bond, share ideas, and make effective decisions? This is an eternal and vital question in the post-pandemic world of (often virtual) work. There is an undeniable power in group process and decision-making, yet the presence and wisdom of the crowd should not be called upon lightly, without reflection, because it comes at a cost. Leaders lead people and use meetings to share their inspirational vision, convey needed information, seek input, and garner buy-in.

The chapter introduces screening tools managers can use to determine which issues are most likely to benefit from a collaborative decision-making process; outlines choices about meeting logistics; explains how to deal with the presence of the media during negotiations and public meetings; examines the skills, characteristics, and habits of effective facilitators; and presents a variety of potential meeting formats from which to choose.

Learning Objectives

- Determine whether a meeting is the best method for meeting desired goals.
- Explain the steps necessary to successfully convene and facilitate a large-group decision-making process.
- Describe the common skills and techniques used by large-group facilitators.
- Understand and describe the ways in which the media can be either an asset or a liability in large-group decision-making processes.
- Understand the benefits of various meeting formats and when/how to apply them.
- Describe and perform the tasks of a successful facilitator.

JOHN AT THE BUREAU OF RECLAMATION

John's agency is plagued by an antiquated system for the management of public meetings and input processes, not unlike many other state and federal government agencies. When a coal mining company seeks to open a new mine or to expand an existing operation, the mining company meets secretly with property owners, slowly buying access to desired properties until all or nearly all the needed plots have been purchased. With each purchase, they require the seller to sign a nondisclosure agreement so that the company's desire to open a new mine does not become public knowledge until all the plots needed have changed hands. Then, the company applies for a mining license from the Bureau of Reclamation. So long as the company has prepared an environmental impact statement, posts the necessary bond (to guard against bankruptcy, which could leave a mess behind), and show they have no outstanding violations on any other mines in the state, the license will be granted. Local members of the community first learn about the mine when the bureau announces the license application in the local paper, as required by state law.

Then, the employees of the Bureau of Reclamation (BR) have the unenviable duty to hold at least one public meeting to record public comments regarding the license application. To be clear, there is almost nothing the public can do to stop the granting of the license, according to state law, yet public comments must be gathered at a public meeting. People come to the meetings with concerns about large trucks on the roads, dust, and noise from blasting, and reduced property values, none of which are within the jurisdictional boundaries of the BR. Most citizens come to these meetings with the idea that their voice will matter. Sometimes they bring petitions with thousands of signatures in the hope that this will halt or delay the issuance of the mining license. It won't. Once the license is granted, another public meeting is required to announce the issuance of the license. The law was written with the explicit input of the mining companies.

Some of the legislative members on the relevant committees have previously worked as employees of the mining committees. Once they leave office, they often go into the lucrative field of lobbying, where their ties to both industry and politicians will serve them well. This is perfectly legal (or imperfectly legal, depending on your perspective). Unless a citizen can show the company is in violation of state or federal rules on one of their other mines, or they can show the company submitted false financial statements, it is nearly impossible to stop the issuance of a coal mining license. For this reason, John and his employees at the BR are generally viewed by citizens as being "in the pocket" of the mining companies. The mining companies know that the BR employees will not hesitate to revoke an existing license or issue a fine for violating any relevant environmental regulations, so they view the BR's employees as "rabid environmentalists."

On the day of the required public meetings, many of John's employees call in sick. Some of them are genuinely ill due to the stress these meetings cause. He consistently has difficulty in getting BR employees to attend the public meetings and record public comments, as required by law. At the public meetings, the BR staff sit at a head table on a raised platform at the front of the building, with computers to record public comment online. Citizens can step up to the microphone and share their concerns for up to five minutes per person. This leads to grandstanding by some local leaders, especially during election season. Usually, the speaker makes a statement against the mine and the audience applauds vigorously, hooting their support, which takes up a lot of the speaker's time. Occasionally, someone will speak in favor of the mine. This is usually someone hoping the mine will bring needed jobs to the town. In other cases, it is an existing employee for the mining company or someone who hopes to sell their property to the mining company. They are usually heckled after the first few sentences and are unable to finish their presentations. To make matters worse, some people wait all evening to speak, but at the end of the 90-minute meeting, some have not yet had their turn and the meeting ends on time.

John is concerned because these meetings leave the public with a negative view of his agency, and they can be dangerous. At the last meeting someone slashed all four tires on his car and the local sheriff had to accompany John and his staff as they left the town hall. Clearly, something needs to change. John has been doing some reading about the management of public disputes and is ready to make some radical changes to the current process— changes that do not require any modification of existing laws.

★ ★ ★

Whether you organize meetings for corporate shareholders, a group of nonprofit volunteers, or a government agency, facilitation skills are indispensable for managers and leaders, yet the majority of leaders fail in this arena. Those who fail to master the skills necessary to lead efficient and productive meetings will encounter low attendance, low levels of attention from those in attendance, and a general sense of dread at the thought of approaching meetings.

When applying alternative dispute resolution (ADR) to large-group decision-making, it is important to understand key terms such as consensus, collaboration, and deliberative democracy as applied to large-group processes. **Consensus** occurs in matters of policy when "the parties have reached a meeting of the minds sufficient to make a decision and carry it out; no one who could block or obstruct the decision or its implementation will exercise that power; and everyone needed to support the decision and put it into effect will do so" (Arthur, Carlson & Moore, 1999, p. 5). In terms of large-group processes, **collaboration** occurs when multiple parties come together to accomplish a common objective due to a shared need, through authentic conversations in which people speak frankly and listen to one another, under norms of reciprocity that require a cooperative give-and-take that enables the group to negotiate effectively (Arthur et al., 1999). **Deliberative democracy**[1] refers to the underlying principle that for laws to have true legitimacy they must be subject to authentic deliberation prior to a majority vote. Authentic deliberation means that decision-makers engage in discussion, debate, and analysis that is free from the influence of unequal power based on wealth, status, or other sources of inequality. The goal of deliberative democracy is to move toward consensus, but decisions can be made based on majority vote once deliberations have occurred and all have had a chance to participate. Deliberative democracy is a founding principle of Western governmental systems, albeit incompletely achieved in practice.

TO MEET OR NOT TO MEET, THAT IS THE QUESTION

Say it with me: Conflict comes from unmet expectations. When you find yourself in a meeting on Friday at 4:45 p.m., frustrated because you believe this meeting was superfluous and inefficient, it is likely that a lack of shared expectations exists among those present on this question: Which form of communication is best for the task at hand? Therefore, in the teams in which you frequently work, it is advisable to spend some time in a face-to-face meeting, if possible, reaching shared expectations about when the team will use different forms of communication to meet different needs and goals (Dhwan, 2021). See Table 13.1 for an example.

It is human nature to make agreements with good intention, then slip back into old habits. Dhwan (2021) suggests assigning two or more people to be "advocates" whose job it is to gently remind teammates of these agreements. They can coach and redirect them as needed, like when someone sends a long text at 7:00 p.m. on a Friday that could have either waited or been an email.

Table 13.1   Team Communication Plan

Communication Medium (tool)	Applies to	Response Time	Norms
Texts	Urgent issues with short responses required.	ASAP.	Don't include unnecessary people. Don't respond to all unless needed. Don't send on weekends or after hours except in dire circumstances.
Email	Routine announcements. Longer questions, concerns than IM.	When convenient unless specified in subject line that "urgent response requested."	When sending attachments. When longer responses are required. Don't respond to all unless needed. Not for social chatter.
Phone Call	Time sensitive. Sensitive matters not to be included in emails. Complicated matters better explained verbally.	Answer phone if available. Leave and return voicemails to share windows of availability for return call and general subject matter.	No recording unless mutually agreed. Describe privacy of your setting if need be. On speaker? Kids in the car?
Video-conference	To share screen or visuals while asking for input or decisions.	Send instant request for urgent matters. Otherwise schedule in advance.	No recording without agreement. Assume to be private unless otherwise disclosed.
F2F meeting	Reach agreement on shared norms, process, or to brainstorm joint problems. Share data and perspectives, and discuss complex issues of joint interest. Public meetings required by law.	Scheduled in advance unless emergency. Not scheduled during lunchtime or after 4:00 p.m. if possible.	Be on time or early (to socialize). Circulate agenda in advance. Attend or send delegate with authority. Minutes will memorialize agreements.

In summary, some meetings should be emails and some decisions require dialogue, perspective sharing, brainstorming, and complex decision-making. During the pandemic, many organizations scheduled more meetings to check in on employees newly working from home to ensure they had needed support and were being productive. Many organizations were overzealous, cluttering every workday with meetings of dubious merit. Reaching consensus about when to meet is the first step to ensuring effective meetings.

PUBLIC AND LARGE-GROUP MEETING DISASTERS

No one comes. Everyone comes. The room is too small. The room is cavernous and there is the faint sound of crickets. Grandstanders monopolize the microphone and shout unhelpful criticisms while those on the podium alternate between disinterest and intimidation. No one speaks at the meeting that was intended to gather input from stakeholders.[2] No clear agenda exists, and the meeting seems to wander wildly off topic. A clear agenda exists, yet the meeting wanders wildly off topic. One person dominates the discussion while seemingly indifferent to the annoyance of the others present. The issues on the agenda were comprised of announcements that could have been disseminated via email, taking people away from more pressing tasks and contributing to burnout. Important decisions could not be made during the meeting because long debates failed to lead to a consensus among decision-makers. Sound familiar? Sitting through poorly designed and executed meetings can feel like torture. Leading such a meeting is even worse. Yet with some planning and preparation, attending or leading group meetings can be invigorating and instrumental to decision-making within an organization or on issues of public policy. Whether you are a wallflower who hates public speaking or are a founding member of Toastmasters, learning the art of skillful meeting design and facilitation will serve both you and your organization well. Not only can some up-front preparation make all the difference; when you find yourself in the middle of a meeting that just isn't working, you can change course mid-stream while being transparent about your observation by saying something like, "It seems this isn't working, let's try it another way."

Why should individual stakeholders and representatives of stakeholder groups be included in decision-making? "Regular" people tend to have intimate knowledge about the problems impacting their lives, communities, and work. They often come up with innovative ideas for problem-solving—innovations that policymakers might not think of on their own. Including stakeholders, as appropriate, into decision-making processes can simply yield better, more sustainable, implementable, politically palatable decisions that uphold the ideals of democracy. As this chapter will show, collaborative processes are most useful and have maximum legitimacy when all relevant stakeholders are engaged in the process and have a voice.

Expert outside neutrals may be brought in to help with these processes or inside manager-leaders may be used. The term *facilitator* is used to refer to the leaders of these large-group processes, but the term *mediator* is also frequently used, especially with smaller groups or when the group's task is to reach a formal agreement. In truth, the terms mediator and facilitator are often used interchangeably in the literature, but for the sake of consistency, this chapter will refer to the leaders of large-group collaborative processes as facilitators. It is the role of facilitators to help "create the conditions for new understandings, solutions, agreements, deals, accords and plans to emerge" (Adler & Fisher, 2007, p. 21).

NEEDS ASSESSMENT/CONFLICT ASSESSMENT STAGE

Before diving in headfirst for a collaborative effort or to convene a group of stakeholders to discuss a contentious issue, it is critical to conduct a thorough assessment of the issue or conflict in order to determine the likelihood of success. A **conflict assessment** or **needs assessment** (two interchangeable terms) is an evaluation of the conflict or issue to determine whether a collaborative process is appropriate. What are the goals of the potential effort? The goals will have a formative impact on the process choices: Is the goal to reach a collaborative decision on an issue of policy? Is the goal to exchange information in two directions (or share information in one direction) between government and the public or between a corporation and its customers? Is the goal to build understanding and community between groups with a history of conflict in order to reduce the incidence of future conflict (such as Catholics and Protestants in Northern Ireland or African American and Korean American communities in Los Angeles)? Each of these goals would necessitate different process choices. Information about the dispute can be gathered through firsthand observation, interviews with stakeholders, reviewing documents and media reports, and so on.

The **process sponsor** is the organization that convenes and usually financially supports the large-group process of decision-making or information exchange. The sponsor is usually a governmental agency, but it can also be a private or nonprofit organization, or the process can be jointly sponsored by more than one organization. The sponsor generally conducts an assessment of the conflict or, ideally, hires an outside consultant to conduct an unbiased assessment. The assessment will determine who the key stakeholders are; their positions, interests, best alternatives to a negotiated agreement—BATNAs (see Chapter 3); the salience of the issue to each stakeholder; and their willingness to participate in a collaborative process.

The assessment will examine the ripeness of the dispute to determine whether the timing is appropriate for a large-group effort. As discussed in Chapter 12, if it is too early in the life cycle of the dispute or issue, there may not be enough information available or an adequate sense of urgency to motivate stakeholder groups to participate. Alternatively, if the issue has risen to the crisis stage and an immediate decision is needed from an authoritative body such as a court or government agency, it may be too late to begin a collaborative process. The conflict assessment must include an analysis of the dispute's ripeness. Related to ripeness, the assessment should examine the timeline available for the group to meet and accomplish its goals. If the group's task is to reach a collaborative decision, then a clear deadline is necessary. Otherwise, the group may talk and talk, with no definite end in sight, putting off difficult decisions because no deadline exists.

During the assessment stage, the sponsor must determine whether sufficient resources exist to support a collaborative process. If a facilitator, mediator, or other expert neutral will be hired, who will pay for those services and how will the resources be found? Will all the key stakeholders be able to send at least one representative to the meetings or will they need some financial support to participate? This is especially important for volunteers who represent civic groups. Participation may mean missed work, thereby making it a burden that is not sustainable for some groups. It may be possible to find grants or government agency funding to enable civic or nonprofit groups to send representatives so their concerns are not overshadowed by commercial and government interests.

If the process would benefit from having a facilitator[3] or other neutral to lead the effort, should that individual come from inside the sponsoring agency, from one of the other stakeholder organizations, or should an outside neutral be hired? The question of whether to hire an outside or inside neutral is not always simple to answer. Outside neutrals will bring process knowledge, experience in handling other complex large-group processes, and an objectivity that comes from *not* being from one of the stakeholder groups. On the other hand, there may be no money to hire an outside neutral, or the group may believe that the technical aspects of the issue are so complex that only someone from one of the stakeholder groups could possibly meet the groups' needs. If the groups decide to use an inside neutral, there needs to be a supermajority (as close to unanimous as possible) for that choice. It needs to be clear as to whether the neutral will give up his advocate role while acting as the neutral or retain his right to share his own comments and preferences. In general, the former seems to work better and with less friction than the latter option. It is also possible to combine the inside/outside neutral role in interesting ways. For example, many large government agencies have trained employees in facilitation and mediation skills. It may be possible to invite a facilitator or mediator from a government agency that is not a party to the current dispute or decision-making process. These "shared neutral" programs are designed to meet the demand for expert neutral facilitators while also saving the expense and contracting process hurdles required when hiring an outside neutral. Stakeholders may decide they wish to hire an outside neutral for the purposes of objectivity and expertise yet pair this person up with one or more inside stakeholders who will serve as a team to make process-related decisions and ensure the facilitator or other neutral has the subject-matter-specific knowledge the group feels is necessary to fully understand the issue under discussion.

What happens if a collaborative decision-making or dialogue process is undertaken, yet one or more key stakeholders were uninvited? The legitimacy of the process becomes immediately suspect. The decisions that result are likely to be seen as skewed toward the interests of those who were invited, and indeed, the resulting decisions will probably reflect the voices of those present more than those who were absent. Imagine the U.S. president is considering new environmental and safety regulations concerning oil pipelines and all the major American oil companies are invited to participate in initial talks on the matter. But the

Sierra Club and other civic groups are not invited. The result of these meetings will be viewed with cynicism by many.

Those who were not invited to participate may seek to block the implementation of any resulting policy change through the courts, claiming that the agency has overstepped its mandate from Congress or has been captured by the interests it is supposed to regulate. Clearly, identifying and recruiting the participation of all key stakeholders is critical to the success of any collaborative effort.

Which groups or individuals get invited? Try using a *snowball sampling method*. Begin by speaking with the obvious stakeholders—organizations from the public, private, and nonprofit sector that are clearly impacted by the issue under discussion. Speak to leaders within those organizations to ascertain their interest and willingness to participate in a collaborative process. Ask them, "Who else should participate?" and "Is there anyone who should not be invited to participate?" Then go to those individuals and organizations who were mentioned by others and ask the same questions. Once you stop hearing new names, it is probable that most or all of the key stakeholders have been identified. Interestingly, the answers to both of these questions are likely to indicate other groups or individuals who need to be invited to participate. Anyone who has the power or incentive to block the implementation of the group's decision is someone who has a stake in the issue. Their voices need to be heard. Remember the advice of the famous Chinese General Sun-Tzu, "Keep your friends close and your enemies closer." By inviting the most cynical or extreme groups, along with the moderate ones, you ensure that no group can later claim the process was tilted against them. More importantly, their views, and the views of all participants, will probably evolve as they take part in the group process. At a minimum, all groups should leave the process with a deeper understanding of the others' concerns and the complexity of the problem itself. These more complete understandings as well as the relationships and rapport formed between negotiators can become the basis of a future agreement and collaboration.

It is common for an individual or organization to appear halfway through the process and insist on joining the group. This happens for three main reasons: (1) a stakeholder group was overlooked during the snowball sampling mentioned above; (2) the group formed recently and now wants to be included; (3) a stakeholder group was invited early in the process but chose not to participate. Now that the process is underway and draft policies or decisions are being formulated, the group has decided that its interests are indeed impacted by the groups' activities, thereby necessitating its late inclusion into the process. In other words, they were hanging back to see what the group was going to do and whether their participation was warranted. In any event, if the process involves issues of public policy, it is best to allow latecomers to participate. This can be frustrating for those who have participated from the outset and may require the neutral to explain the benefits of including all comers, regardless of when and how they arrive.

Screening cases for the appropriateness of an alternative dispute resolution (ADR) process is a key step in the assessment stage. Screening needs to occur on two levels. The sponsoring organization or agency needs to decide whether it is willing and able to engage in a collaborative process, as do the potential participants. Box 13.1 lists the questions commonly asked in a sponsor's assessment. A sponsor should consider a collaborative process when none of the parties is seeking to set a precedent through the courts; when all key stakeholders are willing and able to participate; when adequate time exists along with a reasonably firm deadline for action; when financial and personnel resources exist to support a collaborative process; when the agency is honestly willing to share decision-making power or at least take the group's decision under advisement (and be transparent from the outset what the impact of the group's decision will be); and when ongoing communication and buy-in will be necessary for the implementation of any policy changes resulting from the process. On this last point, it should be noted that when stakeholders believe a policy or rule was created arbitrarily or that it is unreflective of their operational realities, they tend to drag their feet on implementation. Creating new policies or rules is useless if they are not implemented.

BOX 13.1. ASSESSMENT SCREENING QUESTIONS FOR PROCESS SPONSORS

1. Do the issues appear to be negotiable?
2. Are parties framing this as an issue of fundamental rights or moral values that cannot be negotiated?
3. Are parties seeking to establish a legal precedent?
4. Are the interests clearly defined?
5. Where does this issue fall on the spiral of unmanaged conflict? Is this issue a priority for stakeholders?
6. Is there enough time for parties to deliberate or is it an emergency? Is there a deadline that would help avoid endless negotiations?
7. Who are the parties and how is power balanced among them?
8. Are there any parties/stakeholders who can accomplish their goals without negotiation?
9. Power imbalance: Are there issues of race, class, culture, ethnicity, education, or ethnography that will make it difficult for one or more key stakeholders to participate on equal footing? If so, is there anything that can be done to overcome these differences or enable fuller participation?
10. Will the sponsor be able to provide or locate the financial and personnel resources necessary to support this process?
11. Is the agency's leadership truly willing to engage in a good faith effort at shared decision-making?
12. Will the parties, including the sponsor, continue to interact with one another in the future? In other words, are they interdependent? Will any agreement require ongoing participation, collaboration, and buy-in to be fully implemented?

Source: Carpenter & Kennedy (2001, pp. 158–168).

When the sponsor's assessment is complete, create a written summary that identifies the key stakeholders along with their interests, positions, and willingness to negotiate; the substance of the problem itself including various ways to define the problem; the negotiability of the key issues; any ethical dilemmas or values conflicts inherent in the problem; and the various processes that may be used to constructively address the problem. Box 13.2 summarizes the elements of the needs assessment.

In addition to the sponsor's assessment, each potential stakeholder will need to determine for themselves whether their interests and resources are suited to participation in a collaborative process. What will be the impact of sitting it out, while the process may go on without your organization? Are your organization's needs more likely to be met through court action? How important is it to cultivate ongoing collaborative relationships with regulatory agencies and other

---

BOX 13.2. COMMON ELEMENTS IN A NEEDS ASSESSMENT

Substance of the Problem

1. What description is the most constructive way to define the problem?

   a. Conflict focuses on different interests.
   b. Conflict focuses on strongly held values.
   c. Conflict focuses on perceived differences that do not really exist.

2. What is the most constructive way to define the problem?
3. What are the central issues?
4. What are the secondary issues?
5. Are the issues negotiable?
6. What are the key interests of each party?
7. What interests do parties have in common?
8. What positions have been taken?
9. What other options for resolution exist?

Procedures

1. What do parties think about using some form of conflict management? What suggestions do they have?
2. Does a consensus process serve the parties' interests?
3. What constraints might affect the structures of a conflict management process (timing, legal activities, resources)?
4. What other obstacles must a process overcome?
5. Which parties are experienced in using alternative dispute resolution procedures?
6. What are the chances for success?

Source: Carpenter & Kennedy (2001, pp. 158–168).

stakeholders on this issue? How might your brand be impacted by participation or nonparticipation? Will your organization be in a better position to influence the outcome of the decision-making process through participation or nonparticipation? Will implementation of a new policy or regulation be easier as a result of participation in the formulation process? Will your organization learn more about the issue and its competitors or other stakeholders through participation? What is the overall ratio of benefits to costs for participation? Do not forget that the middle ground is always possible: participate now and decide later if participation should be ended.

Convening Stage

Convening is the process of bringing stakeholders together to design the process jointly and begin the dialogue or negotiation. If the needs assessment led to the conclusion that a collaborative process is a good idea, the next phase is to convene the key stakeholders and begin discussions about the process itself. During the assessment phase, key stakeholders were identified and all or most of them were interviewed to learn more about their willingness to participate, their motivation to negotiate in good faith, and any resources they might need to fully participate. Facilitators do not get to choose which individuals serve as delegates from the various stakeholder groups. However, if they can use their influence or make suggestions, "In multi-party cases, mediators must perpetually scan for participants who will imagine the big picture, enhance trust, integrate disparate interests, coordinate tasks and emerge as bridge-builders" (Adler & Fisher, 2007, p. 21).

This is the phase during which primary stakeholders work together to craft the problem statement or task description that will guide the group's time together. The sponsor may seek to suggest the problem statement and task description, but in the end, participants will need to concur with the framing of this statement to consent to participate in the process.

During the convening stage participants work with the facilitator to craft and/or consent to the ground rules and procedures that will guide their time together, including the length and frequency of meetings, rules about who speaks when, and decision rules.

A word about decision rules is in order at this point. While 100% consensus is a wonderful goal, in a large and diverse group it can be nearly impossible to reach. The rule of 100% consensus is well intentioned, but it is only workable in a relatively small group. It gives attention and power to those who seek to undermine collaboration and retain the status quo by acting as spoilers. A **spoiler** is someone who uses his power to sabotage the group's progress in order to gain attention or further his own goals. Spoilers usually hold significantly more extreme views than the majority of process participants and can use consensus processes to stall or sabotage outcomes they wish to avoid.

When leading large-group decision-making processes, consider selecting something short of a 100% consensus rule unless the agreement of every stakeholder is necessary for the implementation of any resulting decision. For example, a "consensus minus one" rule will make it clear to the group that if only one party does not join in on the agreement, it will go forward without their support. Other options include a vote that requires a supermajority. The percentage required to reach agreement is something that can be negotiated among group members. The key is to make decision rules at the outset of the negotiation, rather than waiting until it is time to take a vote or reach a decision. At that point, those who are unhappy with the agreement will insist on 100% consensus and those in favor will prefer a simple majority. This is the first issue to negotiate.

The convening stage is the time to teach basic consensus-building skills, including the difference between interests and positions, listening and framing skills, and techniques for keeping constituents informed regarding the negotiation's progress. In fact, it can be a facilitator's duty to train participants in facilitation skills with the goal of helping them eventually take over the facilitator's role. The best facilitators are those who are able to model and train parties these skills to empower them to create a self-managing group, especially if the group will be together permanently.

During the convening phase it is crucial to build in social and networking time so the participants can get to know each other as people. In most cases, dialogue must come before negotiation—this means the participants simply need to get to know one another, overcome any preexisting stereotypes or assumptions made in the absence of real interactions, and develop the trust necessary to have frank and open discussions.

During the convening stage it is also important to create a timeline for process milestones for the group's work. Some groups work in an ongoing manner, making decisions as necessary to manage shared resources or deal with recurring challenges, rather than having a specific timeline for completion. In these processes it remains important to have timelines for decisions and milestones so as to discourage endless discussions without resulting decisions.

In order to evaluate the efficiency, efficacy, and value of the large-group process it is important to build in evaluation methods from the very beginning. For example, a pretest/posttest may be crafted in order to understand the impact of the process on the management of a resource such as water supply, forest health, hospital quality of care, and so on. The development of evaluation tools will ensure the group has clear goals and methods for evaluating progress toward the goals.

During the Process

Once the meetings or negotiations are underway, the facilitator plays a role in ensuring clear and consistent communication between the negotiators and the constituencies they represent. Any negotiation in which participants represent broader constituency groups is in effect a *two-level game*, to borrow a concept from game theory. In other words, *intra*group negotiations occur to arrive at unified bargaining positions or to respond to offers made. Concurrently, *inter*group negotiations occur between stakeholder groups. While the traditional facilitation role occurs in the intergroup negotiations, facilitators may also be called upon to assist with the intragroup negotiations that must successfully occur in order for a stakeholder group to effectively participate in the larger discussions. Many negotiations fall apart because one or more representatives could not get their constituents to agree upon a negotiating position or agree how to respond to a specific offer. Or worse, the representative commits to a decision that her constituents then refuse to implement. This reduces trust and can end a negotiation permanently.

Be on the lookout for **collaboration fatigue**, which is the weariness that sets in among negotiators after talks have been ongoing for months or even years, especially if progress seems elusive or minimal. The signs of collaboration fatigue include falling meeting attendance, growing impatience or inattentiveness of representatives, and a decreased willingness to financially support the collaborative process. Through the use of ongoing evaluation tools it may be possible to gain feedback from stakeholders that will enable process changes to be made that will help avoid collaboration fatigue.

For public policy decision-making efforts, keep in mind the importance of timing—election cycles, agency leadership changes, funding cycles, and personnel changes. Few large decisions are made or endorsed by politicians just before an election. However, new dialogue or collaborative processes are often endorsed prior to elections, so long as the timeline for decisions occurs comfortably after the election. Politicians and agency leaders may flock to collaborative processes not only because they produce better-quality decisions, but because they provide political cover. A decision reached through a consensus process is likely to occur only if a supermajority of stakeholders reaches agreement. By delegating decision-making authority to a stakeholder group, politicians can give them "credit" and declare the outcome to be reached through a fair and democratic process. Be sure to pay attention to the timing of a collaborative process in order to maximize the chances of finding and sustaining political and leadership support. Yet a collaborative project supported by one politician or agency leader may be abandoned by the next, especially if it is viewed as the "pet project" of the previous administrator. Similarly, each participating organization will have a delegate to the stakeholder group. For long-term negotiations, the group will inevitably need to weather retirements, family leaves, and personnel changes for individual delegates. Recognizing these milestones can become a unifying tradition within the group. Welcoming new members and getting them up to speed can be crucial to the group's continued success, as this story illustrates:

In one case involving proposed development in an environmentally sensitive area, leadership came primarily through the government's lead lawyer. As with most effective negotiators, he was an avid listener who anticipated the other parties' issues, worked hard to figure out potential solutions before they raised concerns, and created a vision for the future that integrated everyone's interests. This resulted in a level of trust that enabled significant progress. Then, overnight, everything changed and his replacement, who had not been involved with the previous discussions, had different ideas and a less collaborative and more adversarial style. He did more talking than listening, the collaboration ended, and the deal fell apart (Adler & Fisher, 2007, p. 21).

While finding and keeping the right people at the table is an ongoing struggle, it is also important to realize that the project is bigger than any individual stakeholder. Stakeholders should be encouraged to keep others from their organization in the wings and in the loop in case they need to step away from the project for any reason. While this is not always possible, anything the manager-facilitator can do to ensure the longevity of the project beyond the career changes of any one person will contribute to the collaboration's ultimate success. Be creative—Raines and Kubala (2011) detail how their collaborative effort lost its main "keeper of the flame" when the project manager left the U.S. Army Corps of Engineers to go to work for a private company. His contribution was so pivotal the group found funds to hire him through his private company to finish the project under his stewardship.

Agreements generally take one of three forms: (1) agreements in principle outline the process through which the problem will be solved, for example "a committee of delegates will select the best person for the position"; (2) each issue is negotiated separately until all issues are resolved (also known as the building block approach); or (3) an entire package of proposals is developed that addresses all issues in a comprehensive manner and is accepted or rejected (Carpenter & Kennedy, 2001). As discussed in Chapter 3, it may be helpful for the group to develop objective criteria against which any proposal can be examined. A plan and timeline for implementation should be part of the agreement, rather than considered as an afterthought. Before any final agreement can be reached, each representative must take the draft agreement back to his or her constituents and gain their approval before a final decision can be made. Once the agreement has been finalized and any required signatures attained, the next step is implementation.

Implementation after Agreement

Once regular meetings cease or become less frequent, and with the expected challenges that come with the implementation of any agreement, it is not unusual for preexisting animosities to return or trust to wane. For implementation to go smoothly, some form of ongoing monitoring will likely be necessary along with a plan to deal with those who fail to fulfill their commitments. Periodic meetings may be necessary to discuss progress regarding implementation, maintain cooperative morale, or even renegotiate parts of the agreement as unexpected circumstances or unforeseen problems arise during the process of implementation. Evaluation of the process and its ongoing impact on the policy issue should continue in order to institutionalize and improve the success of collaborative efforts, while gaining feedback that may be of continued use as the project matures. Process evaluation is an important topic, but beyond the scope of this text. Luckily, there are many useful guides to evaluating large-group decision-making processes from which you can borrow survey questions and ideas for data-gathering (see Emerson et al., 2009; Orr, Emerson & Keyes, 2008).

The Role of the Media in Public Disputes

As discussed in Chapter 12, sunshine laws generally require that decision-making meetings held by government agencies be open to the public, and therefore, the media. In truth, most policymaking meetings are simply not riveting enough to attract media attention, but everyone has become "the media" in that recorded meetings or sound bites get posted on social media sites. Many amateur media buffs seek attention, which can be remedied by pulling them aside one on one and using your ninja negotiation skills (Chapter 3) to learn more about what they want and why. In general, it is best to assume that all conversations, meetings, emails, and texts can become public, and act accordingly.

When an agency is operating smoothly and no crisis exists, the media is notably absent. Yet, when there has been a mistake or a crisis has arisen that necessitates a change in course or new policy action, then the media is more likely to appear. Unlikely as it seems, the media can be a positive asset for collaborative governance and decision-making, but many leaders miss opportunities to develop a positive working relationship with the media or to use them appropriately as a venue for communicating with the public about important policy issues. Chapter 2 presented Maslow's hierarchy of needs. Recall that the most basic needs are for food, shelter, and physical security. Any issue of public policy that deals with these most basic needs is likely to be heated, evoke passionate pleas on all sides of the issue, and therefore pose the greatest likelihood of attracting media attention. These issues may be about jobs, food safety, housing demolition or creation, prices for heating oil or food staples, and so on. People fear losing control over these areas of their lives, hence the pervasive distrust of many governmental institutions that have the power to impact citizens on these issues. The media often oversimplify policy issues into hysteria-producing sound bites that attract an audience to their stories with headlines such as "Is the meat in your refrigerator dangerous?" or "The city government has decided to demolish five homes along the banks of the East River—could yours be next?" Any hint that the government is meeting in secret or withholding information from the media will only feed these fears. The trick in working with the media is the same as it is in working with any other organization or individual—meet needs through interest-based strategies. Help them meet their need for interesting news that attracts an audience and provides the public with accurate, useful information in a timely, preferably written, fashion.

As many public officials and higher-level bureaucrats have learned, contact with the media can result in incomplete and factually inaccurate stories that can embarrass managers and end careers. This can lead managers to try to avoid contact with the media, yet their very avoidance is seen as a challenge to reporters, a sign that the managers are hiding information from the public. What can be done?

First, organizational leaders, upper-level managers, and professional policy facilitators should cultivate positive relationships with media representatives in their regions. If you work for the Department of Education, you should know the names of the reporters who are typically tasked to cover education stories in your city and state. Be careful not to waste their time; they are constantly running under tight deadlines. They will only meet with people who have something of interest to tell them. When you know changes are in store for your organization, set up meetings with relevant reporters to share the news of these impending changes with them. Tell them about your plans to use a collaborative process that engages the public and key stakeholders. Explain to them the reasons your organization is willing to undertake this type of process. Invite them to attend as observers. Observers to the negotiations cannot speak or ask questions unless invited to do so by the facilitators or key stakeholders. Tell them they can funnel questions to you, and you will seek answers from the participants, as time allows. Ask them to refrain from popping in and out during sessions, but instead to be present for the entire work session. This will help avoid their tendency to look for a sound bite to take out of context but is no guarantee. Ask for their advice, since they probably know who the key stakeholders are, as well as some of the history on any contentious public issues. They often have a good feel for the political dimensions of policy issues and may be willing to point out stumbling blocks in advance. Prepare news releases to share with them when important decisions or milestones have been met within the group process. These press releases should include the proper spelling and titles for all participants as well as some background information on the issue itself (for example, "Why is clean water important to our economy?"), define technical terms in layperson's language, and include a brief description of the collaborative process itself. Remember to keep all press releases brief and succinct to maximize the likelihood they will be used as written. These releases should be agreed upon by all key stakeholders or a subcommittee elected by the larger group.

In some contentious policy negotiations, participants may wish to agree upon ground rules for dealing with the media. For example: "We agree not to speak to the media individually until the negotiations are over, but to instead craft mutually agreed-upon press releases." This strategy reduces the incidence of having individual stakeholders trash-talking their fellow negotiators via the media when talks get difficult. Assure the media of your intention to share information with the public, rather than withhold it—especially the information they need to reach informed opinions on policy matters. In some ways, you are educating the reporter about the ways in which she can serve as a conduit for information to the public while developing a deeper level of understanding and analysis on the policy matters relevant to your organization's mission. With a little luck and some finesse, you will turn the media's presence from a liability into an asset. Box 13.3 summarizes these guidelines for working with the media.

BOX 13.3. GUIDELINES FOR WORKING WITH THE MEDIA

1. Cultivate long-term relationships with the reporters in your region who cover issues relevant to your organization's mission.
2. Invite the media to observe, with provisos.
3. Ask for advice.
4. Craft ground rules for communicating with the media.
5. Share information through periodic press releases.
6. Assure reporters they will have opportunities or venues for asking questions or conducting interviews.
7. Partner with media representatives to get needed information to the public.

CHARACTERISTICS OF SUCCESSFUL LARGE-GROUP FACILITATORS

Few organizations have had more experience facilitating group decision-making than the UN member bodies. It is not surprising the United Nations has developed specific advice for their team members who frequently facilitate meetings comprised of culturally diverse stakeholders seeking to collaborate for mutual gain. Box 13.4 paraphrases the characteristics of a successful facilitator, based on the materials developed by the UN Economic and Social Council.

To add to the boxed list, Adler and Fisher (2007) argue for facilitative leaders to "foster better communication, brokering concurrence, taming tough problems and managing the inevitable conflicts that occur in politically charged environments" (p. 21). They add that facilitators do everything from arranging the room and setting out the cookies to addressing the "political choreographies" that address "complex intellectual and emotional moves that are needed to bring a dialogue or negotiation to a productive fruition" (p. 21). Perhaps that is why many observers have noted that successful facilitators seem to exude humility, transparency, and the ability to think on their feet, change course when necessary, maintain healthy emotional boundaries, remain calm in the face of the storm, show empathy, and remain flexible while understanding the need for structure. Facilitators are resilient, adaptive, and proactive at managing positive change and constructive communication between disparate groups and individuals. While individuals may be born with natural endowments that make them great facilitators, these skills and techniques can also be honed through practice and purposeful application.

Habits of an Effective Facilitator

Whether you are leading a meeting of five or five hundred, mastering the skills of facilitation can be key to ensuring productive group performance and decision

---

BOX 13.4. CHARACTERISTICS OF SUCCESSFUL FACILITATORS

1. Belief in your group's capacity to solve their own problems.
2. Well-developed communication skills.
3. Knowledge of the group's needs, expectations, and potentials.
4. The ability to work with a diverse group without forcing your own preferences or beliefs (i.e., low ethnocentricity).
5. Perseverance and patience.
6. Knowledge of multiple approaches and willingness to change an approach that isn't working. (i.e., knowledge and flexibility).
7. Ability to monitor, assess, and summarize the outcomes and impacts of the group's efforts.

Source: http://www.unevoc.unesco.org/ftleadmin/user_upload/docs/04-facilitator _guide.pdf

BOX 13.5. PRIMARY TASKS OF EFFECTIVE FACILITATORS

1. Establish an agenda.
2. Keep the discussion focused on the agenda.
3. Clarify statements.
4. Summarize statements.
5. Explore ideas.
6. Encourage all members to participate.
7. Maintain a calm and positive tone.
8. Enforce the ground rules fairly.
9. Transparently describe what is happening.
10. Offer process suggestions.
11. Supervise record keeping.
12. Test for agreements.
13. Manage communications and activities between meetings.
14. Verify that constituents are informed.

Source: Carpenter & Kennedy (2001, pp. 158–168).

making. The facilitator takes on a mantle of both responsibility and authority. If the facilitator is neutral in regard to the decisions under discussion, she will generally be trusted to be fair, unless her actions lead some parties to believe otherwise. If the facilitator is not neutral regarding the issues under discussion, then trust may need to be earned through a display of fairness, impartiality, and competence. Box 13.5 displays the key tasks of effective facilitators. Some of these tasks require additional elaboration.

A mistake made by many a formal or informal facilitator is the failure to work with the parties in advance to create an agenda around which there is agreement. In advance of the meeting, send around a draft agenda or a request for agenda items. Work with the key stakeholders to ensure the agenda is of sufficient interest to draw players to the table and is manageable based on the available time frame for the meeting. Make sure the meeting's sponsor and facilitator are clear as to the goals of the meeting. Is the goal to make a joint decision? To build rapport among parties? To provide a venue for communication between representatives of different work units or organizations? The goals of the meeting should be clear to all invitees, listed when appropriate.

Once the meeting commences, do your best to stick to the agenda, using good time management skills, while remaining open to addressing critical issues that arise and obstruct progress. Be sure that each agenda item is indeed something that requires discussion, brainstorming, or negotiation during the meeting (see Table 13.1). Announcements can be shared in advance of the meeting via memos or other venues and should not take up the bulk of the time assigned for the meeting. For each agenda item, ask yourself, "Can this be addressed outside a group meeting? If so, how? If not, then is it appropriate fodder for group meeting time?" If a public meeting is required in order to announce a draft policy, then consider using the meeting to accomplish additional goals, such as listening to feedback from stakeholders or gaining input as to potential process choices that may improve the final decision or its implementation.

Occasionally, entirely new items will arise during the meeting that threaten to swamp the groups' ability to address the preexisting agenda items. At that point, it makes sense to ask the group whether they prefer to discard the original agenda for the more pressing issue, or whether a separate meeting should be called to deal with that issue. If the group tends to get off track easily, you may choose to create a "parking lot." A parking lot is a list of issues that one or more of the members wish to discuss but is not on the agenda. By placing these on the parking lot list, the facilitator is putting the issue to the side, temporarily. At the end of the meeting, with whatever time remains, the facilitator will tackle those issues that have made their way to the parking lot list. If time runs out, then the parking lot list will become part of the next meeting agenda or it can be addressed through online discussion boards or other communication used in between the regular meetings. When meetings lack clear agendas, they tend to get bogged down in details or easily sidetracked into nonessential issues. As the adage says, "If you don't know where you are going, you probably won't get there."

Be careful to avoid starting meetings late. While cultural variations should be considered, starting late tends to lead to a slippery slope: The first meeting started five minutes late, so those who were on time come five minutes late to the next meeting. Those who were five minutes late now come ten or more minutes late. Therefore, the second meeting starts ten minutes late. Then, each subsequent meeting gets started later and later. Do not be tempted to skip breaks or shorten the lunch breaks to account for starting late or having an overly packed agenda. These breaks not only provide the respite needed for parties to maintain their patience and stamina; they also provide a venue for building rapport and informal discussions of important issues.

Facilitators serve their group by frequently clarifying the meaning of what group members have said. "If I understand you correctly, you said . . ." This method serves to ensure that everyone present hears and understands the same message, to the extent possible. By summarizing progress that has been made, facilitators highlight areas of consensus that have occurred while organizing the group's focus on the next task at hand. Summarization helps to move the group forward from where they have been to where they are going. When working in large groups, facilitators are faced with some participants who can clearly articulate their thoughts and concerns, and others who have more difficulty in formulating their thoughts into words. Once one individual is embarrassed publicly, it creates a chilling effect on others who may be timid about speaking up and sharing their concerns or ideas. Facilitators often need to invite participants to further explain their concerns and engage in an exploration of those ideas so they feel their participation is welcomed, even if it requires some coaching or assistance on the part of the facilitator: "Can you tell me more about your concern? I'm not sure I understand," or, "It is important that we hear from everyone and understand your needs. Could you give me an example?" This approach will help those quieter members feel able to participate, as will creating multiple mechanisms for input such as the chat function in virtual meetings (Cain, 2012).

Likewise, there may be some who "dominate the airspace" in the room by sharing every thought that comes into their head or responding to every comment made by others. In these situations, it may be necessary to speak to that person during a break and invite them to help create some space for others to participate. It can help to explain that some participants might not speak up until there is a silence to fill, or when they are sure that no one else is trying to get a word in. By "making room for others," the participation of all parties will be possible. Discussing norms or ground rules for sharing the discussion space can be helpful prior to the commencement of the actual dialogue or negotiation in order to set the tone for a discussion in which all participate and none dominate. Introverts have good ideas too. Enforcing the ground rules fairly helps the facilitator maintain trust and the efficiency of the process.

Large-group meetings and collaborative processes can be exhausting. Emotions may be high; listening to others for long periods can be draining. Facilitators can assist by keeping a positive tone, pointing out the progress that has been made, and normalizing the difficulty of decisions such as those under consideration. By emoting a calm, reassuring demeanor, facilitators can help to assure parties that the task ahead of them is indeed "doable."

By being transparent and explaining their techniques and observations, facilitators not only help to build trust with the parties, but they also help to steer the process away from potential pitfalls or icebergs. For example, when the facilitator notices that parties seem to be mentally "checking out," he can say, "It seems like we are getting pretty fatigued at this point. How about a quick break?" or after presiding over bickering between the parties he might say, "I'm not sure the last few minutes have helped us to reach our goal. Let's try breaking into smaller work groups and focus on these remaining questions, okay?" By describing what they are doing and why, and by offering process suggestions, facilitators can assist parties as they navigate the shoals of the dialogue or negotiation process.

Facilitators need to be transparent when they test for agreement, meaning the facilitator affirmatively asks the parties to confirm whether they agree with a particular decision or consensus the group has been working toward. Depending on the group's rules for decision-making, which were discussed at the outset of the group's convening, decisions may require 100% consensus or something less than that. Regardless of the decision rule, facilitators need to ask the group to affirm any decisions made and entered into the minutes.

One of the most important and under-recognized tasks of facilitators is to keep meeting minutes and facilitate communications between meetings. Meeting minutes do not need to be akin to transcripts that show who said what and exactly what was said. In fact, the parties and facilitator may need to negotiate from the outset as to what goes into the minutes. If the meetings are to be frank, it may be better to refrain from identifying speakers in the minutes, but instead stick to a basic summary of the discussions. The minutes should also include a detailing of any agreements reached and action items assigned to parties as a result of the meeting. The minutes should indicate when the next meeting will be held and any activities to occur in the interim.

During the periods between meetings, facilitators can further the success of the group by working to confirm that each stakeholder representative at the negotiations has been communicating with her constituents concerning the direction in which the negotiations are headed and any tentative agreements being made. It is truly devastating to a group process and morale to learn that a stakeholder representative at the negotiations has voiced support for a proposal, only to find out that the group she represents disagrees with that decision and withdraws their support for the decision or for the entire negotiation process. Therefore, one key ground rule for successful large-group decision-making processes is to keep your organizations informed and confirm their support before any decisions or commitments are made by the negotiators at the table.

Be sure to include an evaluation tool to gain feedback as to how to make future meetings as efficient and successful as possible. Consider using an exit survey that participants leave by the door; or for participants within an organization, send around a brief online survey to gather this information. Strive for continual improvement as a facilitator and consensus builder to encourage rather than discourage continued participation from your members.

Choosing among Meeting Formats

The menu of meeting formats is as varied as the decisions undertaken by large groups. Understanding the pros and cons of each format can assist managers as they select the most appropriate process for the issue at hand. This is not an exhaustive list of process options; processes can be custom-made to meet the needs and constraints of each group or issue.

Charrette: A charrette is a method of organizing thoughts from experts and the public into a structured gathering that is conducive to creative problem-solving. A charrette refers to an intensive period of workshop-style meetings that typically occur over one to three days. In a charrette, the group typically divides into smaller working groups and then reports back to the full group at the end of the work session. The findings of each subgroup may become the fodder for additional dialogue for the present or a future charrette. This format allows for maximal input from a large and diverse group of participants and increases the opportunity for creative ideas to arise.

Town Hall Meeting: A town hall meeting is an informal gathering open to all members of a community. Typically, the meeting centers on a specific theme, such as "health-care reform" or "improving public education," and local elected leaders or high-ranking bureaucrats are on hand to answer questions from the audience in a talk-show fashion. These meetings are helpful when a leader wishes to make his or her views known on a particular subject but are less suited to sharing complex information with the public; nor do they engage the public in deliberation or decision-making. If speakers are not screened, it can result in grandstanding by those seeking to compete with the elected officials for the public's attention or votes.

Twenty-First-Century Town Hall Meetings (or Deliberative Democracy Dialogues): A relatively recent hybrid process combines the most important elements of **deliberative democracy** and the old-fashioned town hall meetings. These gatherings occur around specific topics such as "The Walter Reed Re-Use Plan," which examined ways to redevelop and use the campus of the former

Walter Reed Hospital in Washington, DC, or "Listening to the City," which gathered the opinions of New Yorkers concerning the fate of the Ground Zero site. This meeting format involves hundreds of regular citizens and begins with a presentation of various ideas or options along with the pros and cons of each option. Then citizens divide into smaller groups (of up to ten), with one facilitator at each table. Participants are asked to discuss each option, generate any questions, and offer alternative options. These are shared using computers at each table and are grouped into themes by process organizers. These are presented to the whole group and the meeting proceeds in an iterative process. At the end of the meeting, each individual votes on the option they prefer. The outcomes of these gatherings are shared with governmental decision-makers who consider these findings as they make final decisions on these matters. These deliberative dialogues are becoming increasingly popular because they allow the public and relevant stakeholders to learn more about the complexity of policy problems, discuss and debate various approaches to dealing with those problems, and then communicate their preferences back up the decision-making chain. As a positive spillover, these events often increase the sense of community among citizens and build social capital.

Open Space Technology (OST): OST is a process somewhat like the charrette, but with a more specific format and rules. OST is used for strategic planning within organizations as well as for community-based decision-making. An OST process takes one to three days and can be used for anywhere from ten to hundreds of people. The key is that all are invited, with the knowledge that those who come have some interest or passion for the issue under discussion. The beauty of OST is that it creates a format for a group to self-organize, create an agenda for workshop activities, and end with a "next steps" list of action items for group members or committees to pursue after the end of the process (Harrison, 2008). Basically, the convener creates a framing question such as "How can we reinvigorate our local economy?" or "What changes should our company make to maximize our success over the next 10 years?" Participation is voluntary. At the beginning of the gathering, the framing question is posted for all to see. Participants sit in a large circle with a whiteboard or large flip chart at the ready. A *marketplace*, or time and space matrix, is posted with blank spaces awaiting volunteers to post topics for smaller-group discussion (see Table 13.2). Anyone interested in hosting a discussion on a particular idea stakes claim to one of the boxes on the marketplace matrix, acts as facilitator for that discussion, and prepares a summary of discussions to share with the larger group at the end of the day. This is called a marketplace for a specific reason: each topic or idea posted is competing with the others to gather participants for the discussion sessions. If an idea does not appeal to others or is not viewed as important, no one will come. This is itself instructive when one or two people in a group may care passionately about an issue but come to realize they are in the minority on the issue. If two participants post similar discussion topics, no problem—more than one group can address the same issue and see if they arrive at the same or different conclusions.

The OST process has a couple of catchy ground rules, including the *Law of Two Feet*: if you do not like what is happening in a session or feel you are not

Table 13.2 Marketplace Time-Space Matrix

Time	Room A	Room B	Room C	Room D
9:00–10:30				
10:45–12:15				
1:30–3:00				
Reporting Session, 3:30–5:00				

Source: Harrison (2008).

being heard, you simply leave and go to another session. This creates an imperative for discussion facilitators to remain on topic and facilitate a dialogue in which everyone feels heard and respected. Another ground rule is that all are invited and *whoever comes are the right people.* Those who are interested in the topic will likely be there. Don't try to find a perfect time when all can attend; it will delay progress. After the reporting session, the group should prioritize its tasks and develop action items for individuals or groups to work on during and after the OST session. This can be done by simple voting or consensus-building discussions. OST is not an appropriate format for issues of low salience to stakeholders or for those issues in which an authoritative decision-maker is unwilling to share decision-making power with the group. Nothing would be more damaging than for a group of committed stakeholders to engage in a process such as this only to learn their recommendations were disregarded by governmental or organizational leaders.

Traditional Public Meeting Format: As the chapter's opening vignette indicates, one option is to use the old-school traditional public meeting format. In this format, notices are made to announce a public meeting on a particular topic. Agency or organizational leaders sit on a raised dais at the front of the room and record comments raised by members of the public. Anyone who wants to speak can take a turn speaking, usually by signing up on a speaker's list just before the meeting commences. The time for public comments is fixed, commonly at 30 to 60 minutes, with each speaker allowed to speak for between two and five minutes (typically). Depending on the regulations governing the meeting, the leaders at the front of the room may simply record public comments or they may respond to questions or comments. There are a few challenges associated with this format. First, if the matter is contentious, members of the public turn out in droves, seeking to influence the decision being made, but often these meetings occur late in the decision-making process and comments are unlikely to change the outcome. Second, local politicians, members of the media, or irate citizens use their time at the microphone to voice their anger, hurl insults, or stir up the crowd's passions rather than calmly voicing concerns or asking non-rhetorical questions. Third, members of the public rarely understand the purpose of the public meeting and the mission or constraints of the managers leading the meeting. In the mining example used at the beginning of this chapter, members of the public incorrectly believed that if they turned out in large numbers, brought petitions, and had their local officials voice disapproval, then the mining license would not be issued. Because they did not understand the factors that go into the issuance of a mining license, they went to the meeting with the false belief that their opposition mattered. Once they realized their numbers and opposition were immaterial to the factors under which a license could be denied, they became outraged, with negative consequences.

So why do so many organizations stick to the traditional meeting format? It can be useful for one-way information sharing or to fulfill a statutory requirement to hold a public meeting. It may suffice on issues of low salience to stakeholders, as evidenced by traditionally low turnouts. When true input is needed, when an agency or organization needs to share complex information with the public, or when public or stakeholder opinions are strong, this format is generally insufficient and outdated.

Small Group Public Meetings: As in the story from the Bureau of Reclamation in this chapter, sometimes it is important for government agencies or other organizations to both receive information or comments from the public and share information with them. In this case they can consider using the traditional public meeting format or they can consider various alternatives to enhance authentic information sharing between groups. If the issue is likely to evoke strong opinions or it involves complex technical issues, it may be best to consider using a format that breaks the issue and the crowd into more manageable pieces. Consider placing multiple tables around the room with a topic placard clearly visible on each table. In the bureau's example, one table would address "blasting and noise," another would address "water concerns," and still another might address "property values." Place a staff member at each table with either a computer or a pad of paper on which to record comments and questions from each attendee. Staff members can answer questions on a one-on-one basis as they are able and promise an individual response through a follow-up call or email on those issues that need further research. Staff members can share information about the agency's mission, constraints, or mandates as well as redirecting citizens to other agencies or elected officials who can address issues outside their own organization's mandate. By splitting the crowd up into smaller groups with no microphone, managers can avoid the grandstanding and blustering that might otherwise occur, while still ensuring that information is shared between citizens and agency staff. The one-on-one conversations with staff members can better convey the agency's genuine concern and empathy for the situations faced by individual citizens while serving as a conduit for mutual education about the decision-making process and the issue under review.

Visioning Sessions: When developing or redeveloping a public space, consider using a process called *visioning*. In this process community members and leaders are invited to attend one or more visioning sessions in which they seek to create a joint vision for how a section of the neighborhood or community should look once it has been reclaimed or redeveloped. For example, a section of largely abandoned industrial lots along the riverfront in Memphis is slated to be redeveloped into public space, perhaps including a linear park with walking trails and other amenities. Local residents and businesses are invited to a gathering in which they literally draw pictures to show their ideas for what the site should look like once it is finished. A professional artist in attendance takes these individually created drawings, pulls out themes with the help of audience members, and creates a poster to show a shared vision of the space. This vision then becomes the basic plan used for the site's development, perhaps with more public input throughout the process. This hands-on involvement gets community members engaged in shaping their neighborhoods, influencing the ways in which public funds are spent, and involved in dialogue about the trade-offs between various choices between competing visions.

World Café: The World Café defines itself as "a conversational process based on a set of integrated design principles that reveal a deeper living network pattern through which we co-evolve our collective future" (Brown & Isaacs, 2005, p. 2). The unique contribution of the World Café process is that it encourages participants to share information about their own experiences and worldviews with the goal of building interpersonal and intergroup understandings around issues of shared interest. For example, a neighborhood could convene a World Café to discuss local crime, school quality, or economic changes. Through these discussions an agenda for future collaboration may emerge, but the main goal is to build relationships and understandings within and across groups. This is a useful process with groups who have been traditionally distant or at odds with one another. The focal issue of discussion engages the group in an examination of what they have in common, while allowing for the sharing of diverse experiences and perspectives.

CONCLUSION

Managers regularly facilitate meetings, whether they are simply staff meetings, meetings of shareholders, board of directors meetings, or public meetings. This chapter examined several meeting formats and skills designed to assist managers as they improve their facilitation skills. The trick to facilitating productive meetings is that they require careful planning. From agenda setting, to selecting the meeting time and location, to inviting all the key stakeholders, successful meetings are built on a foundation of thoughtful planning. Whether you are a public-sector manager who regularly facilitates public meetings or a manager from the nonprofit or private sector who leads board meetings, skilled facilitation is an indispensable skill to develop and employ as a collaborative manager.

JOHN AT THE BUREAU OF RECLAMATION

It has been six months since the meeting in which the tires on John's car were slashed. A lot has changed. His employees no longer stage a "sick out" on public meeting days. Local residents sometimes even thank them for the work they are doing rather than try to run them out of town. To bring about this enormous change, John made many small changes in the way his agency handles the public involvement issue. First, all of his staff underwent training in listening, framing, and facilitation skills. They use these skills to convey to citizens their sincere empathy for the situations they face and to build rapport. They will even meet concerned citizens one-on-one when possible, to answer their questions and defuse their anger before the public meeting. The BR has developed a brochure explaining their mission, the mining law, and the extent of their authority. While the BR cannot lobby for changes to the mining laws, they have included the contact information for state elected officials on the relevant committees so that if citizens wish to convey their concerns to the appropriate person they can do so. The brochure also includes a list of other agencies the citizens can call with their specific concerns: concerns about trucks and roads go to the state's department of transportation, while concerns about the safety of drinking water go to the state's environmental protection agency, and so on. At the public meeting, the format has been changed. Instead of a head table with a speaker in the middle of the room, the room is set up with round tables that seat six to ten people. At each table, a bureau employee sits ready to record public comments and answer any questions they can about the process of licensing and the public record of the specific mining company that seeks the license, and to refer people to the appropriate agency or individual who can answer questions about groundwater, noise, or other concerns. Instead of holding only one public meeting at the beginning of the process, the BR has set up three meetings so that people can get information when the license application has been received, but also later in the process, as more questions or concerns arise. Bureau employees stay as long as it takes to answer questions, although this rarely exceeds the 90 minutes allotted for these meetings.

Officials from the mining company are invited to attend, meet the local residents, and share information about the ways in which they will be good neighbors, making a positive impact on the community. In fact, this is the accomplishment about which John is proudest. He has asked a number of mining companies around the state to meet with concerned citizens' groups to negotiate voluntary actions that mining companies can take to address some of the citizen's concerns. For example, one mining company, Voltron, has agreed to hold a pancake breakfast for the whole town in which the CEO will shake hands, meet locals, and tell them why the town will be better off after the mine opens. After meeting with concerned residents, Voltron reached an agreement to do the following: no fewer than 70% of the mine's employees will be hired out of the local population rather than brought in from outside, thereby guaranteeing local job creation; Voltron will build a public park with a playground near the mine so that property values will increase for those living closest to the mine rather than decrease; Voltron has agreed not to blast on weeknights after 8:00 p.m., even though state law would allow blasting until 10:00 p.m.; and Voltron has agreed to form a problem-solving task force with the mayor and a representative group of stakeholders to address ongoing problems or issues as they arise, even after the mine is up and running. These changes cost the company very little but did a lot to show their willingness to be a good neighbor. When interviewed for the local paper, the CEO was asked, "Why would you agree to these requests when you clearly didn't have to under current state laws?" He replied, "our managers and employees will be living here too, as neighbors in this community. We want to make this a workable partnership for everyone involved. When we open a mine in another town a few years from now, the residents will hear about our good reputation and know they have nothing to be afraid of. This is the right thing to do and it is good business." As the leader of the Bureau of Reclamation, John's job has become much more pleasant since these changes were implemented. These changes have been noticed by other agencies, who are now asking John for his advice as to how to improve their public engagement processes, too. John is now seen as a leader on public engagement issues, as is Voltron's CEO.

KEY TERMS

collaboration
collaboration fatigue
conflict assessment
consensus
convening

deliberative democracy
needs assessment
process sponsor
spoiler

EXERCISES

1. Think, pair, share: Think back to the most productive meetings you have attended. Make a list of the characteristics that described these meetings and the people leading the meetings. Now, make a list of characteristics to describe the last meeting you led or participated in as a manager. Compare the two. Share these with a classmate or colleague and consider the changes you could implement to implement positive changes.

2. Go to the website of any local, state, or federal government agency to find one or more upcoming public meetings on a topic of interest. Alternatively, if you are a shareholder or manager within a corporate environment, attend a shareholder's meeting. Answer the following questions:

   - How was the meeting advertised? Was it advertised adequately so stakeholders were aware and able to attend?
   - How was the room arranged?
   - What was turnout like? If there were too many or too few participants, was it handled appropriately?
   - Was there a clear agenda and did the facilitator stick to it? Alternatively, if it became clear that the agenda was not working, did the facilitator make reasoned changes?
   - Take the "temperature." What was the level of interest, anxiety, excitement, or anger in the room?
   - Was the decision-making process or the purpose of the meeting clear to attendees? Was their role in that process clear? How was it received?
   - What mechanism was used to gather public input or share information with the public? How effective were these mechanisms?
   - How did the meeting end? Were "next steps" discussed with those present? Will there be minutes shared publicly? Will there be additional opportunities for input or information sharing?
   - What recommendations for process improvements would you make?

3. Select a current "hot topic" of debate in your community, such as the siting of new public facilities, zoning issues, plans to build or widen roads, changes to policies regarding public health or welfare, and so forth. Screen this issue using the screening tools supplied in this chapter to determine whether this issue would be a good candidate for a large-group consensus/collaboration process.

4. Use an online chat or bulletin board to post discussion questions from this chapter with your classmates or colleagues. Take turns facilitating the group discussion online, seeking feedback at the end of the exercise so as to work on continual improvement of your facilitation skills.

GOAL SETTING

1. How are your facilitation skills? Using the content in this chapter, make a list of three things you can do to make your meetings more efficient and implement them in your next meeting.

SUGGESTED SUPPLEMENTAL READINGS

Addor, M. L., Cobb, T. D., Dukes, E. F., Ellerbrock, M., & Smutko, L. S. (2005). Linking theory to practice: A theory of change model of the Natural Resources Leadership Institute. *Conflict Resolution Quarterly, 23*, 203–223.

Cain, S. (2012). *Quiet: The power of introverts in a world that won't stop talking.* Crown.

Emerson, K., Orr, P. J., Keyes, D. L., & Mcknight, K. M. (2009). Environmental conflict resolution: Evaluating performance outcomes and contributing factors. *Conflict Resolution Quarterly, 27*, 27–64.

Fisher, M., & Sablan, T. (2018). Evaluating environmental conflict resolution: Practitioners, projects, and the movement. *Conflict Resolution Quarterly, 36*, 7–19. https://doi.org/10.1002/crq.21222

Orr, P. J., Emerson, K., & Keyes, D. L. (2008). Environmental conflict resolution practice and performance: An evaluation framework. *Conflict Resolution Quarterly, 25*, 283–301.

NOTES

1. The term *deliberative democracy* was originally coined by Joseph M. Bessette in his 1980 work "Deliberative Democracy: The Majority Principle in Republican Government."

2. The term *stakeholders* was defined in Chapter 9: Those who are directly or indirectly impacted by a proposed change—they have a stake in the outcome. Within organizations internal stakeholders include employees at all levels and the legal and human resources departments. External stakeholders could include customers, vendors, shareholders, patients or the affected public, and regulators. For public policy facilitation, primary stakeholders are those most immediately impacted by the policy outcomes while secondary stakeholders are those who are impacted, but for whom the impact is more minor and therefore less salient.

3. See Chapter 4 for a detailed explanation of facilitation versus other types of alternative dispute resolution processes.

Glossary of Key Terms

accommodating style: individuals or organizations that are prone to the use of accommodation in response to conflict (see following term), as said to be employing the accommodating style.

accommodation: occurs when an individual has a preferred outcome but is willing to sacrifice his preference so the other negotiator can realize his own conflicting preference, thereby ensuring no harm enters the relationship. Conflict accommodators care deeply about the feelings of others and seek to maintain harmony in their relationships and work environments.

accuser bias: a form of fundamental attribution error that is "the tendency for an observer negatively affected by an actor's behavior to attribute the behavior to causes under control of the actor" (Allred, 2000, p. 244).

active bystander: anyone who sees unacceptable behavior or a person in distress and takes actions to help. When someone interrupts a problematic or potentially harmful situation, stopping action or comments that promote sexual or discriminatory violence, bullying, harassment, intimidation, or threatening behavior, they are being an **active bystander** (https://www.du.edu/health-and -counseling-center/healthpromotion/gvpe/bi.html).

active listening: refers to a set of techniques often used by counselors and conflict resolution specialists intended to help the listener focus on the speaker, elicit detailed stories related to conflicts or problems, build rapport between the listener and speaker, and form the foundation for later problem-solving efforts.

adjudication: the formal process through which a judge renders a decision in a case before the court.

administrative adjudication: the process through which agencies determine whether an individual or group is guilty of violating administrative rules.

administrative law: "The name given to agencies' rule making and resolution of conflicts regarding their rules" (Harrison, Harris & Tolchin, 2009, p. 479).

administrative rulemaking: the "process by which upper-level bureaucrats use their administrative discretion and their expertise in the policy area to create rules, regulations, and standards that the bureaucracy will then enforce" (Harrison et al., 2009, p. 480).

advocate ombudsmen: ombudsmen whose primary task is to advocate on behalf of aggrieved individuals or groups who are typically vulnerable, such as elders in long-term care facilities or juveniles in detention.

agency capture: occurs when governmental regulatory agencies begin to advocate for the industries or interests they are supposed to regulate, rather than objectively assuring they adhere to all applicable laws and rules.

alternative dispute resolution (ADR): refers to a host of processes that serve as alternatives to costly adversarial litigation, including mediation, arbitration, the use of an ombudsman, and others.

anchoring number: the first proposal made during the negotiation. It tends to create a cognitive anchor against which all subsequent offers are judged.

antisocial personality disorder: characterized by an inability or unwillingness to follow or conform to common social norms, policies, and laws, as well as by impulsive behavior, lying, and the violation of others' rights. Often, these individuals are viewed as criminals or con artists who have a higher risk of incarceration, violence, and fraud.

arbitration: an alternative dispute resolution process in which the parties hire a neutral, expert third-party decision-maker to act as a private judge in their dispute. Arbitration is commonly used to resolve disputes in unionized workplaces, and arbitration decisions can serve as precedent for future similar cases within a union contract. Arbitration rulings do not set a legal precedent in the courts and cannot generally be appealed there except in cases of arbitrator misconduct.

asking price (or **initial offer**): the first proposal shared by each party to the negotiation.

attribution theory explains the ways in which cognitive biases hinder our ability to accurately understand the motivations behind the behaviors of others.

avoiding style: one of the five primary responses to conflict by individuals and organizations. In this style, individuals or groups have evidence that a problem currently exists or will soon exist, but no steps are taken to address the problem. Conflict avoiders refuse to acknowledge the problem exists, hoping it will just go away. This may work for small, nonrecurring problems, or when you lack the authority or power to bring change. This style is unlikely to work for systemic, recurring, or large problems.

backcasting: a problem-solving technique in which the facilitator, mediator, or manager asks the parties to envision a future in which the problem is solved or the relationship is repaired. The parties are asked to "describe what that looks like or feels like." Then the parties are asked to describe the steps that each of them would need to take in order to reach that ideal future state. The parties are asked to focus on the actions that each person can take themselves, rather than focusing on the actions they wish the others would take.

BATNA: an acronym that stands for "best alternative to a negotiated agreement."

bias of the accused: our tendency to downplay our own poor decisions or actions, while attributing them to circumstances beyond our control.

blue-collar jobs: include hourly pay and usually include manual labor. Blue-collar employees may be considered **skilled labor** or **unskilled labor**.

borderline personality disorder: "a serious mental disorder marked by a pattern of instability in moods, behavior, self-image, and functioning. These experiences often result in impulsive actions and unstable relationships. A person with borderline personality disorder may experience intense episodes of anger, depression, and anxiety that may last from only a few hours to days" (NIH, 2018).

boundary setting: a psychological concept referring to a conscious limit between acceptable behaviors that uphold personal dignity versus those behaviors that cause emotional harm. Setting a boundary occurs when one communicates the limits of acceptable behavior. Holding the boundary occurs when there is an appropriate response to a crossed boundary.

brainstorming: an important part of a problem-solving process. During brainstorming all parties agree to think broadly about any and all possible solutions to the problem at hand. It is critical to the success of the brainstorming process that the participants agree to separate the process of generating options from the process of evaluating those options.

bullying/workplace bullying: "Bullying can be considered as a form of coercive interpersonal influence. It involves deliberately inflicting injury or discomfort on another person repeatedly through physical contact, verbal abuse, exclusion, or other negative actions" (Forsyth, 2006, p. 206). The key to this definition is that the behavior must be intentional, repeated over time, and have a negative impact on the target. Bullies wear down their victims over time, usually for more than a year in workplace settings (Einarsen & Skogstad, 1996).

burnout is comprised of three key stress responses: an overwhelming sense of exhaustion, feelings of cynicism and detachment, and a sense of professional ineffectiveness and lack of accomplishment. Burnout results when the balance of deadlines, demands, working hours, and other stressors outstrips rewards, recognition, and relaxation (in Michel, 2016).

business-to-business (B2B): relationships in which the customer is another business.

calculus-based trust (CBT): the parties can be trusted to abide by their agreements because it is in each party's rational self-interest to do so. Often, the penalties for failing to uphold the agreement are detailed in the contract or agreement itself, giving each side incentives to uphold their end of the bargain.

case evaluation: process in which a neutral expert is hired to evaluate the strengths and weaknesses of each side's case and predict for the parties what would happen in court.

claiming value: occurs when a negotiator seeks to gain as much of a fixed resource as possible, leaving less for other negotiators.

classical ombudsmen: receive and investigate complaints and concerns regarding governmental policies and processes. The mandate of these ombuds is generally articulated through statutes and they may be either elected or appointed.

cognitive bias: a pattern of deviation in judgment leading to inaccurate conclusions, distorted perceptions of reality, illogical interpretation of facts or events, and often to irrational behaviors or thought patterns (Kahneman & Tversky, 1972).

collaboration: has four key constituent elements: interdependent stakeholders (i.e., those impacted by a decision); the ability to constructively address differences; joint ownership of decisions; and collective responsibility for the future of the partnership. Collaboration occurs when multiple parties come together to accomplish a common objective due to a shared need, through authentic conversations in which people speak frankly and listen to one another, under norms of reciprocity that require a cooperative give-and-take that enables the group to negotiate effectively.

collaboration fatigue: the weariness that sets in among negotiators after talks have been ongoing for months or even years, especially if progress seems elusive or minimal. The signs of collaboration fatigue include falling meeting attendance, growing impatience or inattentiveness of representatives, and a decreased willingness to financially support the collaborative process.

collaborative monitoring: seeks to engage interested and affected stakeholders, public agencies, and scientific and technical experts in a more direct manner to jointly gather data and information in an ongoing manner. This helps avoid the tendency for each group to gather information on their own which supports their own preferred outcomes.

collaborative public management: defined as "the process of facilitating and operating in multi-organizational arrangements to solve problems that cannot be solved or easily solved by single organizations. Collaborative means to co-labor, to achieve common goals, often working across boundaries and in multi-sector-actor relationships. Collaborative public management may include participatory governance: the active involvement of citizens in government decision-making" (O'Leary & Bingham, 2009, p. 3).

collaborative style: indicates a preference to work together with others to achieve outcomes that meet the needs of all negotiators. This style occurs when two or more individuals work together to share information and make joint decisions.

collective bargaining: a process of negotiation between employers and the employees' representatives aimed at reaching agreements that regulate working conditions and pay.

collective bargaining agreement: the agreement reached between an employees' union and the company, outlining the terms of employment. This agreement covers the initial contract between a group of employees and company leaders, as well as periodic renegotiation of that contract.

collectivist societies (collectivism): where individual identities are based on ties to the group or community and one is expected to make decisions that take into account the best interests of the family, tribe, or community.

competitive style: indicates a preference to "win as much as you can," even at the expense of the other side or the relationship between negotiators.

compromising style: indicates a preference for "splitting the difference" between the negotiators' positions. Compromise can be a quick, efficient way to reach a solution. Compromise tends to be seen as a fair and quick way to reach agreements. Yet it can miss opportunities for more creative problem-solving through collaboration. The compromising style is appropriate when a decision is not highly important, the time for negotiation and discussion is relatively short, and the process needs to be viewed as fair to all parties.

conflict assessment: helps to identify the issues in controversy in a given situation, the affected interests, and the appropriate form(s) of conflict resolution. Also called a "needs assessment," this analysis is used to determine whether an ADR or collaborative process is likely to succeed.

conflict avoidance: occurs when an individual or group has evidence that a problem currently exists or will soon exist, but takes no steps to acknowledge and address the problem. Conflict avoiders refuse to acknowledge that the problem exists, in the hope that it will just go away.

conflict coaching: "a process in which a coach and client communicate one-on-one for the purpose of developing the client's conflict-related understanding, interaction strategies, and interaction skills. Coaches help clients to make sense of conflicts they experience, help them learn to positively manage these conflicts, and help them master specific communication skills and behaviors" (from Jones & Brinkert, 2008, pp. 4–5).

conflict hot spot: a unit within an organization that has a disproportionate amount of unproductive conflict that is revealed through lower-than-average morale, higher turnover, employee disengagement, and rates of litigation. The hot spot may be due to the presence of one or more dysfunctional managers, the presence of disincentives for positive performance, or a negative unit-level culture that breeds negative behaviors and disgruntlement.

conflict management (CM): refers to the systematic prevention of unproductive conflict and proactively addressing those conflicts that cannot be prevented. Every workplace has existing conflict management methods, but these methods have not usually been explicitly discussed, examined, and (re)designed for maximal efficiency and user satisfaction.

conflict prevention: occurs when an individual or group examines the sources of predictable and recurring problems, and then takes reasonable steps to address the root causes of those problems so that they do not occur or recur.

conflict styles inventory (CSI): a personality assessment tool designed to measure the conflict resolution reactions and habits of individuals. This information can be useful to understand one's basic approach to conflict, as well as to learn how to match conflicts with effective response strategies.

consensus: occurs in matters of policy when "the parties have reached a meeting of the minds sufficient to make a decision and carry it out; no one who could block or obstruct the decision or its implementation will exercise that power; and everyone needed to support the decision and put it into effect will do so" (Arthur, Carlson and Moore, 1999, p. 5).

consensus building describes a number of collaborative decision-making techniques in which a facilitator or mediator is used to assist diverse or competing interest groups to reach agreement on policy matters, environmental conflicts, or other issues in controversy affecting a large number of people.

contingent agreements: tend to take this type of format: If X happens by (insert date), then we both agree to do Y. If X does not happen by this date, then we agree instead to do Z. This allows both parties to react to changing future circumstances without needing to renegotiate the contract.

convening: the process of bringing stakeholders together to design the process jointly and begin the dialogue or negotiation.

creating value: when negotiators work together to ensure each of their needs are met by expanding existing value through collaboration, increased efficiency, or creativity.

cultural distance: refers to the extent to which two cultures differ on key factors such as gender role differentiation, the importance of context in verbal communication, views of hierarchy versus equality, and more.

culture: comprised of a set of values, beliefs, and understandings that tell us how to behave and to succeed in our environment. These beliefs are often shared by other members of our cultural group.

customer loyalty programs: this is a method for rewarding return customers by giving them their "13th night free" or a free domestic airline ticket once they accumulate 50,000 frequent flyer miles, etc. These programs may help lure customers back to your business when there are others offering basically the same products and services at similar prices.

customer recovery: refers to the policies and practices put into place to address disgruntled customers with the goal of winning back their loyalty and business. See Chapter 11.

customer satisfaction: defined as "a measure of how a firm's product or service performs compared to customer's expectations" (Zondiros et al., 2007, p. 1086).

customers as business partners: this means organizations should evolve their mindset from a worldview that sees each transaction as a one-time event, to instead seeing each transaction as a chance to build a long-term, mutually beneficial relationship (Witschger, 2011). See Chapter 11.

deliberative democracy: refers to the underlying principle that for laws to have true legitimacy they must be subject to authentic deliberation prior to a majority vote. *Authentic deliberation* means that decision-makers engage in discussion, debate, and analysis that is free from the influence of unequal power based on wealth, status, or other sources of inequality. The goal of deliberative democracy is to move toward consensus, but decisions can be made based on majority vote once deliberations have occurred and all have had a chance to participate. Deliberative democracy is a founding principle of Western governmental systems, albeit incompletely achieved in practice.

denial: occurs when the reality of a situation is so overwhelming as to potentially cause an emotional breakdown. To avoid this potential, one refuses to acknowledge the reality of a situation in order to allow it to sink in slowly (if at all), rather than all at once.

design team (DT): comprised of employees from different parts and levels of the organization who will assist in the development, implementation, and evaluation of the dispute system design.

disassociation: occurs when an individual is emotionally overwhelmed by a situation and therefore has difficulty focusing on that situation. Her mind may wander to more attractive thoughts, such as where to go on vacation, or even drift toward making a mental grocery list—anything seen as safe or pleasant. In layman's terms, they daydream.

displacement: involves changing the topic as another way to avoid dealing directly with a problem or acting upset about one issue when it is really a different issue that has caused one's upset.

dispute system design (DSD) is the "applied art and science of designing the means to prevent, manage, and resolve streams of disputes or conflict" (Blomgren Amsler, Martinez & Smith, 2020, p. 7).

distributive bargaining: also called win-lose or zero-sum negotiations; refers to negotiations between parties with perceived competitive goals. In distributive bargaining situations, resources are fixed and cannot be increased.

distributive justice: deals with perceptions that outcomes and payouts are fairly distributed. Perceptions of distributive justice generally hinge on one of three criteria for determining the fairness of an outcome: equity, equality, or need.

diversity: refers to all the ways in which individuals may differ: gender, race, ethnicity, age, technical or physical abilities and backgrounds, sexual orientation or gender identity, religiosity and religious affiliation, national origin, social class, work style, worldview, and so on.

Dunning-Kruger effect: A cognitive bias that leads people to wrongly overrate their competence in a specific area (Psychology Today, 2022).

EDGE model: stands for "explain, demonstrate, guide, and empower"; a leadership model used to develop subordinates and others by teaching them how to accomplish a task, then setting them free to do so, providing positive encouragement alongside realistic expectations.

emotional intelligence (EI): refers to the ability to perceive, control, and evaluate emotions in oneself and others (Cherry, 2012; Salovey & Mayer, 1990). Emotional intelligence can be further broken down into five facets: self-awareness, self-regulation, motivation, empathy, and social skills.

employee engagement reflects the extent to which employees are fully committed to furthering the organization and its mission.

employee turnover (attrition): employee turnover refers to the rate at which employees leave the organization and should be broken down by rank and location to better isolate the potential root causes. Average rates of employee turnover vary by industry and within organizations.

environmental and public policy conflict resolution (E/PP): the application of alternative dispute resolution methods to public policy issues is referred to as "E/PP."

environmental conflict resolution (ECR): refers to people with differing views and interests working together in a systematic and organized way to find workable solutions to shared problems about environmental issues, usually with the assistance of a neutral third party.

EPM feedback model: Empathize, pinpoint problems with specifics, then move forward to problem-solving together.

equality principle: states that all group members should receive equal amounts of any good or benefit that comes from the labors of the group. Under this version of fairness, all employees would receive the same pay.

equity principle: denotes that benefits should be distributed based on each person's or group's contribution; those who worked harder or contributed greater expertise to a project should receive disproportionate amounts of the fruits of that labor.

ethnocentrism: the belief that one's cultural practices are inherently superior and preferred to those from other cultures.

evaluative (or directive) **mediation**: a mediation style similar to case evaluation or nonbinding arbitration. In this model of mediation, mediators tell parties how a judge or jury would likely decide in their case. They evaluate the strengths and weaknesses of their arguments or evidence and render nonbinding decisions. The parties use this information to inform their settlement negotiations either within or outside mediation. Additionally, mediators work to persuade the parties to step away from unrealistic demands and apply pressure on them to compromise and reach a resolution.

executive or organizational ombudsmen: the most common form of ombuds, commonly used in universities and private-sector companies to receive complaints or queries concerning the actions (or failures to act) by organizational managers, leaders, contractors, or coworkers. The executive (aka organizational) ombuds may work with organizational leaders to improve the performance of the organization by improving organizational culture; assuring fairness in hiring and promotion; bringing allegations of wrongdoing to the attention of organizational leaders (when appropriate); training managers, and others on conflict management and communication skills; and addressing the root causes of problems like employee turnover, low morale, sabotage, harassment, bullying, disengagement, or other organizational challenges that negatively impact mission achievement.

exit interview or **exit surveys**: used to gather information about the reasons the employee is leaving the organization, their perspectives about how the organization could improve as an employer and in the accomplishment of its mission, and various other points of information deemed vital to constant improvement. Employees who have made the choice to leave the organization may be in a position to be more honest about their observations than ongoing employees who may fear reprisals or retribution for speaking out.

external locus of control: an individual with an external locus of control believes that he is controlled by factors external to himself such as a higher power, the environment, political forces, etc.

external stakeholders: could include customers, vendors, shareholders, patients or the affected public, and regulators.

facilitation: a group process in which either an inside or outside neutral leads the discussions in a neutral manner in order to assist in promoting an efficient and civil discussion process that stays on-track (see Chapters 4 and 12 for public policy applications).

facilitative training: a mix of problem identification, targeted training to address those problems, and follow-up to measure any impact of the training on those problems. If those problems include a lack of shared expectations, norms, or understanding of the mission or shared values (the "who are we" questions), then the trainer uses the training period to lead a problem-solving discussion designed to build consensus on the issues at hand. Essentially, this is a mix of facilitation and customized, responsive training.

"failing up" occurs when a "bad" employee is promoted or transferred by their current supervisor to free themselves from the negative impacts of this worker in their unit, then avoiding the opportunity to directly address problematic behaviors or performance. This happens when it is easier to move than terminate an employee.

fairness: variably defined as the quality of being just, equitable, impartial, or even-handed. Fairness can refer to the process through which decisions were made and/or the outcome of those decisions. Depending on one's perspective, there may be many contradictory viewpoints about what comprises a "fair" outcome depending on one's preference for equity, equality, or need-based outcomes.

fallback offer: offer made once the initial offer is rejected. It is somewhere between the initial offer and the resistance point and it may lead to an agreement.

framing refers to the language used to put one's thoughts and conceptualizations into words. See Chapters 1 and 2.

framing effect is a cognitive bias that occurs when the same option is presented in different formats or with different phrasing (it is framed differently), and the choice of format or phrasing influences one's opinions or preferences on the matter (Druckman, 2001). See Chapters 1 and 2.

fundamental attribution error: occurs when we incorrectly attribute someone's behavior to their dispositional or personality characteristics rather than attributing it to a situational factor.

gender role differentiation: refers to the extent to which specific tasks are thought to be appropriate to either men or women such as child rearing, cooking, driving, managing, policing, nursing, teaching, etc. Cultures with low gender role differentiation tend to believe that most tasks can be performed by men or women, compared to cultures with high gender role differentiation in which specific tasks tend to be gendered. Additionally, in cultures with low gender role differentiation, access to power, wealth, and independent decision-making are less dependent upon gender than in cultures with high gender role differentiation.

Great Recession: refers to the period of negative and slow economic growth and high unemployment and underemployment that began in approximately 2007 and continued until at least fall of 2009, yet with lingering workforce impacts well into 2012.

(the) Great Resignation is an economic trend in which employees have voluntarily resigned from their jobs en masse, beginning in early 2021 in the wake of the COVID-19 pandemic. Among the most cited reasons for resigning include wage stagnation amid rising cost of living, limited opportunities for career advancement, hostile work environments, lack of benefits, inflexible remote-work policies, and long-lasting job dissatisfaction. Most likely to quit have been workers in hospitality, health care, and education.

grievance arbitration: a process in which a neutral third party is hired by the disputants to render a binding decision to a dispute between the union and employer, typically determining whether one or both sides failed to abide by the terms of their shared contract. Basically, grievance arbitrators act as private judges to resolve disputes in unionized workplaces.

groupthink: "a pattern of thought characterized by self-deception, forced manufacture of consent, and conformity to group values and ethics" (Merriam-Webster, 2023).

growing pains: the pain that comes from the hard work of resolving conflict, which often results in personal growth and development for the parties involved and results in positive change. Both can be painful, yet necessary and productive.

growth mindset (Dweck, 2007) A growth mindset is the belief that all people can learn and grow, rather than having static potential.

high-context cultures for communication: those in which the majority of meaning is conveyed via nonverbal means such as eye contact, tone, the use of silence, and scripted conversations. "High context" refers to the degree to which one must understand the context of the conversation in order to understand the intended meaning. In high-context cultures the burden of understanding falls to the listener, not the speaker.

histrionic personality disorder: characterized by a need for excessive attention and a high level of emotion when uncalled for. These individuals often dress in ways designed to draw attention to themselves.

identity-based trust (IBT): comes from the human tendency to trust those with whom they share common traits or characteristics such as religion, race, gender, social class, national origin, field of work, etc.

impasse: (pronounced im-pass, not im-pas-say) also known as a stalemate. This means the negotiation concludes with no agreement.

individualistic societies (individualism): those in which the needs, rights, and responsibilities of the individual are prioritized above those of the group or community. In these societies, it is generally considered positive for an individual to stand out from his peers through individual achievements, while in collectivist societies it is less appropriate for individuals to stand out from the crowd.

informal managerial mediation: occurs when a manager facilitates a problem-solving conversation between two or more parties in conflict. It acts as an informal mediator between two or more employees, supervisors, or managers in dispute. As informal mediators, managers listen to each party and encourage both to listen to each other. They engage the parties in a problem-solving discussion with the goal of reaching an agreement that meets the needs of all parties and is superior to continuing the dispute via more formal channels.

informational justice: the quality of explanations about issues, outcomes, and procedures for decision-making.

in-group/out-group theory: (first articulated by Henri Tjafel) states that individuals and groups tend to define themselves in comparison to who they aren't. In-group members tend to elicit better, less conflictual, treatment than out-group members. This theory has three parts: social categorization, social identification, and social comparison.

initial offer: See **asking price**.

integration: occurs when neither group involved in a merger or acquisition dominates the other. While both cultures change due to their interactions, the resulting culture(s) are not dominated by either organization and both retain some distinct cultural aspects.

integrative bargaining: negotiations in which multiple negotiators can achieve their goals without necessarily leaving the others worse off.

interests: tell us of the needs that underlie the positions or demands being made during a negotiation. Position—"I demand a raise." Interest—"I need to earn more money in order to pay my student loans." Understanding the underlying interests of each party allows the negotiation to move away from a zero-sum discussion to one in which all parties leave the negotiation better off than they would be through the use of distributive bargaining techniques.

intergroup conflicts occur between members of distinct groups such as units, teams, identity or ethnic groups, organizations, or even nation-states. These occur when the members of one group believe their interests or values are at odds with those of another group.

internal locus of control: means that an individual believes he is in control of events that effect himself, rather than being controlled by external forces such as God, the environment, or those in powerful positions. Individualistic societies are more likely to espouse a belief in an internal locus of control.

internal stakeholders: internal stakeholders include employees at all levels and the legal and human resources departments. For DSD, internal stakeholders are an organization's members: employees at all levels as well as the legal and human resources departments.

interpersonal conflicts: occur between two or more people. Successful interventions may include facilitated conversations by a third party, such as a manager or mediator. The goal of these conversations is to reach shared expectations designed to address current problem(s) and prevent their recurrence (see 3-step problem-solving in Chapter 7).

interpersonal justice: whether one is treated with dignity, respect, kindness, honesty.

intrapersonal conflicts, also known as intrapsychic conflicts, are those we fight in our own minds as we struggle to accurately make meaning out of facts, in the presence of common cognitive biases such as denial, rationalization, defensiveness, unconscious bias, projection, psychiatric conditions, personality types, the effects of addictions, the impact of past traumas, or conflicting sociocultural norms and expectations. The way in which our brains make meaning out of available information can lead to incomplete or even inaccurate or unhelpful responses. Successful interventions for intrapersonal conflicts often involve coaching or mental health therapy designed to improve self-awareness, coping skills, and the ability to identify and remediate cognitive biases.

joint fact-finding: a process by which interested parties commit to building a mutual understanding of disputed scientific or technical information. Interested parties can select their own experts who presumably reflect differing interpretations of available information. Alternatively, they can also jointly decide on an unassociated third-party expert or a panel of experts. A facilitator/mediator works to clarify and define areas of agreement, disagreement, and uncertainty. The facilitator/mediator can coach the experts to translate technical information into a form that is understandable to all interested parties. The goal is to avoid adversarial or partisan science where competing experts magnify small differences, rather than focusing on points of agreement and/or creating a strategy to provide for a joint conclusion.

leader-member exchange theory: this body of research examines the types of relationships that form between leaders and organizational members, as well as the benefits that accrue to both leaders and members as a result of these relationships. This approach posits that the best managers develop positive relationships with organizational members based on "trust, respect, loyalty, liking, intimacy, support, openness and honesty" (Wilson, Sin & Conlon, 2010, p. 358).

leaders set the strategic direction, curate the culture, fill key positions on the executive team, forge and attend to the relationships necessary for current and future success, and spot opportunities for innovative change. Managers implement the decisions made by leaders and attend to the day-to-day running of the organization. Both leaders and managers need to set goals and measure progress toward them in their own careers, teams, and organizations, yet leaders focus more time on crafting and communicating their vision for the organization. Both need to motivate others to achieve their highest performance and inspire them by connecting each employee's contribution to the accomplishment of the mission.

legislative ombudsman: works to address concerns about potential ethics violations or breaches of trust levied against an elected leader or group of leaders. For example, Arizona and Hawaii both have legislative ombudsmen.

listening to respond: people generally listen to figure out when they can jump into the conversation and get out their view, opinion, and thoughts rather than truly listening to understand.

listening to understand: requires the listener to suspend judgment and their own need to drive the conversation. Instead of listening for her moment to jump into the conversation, the goal of listening to understand is to allow the speaker to completely share his thoughts, concerns, or emotions with the listener, uninterrupted. This calls for active listening.

litigation: the process of filing a court case and taking the necessary procedural steps to prepare that case for adjudication.

low-context culture: one in which most of the meaning is conveyed in the explicit verbal conversation as opposed to being implied through the context, nonverbal cues, or the use of scripted conversations. In low-context cultures the burden for understanding falls on the speaker: If the speaker is clear enough, then the listener will likely understand the intended meaning.

mandatory arbitration clause: a binding pre-dispute contract committing both parties to use arbitration for dispute settlement in the event of a future dispute. By signing a mandatory arbitration clause, both parties give up their right to resort to resolution through the court systems.

Maslow's hierarchy of needs: Abraham Maslow was a psychologist who studied human motivations and behaviors. He is primarily known for his theory of a "hierarchy of needs," which states that humans seek to satisfy their needs in order of importance: Primary needs included the need to breathe, eat, reproduce, etc. The next most pressing needs involve the needs related to safety— physical security of oneself and one's family, employment, and control over one's property. The third group of needs involves meeting the need for belonging in a community and feeling loved. Next comes the need to feel confident, respected, and have self-esteem. Lastly, humans need to be able to express themselves as "self-actualized" individuals, including the ability for creativity, moral choice, and problem-solving.

Media ombudsman: The purpose of the media ombudsman is to promote transparency, accuracy, and neutrality in the reporting of news. This type of ombuds is familiar with journalistic ethics and standards of practice that are meant to ensure fairness, accuracy, and ethical reporting for the public's benefit. For example, National Public Radio (in the United States) has an ombudsman who helps to explain the journalistic process to listeners and help them understand the decisions that go into deciding what stories get reported, which don't, and how the reporting is carried out.

mediation: a process of facilitated negotiation in which the mediator does not act as a judge, but instead assists the parties as they strive to have a civil, productive conversation about how to resolve the dispute and rebuild relationships (if appropriate).

meta-communication: occurs when people communicate about how they communicate to reduce miscommunication by explaining both the intent and the content of a message.

mission statement: a formal summary of the purpose, goals, and vision of an organization, unit, and/or individual. See Chapter 8.

monochronic orientation indicates that one prefers to adhere to strict schedules and deadlines. Time is viewed as something tangible that can be saved, spent, or wasted. This orientation toward time is most common in countries such as Great Britain, Germany, Switzerland, the United States, Australia, and other cultures of Western European origin. People with this orientation may be somewhat less flexible and more driven by deadlines. They may also prefer to get right down to the task at hand rather than spend time building relationships. They tend to believe there is a "right" time for specific activities (e.g., arrive at work by 8:30 a.m., take no more than a one-hour lunch).

monoculturalism: the belief that one identity group (e.g., one gender, race, nation, ethnicity) is the norm and all others vary from that norm. It creates one group as the center around which all others must revolve and to which others must adjust or accommodate. See Chapter 5.

multiculturalism: the "co-existence of diverse cultures, where culture includes racial, religious, or cultural groups and is manifested in customary behaviors, cultural assumptions and values, patterns of thinking, and communicative styles" (ifla.org, 2005).

narcissistic personality disorder: characterized by a "pattern of need for admiration and lack of empathy for others. A person with narcissistic personality disorder may have a grandiose sense of self-importance, a sense of entitlement, take advantage of others or lack empathy" (Psychiatry.org, 2018).

need principle: asserts that more of the goods or benefits should go to those who need more. Therefore, a parent with three young children might receive greater pay or fewer taxes than one with no children at all.

need theories: refer to those explanations for human behavior, including conflict, based on the unmet needs of individuals. More than fifty years ago Abraham Maslow articulated a theory of human motivation that remains crucial to our understanding of conflict today (see Figure 2.1). According to Maslow, people seek to meet their needs, but some needs take precedence over others.

needs assessment phase (aka conflict assessment or organizational assessment): a needs assessment is an evaluation of the conflict, issue, or organization to understand the history, identify the stakeholders, and calculate the costs related to the status quo in order to determine the likely success of changes, including the use of a collaborative process(es) to address dispute(s).

negative settlement range is one in which there is no overlap between the lowest amount the seller is willing to take and the highest amount the buyer is willing to pay. Unless something changes the mind of the buyer or seller, then no agreement will be reached.

negotiated rulemaking (also called "regulatory negotiation" or "reg-neg"): a multiparty consensus process in which a balanced negotiating committee seeks to reach agreement on the substance of a proposed agency rule, policy, or standard. The negotiating committee is composed of representatives of those interests that will be affected by or have an interest in the rule, including the rulemaking agency itself. Affected interests that are represented in the negotiations are expected to abide by any resulting agreement and implement its terms. This agreement-seeking process usually occurs only after a thorough conflict assessment has been conducted and is generally undertaken with the assistance of a skilled, neutral mediator or facilitator.

negotiation: occurs between two or more interdependent parties who have a perceived conflict between their needs and desires yet believe a negotiated outcome is superior to the outcome they could achieve unilaterally.

nonstructural sources of conflict: occur once or rarely, generally as isolated events that could not have been predicted or avoided. These are generally resolved by taking action to resolve the individual problem, rather than creating or changing policies across the organization.

nonverbal communication: includes many contextual cues that convey acknowledgment of power dynamics and emotional ties or lack thereof between individuals or groups. Nonverbal communication is conveyed through tone, body language, eye contact, and even such things as clothing, hairstyles, and demeanor that convey relative social status and dominance or submission within a chain of command.

ombudsman (or ombuds or ombudsperson): an organizational conflict management specialist working to resolve internal disputes with employees or external disputes with customers, vendors, or business partners. Ombudsmen seek to reduce the sources of recurring conflict by recommending changes to policies, procedures, training, and culture to top organizational leaders and by increasing the capacity of organizational members to resolve their own disputes through the provision of coaching services.

online dispute resolution (ODR): the use of technology to provide ADR services or solve disputes.

open-door policy: every manager is open to hearing from every employee. An open-door policy means that any employee with a problem can go to any manager in the organization for help to solve that problem. While there is usually a preference to start lowest on the chain of command and work their way up, ultimately an open-door policy means the employee can choose which manager to approach for help with a problem.

organizational culture: comprised of the values and behaviors that contribute to the unique social and psychological environment of an organization. Organizational culture includes an organization's expectations, experiences, philosophy, and values that hold it together, and is expressed in its self-image, inner workings, interactions with the outside world, and future expectations. It is based on shared attitudes, beliefs, customs, and written and unwritten rules that have been developed over time and are considered valid. Also called corporate culture, it's shown in (1) the ways the organization conducts its business, treats its employees, customers, and the wider community; (2) the extent to which freedom is allowed in decision-making, developing new ideas, and personal expression; (3) how power and information flow through its hierarchy; and (4) how committed employees are toward collective objectives. It also extends to production methods, marketing and advertising practices, and new product creation. Organizational culture is unique for every organization and one of the hardest things to change (Business Dictionary, 2018).

organizational justice: comprised of four components: distributive justice (i.e., whether outcomes and payouts are fairly distributed); procedural justice (i.e., fairness in processes); informational justice (i.e., the quality of explanations about issues, outcomes, and procedures for decision-making); and interpersonal justice (i.e., whether one is treated with dignity, respect, kindness, honesty, etc.). Perceptions of organizational justice are important because they are related to a host of behaviors within organizations that are crucial to mission achievement, including employee turnover, sabotage or embezzlement by employees, shirking, absenteeism, presenteeism (see Chapter 7), and the commitment to caring for customers/clients. See Chapter 9.

ostrich syndrome occurs when individual managers and leaders stick their heads in the metaphorical sand in an attempt to avoid seeing problems.

paranoid personality disorder: "is characterized by a pattern of distrust and suspiciousness where others' motives are seen as mean or spiteful. People with paranoid personality disorder often assume people will harm or deceive them and are reluctant to confide in others or become close to them" (psychiatry.org, 2018).

partnering: a long-term commitment between two or more organizations for the purpose of achieving specific business objectives by maximizing the effectiveness of each participant's resources (Anderson & Polkinghorn, 2008, p. 169).

passion projects are opportunities for community engagement and volunteering, the provision of developmental coaching, and the overall warmth and inclusivity of the working environment (Harrell & Barbato, 2018; Project Oxygen, Google).

patient care advocate (PCA): works either in the emergency department and/or in the other parts of the hospital and is on-call to manage patient complaints, to de-escalate conflict when it arises, and to solve problems early whenever possible. See Chapter 11.

peer review: a process most commonly used within organizational settings to deal with internal employment disputes such as claims of discrimination, wrongful termination, demotions, claims of favoritism or nepotism, or employee appeals of other disciplinary actions. The peer review process is designed to allow employees to decide whether their peers are being treated fairly by the organization and its managers or supervisors.

personality disorder: "a way of thinking, feeling and behaving that deviates from the expectations of the culture, causes distress or problems functioning, and lasts over time" (NIH 2018).

perverse incentives occur when a policy, procedure, or system misaligns the individual's interests against the interests of the organization. Perverse incentives are a pervasive source of conflict within organizations and society.

policy dialogues: processes that bring together representatives of groups with divergent views or interests to tap the collective views of participants in the process. The goals include opening discussion, improving communication and mutual understanding, exploring the issues in controversy to see if participants' different viewpoints can be distilled into general recommendations, and trying to reach agreement on a proposed policy standard or guidelines to be recommended by government. They are often used to address complex environmental conflicts or public policy disputes constructively. See Chapter 12.

polychronic orientation: one believes there are many "right" times to do different activities (e.g., arrive at work anytime between 8:30 and 10:00 a.m., take a flexible lunch break). Polychronic cultures tend to arise nearer the equator, where seasonal differences are smaller (e.g., many Latino and Island cultures). Individuals from polychronic cultures tend to be more comfortable with flexible deadlines and spend time building relationships before attending to tasks.

positional leadership occurs when a leader's power stems from their specific position, a formal title, and derives their influence and authority solely from this position. Conversely, relational leaders are those who act without the formality of a title. This style is often authoritarian, and therefore, likely to increase unproductive conflict in the workplace.

positions: demands that have only one way to be met and lead to win-lose outcomes in which one party's gain comes at the other party's expense.

positive conflict: also called cooperative conflict, it is the healthy sharing of differences of opinion and negotiation necessary to make tough decisions.

positive settlement range: overlap between the acceptable outcomes for the buyer and the seller.

presenteeism: also known as **quiet quitting**, occurs when an employee wishes to leave the organization but hasn't done so yet. While remaining in the job the employee is less committed to the organization, its customers, and its other employees. This lack of commitment is displayed through lower productivity and occasionally through acts of sabotage, theft, or embezzlement.

primary stakeholders: those most immediately impacted by the policy outcomes, while secondary stakeholders are those who are impacted, but for whom the impact is more minor and therefore less salient.

privilege: refers "to a right or immunity granted as a peculiar benefit, advantage, or favor. Within American and other Western societies, these privileged social identities—of people who have historically occupied positions of dominance over others—include whites, males, heterosexuals, Christians, and the wealthy, among others." (Garcia, 2018).

procedural justice: deals with the fairness of the process used for reaching a decision or resolving a conflict. Individuals tend to perceive that a process is fair when it is transparent, respectful, and allows them to be heard during the decision-making process.

process sponsor: the organization that convenes and usually financially supports the large-group process of decision-making or information exchange. The sponsor is usually a governmental agency, but it can also be a private or non-profit organization, or the process can be jointly sponsored by more than one organization. The sponsor generally conducts an assessment of the conflict or, ideally, hires an outside consultant to conduct an unbiased assessment.

projection is related to denial and involves misinterpreting undesirable feelings or behaviors as coming from someone else rather than acknowledging or dealing with them in oneself. By focusing oneself on the faults of others, one does not need to address them in oneself.

psychological safety: "Psychological safety refers to an individual's perception of the consequences of taking an interpersonal risk or a belief that a team is safe for risk taking in the face of being seen as ignorant, incompetent, negative, or disruptive" (Duhigg, 2016); see Chapter 8.

public disputes: complex, multiparty, decision-making or consensus building processes impacting the public interest or policy that involve complicated networks of interests, unequal accountability among stakeholders, and strongly held values, and are highly influenced by governmental rules and regulations.

public goods: something that, by its nature, is either supplied to all people or to none, regardless of whether each individual has paid his fair share for the enjoyment of that good. For example, national defense, clean air, public roads, and public libraries are all public goods: If they exist for anyone, then they exist for everyone.

quiet quitting: See **presenteeism**.

rationalization: refers to the psychological tendency that individuals have to find rational reasons why their own behaviors make sense under the prevailing circumstances that were beyond their control.

reactive devaluation: occurs when an offer in a negotiation is discounted or disregarded due to a lack of trust in the person making the offer, even though the same offer might be accepted or seriously considered if it came from a neutral or trusted source, such as a mediator; a form of attribution bias (see Chapter 2), specific to negotiation and can lead to higher rates of impasse than would be objectively predicted based on the interests of the parties to the negotiation.

reframing refers to the language used to summarize, paraphrase, and reflect on what a party has said but using different words or conceptualizations than originally intended with the goal of altering the course of the communication and interaction between two or more parties. See Chapters 1 and 2.

regulatory agencies: usually a part of the executive branch of the government at the federal or state level, or they have statutory authority to perform their functions with oversight from the legislative branch. Regulatory authorities are commonly set up to enforce standards and safety, regulate commerce, or oversee public goods such as national defense or clean air. Regulatory agencies deal in the area of administrative law—regulation or rulemaking.

relational leadership is a "model of leadership that suggests the effectiveness of a leader and relates their ability to develop positive relationships within an organization. It also relates to the process of people working together to achieve the greater good or accomplish a positive change in the workplace. Relational leaders use empathy skills to empower their teams to build strength in their current skills and develop new skills" (Indeed Editorial Team, 2022).

relationship-based conflict: occurs when two or more people experience non-structural conflict stemming from a lack of rapport or personality conflicts between team members. Relationship conflict is associated with negative impacts on the team's ability to accomplish its tasks (Farh, Lee & Farh, 2010).

relationship-based trust (RBT): built upon the parties' history from past interactions or negotiations. If one's negotiating partner has behaved honorably in past negotiations, then there is "positive relationship-based trust," while a disappointing history leads to negative relationship-based trust.

relationship management: refers to the specific techniques used to court and retain valued customers and partners over a long period of time.

resistance point: while the target point is the goal, the resistance point is the "bottom line." For example, if a merchant purchases his stock wholesale at a cost of $5.00 per unit, his resistance point will generally be somewhere above $5.00. The resistance point is the smallest amount he or she will settle for and is sometimes referred to as the "reservation price" (Lewicki et al., 2010).

resource-based conflict: occurs when two or more people, units, organizations, or even nations compete over perceived limited resources.

restorative justice: a process that defines crime as doing harm to victims, the community, and the wrongdoer, so all of these individuals and groups must be included in efforts to put things right by creating opportunities to encounter each other and really listen. Then, with the help of the mediator, they negotiate amends while seeking to support the offender during and after the process to avoid recidivism and reintegrate him or her back into the community.

revolving door: refers to the fact that government bureaucrats often leave their government careers behind and go to work for the agencies they used to regulate. Similarly, members of Congress often become lobbyists when they leave elected office. The powerful ties between industry, Congress, and government regulatory agencies mean that a relatively small, tight-knit group of powerful decision-makers is usually involved in rulemaking within each agency's issue area. This reduces the number and variety of voices heard when important decisions are being made and increases the public's distrust of many decision-making processes. See Chapter 12.

ripeness: when a dispute is ripe, the timing for intervention is ideal because the parties perceive a mutually hurting stalemate and the possibility of an outcome that is superior to continuing the conflict with the status quo (Coleman et al., 2008a). If intervention occurs too late, tempers are high, resources have been committed that make it hard to walk away or agree to small settlements. At the opposite end of the spectrum, before a conflict is ripe for intervention, it may not be viewed as important, or the parties and issues may be unclear. The goal is to intervene as early as possible, once the parties, issues, and possible options are known but before the sides become so entrenched in an adversarial posture that settlement becomes less likely.

role-based conflict: occurs when someone behaves in a way that is different from what one would anticipate based on their role. For example, if a peer begins issuing directions to colleagues, it could cause conflict out of a belief that it is not their role to issue orders or directions because they are not a superior in the chain of command.

scripted conversation: one in which both parties understand what they are expected to say due to prevailing cultural norms that dictate appropriate and inappropriate responses during the conversation.

secondary stakeholders: individuals or groups who are indirectly impacted by the decisions or actions of an organization.

separation: occurs when little or no culture change comes to either organization, with each having little interaction with the other and no significant cultural changes resulting from the M&A process.

settlement point: the spot within the settlement range where the negotiators reach agreement on settlement terms. The goal in distributive bargaining is to reach an agreement that is close to the other side's resistance point.

settlement range (or the zone of agreement): the space between two resistance points. For example, the buyer's initial offer is $5,000 and her resistance point is $8,000. The seller's initial offer is $9,000 but his resistance point is $6,000. Then the settlement range will be between $6,000 and $8,000.

sexual harassment: according to the U.S. Equal Employment Opportunity Commission, it is unlawful to harass a person (an applicant or employee) because of that person's sex. Harassment can include "sexual harassment" or unwelcome sexual advances, requests for sexual favors, and other verbal or physical harassment of a sexual nature. Harassment does not have to be of a sexual nature, however, and can include offensive remarks about a person's sex. For example, it is illegal to harass a woman by making offensive comments about women in general. Both victim and harasser can be either a woman or a man, and the victim and harasser can be the same sex.

Although the law doesn't prohibit simple teasing, offhand comments, or isolated incidents that are not very serious, harassment is illegal when it is so frequent or severe that it creates a hostile or offensive work environment or when it results in an adverse employment decision (such as the victim being fired or demoted). The harasser can be the victim's supervisor, a supervisor in another area, a coworker, or someone who is not an employee of the employer, such as a client or customer (Equal Employment Opportunity Commission, 2018c).

shared mental model: those aspects of knowledge known by each team member collectively (see Chapter 8).

shirking (also known as **social loafing**): occurs when an employee chooses not to do their share of the collective workload. As a result, other members of the team have to work harder to make up for the employee(s) who is not doing their fair share. Shirkers lead others in the organization to feel disgruntled, overworked, and taken advantage of.

sick-outs (also known as the blue flu): occur when unionized employees stage massive work stoppages by calling in sick for work to show their solidarity and bargaining strength. These sick-outs have sometimes been called the "blue flu" because police officers' unions have used them to overcome laws against labor strikes by first responders and other essential public employees.

skilled labor: that which requires special training, knowledge, and often an apprenticeship, such as plumbers, electricians, or carpenters. Traditionally, the labor market has had a larger surplus of unskilled than skilled laborers, making the former more vulnerable to poverty and at a bargaining disadvantage in terms of their ability to press employers for higher wages or better working conditions.

social categorization: refers to the human tendency to apply labels or categories to individuals in order to better understand them and predict their behavior. For example: Republican/Democrat, black/white, professor/student.

social comparison: once we categorize ourselves as a group member and identify with that group, then we compare our group to other groups. To protect or increase our self-esteem, humans tend to seek out information that confirms the superiority or positivity of their in-group compared to out-groups. This is the root cause of prejudice, discrimination, and even genocide.

social identification: refers to our tendency to model our behaviors and values upon those in our in-group. Meeting the expectations of our in-group is central to positive self-esteem.

social loafing: See **shirking**.

spoiler: someone who uses his power to sabotage the group's progress in order to gain attention or further his own goals. Spoilers usually hold significantly more extreme views than the majority of process participants and can use consensus processes to stall or sabotage outcomes they wish to avoid.

stakeholders: those who are directly or indirectly impacted by a proposed change—they have a stake in the outcome. Within organizations internal stakeholders include employees at all levels and the legal and human resources departments. External stakeholders could include customers, vendors, shareholders, patients or the affected public, and regulators. For public policy facilitation, primary stakeholders are those most immediately impacted by the policy outcomes while secondary stakeholders are those who are impacted, but for whom the impact is more minor and therefore less salient.

strategic leadership: the ability to articulate a vision, set an example, and balance multiple competing demands in ways that promote the best interests of the organization, its people, and the leader himself or herself. Strategic leaders understand the current state of their organization and while predicting future threats or opportunities.

structural sources of conflict: include unfair, unclear, or inefficient policies, procedures, organizational cultures, or ingrained practices that repeatedly give rise to disputes irrespective of personnel changes.

structural violence: refers to "systematic ways in which social structures harm or otherwise disadvantage individuals" (partial definition borrowed from Structural Violence.org, http://www.structuralviolence.org/structural-violence) or groups, usually based on an identity category such as race, culture, gender, national origin, age, sexual orientation, physical ability, etc.

summary jury trials (SJTs): mock trials. In advance of the process, the attorneys and parties in the case reach agreements related to the types of evidence to be admitted, the length of the trial (usually one to three days), and whether the verdict will be binding or advisory. If the process is advisory, it is used as a settlement tool to enable both sides to see the weaknesses in their case and get the jury's objective perspective on the matter. SJTs are most useful for cases that are complex and would take weeks or months to try in court.

sunshine laws: refers to federal, state, and local laws that require regulatory meetings, decisions, and records to be open to the public.

system-level conflicts occur when policies, procedures, institutions, or systems such as economic or justice systems work to the benefit of one or more groups at the expense of one or more other groups. The tendency is to blame individuals for behaviors that are encouraged or required by a broader system. By blaming individuals for systemic problems, the system can continue to function unchanged. For example, when Wells Fargo created unreachable sales goals for employees, the employees responded by opening accounts without the permission of the impacted customers. While individually unethical, it was an open secret that thousands of employees were engaging in this fraudulent activity to keep their jobs (Kelly, 2020). Firing employees would not be sufficient to prevent the recurrence of this problem. Instead, the company's culture and systems must change to ensure the problem is fully resolved. See Chapter 2.

target point: the negotiator's end goal or preferred outcome for the negotiation.

task-based conflict: task conflict occurs when the group disagrees about the best ways to accomplish its tasks. Moderate levels of task conflict are associated with greater creativity and better outcomes, while relationship conflicts are associated with reduced productivity and morale.

team cognition: the ability to think like a team.

team mental model (TMM): a set of jointly held information within a group.

10–80–10 rule: ten percent of employees won't steal or behave unethically under any circumstances. Another 10% are unethical and nothing can be done to change their behaviors other than monitoring and sanctioning them. The other 80% will be influenced by the workplace culture and the thoughts of their peers on the matter. Therefore, the key to reducing workplace theft, ethics violations, and malfeasance is to create a workplace culture in which employees feel loyalty toward their organizations and where cultural norms mitigate against such behaviors.

theory of relative deprivation: states that a sense of injustice can arise when one compares one's distribution to others in a competitive environment and sees that others are receiving more.

transaction costs: every negotiation entails transaction costs, which include the time, energy, and money necessary to facilitate the negotiation and the deal itself.

transactional leadership is "a managerial style that relies on attaining goals through structure, supervision and a system of rewards and punishments. This results-oriented approach works well with self-motivated employees. Transactional leadership doesn't focus on changing or improving the organization, but instead, aims to hit short-term goals while establishing unity and conformity with the company. The rewards or punishments are, therefore, referred to as the 'transaction'" (Indeed Editorial Team, 2022).

transactive memory system (TMS): a mental map disseminating the information held by individual members of a team and clarifying who knows what within the team.

transformational leadership is a theory of leadership in which the leader works with followers to go beyond their self-interest to adopt a collective identity as a team and organization to identify needed change, create a vision to guide the change through influence and inspiration, and executing the change in tandem with committed members of a group. Transformational leadership enhances motivation, morale, and the performance of employees by connecting their sense of identity to the organization; being a role model who inspires them and raises their interest in the mission; challenging employees to take greater ownership for their work; and understanding the strengths and weaknesses of team members, which allows the leader to align employees with tasks that enhance their performance. Transformational leaders are strong in the abilities to adapt to different situations, share a collective consciousness, self-manage, and be inspirational while leading a group.

union grievance: any alleged violation of the "contract, past practice, employer rules, previous grievance or arbitration settlements [which set precedence for the contract's interpretation], or any violation of laws such as Occupational Health and Safety, Americans with Disabilities Act, Family Medical Leave Act, or EEOC regulations on race, age or sex discrimination" (UE Information for Workers, 2011).

union steward: the first point of contact for each rank-and-file union member when a grievance arises. The union steward is usually a position elected by the union members, someone who is generally liked and trusted by the employees. The steward can advise the union member as to whether the complaint is an actual violation of the union contract and offer information about the available dispute resolution options. The union steward may also accompany the employee to any grievance process such as mediation or arbitration and represent them in that process. The steward can provide information about the contents of the collective bargaining agreement and those issues that may or may not fall under its terms.

unskilled labor: those whose jobs require little training and education, making workers easily replaced at a lower cost to employers. Traditionally, the labor market has had a larger surplus of unskilled than skilled laborers, making the former more vulnerable to poverty and at a bargaining disadvantage in terms of their ability to press employers for higher wages or better working conditions.

values conflict: occurs when two or more people have differing views about what is right and wrong, sacred or profane, important or unimportant based on different perspectives, viewpoints, identity categories, and/or religious upbringing.

vertical sex segregation refers to the gendered division of labor in which women are more commonly represented at the lowest levels of a corporation and more absent at the highest levels (see Nemoto, 2017).

whistleblowers report illegal, unethical, or counter-policy actions committed by their organization or its leaders. These reports may be made internally to persons of authority within the organization, or they may be made externally to law enforcement agencies, government regulators, or other possible sources of redress. Usually, whistleblowers act in the public or national security interests, at great risk of reprisal or retaliation.

white collar: a term used to describe skilled workers who do not usually wear uniforms, who undertake intellectual rather than physical work, and who have generally pursued education beyond secondary school (meaning they have attended college or university). These employees generally include supervisors and managers. The labels of white versus blue collar are loosely defined, with many jobs meeting one or more of these conditions but not all. For example, nurses wear uniforms but their level of education and pay places them among the white-collar rather than blue-collar workforce.

"win-win": viewpoint, meaning that for one person to win in a negotiation or conflict, the other person's needs must also be met (meaning they must also win).

zero-sum negotiations: also called distributive negotiation situations, in zero-sum negotiations, there is only one winner at the end of the negotiation. Each gain made by one negotiator comes at the expense of another negotiator.

References

Adelson, E. (2017). Power of kneeling Kennesaw State cheerleaders revealed in president's resignation. *Yahoo! Sports.* https://sports.yahoo.com/power-kneeling-kennesaw-state-cheerleaders-revealed-presidents-resignation-224610819.html

Adler, P. S., & Fisher, R. C. (2007). Leading from behind: The un-heroic challenge of leading leaders. *ACResolution,* Summer, 18–21.

ADR.gov. (2023, May 11). *Environmental conflict resolution.* https://adr.gov/about-adr/environmental-conflict-resolution/

Alexander, M. (1999). *Transforming your workplace: A model for implementing change and labour-management cooperation.* IRC Press.

Allen, D. G. (2008). *Retaining talent: A guide to analyzing and managing employee turnover.* SHRM Foundation. http://www.shrm.org/about/foundation/research/Documents/Retaining%20Talent-%20Final.pdf

Alliance for Board Diversity. (2018, March 16). *Despite modest gains, women and minorities see little change in representation on Fortune 500 boards.* https://hacr.org/2017/02/06/despite-modest-gains-women-and-minorities-see-little-change/

Allred, K. G. (2000). Anger and retaliation in conflict: The role of attribution. In M. Deutsch & P. Coleman (Eds.), *The handbook of conflict resolution: Theory and practice* (pp. 236–255). Jossey-Bass.

Althen, G., & Bennett, J. (2011). *American ways: A guide for foreigners in the United States* (4th ed.). Intercultural Press.

Amanatullah, E. T., & Morris, M. W. (2010). Negotiating gender roles: Gender differences in assertive negotiating are mediated by women's fear of backlash and attenuated when negotiating on behalf of others. *Journal of Personality and Social Psychology, 98*(2), 256–267.

Amble, B. (2006, May 26). Poor conflict management costs business billions. *Management Issues Ltd.* https://www.management-issues.com/news/3262/poor-conflict-management-costs-business-billions/

Anderson, L. L., Jr., & Polkinghorn, B. (2008). Managing conflict in construction megaprojects: Leadership and third-party principles. *Conflict Resolution Quarterly, 26*(2), 167–198.

Angier, T. (2009, November 23). The biology behind the milk of human kindness. *New York Times,* p. D2.

Arruda, W. (2016, November 16). 9 differences between being a leader and a manager. *Forbes*. https://www.forbes.com/sites/williamarruda/2016/11/15/9-differences-between-being-a-leader-and-a-manager/?sh=6596e9346096

Arthur, J., Carlson, C., & Moore, J. (1999). *A practical guide to consensus*. Policy Consensus Initiative.

Association of Certified Fraud Examiners (CFE). (2004). *2004 report to the nation on occupational fraud and abuse*. http://www.acfe.com/uploadedFiles/ACFE_Website/Content/documents/2004RttN.pdf

Austin, J. R. (2003). Transactive memory in organizational groups: The effects of content, consensus, specialization, and accuracy on group performance. *Journal of Applied Psychology, 88*(5), 866–878.

Babiak, P., & Hare, R. D. (2006). *Snakes in suits: When psychopaths go to work*. HarperCollins.

Baghat, S., Brickley, J. A., & Coles, J. L. (1994). The costs of inefficient bargaining and financial distress: Evidence from corporate lawsuits. *Journal of Financial Economics, 35*(2), 221–247.

Bandura, A. (1973). *Aggression: A social learning analysis*. Prentice Hall.

Baracz, S., & Buisman-Pijlman, F. (2017, October 16). *How childhood trauma changes our hormones, and thus our mental health, into adulthood*. The Conversation. https://theconversation.com/how-childhood-trauma-changes-our-hormones-and-thus-our-mental-health-into-adulthood-84689

Baril, M. B. (2021, February 16). The high cost of unmanaged conflict in your organization. *Forbes*. https://www.forbes.com/sites/forbescoachescouncil/2021/02/16/the-high-costs-of-unmanaged-conflict-in-your-organization/?sh=32e1b621ca9a

Barrett, J. T. (2007). Labor-management golden years: A foundation for today's ADR. *ACResolution*, Summer, 4.

Barween, A. K., Alshurideh, M., & Alnaser, A. (2020). The impact of employee satisfaction on customer satisfaction: Theoretical and empirical underpinning. *Management Science Letters, 10*(15), 3561–3570.

Bass, B., & Bass, R. (2009). *The handbook of leadership: Theory, research, and managerial applications*. Free Press.

Bastian, R. (2019, March 8). Personality-based performance reviews are fine to give women—As long as men get them too. *Forbes*. https://www.forbes.com/sites/rebekahbastian/2019/03/08/personality-based-performance-reviews-are-fine-to-give-women-as-long-as-men-get-them-too/?sh=642746e31667

Bazerman, M. H., & Neale, M. A. (1992). *Negotiating rationally*. Free Press.

BBC News. (2017, July 20). *What is India's caste system?* https://www.bbc.com/news/world-asia-india-35650616

Bean, S. (2018, April 6). *Women are happier and more engaged at work than men, despite the gender pay gap*. https://workplaceinsight.net/women-happier-at-work-than-men-despite-the-gender-pay-gap/

Bednarek, R., & Smith, W. K. (2023). "What may be": Inspiration from Mary Parker Follett for paradox theory. *Strategic Organization, 0*(0). https://doi.org/10.1177/14761270231151734

Beierle, T. C., & Cayford, J. (2002). *Democracy in practice: Public participation in environmental decisions*. RFF Press.

Bendick, M., & Nunes, A. P. (2012). Developing the research basis for controlling bias in hiring. *Journal of Social Issues, 68*, 238–262. https://doi.org/10.1111/j.1540-4560.2012.01747.x

Beng-Chong, L., & Klein, K. J. (2006). Team mental models and team performance: A field study of the effects of team mental model similarity and accuracy. *Journal of Organizational Behavior, 27*(4), 403.

Bennhold, K. (2010, January 17). In Germany, a tradition falls, and women rise. *New York Times.* https://www.nytimes.com/2010/01/18/world/europe/18iht-women.html

Bennhold, K. (2011, June 28). Women nudged out of German workforce. *New York Times.* https://www.nytimes.com/2011/06/29/world/europe/29iht-FFgermany29.html

Bens, I. (2005). *Facilitating with ease! Core skills for facilitators, team leaders and members, managers, consultants, and trainers.* Jossey-Bass.

Bernstein, J. (2017, August 24). Bend the trend: Reviving unionization in America. *Washington Post.* https://www.washingtonpost.com/news/posteverything/wp/2017/08/24/bend-the-trend-reviving-unionization-in-america/?noredirect=on&utm_term=.1bfae0be9e62

Bessette, J. M. (1980). Deliberative democracy: The majority principle in Republican government. In R. Goldwin & W. Shambra (Eds.), *How democratic is the Constitution?* (pp. 102–116). AEI Press.

Bingham, L. B. (2004). Employment dispute resolution: The case for mediation. *Conflict Resolution Quarterly, 22*(1–2), 145–174.

Bingham, L. B. (2008). Designing justice: Legal institutions and other systems for managing conflict. *Ohio State Journal on Dispute Resolution, 24,* 1–51.

Bingham, L. B., Hedeen, T., Napoli, L. M., & Raines, S. S. (2003). *A tale of three cities: Before and after REDRESS.* Unpublished manuscript.

Bingham, L. B., Kim, K., & Raines, S. S. (2002). Exploring the role of representation in employment mediation at the U.S.P.S. *Ohio State Journal on Dispute Resolution, 17,* 341–378.

Bingham, L. B., Nabatchi, T., Senger, J., & Jackman, M. S. (2009). Dispute resolution and the vanishing trial: Comparing federal government litigation and ADR outcomes. *Ohio State Journal of Dispute Resolution, 24,* 225–262.

Bingham, L. B., & Novac, M. C. (2001). Mediation's impact on formal discrimination complaint filing: Before and after the REDRESS program at the USPS. *Review of Public Personnel Administration, 21,* 308–331.

Birkinshaw, J., Bresman, H., & Hakanson, L. (2000). Managing the post-acquisition integration process: How the human integration and task integration processes interact to foster value creation. *Journal of Management Studies, 37*(3), 395–425.

Birt, J., Herrity, J., & Esparza, E. (2022, June 7). *7 characteristics about Generation Z in the workplace.* Indeed.com.

Black, D. W. (2015, July). The natural history of anti-social personality disorder. *Canadian Journal of Psychiatry, 60*(7), 309–314.

Blackard, K. (2000). *Managing change in a unionized workplace: Countervailing collaboration.* Greenwood.

Bland, V. (2004). Keeping customers (satisfied). *NZBusiness, 18*(8), 16–20.

Blank, A. (2016, May 24). Jolt your corporate board with a millennial like Starbucks. *Forbes.* https://www.forbes.com/sites/averyblank/2016/05/24/jolt-your-corporate-board-with-a-millennial-like-starbucks/?sh=7659215166a3

Blodget, H. (2011, March 20). *Eight habits of highly effective Google managers.* Business Insider. https://www.businessinsider.com/8-habits-of-highly-effective-google-managers-2011-3

Blomgren Amsler, L., Martinez, J. K., and Smith, S. E. (2020). *Dispute system design: Preventing, managing, & resolving conflict.* Stanford University Press.

Bolman, D. G., & Deal, T. E. (2017). *Reframing organizations: Artistry, choice and leadership* (6th ed.). Jossey-Bass.

Bonnivier, B. M., Brooke-Lander, M. C., & Lewis, M. R. (2015, March 16–18). *The organizational ombuds office and corporate social responsibility: Driving values in an organization* [Conference presentation]. Society for Petroleum Engineers, Denver, CO.

Brasor, P., & Tsubuko, M. (2018, July 13). Poverty in Japan: Underclass struggles to achieve upward mobility. *Japan Times*. https://www.japantimes.co.jp/news/2018/07/13/business/poverty-japan-underclass-struggles-achieve-upward-mobility/#. XBuZgFVKjIU

Braun, S. (2017). Leader narcissism and outcomes in organizations: A review at multiple levels of analysis and implications for future research. *Frontiers in Psychology, 8*, 773.

Bridges, W. (1991). *Managing change in a unionized workplace: Countervailing collaboration*. Greenwood.

Brosnan, M., Turner-Cobb, J., Munro-Naan, Z., & Jessop, D. (2009). Absence of a normal cortisol awakening response (CAR) in adolescent males with Asperger Syndrome (AS). *Psychoneuroendocrinology, 34*(7), 1095–1100. http://opus.bath.ac.uk/13807/

Brown, B. (2018). *Dare to lead: Brave work, tough conversations, whole hearts*. Random House.

Brown, J., & Isaacs, D. (2005). *The world café: Shaping our futures through conversations that matter*. Berrett-Koehler.

Bruner, R. F. (2005). *M&A lessons that rise above the ashes: Deals from hell*. Wiley.

Bryant, A. (2011, March 13). The quest to build a better boss. *New York Times*. http://query.nytimes.com/gst/fullpage.html?res=9503E3DD173EF930A25750C0A9679D8B63&scp=2&sq=Google%27s%20Quest%20to%20Build%20a%20Better%20Boss&st=cse

Burnett, B., & Evans. D. (2016). *Designing your life: How to lead a well-built, joyful life*. Knopf.

Bush, R. A., & Folger, J. P. (1994). *The promise of mediation: The transformative approach to conflict*. Jossey-Bass.

Business Dictionary. (2018). *Definition: Organizational culture*. http://www.businessdictionary.com/definition/organizational-culture.html

Callahan, R. (2023, March 18). Personal interview.

Captain, S. (2017, July 31). *Workers win only 1% of civil rights lawsuits at trial*. Fast Company.

Carpenter, S. L., & Kennedy, W. J. (2001). *Managing public disputes: A practical guide for government, business and citizen's groups*. Jossey-Bass.

Carson, B., & Gould, S. (2017, June 26). Uber's bad year: The stunning string of blows that upended the world's most valuable startup. https://www.businessinsider.com/uber-scandal-crisis-complete-timeline-2017-6.

Cartwright, S., & Cooper, C. L. (1994). The human effects of mergers and acquisitions. *Journal of Organizational Behavior, 1*, 47–61.

Census.gov. (2021). *2020 U.S. population more racially and ethnically diverse than measured in 2010*. https://www.census.gov/library/stories/2021/08/2020-united-states-population-more-racially-ethnically-diverse-than-2010.html

Chan, K. W., Huang, X., & Ng, P. M. (2008). Managers' conflict management styles and employee attitudinal outcomes: The mediating role of trust. *Asia Pacific Journal Management, 25*(2), 277–295.

Chapman, G. (2010). *The five love languages: The secret to love that lasts*. Gale Cengage.

Charkoudian, L., Eisenberg, D. T., & Walter, J. L. (2017). What difference does ADR make? Comparison of ADR and trial outcomes in small claims court. *Conflict Resolution Quarterly, 35*, 7–45.

Charkoudian, L., Eisenberg, D. T., Walter, J. L. (2019). What works in alternative dispute resolution? The impact of third-party neutral strategies in small claims cases. *Conflict Resolution Quarterly, 37*, 101–121. https://doi.org/10.1002/crq.21264

Charkoudian, L., & Wilson, C. (2006). Factors affecting individuals' decisions to use community mediation. *Review of Policy Research, 23*, 865–885.

Chaykowski, R., Cutcher-Gershenfeld, J., Kochan, T., & Sickles Merchant, C. (2001). Facilitating resolution in union-management relationships: A guide for neutrals. *Soci-*

ety for Professionals in Dispute Resolution. http://digitalcommons.ilr.cornell.edu/cgi /viewcontent.cgi?article=1002&context=icrpubs

Cherry, K. (2012). *What is emotional intelligence? Definition, history and measures of emotional intelligence.* About.com Psychology. http://psychology.about.com/od /personalitydevelopment/a/emotionalintell.htm

Children's Healthcare of Atlanta (CHOA). (2011). *Facts about children's awards: A model for pediatric care.* http://www.choa.org/About-Childrens/Awards-and-Recognition/Facts -and-Figures

Cianci, R., & Gambrel, P. A. (2003). Maslow's hierarchy of needs: Does it apply in a collectivist culture? *Journal of Applied Management and Entrepreneurship, 8*(2), 143–161.

Cloke, K., & Goldsmith, J. (1997). *The end of management and the rise of organizational democracy.* Jossey-Bass.

Cloke, K., & Goldsmith, J. (2003). *The art of waking people up: Cultivating awareness and authenticity at work.* Jossey-Bass.

Cole, M. S., Walter, F., & Bruch, H. (2008). The affective mechanisms linking dysfunctional behavior to performance in work teams: A moderated mediation study. *Journal of Applied Psychology, 93,* 945–958.

Coleman, D. (1992). How to achieve a productive partnership. *Journal of Accountancy, 173*(5), 113–118.

Coleman, P. T., Fisher-Yoshida, B., Stover, M. A., Hacking, A. G., & Bartoli, A. (2008b). Reconstructing ripeness II: Models and methods for fostering constructive stakeholder engagement across protracted divides. *Conflict Resolution Quarterly, 26,* 43–69. https://doi.org/10.1002/crq.223

Coleman, P. T., Hacking, A. G., Stover, M. A., Fisher-Yoshida, B., & Nowak, A. (2008a). Reconstructing ripeness I: A study of constructive engagement in protracted social conflicts. *Conflict Resolution Quarterly, 26,* 3–42. https://doi.org/10.1002/crq.222

Colquitt, J. A., Conlon, D. E., Wesson, M. J., Porter, C., & Ng, K. Y. (2001). Justice at the millennium: A meta-analytic review of 25 years of organizational justice research. *Journal of Applied Psychology, 86,* 425–445.

Colvin, A. (2004). The relationship between employee involvement and workplace dispute resolution. *Relations Industrielles, 59*(4), 681–704.

Comaford, C. (2016, August 21). 75% of workers are affected by workplace bullying: Here's what to do about it. *Forbes.* https://www.forbes.com/sites/christinecomaford /2016/08/27/the-enormous-toll-workplace-bullying-takes-on-your-bottom-line/#146 b2ab25595

Commisceo Global. (2018). South Korea Management Guide. *International Management Guides.* https://www.commisceo-global.com/resources/management-guides/south-ko rea-management-guide

Constantino, C. A., & Merchant, C. S. (1996). *Designing conflict management systems: A guide to creating productive and healthy organizations.* Jossey-Bass.

Cooke, N. J., Gorman, J. C., Duran, J. L., & Taylor, A. R. (2007). Team cognition in experienced command-and-control teams. *Journal of Experimental Psychology, 13*(3), 146–157.

Covey, S. M. R. (2008). *The speed of trust.* Simon & Schuster.

Cox, D. (2010). *An examination of the impact of culture and human resources on cross-border M&A transactions* (Unpublished master's thesis). Kennesaw State University.

CPR Institute for Dispute Resolution. (2002). New skills and renewed challenges: Building better negotiation skills. *Alternatives, 20*(8), 1–22.

Crothers, L. M. (2009). Cliques, rumors, and gossip by the water cooler: Female bullying in the workplace. *Psychologist-Manager Journal, 12,* 97–100.

Dana, D. (2001). *The Dana measure of financial cost of organizational conflict.* Mediation Training Institute. http://www.mediationworks.com/dmi/toolbox.htm

Danning, S. (2018, July 26). How to fix stagnant wages: Dump the world's dumbest idea. *Forbes.* https://www.forbes.com/sites/stevedenning/2018/07/26/how-to-fix-stagnant-wages-dump-the-worlds-dumbest-idea/#7bf9be381abc

DeChurch, L. A., & Marks, M. A. (2001). Maximizing the benefits of task conflict: The role of conflict management. *International Journal of Conflict Management, 12*(1), 4.

DeChurch, L. A., & Mesmer-Magnus, J. (2010). The cognitive underpinnings of effective teamwork: A meta-analysis. *Journal of Applied Psychology, 95*(1), 32–53.

DeCusatis, C. (2008). Creating, growing and sustaining efficient innovation teams. *Creativity and Innovation Management, 17*(2), 155.

Deloitte. (2017). *2017 board diversity report: Seeing is believing.* https://www2.deloitte.com/us/en/pages/about-deloitte/articles/board-diversity-survey.html

Denning, D. (2011, July 23). An organization's culture comprises an interlocking set of goals, roles, processes, values, communications practices, attitudes and assumptions. *Forbes.* https://www.forbes.com/sites/stevedenning/2011/07/23/how-do-you-change-an-organizational-culture/#699a017b39dc

Department of Defense. (2022, September 1). Department of Defense releases fiscal year 2021 annual report on sexual assault in the military. https://www.defense.gov/News/Releases/Release/Article/3147042/department-of-defense-releases-fiscal-year-2021-annual-report-on-sexual-assault/

Desilver, D. (2018, August 7). *For most U.S. workers, real wages have barely budged in decades.* Pew Research Center. http://www.pewresearch.org/fact-tank/2018/08/07/for-most-us-workers-real-wages-have-barely-budged-for-decades/

Deutsch, M. (2000). Justice and conflict. In M. Deutsch & P. Coleman (Eds.), *The handbook of conflict resolution: Theory and practice* (pp. 41–64). Jossey-Bass.

Deutsch, M., Coleman, P., & Marcus, E. C. (Eds.). (2006). *The handbook of conflict resolution: Theory and practice.* Jossey-Bass.

Devasagayam, R., & DeMars, J. (2004). Consumer perceptions of alternative dispute resolution mechanisms in financial transactions. *Journal of Financial Services Marketing, 8*(4), 378.

Dhwan, E. (2021, March 7). Did you get my slack/email/text? *Harvard Business Review.* https://hbr.org/2021/05/did-you-get-my-slack-email-text

Diaz, J. (2022, August 31). *Support for labor unions in the US is at a 57 year high.* National Public Radio. https://www.npr.org/2022/08/31/1120111276/labor-union-support-in-us

Dictionary.com. (2019). Personality disorder. https://www.dictionary.com/browse/personality-disorder

Dirks, K. T. (1999). The effects of interpersonal trust on work group performance. *Journal of Applied Psychology, 84*(3), 445–455.

DOJ. (2018). *Alternative dispute resolution at the Department of Justice.* https://www.justice.gov/olp/alternative-dispute-resolution-department-justice

Doran, G. T. (1981). There's a S.M.A.R.T. way to write management's goals and objectives. *Management Review, 70* (11), 35–36.

Drahozal, C. R., & Ware, S. J. (2010). Why do businesses use (or not use) arbitration clauses? *Ohio State Journal on Dispute Resolution, 25*(2), 433–476.

Drucker, P. F. (2002). They're not employees, they're people. *Harvard Business Review, 80*(2), 70–77.

Druckman, J. (2001). Evaluating framing effects. *Journal of Economic Psychology, 22,* 96–101.

Duarte, M., & Davies, G. (2003). Testing the conflict—Performance assumption in business-to-business relationships. *Industrial Marketing Management, 32*(2), 91–99.

Duckworth, A. (2016). *Grit: The power of passion & perseverance.* Scribner.

Duffy, J. (2010). Empathy, neutrality and emotional intelligence: A balancing act for the emotional Einstein. *Queensland University of Technology Law & Justice Journal,* 10(1), 44–61.

Duhigg, C. (2016, February 25). What Google learned from its quest to build the perfect team: New research reveals surprising truths about why some work groups thrive while others falter. *New York Times.* https://www.nytimes.com/2016/02/28/magazine/what -google-learned-from-its-quest-to-build-the-perfect-team.html

Duxbury, L., & Higgins, C. (2003). *Work-life conflict in Canada in the new millennium: A status report.* Public Health Agency of Canada. http://www.phac-aspc.gc.ca/publicat /work-travail/report2/index-eng.php

Dweck, C. (2007). *Mindset: The new psychology of success. How we can learn to fulfill our success.* Ballentine Books.

The Economist. (2016, June 11). *South Korea's working women: Of careers and carers* (Print edition). Seoul, Korea. https://www.economist.com/asia/2016/06/11/of-careers -and-carers

Eddy, B. (2016). *High conflict people in legal disputes.* Unhooked Books.

Eddy, B., & DiStefano, L. G. (2015). *It's all your fault at work: Managing narcissists and other high-conflict people.* Unhooked Books.

Egan, M. (2016, September 9). *5300 Wells Fargo employees fired over 2 million phony accounts.* CNN Business. https://money.cnn.com/2016/09/08/investing/wells-fargo -created-phony-accounts-bank-fees/index.html

Egan, M. (2018, September 7). The two-year Wells Fargo horror story that just won't end. *CNN Business.* https://money.cnn.com/2018/09/07/news/companies/wells-fargo -scandal-two-years/index.html

Einarsen, S., Hoel, H., Zapf, D., & Cooper, C. L. (2003). The concept of bullying at work: The European tradition. In S. Einarsen, H. Hoel, D. Zapf, & C. L. Cooper (Eds.), *Bullying and emotional abuse in the workplace* (pp. 3–30). Taylor & Francis.

Einarsen, S., & Skogstad, A. (1996). Bullying at work: Epidemiological findings in public and private organizations. *European Journal of Work and Organizational Psychology,* 5(2), 185–201.

Emerson, K., Orr, P. J., Keyes, D. L., & Mcknight, K. M. (2009). Environmental conflict resolution: Evaluating performance outcomes and contributing factors. *Conflict Resolution Quarterly, 27,* 27–64.

Engaging employees through social responsibility. (2007). *Leader to Leader, 46,* 56–58. http://www.sirota.com/pdfs/Engaging_Employees_through_Social_Responsibility.pdf

Environmental Protection Agency (EPA). (2000, May). *Resource guide: Resolving environmental conflicts in communities.* https://www.epa.gov/sites/default/files/2015-09 /documents/resguide.pdf

Equal Employment Opportunity Commission (EEOC). (2009). *EEOC mediation statistics FY 1999 through FY 2007.* US Equal Employment Opportunity Commission. http:// www.eeoc.gov/mediate/mediation_stats.html

Equal Employment Opportunity Commission (EEOC). (2010). *EEOC reports job bias charges hit record high of nearly 100,000 in fiscal year 2010.* News release. http://www .eeoc.gov/eeoc/newsroom/release/1-11-11.cfm

Equal Employment Opportunity Commission (EEOC). (2018a). *All charges alleging harassment (Charges filed with EEOC) FY 2010–FY 2017.* https://www.eeoc.gov/eeoc /statistics/enforcement/all_harassment.cfm

Equal Employment Opportunity Commission (EEOC). (2018b). *Sexual harassment.* https://www.eeoc.gov/laws/types/sexual_harassment.cfm

Equal Employment Opportunity Commission (EEOC). (2018c). *What you can expect after you file a charge.* https://www.eeoc.gov/employees/process.cfm

Equal Employment Opportunity Commission (EEOC). (2022, February 21). *EEOC Releases fiscal year 2020 enforcement and litigation data.* https://www.eeoc.gov/news room/eeoc-releases-fiscal-year-2020-enforcement-and-litigation-data

Ewing, J. (2018, July 25). Wages are rising in Europe. But economists are puzzled. *New York Times.* https://www.nytimes.com/2018/07/25/business/europe-ecb-wages-infla tion.html

Expatica. (2018). *Understanding German business culture.* https://www.expatica.com /de/employment/Understanding-German-business-culture_100983.html

Farh, J., Lee, C., & Farh, C. I. (2010). Task conflict and team creativity: A question of how much and when. *Journal of Applied Psychology, 95*(6), 1173–1180.

Farrell, L. U. (2002, March 18). Workplace bullying's high cost: $180m in lost time, productivity. *Orlando Business Journal.* http://orlando.bizjournals.com/orlando/sto ries/2002/03/18/focus1.html

Farrugia, J. D. (2022, September 13). *7 statistics on employee turnover in 2022 every HR manager should be aware of employee engagement.* https://workforce.com/news/7 -statistics-on-employee-turnover-in-2022-every-hr-manager-should-be-aware-of

Fedor, D. B., & Herold, D. M. (2008). *Change the way you lead change.* Stanford Business Books.

Fisher, R., & Ury, W. (1981). *Getting to yes: Negotiating agreement without giving in.* Penguin.

Folger, J. P., Poole, M. S., & Stutman, R. K. (2000). *Working through conflict: Strategies for relationships, groups, and organizations* (4th ed.). Longman.

Follett, M. P. (1942). In M. Follett & L. Urwick (Eds.), *Dynamic administration: The collected papers of Mary Parker Follett: Early sociology of management and organizations* (Vol. 3). Taylor & Francis. November 2003 (republished).

Follett, M. P. (1973). Constructive conflict. In E. M. Fox & L. Urwick (Eds.), *Dynamic administration: The collected papers of Mary Parker Follett* (pp. 1–20). Pitman. http:// www.columbia.edu/~mwm82/negotiation/FollettConstructiveConflict.pdf

Ford, J. (2000). *Workplace conflict: Facts and figures.* http://www.mediate.com/articles /Ford1.cfm

Forsyth, D. R. (2006). *Group dynamics* (4th ed.). Thomson Wadsworth.

Fowler, E. (2011, July 28). *State attorney general questions Cobb School Board's emails.* SouthCobbPatch. http://southcobb.patch.com/articles/state-attorney-general-ques tions-cobb-school-boards-emails-2

Friedlander, F. (1970). The primacy of trust as a facilitator of further group accomplishment. *Journal of Applied Behavioral Science, 6*(4), 387–400.

Garcia, J. D. (2018). *Privilege (social inequality).* Salem Press Encyclopedia.

Garland's Digest. (2012). *Hooters of America, Inc. v. Phillips,* 173 F.3d 933; 4th Cir. April 8, 1999. http://www.garlands-digest.com/cs/4th/1990s/99/040499ho.html

Garrett, H. J. (2018, December 28). The kernel of human (or rodent) kindness: What we can learn from lab rats that don't show empathy for other rats. *New York Times.* https:// www.nytimes.com/2018/12/28/opinion/empathy-research-morality-rats.html

Gault, D. (2011). *Creating respectful, violence-free productive workplaces: A community level response to workplace violence.* Ramsey County Department of Public Health. http://www.tandfonline.com/doi/abs/10.1300/J135v04n03_08#preview

Gerzon, M. (2006). *Leading through conflict.* Harvard Business Press.

Gevers, J. M., & Peeters, M. (2009). A pleasure working together? The effects of dissimilarity in team member conscientiousness on team temporal processes and individual satisfaction. *Journal of Organizational Behavior, 30*(3), 379–400.

Gillespie, B. M., Chaboyer, W., & Murray, P. (2010, December). Enhancing communication in surgery through team training interventions: A systematic literature review. *AORN Journal, 92*(6), 642–657.

Gilmer v. Interstate/Johnson Corporation. (1991). https://supreme.justia.com/cases/fed eral/us/500/20/

Global Affairs Canada. (2018). *Cultural information for work in Japan.* https://www.inter national.gc.ca/cil-cai/country_insights-apercus_pays/ci-ic_jp.aspx?lang=eng

Globe. (2020). *Global leadership and organizational effectiveness.* https://globeproject .com/studies

Godt, P. T. (2005). Additional tips for dealing with "difficult" people. *Illinois Reading Council Journal, 33*(3), 57–59.

Gottman, J. (2014). *Principia amoris: The new science of love.* Routledge.

Gottman, J., & Schwartz Gottman, J. (2022). *The love prescription: Seven days to more intimacy, connection, and joy.* Penguin Life.

Goudreau, J. (2011). Disappearing middle class jobs. *Forbes.* http://www.forbes.com/sites /jennagoudreau/2011/06/22/disappearing-middle-class-jobs/

Gray, B. (1989). *Collaborating: Finding common ground for multiparty problems.* Jossey-Bass.

Green, K. (2017). *Life coach.* Bureau of Labor Statistics: U.S. Department of Labor. https:// www.bls.gov/careeroutlook/2017/youre-a-what/life-coach.htm

Greenberg, J. (1990). Looking fair vs. being fair: Managing impressions of organizational justice. In B. M. Staw & L. L. Cummings (Eds.), *Research in organizational behavior* (Vol. 12, pp. 111–157). JAI Press.

Greengard, S. (2003). Keeping the customer satisfied. *CIO Insight, 109,* 32–35.

"Groupthink." *Merriam-Webster.com Dictionary.* https://www.merriam-webster.com /dictionary/groupthink.

Gulati, R., Mayo, A. J., & Nohria, N. (2017). *Management: An integrated approach.* Cengage Publishing.

Gunnar, M. R., & Fisher, P. A. (2006). Bringing basic research on early experience and stress neurobiology to bear on preventive interventions for neglected and maltreated children. *Development and Psychopathology, 18*(3), 651–677.

Gurchiek, K. (2016, May 9) *What motivates your workers? It depends on their generation.* Society for Human Resource Management (SHRM). https://www.shrm.org/ResourcesAnd Tools/hr-topics/behavioral-competencies/global-and-cultural-effectiveness/Pages/What -Motivates-Your-Workers-It-Depends-on-Their-Generation.aspx#:~:text=AbelLanier%20 recommended%20the%20following%20ways%20to%20motivate%20a,strengths%20 through%20a%20mentorship%20program.%20...%20More%20items

Hallberlin, C. J. (2001). Transforming workplace culture through mediation: Lessons learned from swimming upstream. *Hofstra Labor & Employment Law Journal, 18,* 375–383.

Hamilton, W. D. (1964). The genetical evolution of social behaviour I and II. *Journal of Theoretical Biology, 7,* 1–52.

Handelsblatt Global. (2018, November 23). *Why Germans take vacations so seriously.* https://global.handelsblatt.com/politics/why-germans-take-their-vacations-so -seriously-807331

Harms, P. D., & Credé, M. (2010). Emotional intelligence and transformational and transactional leadership: A meta-analysis. *Journal of Leadership & Organizational Studies, 17*(1), 5–17.

Harrell, M., & Barbato, L. (2018, February 28). *Great managers still matter: The evolution of Google's Project Oxygen.* re:Work. https://rework.withgoogle.com/blog/the -evolution-of-project-oxygen/

Harrison, B. C., Harris, J. W., & Tolchin, S. J. (2009). *American democracy now.* McGraw-Hill.

Harrison, O. (2008). *Open space technology: A user's guide* (3rd ed.). Barrett-Koehler.

Hayes, J. (2008). Foreword. In CCP GLOBAL, *Workplace conflict and how businesses can harness it to thrive.* http://img.en25.com/Web/CPP/Conflict_report.pdf

Haynes, C. (2009). *Conflict management for mergers, acquisitions and downsizing* (Unpublished master's thesis). Kennesaw State University.

Health Canada. (1998). *Workplace health system.* Canadian Fitness and Lifestyle Research Institute. http://www.hc-sc.gc.ca/ewh-semt/pubs/occup-travail/absenteeism/index-eng.php

Hedeen, T., Rowe, M., & Schneider, A. (2018). *International ombudsman association 2017 compensation report.* International Ombudsman Association, p. 14.

Hempel, P. S., Zhang, Z., & Tjosvold, D. (2009). Conflict management between and within teams for trusting relationships and performance in China. *Journal of Organizational Behavior, 30*(1), 41–65.

Herrera, T. (2018, April 8). Three steps to avoid giving biased feedback. *New York Times.* https://www.nytimes.com/2018/04/08/smarter-living/give-better-feedback.html

Hersh, E. (2017). *Why diversity matters: Women on boards of directors.* Harvard School of Public Health. https://www.hsph.harvard.edu/ecpe/why-diversity-matters-women-on-boards-of-directors/

Hess, A. (2018, July 6). *Here's how many paid vacation days the average American worker gets.* CNBC. https://www.cnbc.com/2018/07/05/heres-how-many-paid-vacation-days-the-typical-american-worker-gets-.html

Hickok, T. A. (1998). Downsizing organizational culture. *Journal of Public Administration and Management, 3*(3).

Hippensteele, S. K. (2009). Revisiting the promise of mediation for employment discrimination claims. *Pepperdine Dispute Resolution Law Journal, 9,* 211.

Hirsch, B. (2006). *Wage determination in the US airline industry: Union power under product market constraints.* Institute for the Study of Labor. http://ftp.iza.org/dp2384.pdf

Hofstede, G. (1984, January). Cultural dimensions in management and planning. *Asia Pacific Journal of Management, 1*(2), 81–99.

Hooters of America v. Phillips. (1999). http://www.lawschoolcasebriefs.net/2013/12/hooters-of-america-inc-v-phillips-case.html

House, R. J., Hanges, P. J., Javidan, M., Dorfman, P. W., & Gupta, V. (2004). *Culture leadership and organizations: The GLOBE study of 62 societies.* Sage.

Howard, W. M. (1995, October–December). Arbitrating claims of employment discrimination: What really does happen? What really should happen? *Dispute Resolution Journal,* 40–50.

Huang, Q., & Gamble, J. (2015). Social expectations, gender and job satisfaction: Frontline employees in China's retail sector. *Human Resource Management Journal, 25*(3), 331–347.

Hughes, R. (1996, June 10). Modernism's patriarchy. *Time.*

Hughes, S., & Bennett, M. (2005). *The art of mediation* (2nd ed.). National Institute for Trial Advocacy.

Hughes, V. (2022, September 16). How to change minds? A study makes the case for talking it out. *New York Times.* https://www.nytimes.com/2022/09/16/science/group-consensus-persuasion-brain-alignment.html?smid=url-share

Hunt, J. (2018). *University of Nike: How corporate cash bought American higher education.* Melville House.

ifla.org. (2005). "Multiculturalism." https://repository.ifla.org/bitstream/123456789/1608/1/publication_multiculturalism_mcultp_2005.pdf

Illinois Legal Aid. (2006). *How to represent yourself at an EEOC mediation.* http://www
.illinoislegalaid.org/index.cfm?fuseaction=home.dsp_Content&contentID=5346

Indeed Editorial Team. (2022, June 3). What is relational leadership? (Definition & Tips).
https://www.indeed.com/career-advice/career-development/relational-leadership

International Court of Arbitration. (n.d.). *Sample arbitration clauses.* http://www.dispute
.it/?page_id=7

International Ombuds Association (IOA). (2023). *Generic academic ombudsman position
description.* https://www.ombudsassociation.org/Academic-PD

Isaac, M. (2017a, February 22). Inside Uber's unrestrained, aggressive workplace culture.
New York Times. https://www.nytimes.com/2017/02/22/technology/uber-workplace
-culture.html?module=inline

Isaac, M. (2017b). Uber founder Travis Kalanick resigns as CEO. *New York Times.* https://
www.nytimes.com/2017/06/21/technology/uber-ceo-travis-kalanick.html?_r=0

Jacobs, Hendel, H. (2020, January 16). Rupture and repair: Emotional communication,
breakdown, and connection from infancy through adulthood. *Psychology Today.*
https://www.psychologytoday.com/us/blog/emotion-information/202001/rupture-and
-repair

Jawahar, I. M. (2006). Correlates of satisfaction with performance appraisal feedback. *Journal of Labor Research, 27*(2), 213–236.

Jehn, K. A., Greer, L., Levine, S., & Szulanski, G. (2008). The effects of conflict types,
dimensions, and emergent states on group outcomes. *Group Decision & Negotiation,
17*(6), 465–495.

Johnson, S. (2018, September 1). How to make a big decision: Have no fear. An emerging
science can help you choose. *New York Times.* https://www.nytimes.com/2018/09/01
/opinion/sunday/how-make-big-decision.html

Jones, T., & Brinkert, R. (2008). *Conflict coaching: Conflict management strategies and
skills for the individual.* Sage.

Jouany, V., & M. Mäkipää. (2023). *8 employee engagement statistics you need to know
in 2023.* Haiilo. https://haiilo.com/blog/employee-engagement-8-statistics-you-need-to
-know/#:~:text=According%20to%20Gallup's%20State%20of,little%20to%20no%20
emotional%20attachment

Jules, S. (2019, October 25). *Top reasons why employees stay or leave.* LinkedIn Research.
https://www.linkedin.com/pulse/top-reasons-why-employees-stay-leave-alie-jules/

Jung-a, S. (2013, June 11). *South Korean women struggle in the workforce.* CNBC. https://
www.cnbc.com/id/100808174

Kaboulian, L., & Sutherland, P. (2005). *Win-win labor-management collaboration in
education: Breakthrough practices to benefit students, teachers and administrators.*
Education Week Press.

Kahneman, D., & Tversky, A. (1972). Subjective probability. A judgment of representa-
tiveness. *Cognitive Psychology, 3*(3), 430–454.

Kaplan, D. A. (2006, September 17). Suspicions and spies in Silicon Valley. *Newsweek.*
https://www.newsweek.com/suspicions-and-spies-silicon-valley-109827

Kastelle, T. (2013, November 20). Hierarchy is overrated. *Harvard Business Review.*
https://hbr.org/2013/11/hierarchy-is-overrated

Katz, T. Y., & Block, C. J. (2000). Process and outcome goal orientations in conflict situations: The importance of framing. In M. Deutsch & P. Coleman (Eds.), *The handbook
of conflict resolution: Theory and practice* (pp. 279–288). Jossey-Bass.

Kelly, J. (2020, February 24). Wells Fargo forced to pay $3 billion for the bank's fake ac-
count scandal. *Forbes.* https://www.forbes.com/sites/jackkelly/2020/02/24/wells-fargo
-forced-to-pay-3-billion-for-the-banks-fake-account-scandal/?sh=5a124e6c42d2

Keyton, J. (1999). Analyzing interaction patterns in dysfunctional teams. *Small Group Research, 30*(4), 491–518.

Khazan, O. (2015, February 15). How often people in various countries shower: Amidst the no-shampoo revolution, a look at global hygiene habits. *The Atlantic.* https://www.theatlantic.com/health/archive/2015/02/how-often-people-in-various-countries-shower/385470/

Kilborn, P. T. (1991, June 3). Americans complain of bias by Japanese bosses in the US. *New York Times.* https://www.nytimes.com/1991/06/03/us/americans-complain-of-bias-by-japanese-bosses-in-us.html

Kim, S. (2023, February 3). More than one-third of Americans are "quiet quitting." *Newsweek.* https://www.msn.com/en-us/health/other/more-than-a-third-of-americans-are-quiet-quitting/ar-AA174yTO

King, E. B., Hebl, M. R., & Beal, D. J. (2009). Conflict and cooperation in diverse workgroups. *Journal of Social Issues, 65,* 261–285.

Klimoski, R. J., & Karol, B. L. (1976). The impact of trust on creative problem-solving groups. *Journal of Applied Psychology, 61*(5), 630–633.

Klinger, S. (2021, September 24) Why both employee and customer satisfaction matter to your bottom line. *Forbes.* https://www.forbes.com/sites/forbeshumanresourcescouncil/2021/09/24/why-both-employee-and-customer-satisfaction-matter-to-your-bottom-line/?sh=71dbd5611487

Knight, J. (2004, August 17). Bullied workers suffer "battle stress." *BBC News Online.* http://news.bbc.co.uk/2/hi/business/3563450.stm

Konigsburg, D., & Thorne, S. (2022, March 5). Women in the boardroom: 2022 update. *Harvard Law School Forum on Corporate Governance.* https://corpgov.law.harvard.edu/2022/03/05/women-in-the-boardroom-2022-update/

Kotter, J. P. (1996). *Leading change.* Harvard Business School Press.

Kozlowski, S. W., & Ilgen, D. R. (2006). Enhancing the effectiveness of work groups and teams. *Psychological Science in the Public Interest, 7*(3), 77–124.

Kreps, D. M. (2017). *The motivation toolkit.* Norton.

Kuypers, J. (2006). *Bush's war: Media bias and justifications for war in a terrorist age.* Rowman & Littlefield.

Kyckelhahn, T., & Cohen, T. H. (2008). *Civil rights complaints in U.S. District Courts, 1990–2006* (Report No. NCJ 222989). United States Department of Justice, Office of Justice Programs, Bureau of Justice Statistics.

Langan-Fox, J. (2004). Mental models, team mental models, and performance: Process, development, and future directions. *Human Factors & Ergonomics in Manufacturing, 14*(4), 331–352.

Lastauskaite, A. (2015, October 26). *Japanese work etiquette: Tips to survive.* Linked In. https://www.linkedin.com/pulse/japanese-work-etiquette-tips-survive-aiste-lastauskaite/

Lauszat, B. (2014). *Challenges and advantages when working with Germans.* Search Laboratory. https://www.searchlaboratory.com/us/2014/07/challenges-and-advantages-when-working-with-germans/

Lee, M. (2010, April 28). *Finding, minding, binding and grinding.* https://bookmarklee.co.uk/finding-minding-binding-grinding/

Leech, M. (2022, August 3). *Report finds a continued lack of diversity on boards of Fortune 500 companies.* BizWomenJournal. https://www.bizjournals.com/bizwomen/news/latest-news/2022/08/mogul-women-boards.html?page=all#:~:text=Mogul's%20Board%20Diversity%20in%202022,on%20them%2C%20male%20or%20female

Legal Information Institute. (2012). *Gilmer v. Insterstate/Johnson Lane Corporation.* Cornell University Law School. http://www.law.cornell.edu/supct/html/90-18.ZS.html

Lencioni, P. (2002). *The five dysfunctions of a team: A leadership fable*. Jossey-Bass.

Lewicki, R. S. (2006). Trust, trust development, and repair. In M. Deutsch, P. T. Coleman, & E. C. Marcus (Eds.), *The handbook of conflict resolution: Theory and practice* (2nd ed.). Jossey-Bass.

Lewicki, R., Barry, B., & Saunders, D. (2010). *Essentials of negotiation*. McGraw-Hill.

Lewis, L. (2015, July 6). Japan: Women in the workforce. *Financial Times*. https://www.ft.com/content/60729d68-20bb-11e5-aa5a-398b2169cf79

Linden, R. (2003). The discipline of collaboration. *Leader to Leader, 29*, 41–47.

Lipman, V. (2013, April 25). The disturbing link between psychopathy and leadership. *Forbes*. https://www.forbes.com/sites/victorlipman/2013/04/25/the-disturbing-link-between-psychopathy-and-leadership/#6c76ce234104

Lu, M. (2020, September 2). *Is the American dream over? Here is what the data says*. World Economic Forum. https://www.weforum.org/agenda/2020/09/social-mobility-upwards-decline-usa-us-america-economics/

Lutgen-Sandvik, P., Tracy, S. J., & Alberts, J. K. (2007). Burned by bullying in the American workplace: Prevalence, perception, degree and impact. *Journal of Management Studies, 44*, 837–862.

MacBriade-King, J. L., & Bachmann, K. (1999). *Solutions for the stressed-out worker*. Conference Board of Canada, Ontario.

Maden, C. (2011). Dark side of mergers & acquisitions: Organizational interventions and survival strategies. *Journal of American Academy of Business, 17*(1), 188–195.

Magee, J. C., Galinsky, A. D., & Gruenfeld, D. (2007). Power, propensity to negotiate, and moving first in competitive interactions. *Personality and Social Psychology Bulletin, 33*(2), 200–212.

Malin, D. M. (2004). Johnson & Johnson's dispute resolution program: A new formula for achieving common ground. In S. Estreicher & D. Sherwyn (Eds.), *Alternative dispute resolution in the employment arena*. Kluwer Law International.

Mallick, D. L. (2007). *Don't think twice, mediation's alright: U.S. corporations should implement in-house mediation programs into their business plans to resolve disputes*. Harvard Negotiation Law Review. http://www.hnlr.org/2009/03/us-corporations-should-implement-in-house-mediation-programs-into-their-business-plans-to-resolve-disputes/

Markey, S. (2003, September 17). *Monkeys show sense of fairness, study says*. National Geographic. http://news.nationalgeographic.com/news/2003/09/0917_030917_monkeyfairness_2.html

Marks, M. L., & Mirvis, P. H. (2010). *Joining forces: Making one plus one equal three in mergers, acquisitions and alliances*. Jossey-Bass.

Maslow, A. (1954). *Motivation and personality*. Harper and Row.

Matthews, D. (2017, April 17). *Europe could have the secret to saving America's unions*. Vox. https://www.vox.com/policy-and-politics/2017/4/17/15290674/union-labor-movement-europe-bargaining-ftght-15-ghent

Matthiesen, S. B., & Einarsen, S. (2007). Perpetrators & targets of bullying at work: Role stress and individual differences. *Violence and Victims, 22*(6), 735–753.

McCarthy, J. (2022). *What percentage of US workers belong to unions?* Gallup. https://news.gallup.com/poll/265958/percentage-workers-union-members.aspx

McDermott, P., Obar, R., Jose, A., & Bowers, M. (2000, September 20). *An evaluation of the Equal Employment Opportunity Commission mediation program* (EEOC Order No. 9/0900/7632/2). U. S. Equal Employment Opportunity Commission. http://www.eeoc.gov/eeoc/mediation/report/index.html

McEwen, C. (1994). *An evaluation of the Equal Employment Opportunity Commission's pilot mediation program*. Center for Dispute Settlement.

McGown, A. (2009). Keeping customers satisfied. *Retail Merchandiser, 49*(3), 66–67.

McGregor, J. (2018, April 24). Corporate boards are still mostly white, mostly male—and getting even older. *Washington Post.* https://www.washington-post.com/news/on-leadership/wp/2018/04/24/corporate-boards-are-still-mostly-white-mostly-male-and-getting-even-older/?utm_term=.7b5a71ffa47a

Merchant, N. (2011, March 22). Culture trumps strategy every time. *Harvard Business Review.* https://hbr.org/2011/03/culture-trumps-strategy-every

Merchant, Y. S. (2018, April 5). 5 major differences between Japanese and American workplaces. *Business Insider.* https://www.businessinsider.com/differences-between-japanese-and-american-work-culture-2018-3

Merecz, D., Drabek, M., & Mościcka, A. (2009). Aggression at the workplace—Psychological consequences of abusive encounters with coworkers and clients. *International Journal of Occupational Medicine & Environmental Health, 22*(3), 243–260.

Meyer, C. B., & Altenborg, E. (2008). Incompatible strategies in international mergers: The failed merger between Telia and Telenor. *Journal of International Business Studies, 39*(3), 508–525.

Michel, A. (2016, January 29). *Burnout and the brain.* Association for Psychological Sciences. https://www.psychologicalscience.org/observer/burnout-and-the-brain

Miles, M. (2022, July 19). *Project Oxygen: An inside look at what makes a good manager.* BetterUp. https://www.betterup.com/blog/project-oxygen#:~:text=8%20findings%20about%20good%20managers%20from%20Google%E2%80%99s%20Project,that%20help%20him%20or%20her%20advise%20the%20team

Miller, L. M. (1990). *Barbarians to bureaucrats: Corporate life cycle strategies.* Fawcett.

Minson, J. A., & Chen, F. S. (2022). Receptiveness to opposing views: Conceptualization and integrative review. *Personality and Social Psychology Review, 26*(2), 93–111. https://doi.org/10.1177/10888683211061037

Monahan, C. (2008). Faster, cheaper, and unused: The paradox of grievance mediation in unionized environments. *Conflict Resolution Quarterly, 25*, 479–496. https://doi.org/10.1002/crq.218

Moore, C. (2003). *The mediation process: Practical strategies for resolving conflict* (3rd ed.). Jossey-Bass.

Moorman, R. H. (1991). Relationship between justice and organizational citizenship behaviors: Do fairness perceptions influence employee citizenship? *Journal of Applied Psychology, 76*, 845–855.

Morrow, A. (2022, December 22). *Can Wells Fargo save itself?* CNN Business. https://www.cnn.com/2022/12/20/business/nightcap-wells-fargo-scandals/index.html

Moye, N. A., & Langfred, C. W. (2004). Information sharing and group conflict: Going beyond decision making to understand the effects of information sharing on group performance. *International Journal of Conflict Management, 15*(4), 381–410.

Mueller, S. L., & Thomas, A. S. (2001). Culture and entrepreneurial potential: A nine country study of locus of control and innovativeness. *Journal of Business Venturing, 16*(1), 51–75.

Nabatchi, T., & Bingham, L. B. (2010). From postal to peaceful: Dispute system design in the USPS REDRESS program. *Review of Public Personnel Administration, 30*(2), 211–234.

Namie, G. (2021). *US workplace bullying survey.* Workplace Bullying Institute. https://workplacebullying.org/wp-content/uploads/2021/04/2021-Full-Report.pdf?_ga=2.210014677.1794564928.1675875624-481941402.1675875624

Namie, G., & Namie, R. (2003). *The bully at work: What you can do to stop the hurt and reclaim the dignity in your job.* Sourcebooks.

National Institutes of Mental Health. (2022). *Personality disorders.* https://www.nimh.nih.gov/health/statistics/personality-disorders.shtml

Nemoto, K. (2017, October 3). *Why gender equality persists in Japan*. Work in Progress: Sociology on the Economy, Work and Inequality. https://workinprog-ress.oowsection .org/2017/10/03/why-gender-inequality-persists-in-corporate-japan/

Neuliep, J. W. (2009). *Intercultural communication: A contextual approach* (4th ed.). Sage.

Neuliep, J. W. (2017). *Intercultural communications: An intercultural approach* (7th ed.). Sage.

Nielson, L. B., & Beim, A. (2004). Media misrepresentation: Title VII, print media, and public perceptions of discrimination litigation. *Stanford Law & Policy Review, 15*, 237.

Nowak, M., & Sigmund, K. (2005). Evolution of indirect reciprocity. *Nature, 437*(7063), 1291–1298.

Occupational Safety & Health Administration (OSHA). (2023, January 16). *Workplace violence*. https://www.osha.gov/workplace-violence

O'Donnell, N., Towey, M., Steve, K. & Verdugo, A. (2021, November 8). The military is failing to comply with federal law in sexual assault cases, new watchdog report finds. *CBS News*. https://www.cbsnews.com/news/pentagon-federal-law-sex-assault-cases -watchdog-report/

O'Donovan, E. (2007). Dealing with difficult people. *District Administration, 43*(9), 70.

O'Leary, R., & Blomgren Bingham, L. (2009). *The collaborative public manager: New ideas for the twentieth century*. Georgetown University Press.

Orr, P. J., Emerson, K., & Keyes, D. L. (2008). Environmental conflict resolution practice and performance: An evaluation framework. *Conflict Resolution Quarterly, 25*, 283–301.

Overman, S. (2011). Can a hybrid union/professional association give white-collar employees a voice at work without the power of collective bargaining? *Fortune*. https:// fortune.com/2011/09/02/not-quite-the-union-label/

Palmer, E. J., & Thakordas, V. (2005). Relationship between bullying and scores on the Buss-Perry aggression questionnaire among imprisoned male offenders. *Aggressive Behavior, 31*, 55–66.

Parker, K., & Horowitz, J. M. (2022, March 9). *Majority of workers who quit a job in 2021 cite low pay, no opportunities for advancement, feeling disrespected*. Pew Research Center. https://www.pewresearch.org/fact-tank/2022/03/09/majority-of-workers -who-quit-a-job-in-2021-cite-low-pay-no-opportunities-for-advancement-feeling-dis respected/#:~:text=Overall%2C%20about%20one%2Din%2D,a%20temporary%20 job%20had%20ended

Pearsall, M. J., Christian, M. S., & Ellis, A. J. (2010). Motivating interdependent teams: Individual rewards, shared rewards, or something in between? *Journal of Applied Psychology, 95*(1), 183–191.

Peck, E. (2022, June 17). *Asian and white men more likely to be described as "genius" in performance reviews*. Axios. https://www.axios.com/2022/06/17/performance-reviews -bias-racism-sexism

Pelusi, N. (2006). Dealing with difficult people. *Psychology Today, 39*(5), 68–69.

Perhach, P. (2023, January 14). How to ask for a raise without alienating your boss along the way. *New York Times*.

Phillips, D. T. (1990, December). The price tag of turnover. *Personnel Journal*, 58.

Poitras, J., & Raines, S. (2013). *Expert mediators: Overcoming mediation challenges in workplace, family and community disputes*. Rowman & Littlefield.

Preston, P. (2005). Dealing with "difficult" people. *Journal of Healthcare Management, 50*(6), 367–370.

Projections (2023, February 13). Who is unionizing? A breakdown of unionization trends by demographics for 2023. https://projectionsinc.com/2023-unionization-trends/

Psychiatry.org. (2018). *Personality disorders.* https://www.psychiatry.org/patients-fami lies/personality-disorders/what-are-personality-disorders

Psychology Today. (2022). *Dunning-Kruger effect.* https://www.psychologytoday.com/us /basics/dunning-kruger-effect

Quinn, R. (2004). *Building the bridge as you walk on it: A guide for leading change* (2nd ed.). Jossey-Bass.

Quinn, R. E. (2012). *The deep change field guide: A personal course to discover the leader within.* Jossey-Bass.

Rafenstein, M. (2000). Dealing with difficult people on the job. *Current Health 2(2),* 5.

Raines, S. (2002). *Unheard voices in international environmental relations* (Doctoral dissertation). Indiana University.

Raines, S. S. (2005). Can online mediation be transformative? Tales from the front. *Conflict Resolution Quarterly, 22,* 2.

Raines, S. S. (2006). Mediating in your pajamas: The benefits and challenges for ODR practitioners. *Conflict Resolution Quarterly, 23(3).* https://doi.org/10.1002/crq.143

Raines, S., Albert, A. S., Davis, C., & Johnson, J. (2023). Comparing the performance of attorney vs. non-attorney mediators: Policy implications for court-connected mediation. *Journal of Mediation Theory & Practice.*

Raines, S., & Harrison, T. (2020). Overcoming Groundhog Day: Changing organizational culture while institutionalizing the ombudsman role. *Journal of the International Ombudsman Association.*

Raines, S., & Kubala, D. (2011). Environmental conflict resolution by water utilities: Applications and lessons learned. *Journal of the American Water Works Association, 103(6),* 61–70.

Raines, S., & O'Leary, R. (2000). Evaluating the use of alternative dispute resolution in U.S. Environmental Protection Agency enforcement cases: Views of agency attorneys. *Pace Environmental Law Review, 18(1),* 119.

Rajagopal, A. (2006). *Trust and cross-cultural dissimilarities in corporate environment.* http://papers.ssrn.com/sol3/papers.cfm?abstract_id=916023

Randstad Research. (2022, July 20). *Top reasons why employees leave their jobs in 2022.* https://www.randstad.co.uk/market-insights/staff-retention/top-reasons-why-employ ees-leave-their-jobs-2022/

Rehfeld, J. E. (1990). What working for a Japanese company taught me. *Harvard Business Review.* https://hbr.org/1990/11/what-working-for-a-japanese-company-taught-me

Reyes, G. (2019, September 23). The ROI of diversity: Delivering business success. *Forbes.* https://www.forbes.com/sites/forbesfinancecouncil/2019/09/23/the-roi-of-diversity-de livering-business-success/?sh=7ef2cd21d78f

Rigge, M. (1997). NHS—Keeping the customer satisfied. *Health Service Journal, 107(5577),* 24–27.

Robbennolt, J. K. (2003). Apologies and legal settlement: An empirical examination. *Michigan Law Review, 102,* 460.

Roberts, D. (2018, March 15). Senator demands Wells Fargo CEO should be fired, criticizes his "big, fat raise." *Charlotte Observer.* https://www.charlotteobserver.com/news/busi ness/banking/article205382969.html

Rohlander, D. G. (1999). Effective team building. *IIE Solutions, 31(9),* 22.

Rowe, M. (2018). Effectiveness of the organizational ombudsman. In *The handbook of the International Association of Ombudsmen.* http://mitsloan.mit.edu/shared/ods /documents/?DocumentID=4391

Rowe, M., Hedeen, T., & Scheider, J. (2020). *What do organizational ombudsmen do? And not do?* (Working Paper). International Ombudsman Association. https://mitsloan.mit .edu/shared/ods/documents?PublicationDocumentID=7572

Salovey, P., & Mayer, J. (1990). Emotional intelligence. *Imagination, Cognition & Personality, 9*, 185–211.

Sander, F. E. A., and Goldberg, S. B. (1994). Fitting the forum to the fuss: A user-friendly guide to selecting an ADR procedure. *Negotiation Journal, 10*(1), 49–68. https://doi.org/10.1111/j.1571-9979.1994.tb00005.x

Sandy, S. V., Boardman, S. K., & Deutsch, M. (2000). Personality and conflict. In M. Deutsch & P. Coleman (Eds.), *The handbook of conflict resolution: Theory and practice* (pp. 289–315). Jossey-Bass.

Schenck, A., & Zinsser, J. (2014). Prepared to be valuable: Positioning ombuds programs. *Journal of the International Ombuds Association, 7*(1), 23–44. http://www.ombudsassociation.org/IOA_Main/media/SiteFiles/docs/JIOA-14-V7-1_FINAL_0.pdf

Schultz, J. R. (2015). To improve performance, replace annual assessment with ongoing feedback. *Global Business & Organizational Excellence, 34*(5), 13–20. https://doi.org/10.1002/joe.2162

Schwantes, M. (2022, December 12). *Google spent one year researching great managers. The most successful ones shared these 5 traits.*

Schweiger, D. M., & Goulet, P. K. (2000). Integrating mergers and acquisitions: An international research review (1st ed.). In *Advances in mergers & acquisitions* (Vol. 1, pp. 61–91). Emerald Group Publishing.

Science Daily. (2008, October 5). Antisocial behavior may be caused by low stress hormone levels. https://www.sciencedaily.com/releases/2008/10/081001093506.htm

Scott, G. (2008). Take emotion out of conflict resolution. *T + D, 62*(2), 84.

Shelton, B. (2021). *Overestimating your leadership: The Dunning-Kruger Effect.* ADI. https://www.aubreydaniels.com/blog/overestimating-your-leadership-the-dunning-kruger-effect

Sherman, N. (2018, May 3). Diesel admissions scandal: Ex-VW boss Winterkorn charged in the US. *BBC News.* https://www.bbc.com/news/business-43995167

Shonk, K. (2022, October 10). *3 types of conflict and how to address them.* Program on Negotiation, Harvard Law School Blog. https://www.pon.harvard.edu/daily/conflict-resolution/types-conflict/

SHRM. (2011). *Employee recognition programs survey findings.* http://www.shrm.org/Research/SurveyFindings/Articles/Pages/EmployeeRecognitionProgramsSurveyFindings.aspx

SHRM. (2016). *Research overview: Employee engagement.* https://www.shrm.org/hr-today/trends-and-forecasting/special-reports-and-expert-views/Documents/Research%20Overview%20Employee%20Engagement.pdf

Sims, R. L. (2010). A study of deviance as a retaliatory response to organizational power. *Journal of Business Ethics, 92*(4), 553–563. http://www.jstor.org/stable/40605316

Sipe, N., & Stiftel, B. (1995). Mediating environmental enforcement disputes: How well does it work? *Environmental Impact Assessment Review, 15*(2), 139.

Skilton, P. F., & Dooley, K. J. (2010). The effects of repeat collaboration on creative abrasion. *Academy of Management Review, 35*(1), 118–134.

Smith, A., & Garza, E. (2021, December 19). *4 different parenting styles and how they can trigger anxiety.* Brillia. https://discoverbrillia.com/blogs/articles/four-different-parenting-styles-and-anxiety

Solomon, R. C., & Flores, F. (2001). *Building trust in business, politics, relationships and life.* Oxford University Press.

Solovic, S. W. (2018). *Turning an unhappy customer into a happy one is a powerful business strategy.* AllBusiness. https://www.allbusiness.com/turning-an-unhappy-customer-into-a-happy-one-is-a-powerful-business-strategy-11599156-1.html

Sourry, A. (2018, July 20). *The moral and business need for diversity and inclusion in the workplace.* Huffington Post.

Southwest Airlines. (2008). *Southwest Airlines annual report.*

Stafford, D. (2011, September 4). Union organizing shifts to white collar jobs, especially in hospitals. *Kansas City Star.* http://www.kansascity.com/2011/09/04/3121350/orga nized-labor-goes-to-the-hospital.html

Strauss, K. (2018, January 25). More evidence that company diversity leads to better profits. *Forbes.* https://www.forbes.com/sites/karstenstrauss/2018/01/25/more-evidence -that-company-diversity-leads-to-better-profits/#3488c3711bc7

Sullivan, A. (2018, May 5). *Report highlights lack of female leaders in German business.* DW. https://p.dw.com/p/2xYjA

Sulzmann, J. (2018). *How the ombuds add value to Oregon State University.* Internal Program Evaluation. https://ombuds.oregonstate.edu/sites/ombuds.ore-gonstate.edu /ftles/ombuds_value-year_5_4-14-17.pdf

Surowiecki, J. (2004). *The wisdom of crowds: Why the many are smarter than the few and how collective wisdom shapes business, economies, societies and nations.* Knopf Doubleday.

Tajfel, H., & Turner, J. (2001). An integrative theory of intergroup conflict. In M. A. Hogg & D. Abrams (Eds.), *Key readings in social psychology. Intergroup relations: Essential readings* (pp. 94–109). Psychology Press.

Tanous, O. (2021). Structural violence and its effects on children living in war and armed conflict zones: A Palestinian perspective. *International Journal of Social Determinants of Health and Health Services, 52*(1). https://doi.org/10.1177/00207314211039096

TechFunnel. (2019, November 21). How to prevent harassment and violence in the workplace? https://www.techfunnel.com/hr-tech/prevent-workplace-violence -harassment/#:~:text=12%20Tips%20for%20Workplace%20Violence%20and%20Ha rassment%20Prevention,where%20employees%20could%20be%20vulnerable%20 ...%20More%20items

Thorbecke, C. (2022, November 17). *Airbnb CEO on the tech downturn: "It's like we're all in a nightclub and the lights just came on."* CNN Business. https://www.cnn .com/2022/11/17/tech/brian-chesky-airbnb/index.html

Tidwell, A. (1997). Problem solving for one. *Mediation Quarterly, 14,* 309–317.

Tierney, J. (2010, March 22). Moral lessons, down aisle 9. *New York Times.* http://www .nytimes.com/2010/03/23/science/23tier.html

Tierney, M. (2011, April 16). Executive Q & A: The best in business. *Atlanta Journal-Constitution.* http://www.ajc.com/business/topworkplaces/executive-q-a-911507.html

Tiffan, B. (2009). Dealing with difficult people. *Physician Executive, 35*(5), 86–89.

Tilghman, A. (2016, May 5). Military sex assault: Just 4% of complaints result in convictions. https://www.militarytimes.com/veterans/2016/05/05/military-sex-assault-just -4-percent-of-complaints-result-in-convictions/

Timpano, K. R., Keough, M. E., Mahaffey, B., Schmidt, N. B., & Abramowitz, J. (2010). Parenting and obsessive-compulsive symptoms: Implications for authoritarian parenting. *Journal of Cognitive Psychotherapy, 24*(3). https://doi.org/10.1891/0889-8391.24.3.151

Tjosvold, D. (2008). The conflict-positive organization: It depends upon us. *Journal of Organizational Behavior, 29,* 19–28.

Trivers, R. L. (1971). The evolution of reciprocal altruism. *Quarterly Review of Biology, 46*(35), 57.

Tuchman, B. W., & Jensen, M. A. (1977). Stages of small-group development revisited. *Group & Organization Studies, 2*(4), 419.

Tugend, A. (2023, January 23). Calling it quits: Why is assessing job satisfaction so hard? *New York Times.* https://www.nytimes.com/2023/01/30/business/companies-job-satis faction-surveys.html?smid=nytcore-ios-share&referringSource=articleShare.

12 Manage: The Executive Fast Track. (2018). *The Kaizen method.* https://www.12manage .com/methods_kaizen.html

UE Information for Workers. (2011). *Step one of the grievance procedure.* http://www .ueunion.org/stwd_grstep1.html

Ullrich, J., & Van Dick, R. (2007). The group psychology of mergers & acquisitions: Lessons from the social identity approach. In C. L. Cooper and S. Finkelstein (Eds.), *Advances in mergers and acquisitions* (pp. 1–15). Emerald Group Publishing.

University of Chicago Medical Center. (2000, January 20). Low levels of salivary cortisol associated with aggressive behavior. *ScienceDaily.* http://www.sciencedaily.com/re leases/2000/01/000120073039.htm#

University of Iowa. (2011). *Child labor public education project.* http://www.continue tolearn.uiowa.edu/laborctr/child_labor/about/us_history.html

Ury, W., Brett, J., & Goldberg, S. (1988). *Getting disputes resolved: Designing systems to cut the cost of conflict.* Jossey-Bass.

U.S. Bureau of Labor Statistics. (2022, January 25). *Union membership rate declines in 2021, returns to 2019 rate of 10.3 percent.* https://www.bls.gov/opub/ted/2022/union -membership-rate-declines-in-2021-returns-to-2019-rate-of-10-3-percent.htm

U.S. Governmental Accountability Office (GAO). (1997). *U.S. Postal Service: Little progress made in addressing persistent labor-management problems.* https://www.gao.gov /products/ggd-98-1

Van der Kolk, B. (2015). *The body keeps the score: Brain, mind and body in the healing of trauma.* Penguin.

Varettoni, W. (2005). Success overdue at the Quincy library group. *PERC Reports, 23*(2). https://www.perc.org/2005/06/01/success-overdue-at-the-quincy-library/

Vedantam, S. (2007). If it feels good to be good, it might be only natural. *Washington Post.* http://www.washingtonpost.com/wp-dyn/content/article/2007/05/27 /AR2007052701056.html

Vogel, G. (2004, February 20). The evolution of the "golden rule." *Science, 303*(5661), 1128–1131.

von Neumann, J. (1944). *The theory of games and economic behavior.* Princeton University Press.

Wahab, M. A., Katsh, E., & Rainey, D. (Eds.). (2013). *Online dispute resolution theory and practice.* Eleven Publishing.

Warner, J., & Corley, C. (2017, May 21). *The women's leadership gap: Women's leadership by the numbers.* Center for American Progress. https://www.americanprogress.org/is sues/women/reports/2017/05/21/432758/womens-leadership-gap/

WarrenShepel. (2005). *Research-based database.* http://www.shepellfgiservices.com /research/iresearch.asp

Watson, C., & Hoffman, R. L. (1996). Managers as negotiators: A test of power versus gender as predictors of feelings, behavior, and outcomes. *Leadership Quarterly, 7*(1), 63–85.

Wecker, K. (2015, May 4). New German law: A woman's place should be on corporate boards. *USA Today.* https://www.usatoday.com/story/money/2015/05/04/berlin-ger many-women-corporate-boards/26831917/

Westwood, C. (2010, October). Managing difficult behavior. *Nursing Manager (Harrow), 17*(6), 20–21.

Wiedmer, T. L. (2011). Workplace bullying: Costly and preventable. *Delta Kappa Gamma Bulletin, 77*(2), 35–41.

Willink, J., & Babin, L. (2015). *Extreme ownership: How U.S. Navy SEALS lead and win*. St. Martin's Press.

Wilmot, W. W., & Hocker, J. L. (2001). *Interpersonal conflict* (6th ed.). McGraw-Hill.

Wilson, K. S., Sin, H., & Conlon, D. E. (2010). What about the leader in leader-member exchange? The impact of resource exchanges and substitutability on the leader. *Academy of Management Review, 35*(3), 358.

Winfrey, O., & Perry, B. 2021. *What happened to you? Conversations on trauma, resilience, and healing*. Macmillan.

Wissler, R. L. (2002). Court-connected mediation in general civil cases: What we know from empirical research. *Ohio State Journal on Dispute Resolution, 17*(3), 641–703.

Witschger, J. D. (2011). Our customers, our partners. *American Salesman, 56*(4), 27–30.

World Bank. (2011). *Respectful workplace advisors program*. https://www.worldbank.org/en/about/unit/respectful-workplace-advisors

World Bank Administrative Tribunal. (2023, May 11). *Frequently asked questions*. https://tribunal.worldbank.org/faq

World Business Culture. (2018). *Business culture in South Korea*. https://www.worldbusinessculture.com/country-proftles/south-korea/culture/management-style/

Yarrington, Y. (2017). *UNM ombuds services for staff. Annual report*. https://ombuds-forstaff.unm.edu/common/images/documents/costsofconflict.pdf

Yerkes Primate Research Center at Emory University. (2003). *Yerkes researchers first to recognize sense of fairness in non-human primates*. http://www2.gsu.edu/~wwwcbs/pdf/Senseoffairness.pdf

Young, C., Stumpf, S., & Arnone, M. (1995). Managing change: Strategic response, organizational realities, and overcoming resistance. In *Challenges for Management: Total Quality Management as a Success Strategy* (Vol. 2). Springer-Verlag.

Zapf, D., & Einarsen, S. (2003). Individual antecedents of bullying. In S. Einarsen, H. Hoel, D. Zapf, & C. L. Cooper (Eds.), *Bullying and emotional abuse in the workplace* (pp. 165–184). Taylor & Francis.

Zondiros, D., Konstantopoulos, N., & Tomaras, P. (2007). A simulation model for measuring customer satisfaction through employee satisfaction. *AIP Conference Proceedings, 963*(2), 1086–1089.

Zullo, R. (2011). *The effect of interest arbitration on fire fighter wage increases: Evaluating Michigan's Act 312*. Institute for Research on Labor, Employment and the Economy. University of Michigan, Kalamazoo.

Index

About the Author

Susan S. Raines, PhD, is a foreign service officer with the U.S. Department of State.* For more than 20 years she was a professor of conflict management in the Graduate School of Conflict Management, Peacebuilding & Development at Kennesaw State University (KSU), in suburban Atlanta. She is the president of Collaboration Services, a consulting firm that works with public, private, and nonprofit organizations to prevent and proactively manage conflict and collaboration. She has mediated more than 17,000 cases within and outside the court system and served as an alternative dispute resolution reservist for the U.S. Federal Emergency Management Agency (FEMA). Through the provision of training, one-on-one performance coaching, program evaluation, culture change initiatives, strategic planning, and crisis intervention, she has assisted organizations such as the International Monetary Fund, United Nations International Organization for Migration, Florida and Georgia Supreme Courts, Volkswagen North America, Coca-Cola, YKK, the DeKalb County Multi-Door Courthouse, the Maryland Association for Conflict Resolution, the U.S. Army Corps of Engineers, Florida Medical Association, George Physician Leadership Association, American Association of Chemists, New York State Agricultural Mediation Program (NYSAMP), CureViolence Global, and many more. She is the coauthor of *Expert Mediators* (2013) and is author and coauthor of more than 60 peer-reviewed publications, and she served as the editor in chief of *Conflict Resolution Quarterly* for 12 years.

---

*The views expressed in the book are my own and not those of the U.S. Department of State.